STUDENT'S SOLUTIONS MANUAL

JOHN R. MARTIN

Tarrant County College, Northeast Campus

BASIC TECHNICAL MATHEMATICS

EIGHTH EDITION

AND

BASIC TECHNICAL MATHEMATICS WITH CALCULUS

EIGHTH EDITION

Allyn J. Washington

Dutchess Community College

PEARSON

Addison
Wesley

Boston San Francisco New York
London Toronto Sydney Tokyo Singapore Madrid
Mexico City Munich Paris Cape Town Hong Kong Montreal

Reproduced by Pearson Addison-Wesley from electronic files supplied by the author.

Copyright © 2005 Pearson Education, Inc.
Publishing as Pearson Addison-Wesley, 75 Arlington Street, Boston, MA 02116

ISBN   0-321-19742-9

4 5 6 BB 07 06

PEARSON

Addison
Wesley

CONTENTS

Acknowledgments

The author gratefully acknowledges the contributions of the following individuals: Judy Martinez for the word processing, John Garlow for the art work, and Susan Schroder for the proofing. Their attention to detail and cooperation were of great assistance in preparing this manual.

John R. Martin
Tarrant County College, NE Campus
Hurst, Texas
2004

Chapter 1

BASIC ALGEBRAIC OPERATIONS

1.1 Numbers

1. The numbers -3 and 14 are integers. They are also rational numbers since they can be written as $\dfrac{-3}{1}$ and $\dfrac{14}{1}$.

5. 3 is an integer (whole number); 3 is rational (may be written as a ratio of integers, $3/1$); 3 is real (not the square root of a negative number). $-\pi$ is irrational; it is not a ratio of integers; $-\pi$ is real.

9. $|3| = 3.$ $\left|\dfrac{7}{2}\right| = \dfrac{7}{2}$

13. $6 < 8$

17. $-|-3| = -3 \Rightarrow -4 < -3 = -|-3|$

21. The reciprocal of $3 = \frac{1}{3}$. The reciprocal of

$-\frac{1}{3} = \dfrac{1}{-\frac{1}{3}} = -3.$

25.

$$\underline{-\tfrac{1}{2}2.5}$$
$$-2 \quad -1 \quad | \quad 0 \quad 1 \quad 2 \quad | \quad 3 \quad 4$$

29. An absolute value is not always positive, $|0| = 0$ which is not positive.

33. Since $0.13 = \dfrac{13}{100} \cdot \dfrac{\frac{3}{13}}{\frac{3}{13}} = \dfrac{3}{\frac{300}{13}} = \dfrac{3}{23.0769\cdots} <$

$\dfrac{3}{23} = \dfrac{3}{23} \cdot \dfrac{\frac{14}{3}}{\frac{14}{3}} = \dfrac{14}{107.\overline{3}} < \dfrac{14}{100} = 0.14$

$\dfrac{3}{23}$ is a rational number between 0.13 and 0.14 with numerator 3 and an integer, 23, in the denominator.

37. **(a)** $b - a; b > a$, positive integer

   (b) $a - b; b > a$, negative integer

   (c) $\dfrac{b - a}{b + a}$, positive rational number less than 1

41. **(a)** x is a positive number located to the right of 0.

   (b) x is a negative number located to the left of -4.

45. $L = \dfrac{a}{t}$, L, t are variables and a is constant.

49. $\mathrm{N} = \dfrac{a \text{ bits}}{\text{byte}} \dfrac{1000 \text{ bytes}}{\text{kilobytes}} \cdot n\text{kilobytes}$

   $= 1000an \text{ bits}$

1.2 Fundamental Operations of Algebra

1. $16 - 2 \times (-3) = 16 - (-6) = 22$

5. $8 + (-4) = 8 - 4 = 4$

9. $-19 - (-16) = -19 + 16 = -3$

13. $-7(-5) = 35$

17. $-2(4)(-5) = (-8)(-5) = 40$

21. $9 - 0 = 9$

25. $8 - 3(-4) = 8 - (-12) = 8 + 12 = 20$

29. $30(-6)(-2) \div (0 - 40) = 360 \div (-40) = -9$

33. $-7 - \dfrac{|-14|}{2(2-3)} - 3(8-6) = -7 - \dfrac{14}{2(-1)} - 3(2)$

   $= -7 - \dfrac{14}{-2} - 6$

   $= -7 - (-7) - 6$
   $= 0 - 6$
   $= -6$

37. $6(7) = 7(6)$ demonstrates the commutative law of multiplication.

41. $3 + (5 + 9) = (3 + 5) + 9$ demonstrates the associative law of addition.

45. $-a + (-b) = -a - b$ which is expression (d).

49. (a) The product of an even number of negative numbers is positive.

(b) The product of an odd number of negative numbers is negative.

53. $2.1 - 1.5(3) = -2.4$ kW·h

57. 100 m + 200 m = 200 m + 100 m illustrates the commutative law of addition.

1.3　Calculators and Approximate Numbers

1. Yes, 0.390 has three significant digits since the 0 after the 9 is not needed to locate the decimal.

5. 8 cylinders is exact because they can be counted. 55 mi/h is approximate since it is measured.

9. 107 has 3 significant digits. 3004 has 4 significant digits.

13. 3000 has 1 significant digit. 3000.1 has 5 significant digits.

17. (a) Both numbers have the same precision with digits in the tenths place.

(b) 78.0 with 3 significant digits is more accurate than 0.1 with 1 significant digit.

21. (a) $4.936 = 4.94$ rounded to 3 significant digits.

(b) $4.936 = 4.9$ rounded to 2 significant digits.

25. (a) $9549 = 9550$ rounded to 3 significant digits.

(b) $9549 = 9500$ rounded to 2 significant digits.

29. (a) Calculator: $3.8 + 0.154 + 47.26 = 51.2$.

(b) Estimate: $4 + 0 + 47 = 51$

33. (a) Calculator: $0.0350 - \dfrac{0.0450}{1.909} = 0.0114$

(b) Estimate: $0.04 - \dfrac{0.05}{2} = 0.015$

37. (a) Calculator: $\dfrac{23.962 \times 0.01537}{10.965 - 8.249} = 0.1356$

(b) Estimate: $\dfrac{20 \times 0.02}{10 - 8} = 0.2$

41. $0.9788 + 14.9 = 15.8788$ since 4 is the number of decimal places in the least precise number.

45. 2.745 MHz and 2.755 MHz are the least possible and greatest possible frequencies respectively.

49. (a) $2.2 + 3.8 \times 4.5 = 19.3$

(b) $(2.2 + 3.8) \times 4.5 = 27$

53. (a) $\dfrac{8}{33} = 0.242424\cdots = 0.\overline{24}$

(b) $\pi = 3.141592653589873\cdots$

57. 1 K = 1024 bytes
256 K $= 256 \times 1024 = 262{,}144$ bytes

1.4　Exponents

1. $(-x^3)^2 = \left[(-1)x^3\right]^2 = (-1)^2(x^3)^2 = x^{3(2)} = x^6$

5. $x^3 \cdot x^4 = x^{3+4} = x^7$

9. $\dfrac{m^5}{m^3} = m^{5-3} = m^2$

13. $(P^2)^4 = P^{2\cdot4} = P^8$

17. $(2n)^3 = 2^3 \cdot n^3 = 8n^3$

21. $\left(\dfrac{2}{b}\right)^3 = \dfrac{2^3}{b^3} = \dfrac{8}{b^3}$

25. $7^0 = 1$

29. $6^{-1} = \dfrac{1}{6^1} = \dfrac{1}{6}$

33. $(-t^2)^7 = -t^{2\cdot7} = -t^{14}$

37. $(4xa^{-2})^0 = 1$

41. $\dfrac{2v^4}{(2v)^4} = \dfrac{2v^4}{2^4v^4} = \dfrac{1}{2^3} = \dfrac{1}{8}$

45. $(5^0x^2a^{-1})^{-1} = 1\cdot x^{2\cdot(-1)}\cdot a^{(-1)(-1)} = x^{-2}\cdot a^1 = \dfrac{a}{x^2}$

49. $(-8gs^3)^2 = (-8)^2 \cdot g^2 \cdot (s^3)^2 = 64g^2s^{3\cdot2} = 64g^2s^6$

53. $7(-4) - (-5)^2 = -28 - 25 = -53$

57. $\dfrac{3.07(-1.86)}{(-1.86)^4 + 1.596} = \dfrac{-5.71}{11.97 + 1.596}$

$$= \dfrac{-5.71}{13.57} = -0.421$$

61. $\left(\dfrac{1}{x^{-1}}\right)^{-1} = \dfrac{1^{-1}}{x^{-1(-1)}} = \dfrac{1}{x} = $ reciprocal of x, yes.

65. $\pi\left(\dfrac{r}{2}\right)^3\left(\dfrac{4}{3\pi r^2}\right) = \pi \cdot \dfrac{r^3}{8} \cdot \dfrac{4}{3\pi r^2} = \dfrac{r}{6}$

1.5　Scientific Notation

1. $8.06 \times 10^3 = 8060$

5. $2.01 \times 10^{-3} = 0.00201$; move decimal point 3 places to the left by adding 2 zeros.

9. $1.86 \times 10 = 18.6$; move decimal point 1 place to the right.

13. $0.0087 = 8.7 \times 10^{-3}$; move decimal point to the right 3 places.

17. $0.063 = 6.3 \times 10^{-2}$; move decimal point 2 places to the right.

21. $28,000(2,000,000,000) = 2.8 \times 10^4(2 \times 10^9)$
$$= 5.6 \times 10^{13}$$

25. $2 \times 10^{-35} + 3 \times 10^{-34} = 0.2 \times 10^{-34} + 3 \times 10^{-34}$
$$= 3.2 \times 10^{-34}$$

29. $1280(865,000)(43.8) = 4.85 \times 10^{10}$

33. $(3.642 \times 10^{-8})(2.736 \times 10^5) = 9.965 \times 10^{-3}$

37. $6,500,000 \text{ kW} = 6.5 \times 10^6 \text{ kW}$

41. $10^{30}{}^{\circ}\text{C}$
$$= 1,000,000,000,000,000,000,000,000,000,000{}^{\circ}\text{C}$$

45. $\dfrac{7.5 \times 10^{-15} \text{ s}}{\text{addition}} \cdot 5.6 \times 10^6 \text{ additions}$
$$= 4.2 \times 10^{-8} \text{ s}$$

49. $37,000,000,000 \dfrac{\text{disintigrations}}{\text{s}} \cdot \dfrac{3600 \text{ s}}{1.0 \text{ h}}$
$$= 1.3 \times 10^{14} \text{ disintegrations}$$

1.6　Roots and Radicals

1. $-\sqrt[3]{64} = -4$ since $(-4)^3 = -64$

5. $\sqrt{81} = 9$

9. $-\sqrt{49} = -7$

13. $\sqrt[3]{125} = 5$

17. $\left(\sqrt{5}\right)^2 = 5$

21. $\left(-\sqrt{18}\right)^2 = 18$

25. $2\sqrt{84} = 2\sqrt{4 \cdot 21} = 2 \cdot 2\sqrt{21} = 4\sqrt{21}$

29. $\sqrt[3]{8^2} = \sqrt[3]{64} = 4$

33. $\sqrt{36 + 64} = \sqrt{100} = 10$

37. $\sqrt{85.4} = 9.24$

41. (a) $\sqrt{1296 + 2304} = \sqrt{3600} = 60.00$

　　　(b) $\sqrt{1296} + \sqrt{2304} = 36.00 + 48.00 = 84.00$

45. $\sqrt{24s} = \sqrt{(24)(150)} = \sqrt{3600} = 60 \text{ mi/h}$

49. $d = \sqrt{w^2 + h^2} = \sqrt{15.2^2 + 11.4^2}$
$$= \sqrt{361}$$
$$= 19.0 \text{ in.}$$

1.7　Addition and Subtraction of Algebraic Expressions

1. $3x + 2y - 5y = 3x - 3y$

5. $5x + 7x - 4x = 12x - 4x = 8x$

9. $2F - 2T - 2 + 3F - T = 5F - 3T - 2$

13. $s + (4 + 3s) = s + 4 + 3s = 4s + 4$

17. $2 - 3 - (4 - 5a) = -1 - 4 + 5a$
$$= -5 + 5a$$
$$= 5a - 5$$

21. $-(t - 2u) + (3u - t) = -t + 2u + 3u - t = 5u - 2t$

25. $-7(6 - 3j) - 2(j + 4) = -42 + 21j - 2j - 8$
$$= 19j - 50$$

29. $2[4 - (t^2 - 5)] = 2[4 - t^2 + 5] = 2[9 - t^2]$
$$= 18 - 2t^2$$

33. $a\sqrt{LC} - [3 - (a\sqrt{LC} + 4)]$
$$= a\sqrt{LC} - [3 - a\sqrt{LC} - 4]$$
$$= a\sqrt{LC} - [-1 - a\sqrt{LC}]$$
$$= a\sqrt{LC} + 1 + a\sqrt{LC}$$
$$= 2a\sqrt{LC} + 1$$

37. $5p - (q - 2p) - [3q - (p - q)]$
$$= 5p - q + 2p - [3q - p + q]$$
$$= 7p - q - [4q - p]$$
$$= 7p - q - 4q + p$$
$$= 8p - 5q$$

41. $5V^2 - (6 - (2V^2 + 3)) = 5V^2 - (6 - 2V^3 - 3)$
$$= 5V^2 - (3 - 2V^2)$$
$$= 5V^2 - 3 + 2V^2$$
$$= 7V^2 - 3$$

45. $-4[4R - 2.5(Z - 2R) - 1.5(2R - Z)]$
$$= -4[4R - 2.5Z + 5R - 3R + 1.5Z]$$
$$= -4[6R - Z]$$
$$= -24R + 4Z$$
$$= 4Z - 24R$$

49. $-4(b - c) - 3(a - b) = -4b + 4c - 3a + 3b$
$$= -b + 4c - 3a$$

1.8 Multiplication of Algebraic Expressions

1. $2s^3(-st^4)^3(4s^2t) = 2s^3(-s)^3(t^4)^3(4s^2t)$
$$= -2s^6t^{12}(4s^2t)$$
$$= -8s^8t^{13}$$

5. $(a^2)(ax) = a^{2+1}x = a^3x$

9. $(2ax^2)^2(-2ax) = 4a^2x^4(-2ax) = -8a^3x^5$

13. $i^2(R + r) = i^2R + i^2r$

17. $5m(m^2n + 3mn) = 5m^3n + 15m^2n$

21. $ab^2c^4(ac - bc - ab) = a^2b^2c^5 - ab^3c^5 - a^2b^3c^4$

25. $(x - 3)(x + 5) = x^2 + 5x - 3x - 15 = x^2 + 2x - 15$

29. $(2a - b)(3a - 2b) = 6a^2 - 4ab - 3ab + 2b^2$
$$= 6a^2 - 7ab + 2b^2$$

33. $(x^2 - 1)(2x + 5) = 2x^3 + 5x^2 - 2x - 5$

37. $(x + 1)(x^2 - 3x + 2) = x^3 - 3x^2 + 2x + x^2 - 3x + 2$
$$= x^3 - 2x^2 - x + 2$$

41. $2(a + 1)(a - 9) = 2(a^2 - 8a - 9) = 2a^2 - 16a - 18$

45. $2L(L + 1)(L - 4) = 2L(L^2 - 4L + L - 4)$
$$= 2L(L^2 - 3L - 4)$$
$$= 2L^3 - 6L^2 - 8L$$

49. $(x_1 + 3x_2)^2 = (x_1 + 3x_2)(x_1 + 3x_2)$
$$= x_1^2 + 3x_1x_2 + 3x_1x_2 + 9x_2^2$$
$$= x_1^2 + 6x_1x_2 + 9x_2^2$$

53. $2(x + 8)^2 = 2(x + 8)(x + 8)$
$$= 2(x^2 + 8x + 8x + 64)$$
$$= 2(x^2 + 16x + 64)$$
$$= 2x^2 + 32x + 128$$

57. $3T(T + 2)(2T - 1) = (3T^2 + 6T)(2T - 1)$
$$= 6T^3 - 3T^2 + 12T^2 - 6T$$
$$= 6T^3 + 9T^2 - 6T$$

61. Let $1 < n < 9$, $n^2 - 1 = (n - 1)(n + 1)$ which shows the square of the integer minus $1 =$ product of integer before n and the integer after n.

65. $(n + 100)^2 = n^2 + 200n + 100^2$
$$= n^2 + 200n + 10{,}000$$

1.9 Division of Algebraic Expressions

1. $\dfrac{-6a^2xy^2}{-2a^2xy^5} = 3y^{2-5} = 3y^{-3} = \dfrac{3}{y^3}$

5. $\dfrac{8x^3y^2}{-2xy} = -4x^2y$

9. $\dfrac{(15x^2)(4bx)(2y)}{30bxy} = 4x^2$

13. $\dfrac{a^2x + 4xy}{x} = \dfrac{a^2x}{x} + \dfrac{4xy}{x}$
$$= a^2 + 4y$$

17. $\dfrac{4pq^3 + 8p^2q^2 - 16pq^5}{4pq^2}$
$$= \dfrac{4pq^3}{4pq^2} + \dfrac{8p^2q^2}{4pq^2} - \dfrac{16pq^5}{4pq^2}$$
$$= q + 2p - 4q^3$$

21. $\dfrac{3ab^2 - 6ab^3 + 9a^2b^2}{9a^2b^2}$
$$= \dfrac{3ab^2}{9a^2b^2} - \dfrac{6ab^3}{9a^2b^2} + \dfrac{9a^2b^2}{9a^2b^2}$$
$$= \dfrac{1}{3a} - \dfrac{2b}{3a} + 1$$

25.
$$\require{enclose}
\begin{array}{r}
2x + 1 \\
x + 3 \enclose{longdiv}{2x^2 + 7x + 3} \\
\underline{2x^2 + 6x} \\
x + 3 \\
\underline{x + 3} \\
0
\end{array}$$

29.
$$\require{enclose}
\begin{array}{r}
4x^2 - x - 1 \\
2x - 3 \enclose{longdiv}{8x^3 - 14x^2 + x + 0} \\
\underline{8x^3 - 12x^2} \\
-2x^2 + x \\
\underline{-2x^2 + 3x} \\
-2x + 0 \\
\underline{-2x + 3} \\
-3
\end{array}$$

33.

$$
\begin{array}{r}
x^2 + x - 6 \\
x + 2)\overline{x^3 + 3x^2 - 4x - 12} \\
\underline{x^3 + 2x^2} \\
x^2 - 4x \\
\underline{x^2 + 2x} \\
-6x - 12 \\
\underline{-6x - 12} \\
0
\end{array}
$$

37.

$$
\begin{array}{r}
x^2 - 2x + 4 \\
x + 2)\overline{x^3 + 0x^2 + 0x + 8} \\
\underline{x^3 + 2x^2} \\
-2x^2 + 0x \\
\underline{-2x^2 - 4x} \\
4x + 8 \\
\underline{4x + 8} \\
0
\end{array}
$$

41.

$$
\begin{array}{r}
E + 3 \\
5E^2 - 7E - 2)\overline{5E^3 + 8E^2 - 23E - 1} \\
\underline{5E^3 - 7E^2 - 2E} \\
15E^2 - 21E - 1 \\
\underline{15E^2 - 21E - 6} \\
5
\end{array}
$$

$$\frac{5E^3 + 8E^2 - 23E - 1}{5E^2 - 7E - 2} = E + 3 + \frac{5}{5E^2 - 7E - 2}$$

45. $\dfrac{GMm[(R + r) - (R - r)]}{2rR}$

$$= \frac{GMm[R + r - R + r]}{2rR}$$

$$= \frac{GMm[2r]}{2rR} = \frac{GMm}{R}$$

1.10   Solving Equations

1. (a)
$$x - 3 = -12$$
$$x - 3 + 3 = -12 + 3$$
$$x = -9$$

(b)
$$x + 3 = -12$$
$$x + 3 - 3 = -12 - 3$$
$$x = -15$$

(c)
$$\frac{x}{3} = -12$$
$$3\left(\frac{x}{3}\right) = 3(-12)$$
$$x = -36$$

(d)
$$3x = -12$$
$$\frac{3x}{3} = \frac{-12}{3}$$
$$x = -4$$

5. $x - 2 = 7$
$$x = 7 + 2$$
$$x = 9$$

9. $\dfrac{t}{2} = 5$
$$t = 2 \cdot 5$$
$$t = 10$$

13. $3t + 5 = -4$
$$3t = -4 - 5$$
$$3t = -9$$
$$t = -3$$

17. $3x + 7 = x$
$$3x - x = -7$$
$$2x = -7$$
$$x = \frac{-7}{2}$$

21. $6 - (r - 4) = 2r$
$$6 - r + 4 = 2r$$
$$-3r = -10$$
$$r = \frac{10}{3}$$

25. $0.1x - 0.5(x - 2) = 2$
$$x - 5(x - 2) = 20$$
$$x - 5x + 10 = 20$$
$$-4x = 10$$
$$x = -2.5$$

29. $\dfrac{4x - 2(x - 4)}{3} = 8$
$$4x - 2(x - 4) = 24$$
$$4x - 2x + 8 = 24$$
$$2x = 16$$
$$x = 8$$

33. $5.8 - 0.3(x - 6.0) = 0.5x$
$$5.8 - 0.3x + 1.8 = 0.5x$$
$$7.6 = 0.8x$$
$$x = 9.5$$

37. $\dfrac{x}{2.0} = \dfrac{17}{6.0}$
$$x = \frac{34}{6.0}$$
$$x = 5.7$$

41. $1.1 = \dfrac{T - 76}{40}$
$$44 = T - 76$$
$$T = 120°\text{C}$$

45. $\dfrac{x}{150} = \dfrac{2}{5}$
$$x = \frac{300}{5}$$
$$x = 60 \text{ mg}$$

1.11   Formulas and Literal Equations

1. $v = v_o + at$

$v - v_o = at$

$$a = \frac{v - v_o}{t}$$

5. $E = IR$

$$\frac{E}{I} = \frac{IR}{I}$$

$$R = \frac{E}{I}$$

9. $Q = SLd^2$

$$L = \frac{Q}{Sd^2}$$

13. $A = \dfrac{Rt}{PV}$

$Rt = APV$

$$t = \frac{APV}{R}$$

17. $T = \dfrac{c + d}{v}$

$Tv = c + d$

$d = Tv - c$

21. $a = \dfrac{2mg}{M + 2m}$

$aM + 2ma = 2mg$

$aM = 2mg - 2ma$

$$M = \frac{2mg - 2ma}{a}$$

25. $P = n(p - c)$

$P = np - nc$

$P + nc = np$

$$p = \frac{P + nc}{n}$$

29. $Q_1 = P(Q_2 - Q_1)$

$Q_1 = PQ_2 - PQ_1$

$Q_1(1 + P) = PQ_2$

$$Q_2 = \frac{Q_1 + PQ_1}{P}$$

33. $L = \pi(r_1 + r_2) + 2x_1 + x_2$

$L = \pi r_1 + \pi r_2 + 2x_1 + x_2$

$\pi r_1 = L - \pi r_2 - 2x_1 - x_2$

$$r_1 = \frac{L - \pi r_2 - 2x_1 - x_2}{\pi}$$

37. $C = \dfrac{2eAk_1k_2}{d(k_1 + k_2)}$

$Cd(k_1 + k_2) = 2eAk_1k_2$

$$e = \frac{Cd(k_1 + k_2)}{2Ak_1k_2}$$

41. $F = \dfrac{9}{5}C + 32$

$$90.2 = \frac{9}{5}C + 32$$

$$\frac{5}{9}(90.2 - 32) = C$$

$$C = \frac{5}{9} \times 58.2$$

$$C = 32.3°C$$

1.12   Applied Word Problems

1. $x = $ number of 1.5 Ω resistors

$34 - x = $ number of 2.5 Ω resistors

$$1.5x + 2.5(34 - x) = 56$$
$$1.5x + 85 - 2.5x = 56$$
$$-1.0x = -29$$
$$x = 29$$
$$34 - x = 5$$

29 1.5 Ω resistors

5 2.5 Ω resistors

5. $x = $ cost 6 years ago

$x + 5000 = $ cost today

$$x + (x + 5000) = 49{,}000$$
$$2x + 5000 = 49{,}000$$
$$2x = 44{,}000$$
$$x = 22{,}000$$
$$x + 5000 = 27{,}000$$

$22,000 six years ago.

$27,000 is cost today.

9. Let $x = $ number of acres @ $20,000

$$20{,}000 \cdot x + 10{,}000 \cdot (70 - x) = 900{,}000$$
$$2x + 70 - x = 90$$
$$x = 20 \text{ acres @ } \$20{,}000$$
$$70 - x = 50 \text{ acres @ } \$10{,}000$$

15. $x + 2x + (x + 9.2) = 0$

$4x = -9.2 \Rightarrow x = -2.3 \ \mu A$ for the first current

$2x = -4.6 \ \mu A$ for the second current

$x + 9.2 = 6.9 \ \mu A$ for the third current

19.
$$x = \text{number of adults}$$
$$2002 - x = \text{number of children}$$

$$48x + 30(2002 - x) = 81{,}480$$
$$48x + 60{,}060 - 30x = 81{,}480$$
$$18x = 21{,}420$$
$$x = 1190 \text{ adults}$$
$$2002 - x = 812 \text{ children}$$

25. Let $x - 30 = $ time first car started race;
$x = $ time second car started race

$$260(x - 30) = 240(x)$$
$$260x - 7800 = 240x$$
$$20x = 7800$$
$$x = 390 \text{ s}$$

8 laps $= 2.50 \times 8 = 20$ mi, 105 600 ft, total distance
$d = vt = 260 \times 390 = 101{,}400$ ft $< 105{,}600$ ft
So, the first car is ahead after 8 laps.

29. $x = $ number of liters of pure antifreeze
added
$x = $ number of liters of 50% antifreeze
drained

$$0.25(12 - x) + x = 0.50(12)$$
$$3.0 - 0.25x + x = 6.0$$
$$0.75x = 3.0$$
$$x = 4.0 \text{ L}$$

Chapter 1 Review Exercises

1. $(-2) + (-5) - 3 = -7 - 3$
$$= -10$$

5. $-5 - |2(-6)| + \dfrac{-15}{3} = -5 - |-12| + (-5)$
$$= -5 - 12 - 5$$
$$= -17 - 5$$
$$= -22$$

9. $\sqrt{16} - \sqrt{64} = 4 - 8 = -4$

13. $(-2rt^2)^2 = 4r^2(t^2)^2 = 4r^2t^4$

17. $\dfrac{-16N^{-2}(NT^2)}{-2N^0T^{-1}} = 8N^{-2+1}T^{2-(-1)}$
$$= 8N^{-1}T^3$$
$$= \dfrac{8T^3}{N}$$

21. (a) 8840 has 3 significant digits
(b) 8840 rounded to 2 significant digits is 8800

25. $37.3 - 16.92(1.067)^2 = 18.03676612$ on a calculator; 18.0

29. $a - 3ab - 2a + ab = a - 2a - 3ab + ab = -a - 2ab$

33. $(2x - 1)(x + 5) = 2x^2 + 10x - x - 5$
$$= 2x^2 + 9x - 5$$

37. $\dfrac{2h^3k^2 - 6h^4k^5}{2h^2k} = \dfrac{2h^3k^2}{2h^2k} - \dfrac{6h^4k^5}{2h^2k}$
$$= hk - 3h^2k^4$$

41. $2xy - \{3z - [5xy - (7z - 6xy)]\}$
$$= 2xy - \{3z - [5xy - 7z + 6xy[\}$$
$$= 2xy - \{3z - [11xy - 7z]\}$$
$$= 2xy - \{3z - 11xy + 7z\}$$
$$= 2xy - \{10z - 11xy\}$$
$$= 2xy - 10z + 11xy$$
$$= 13xy - 10z$$

45. $-3y(x - 4y)^2 = -3y(x^2 - 8xy + 16y^2)$
$$= -3x^2y + 24xy^2 - 48y^3$$

49. $\dfrac{12p^3q^2 - 4p^4q + 6pq^5}{2p^4q} = \dfrac{12p^3q^2}{2p^4q} - \dfrac{4p^4q}{2p^4q} + \dfrac{6pq^5}{2p^4q}$
$$= \dfrac{6q}{p} - 2 + \dfrac{3q^4}{p^3}$$

53.
$$
\begin{array}{r}
x^2 - 2x + 3 \\
3x - 1 \overline{)3x^3 - 7x^2 + 11x - 3} \\
\underline{3x^3 - x^2} \\
-6x^2 + 11x \\
\underline{-6x^2 + 2x} \\
9x - 3 \\
\underline{9x - 3}
\end{array}
$$

57. $-3\{(r + s - t) - 2[(3r - 2s) - (t - 2s)]\}$
$$= -3\{(r + s - t) - 2[3r - 2s - t + 2s]\}$$
$$= -3\{r + s - t - 2[3r - t]\}$$
$$= -3\{r + s - t - 6r + 2t\}$$
$$= -3\{-5r + s + t\}$$
$$= 15r - 3s - 3t$$

61. $3x + 1 = x - 8$
$$3x - x = -8 - 1$$
$$2x = -9$$
$$x = \dfrac{-9}{2}$$

65. $6x - 5 = 3(x - 4)$
$$6x - 5 = 3x - 12$$
$$3x = -7$$
$$x = \dfrac{-7}{3}$$

69.
$$3t - 2(7 - t) = 5(2t + 1)$$
$$3t - 14 + 2t = 10t + 5$$
$$5t - 14 = 10t + 5$$
$$-5t = 19$$
$$t = \frac{-19}{5}$$

73. $16{,}000 \text{ Pa} = 1.6 \times 10^4 \text{ Pa}$

77. $2.53 \times 10^{13} \text{ mi} = 25{,}300{,}000{,}000{,}000 \text{ mi}$

81. $1.5 \times 10^{-1} \text{ Bq/L} = 0.15 \text{ Bq/L}$

85.
$$P = \frac{\pi^2 E I}{L^2}$$
$$E = \frac{P L^2}{\pi^2 I}$$

89.
$$m = dV(1 - e)$$
$$\frac{m}{dV} = 1 - e$$
$$e = 1 - \frac{m}{dV}$$

93.
$$R = \frac{A(T_2 - T_1)}{H}$$
$$RH = AT_2 - AT_1$$
$$AT_2 = RH + AT_1$$
$$T_2 = \frac{RH + AT_1}{A}$$

97. $108 + 89.7 + 210 = 410 \text{ ft}$

101. $\dfrac{R_1 R_2}{R_1 + R_2} = \dfrac{0.0275(0.0590)}{0.0275 + 0.0590} = 0.0188 \, \Omega$

105. $4(t + h) - 2(t + h)^2 = 4t + 4h - 2(t^2 + 2th + h^2) =$
$4t + 4h - 2t^2 - 4th - 2h^2$

109.
$$x = \text{volume produced by second,}$$
$$2x = \text{volume produced by first, and}$$
$$2(2x) = \text{volume produced by third.}$$

$$x + 2x + 2(2x) = 560$$
$$7x = 560$$
$$x = 80 \text{ cm}^3 \text{ produced by second}$$
$$2x = 160 \text{ cm}^3 \text{ produced by first}$$
$$2(2x) = 320 \text{ cm}^3 \text{ produced by third}$$

113. $\dfrac{5.0 \text{ ft}}{1.7 \text{ lb}} = \dfrac{27 \text{ ft}}{x} \Rightarrow 5.0x = 46 \Rightarrow x = 9.2 \text{ lb}$

117. Let $\quad x =$ the number of liters of 0.50%
mixture.
$100 - x =$ the number of liters of 0.75%
mixture.

$$0.50\% \cdot x + 0.75\%(1000 - x) = 0.65\% \cdot 1000$$
$$50x + 75(1000 - x) = 65{,}000$$
$$50x + 75{,}000 - 75x = 65{,}000$$
$$25x = 10{,}000$$
$$x = 400 \text{ L of the } 0.50\% \text{ mixture}$$
$$1000 - x = 600 \text{ L of the } 0.75\% \text{ mixture}$$

121. Answers will vary.

Chapter 2

GEOMETRY

2.1   Lines and Angles

1. $\angle ABE = 90°$

5. $\angle EBD$ and $\angle DBC$ are acute angles.

9. The complement of $\angle CBD = 65°$ is $25°$.

13. $\angle AOB = 90° + 50° = 140°$

17. $\angle 1° = 62°$

21. $\angle BDE = 90° - 44° = 46°$
$\angle BDF = 180° - 46° = 134°$

25. $\dfrac{a}{4.75} = \dfrac{3.05}{3.20} \Rightarrow a = 4.75 \cdot \dfrac{3.05}{3.20} = 4.53$ m

29. $\angle BCD = 180° - 47°$
$= 133°$

2.2   Triangles

1. $\angle 5 = 45° \Rightarrow \angle 3 = 45°$
$\angle 2 = 180° - 70° - 45° = 65°$

5. $\angle A = 180° - 84° - 40° = 56°$

9. $p = 3.5 + 2.3 + 4.1 = 9.9$ ft

13. $A = \dfrac{1}{2}bh = \dfrac{1}{2}(7.6)(2.2) = 8.4$ ft^2

17. $A = \dfrac{1}{2}bh = \dfrac{1}{2}(3.46)(2.55) = 4.41$ ft^2

21. $c = \sqrt{13.8^2 + 22.7^2} = 26.6$ ft

25. $\angle B = 90° - 23° = 67°$

29. $\angle LMK$ and $\angle OMN$ are vertical angles and thus equal $\Rightarrow \angle KLM = \angle MON$.
The corresponding angles are equal and the triangles are similar.

33. An equilateral triangle.°

37. $s = \dfrac{2(76.6) + 30.6}{2} = 91.9$
$A = \sqrt{91.9(91.9 - 76.6)^2(91.6 - 30.6)}$
$A = 1150$ cm^2

41.

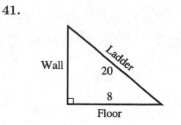

distance up wall $= \sqrt{20^2 - 8^2}$
$= \sqrt{336}$
$= 18.3$ ft

45.

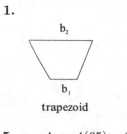

$\dfrac{4.5}{z} = \dfrac{5.4}{1.2 + z}$

$z = 6.0$ m
$x^2 = z^2 + 4.5^2$
$x = 7.5$ m
$y^2 = (1.2 + 6)^2 + 5.4^2$
$y = 9.0$ m

2.3   Quadrilaterals

1.

trapezoid

5. $p = 4s = 4(65) = 260$ m

9. $p = 2\ell + 2w = 2(3.7) + 2(2.7) = 12.8$ m

13. $A = s^2 = 2.7^2 = 7.3$ mm^2

17. $A = bh = 3.7(2.5) = 9.3$ m^2

21. $p = 2b + 4a$

25. The parallelogram is a rectangle.

29. For the courtyard: $s = \dfrac{p}{4} = \dfrac{320}{4} = 80$. For the outer edge of the walkway: $p = 4s = 4(80 + 6) = 344$ m.

33. $A = 2(\text{area of trapezoid} - \text{area of window}) = 2\left(\dfrac{1}{2}(28 + 16) \cdot 8 - 12(3.5)\right) = 268$ ft^2

$$\dfrac{1 \text{ gal}}{320 \text{ ft}^2} = \dfrac{x}{268 \text{ ft}^2} \qquad \text{ht of trapezoid} = \sqrt{10^2 - \left(\dfrac{28 - 16}{2}\right)^2} = 8.0 \text{ ft}$$

$$x = 0.84 \text{ gal}$$

2.4 Circles

1. $\angle OAB + \angle OBA + \angle AOB = 180°$
$\angle OAB + 90° + 72° = 180°$
$\angle OAB = 18°$

5. (a) AD is a secant line.

    (b) AF is a tangent line.

9. $c = 2\pi r = 2\pi(275) = 1730$ ft

13. $A = \pi r^2 = \pi(0.0952^2) = 0.0285$ yd^2

17. $\angle CBT = 90° - \angle ABC = 90° - 65° = 25°$

21. ARC BC $= 2(60°) = 120°$

25. $22.5°\left(\dfrac{\pi}{180°}\right) = 0.393$ rad

29. $P = \dfrac{1}{4}(2\pi r) + 2r = \dfrac{\pi r}{2} + 2r$

33. All are on the same diameter

37. $\dfrac{A_{\text{basketball}}}{A_{\text{hoop}}} = \dfrac{\pi\left(\dfrac{12.0}{2}\right)^2}{\pi\left(\dfrac{18.0}{2}\right)^2} = \dfrac{4}{9}$

41. $A = \dfrac{\pi}{2}(90^2 - 45^2)$

$A = 9500$ cm^2

2.5 Measurement of Irregular Areas

1. $A = \dfrac{52.0}{2}[0.0 + 2(52.1) + 2(60.4) + 2(73.9) + 2(75.5) + 2(86.1) + 0.0]$

$A = 18{,}100$ km^2

5. $A_{\text{trap}} = \dfrac{2.0}{2}[0.0 + 2(6.4) + 2(7.4) + 2(7.0) + 2(6.1) + 2(5.2) + 2(5.0) + 2(5.1) + 0.0]$

$A_{\text{trap}} = 84.4 = 84$ m^2 to two significant digits

9. $A_{\text{trap}} = \dfrac{0.5}{2}[0.6 + 2(2.2) + 2(4.7) + 2(3.1) + 2(3.6) + 2(1.6) + 2(2.2) + 2(1.5) + 0.8]$

$A_{\text{trap}} = 9.8$ mi^2

13. $A_{\text{trap}} = \dfrac{45}{2}[170 + 2(360) + 2(420) + 2(410) + 2(390) + 2(350) + 2(330) + 2(290) + 230]$

$A_{\text{trap}} = 120{,}000$ ft^2

17. $A_{\text{trap}} = \dfrac{0.500}{2}[0.0 + 2(1.732) + 2(2.000) + 2(1.732) + 0.0] = 2.73$ in.^{2}

This value is less than 3.14 in^2 because all of the trapezoids are inscribed.

2.6 Solid Geometric Figures

1. $V_1 = lwh$, $V_2 = (2l)(w)(2h) = 4lwh = 4V_1$
The volume is four times as much.

5. $V = e^3 = 7.15^3 = 366$ ft^3

9. $V = \dfrac{4}{3}\pi r^3 = \dfrac{4}{3}\pi(0.877^3) = 2.83$ yd^3

13. $V = \dfrac{1}{3}Bh = \dfrac{1}{3}(76^2)(130) = 250{,}000$ in.^{3}

17. $V = \dfrac{1}{2}\left(\dfrac{4}{3}\pi r^3\right) = \dfrac{2}{3}\pi\left(\dfrac{0.83}{2}\right)^3 = 0.15$ yd^3

21. $\dfrac{V_{\text{cylinder}}}{V_{\text{cone}}} = \dfrac{\pi(2r)^2\frac{h}{2}}{\frac{1}{3}\pi r^2 h} = \dfrac{6}{1}$

25. $A = 2lh + 2lw + 2wh$
$= 2(12.0)(8.75) + 2(12.0)(9.50) + 2(9.50)(8.75)$
$A = 604$ in.^{2}

29. $V = \dfrac{1}{3}BH = \dfrac{1}{3}(250^2)(160) = 3{,}300{,}000$ yd^3

33. $A = l^2 + \dfrac{1}{2}ps = 16^2 + \dfrac{1}{2}(4)(16)\sqrt{8^2 + 40^2} = 1560$ mm^2

Chapter 2 Review Exercises

1. $\angle CGE = 180° - 148° = 32°$

5. $c = \sqrt{9^2 + 40^2} = 41$

9. $c = \sqrt{6.30^2 + 3.80^2} = 7.36$

13. $P = 3s = 3(8.5) = 25.5$ mm

17. $C = \pi d = \pi(98.4) = 309$ mm

21. $V = Bh = \dfrac{1}{2}(26.0)(34.0)(14.0) = 6190$ cm^3

25. $A = 6e^2 = 6(5.20^2) = 162$ m^2

29. $\angle BTA = \dfrac{50°}{2} = 25°$

33. $\angle ABE = 90° - 37° = 53°$

37. $P = b + \sqrt{b^2 + (2a)^2} + \dfrac{1}{2}\pi(2a) = b + \sqrt{b^2 + 4a^2} + \pi a$

41. A square is a rectangle with four equal sides and a rectangle is a parallelogram with perpendicular intersecting sides so a square is a parallelogram. A rhombus is a parallelogram with four equal sides and since a square is a parallelogram, a square is a rhombus.

45. $P = 6s = 6(2) = 12$ cm

49. $L = \sqrt{1.2^2 + 7.8^2} = 7.9$ m

53. $s = \dfrac{18.0 + 15.5 + 7.50}{2} = 20.5$, $A = lw + \sqrt{s(s-a)(s-b)(s-c)}$

$A = 18.0(8.75) + \sqrt{20.5(20.5 - 18.0)(20.5 - 15.5)(20.5 - 7.50)} = 215$ ft^2

57. $c = \pi D = \pi(7920 + 2(210)) = 26{,}200$ mi

61. $A = \dfrac{250}{3}\,[220 + 4(530) + 2(480) + 4(320 + 190 + 260) + 2(510) + 4(350) + 2(730) + 4(560) + 240]$

$A = 1{,}000{,}000 \text{ m}^2$

65. $\sqrt{(500.10)^2 - 500^2} = 10$ ft

69. Label the vertices of the pentagon ABCDE. The area is the sum of the areas of three triangles, one with sides 921, 1490, and 1490 and two with sides 921, 921, and 1490. The semi-perimeters are given by

$$s_1 = \frac{921 + 921 + 1490}{2} = 1666 \quad \text{and} \quad s_2 = \frac{921 + 1490 + 1490}{2} = 1950.5.$$

$$A = 2\sqrt{1666(1666 - 921)(1666 - 921)(1666 - 1490)} + \sqrt{1950.5(1950.5 - 1490)(1950.5 - 1490)(1950.5 - 921)}$$
$$= 1{,}460{,}000 \text{ ft}^2$$

FUNCTIONS AND GRAPHS

3.1 Introduction to Functions

1. $f(x) = 3x - 7$
   $f(-2) = 3(-2) - 7 = -13$

5. (a) $A(r) = \pi r^2$

   (b) $A(d) = \pi \left(\dfrac{d}{2}\right)^2 = \dfrac{1}{4}\pi d^2$

9. From geometry, $A = s^2$
   $$\sqrt{A} = \sqrt{s^2}$$
   $$s = \sqrt{A}$$

13. $f(x) = 2x + 1; f(1) = 2(1) + 1 = 3;$
    $f(-1) = 2(-1) + 1 = -1$

17. $\phi(\pi) = \dfrac{6 - \pi^2}{2\pi}$

    $\phi(-2) = \dfrac{6 - (-2)^2}{2 \cdot (-2)} = \dfrac{2}{-4} = -\dfrac{1}{2}$

21. $K(s) = 3s^2 - s + 6;$
    $K(-s) = 3(-s)^2 - (-s) + 6 = 3s^2 + s + 6$
    $K(2s) = 3(2s)^2 - 2s + 6 = 12s^2 - 2s + 6$

25. $f(x) = 5x^2 - 3x; f(3.86) = 5 \cdot 3.86^2 - 3 \cdot 3.86 = 62.9$
    $f(-6.92) = 5 \cdot (-6.92)^2 - 3 \cdot (-6.92) = 260$

29. $f(x) = x^2 + 2$: square x and add 2 to the result.

33. Take 3 times the sum of twice the independent variable and 5, then subtract 1.

37. $A = 5e^2$
    $f(e) = 5e^2$

41. $s = f(t) = 17.5 - 4.9t^2; f(1.2) = 17.5 - 4.9 \cdot (1.2)^2$
    $s = 10.4$ m

3.2 More About Functions

1. $f(x) = -x^2 + 2$ is defined for all real values of x; the domain is all real numbers. Since $-x^2 + 2 \le 2$ the range is all real numbers $f(x) \le 2$.

5. The domain and range of $f(x) = x + 5$ is all real numbers.

9. The domain of $f(s) = \dfrac{2}{s^2}$ is all real numbers except zero since it gives a division by zero. The range is all positive real numbers because $\frac{2}{s^2}$ is always positive.

13. The domain of $Y(y) = \dfrac{y+1}{\sqrt{y-2}}$ is $y > 2$ because the square root requires $y - 2 \ge 0$ or $y \ge 2$ and to avoid a division by zero, $y > 2$ is required.

17. $F(t) = 3t - t^2$ for $t \le 2$; $F(2) = 3 \cdot 2 - 2^2 = 2$; $F(3)$ does not exist.

21. $d(t) = 40(2) + 55t = 80 + 55t$

25. $m(h) = \begin{cases} 110 \text{ for } h \le 1000 \\ 110 + 0.5(h - 1000) \text{ for } h > 1000 \end{cases}$

29. (a) $0.1x + 0.4y = 1200 \Rightarrow y(x) = \dfrac{1200 - 0.1x}{0.4}$

    (b) $y(400) = \dfrac{1200 - 0.1 \cdot 400}{0.4} = 2900$ L

33. $d = f(h)$
    $120^2 + h^2 = d^2$
    $d = \sqrt{14{,}400 + h^2}$

    Range: $d \ge 120$ m since $d = 120$ when $h = 0$.
    Domain: $h \ge 0$ since distance above ground is nonnegative.

37. The domain of $f = \dfrac{1}{2\pi\sqrt{C}}$ is $C > 0$ because C must be ≥ 0 to avoid taking the square root of a negative and > 0 to prevent division by zero.

13

41. (a) $V = lwh$

$V = (2w - 4)(w - 4)(2)$

$V = (2w^2 - 12w + 16)(2)$

$V = 4w^2 - 24w + 32$

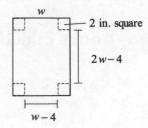

(b)   Domain: $w > 4$ in.

3.3   Rectangular Coordinates

1. $A(-1, -2)$, $B(4, -2)$, $C(4, 1)$

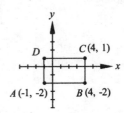

D, the fourth vertex has coordinates $(-1, 1)$.

5.

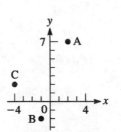

9. Rectangle

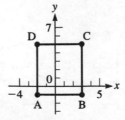

13. In order for the x-axis to be the perpendicular bisector of the line segment join P and Q, Q must be $(3, -2)$.

---

17. All points $(x, 3)$, where x is any real number, are points on a line parallel to the x-axis, 3 units above it.

21. Abscissas are x-coordinates; thus the abscissa of all points on the y-axis is zero.

25. All points which lie to the left of a line that is parallel to the y-axis, one unit to the left have $x < -1$.

29. $xy = 0$ for $x = 0$ (y-axis) or $y = 0$ (x-axis)

$xy = 0$ on either axis

3.4   The Graph of a Function

1. $f(x) = 3x + 5$

x	y
-3	-4
-2	-1
-1	2
0	5
1	8

5. $y = 3x$

x	y
-1	-3
0	0
1	3

9. $y = 7 - 2x$

x	y
-1	9
0	7
1	5

13. $y = x^2$

x	y
-2	4
-1	1
0	0
1	1
2	4

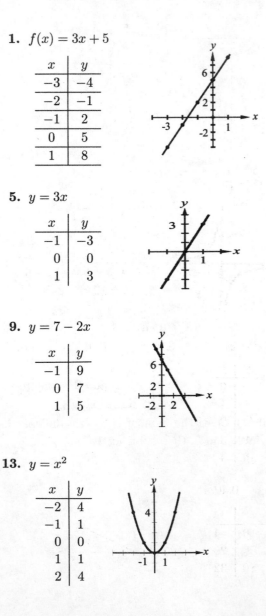

17. $y = \frac{1}{2}x^2 + 2$

x	y
-4	10
-2	4
0	2
2	4
4	10

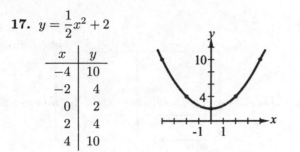

21. $y = x^2 - 3x + 1$

x	y
3	1
2	-1
1.5	-1.25
1	-1
0	1

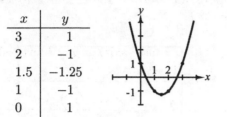

25. $y = x^3 - x^2$

x	y
-2	-12
-1	-2
0	0
$\frac{2}{3}$	$-\frac{4}{27}$
1	0
2	4

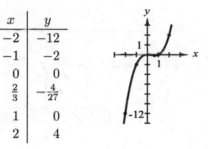

29. $P = \dfrac{1}{V}$

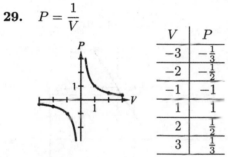

V	P
-3	$-\frac{1}{3}$
-2	$-\frac{1}{2}$
-1	-1
1	1
2	$\frac{1}{2}$
3	$\frac{1}{3}$

33. $y = \sqrt{x}$

x	y
0	0
1	1
4	2
9	3
16	4

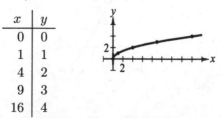

37. $n = 0.40m$

m	n
10	4
50	20
80	32

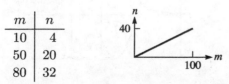

41. $H = 240I^2$

I	H
0	0
0.2	9.6
0.4	38.4
0.6	86.4
0.8	153.6

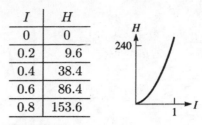

45. $P = 0.004v^3$

v	P
0	0
5	0.5
10	4.0
15	13.5
20	32.0

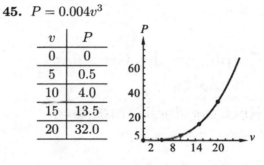

49. $P = 2l + 2w = 200 \Rightarrow l = 100 - w$
$A = lw = (100 - w)w = 100w - w^2$
for $30 \le w \le 70$

w	30	40	50	60	70
A	2100	2400	2500	2400	2100

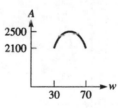

53. $S = \dfrac{5n}{4 + n}$

n	S
0	0
2	5/3
4	5/2
6	3
8	10/3

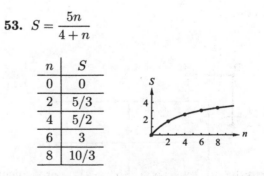

Only integral values of n have meaning.

57. $f(x) = \begin{cases} 3 - x & x < 1 \\ x^2 + 1 & x \geq 1 \end{cases}$

x	y
-2	5
-1	4
0	3
1	2
2	5
3	10

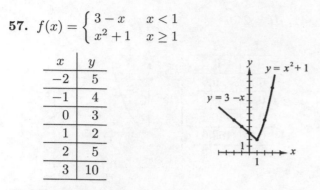

61. The graph passes the vertical line test and is, therefore, a function.

3.5   Graphs on the Graphing Calculator

1. $x^2 + 2x = 1 \Rightarrow x^2 + 2x - 1 = 0$. Graph $y = x^2 + 2x - 1$.

x	y
-4	7
-3	2
-2	-1
-1	-2
0	-1
1	2
2	7

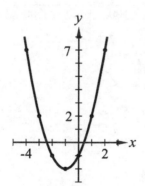

$x = -2.4, x = 0.4$

5. $y = 3x - 1$

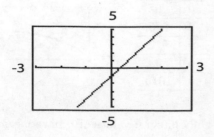

9. $y = 6 - x$

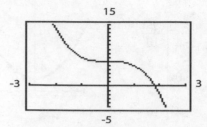

13. Graph $y = x^2 + x - 5$ and use the zero feature to solve.

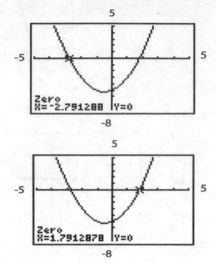

$x = -2.8, x = 1.8$

17. $\sqrt{5R + 2} = 3 \Rightarrow \sqrt{5R + 2} - 3 = 0$

Graph $y = \sqrt{5x + 2} - 3$ and use zero feature to solve.

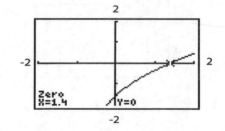

$x = 1.4$

21. From the graph, $y = \dfrac{4}{x^2 - 4}$ has range $y \leq -1$ or $y > 0$.

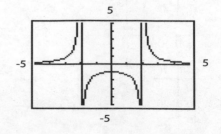

25. Graph $y = \dfrac{x+1}{\sqrt{x-2}}$ on graphing calculator and use the minimum feature, then from the graph, $Y(y) = \dfrac{y+1}{\sqrt{y-2}}$ has range $Y(y) \geq 3.464$.

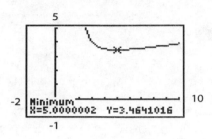

29. function: $y = 3x$
function shifted up 1: $y = 3x + 1$

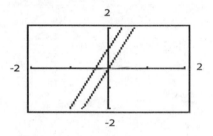

33. function; $y = -2x^2$
function shifted down 3, left 2: $y = -2(x+2)^2 - 3$

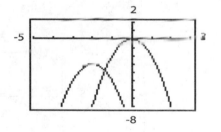

37. $i = 0.1v - 0.06$, graph $y = 0.01x - 0.06$
From the graph, $v = 6.0\,V$ for $i = 0$.

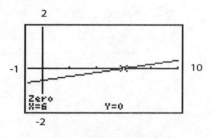

41. $A = 520 = lw = (w+12)w = w^2 + 12w \Rightarrow w^2 + 12w - 520 = 0$

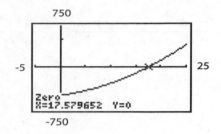

The approximate dimensions, in cm, to 2 significant digits are $w \approx 18$ cm, $l \approx 30$ cm.

45. $x^2 - 2x = 1 \Rightarrow x^2 - 2x - 1 = 0$

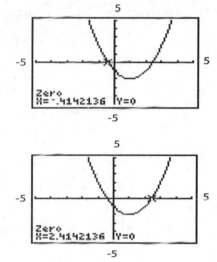

$x = -0.4142,\ x = 2.4142$

49. (a) Since V is increasing at a constant rate and $V = \dfrac{4}{3}\pi r^3$ it seems reasonable that r^3 should be increasing at a constant rate. Thus, r should be proportional to the cube root of time, $r = k\sqrt[3]{t}$.

(b) $r = \sqrt[3]{3t}$ would be a typical situation.

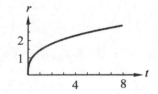

3.6   Graphs of Functions Defined by Tables of Data

1.

Week	1	2	3	4	5	6	7	8
Production	765	780	840	850	880	840	760	820

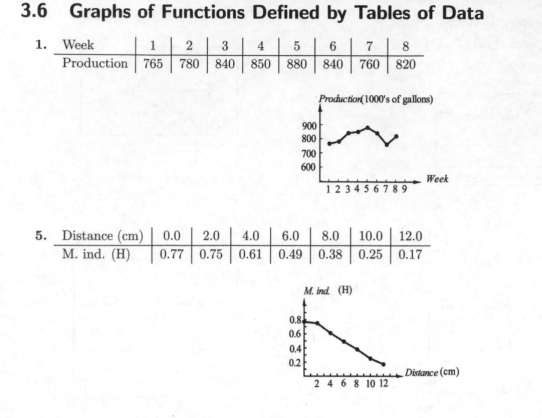

5.

Distance (cm)	0.0	2.0	4.0	6.0	8.0	10.0	12.0
M. ind. (H)	0.77	0.75	0.61	0.49	0.38	0.25	0.17

9. (a) Reading from the graph, $T = 132°C$ for $t = 4.3$ min.

(b) Reading from the graph, $t = 0.7$ min for $T = 145.0°C$.

13.

$$2 \left[1.2 \begin{array}{cc} \begin{bmatrix} 8.0 & 0.38 \\ 9.2 & ? \\ 10.0 & 0.25 \end{bmatrix} & x \end{array} \right] -0.13$$

$$\frac{1.2}{2} = \frac{x}{-0.13}, x = -0.78$$

Therefore $M = 0.38 - 0.078 = 0.30$ H

17.

Height (ft)	0	1.0	2.0	4.0	6.0	8.0	12
Rate (ft^3/s)	0	10	15	22	27	31	35

(a) For $R = 20$ ft^3/s, $H = 3.4$ ft   **(b)** For $H = 2.5$ ft, $R = 17$ ft^3/s

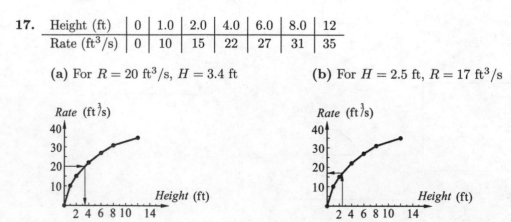

21. $10 \begin{bmatrix} 6 & \begin{bmatrix} 30 & 0.30 \\ 46 & ? \\ 40 & 0.37 \end{bmatrix} & x \end{bmatrix} 0.07$

$\dfrac{6}{10} = \dfrac{x}{0.07}, \; x = 0.042$

Therefore, $f = 0.30 + 0.042 = 0.34$

25. The graph is extended using a straight line segment. $T \approx 130.3°C$ for $t = 5.3$ min

Chapter 3 Review Exercises

1. $A = \pi r^2 = \pi(2t)^2$
$A = 4\pi t^2$

5. $f(x) = 7x - 5$
$f(3) = 7(3) - 5 = 21 - 5 = 16$
$f(-6) = 7(-6) - 5 = -42 - 5 = -47$

9. $f(x) = 3x^2 - 2x + 4$

$f(x+h) - f(x) = 3(x+h)^2 - 2(x+h) + 4 - (3x^2 - 2x + 4)$
$= 3(x^2 + 2xh + h^2) - 2x - 2h + 4 - 3x^2 + 2x - 4$
$= 3x^2 + 6xh + 3h^2 - 2x - 2h + 4 - 3x^2 + 2x - 4$
$= 6xh + 3h^2 - 2h$

13. $f(x) = 8.07 - 2x$
$f(5.87) = 8.07 - 2 \cdot 5.87 = -3.67$
$f(-4.29) = 8.07 - 2(-4.29) = 16.65 \approx 16.7$

17. The domain of $f(x) = x^4 + 1$ is $-\infty < x < \infty$. The range is $y \geq 1$.

21. The graph of $y = 4x + 2$ is

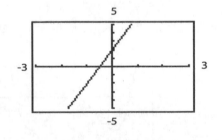

25. The graph of $y = 3 - x - 2x^2$ is

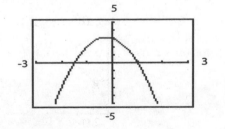

29. The graph of $y = 2 - x^4$ is

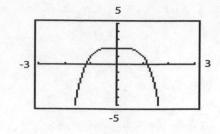

33. $7x - 3 = 0$

Graph $y = 7x - 3$ and use the zero feature to solve.

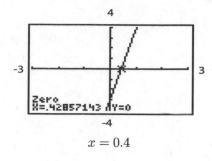

$x = 0.4$

37. $x^3 - x^2 = 2 - x \Rightarrow x^3 - x^2 + x - 2 = 0$

Graph $y = x^3 - x^2 + x - 2$ use the zero feature to solve.

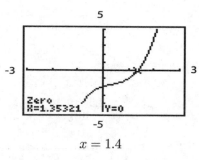

$x = 1.4$

41. Graph $y = x^4 - 5x^2$ and use the minimum feature, then from the graph, the range is $y \geq -6.25$.

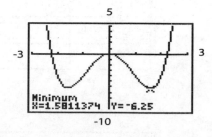

45. $A(a, b) = A(2, -3)$ is in QIV while $B(b, a) = B(-3, 2)$ is in QII.

49. $\left| \dfrac{y}{x} \right| > 0$ for $\dfrac{y}{x} \neq 0 \Rightarrow$ all (x, y) not on x-axis or y-axis.

53. $y = \sqrt{x - 1}$ shifted left 2 and up 1 is
$y = \sqrt{(x + 2) - 1} + 1$
$y = \sqrt{x + 1} + 1$

57. $I = f(m) = 12.5\sqrt{1 + 0.5m^2}$

$f(0.55) = 12.5\sqrt{1 + 0.5(0.55)^2} = 13.41203983\ldots \approx 13.4$

61. $T = f(t) = 28.0 + 0.15t,\ 0 \le t \le 30$

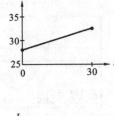

65. $L = 2\pi r + 12$

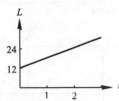

69. $P = f(i) = 1.5 \times 10^{-6}i^3 - 0.77,\ 80 \le i \le 140$

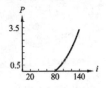

73. $d = f(D)$

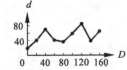

77. $d = f(t) = 250 - 60y,\ 0 \le t \le 2;\ d = f(t) = 130 - 40(t - 2),\ 2 < t < 5.25$

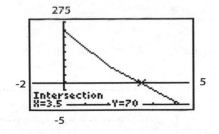

The person is 70 mi from home after 3.5 hours.

81. $v = 7.6x - 2.1x^2,\ 0 \le x \le 1.75$

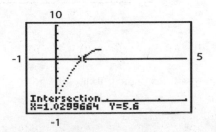

$x = 1.0299664 \approx 1.03$ ft for $v = 5.6$ ft/s

85. $V = \pi r^2 h = 250.0 \Rightarrow h = \dfrac{250.0}{\pi r^2}$

$A = A_{\text{base}} + A_{\text{side}} = \pi r^2 + 2\pi r h = \pi r^2 + 2\pi r \cdot \dfrac{250.0}{\pi r^2} = \pi r^2 + \dfrac{500.0}{r}$

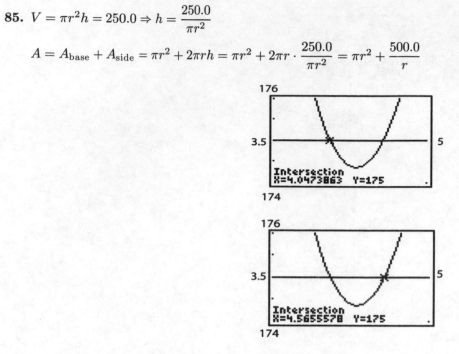

$r = 4.047$ cm, $r = 4.566$ cm when $A = 175.0$ cm^2.

THE TRIGONOMETRIC FUNCTIONS

4.1 Angles

1. $145.6° + 2(360°) = 865.6°$

5.

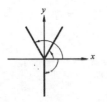

9. positive: $45° + 360° = 405°$
negative: $45° - 360° = -315°$

13. positive: $70°30' + 360 = 430°30'$
negative: $70°30' - 360° = -289°30'$

17. To change 0.265 rad to degrees multiply by $\dfrac{180}{\pi}$,

$0.265 \text{ rad} \left(\dfrac{180°}{\pi \text{ rad}} \right) \approx 15.18°$

21. $0.329 \text{ rad} \approx 18.85°$

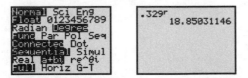

25. $56.0° = 0.977$ rad to three significant digits

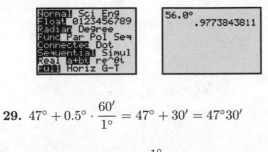

29. $47° + 0.5° \cdot \dfrac{60'}{1°} = 47° + 30' = 47°30'$

33. $15°12' = 15° + 12' \cdot \dfrac{1°}{60'} = 15.2°$

37. Angle in standard position terminal side passing through (4, 2).

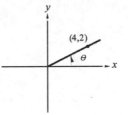

41. Angle in standard position terminal side passing through $(-7, 5)$.

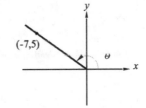

45. $31°$, QI; $310°$, QIV

49. 1 rad, QI; 2 rad, QII

53. $21°42'36''$

$= 21° + 42' \cdot \dfrac{1°}{60'} + 36'' \cdot \dfrac{1°}{60''} \cdot \dfrac{1°}{60'}$

$= 21.710°$

4.2 Defining the Trigonometric Functions

1. $r = \sqrt{4^2 + 3^2} = \sqrt{25} = 5$

$\sin \theta = \dfrac{3}{5}$

$\cos \theta = \dfrac{4}{5}$

$\tan \theta = \dfrac{3}{4}$

$\csc \theta = \dfrac{5}{3}$

$\sec \theta = \dfrac{5}{4}$

$\cot \theta = \dfrac{4}{3}$

5. $r = \sqrt{15^2 + 8^2} = \sqrt{289} = 17$

$$\sin\theta = \frac{y}{r} = \frac{8}{17}$$

$$\cos\theta = \frac{x}{r} = \frac{15}{17}$$

$$\tan\theta = \frac{y}{x} = \frac{8}{15}$$

$$\csc\theta = \frac{r}{y} = \frac{17}{8}$$

$$\sec\theta = \frac{r}{x} = \frac{17}{15}$$

$$\cot\theta = \frac{x}{y} = \frac{15}{8}$$

9. $r = \sqrt{1 + 15} = \sqrt{16} = 4$

$$\sin\theta = \frac{y}{r} = \frac{\sqrt{15}}{4}$$

$$\cos\theta = \frac{x}{r} = \frac{1}{4}$$

$$\tan\theta = \frac{y}{x} = \sqrt{15}$$

$$\csc\theta = \frac{r}{y} = \frac{4}{\sqrt{15}}$$

$$\sec\theta = \frac{r}{x} = 4$$

$$\cot\theta = \frac{x}{y} = \frac{1}{\sqrt{15}}$$

13. $r = \sqrt{5^2 + 2^2} = \sqrt{29}$

$$\sin\theta = \frac{y}{r} = \frac{2}{\sqrt{29}}$$

$$\cos\theta = \frac{x}{r} = \frac{5}{\sqrt{29}}$$

$$\tan\theta = \frac{y}{x} = \frac{2}{5}$$

$$\csc\theta = \frac{r}{y} = \frac{\sqrt{29}}{2}$$

$$\sec\theta = \frac{r}{x} = \frac{\sqrt{29}}{5}$$

$$\cot\theta = \frac{x}{y} = \frac{5}{2}$$

17. $\cos\theta = \frac{12}{13} \Rightarrow x = 12$ and $r = 13$ with θ in QI.

$$r^2 = x^2 + y^2 \Rightarrow 169 = 144 + y^2 \Rightarrow y^2 = 25$$
$$y = 5$$

$$\sin\theta = \frac{y}{r} = \frac{5}{13}, \cot\theta = \frac{x}{y} = \frac{12}{5}.$$

21. $\sin\theta = 0.750 \Rightarrow y = 0.750$ and $r = 1$ with θ in QI.

$$r^2 = x^2 + y^2 \Rightarrow 1^2$$
$$= x^2 + 0.750^2 \Rightarrow x^2$$
$$= 0.4375 \Rightarrow x = 0.661$$

$$\cot\theta = \frac{x}{y} = \frac{0.661}{0.750} = 0.881.$$

$$\csc\theta = \frac{r}{y} = \frac{1}{0.750} = 1.333.$$

25. For $(3, 4)$, $r = 5$,

$$\sin\theta = \frac{y}{r} = \frac{4}{5} \text{ and } \tan\theta = \frac{y}{x} = \frac{4}{3}.$$

For $(6, 8)$, $r = 10$,

$$\sin\theta = \frac{y}{r} = \frac{8}{10} = \frac{4}{5} \text{ and } \tan\theta = \frac{y}{x} = \frac{8}{6} = \frac{4}{3}.$$

For $(4.5, 6)$, $r = 7.5$,

$$\sin\theta = \frac{y}{r} = \frac{6}{7.5} = \frac{4}{5} \text{ and } \tan\theta = \frac{y}{x} = \frac{6}{4.5} = \frac{4}{3}.$$

29. $\sin^2\theta + \cos^2\theta = \left(\frac{3}{5}\right)^2 + \left(\frac{4}{5}\right)^2$

$$= \frac{9}{25} + \frac{16}{25}$$

$$= \frac{25}{25} = 1$$

33. $\tan\theta = \frac{y}{x} = \frac{6}{-2} = \frac{4}{x+1}$

$$6x + 6 = -8$$
$$6x = -14$$
$$x = -\frac{7}{3}$$

4.3   Values of the Trigonometric Functions

1. $\sin\theta = 0.3527$

$\theta = 20.65°$

```
sin⁻¹(0.3527)
        20.65254838
```

5. Answers may vary in exercises 5, 6, 7, 8. One set of measurements gives $x = 7.6$ and $y = 6.5$.

$$\sin 40° = \frac{6.5}{10} = 0.65$$

$$\cos 40° = \frac{7.6}{10} = 0.76$$

$$\tan 40° = \frac{6.5}{7.6} = 0.86$$

$$\csc 40° = \frac{10}{6.5} = 1.54$$

$$\sec 40° = \frac{10}{7.6} = 1.32$$

$$\cot 40° = \frac{7.6}{6.5} = 1.17$$

9. $\sin 22.4° = 0.381$

13. $\cos 15.71° = 0.9626$

17. $\cot 67.78° = 0.4085$

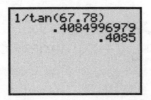

21. $\csc 49.3° = 1.32$

25. $\cos \theta = 0.3261$
$\theta = 70.97°$

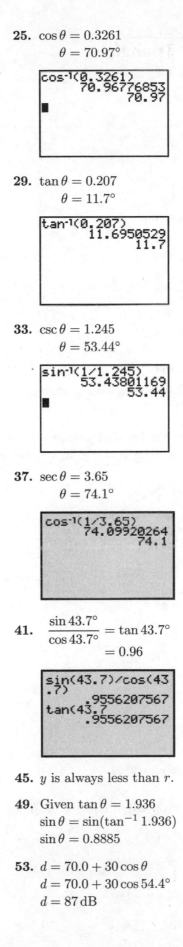

29. $\tan \theta = 0.207$
$\theta = 11.7°$

33. $\csc \theta = 1.245$
$\theta = 53.44°$

37. $\sec \theta = 3.65$
$\theta = 74.1°$

41. $\dfrac{\sin 43.7°}{\cos 43.7°} = \tan 43.7°$
$= 0.96$

45. y is always less than r.

49. Given $\tan \theta = 1.936$
$\sin \theta = \sin(\tan^{-1} 1.936)$
$\sin \theta = 0.8885$

53. $d = 70.0 + 30 \cos \theta$
$d = 70.0 + 30 \cos 54.4°$
$d = 87 \text{ dB}$

4.4   The Right Triangle

1.

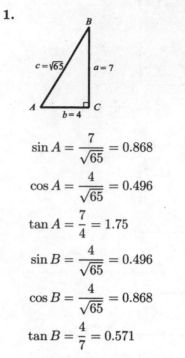

$$\sin A = \frac{7}{\sqrt{65}} = 0.868$$

$$\cos A = \frac{4}{\sqrt{65}} = 0.496$$

$$\tan A = \frac{7}{4} = 1.75$$

$$\sin B = \frac{4}{\sqrt{65}} = 0.496$$

$$\cos B = \frac{4}{\sqrt{65}} = 0.868$$

$$\tan B = \frac{4}{7} = 0.571$$

5. A 60° angle between sides of 3 in and 6 in determines the unique triangle shown in the figure below.

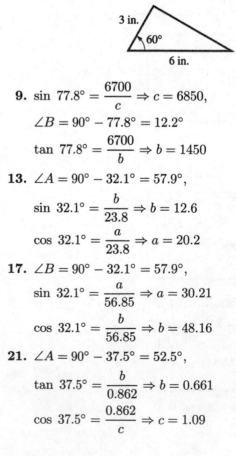

9. $\sin 77.8° = \dfrac{6700}{c} \Rightarrow c = 6850,$

  $\angle B = 90° - 77.8° = 12.2°$

  $\tan 77.8° = \dfrac{6700}{b} \Rightarrow b = 1450$

13. $\angle A = 90° - 32.1° = 57.9°,$

  $\sin 32.1° = \dfrac{b}{23.8} \Rightarrow b = 12.6$

  $\cos 32.1° = \dfrac{a}{23.8} \Rightarrow a = 20.2$

17. $\angle B = 90° - 32.1° = 57.9°,$

  $\sin 32.1° = \dfrac{a}{56.85} \Rightarrow a = 30.21$

  $\cos 32.1° = \dfrac{b}{56.85} \Rightarrow b = 48.16$

21. $\angle A = 90° - 37.5° = 52.5°,$

  $\tan 37.5° = \dfrac{b}{0.862} \Rightarrow b = 0.661$

  $\cos 37.5° = \dfrac{0.862}{c} \Rightarrow c = 1.09$

25. $\tan A = \dfrac{591.87}{264.93} \Rightarrow A = 65.89°;$

  $\tan B = \dfrac{264.93}{591.87} \Rightarrow B = 24.11°$

  $c = \sqrt{264.93^2 + 591.87^2} = 648.46$

29. $\sin 61.7° = \dfrac{3.92}{x} \Rightarrow x = \dfrac{3.92}{\sin 61.7°} = 4.45$

33.

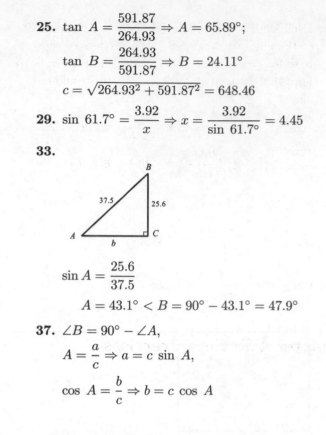

$$\sin A = \frac{25.6}{37.5}$$

  $A = 43.1° < B = 90° - 43.1° = 47.9°$

37. $\angle B = 90° - \angle A,$

  $A = \dfrac{a}{c} \Rightarrow a = c \sin A,$

  $\cos A = \dfrac{b}{c} \Rightarrow b = c \cos A$

4.5   Applications of Right Triangles

1. $90° - 62.1° = 27.9°$

  $d = 2090 \text{ ft}$

5. $\tan 62.6° = \dfrac{h}{22.8}$

  $h = 22.8 \tan 62.6° = 44.0 \text{ ft}$

9. $\cos 76.67° = \dfrac{196.0}{h}$

  $h = \dfrac{196.0}{\cos 76.67°} = 850.1 \text{ cm}$

13.

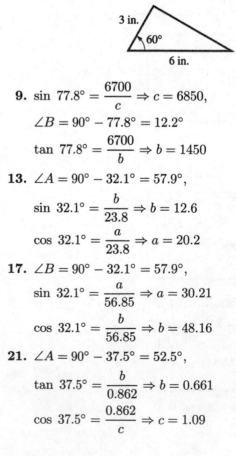

$$\tan 1.2° = \frac{h}{9.8}$$

  $h = 9.8 \tan 1.2°$

  $h = 0.21 \text{ mi}$

17. $\theta = \tan^{-1} \dfrac{6.0}{100} = 3.4°$

21. $\theta = \sin^{-1} \dfrac{12.0}{85.0} = 8.1°$

25. Each angle of the pentagon is $\frac{360°}{5} = 72°$. Radii drawn from the center of the pentagon (which is also the center of the circle) through adjacent vertices of the pentagon outward to the fence form an isosceles triangle with base 92.5 and equal sides x. A $\perp$ bisector from the center of the pentagon to the base this isosceles triangle forms a right triangle with hypotenuse x and base 46.25. The base angle of this right triangle is $\frac{180°-72°}{2} = 54°$. Thus,

$$\cos(54°) = \frac{46.25}{x} \Rightarrow x = \frac{46.25}{\cos 54°} \text{ and } C = 2\pi(x + 25)$$

$$C = 2\pi\left(\frac{46.25}{\cos 54°} + 25\right) = 651 \text{ ft}$$

29. $\qquad \frac{1}{2}C = \frac{1}{2}[2\pi(11.8 + 1)] = 12.8\pi$

$$\cos 31.8° = \frac{12.8\pi}{l} \Rightarrow l = 47.3 \text{ m}$$

33. $\tan\frac{\theta}{2} = \frac{\frac{d}{2}}{x} = \frac{\frac{d}{2}}{\tan\frac{\theta}{2}} = 0.5d\cot\frac{\theta}{2}$

Chapter 4 Review Exercises

1. $17.0° + 360.0° = 377.0°, \quad 17.0 - 360.0° = -343.0°$
 5. and 9. $31°54' = 31.9°, 17.5° = 17°30'$

13. $\quad r = \sqrt{x^2 + y^2} = \sqrt{24^2 + 7^2} = \sqrt{625} = 25$

$$\sin\theta = \frac{y}{r} = \frac{7}{25} \qquad\qquad \csc\theta = \frac{r}{y} = \frac{25}{7}$$

$$\cos\theta = \frac{x}{r} = \frac{24}{25} \qquad\qquad \sec\theta = \frac{r}{x} = \frac{25}{24}$$

$$\tan\theta = \frac{y}{x} = \frac{7}{24} \qquad\qquad \cot\theta = \frac{x}{y} = \frac{24}{7}$$

17. $r^2 = x^2 + y^2 \Rightarrow 13^2 = x^2 + 5^2 \Rightarrow x = 12$

$$\cos\theta = \frac{x}{r} = \frac{12}{13} = 0.923$$

$$\cot\theta = \frac{x}{y} = \frac{12}{5} = 2.40$$

21. $\sin 72.1° = 0.952$

25. $\sec 18.4° = 1.05$

Note: image 1 (graphing calculator display) shows:
```
31°54'
                31.9
17.5▸DMS
          17°30'0"
```

Note: image 2 (graphing calculator display) shows:
```
sin(72.1)
      .9515944039
            .952
```

The image for exercise 25 (graphing calculator display) shows:
```
1/cos(18.4)
      1.053878471
            1.05
```

29. $\cos \theta = 0.950$
$\theta = 18.2°$

```
cos⁻¹(0.950)
       18.19487234
              18.2
```

33. $\csc \theta = 4.713$
$\theta = 12.3°$

```
sin⁻¹(1/4.713)
       12.25008249
              12.3
```

37. $\angle B = 90.0° - 17.0° = 73.0°$ $\tan 17.0° = \dfrac{a}{6.00} \Rightarrow a = 1.83$

$\cos 17.0° = \dfrac{6.00}{c} \Rightarrow c = \dfrac{6.00}{\cos 17.0°} = 6.27$

41. $\angle B = 90.0° - 37.5° = 52.5°$ $\tan 37.5° = \dfrac{12.0}{b} \Rightarrow b = 15.6$

$\sin 37.5° = \dfrac{12.0}{c} \Rightarrow c = \dfrac{12.0}{\sin 37.5°} = 19.7$

45. $\angle B = 90.00° - 49.67° = 40.33°$ $\sin 49.67° = \dfrac{a}{0.8253} \Rightarrow a = 0.6292$

$\cos 49.67° = \dfrac{b}{0.8253} \Rightarrow b = 0.5341$

49.

$90° - 25° = 65°$

$\tan 65° = \dfrac{x}{d} \Rightarrow d = \dfrac{x}{\tan 65°}$

$\tan 25° = \dfrac{x}{12 - d} = \dfrac{x}{12 - \dfrac{x}{\tan 65°}}$

$x = \left(12 - \dfrac{x}{\tan 65°}\right) \tan 25°$

$x = 12 \tan 25° - x \cdot \dfrac{\tan 25°}{\tan 65°}$

$x \left(1 + \dfrac{\tan 25°}{\tan 65°}\right) = 12 \tan 25°$

$x = \dfrac{12 \tan 25°}{1 + \dfrac{\tan 25°}{\tan 65°}}$

$x = 4.6$

53.

$$\tan\theta = \frac{2}{3} = \frac{7}{x}$$

$$2x = 21$$

$$x = 10.5$$

57. $e = E\cos\alpha \Rightarrow 56.9 = 339\cos\alpha \Rightarrow \alpha = \cos^{-1}\frac{56.9}{339} = 80.3°$

61. (a) A triangle with angle θ included between sides a and b, the base, has an altitude of $a\sin\theta$. The area, A, is $A = \frac{1}{2} \cdot b \cdot a\sin\theta$.

(b) The area of the tract is $A = \frac{1}{2} \cdot 31.96 \cdot 47.25\sin 64.09° = 679.2 \text{ m}^2$.

65.

$$A = lw$$

$$A = \frac{1.50}{\cos 42.5°}(4.80)$$

$$A = 9.77 \text{ ft}^2$$

69. $d = a + b = \dfrac{1.85}{\tan 28.3°} + \dfrac{1.85}{\tan(90.0° - 28.3°)} = 4.43 \text{ m}$

73. $\sin 31.0° = \dfrac{d}{x} \Rightarrow \sin 31.0° = \dfrac{14.2\sin 21.8°}{x} \Rightarrow x = \dfrac{14.2\sin 21.8°}{\sin 31.0°} = 10.2 \text{ in}$

77. Each angle of a regular pentagon is $\frac{(5-2)\cdot 180}{5} = 108°$. A regular pentagon with a side of 45.0 mm consists of 5 triangles of base 45.0 and altitude of $22.5\tan 54°$. The area of 12 such pentagons is $12 \cdot 5 \cdot \frac{1}{2} \cdot 45.0 \cdot 22.5\tan 54°$ or 41,807.60083 mm². Each angle of a regular hexagon is $\frac{(6-2)\cdot 180}{6} = 120°$. A regular hexagon with a side of 45.0 mm consists of 6 triangles of base 45.0 and an altitude of $22.5\tan 60°$. The area of 20 such hexagons is

$$20 \cdot 6 \cdot \frac{1}{2} \cdot 45 \cdot 22.5\tan 60° = 105,222.0866 \text{ mm}^2.$$

Thus, the area of 12 regular pentagons of side 45.0 mm and 20 regular hexagons of side 45.0 mm is 147,029.6874 mm² (147,000 mm² rounded off). Since this is the area of a flat surface it approximates the area of the spherical soccer ball which is given by

$$4\pi r^2 = 4\pi \cdot \left(\frac{222}{2}\right)^2 = 154,830.2523 \text{ mm}^2 \text{ (155,000 mm}^2 \text{ rounded off).}$$

81. $h = a + b = 375 \sin 25° + d \tan 42°$
$\qquad\qquad = 375 \sin 25° + 375 \cos 25° \tan 42°$
$\qquad\qquad = 464 \text{ m}$

85. For small angles, such as 2.3°, the sine and tangent are approximately equal.

$$\sin \ 2.3° = 0.0401317925 \approx \tan \ 2.3° = 0.040164149.$$

Chapter 5

SYSTEMS OF LINEAR EQUATIONS; DETERMINANTS

5.1 Linear Equations

1. $x - \dfrac{y}{6} + z - 4w = 7 \Rightarrow x - \dfrac{1}{6}y + z - 4w = 7$ is linear.

5. The coordinates of the point $(3, 1)$ do not satisfy the equation since $2(3) + 3(1) = 6 + 3 = 9$.
The coordinates of the point $(5, 1/3)$ do not satisfy the equation since $2(5) + 3\left(\dfrac{1}{3}\right) = 10 + 1 = 11 \neq 9$.

9. $3(2) - 2y = 12;\ 2y = 6 - 12 = -6;\ y = -3$
$3(-3) - 2y = 12;\ 2y = -9 - 12 = -21;\ y = -\dfrac{21}{2}$

13. $4\left(\dfrac{2}{3}\right) - 9y = 8;\ 9y = \dfrac{8}{3} - 8 = -\dfrac{16}{3};\ y = -\dfrac{16}{27}$

$4\left(-\dfrac{1}{2}\right) - 9y = 8;\ 9y = -2 - 8 = -10;\ y = \dfrac{-10}{9}$

17. If the values $A = -2$ and $B = 1$ satisfy both equations, they are a solution.

$-2 + 5(1) = 3 \neq -7;\ 3(-2) - 4(1) = -10 \neq -4$

Since the given values do not satisfy both equations, they are not a solution.

21. If the values $x = 0.6$ and $y = -0.2$ satisfy both equations, they are a solution.

$3(0.6) - 2(-0.2) = 2.2;\ 5(0.6) - 0.2 = 2.8$

Therefore the given values are a solution.

25. If $p = 260$ mi/h and $w = 40$ mi/h, then

$p + w = 260 + 40 = 300$ mi/h
$p - w = 260 - 40 = 220$ mi/h

The speeds are 260 mi/h and 40 mi/h.

5.2 Graphs of Linear Functions

1. $(-1, -2), (3, -1)$

$m = \dfrac{-1 - (-2)}{3 - (-1)} = \dfrac{1}{4}$. The line rises 1 unit for each 4 units in going from left to right.

5. By taking $(3, 8)$ as (x_2, y_2) and $(1, 0)$ as (x_1, y_1)

$$m = \frac{8 - 0}{3 - 1} = \frac{8}{2} = 4$$

9. By taking $(-2, -5)$ as (x_2, y_2) and $(5, -3)$ as (x_1, y_1)

$$m = \frac{-5 - (-3)}{-2 - 5} = \frac{-5 + 3}{-7} = \frac{2}{7}$$

13. $m = 2,\ (0, -1)$

Plot the y-intercept point $(0, -1)$. Since the slope is 2/1, from this point, go over 1 unit and up 2 units, and plot a second point. Sketch the line between the 2 points.

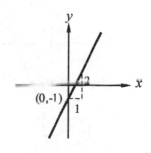

17. $m = \dfrac{1}{2},\ (0, 0)$

Plot the y-intercept point $(0, 0)$. Since the slope is $\dfrac{1}{2}$, from this point, go over 2 units and up 1 unit, and plot a second point. Sketch the line between the 2 points.

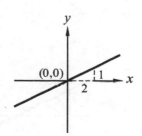

21. $y = -2x + 1$, $m = -2$, $b = 1$

Plot the y-intercept point $(0, 1)$. Since the slope is $-2/1$, from this point, go over 1 unit and down 2 units, and plot a second point. Sketch the line between the 2 points.

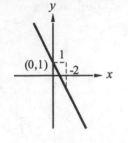

25. $5x - 2y = 40 \Rightarrow y = \dfrac{5}{2}x - 20$, $m = \dfrac{5}{2}$, $b = -20$

Plot the y-intercept point $(0, -20)$. Since the slope is $5/2$, from this point, go over 2 units and up 5 units, and plot a second point. Sketch the line between these 2 points.

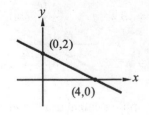

29. $x + 2y = 4|_{x=0} \Rightarrow 0 + 2y = 4 \Rightarrow y\text{-int} = 2$

$x + 2y = 4|_{y=0} \Rightarrow x + 2 \cdot 0 = 4 \Rightarrow x\text{-int} = 4$

Plot the y-intercept point $(4, 0)$ and the y-intercept point $(0, 2)$. Sketch the line between these 2 points. A third point is found as a check. Let $x = -2$, $-2 + 2y = 4$, $2y = 6$, $y = 3$. Therefore the point $(-2, 3)$ should lie on the line.

33. $y = 3x + 6|_{x=0} \Rightarrow y = 3 \cdot 0 + 6 \Rightarrow y\text{-int} = 6$

$y = 3x + 6|_{y=0} \Rightarrow 0 = 3x + 6 \Rightarrow x\text{-int} = -2$

Plot the x-intercept point $(-2, 0)$ and the y-intercept point $(0, 6)$. Sketch the line between these 2 points. A third point is found as a check. Let $x = 1$, $y = 3(1) + 6 = 9$. Therefore the point $(1, 9)$ should lie on the line.

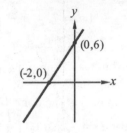

37. $d = 0.2l + 1.2$

"The d-intercept is $(0, 1.2)$. Since the slope is $2/10$, from the d-intercept go over 10 units and up 2 units the point $(10, 3.2)$ and plot a second point. Sketch the line between these 2 points."

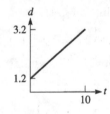

5.3   Solving Systems of Two Linear Equations in Two Unknowns Graphically

1. $2x + 5y = 10$. Let $x = 0$, $y = 0$ to find intercepts of $(0, 2)$, $(5, 0)$. A third point is $\left(1, \dfrac{8}{5}\right)$.

$3x + y = 6$. Let $x = 0, y = 0$ to find intercepts of $(0, 6)$, $(2, 0)$. A third point is $(1, 3)$.

From the graph the solution is approximately $x = 1.5$, $y = 1.4$.

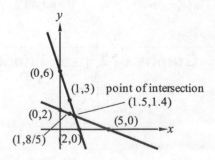

5. $y = 2x - 6$; $y = -\left(\dfrac{1}{3}\right)x + 1$

The slope of the first line is 2, and the y-intercept is -6. The slope of the second line is $-1/3$, and the y-intercept is 1. From the graph, the point of intersection is $(3.0, 0.0)$. Therefore, the solution of the system of equations is $x = 3.0$, $y = 0.0$.

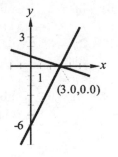

9. $2x - 5y = 10$; $3x + 4y = -12$

The intercepts of the first line are $(5, 0), (0, -2)$. A third point is $(1, -\frac{8}{5})$.

The intercepts of the second line are $(-4, 0), (0, -3)$. A third point is $(\frac{4}{3}, 4)$.

From the graph, the point of intersection is $x = -0.9$, $y = -2.3$.

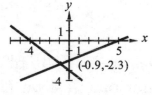

13. $y = -x + 3$; $y = -2x + 3$

The intercepts of the first line are $(3, 0), (0, 3)$. A third point is $(2, 1)$.
The intercepts of the second line are $(\frac{3}{2}, 0), (0, 3)$. A third point is $(1, 1)$.
From the graph, the point of intersection is $(0.0, 3.0)$. The solution of the system of equations is $x = 0.0$, $y = 3.0$.

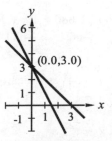

17. $-2r_1 + 2r_2 = 7$; $4r_1 - 2r_2 = 1$

The intercepts of the first line are $(-\frac{7}{2}, 0)(0, \frac{7}{2})$. A third point is $(-2, \frac{3}{2})$.
The intercepts of the second line are $(\frac{1}{4}, 0), (0, -\frac{1}{2})$. A third point is $(1, \frac{3}{2})$.
From the graph, the point of intersection is $(4.0, 7.5)$, and the solution of the system of equations is $r_1 = 4.0$, $r_2 = 7.5$.

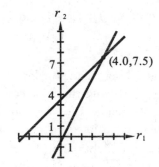

21. $x = 4y + 2 \Leftrightarrow y = \dfrac{x - 2}{4}$ and

$3y = 2x + 3 \Leftrightarrow y = \dfrac{2x + 3}{3}$

On a graphing calculator let $y_1 = \dfrac{x - 2}{4}$ and $y_2 = \dfrac{2x + 3}{3}$. Using the intersect feature, the point of intersection is $(-3.6, -1.4)$, and the solution of the system of equations is $x = -3.6$, $y = -1.4$.

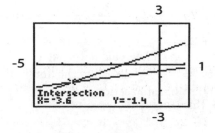

25. $x - 5y = 10 \Leftrightarrow y = \dfrac{x - 10}{5}$ and

$2x - 10y = 20 \Leftrightarrow y = \dfrac{x - 10}{5}$

On a graphing calculator let $y_1 = \frac{x-10}{5}$ and $y_2 = \frac{x-10}{5}$. From the graph the lines are the same.

The system is dependent.

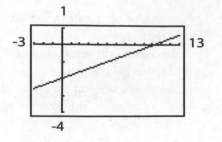

29. $5x - y = 3 \Leftrightarrow y = 5x - 3$ and

$$4x = 2y - 3 \Leftrightarrow y = \frac{4x + 3}{2}$$

On a graphing calculator let $y_1 = 5x - 3$ and $y_2 = \frac{4x+3}{2}$. Using the intersect feature, the point of intersection is $(1.5, 4.5)$, and the solution to the system of equations is $x = 1.5$, $y = 4.5$.

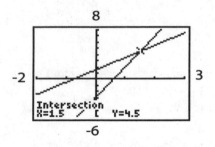

33. $0.8T_1 - 0.6T_2 = 12 \Leftrightarrow$

$$T_2 = \frac{0.8T_1 - 12}{0.6} \Rightarrow y = \frac{0.8x - 12}{0.6}$$

$0.6T_1 + 0.8T_2 = 68 \Leftrightarrow$

$$T_2 = \frac{68 - 0.6T_1}{0.8} \Rightarrow y = \frac{68 - 0.6x}{0.8}$$

On a graphing calculator let $y_1 = \frac{0.8x-12}{0.6}$ and $y_2 = \frac{68-0.6x}{0.8}$. Using the intersect feature, the point of intersection is $(50, 47)$. The tensions are $T_1 = 50$ N, $T_2 = 47$ N.

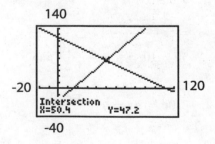

5.4 Solving Systems of Two Linear Equations in Two Unknowns Algebraically

1. (1) $x - 3y = 6 \Rightarrow x = 3y + 6$
  (2) $2x - 3y = 3$

  $2(3y + 6) - 3y = 3$ substitute x from
          (1) into (2)

  $6y + 12 - 3y = 3$
     $3y = -9$
      $y = -3$
  $x - 3(-3) = 6$ substitute -3 for
         y in (1)

   $x + 9 = 6$
     $x = -3$

5. (1) $x = y + 3$
  (2) $x - 2y = 5$

  $(y + 3) - 2y = 5$ substitute x from
          (1) into (2)

    $-y = 2$
     $y = -2$ substitute -2 for
         y in (1)
  $x = -2 + 3 = 1$

9. (1) $x + y = -5, y = -x - 5$
  (2) $2x - y = 2$

  $2x - (-x - 5) = 2$ substitute y from
          (1) into (2)

    $3x = -3$
     $x = -1$
  $-1 + y = -5$ substitute -1
        for x in (1)
    $y = -4$

13. (1) $33x + 2y = 34 \Rightarrow y = -\dfrac{33}{2}x + 17$

  (2) $40y = 9x + 11$

  $40\left(-\dfrac{33}{2}x + 17\right) = 9x + 11$ substitute y from
             (1) in (2)

  $-660x + 680 = 9x + 11$
    $-669x = -669$
      $x = 1$

  $33(1) + 2y = 34$ substitute 1 for x in (1)
    $2y = 1$

     $y = \dfrac{1}{2}$

17. $x + 2y = 5$
$\underline{x - 2y = 1}$
$\quad 2x = 6$
$\quad\quad x = 3$
$3 + 2y = 5$
$\quad 2y = 2$
$\quad\quad y = 1$
$(3, 1)$

21. (1) $12t + 9y = 14 \Rightarrow \quad 12t + \ 9y = \ 14$
(2) $6t = 7y - 16 \Rightarrow \underline{-12t + 14y = +32}$ add
$\quad\quad\quad\quad\quad\quad\quad\quad\quad 23y = \ 46$
$\quad\quad\quad\quad\quad\quad\quad\quad\quad\quad y = 2$

$12t + 9(2) = 14$ substitute 2 for y in (1)
$\quad 12t = -4$

$\quad\quad t = -\dfrac{1}{3}$

25. (1) $2x - 3y - 4 = \quad 0$
(2) $\quad\quad 3x + 2 = \ 2y$ put (1) in standard form
(3) $\quad\quad 2x - 3y = \quad 4$ recopy (2)
(4) $\quad\quad 3x - 2y = -2$ put (2) in standard form
(5) $\quad\quad 6x - 9y = \quad 12$ (3) multiplied by 3
(6) $\underline{-6x + 4y = \quad 4}$ (4) multiplied by -2
$\quad\quad\quad\quad -5y = 16$

$\quad\quad\quad\quad y = -\dfrac{16}{5}$

from (1) $x = \dfrac{3y + 4}{2} = \dfrac{3\left(-\dfrac{16}{5}\right) + 4}{2} = -\dfrac{14}{5}$,
$\left(-\dfrac{14}{5}, -\dfrac{16}{5}\right)$ is the solution.

29. (1) $2x - y = 5, y = 2x - 5$
(2) $6x + 2y = -5$
$6x + 2(2x - 5) = -5$ substitute y from
$\quad\quad\quad\quad\quad\quad\quad\quad$ (1) into (2)
$\quad\quad 10x = 5$

$\quad\quad\quad x = \dfrac{1}{2}$
$y = 2\left(\dfrac{1}{2}\right) - 5 = -4$ substitute $\dfrac{1}{2}$
$\quad\quad\quad\quad\quad\quad\quad\quad$ for x in (1)

$x = \dfrac{1}{2}$, from (1) $y = 2x - 5 = 2 \cdot \dfrac{1}{2} - 5 = 1 - 5 = -4$

$\left(\dfrac{1}{2}, -4\right)$

33. (1) $15x + 10y = 11 \Rightarrow \quad 75x + 50y = 55$
(2) $20x - 25y = \ 7 \Rightarrow \underline{40x - 50y = 14}$ add
$\quad\quad\quad\quad\quad\quad\quad\quad\quad 115x \quad\quad = 69$

$\quad\quad\quad\quad\quad\quad\quad x = \dfrac{3}{5}$

$15\left(\dfrac{3}{5}\right) + 10y = 11$ substitute $\frac{3}{5}$ for x in (1)
$\quad\quad\quad 10y = 2$

$\quad\quad\quad\quad y = \dfrac{1}{5}$

37. (1) $44A = 1 - 15B \Rightarrow \quad 44A + 15B = \quad 1$
(2) $5B = 22 + 7A \Rightarrow \quad 7A - \ 5B = -22$

(1) $44A + 15B = \quad 1$
(2) $\underline{21A - 15B = -66}$ multiply (2) by 3
$\quad 65A \quad\quad = -65$
$\quad\quad A = -1$

$5B = 22 + 7(-1)$ substitute (-1) for A in (2)
$5B = 15$
$\ B = 3$

41. $V_1 + V_2 = 15$
$\underline{V_1 - V_2 = 3}$
$2V_1 = 18$
$V_1 = 9\ V$

$9 + V_2 = 15 \Rightarrow V_2 = 6$, the solution is $V_1 = 9$ and $V_2 = 6\ V$

45. $W_r + W_f = 17{,}700$

$\dfrac{W_r}{W_f} = 0.847 \Rightarrow W_r = 0.847 W_f$

$0.847 W_f + W_f = 17{,}700$

$\quad\quad W_f = \dfrac{17{,}700}{1 + 0.847}$

$\quad\quad W_f = 9580\ N$

$W_r = 0.847 W_f$

$\quad = \left(\dfrac{17{,}700}{1 + 0.847}\right)$

$W_r = 8120\ N$

49. w = capacity of windmill in kW,
g = capacity of generator in kW

(1) $\quad 0.45w(10 \cdot 24) + g(10 \cdot 24) = 3010$
for first 10 day period

(2) $\quad\quad\quad\quad 108w + 240g = 3010$

(3) $\quad\quad\quad\quad 54w + 120g = 1505$

(4) $\quad 0.72w(10 \cdot 24) + g(10 \cdot 24 - 60) = 2900$
for second 10 day period

(5) $\quad\quad\quad\quad 172.8w + 180g = 2900$

Solving (3) and (5) gives $w = 7.00$ kW,
$g = 9.39$ kW

53. Let $x =$ the amount of sales; $x + 8000$
$\quad\quad = $ this month.
$\quad\quad x =$ last month

so $x + 8000 + x = 4000 - 2x$
$\quad\quad 2x + 8000 = 4000 - 2x$

$0 = 4000$ inconsistent; incorrect conclusion or error in sales figures.

5.5 Solving Systems of Two Linear Equations in Two Unknowns by Determinants

1. $\begin{vmatrix} 4 & -6 \\ 3 & 17 \end{vmatrix} = 4(17) - 3(-6) = 68 + 18 = 86$

5. $\begin{vmatrix} 2 & 4 \\ 3 & 1 \end{vmatrix} = (2)(1) - (3)(4) = 2 - 12 = -10$

9. $\begin{vmatrix} 8 & -10 \\ 0 & 4 \end{vmatrix} = (8)(4) - (0)(-10) = 32 - 0 = 32$

13. $\begin{vmatrix} 0.75 & -1.32 \\ 0.15 & 1.18 \end{vmatrix} = 0.75(1.18) - (0.15)(-1.32)$
$\quad\quad\quad\quad\quad\quad = 0.885 + 0.198 = 1.083$

17. $x + 2y = 5$
$\quad\ x - 2y = 1$

$x = \dfrac{\begin{vmatrix} 5 & 2 \\ 1 & -2 \end{vmatrix}}{\begin{vmatrix} 1 & 2 \\ 1 & -2 \end{vmatrix}} = \dfrac{(5)(-2) - (1)(2)}{(1)(-2) - (1)(2)}$
$\quad = \dfrac{-10 - 2}{-2 - 2} = 3$

$y = \dfrac{\begin{vmatrix} 1 & 5 \\ 1 & 1 \end{vmatrix}}{-4} = \dfrac{(1)(1) - (1)(5)}{-4}$
$\quad = \dfrac{1 - 5}{-4} = 1$

21. Rewrite the system with both equations in standard form.

$12t + 9y = 14$
$\ 6t - 7y = -16$

$t = \dfrac{\begin{vmatrix} 14 & 9 \\ -16 & -7 \end{vmatrix}}{\begin{vmatrix} 12 & 9 \\ 6 & -7 \end{vmatrix}} = \dfrac{46}{-138} = -\dfrac{1}{3},$

$y = \dfrac{\begin{vmatrix} 12 & 14 \\ 6 & -16 \end{vmatrix}}{-138} = \dfrac{-276}{-138} = 2$

25. -3 Rewrite the system with both equations in standard form.

$2x - 3y = 4$
$3x - 2y = -2$

$x = \dfrac{\begin{vmatrix} 4 & -3 \\ -2 & -2 \end{vmatrix}}{\begin{vmatrix} 2 & -3 \\ 3 & -2 \end{vmatrix}} = -2.8 = -\dfrac{14}{5}$

$y = \dfrac{\begin{vmatrix} 2 & 4 \\ 3 & -2 \end{vmatrix}}{\begin{vmatrix} 2 & -3 \\ 3 & -2 \end{vmatrix}} = -3.2 = \dfrac{-16}{5}$

29. $2.1x - 1.0y = 5.2$
$\quad\ 5.8x + 1.6y = -5.4$

$x = \dfrac{\begin{vmatrix} 5.2 & -1.0 \\ -5.4 & 1.6 \end{vmatrix}}{\begin{vmatrix} 2.1 & -1.0 \\ 5.8 & 1.6 \end{vmatrix}} = 0.32$

$y = \dfrac{\begin{vmatrix} 2.1 & 5.2 \\ 5.8 & -5.4 \end{vmatrix}}{\begin{vmatrix} 2.1 & -1.0 \\ 5.8 & 1.6 \end{vmatrix}} = -4.5$

33. $301x - 529y = 1520$
$385x - 741 = 2540$

$$x = \frac{\begin{vmatrix} 1520 & -529 \\ 2540 & -741 \end{vmatrix}}{\begin{vmatrix} 301 & -529 \\ 385 & -741 \end{vmatrix}} = -11.2$$

$$y = \frac{\begin{vmatrix} 301 & 1520 \\ 385 & 2540 \end{vmatrix}}{\begin{vmatrix} 301 & -529 \\ 385 & -741 \end{vmatrix}} = -9.26$$

37. Rewrite the system with both equations in standard form.

$F_1 + F_2 = 21$
$2F_1 - 5F_2 = 0$

$$F_1 = \frac{\begin{vmatrix} 21 & 1 \\ 0 & -5 \end{vmatrix}}{\begin{vmatrix} 1 & 1 \\ 2 & -5 \end{vmatrix}} = 15 \text{ lb}$$

$$F_2 = \frac{\begin{vmatrix} 1 & 21 \\ 2 & 0 \end{vmatrix}}{\begin{vmatrix} 1 & 1 \\ 2 & -5 \end{vmatrix}} = 6 \text{ lb}$$

41. x = number of phones, y = number of detectors

(1) $x + y = 320$
(2) $110x + 160y = 40,700$

Solving (1) and (2) gives $x = 210$ phones, $y = 110$ detectors

45. Convert 24 minutes to hours.
24 min = 0.4 h

$t_2 = t_1 - 0.4 \Leftrightarrow t_1 - t_2 = 0.4$

$42t_1 = 50t_2 \Leftrightarrow 42t_1 - 50t_2 = 0$

$$t_1 = \frac{\begin{vmatrix} 0.4 & -1 \\ 0 & -50 \end{vmatrix}}{\begin{vmatrix} 1 & -1 \\ 42 & -50 \end{vmatrix}} = 2.5 \text{ h}$$

$$t_2 = \frac{\begin{vmatrix} 1 & 0.4 \\ 42 & 0 \end{vmatrix}}{\begin{vmatrix} 1 & -1 \\ 42 & -50 \end{vmatrix}} = 2.1 \text{ h}$$

5.6   Solving Systems of Three Linear Equations in Three Unknowns Algebraically

1.
(1)	$4x + y + 3z = 1$	
(2)	$2x - 2y + 6z = 12$	
(3)	$-6x + 3y + 12z = -14$	
(4)	$8x + 2y + 6z = 2$	(1) multiplied by 2
(2)	$2x - 2y + 6z = 12$	add
(5)	$10x + 12z = 14$	
(6)	$12x + 3y + 9z = 3$	(1) multiplied by 3
(3)	$-6x + 3y + 12z = -14$	subtract
(7)	$18x - 3z = 17$	
(8)	$72x - 12z = 68$	
(5)	$10x + 12z = 14$	add
(9)	$82x = 82$	
(10)	$x = 1$	
(11)	$18(1) - 3z = 17$	substituting $x = 1$ into (7)
(12)	$-3z = -1$	
(13)	$z = \dfrac{1}{3}$	
(14)	$4(1) + y + 3\left(\dfrac{1}{3}\right) = 1$	substitute $x = 1$ and $z = \dfrac{1}{3}$ into (1)
(15)	$4 + y + 1 = 1$	
(16)	$y = -4$	

Thus, the solution is $x = 1$, $y = -4$, $z = \dfrac{1}{3}$

5.
(1) $2x + 3y + z = 2$
(2) $-x + 2y + 3z = -1$
(3) $-3x - 3y + z = 0$
(4) $-2x + 4y + 6z = -2$ multiply (2) by 2
(5) $7y + 7z = 0$ add (1) and (4)
(6) $y = -z$
(7) $-x + 2(-z) + 3z = -1$ substitute (5) in (2)
(8) $-x - z = -1$
(9) $-3x - 3(-z) + z = 0$ substitute (5) in (3)
(10) $-3x + 4z = 0$
$3x = 4z$
$$x = \frac{4}{3}z$$

(11) $2\left(\dfrac{4}{3}z\right) + 3(-z) + z = 2$ $\quad$ substitute (10),
$\qquad\qquad\qquad\qquad\qquad$ (6) in (1)

$$\dfrac{8}{3}z - 3z + z = 2$$

$$\left(\dfrac{8}{3} - \dfrac{9}{3} + \dfrac{3}{3}\right)z = 2$$

$$\dfrac{2}{3}z = 2$$

$$z = 2$$

The solution is $x = 4, y = -3, z = 3$.

9. $\quad$ (1) $2x - 2y + 3z = 5$
$\qquad$ (2) $2x + y - 2z = -1$
$\qquad$ (3) $4x - y - 3z = 0$
$\qquad$ (4) $-3y + 5z = 6$ $\qquad$ subtract (1) and (2)
$\qquad$ (5) $4x + 2y - 4z = -2$ $\quad$ multiply (2) by 2
$\qquad$ (6) $-3y + z = 2$ $\qquad$ subtract (5) and (3)
$\qquad\qquad\qquad 4z = 4$
$\qquad\qquad\qquad\; z = 1$

$\qquad$ (10) $2x - 2\left(-\dfrac{1}{3}\right) + 3(1) = 5$ $\quad$ substitute (9),
$\qquad\qquad\qquad\qquad\qquad\qquad\qquad$ (6) into (1)

$$2x + \dfrac{2}{3} + 3 = 5$$

$$2x = \dfrac{15}{3} - \dfrac{11}{3}$$

$$2x = \dfrac{4}{3}$$

$$x = \dfrac{2}{3}$$

(7) $2x - 2y + 3(1) = 5$ $\quad$ substitute (6) in (1)
$\qquad\quad 2x - 2y = 2$

(8) $2x + y - 2(1) = -1$ $\quad$ substitute (6) in (2)
$\qquad\quad 2x + y = 1$

(9) $-3y = 1$ $\qquad\qquad$ subtract (7) and (8)

$$y = -\dfrac{1}{3}$$

The solution is $x = 2/3, y = -1/3, z = 1$.

13. $\quad$ (1) $p + 2q + 2r = 0$
$\qquad$ (2) $2p + 6q - 3r = -1$
$\qquad$ (3) $4p - 3q + 6r = -8$
$\qquad$ (4) $2p + 4q + 4r = 0$ $\qquad$ multiply (1) by 2
$\qquad$ (5) $2q - 7r = -1$ $\qquad$ subtract (4) and (2)
$\qquad$ (6) $4p + 8q + 8r = 0$ $\qquad$ multiply (1) by 4
$\qquad$ (7) $-11q - 2r = -8$ $\qquad$ subtract (3) and (6)
$\qquad$ (8) $22q - 77r = -11$ $\quad$ multiply (5) by 11
$\qquad$ (9) $-22q - 4r = -16$ $\quad$ multiply (7) by 2
$\qquad$ (10) $81r = 27$ $\qquad\qquad$ add (8) and (9)

$\qquad$ (11) $r = \dfrac{27}{81} = \dfrac{1}{3}$

(12) $-11q - 2\left(\dfrac{1}{3}\right) = -8$ $\quad$ substitute
$\qquad\qquad\qquad\qquad\qquad\qquad$ (11) into 7

$$-11q - \dfrac{2}{3} = -8$$

$$-11q = -\dfrac{22}{3}$$

$$q = \dfrac{2}{3}$$

(13) $p + 2\left(\dfrac{2}{3}\right) + 2\left(\dfrac{1}{3}\right) = 0$ $\quad$ substitute (11),
$\qquad\qquad\qquad\qquad\qquad\qquad\qquad$ (12) into (1)

$$p + \dfrac{4}{3} + \dfrac{2}{3} = 0$$

$$p = -\dfrac{6}{3} = -2$$

The solution is $p = -2, \; q = \dfrac{2}{3}, \; r = \dfrac{1}{3}$.

17.

(1) $r - s - 3t - u = 1$

(2) $2r + 4s - 2u = 2$

(3) $3r + 4s - 2t = 0$

(4) $r + 2t - 3u = 3$

(5) $-s - 5t + 2u = -2$ subtract (1) and (4)

(6) $6r + 12s - 6u = 6$ multiply (2) by 3

(7) $6r + 8s - 4t = 0$ multiply (3) by 2

(8) $4s - 6u + 4t = 6$ subtract (6) and (7)

(9) $-3s + 6u - 15t = -6$ multiply (5) by 3

(10) $s - 11t = 0$ add (8) and (9)

(11) $s = 11t$

(12) $3r + 4(11t) - 2t = 0$ substitute (11) into 3

$$3r + 42t = 0$$

$$3r = -42t$$

(13) $r = -14t$

(14) $-14t - 11t - 3t - u = 1$ substitute (11), (13) into (1)

(15) $-28t - u = 1$

(16) $-14t + 2t - 3u = 3$ substitute (11), (13) into (4)

(17) $-16t - 3u = 3$

(18) $-84t - 3u = 3$ multiply (15) by 3

(19) $68t = 0$ subtract (17) and (18)

(20) $t = 0$

(21) $s - 11(0) = 0$

(22) $r = -14(0) = 0$

(23) $-u = 1$ substitute (20), (21), (22) into (1)

(24) $u = -1$

The solution is $r = s = t = 0$, $u = -1$.

21.

(1) $0.707F_1 - 0.800F_2 = 0$

(2) $0.707F_1 + 0.600F_2 - F_3 = 10.0$

(3) $3.00F_2 - 3.00F_3 = 20.0$

(4) $-1.4F_2 + F_3 = -10.0$ subtract (1) and (2)

(5) $-4.2F_2 + 3.00F_3 = -30.0$ multiply (4) by 3

(6) $-1.2F_2 = -10.0$ add (3) and (5)

(7) $F_2 = 8.33$

(8) $-1.4(8.33) + F_3 = -10.0$ substitute (7) into (4)

$$F_3 = -10.0 + 11.662$$

(9) $F_3 = 1.67$

(10) $0.707F_1 - 0.800(8.33) = 0$ substitute (7) into (1)

(11) $F_1 = \dfrac{6.66}{0.707} = 9.43$

The solution is $F_1 = 9.43$ N, $F_2 = 8.33$ N, $F_3 = 1.67$ N.

25. Letting $t = 1, 3, 5$ and $\theta = 19, 30.9, 19.8$ in $at^3 + bt^2 + ct = \theta$ gives

(1) $a + b + c = 19$

(2) $27a + 9b + 3c = 30.9$

(3) $125a + 25b + 5c = 19.8$. Solving (1) for $c = 19 - a - b$ and substituting into (2) and (3) gives

(4) $24a + 6b = -26.1$ and (5) $120a + 20b = -75.2$. From (4), (6) $b = \dfrac{-26.1 - 24a}{6}$.

Substituting in (5) gives

(7) $120a + 20\left(\dfrac{-26.1 - 24a}{6}\right) = -75.2 \Rightarrow a = 0.295$

(6) $b = \dfrac{-26.1 - 24(0.295)}{6} = -5.53$

From (1) $c = 19 - 0.295 - (-5.53) = 24.235$.

The solution is $a = 0.295$, $b = -5.53$, and $c = 24.235$.

$\theta = 0.295t^3 - 5.53t^2 + 24.2t$

29. (1) $x - 2y - 3z = 2 \Rightarrow x = 2y + 3z + 2$ substituted in (2) and (3) gives

(2) $x - 4y - 13z = 14 \Rightarrow 2y + 3z + 2 - 4y - 13z = 14 \Rightarrow -2y - 10z = 12 \Rightarrow$

(4) $y + 5z = -6$

(3) $-3x + 5y + 4z = 0 \Rightarrow -3(2y + 3z + 2) + 5y + 4z = 0 \Rightarrow y + 5z = -6$ which is (4).

Thus, $y = -6 - 5z$ and from (1) $x - 2(-6 - 5z) - 3z = 2 \Rightarrow x = -7z - 10$. The solution is $x = -7z - 10, y = -5z - 6, z = z$. Letting $z = 0, x = -10, y = -6, z = 0$.

5.7 Solving Systems of Three Linear Equations in Three Unknowns by Determinants

1. $\begin{vmatrix} -2 & 3 & -1 \\ 1 & 5 & 4 \\ 2 & -1 & 5 \end{vmatrix} \begin{matrix} -2 & 3 \\ 1 & 5 \\ 2 & -1 \end{matrix} = -2(5)(5) + 3(4)(2) + (-1)(1)(-1) - 2(5)(-1) - (-1)(4)(-2) - 5(1)(3)| = -38$

5. $\begin{vmatrix} 8 & 9 & -6 \\ -3 & 7 & 2 \\ 4 & -2 & 5 \end{vmatrix} \begin{matrix} 8 & 9 \\ -3 & 7 \\ 4 & -2 \end{matrix} = 280 - (-32) + 72 - (-135) + (-36) - (-168) = 651$

9. $\begin{vmatrix} 4 & -3 & -11 \\ -9 & 2 & -2 \\ 0 & 1 & -5 \end{vmatrix} \begin{matrix} 4 & -3 \\ -9 & 2 \\ 0 & 1 \end{matrix} = -40 - (-8) + 0 - (-135) + 99 - 0 = 202$

13. $\begin{vmatrix} 0.1 & -0.2 & 0 \\ -0.5 & 1 & 0.4 \\ -2 & 0.8 & 2 \end{vmatrix} \begin{matrix} 0.1 & -0.2 \\ -0.5 & 1 \\ -2 & 0.8 \end{matrix} = 0.2 - 0.032 + 0.16 - 0.2 + 0 - 0 = 0.128$

17. $x = \dfrac{\begin{vmatrix} 2 & 1 & 1 \\ 1 & 0 & -1 \\ 1 & 1 & 0 \end{vmatrix} \begin{matrix} 2 & 1 \\ 1 & 0 \\ 1 & 1 \end{matrix}}{\begin{vmatrix} 1 & 1 & 1 \\ 1 & 0 & -1 \\ 1 & 1 & 0 \end{vmatrix} \begin{matrix} 1 & 1 \\ 1 & 0 \\ 1 & 1 \end{matrix}} = \dfrac{0 - (-2) + (-1) - 0 + 1 - 0}{0 - (-1) + (-1) - 0 + 1 - 0} = \dfrac{2}{1} = 2$

$y = \dfrac{\begin{vmatrix} 1 & 2 & 1 \\ 1 & 1 & -1 \\ 1 & 1 & 0 \end{vmatrix} \begin{matrix} 1 & 2 \\ 1 & 1 \\ 1 & 1 \end{matrix}}{1} = \dfrac{0 - (-1) + (-2) - 0 + 1 - 1}{1} = \dfrac{-1}{1} = -1$

$z = \dfrac{\begin{vmatrix} 1 & 1 & 2 \\ 1 & 0 & 1 \\ 1 & 1 & 1 \end{vmatrix} \begin{matrix} 1 & 1 \\ 1 & 0 \\ 1 & 1 \end{matrix}}{1} = \dfrac{0 - 1 + 1 - 1 + 2 - 0}{1} = \dfrac{1}{1} = 1$

21. $l = \dfrac{\begin{vmatrix} 6 & 6 & -3 \\ -3 & -7 & -2 \\ 1 & 1 & -7 \end{vmatrix}\begin{matrix} 6 & 6 \\ -3 & -7 \\ 1 & 1 \end{matrix}}{\begin{vmatrix} 5 & 6 & -3 \\ 4 & -7 & -2 \\ 3 & 1 & -7 \end{vmatrix}\begin{matrix} 5 & 6 \\ 4 & -7 \\ 3 & 1 \end{matrix}} = \dfrac{294 + 12 - 12 - 126 + 9 - 21}{245 + 10 - 36 + 168 - 12 - 63} = \dfrac{156}{312} = \dfrac{1}{2}$

$w = \dfrac{\begin{vmatrix} 5 & 6 & -3 \\ 4 & -3 & -2 \\ 3 & 1 & -7 \end{vmatrix}\begin{matrix} 5 & 6 \\ 4 & -3 \\ 3 & 1 \end{matrix}}{312} = \dfrac{105 + 10 - 36 + 168 - 12 - 27}{312} = \dfrac{208}{312} = \dfrac{2}{3}$

$h = \dfrac{\begin{vmatrix} 5 & 6 & -3 \\ 4 & -3 & -2 \\ 3 & 1 & -7 \end{vmatrix}\begin{matrix} 5 & 6 \\ 4 & -3 \\ 3 & 1 \end{matrix}}{312} = \dfrac{-35 + 15 - 54 - 224 + 24 + 126}{312} = \dfrac{52}{312} = \dfrac{1}{6}$

25. $x = \dfrac{\begin{vmatrix} 6 & -7 & 3 \\ 1 & 3 & 6 \\ 5 & -5 & 2 \end{vmatrix}\begin{matrix} 6 & -7 \\ 1 & 3 \\ 5 & -5 \end{matrix}}{\begin{vmatrix} 3 & -7 & 3 \\ 3 & 3 & 6 \\ 5 & -5 & 2 \end{vmatrix}\begin{matrix} 3 & -7 \\ 3 & 3 \\ 5 & -5 \end{matrix}} = \dfrac{36 + 180 - 210 + 14 - 15 - 45}{18 + 90 - 210 + 42 - 45 - 45} = \dfrac{-40}{-150} = \dfrac{4}{15}$

$y = \dfrac{\begin{vmatrix} 3 & 6 & 3 \\ 3 & 1 & 6 \\ 5 & 5 & 2 \end{vmatrix}\begin{matrix} 3 & 6 \\ 3 & 1 \\ 5 & 5 \end{matrix}}{-150} = \dfrac{6 - 90 + 180 - 36 + 45 - 15}{-150} = \dfrac{90}{-150} = -\dfrac{3}{5}$

$z = \dfrac{\begin{vmatrix} 3 & -7 & 6 \\ 3 & 3 & 1 \\ 5 & -5 & 5 \end{vmatrix}\begin{matrix} 3 & -7 \\ 3 & 3 \\ 5 & -5 \end{matrix}}{-150} = \dfrac{45 + 15 - 35 + 105 - 90 - 90}{-150} = \dfrac{-50}{-150} = \dfrac{1}{3}$

29. $x = \dfrac{\begin{vmatrix} 10.5 & 4.5 & -7.5 \\ 1.2 & -3.6 & -2.4 \\ 1.5 & -0.5 & 2.0 \end{vmatrix}\begin{matrix} 10.5 & 4.5 \\ 1.2 & -3.6 \\ 1.5 & -0.5 \end{matrix}}{\begin{vmatrix} 3.0 & 4.5 & -7.5 \\ 4.8 & -3.6 & -2.4 \\ 4.0 & -0.5 & 2.0 \end{vmatrix}\begin{matrix} 3.0 & 4.5 \\ 4.8 & -3.6 \\ 4.0 & -0.5 \end{matrix}} = \dfrac{-75.6 - 12.6 - 16.2 - 10.8 + 4.5 - 40.5}{-21.6 - 3.6 - 43.2 - 43.2 + 18 - 108} = \dfrac{-151.2}{-201.6} = \dfrac{3}{4}$

$y = \dfrac{\begin{vmatrix} 3.0 & 10.5 & -7.5 \\ 4.8 & 1.2 & -2.4 \\ 4.0 & 1.5 & 2.0 \end{vmatrix}\begin{matrix} 3.0 & 10.5 \\ 4.8 & 1.2 \\ 4.0 & 1.5 \end{matrix}}{-201.6} = \dfrac{7.2 + 10.8 - 100.8 - 100.8 - 54 + 36}{-201.6}\dfrac{-201.6}{-201.6} = 1$

$z = \dfrac{\begin{vmatrix} 3.0 & 4.5 & 10.5 \\ 4.8 & -3.6 & 1.2 \\ 4.0 & -0.5 & 1.5 \end{vmatrix}\begin{matrix} 3.0 & 4.5 \\ 4.8 & -3.6 \\ 4.0 & -0.5 \end{matrix}}{-201.6} = \dfrac{-16.2 + 1.8 + 21.6 - 32.4 - 25.2 + 151.2}{-201.6} = \dfrac{100.8}{-201.6} = -\dfrac{1}{2}$

33.
$$s_o + 2v_o + 2a = 20$$
$$s_o + 4v_o + 8a = 54$$
$$s_o + 6v_o + 18a = 104$$

$$s_o = \dfrac{\begin{vmatrix} 20 & 2 & 2 \\ 54 & 4 & 8 \\ 104 & 6 & 18 \end{vmatrix}}{\begin{vmatrix} 1 & 2 & 2 \\ 1 & 4 & 8 \\ 1 & 6 & 18 \end{vmatrix}} = \dfrac{16}{8} = 2 \text{ ft}$$

$$v_o = \dfrac{\begin{vmatrix} 1 & 20 & 2 \\ 1 & 54 & 8 \\ 1 & 104 & 18 \end{vmatrix}}{8} = \dfrac{40}{8} = 5 \text{ ft/s}$$

$$a = \dfrac{\begin{vmatrix} 1 & 2 & 20 \\ 1 & 4 & 54 \\ 1 & 6 & 104 \end{vmatrix}}{8} = \dfrac{32}{8} = 4 \text{ ft/s}^2$$

37.
$x = $ percent of nickel
$y = $ percent of iron
$z = $ percent of molybdenum

$$x + y + z = 100$$
$$x - 5y = -1$$
$$y - 3z = 1$$

$$x = \dfrac{\begin{vmatrix} 100 & 1 & 1 \\ -1 & -5 & 0 \\ 1 & 1 & -3 \end{vmatrix}}{\begin{vmatrix} 1 & 1 & 1 \\ 1 & -5 & 0 \\ 0 & 1 & -3 \end{vmatrix}} = \dfrac{1501}{19} = 79\% \text{ nickel}$$

$$y = \dfrac{\begin{vmatrix} 1 & 100 & 1 \\ 1 & -1 & 0 \\ 0 & 1 & -3 \end{vmatrix}}{19} = \dfrac{304}{19} = 16\% \text{ iron}$$

$$z = \dfrac{\begin{vmatrix} 1 & 1 & 100 \\ 1 & -5 & -1 \\ 0 & 1 & 1 \end{vmatrix}}{19} = \dfrac{95}{19} = 5\% \text{ molybdenum}$$

Chapter 5 Review Exercises

1. $\begin{vmatrix} -2 & 5 \\ 3 & 1 \end{vmatrix} = (-2)(1) - (3)(5) = -2 - 15 = -17$

5. $m = \dfrac{y_2 - y_1}{x_2 - x_1} = \dfrac{-8 - 0}{4 - 2} = \dfrac{-8}{2} = -4$

9. Comparing $y = -2x + 4$ to $y = mx + b$ gives a slope of -2 and y-int of 4.

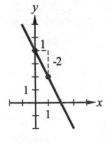

13.

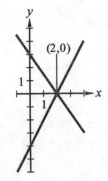

17. $7x = 2y + 14 \Rightarrow y = \dfrac{7x - 14}{2}$

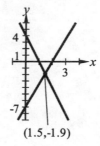

(1.5,-1.9)

21. (1) $x + 2y = 5 \Rightarrow x = 5 - 2y$ which substitutes into (2) $x + 3y = 7$ to give
$5 - 2y + 3y = 7 \Rightarrow y = 2$. From (1) $x = 5 - 2 \cdot 2 = 1$. The solution is $(1, 2)$.

25. $i = \dfrac{\begin{vmatrix} 29 & -27 \\ 69 & 33 \end{vmatrix}}{\begin{vmatrix} 10 & -27 \\ 40 & 33 \end{vmatrix}} = \dfrac{2820}{1410} = 2$

$v = \dfrac{\begin{vmatrix} 10 & 29 \\ 40 & 69 \end{vmatrix}}{1410} = \dfrac{-470}{1410} = -\dfrac{1}{3}$

The solution is $i = 2$, $v = -\dfrac{1}{3}$.

29. (1) $0.9x - 1.1y = 0.4 \Rightarrow x = \dfrac{11y + 4}{9}$ which substitutes into (2) $0.6x - 0.3y = 0.5$ to give

$6\dfrac{11y + 4}{9} - 3y = 5 \Rightarrow y = \dfrac{7}{13}$. From (1) $x = \dfrac{11 \cdot \frac{7}{13} + 4}{9} = \dfrac{43}{39}$. The solution is $\left(\dfrac{43}{39}, \dfrac{7}{13}\right)$.

33. (1) $y = 2x - 3$ substitute into (2) $4x + 3y = -4$ gives $4x + 3(2x - 3) = -4 \Rightarrow x = \dfrac{1}{2}$. From (1) $y = 2 \cdot \dfrac{1}{2} - 3 = -2$.
The solution is $\left(\dfrac{1}{2}, -2\right)$.

37. (1) $7x = 2y - 6 \Rightarrow x = \dfrac{2y - 6}{7}$ which substitutes into (2) $7y = 12 - 4x$ to give

$7y = 12 - 4 \cdot \dfrac{2y - 6}{7} \Rightarrow y = \dfrac{36}{19}$. From (1) $x = \dfrac{2 \cdot \frac{36}{19} - 6}{7} = -\dfrac{6}{19}$. The solution is $\left(-\dfrac{6}{19}, \dfrac{36}{19}\right)$.

41. Exercise 33 is most easily solved by substitution because the second equation is already solved for y.

45. $\begin{vmatrix} 4 & -1 & 8 \\ -1 & 6 & -2 \\ 2 & 1 & -1 \end{vmatrix} = 4(-6 + 2) + (1 + 4) + 8(-1 - 12) = -115$

49.
(1) $2x + y + z = 4$ mulltiplied by 2 $4x + 2y + 2z = 8$
(2) $x - 2y - z = 3$ adding   (3) $\dfrac{3x + 3y - 2z = 1}{}$ adding
(4) $3x - y = 7$ (5) $7x + 5y = 9$
                 (4) multiplied by 5 $\dfrac{15x - 5y = 35}{22x = 44 \Rightarrow x = 2}$ adding

From (4) $y = 3 \cdot 2 - 7 = -1$. From (1) $z = 4 - (-1) - 2(2) = 1$. The solution is $(2, -1, 1)$.

53. Multiply both sides of all three equations by 10 to clear decimals.

(1) $36x + 52y - 10z = -22$ solved for z : (4) $z = \dfrac{36x + 52y + 22}{10}$

(2) $32x - 48y + 39z = 81$

(3) $64x + 41y + 23z = 51$

(5) $32x - 48y + 39 \cdot \dfrac{36x + 52y + 22}{10} = 81$ (2) with z from (4) which simplifes to

(5) $1724x + 1548y = -48 \Rightarrow y = \dfrac{-48 - 1724x}{1548}$

(6) $64x + 41y + 23 \cdot \dfrac{36x + 52y + 22}{10} = 51$ (3) with z from (4) which simplites to

(6) $1468x + 1606 \cdot \dfrac{-48 - 1724x}{1548} = 4 \Rightarrow x = -0.1678084952$. From (5)

$y = \dfrac{-48 - 1724x}{1548} = 0.1558797453$. From (4)

$z = \dfrac{36x + 52y + 22}{10} = 2.406464093$. The solution is $(-0.17, 0.16, 2.4)$.

57. $r = \dfrac{\begin{vmatrix} 8 & 1 & 2 \\ 5 & -2 & -4 \\ -3 & 3 & 4 \end{vmatrix}}{\begin{vmatrix} 2 & 1 & 2 \\ 3 & -2 & -4 \\ -2 & 3 & 4 \end{vmatrix}} = \dfrac{42}{14} = 3, \qquad s = \dfrac{\begin{vmatrix} 2 & 8 & 2 \\ 3 & 5 & -4 \\ -2 & -3 & 4 \end{vmatrix}}{14} = \dfrac{-14}{14} = -1$

$t = \dfrac{\begin{vmatrix} 2 & 1 & 8 \\ 3 & -2 & 5 \\ -2 & 3 & -3 \end{vmatrix}}{14} = \dfrac{21}{14} = \dfrac{3}{2}$. The solution is $\left(3, -1, \dfrac{3}{2}\right)$.

61. $\begin{vmatrix} 2 & 5 \\ 1 & x \end{vmatrix} = 3 \Rightarrow 2x - 5 = 3 \Rightarrow 2x = 8 \Rightarrow x = 4$

65. (1) $\dfrac{1}{x} - \dfrac{1}{y} = \dfrac{1}{2} \Rightarrow u - v = \dfrac{1}{2}$

(2) $\dfrac{1}{x} + \dfrac{1}{y} = \dfrac{1}{4} \Rightarrow u + v = \dfrac{1}{4}$

Adding (1), (2) $2u = \dfrac{3}{4} \Rightarrow u = \dfrac{3}{8} \Rightarrow x = \dfrac{8}{3}$, from (2) $v = \dfrac{1}{4} - \dfrac{3}{8} = -\dfrac{1}{8}$, $y = -8$. The solution is $\left(\dfrac{8}{3}, -8\right)$.

69. (1) $3x - ky = 6$
(2) $x + 2y = 2$. Multiplying (2) by 3 gives $3x + 6y = 6$ which is (1) with $k = -6$. A k-value of -6 makes the system dependent.

73. $F_1 = \dfrac{\begin{vmatrix} 280 & 2.0 & 0 \\ 0 & 0 & -1 \\ 600 & -4.0 & 0 \end{vmatrix}}{\begin{vmatrix} 1 & 2.0 & 0 \\ 0.87 & 0 & -1 \\ 3.0 & -4.0 & 0 \end{vmatrix}} = \dfrac{-2320}{-10} = 232 = 230 \text{ lb}$

$F_2 = \dfrac{\begin{vmatrix} 1 & 280 & 0 \\ 0.87 & 0 & -1 \\ 3.0 & 600 & 0 \end{vmatrix}}{-10} = \dfrac{-240}{-10} = 24 \text{ lb}$

$F_3 = \dfrac{\begin{vmatrix} 1 & 2.0 & 280 \\ 0.87 & 0 & 0 \\ 3.0 & -4 & 600 \end{vmatrix}}{-10} = \dfrac{-2018.4}{-10} = 201.84 = 200 \text{ lb}$

77. $x =$ number of tons of 6% copper ore

$y =$ number of tons of 2.4% copper ore

$$x + y = 42$$
$$0.06x + 0.024y = 2$$

$x = \dfrac{\begin{vmatrix} 42 & 1 \\ 2 & 0.024 \end{vmatrix}}{\begin{vmatrix} 1 & 1 \\ 0.06 & 0.024 \end{vmatrix}} = \dfrac{-0.992}{-0.036} = 27.\overline{5}$

$y = \dfrac{\begin{vmatrix} 1 & 42 \\ 0.06 & 2 \end{vmatrix}}{-0.036} = \dfrac{-0.52}{-0.036} = 14.\overline{4}$

Use 28 tons of 6% copper and 14 tons of 2.4% copper.

81. (1) $V + v = 24,200$

(2) $\underline{V - v = 21,400}$ adding

$2V = 45,600 \Rightarrow V = 22,800$ km/h is the speed of the shuttle.

(1) $22,800 + v = 24,200 \Rightarrow v = 1400$ km/h is the speed of the satellite.

85. (1) $2w = 8L \Rightarrow w = 4L$ which may be subsituted into (2)

(2) $4L \cdot 8 = 2w + 20 \cdot 12$ to obtain $32L = 2 \cdot 4L + 240 \Rightarrow L = 10$ lb

$w = 4 \cdot 10 = 40$ lb

89. Reasons for choosing a particular method may vary.

Let Q_1, Q_2 be the ft^3/h removed by each pump. Then $2.2Q_1 + 2.7Q_2 = 1100$
and $1.4Q_1 + 2.5Q_2 = 840$ describes the situation.

The solution is $Q_1 = 280$ ft^3/h and $Q_2 = 180$ ft^3/h.

FACTORING AND FRACTIONS

6.1 Special Products

1. $(3r - 2s)(3r + 2s) = (3r)^2 - (2s)^2$
$$= 9r^2 - 4s^2$$

5. $40(x - y) = 40x - 40y$

9. $(y + 6)(y - 6) = y^2 - 6^2 = y^2 - 36$

13. $(4x - 5y)(4x + 5y) = (4x)^2 - (5y)^2$
$$= 16x^2 - 25y^2$$

17. $(5f + 4)^2 = (5f)^2 + 2(5f)(4) + 4^2$
$$= 25f^2 + 40f + 16$$

21. $(L^2 - 1)^2 = (L^2)^2 - 2 \cdot L^2 \cdot 1 + 1^2$
$$= L^4 - 2L^2 + 1$$

25. $(0.6s - t)^2 = (0.6s)^2 - 2(0.6s)(t) + t^2$
$$= 0.36s^2 - 1.2st + t^2$$

29. $(3 + C^2)(6 + C^2) = 18 + (3C^2 + 6C^2) + (C^2)^2$
$$= 18 + 9C^2 + C^4$$

33. $(5v - 3)(4v + 5) = 20v^2 + 13v - 15$

37. $2(x - 2)(x + 2) = 2(x^2 - 4) = 2x^2 - 8$

41. $6a(x + 2b)^2 = 6a(x^2 + 4bx + 4b^2)$
$$= 6ax^2 + 24abx + 24ab^2$$

45. $[(2R + 3r)(2R - 3r)]^2 = [4R^2 - 9r^2]^2$
$$= 16R^4 - 72R^2r^2 + 81r^4$$

49. $[3 - (x + y)^2] = 9 - 6(x + y) + (x + y)^2$
$$= 9 - 6x - 6y + x^2 + 2xy + y^2$$

53. $(3L + 7R)^3$
$$= (3L)^3 + 3(3L)^2(7R) + 3(3L)(7R)^2 + (7R)^3$$
$$= 27L^3 + 189L^2R + 441LR^2 + 343R^3$$

57. $(x + 2)(x^2 - 2x + 4) = x^3 - 2x^2 + 4x + 2x^2 - 4x + 8$
$$= x^3 + 8$$

61. $(x + y)^2(x - y)^2 = (x^2 + 2xy + y^2)(x^2 - 2xy + y^2)$
$$= x^4 - 2x^3y + x^2y^2$$
$$+ 2x^3y - 4x^2y^2 + 2xy^3$$
$$+ x^2y^2 - 2xy^3 + y^4$$
$$= x^4 - 2x^2y^2 + y^4$$

65. $4(p + DA)^2 = 4(p^2 + 2pDA + D^2A^2)$
$$= 4p^2 + 8pDA + 4D^2A^2$$

69. $\dfrac{L}{6}(x - a)^3 = \dfrac{L}{6}[x^3 - 3x^2a + 3xa^2 - a^3]$
$$= \dfrac{L}{6}x^3 - \dfrac{L}{2}ax^2 + \dfrac{L}{2}a^2x - \dfrac{L}{6}a^3$$

73.

$$A = (2x + 3)(2x - 3) = 4x^2 - 9$$

6.2 Factoring: Common Factor and Difference of Squares

1. $4ax^2 - 2ax = 2ax(2x - 1)$

5. $6x + 6y = 6(x + y)$
(6 is a common monomial factor, c.m.f.)

9. $3x^2 - 9x = 3x(x - 3)(3x$ is a c.m.f.)

13. $72n^2 + 6n = 6n(12n + 1)(6n$ is a c.m.f.)

17. $3ab^2 - 6ab + 12ab^3 = 3ab(b - 2 + 4b^2)$
($3ab$ is a c.m.f.)

21. $2a^2 - 2b^2 + 4c^2 - 6d^2 = 2(a^2 - b^2 + 2c^2 - 3d^2)$
(2 is a c.m.f.)

25. $100 - 9A^2 = (10 - 3A)(10 + 3A)$
(because $-30A + 30A = 0A = 0$)

29. $81s^2 - 25t^2 = (9s - 5t)(9s + 5t)$
(because $-45st + 45st = 0st = 0$)

33. $(x + y)^2 - 9 = (x + y - 3)(x + y + 3)$

37. $3x^2 - 27z^2 = 3(x^2 - 9z^2)$
$$= 3(x - 3z)(x + 3z)$$

41. $x^4 - 16 = (x^2 - 4)(x^2 + 4)$
$$= (x - 2)(x + 2)(x^2 + 4)$$

45. Solve $2a - b = ab + 3$ for a.
$$2a - ab = b + 3$$
$$a(2 - b) = b + 3$$
$$a = \frac{b + 3}{2 - b}$$

49. $3x - 3y + bx - by = 3(x - y) + b(x - y)$
$$= (x - y)(b + 3)$$

53. $x^3 + 3x^2 - 4x - 12 = x^2(x + 3) - 4(x + 3)$
$$= (x + 3)(x^2 - 4)$$
$$= (x + 3)(x + 2)(x - 2)$$

57. $\dfrac{8^9 - 8^8}{7} = \dfrac{8^8(8 - 1)}{7} = 8^8 = 16{,}777{,}216$

61. $Rv + Rv^2 + Rv^3 = Rv(1 + v + v^2)$

65.

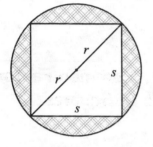

$$s^2 + s^2 = (2r)^2$$
$$2s^2 = 4r^2$$
$$s^2 = 2r^2 = \text{area of square}$$

Area left = Area of circle $-$ Area of square
$$= \pi r^2 - 2r^2$$
$$= r^2(\pi - 2)$$

69.
$$3BY + 5Y = 9BS$$
$$3BY - 9BS = -5Y$$
$$B(3Y - 9S) = -5Y$$
$$B = \frac{-5Y}{3Y - 9S} = \frac{5Y}{3(3S - Y)}$$

6.3 Factoring Trinomials

1. $x^2 + 4x + 3 = (x + 3)(x + 1)$

5. $2x^2 + 6x - 36 = 2(x^2 + 3x - 18)$
$$= 2(x + 6)(x - 3)$$

9. $s^2 - s - 42 = (s - 7)(s + 6)$
(because $-s = -7s + 6s$)

13. $x^2 + 2x + 1 = (x + 1)(x + 1) = (x + 1)^2$
(because $2x = x + x$)

17. $3x^2 - 5x - 2 = (3x + 1)(x - 2)$
(because $-5x = -6x + x$)

21. $2s^2 + 13s + 11 = (2s + 11)(s + 1)$
(because $13s = 2s + 11s$)

25. $2t^2 + 7t - 15 = (2t - 3)(t + 5)$
(because $7t = 10t - 3t$)

29. $4x^2 - 3x - 7 = (4x - 7)(x + 1)$
(because $-3x = 4x - 7x$)

33. $4m^2 + 20m + 25 = (2m + 5)(2m + 5) = (2m + 5)^2$
(because $20m = 10m + 10m$)

37. $9t^2 - 15t + 4 = (3t - 4)(3t - 1)$
(because $-15t = -3t - 12t$)

41. $4p^2 - 25pq + 6q^2 = (4p - q)(p - 6q)$
(because $-25pq = -24pq - pq$)

45. $2x^2 - 14x + 12 = 2(x^2 - 7x + 6) = 2(x - 1)(x - 6)$
(because $-7x = -6x - x$)

49. $ax^3 + 4a^2x^2 - 12a^3x = ax(x^2 + 4ax - 12a^2)$
$$= ax(x + 6a)(x - 2a)$$

53. $25a^2 - 25x^2 - 10xy - y^2$
$$= 25a^2 - (25x^2 + 10xy + y^2)$$
$$= 25a^2 - (5x + y)^2$$
$$= (5a + 5x + y)(5a - 5x - y)$$

57. $3p^2 + 9p - 54 = 3(p^2 + 3p - 18)$
$$= 3(p + 6)(p - 3)$$

61. $200n^2 - 2100n - 3600 = 100(2n^2 - 21 - 36)$
$$= 100(2n + 3)(n - 12)$$

65. $wx^4 - 5wLx^3 + 6wL^2x^2 = wx^2(x^2 - 5Lx + 6L^2)$
$$= wx^2(x - 3L)(x - 2L)$$

69. $x^4 + 4 = x^4 + 4 - 4x^2 + 4x^2$
$$= x^4 + 4x^2 + 4 - 4x^2$$
$$= (x^2 + 2)^2 - 4x^2$$
$$= (x^2 + 2)^2 - (2x)^2$$
$$= (x^2 + 2 - 2x)(x^2 + 2 + 2x)$$
$$= (x^2 - 2x + 2)(x^2 + 2x + 2)$$

6.4　The Sum and Difference of Cubes

1. $x^3 - 8 = x^3 - 2^3 = (x-2)(x^2 + 2x + 2^2) = (x-2)(x^2 + 2x + 4)$

5. $8 - t^3 = 2^3 - t^3 = (2-t)(4 + 2t + t^2)$

9. $2x^3 + 16 = 2(x^3 + 8) = 2(x+2)(x^2 - 2x + 4)$

13. $6x^3 y - 6x^3 y^4 = 6x^3 y(1 - y^3) = 6x^3 y(1-y)(1 + y + y^2)$

17. $3a^6 - 3a^2 = 3a^2(a^4 - 1) = 3a^2(a^2 - 1)(a^2 + 1) = 3a^2(a+1)(a-1)(a^2 + 1)$

21. $27L^6 + 216L^3 = 27L^3(L^3 + 8) = 27L^3(L+2)(L^2 - 2L + 4)$

25. $64 - x^6 = 4^3 - (x^2)^3 = (4 - x^2)(16 + 4x^2 + x^4) = (2+x)(2-x)(16 + 4x^2 + x^4)$

29. $D^4 - d^3 D = D(D^3 - d^3) = D(D-d)(D^2 + Dd + d^2)$

33.

$$
\require{enclose}
\begin{array}{r}
x^4 \;\;+ x^3 y \;\;+ x^2 y^2 + \;\;xy^3 + \;\;y^4 \phantom{{}-y^5} \\[2pt]
x - y \enclose{longdiv}{x^5 \; - y^5} \\[2pt]
\underline{x^5 - x^4 y \phantom{{}+ x^2y^2 + xy^3 + y^4 - y^5}} \\[2pt]
x^4 y \phantom{{}+ x^2y^2 + xy^3 + y^4 - y^5} \\[2pt]
\underline{x^4 y - x^3 y^2 \phantom{{}+ xy^3 + y^4 - y^5}} \\[2pt]
x^3 y^2 \phantom{{}+ xy^3 + y^4 - y^5} \\[2pt]
\underline{x^3 y^2 - x^2 y^3 \phantom{{}+ y^4 - y^5}} \\[2pt]
x^2 y^3 \phantom{{}+ y^4 - y^5} \\[2pt]
\underline{x^2 y^3 - xy^4 \phantom{{}- y^5}} \\[2pt]
xy^4 - y^5 \\[2pt]
\underline{xy^4 - y^5}
\end{array}
$$

$(x^5 - y^5) \div (x - y) = x^4 + x^3 y + x^2 y^2 + xy^3 + y^4$
$x^5 - y^5 = (x-y)(x^4 + x^3 y + x^2 y^2 + xy^3 + y^4)$

$(x^7 - y^7) \div (x - y) = x^6 + x^5 y + x^4 y^2 + x^3 y^3 + x^2 y^4 + xy^5 + y^6$
$x^7 - y^7 = (x-y)(x^6 + x^5 y + x^4 y^2 + x^3 y^3 + x^2 y^4 + xy^5 + y^6)$

6.5　Equivalent Fractions

1. $\dfrac{18abc^6}{24ab^2 c^5} = \dfrac{6abc^5(3c)}{6abc^5(4b)} = \dfrac{3c}{4b}$

5. $\dfrac{2}{3} \cdot \dfrac{7}{7} = \dfrac{14}{21}$

9. $\dfrac{2}{(x+3)} \cdot \dfrac{(x-2)}{(x-2)} = \dfrac{2(x-2)}{(x+3)(x-2)}$

$\phantom{\dfrac{2}{(x+3)} \cdot \dfrac{(x-2)}{(x-2)}} = \dfrac{2x-4}{x^2 + x - 6}$

13. $\dfrac{28}{44} = \dfrac{\frac{28}{4}}{\frac{44}{4}} = \dfrac{7}{11}$

17. $\dfrac{2(R-1)}{(R-1)(R+1)} = \dfrac{\frac{2(R-1)}{(R-1)}}{\frac{(R-1)(R+1)}{(R-1)}} = \dfrac{2}{R+1}$

21. $\dfrac{A}{6y^2} = \dfrac{3x}{2y} \cdot \dfrac{3y}{3y}$

$\phantom{\dfrac{A}{6y^2}} = \dfrac{9xy}{6y^2} \Rightarrow A = 9xy$

25. $\dfrac{A}{x^2-1} = \dfrac{2x^3+2x}{x^4-1}$

$\qquad = \dfrac{2x(x^2+1)}{(x^2+1)(x^2-1)}$

$\qquad = \dfrac{2x}{x^2-1} \Rightarrow A = 2x$

29. $\dfrac{2a}{8a} = \dfrac{2a}{2a\cdot 4} = \dfrac{1}{4}$

33. $\dfrac{a+b}{5a^2+5ab} = \dfrac{(a+b)}{5a(a+b)} = \dfrac{1}{5a}$

37. $\dfrac{4x^2+1}{4x^2-1} = \dfrac{4x^2+1}{(2x-1)(2x+1)}$

Since no cancellations can be made the fraction cannot be reduced.

41. $\dfrac{2y+3}{4y^3+6y^2} = \dfrac{(2y+3)}{2y^2(2y+3)}$

$\qquad = \dfrac{1}{2y^2}$

45. $\dfrac{2w^4+5w^2-3}{w^4+11w^2+24} = \dfrac{(2w^2-1)(w^2+3)}{(w^2+8)(w^2+3)}$

$\qquad = \dfrac{2w^2-1}{w^2+8}$

49. $\dfrac{N^4-16}{N+2} = \dfrac{(N^2+4)(N^2-4)}{(N+2)}$

$\qquad = \dfrac{(N^2+4)(N+2)(N-2)}{(N+2)}$

$\qquad = (N^2+4)(N-2)$

53. $\dfrac{(x-1)(3+x)}{(3-x)(1-x)} = \dfrac{(x-1)(3+x)}{-(3-x)(x-1)}$

$\qquad = \dfrac{3+x}{-(3-x)} = \dfrac{x+3}{x-3}$

57. $\dfrac{2x^2-9x+4}{4x-x^2} = \dfrac{(2x-1)(x-4)}{-x(x-4)}$

$\qquad = \dfrac{-(2x-1)}{x}$

61. $\dfrac{x^3+y^3}{2x+2y} = \dfrac{(x+y)(x^2-xy+y^2)}{2(x+y)} = \dfrac{x^2-xy+y^2}{2}$

65. (a) $\dfrac{x^2(x+2)}{x^2+4}$ will not reduce further since x^2+4 does not factor.

(b) $\dfrac{x^4+4x^2}{x^4-16} = \dfrac{x^2(x^2+4)}{(x^2+4)(x^2-4)} = \dfrac{x^2}{x^2-4}$

$\qquad = \dfrac{x^2}{(x+2)(x-2)}$

69. $\dfrac{mu^2-mv^2}{mu-mv} = \dfrac{m(u^2-v^2)}{m(u-v)}$

$\qquad = \dfrac{(u-v)(u+v)}{(u-v)} = u+v$

6.6 Multiplication and Division of Fractions

1. $\dfrac{4x+6y}{(x-y)^2} \times \dfrac{(x^2-y^2)}{6x+9y} = \dfrac{2(2x+3y)(x+y)(x-y)}{(x-y)(x-y)\cdot 3(2x+3y)}$

$\qquad = \dfrac{2(x+y)}{3(x-y)}$

5. $\dfrac{3}{8}\cdot\dfrac{2}{7} = \dfrac{3}{4}\cdot\dfrac{1}{7} = \dfrac{3}{28}$

(divide out a common factor of 2)

9. $\dfrac{2}{9}\div\dfrac{4}{7} = \dfrac{2}{9}\cdot\dfrac{7}{4} = \dfrac{1}{9}\cdot\dfrac{7}{2} = \dfrac{7}{18}$

(divide out a common factor of 2)

13. $\dfrac{4x+12}{5}\cdot\dfrac{15t}{3x+9} = \dfrac{4(x+3)}{5}\cdot\dfrac{5(3t)}{3(x+3)}$

$\qquad = 4t$

(divide out a common factors of $15(x+3)$)

17. $\dfrac{2a+8}{15}\div\dfrac{a^2+8a+16}{25}$

$\qquad = \dfrac{2(a+4)}{3\cdot 5}\cdot\dfrac{5\cdot 5}{(a+4)(a+4)}$

$\qquad = \dfrac{10}{3(a+4)}$

(divide out a common factor of $5(a+4)$)

21. $\dfrac{3ax^2-9ax}{10x^2+5x}\cdot\dfrac{2x^2+x}{a^2x-3a^2} = \dfrac{3ax(x-3)}{5x(2x+1)}\cdot\dfrac{x(2x+1)}{a^2(x-3)}$

$\qquad = \dfrac{3x}{5a}$

(divide out a common factor of $ax(2x+1)(x-3)$)

25. $\dfrac{ax+x^2}{2b-cx}\div\dfrac{a^2+2ax+x^2}{2bx-cx^2}$

$\qquad \dfrac{x(a+x)}{(2b-cx)}\cdot\dfrac{x(2b-cx)}{(a+x)(a+x)} = \dfrac{x^2}{a+x}$

(divide out common factor $(a+x)(2b-cx)$)

29. $\dfrac{x^2 - 6x + 5}{4x^2 - 17x - 15} \cdot \dfrac{6x + 21}{2x^2 + 5x - 7}$

$\qquad = \dfrac{(x - 5)(x - 1)}{(4x + 3)(x - 5)} \cdot \dfrac{3(2x + 7)}{(2x + 7)(x - 1)}$

$\qquad = \dfrac{3}{4x + 3}$

(divide out common factor $(x - 5)(x - 1)(2x + 7)$)

33. $\dfrac{7x^2}{3a} \div \left(\dfrac{a}{x} \cdot \dfrac{a^2 x}{x^2} \right) = \dfrac{7x^2}{3a} \div \dfrac{a^3}{x^2} = \dfrac{7x^2}{3a} \cdot \dfrac{x^2}{a^3}$

$\qquad = \dfrac{7x^4}{3a^4}$

(divide out a common factor of x)

37. $\dfrac{x^3 - y^3}{2x^2 - 2y^2} \cdot \dfrac{x^2 + 2xy + y^2}{x^2 + xy + y^2}$

$\qquad = \dfrac{(x - y)(x^2 + xy + y^2)}{2(x - y)(x + y)} \cdot \dfrac{(x + y)(x + y)}{(x^2 + xy + y^2)}$

$\qquad = \dfrac{x + y}{2}$

(divide out common factor
$(x - y)(x + y)(x^2 + xy + y^2)$)

41. $\dfrac{x}{2x + 4} \times \dfrac{x^2 - 4}{3x^2} = \dfrac{x(x + 2)(x - 2)}{2(x + 2) \cdot 3x^2}$

$\qquad = \dfrac{x - 2}{6x}$

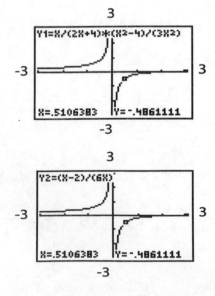

Graph y_1 = original expression and y_2 = final expression and use TRACE feature to show they are the same.

45. $\dfrac{d}{2} \div \dfrac{v_1 d + v_2 d}{4v_1 v_2} = \dfrac{d}{2} \cdot \dfrac{4v_1 v_2}{d(v_1 + v_2)} = \dfrac{2v_1 v_2}{v_1 + v_2}$

(divide out common factor $2d$)

6.7   Addition and Subtraction of Fractions

1. $4a^2 b = 2 \cdot 2 \cdot a \cdot a \cdot b$

$\quad 6ab^3 = 2 \cdot 3 \cdot a \cdot b \cdot b \cdot b$

$\quad 4a^2 b^2 = 2 \cdot 2 \cdot a \cdot a \cdot b \cdot b$

$\quad$ L.C.D.: $2^2 \cdot 3 \cdot a^2 \cdot b^3 = 12a^2 b^3$

5. $\dfrac{3}{5} + \dfrac{6}{5} = \dfrac{3 + 6}{5} = \dfrac{9}{5}$

9. $\dfrac{1}{2} + \dfrac{3}{4} = \dfrac{2}{4} + \dfrac{3}{4} = \dfrac{2 + 3}{4} = \dfrac{5}{4}$

13. $\dfrac{a}{x} - \dfrac{b}{x^2} = \dfrac{ax}{x^2} - \dfrac{b}{x^2} = \dfrac{ax - b}{x^2}$

17. $\dfrac{2}{5a} + \dfrac{1}{a} - \dfrac{a}{10} = \dfrac{4}{10a} + \dfrac{10}{10a} - \dfrac{a^2}{10a}$

$\qquad\qquad = \dfrac{4 + 10 - a^2}{10a}$

$\qquad\qquad = \dfrac{14 - a^2}{10a}$

21. L.C.D. $= 2(2x - 1)$

$\dfrac{3}{2x - 1} + \dfrac{1}{4x - 2} = \dfrac{3}{(2x - 1)} \cdot \dfrac{2}{2} + \dfrac{1}{2(2x - 1)}$

$\qquad\qquad\qquad = \dfrac{6 + 1}{2(2x - 1)} = \dfrac{7}{2(2x - 1)}$

25. L.C.D $= 4(s - 3)$

$\dfrac{s}{2s - 6} + \dfrac{1}{4} - \dfrac{3s}{4s - 12}$

$\quad = \dfrac{s}{2(s - 3)} \cdot \dfrac{2}{2} + \dfrac{1}{4} \cdot \dfrac{(s - 3)}{(s - 3)}$

$\quad - \dfrac{3s}{4(s - 3)} = \dfrac{2s + (s - 3) - 3s}{4(s - 3)} = \dfrac{-3}{4(s - 3)}$

29. L.C.D $= (x - 4)(x - 4) = (x - 4)^2$

$\dfrac{3}{x^2 - 8x + 16} - \dfrac{2}{4 - x}$

$\quad = \dfrac{3}{(x - 4)(x - 4)} + \dfrac{2}{(x - 4)} \cdot \dfrac{(x - 4)}{(x - 4)}$

$\quad = \dfrac{3 + 2(x - 4)}{(x - 4)(x - 4)} = \dfrac{3 + 2x - 8}{(x - 4)(x - 4)}$

$\quad = \dfrac{2x - 5}{(x - 4)(x - 4)} = \dfrac{2x - 5}{(x - 4)^2}$

33. L.C.D. $= (3x - 1)(x - 4)$

$$\frac{x-1}{3x^2 - 13x + 4} - \frac{3x+1}{4-x} = \frac{(x-1)}{(3x-1)(x-4)} + \frac{(3x+1)}{(x-4)} \cdot \frac{(3x-1)}{(3x-1)} = \frac{x-1+9x^2-1}{(3x-1)(x-4)} = \frac{9x^2+x-2}{(3x-1)(x-4)}$$

37. $L.C.D. = (w+1)(w^2 - w + 1)$

$$\frac{1}{w^3+1} + \frac{1}{w+1} - 2 = \frac{1}{(w+1)(w^2-w+1)} + \frac{(w^2-w+1)}{(w+1)(w^2-w+1)} - \frac{2(w+1)(w^2-w+1)}{(w+1)(w^2-w+1)}$$

$$= \frac{1+w^2-w+1-2(w+1)(w^2-w+1)}{(w+1)(w^2-w+1)} = \frac{w^2-w+2-2w^3-2}{(w+1)(w^2-w+1)}$$

$$= \frac{-2w^3+w^2-w}{(w+1)(w^2-w+1)}$$

41. $\dfrac{\dfrac{x}{y} - \dfrac{y}{x}}{1 + \dfrac{y}{x}} \cdot \dfrac{xy}{xy} = \dfrac{x^2 - y^2}{xy + y^2} = \dfrac{(x+y)(x-y)}{y(x+y)} = \dfrac{x-y}{y}$

45. $\dfrac{\dfrac{3}{x} + \dfrac{1}{x^2+x}}{\dfrac{1}{x+1} - \dfrac{1}{x-1}} = \dfrac{\dfrac{3}{x} + \dfrac{1}{x(x+1)}}{\dfrac{1}{x+1} - \dfrac{1}{x-1}} \cdot \dfrac{x(x+1)(x-1)}{x(x+1)(x-1)} = \dfrac{3(x+1)(x-1) + (x-1)}{x(x-1) - x(x+1)}$

$$= \frac{3x^2 - 3 + x - 1}{x^2 - x - x^2 - x} = \frac{3x^2 + x - 4}{-2x} = -\frac{(3x+4)(x-1)}{2x}$$

49.
$$f(x) = \frac{1}{x^2}$$

$$f(x+h) = \frac{1}{(x+h)^2}$$

$$f(x+h) - f(x) = \frac{1}{(x+h)^2} - \frac{1}{x^2} = \frac{x^2 - (x^2 + 2xh + h^2)}{x^2(x+h)^2} = \frac{x^2 - x^2 - 2xh - h^2}{x^2(x+h)^2}$$

$$= \frac{-2xh - h^2}{x^2(x+h)^2}$$

53. $f(x) = 2x - x^2$

$$f\left(\frac{1}{a}\right) = 2\left(\frac{1}{a}\right) - \left(\frac{1}{a}\right)^2 = \frac{2}{a} - \frac{1}{a^2} = \frac{2a-1}{a^2}$$

57. $\dfrac{a+b}{\dfrac{1}{a} + \dfrac{1}{b}} = \dfrac{a+b}{\dfrac{b+a}{ab}} = (a+b) \times \dfrac{ab}{(a+b)} = ab$

61. $\dfrac{2n^2 - n - 4}{2n^2 + 2n - 4} + \dfrac{1}{n-1} = \dfrac{2n^2 - n - 4 + 2(n+2)}{2(n-1)(n+2)} = \dfrac{2n^2 - n - 4 + 2n + 4}{2(n-1)(n+2)}$

$$= \frac{2n^2 + n}{2(n-1)(n+2)} = \frac{n(2n+1)}{2(n-1)(n+2)}$$

65. $\dfrac{\dfrac{L}{C}+\dfrac{R}{sC}}{sL+R+\dfrac{1}{sC}} = \dfrac{\dfrac{Ls+R}{sC}}{\dfrac{(sL+R)sC+1}{sC}}$

$= \dfrac{\dfrac{Ls+R}{sC}}{\dfrac{s^2CL+CRs+1}{sC}}$

$= \dfrac{Ls+R}{Cs} \times \dfrac{Cs}{CLs^2+CRs+1}$

$= \dfrac{Ls+R}{CLs^2+CRs+1}$

6.8   Equations Involving Fractions

1. $\dfrac{x}{2}-\dfrac{1}{b}=\dfrac{x}{2b}$

$xb-2=x$
$x(b-1)=2$

$x=\dfrac{2}{b-1}$

5. $\dfrac{x}{2}+6=2x$

$x+12=4x$
$3x=12$
$x=4$

9. $\dfrac{1}{2}-\dfrac{t-5}{6}=\dfrac{3}{4}$

Multiply both sides by L.C.D. = 12

$6-2(t-5)=9$
$6-2t+10=9$
$2t=7$

$t=\dfrac{7}{2}$

13. $\dfrac{3}{T}+2=\dfrac{5}{3}$

Multiply both sides by L.C.D. = $3T$

$9+6T=5T$
$T=-9$

17. $\dfrac{2y}{y-1}=5$

Multiply both sides by L.C.D. = $y-1$

$2y=5y-5$
$3y=5$

$y=\dfrac{5}{3}$

21. $\dfrac{5}{2x+4}+\dfrac{3}{x+2}=2$

Multiply both sides by L.C.D. = $2(x+2)$

$\dfrac{5}{2(x+2)}+\dfrac{3}{(x+2)}=2$

$5+6=2\cdot 2(x+2)$
$11=4x+8$
$4x=3$

$x=\dfrac{3}{4}$

25. $\dfrac{1}{x}+\dfrac{3}{2x}=\dfrac{2}{x+1}$

Multiply both sides by L.C.D. = $2x(x+1)$

$2(x+1)+3(x+1)=2\cdot 2x$
$2x+2+3x+3=4x$
$x=-5$

29. $\dfrac{1}{x^2-x}-\dfrac{1}{x}=\dfrac{1}{x-1}$

Multiply both sides by L.C.D. = $x(x-1)$

$\dfrac{1}{x(x-1)}-\dfrac{1}{x}=\dfrac{1}{(x-1)}$

$1-(x-1)=x$
$1-x+1=x$
$2x=2$
$x=1$, no solution

33. $2-\dfrac{1}{b}+\dfrac{3}{c}=0$, for c

Multiply both sides by L.C.D. = bc

$2bc-c+3b=0$
$c(2b-1)=-3b$

$c=\dfrac{3b}{1-2b}$

37. $\dfrac{s-s_0}{t}=\dfrac{v+v_0}{2}$ for v

Multiply both sides by L.C.D. = $2t$

$2(s-s_0)=t(v+v_0)$
$2(s-s_0)=tv+tv_0$
$2(s-s_0)-tv_0=tv$

$v=\dfrac{2(s-s_0)-t_0v_0}{t}$

41. $z = \dfrac{1}{g_m} - \dfrac{jX}{g_m R}$ for R

$$g_m R z = R - jX$$
$$g_m R z - R = -jX$$
$$R(g_m z - 1) = -jX$$
$$R = \dfrac{jX}{1 - g_m z}$$

45. $\dfrac{1}{R_1} = \dfrac{N_2^2}{N_1^2 R_2} + \dfrac{N_3^2}{N_1^2 R_3}$ for R_1

$$\dfrac{1}{R_1} = \dfrac{N_2^2 R_3}{N_1^2 R_2 R_3} + \dfrac{N_3^2 R_2}{N_1^2 R_2 R_3}$$
$$\dfrac{1}{R_1} = \dfrac{N_2^2 R_3 + N_3^2 R_2}{N_1^2 R_2 R_3}$$
$$R_1 = \dfrac{N_1^2 R_2 R_3}{N_2^2 R_3 + N_3^2 R_2}$$

49. $\dfrac{1}{4} \cdot t + \dfrac{1}{6} \cdot t = 1$

$$\dfrac{5}{12} \cdot t = 1$$
$$t = \dfrac{12}{5}$$
$$t = 2.4 \text{ h}$$

53. $d = 2.0 t_1$ for trip up
$d = 2.2 t_2$ for trip down

$$t_1 + t_2 + 90 = 5.0(60)$$
$$\dfrac{d}{2.0} + \dfrac{d}{2.2} + 90 = 5(60)$$
$$d = 220 \text{ m}$$

57. $\dfrac{V}{R_1} + \dfrac{V}{R_2} = i$

$$\dfrac{V}{2.7} + \dfrac{V}{6.0} = 1.2$$
$$V = 2.2 \text{ V}$$

Chapter 6 Review Exercises

1. $3a(4x + 5a) = 12ax + 15a^2$

5. $(2a + 1)^2 = 4a^2 + 4a + 1$

9. $(2x + 5)(x - 9) = 2x^2 - 13x - 45$

13. $3s + 9t = 3(s + 3t)$

17. $W^2 - 144 = (W + 12)(W - 12)$

21. $9t^2 - 6t + 1 = (3t - 1)(3t - 1) = (3t - 1)^2$

25. $x^2 + x - 56 = (x + 8)(x - 7)$

29. $2k^2 - k - 36 = (2k - 9)(k + 4)$

33. $10b^2 + 23b - 5 = (5b - 1)(2b + 5)$

37. $250 - 16y^6 = 2(125 - 8y^6)$
$$= 2(5^3 - (2y^2)^3)$$
$$= 2(5 - 2y^2)(25 + 10y^2 + 4y^4)$$

41. $ab^2 - 3b^2 + a - 3 = b^2(a - 3) + (a - 3)$
$$= (a - 3)(b^2 + 1)$$

45. $\dfrac{48ax^3 y^6}{9a^3 xy^6} = \dfrac{16x^2}{3a^2}$

49. $\dfrac{4x + 4y}{35x^2} \cdot \dfrac{28x}{x^2 - y^2} = \dfrac{4(x + y)}{35x^2} \cdot \dfrac{28x}{(x + y)(x - y)}$
$$= \dfrac{4 \cdot 7 \cdot 4}{7 \cdot 5x(x - y)}$$
$$= \dfrac{16}{5x(x - y)}$$

53. $\dfrac{\dfrac{3x}{7x^2 + 13x - 3}}{\dfrac{6x^2}{x^2 + 4x + 4}}$
$$= \dfrac{3x}{(7x - 1)(x + 2)} \cdot \dfrac{(x + 2)(x + 2)}{3 \cdot 2x^2}$$
$$= \dfrac{x + 2}{2x(7x - 1)}$$

57. $\dfrac{4}{9x} - \dfrac{5}{12x^2} = \dfrac{4}{9x} \cdot \dfrac{4x}{4x} - \dfrac{5}{12x^2} \cdot \dfrac{3}{3}$
$$= \dfrac{16x - 15}{36x^2}$$

61. $\dfrac{a + 1}{a + 2} - \dfrac{a + 3}{a} = \dfrac{(a + 1)}{(a + 2)} \cdot \dfrac{a}{a} - \dfrac{(a + 3)}{a} \cdot \dfrac{(a + 2)}{(a + 2)}$
$$= \dfrac{a(a + 1) - (a + 3)(a + 2)}{a(a + 2)}$$
$$= \dfrac{a^2 + a - a^2 - 5a - 6}{a(a + 2)}$$
$$= \dfrac{-4a - 6}{a(a + 2)} = \dfrac{-2(a + 3)}{a(a + 2)}$$

65. $\dfrac{3x}{2x^2-2} - \dfrac{2}{4x^2-5x+1} = \dfrac{3x}{2(x+1)(x-1)} \cdot \dfrac{(4x-1)}{(4x-1)} - \dfrac{2}{(4x-1)(x-1)} \cdot \dfrac{2(x+1)}{2(x+1)}$

$$= \dfrac{3x(4x-1)-4(x+1)}{2(4x-1)(x+1)(x-1)} = \dfrac{12x^2-3x-4x-4}{2(4x-1)(x+1)(x-1)}$$

$$= \dfrac{12x^2-7x-4}{2(4x-1)(x+1)(x-1)}$$

69. $\dfrac{6x^2-7x-3}{4x^2-8x+3} = \dfrac{(2x-3)(3x+1)}{(2x-1)(2x-3)} = \dfrac{3x+1}{2x-1}$

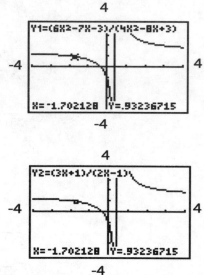

73. $x^2-5 = (x+\sqrt{5})(x-\sqrt{5})$

77. $\dfrac{x}{2} - 3 = \dfrac{x-10}{4}$

$2x - 12 = x - 10$

$x = 2$

81. $\dfrac{2x}{2x^2-5x} - \dfrac{3}{x} = \dfrac{1}{4x-10}$

$\dfrac{2x}{x(2x-5)} - \dfrac{3}{x} = \dfrac{1}{2(2x-5)}$

$4x - 6(2x-5) = x$

$4x - 12x + 30 = x$

$9x = 30$

$x = \dfrac{10}{3}$

85. $\dfrac{1}{4}[(x+y)^2-(x-y)^2] = \dfrac{1}{4}[x^2+2xy+y^2-(x^2-2xy+y^2)] = \dfrac{1}{4}[x^2+2xy+y^2-x^2+2xy-y^2] = \dfrac{1}{4}[4xy] = xy$

89. $kr(R-r) = krR - kr^2$

93. $4s^3 + 56s^2 + 96s = 4s(s^2+14s+24) = 4s(s+12)(s+2)$

97. $(n+1)^3(2n+1)^3 = (n^3+3n^2+3n+1)(8n^3+12n^2+6n+1)$

$= 8n^6 + 12n^5 + 6n^4 + n^3 + 24n^5 + 36n^4 + 18n^3 + 3n^2 + 24n^4 + 36n^3 + 18n^2 + 3n$

$\quad + 8n^3 + 12n^2 + 6n + 1$

$= 8n^6 + 36n^5 + 66n^4 + 63n^3 + 33n^2 + 9n + 1$

101. increase in volume $= (x + 4)^3 - x^3 = x^3 + 12x^2 + 48x + 64 - x^3 = 12x^2 + 48x + 64 = 4(3x^2 + 12x + 16)$

105. $\dfrac{\dfrac{\pi k a}{2}(R^4 - r^4)}{\pi k a (R^2 - r^2)} = \dfrac{1(R^2 + r^2)(R^2 - r^2)}{2(R^2 - r^2)} = \dfrac{R^2 + r^2}{2}$

109. $\dfrac{N + n}{2} + \dfrac{(N - n)^2}{4\pi^2 C} = \dfrac{4\pi^2 C(N + n) + 2(N - n)^2}{8\pi^2 C} = \dfrac{2\pi^2 CN + 2\pi^2 Cn + N^2 - 2Nn + n^2}{4\pi^2 C}$

113. $\dfrac{\dfrac{u^2}{2g} - x}{\dfrac{1}{2gc^2} - \dfrac{u^2}{2g} + x} \cdot \dfrac{2gc^2}{2gc^2} = \dfrac{u^2 c^2 - 2gc^2 x}{1 - u^2 c^2 + 2gc^2 x}$

117. $$R = \frac{wL}{H(w + L)}$$

$$RHw + RHL = wL$$
$$wL - RHL = RHw$$
$$L(w - RH) = RHw$$
$$L = \frac{RHw}{w - RH}$$

121. $$s^2 + \frac{cs}{m} + \frac{kL^2}{mb^2} = 0$$

$$s^2 mb^2 + csb^2 + kL^2 = 0$$
$$csb^2 = -s^2 mb^2 - kL^2$$
$$c = \frac{-s^2 mb^2 - kL^2}{sb^2}$$

125. $\dfrac{1}{4} \cdot t + \dfrac{1}{24} \cdot t = 1$

$\quad\quad \dfrac{7}{24} \cdot t = 1$

$\quad\quad\quad t = 3.4 \text{ h}$

129. $d = \dfrac{w_a}{w_a - w_w} = \dfrac{1.097 w_w}{1.097 w_w - w_w} = \dfrac{1.097}{1.097 - 1} = 11.3$

133. $\dfrac{2r^2 + 5r - 3}{2r^2 + 7r + 3} = \dfrac{(r + 3)(2r - 1)}{(r + 3)(2r + 1)} = \dfrac{2r - 1}{2r + 1}$

When you "cancel", the basic operation being performed is division.

Chapter 7

QUADRATIC EQUATIONS

7.1 Quadratic Equations; Solution by Factoring

1. $2N^2 - 7N - 4 = 0$
$(2N + 1)(N - 4) = 0$ factor
$2N + 1 = 0$ or $N - 4 = 0$
$2N = -1$ or $N = 4$ Set each factor
$N = -\dfrac{1}{2}$ or $N = 4$ equal to zero and solve

The roots are $N = -\dfrac{1}{2}$ and $N = 4$.

5. $x^2 = (x + 2)^2$
$x^2 = x^2 + 4x + 4$

$4x + 4 = 0$, no x^2 term, not quadratic

9. $x^2 - 4 = 0$
$(x + 2)(x - 2) = 0$
$x + 2 = 0$ or $x - 2 = 0$
$x = -2$ $x = 2$

13. $x^2 - 8x - 9 = 0$
$(x - 9)(x + 1) = 0$
$x - 9 = 0$ or $x + 1 = 0$
$x = 9$ $x = -1$

17. $40x - 16x^2 = 0$
$2x^2 - 5x = 0$
$x(2x - 5) = 0$
$x = 0$ or $2x - 5 = 0$
$2x = 5$
$x = \dfrac{5}{2}$

21. $3x^2 - 13x + 4 = 0$
$(3x - 1)(x - 4) = 0$
$3x - 1 = 0$ or $x - 4 = 0$
$3x = 1$ $x = 4$
$x = \dfrac{1}{3}$

25. $6x^2 = 13x - 6$
$6x^2 - 13x + 6 = 0$
$(3x - 2)(2x - 3) = 0$
$3x - 2 = 0$ or $2x - 3 = 0$
$3x = 2$ $2x = 3$
$x = \dfrac{2}{3}$ $x = \dfrac{3}{2}$

29. $x^2 - x - 1 = 1$
$x^2 - x - 2 = 0$
$(x - 2)(x + 1) = 0$
$x - 2 = 0$ or $x + 1 = 0$
$x = 2$ $x = -1$

33. $8s^2 + 16s = 90$
$8s^2 + 16s - 90 = 0$
$(4s - 10)(2s + 9) = 0$
$4s - 10 = 0$ or $2s + 9 = 0$
$4s = 10$ $2s = -9$
$s = \dfrac{5}{2}$ $s = -\dfrac{9}{2}$

37. $(x + a)^2 - b^2 = 0$
$(x - a - b)(x + a + b) = 0$
$x + a - b = 0$ or $x + a + b = 0$
$x = b - a$ $x = -b - a$

41. $P = 4h^2 - 48h + 744$
$P = 664 = 4h^2 - 48h + 774$
$4h^2 - 48h + 80 = 0$
$4(h^2 - 12h + 20) = 0$
$4(h - 10)(h - 2) = 0$
$h - 2 = 0$ or $h = 2$
$h - 10 = 0$ $h = 10$

The power is 664 MW at 2 A.M. and 10 A.M.

45. $\dfrac{1}{x-3} + \dfrac{4}{x} = 2$ L.C.D $= x(x-3)$; multiply each term by L.C.D.

$$x + 4(x-3) = 2x(x-3)$$
$$x + 4x - 12 = 2x^2 - 6x$$
$$2x^2 - 11x + 12 = 0$$
$$(x-4)(2x-3) = 0$$
$$x - 4 = 0 \quad \text{or} \quad 2x - 3 = 0$$
$$x = 4 \qquad\qquad 2x = 3$$
$$x = \dfrac{3}{2}$$

49. $\dfrac{1}{k_c} = \dfrac{1}{k_1} + \dfrac{1}{k_2} \Rightarrow \dfrac{1}{2} = \dfrac{1}{k} + \dfrac{1}{k+3}$

$$k(k+3) = 2(k+3) + 2k$$
$$k^2 + 3k = 2k + 6 + 2k$$
$$k^2 - k - 6 = 0$$
$$(k-3)(k+2) = 0$$
$$k - 3 = 0 \quad \text{or} \quad k + 2 = 0$$
$$k = 3 \qquad\qquad k = -2, \text{ reject since } k > 0.$$
$$k + 3 = 6$$

The spring constants are 3 N/cm and 6 N/cm.

7.2   Completing the Square

1. $x^2 + 6x - 8 = 0$
$$x^2 + 6x = 8$$
$$x^2 + 6x + 9 = 8 + 9$$
$$(x+3)^2 = 17$$
$$x + 3 = \pm\sqrt{17}$$
$$x = -3 \pm \sqrt{17}$$

5. $x^2 = 7$
$$\sqrt{x^2} = \pm\sqrt{7}$$
$$x = \sqrt{7} \text{ or } x = -\sqrt{7}$$

9. $(x+3)^2 = 7$
$$\sqrt{(x+3)^2} = \pm\sqrt{7}$$
$$x + 3 = \pm\sqrt{7} \text{ or } x = -3 \pm \sqrt{7}$$

13. $D^2 + 3D + 2 = 0$
$$D^2 + 3D = -2$$
$$D^2 + 3D + \dfrac{9}{4} = -2 + \dfrac{9}{4}$$
$$\left(D + \dfrac{3}{2}\right)^2 = \dfrac{1}{4}$$

$$D + \dfrac{3}{2} = -\dfrac{1}{2} \quad \text{or} \quad D + \dfrac{3}{2} = \dfrac{1}{2}$$
$$D = -\dfrac{4}{2} \qquad\qquad D = -\dfrac{2}{2}$$
$$= -2 \qquad\qquad\quad = -1$$

17. $v(v+2) = 15$
$$v^2 + 2v = 15$$
$$v^2 + 2v - 15 = 0$$
$$v^2 + 2v = 15$$
$$v^2 + 2v + 1 = 15 + 1$$
$$(v+1)^2 = 16$$
$$v + 1 = \pm 4$$
$$v = -4 - 1 = -5$$
$$v = 4 - 1 = 3$$

21. $3y^2 = 3y + 2$
$$3y^2 - 3y - 2 = 0$$
$$y^2 - y = \dfrac{2}{3}$$
$$y^2 - y + \dfrac{1}{4} = \dfrac{2}{3} + \dfrac{1}{4}$$
$$\left(y - \dfrac{1}{2}\right)^2 = \dfrac{11}{12}$$
$$y - \dfrac{1}{2} = \pm\sqrt{\dfrac{11}{12}}$$
$$y = \dfrac{1}{2} \pm \dfrac{1}{2}\sqrt{\dfrac{11}{3}} = \dfrac{1}{2} \pm \dfrac{1}{2}\dfrac{\sqrt{33}}{3}$$
$$= \dfrac{1}{2} \pm \dfrac{1}{6}\sqrt{33} = \dfrac{1}{6}(3 \pm \sqrt{33})$$

25. $5T^2 - 10T + 4 = 0$
$$5(T^2 - 2T + 1) = -4 + 5$$
$$5(T-1)^2 = 1$$
$$(T-1)^2 = \dfrac{1}{5}$$
$$T = 1 \pm \dfrac{\sqrt{5}}{5}$$

29. $x^2 + 2bx + c = 0$
$$x^2 + 2bx = -c$$
$$x^2 + 2bx + b^2 = -c + b^2$$
$$(x+b)^2 = -c + b$$
$$x + b = \pm\sqrt{b^2 - c}$$
$$x = -b \pm \sqrt{b^2 - c}$$

7.3   The Quadratic Formula

1. $x^2 + 5x + 6 = 0$, $a = 1$, $b = 5$, $c = 6$

$$x = \frac{-5 \pm \sqrt{5^2 - 4(1)(6)}}{2(1)} = \frac{-5 \pm \sqrt{1}}{2} = \frac{-5 \pm 1}{2}$$

$$x = \frac{-5 + 1}{2} = -2 \text{ or } x = \frac{-5 - 1}{2} = -3$$

5. $x^2 + 2x - 8 = 0$; $a = 1$, $b = 2$, $c = -8$

$$x = \frac{-2 \pm \sqrt{2^2 - 4(1)(-8)}}{2(1)}$$

$$= \frac{-2 \pm \sqrt{36}}{2}$$

$$= \frac{-2 \pm 6}{2}$$

$$x = 2 \quad \text{or} \quad x = -4$$

9. $x^2 - 4x + 2 = 0$; $a = 1$, $b = -4$, $c = 2$

$$x = \frac{-(-4) \pm \sqrt{(-4)^2 - 4(1)(2)}}{2}$$

$$= \frac{4 \pm \sqrt{8}}{2}$$

$$= \frac{4 \pm 2\sqrt{2}}{2}$$

$$= 2 \pm \sqrt{2}$$

13. $2s^2 + 5s = 3$

$2s^2 + 5s - 3 = 0$; $a = 2$, $b = 5$, $c = -3$

$$s = \frac{-5 \pm \sqrt{5^2 - 4(2)(-3)}}{2(2)}$$

$$= \frac{-5 \pm \sqrt{49}}{4}$$

$$= \frac{-5 \pm 7}{4}$$

$$s = \frac{1}{2} \quad \text{or} \quad s = -3$$

17. $2y^2 - y - 2 = 0$

$2y^2 - y - 2 = 0$; $a = 2$, $b = -1$, $c = -2$

$$y = \frac{-(-1) \pm \sqrt{(-1)^2 - 4(2)(-2)}}{2(2)}$$

$$= \frac{1 \pm \sqrt{17}}{4}$$

21. $\quad 8t^2 + 61t = -120$

$8t^2 + 61t + 120 = 0$; $a = 8$, $b = 61$, $c = 120$

$$t = \frac{-61 \pm \sqrt{61^2 - 4(8)(120)}}{2(8)}$$

$$= \frac{-61 \pm \sqrt{-119}}{16}$$

25. $25y^2 - 121 = 0$; $a = 25$, $b = 0$, $c = -121$

$$y = \frac{-0 \pm \sqrt{0^2 - 4(25)(-121)}}{2(25)}$$

$$y = \frac{\pm\sqrt{12{,}100}}{50}$$

$$= \frac{\pm 110}{50}$$

$$y = \pm\frac{11}{5}$$

29. $x^2 - 0.20x - 0.40 = 0$; $a = 1$, $b = -0.20$, $c = -0.40$

$$x = \frac{-(-0.20) \pm \sqrt{(-0.20)^2 - 4(1)(-0.40)}}{2(1)}$$

$$= \frac{0.2 \pm \sqrt{1.64}}{2}$$

$$x = -0.54 \quad \text{or} \quad x = 0.74$$

33. $x^2 + 2cx - 1 = 0$

$$x = \frac{-2c \pm \sqrt{(2c)^2 - 4(1)(-1)}}{2(1)}$$

$$= \frac{-2c \pm \sqrt{4c^2 + 4}}{2}$$

$$= \frac{-2c \pm 2\sqrt{c^2 + 1}}{2}$$

$$x = -c \pm \sqrt{c^2 + 1}$$

37. $\quad 2x^2 - 7x = -8$

$2x^2 - 7x + 8 = 0$; $a = 2$, $b = -7$, $c = 8$

$D = \sqrt{(-7)^2 - 4(2)(8)} = \sqrt{-15}$,

unequal imaginary roots

41. $\dfrac{-b + \sqrt{b^2 - 4ac}}{2a} = \dfrac{1}{\dfrac{-b - \sqrt{b^2 - 4ac}}{2a}}$

$$\frac{-b + \sqrt{b^2 - 4ac}}{2a} = \frac{2a}{\sqrt{-b - b^2 - 4ac}}$$

$$4a^2 = b^2 + b\sqrt{b^2 - 4ac} - b\sqrt{b^2 - 4ac}$$
$$- b^2 + 4ac$$

$$a = c$$

45. $\dfrac{l}{w} = \dfrac{l+w}{l} \Rightarrow l^2 = lw + w^2$

$l^2 - wl - w^2 = 0;\ a = 1,\ b = -w,\ c = -w^2$

$l = \dfrac{-(-w) \pm \sqrt{(-w)^2 - 4(1)(-w^2)}}{2(1)}$

$ = \dfrac{w + w\sqrt{5}}{2}$ where $+$ is chosen to make $l > 0$

$\dfrac{l}{w} = \dfrac{1 + \sqrt{5}}{2} = 1.618$

49.

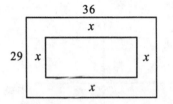

A edge $= 0.44(29)(36)$
$2(29)x + 2(36 - 2x)x = 0.44(29)(36)$
$-4x^2 + 130x - 459.36 = 0;\ a = -4,\ b = 130,$
$c = -459.36$

$x = \dfrac{-130 \pm \sqrt{130^2 - 4(-4)(-459.36)}}{2(-4)}$

$x = 4.0$ cm

53. $A = b \times h = 12 \times 16 = 192$ ft^2
$A_{\text{new}} = 192 + 80 = 272$ ft^2
$272 = (12 + r)(16 + r)$
$272 = r^2 + 28r + 192$

$r^2 + 28r - 80 = 0;\ a = 1,\ b = 28,\ c = -80$

$r = \dfrac{-28 \pm \sqrt{784 - 4(1)(-80)}}{2(1)} = \dfrac{-28 \pm \sqrt{1104}}{2}$

$= 2.6$ ft (ignore negative dimension)

7.4   The Graph of the Quadratic Function

1. $y = 2x^2 + 8x + 6;\ a = 2,\ b = 8,\ c = 6$

x-coordinate of vertex $= \dfrac{-b}{2a}$

$\phantom{x\text{-coordinate of vertex}} = \dfrac{-8}{2(2)} = -2$

y-coordinate of vertex $= 2(-2)^2 + 8(-2) + 6$

$\phantom{y\text{-coordinate of vertex}} = -2$

The vertex is $(-2, -2)$ and since $a > 0$, it is a minimum. Since $c = 6$, the y-intercept is $(0, 6)$ and the sketch is

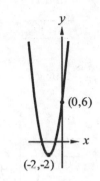

5. $y = -3x^2 + 10x - 4;\ a = -3,\ b = 10.$

This means that the x-coordinate of the extreme point is

$$\dfrac{-b}{2a} = \dfrac{-10}{2(-3)} = \dfrac{10}{6} = \dfrac{5}{3}$$

and the y-coordinate is

$$y = -3\left(\dfrac{5}{3}\right)^2 + 10\left(\dfrac{5}{3}\right) - 4 = \dfrac{13}{3}.$$

Thus the extreme point is $\left(\dfrac{5}{3}, \dfrac{13}{3}\right)$.

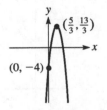

Since $a < 0$, it is a maximum point. Since $c = -4$, the y-intercept is $(0, -4)$. Use maximum point $\left(\dfrac{5}{3}, \dfrac{13}{3}\right)$, and the y-intercept $(0, -4)$, and the fact that the graph is a parabola, to sketch the graph.

9. $y = x^2 - 4 = x^2 + 0x - 4$; $a = 1$, $b = 0$, $c = -4$
The x-coordinate of the extreme point is

$$\frac{-b}{2a} = \frac{-0}{2(1)} = 0,$$ and the y-coordinate is

$y = 0^2 - 4 = -4$.
The extreme is $(0, -4)$.

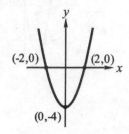

Since $a > 0$ it is a minimum. Since $c = -4$, the y-intercept is $(0, -4)$. $x^2 - 4 = 0$, $x^2 = 4$, $x = \pm 2$ are the x-intercepts. Use minimum points and intercepts to sketch the graph.

13. $y = 2x^2 + 3 = 2x^2 + 0x + 3$; $a = 2$, $b = 0$, $c = 3$
The x-coordinate of the extreme point is

$$\frac{-b}{2a} = \frac{-0}{2(2)} = 0,$$ and the y-coordinate is

$y = 2(0)^2 + 3 = 3$.
The extreme point is $(0, 3)$. Since $a > 0$ it is a minimum point.

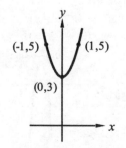

Since $c = 3$, the y-intercept is $(0, 3)$ there are no x-intercepts, $b^2 - 4ac = -24$. $(-1, 5)$ and $(1, 5)$ are on the graph. Use the three points to sketch the graph.

17. $2x^2 - 3 = 0$. Graph $y = 2x - 3$ on graphing calculator and use zero feature to find roots.
$x = -1.2$ and $x = 1.2$

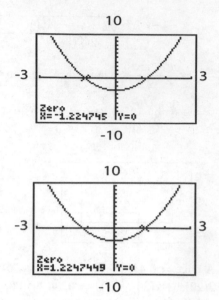

21. $x(2x - 1) = -3$. Graph $y = x(2x - 1) + 3$ on graphing calculator and use zero feature to find roots.

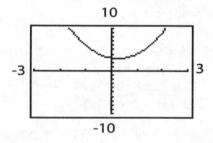

As the graph shows there are no real solutions.

25. **(a)** $y = x^2$ **(b)** $y = x^2 + 3$
(c) $y = x^2 - 3$

The parabola $y = x^2 + 3$ is shifted up $+3$ units (minimum point $(0, 3)$).
The parabola $y = x^2 - 3$ is shifted down -3 units (minimum point $(0, -3)$).

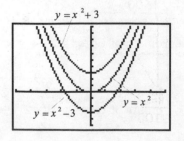

29. (a) $y = x^2$ **(b)** $y = 3x^2$ **(c)** $y = \frac{1}{3}x^2$

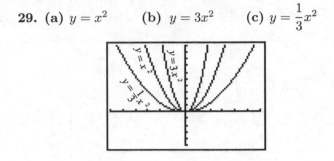

The graph of $y = 3x^2$ is the graph of $y = x^2$ narrowed. The graph of $y = \frac{1}{3}x^2$ is the graph of $y = x^2$ broadened.

33. Graph $y = x(8 - x)$ for $0 > x > 8$.

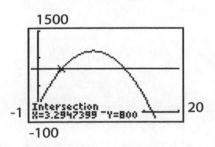

37.

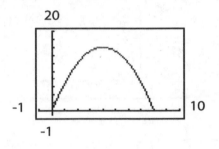

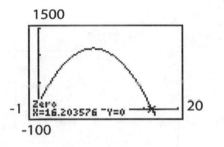

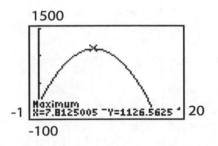

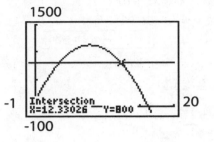

From the graphs:

(a) the missile will hit the ground after 16.2 s

(b) the missile will reach a maximum height of 1130 ft

(c) the missile will have a height of 800 ft at 3.3 s and 12.3 s

Chapter 7 Review Exercises

1. $x^2 + 3x - 4 = 0$
$(x + 4)(x - 1) = 0$
$x + 4 = 0$ or $x - 1 = 0$
$x = -4$ $x = 1$

5. $3x^2 + 11x = 4$
$3x^2 + 11x - 4 = 0$
$(3x - 1)(x + 4) = 0$
$3x - 1 = 0$ or $x + 4 = 0$
$3x = 1$ $x = -4$
$x = \frac{1}{3}$

9. $6s^2 = 25s$
$6s^2 - 25s = 0$
$s(6s - 25) = 0$
$s = 0$ or $6s - 25 = 0$
$6s = 25$
$s = \frac{25}{6}$

13. $x^2 - x - 110 = 0$
$x = \dfrac{-(-1) \pm \sqrt{(-1)^2 - 4(1)(-110)}}{2(1)}$
$= \dfrac{1 \pm 21}{2}$
$x = -10$ or $x = 11$

17.
$$2x^2 - x = 36$$
$$2x^2 - x - 36 = 0$$
$$x = \frac{-(-1) \pm \sqrt{(-1)^2 - 4(2)(-36)}}{2(2)}$$
$$= \frac{1 \pm \sqrt{289}}{4}$$
$$= \frac{1 \pm 17}{4}$$
$$x = \frac{9}{2} \quad \text{or} \quad x = -4$$

21. $2.1x^2 + 2.3x + 5.5 = 0$
$$x = \frac{-2.3 \pm \sqrt{2.3^2 - 4(2.1)(5.5)}}{2(2.1)}$$
$$= \frac{-23 \pm \sqrt{-4091}}{42} = \frac{-23 \pm \sqrt{-4091}}{42}$$
there are two unequal imaginary roots.

25. $x^2 + 4x - 4 = 0$
$$x = \frac{-4 \pm \sqrt{4^2 - 4(1)(-4)}}{2(1)}$$
$$= \frac{-4 \pm \sqrt{32}}{2}$$
$$= \frac{-4 \pm 4\sqrt{2}}{2}$$
$$x = -2 \pm 2\sqrt{2}$$

29.
$$4v^2 = v + 5$$
$$4v^2 - v - 5 = 0$$
$$(v + 1)(4v - 5) = 0$$
$$v + 1 = 0 \quad \text{or} \quad 4v - 5 = 0$$
$$v = -1 \qquad\qquad 4v = 5$$
$$v = \frac{5}{4}$$

33. $a^2x^2 + 2ax + 2 = 0$
$$x = \frac{-2a \pm \sqrt{(2a)^2 - 4(a^2)(2)}}{2(a^2)}$$
$$x = \frac{-2a \pm \sqrt{-4a^2}}{2a^2} \quad \text{and for } a > 0,$$
$$x = \frac{-2a \pm 2a\sqrt{-1}}{2a^2}$$
$$x = \frac{-1 \pm \sqrt{-1}}{a}$$

37. $x^2 - x - 30 = 0$
$$x^2 - x + \frac{1}{4} = 30 + \frac{1}{4} = \frac{121}{4}$$
$$\left(x - \frac{1}{2}\right)^2 = \frac{121}{4}$$
$$x - \frac{1}{2} = \frac{\pm 11}{2}$$
$$x = \frac{1}{2} \pm \frac{11}{2}$$
$$x = -5 \quad \text{or} \quad x = 6$$

41.
$$\frac{x - 4}{x - 1} = \frac{2}{x}$$
$$x(x - 4) = 2(x - 1)$$
$$x^2 - 4x = 2x - 2$$
$$x^2 - 6x + 2 = 0$$
$$x = \frac{-(-6) \pm \sqrt{(-6)^2 - 4(1)(2)}}{2(1)}$$
$$= \frac{6 \pm \sqrt{28}}{2}$$
$$= \frac{6 \pm \sqrt{4 \cdot 7}}{2}$$
$$= \frac{6 \pm 2\sqrt{7}}{2}$$
$$x = 3 \pm \sqrt{7}$$

45. $y = 2x^2 - x - 1; \; a = 2, \; b = -1, \; c = -1$
$$c = -1 \Rightarrow y\text{-int} = -1$$
$$2x^2 - x - 1 = 0 \Rightarrow x = -\frac{1}{2}, \; x = 1, \text{ the } x\text{-intercepts}$$
$$x \text{ vertex} = \frac{-b}{2a} = \frac{-(-1)}{2(2)} = \frac{1}{4}$$
$$y \text{ vertex} = 2\left(\frac{1}{4}\right)^2 - \left(\frac{1}{4}\right) - 1 = -\frac{9}{8}$$

x	y
$\frac{1}{4}$	$-\frac{9}{8}$
0	-1
$-\frac{1}{2}$	0
1	0
-2	9
-1	2
2	5

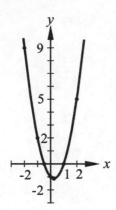

65. $p_2 = p_1 + rp_1(1 - p_1)$

$p_2 = p_1 + rp_1 - rp^2.$

$rp_1^2 - (r + 1)p_1 + p_2 = 0;\ a = r,\ b = -(r + 1),$

$c = p_2$

$$p_1 = \frac{-[-(r + 1)] \pm \sqrt{[-(r + 1)]^2 - 4rp_2}}{2r}$$

$$p_1 = \frac{r + 1 \pm \sqrt{(r + 1)^2 - 4rp_2}}{2r}$$

49. Graph $y = 2x^2 + x - 4$ and find roots.

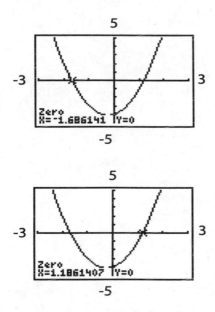

$x = -1.7, 1.2$

53. $M = 0.5wLx - 0.5wx^2$

$M = 0.5wx(L - x)$

$M = 0$ for $x = 0$ and $x = L$

57. $T^2 + 520T - 5300 = 0$

$(T - 10)(T + 530) = 0$

$T - 10 = 0$

$T = 10$

$212 - 10 = 202°F$

61. $\dfrac{n^2}{500,000} = 144 - \dfrac{n}{500}$

$n^2 + 1000n - 72,000,000 = 0$

$(n + 9000)(n - 8000) = 0$

$n - 8000 = 0$ or $n + 9000 = 0$

$n = 8000$ $n = -9000$

reject since $n > 0$

69. $100x + x(80 - x) = 3000$

$100x + 80x - x^2 = 3000$

$x^2 - 180x + 3000 = 0;\ a = 1,\ b = -180,$

$c = 3000$

The quadratic formula gives $x = 19$ or $x = 161$. The original dimensions are $80 - 19 = 61$ m and $100 - 19 = 81$ m.

73.

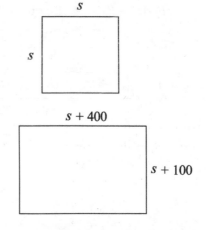

$(s + 400)(s + 100) = 2 \cdot s^2$

$s^2 + 500s + 40,000 = 2s^2$

$s^2 - 500s - 40,000 = 0;\ a = 1,\ b = -500,$

$c = -40,000$

The quadratic formula gives $s = 570$

The dimensions of the square: 570 m by 570 m.

The dimensions of the rectangle: 670 m by 970 m.

77. Suppose n poles are placed along the road for a distance of 1 km and x is the distance, in km, between the poles, then $n \cdot x = 1$. Increasing the distance between the poles to $x + 0.01$ and decreasing the number of poles to $n - 5$ gives $(n-5)(x+0.01) = 1$. Substitution gives

$$(n-5)\left(\frac{1}{n} + 0.01\right) = 1$$

$$1 + 0.01n - \frac{5}{n} - 0.05 = 1$$

$$0.01n^2 - 0.05n - 5 = 0$$
$$n^2 - 5n - 500 = 0$$
$$(n+20)(n-25) = 0$$
$$= 0$$
$$n + 20 = 0 \qquad \text{or} \qquad n - 25 = 0$$
$$n = -20, \quad \text{reject} \qquad n = 25$$

There are 25 poles being placed each kilometer.

81. $$\frac{1}{R_T} = \frac{1}{R} + \frac{1}{R+1}$$

$$R(R+1) = R_T(R+1) + RR_T$$
$$R^2 + R = R_T R + R_T + RR_T$$
$$R^2 - 2R_T R + R - R_T = 0$$
$$R^2 + (1 - 2R_T)R - R_T = 0, \text{ use quadratic formula}$$

$$R = \frac{-(1 - 2R_T) \pm \sqrt{(1-2R_T)^2 - 4(1)(-R_T)}}{2(1)}$$

$$R = \frac{2R_T - 1 \pm \sqrt{1 - 4R_T + 4R_T^2 + 4R_T}}{2}$$

$$R = \frac{2R_T - 1 \pm \sqrt{1 + 4R_T^2}}{2}$$

TRIGONOMETRIC FUNCTIONS OF ANY ANGLE

8.1 Signs of the Trigonometric Functions

1. (a) $\sin(150° + 90°)$ is $-$
   $\cos(290° + 90°)$ is $+$
   $\tan(190° + 90°)$ is $-$
   $\cot(260° + 90°)$ is $-$
   $\sec(350° + 90°)$ is $+$
   $\csc(100° + 90°)$ is $-$

   (b) $\sin(300° + 90°)$ is $+$
   $\cos(150° + 90°)$ is $-$
   $\tan(100° + 90°)$ is $+$
   $\cot(300° + 90°)$ is $+$
   $\sec(200° + 90°)$ is $+$
   $\csc(250° + 90°)$ is $-$

5. $\csc 98°$ is positive since $98°$ is in Quad II, where $\csc \theta$ is positive.
   $\cot(82°)$ is positive since $82°$ is in Quad I, where $\cot \theta$ is positive.

9. $\cos(348°)$ is positive since $348°$ is in Quad IV, where $\cos \theta$ is positive.
   $\csc 238°$ is negative since $238°$ is in Quad III, where $\csc \theta$ is negative.

13. $\cot(-2°)$ is negative since $-2°$ is in Quad IV where $\cot \theta$ is negative..
    $\cos(710°) = \cos(710° - 360°) = \cos(350°)$ which is positive since $350°$ is in Quad IV where $\cos \theta$ is positive.

17. $(-2, -3)$; $x = -2, y = -3, r = \sqrt{x^2 + y^2} = \sqrt{13}$

$$\sin \theta = \frac{y}{r} = \frac{-3}{\sqrt{13}}$$

$$\cos \theta = \frac{x}{r} = \frac{-2}{\sqrt{13}}$$

$$\tan \theta = \frac{y}{x} = \frac{-3}{-2} = \frac{3}{2}$$

$$\csc \theta = \frac{r}{y} = -\frac{\sqrt{13}}{3}$$

$$\sec \theta = \frac{r}{x} = -\frac{\sqrt{13}}{2}$$

$$\cot \theta = \frac{x}{y} = \frac{-2}{-3} = \frac{2}{3}$$

21. $(50, -20)$; $x = 50,$
    $y = -20, r = \sqrt{x^2 + y^2} = 10\sqrt{29}$

$$\sin \theta = \frac{y}{r} = \frac{-20}{10\sqrt{29}} = \frac{-2}{\sqrt{29}}$$

$$\cos \theta = \frac{x}{r} = \frac{50}{10\sqrt{29}} = \frac{5}{\sqrt{29}}$$

$$\tan \theta = \frac{y}{x} = \frac{-20}{50} = -\frac{2}{5}$$

$$\csc \theta = \frac{r}{y} = \frac{10\sqrt{29}}{-20} = -\frac{\sqrt{29}}{2}$$

$$\sec \theta = \frac{r}{x} = \frac{10\sqrt{29}}{50} = \frac{\sqrt{29}}{5}$$

$$\cot \theta = \frac{x}{y} = \frac{50}{-20} = -\frac{5}{2}$$

25. $\tan \theta = 1.500 \Rightarrow$ QI, QIII

29. $\sin \theta$ is positive and $\cos \theta$ is negative
    $\sin \theta$ positive in QI and QII
    $\cos \theta$ negative in QII and QIII. The terminal side of θ is in QII.

33. $\csc \theta$ negative and $\tan \theta$ negative
    $\csc \theta$ negative in QIII and QIV
    $\tan \theta$ negative in QII and QIV.
    The terminal side of θ is in QIV.

37. $\tan \theta$ negative, $\cos \theta$ positive
    $\tan \theta$ is negative in QII and QIV
    $\cos \theta$ is positive in QI and QIV.
    The terminal side of θ is in QIV.

8.2   Trigonometric Functions of Any Angle

1. $\sin 200° = -\sin 20° = -0.3420$
   $\tan 150° = -\tan 30° = -0.5774$
   $\cos 265° = -\cos 85° = -0.0872$
   $\cot 300° = -\cot 60° = -0.5774$
   $\sec 344° = \sec 16° = 1.040$
   $\sin 397° = \sin 37° = 0.6018$

5. $\sin 160° = \sin(180° - 160°)$
   $\qquad = \sin\ 20°$

   $\cos\ 220° = \cos(180° + 40°)$
   $\qquad\quad = -\cos\ 40°$

9.

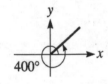

   $\cos\ 400° = \cos(360° + 40°)$
   $\qquad\quad = \cos 40°$

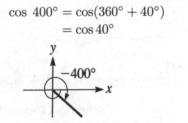

   $\tan(-400°) = \tan(-360° - 40°)$
   $\qquad\qquad = \tan(-40°)$
   $\qquad\qquad = -\tan\ 40°$

13. $\cos 106.3° = -\cos 73.7° = -0.281$

17. $\tan(-31.5°) = -\tan 31.5° = -0.613$

21. $\sin 310.36° = -0.7620$

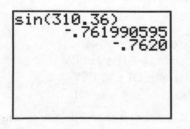

25. $\cos(-72.61°) = 0.2989$

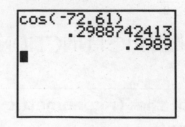

29. $\cos\theta = 0.4003,$
   $\theta_{\text{ref}} = \cos^{-1}(0.4003) = 66.4°.$
   Since $\cos\theta$ is positive, θ is in QI or QIV. Therefore,
   $\theta = 66.4°$ or
   $\theta = 293.6°$
   $0^0 \le \theta < 360°$

33. $\sin\theta = 0.870, \theta_{\text{ref}} = \sin^{-1}(0.870) = 60.4°$
   Since $0^0 \le \theta < 360°$, $\cos\theta < 0$, θ is in QII and
   $\theta = 119.5°$

37. $\tan\theta = -1.366, \theta_{\text{ref}} = \tan^{-1}(-1.366) = -53.8°$
   Since $0^0 \le \theta < 360°$, $\cos\theta > 0$, θ is in QIV and
   $\theta = 306.2°$

41. $\sin\theta = -0.5736, \theta_{\text{ref}} = \sin^{-1}(-0.5736) = -35°.$
   Since $\cos\theta > 0$, θ is in QIV.
   $\theta = 325° + k \cdot 360°$
   where $k = 0, \pm 1, \pm 2, \cdots$
   $\tan\theta = -0.7003$

45. $\sin\ 90° = 1, 2\ \sin\ 45° = 2 \cdot \dfrac{\sqrt{2}}{2} = \sqrt{2}$
   $\qquad\qquad 1 < \sqrt{2}$
   $\sin\ 90° < 2\ \sin\ 45°$

49. $i = i_m\ \sin\theta$
   $i = 0.0259 \cdot \sin\ 495.2°$
   $i = 0.0183\ \text{A}$

8.3   Radians

1. $2.80 = \left(\dfrac{180°}{\pi}\right)(2.80) = 160$

5. $15° = \dfrac{\pi}{180°}(15) = \dfrac{\pi}{12}$

   $150° = \dfrac{\pi}{180°}(150) = \dfrac{5\pi}{6}$

9. $210° = \dfrac{\pi}{180°}(210) = \dfrac{7\pi}{6}$

   $270° = \dfrac{\pi}{180°}(270) = \dfrac{3\pi}{2}$

13. $\dfrac{2\pi}{5} = \dfrac{180°}{\pi}\left(\dfrac{2\pi}{2}\right) = 72°$

$\dfrac{3\pi}{2} = \dfrac{180°}{\pi}\left(\dfrac{3\pi}{2}\right) = 270°$

17. $\dfrac{17\pi}{18} = \dfrac{180°}{\pi}\left(\dfrac{17\pi}{18}\right) = 170°$

$\dfrac{5\pi}{3} = \dfrac{180°}{\pi}\left(\dfrac{5\pi}{3}\right) = 300°$

21. $23° = \dfrac{\pi}{180°}(23) = 0.401$

25. $333.5° = \dfrac{\pi}{180°}(333.5) = 5.821$

29. $0.750 = \dfrac{180°}{\pi}(0.750) = 43.0°$

33. $12.4 = \dfrac{180°}{\pi}(12.4) = 710°$

37. $\sin\dfrac{\pi}{4} = \sin\left[\left(\dfrac{\pi}{4}\right)\left(\dfrac{180}{\pi}\right)\right] = \sin 45°$

$= 0.7071$

41. $\cos\dfrac{5\pi}{6} = \cos\left[\left(\dfrac{5\pi}{6}\right)\left(\dfrac{180}{\pi}\right)\right] = \cos 150°$

$= -0.8660$

45. $\tan 0.7359 = 0.9056$

49. $\sec 2.07 = \dfrac{1}{\cos 2.07}$

$= -2.1$

53. $\sin\theta = 0.3090,\ \theta = 0.3141$
$\sin\theta$ is positive, θ is in QI and QII
In QI, $\theta = 0.3141$
In QII $\theta = \pi - 0.3141 = 2.827$

57. $\cos\theta = 0.6742,\ \theta = 0.8309$
$\cos\theta$ is positive, θ is in QI and QIV.
In QI, $\theta = 0.8309$
In QIV, $\theta = 2\pi - 0.8309 = 5.452$

61. $\dfrac{34.4}{360}\cdot\dfrac{1}{\dfrac{1}{6400}} = 612$ mil

65. $V = \dfrac{1}{2}Wb\theta^2$

$V = \dfrac{1}{2}(8.75)(0.75)\left(5.5°\dfrac{\pi}{180°}\right)^2$

$V = 0.030\ \text{ft}\cdot\text{lb}$

8.4 Applications of Radian Measure

1. $s = \left(\dfrac{\pi}{4}\right)(3.00) = 2.36$ in.

5. $s = r\theta = (3.30)\left(\dfrac{\pi}{3}\right) = 3.46$ in.

9. $\theta = \dfrac{s}{r} = \dfrac{0.3913}{0.9449} = 0.4141 = 23.73°$

$A = \dfrac{1}{2}\theta r^2 = \dfrac{1}{2}(0.4141)(0.9449)^2 = 0.1849\ \text{mi}^2$

13. $A = \dfrac{1}{2}r^2\theta \Rightarrow r = \sqrt{\dfrac{2A}{\theta}} = \sqrt{\dfrac{2(0.0119)}{326°\dfrac{\pi}{180}}}$

$r = 0.0647$ ft

17. $s = r\theta = 3.30\cdot\left(820°\cdot\dfrac{\pi}{180°}\right) = 47.2$

47.2 cm of tape is played.

21. From $\theta = wt$,

hour hand: $\theta = \dfrac{2\pi}{12}t$

minute hand: $\theta + \pi = \dfrac{2\pi}{1}t$, t in hours

$\dfrac{\pi}{6}t + \pi = 2\pi t \Rightarrow t = \dfrac{6}{11}$ hour $= 32.73$ minutes

$t = 32$ minutes 44 seconds

at 32 minutes and 44 seconds after noon the hour and minute hands will be at 180°.

25. $w = \dfrac{\theta}{t} = \dfrac{\pi}{6.0}$ rad/s $= 0.52$ rad/s

29.

From $S = r\theta$

$S_1 = 93.67(28.0°)\dfrac{\pi}{180°}$

$S_1 = 45.78$

$S_2 = (93.67 + 4.71)(28.0°)\dfrac{\pi}{180°}$

$S_2 = 48.08$

$S_2 - S_1 = 2.30$ ft. Outer rail is 2.30 ft longer

33. $V = At = \left[\frac{1}{2}r_1^2\theta - \frac{1}{2}r_2^2\theta\right]t = \frac{1}{2}\theta\left(r_1^2 - r_2^2\right)t$

$V = \frac{1}{2}(15.6°)\frac{\pi}{180°}((285 + 15.2)^2 - 285^2)(0.305)$

$V = 369 \text{ m}^3$

37. $v = rw = 8.5(20)(2\pi) = 1070 \text{ ft/min}$

41. $v = rw$

$15\dfrac{\text{mi}}{\text{h}}\dfrac{\text{h}}{60 \text{ min}}\dfrac{5280 \text{ ft}}{\text{mi}}\dfrac{12 \text{ in.}}{\text{ft}} = 14 \text{ in. } w_1$

$w_1 = 1130 \text{ rad/min}$

$w_2 = \dfrac{2}{5}w_1 = \dfrac{2}{5}(1130 \text{ rad/min})\dfrac{\text{r}}{2\pi}$

$w_2 = 72.0 \text{ r/min}$

45. $v = 1200\dfrac{\text{r}}{\text{min}}\left(\dfrac{3}{16} \text{ in.}\right)\dfrac{2\pi}{1 \text{ r}}$

$= 1400 \text{ in/min}$

49. $v = 40.0\dfrac{\text{r}}{\text{min}}(35)\dfrac{2\pi}{1 \text{ r}} = 8800 \text{ ft/min}$

53. $v = rw = \dfrac{d}{2}w$

$v = \dfrac{1.2 \text{ m}}{2}(250 \text{ r/s})\dfrac{2\pi}{\text{r}}$

$v = 940 \text{ m/s}$

57.

θ	$\dfrac{\sin\theta}{\theta}$	$\dfrac{\tan\theta}{\theta}$
0.0001	0.9999999983	1.000000003
0.001	0.9999998333	1.000000333
0.01	0.9999833334	1.000033335
0.1	0.9983341665	1.003346721

For small θ, in rad, $\theta \approx \sin\theta \approx \tan\theta$

Chapter 8 Review Exercises

1. $r = \sqrt{6^2 + 8^2} = 10$ for $(6, 8)$

$\sin\theta = \dfrac{y}{r} = \dfrac{8}{10} = \dfrac{4}{5}$

$\cos\theta = \dfrac{x}{r} = \dfrac{6}{10} = \dfrac{3}{5}$

$\tan\theta = \dfrac{y}{x} = \dfrac{8}{6} = \dfrac{4}{3}$

$\csc\theta = \dfrac{r}{y} = \dfrac{5}{4}$

$\sec\theta = \dfrac{r}{x} = \dfrac{5}{3}$

$\cot\theta = \dfrac{x}{y} = \dfrac{3}{4}$

5. $\cos 132° = -\cos(180° - 132) = -\cos 48°$

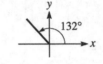

$\tan 194° = \tan(194° - 180°) = \tan 14°$

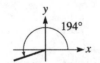

9. $40° \cdot \dfrac{\pi}{180°} = \dfrac{2\pi}{9}$

$153° \cdot \dfrac{\pi}{180°} = \dfrac{17\pi}{20}$

13. $\dfrac{7\pi}{5} \cdot \dfrac{180°}{\pi} = 252°$; $\dfrac{13\pi}{18} \cdot \dfrac{180°}{\pi} = 130°$

17. $0.560 \cdot \dfrac{180°}{\pi} = 32.1°$

21. $102° \cdot \dfrac{\pi}{180°} = 1.78$

25. $262.05° \cdot \dfrac{\pi}{180°} = 4.5736$

29. $\cos 245.5° = -0.415$

33. $\csc 247.82° = -1.080$

37. $\tan 301.4° = -1.64$

41. $\sin \dfrac{9\pi}{4} = -0.5878$

45. $\sin 0.5906 = 0.5569$

49. $\tan \theta = 0.1817, \ 0 \le \theta < 360°$
$\theta = \tan^{-1}(0.1817) = 10.3°$ in QI
$\theta = 180° + 10.3° = 190.3°$ in QIII

53. $\cos \theta = 0.8387, \ 0 \le \theta < 2\pi$
$\theta = \cos^{-1}(0.8387) = 0.5759$ in QI
$\theta = 2\pi - 0.5759 = 5.707$ in QIV

57. $\cos \theta = -0.7222, \ \sin \theta < 0$ for $0° \le \theta < 360° \Rightarrow \theta$ in QIII
$\theta = \cos^{-1}(-0.7222) = 136.2364165$ from calculator
reference angle $= 180° - \theta = 43.76°$
QIII angle $= 180° + $ reference angle $= 223.76°$.

61. $r = \dfrac{s}{\theta} = \dfrac{20.3 \text{ in.}}{107.5° \cdot \dfrac{\pi}{180°}} = 10.8 \text{ in.}$

65. $s = r\theta = r\dfrac{2A}{r^2} = \dfrac{2A}{r}$

$s = \dfrac{2(32.8)}{4.62} = 14.2 \text{ m}$

69. $p = P_m \sin^2 377 \cdot t = 0.120 \sin^2(377 \cdot 2 \cdot 10^{-3})$
$p = 0.0562 \ W$

73. $w = \dfrac{v}{r} = \dfrac{3.5 \text{ mi/h}}{2.4 \text{ ft}} \dfrac{5280 \text{ ft}}{\text{mi}} \dfrac{r}{2\pi \text{ rad}} \dfrac{h}{60 \text{ min}}$
$w = 20.4 \text{ r/min}$

77. (a) $3960 \cdot 60° \cdot \dfrac{\pi}{180°} = 3960 \cdot \dfrac{\pi}{3}$ over with pole, 4150 mi

(b) $3960 \cdot \sin 30° \cdot \pi = 3960 \cdot \dfrac{\pi}{2}$ along 60°N latitude arc, 6220 mi

The distance over the north pole is shorter.

81.

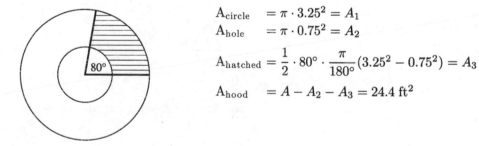

$A_{\text{circle}} = \pi \cdot 3.25^2 = A_1$
$A_{\text{hole}} = \pi \cdot 0.75^2 = A_2$

$A_{\text{hatched}} = \dfrac{1}{2} \cdot 80° \cdot \dfrac{\pi}{180°}(3.25^2 - 0.75^2) = A_3$

$A_{\text{hood}} = A - A_2 - A_3 = 24.4 \text{ ft}^2$

85. $A = \underbrace{\dfrac{1}{2} \cdot 15^2 \cdot 60° \cdot \dfrac{\pi}{180°}}_{\substack{\text{area of sector} \\ \text{formed by one arc}}} + (\dfrac{1}{2} \cdot 15^2 \cdot 60° \cdot \dfrac{\pi}{180°} - \underbrace{\dfrac{1}{2} \cdot 15 \cdot 15 \sin 60°)}_{\substack{\text{area of equilateral} \\ \text{triangle inside} \\ \text{one sector}}}$

$A = 138 \text{ m}^2$

89. $v = r \cdot w = (1080 \text{ mi} + 70.0 \text{ mi}) \cdot \dfrac{1 \text{ r}}{1.95 \text{ h}} \cdot \dfrac{2\pi \text{ rad}}{r}$

$v = 3705.5 \text{ mi/h}$

VECTORS AND OBLIQUE TRIANGLES

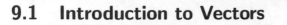

9.1   Introduction to Vectors

1.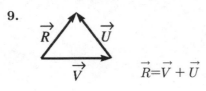

5. **(a)** scalar, no direction given
   (b) vector, magnitude and direction both given

9.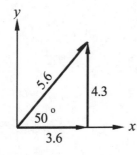

    $\vec{R} = \vec{V} + \vec{U}$

13.   5.6 cm, 50°

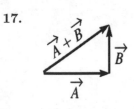

17.

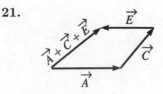

21.

25.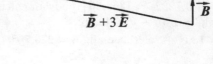

29.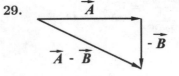

33.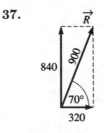

37.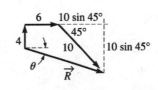

    from drawing $\vec{R}$ is approximately 900 lb at 70

41.

    From drawing,

    $R = 13$ mi

    $\theta = 13°$

9.2   **Components of Vectors**

1.

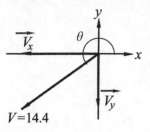

$V_x = V \cos \theta$
$V_x = 14.4 \cos 216° = -11.6$
$V_y = V \sin \theta$
$V_y = 14.4 \sin 216° = -8.46$

5. $V_x = -750 \cos 62.3° = 750 \cos 242.3° = -349$
$V_y = -750 \sin 62.3° = 750 \sin 242.3° = -664$

9. Let $V = 76.8$

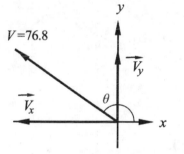

$V_x = V \cos 145.0° = 76.8(-0.819) = -62.9$ m/s
$V_y = V \sin 145.0° = 76.8(0.574) = 44.1$ m/s

13. Let $V = 2.65$

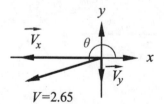

$V_x = V \cos 197.3° = 2.65(-0.955) = -2.53$ mN
$V_y = V \sin 197.3° = 2.65(-0.297) = -0.788$ mN

17.

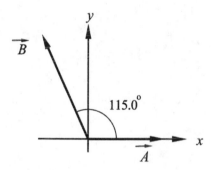

Surface

17.3°

25.0

$V_x = 25.0 \cos 17.3°$
$\quad = 23.9$ km/h
$V_y = 25.0 \sin 17.3°$
$\quad = 7.43$ km/h

21. $F_x = F \cos 78.6° = 3.50(0.198) = 0.692$ ft
$\quad F_y = F \sin 78.6° = 3.50(0.980) = 3.43$ ft

25. $80 \cos 20° = 75$ lb

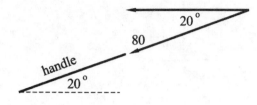

20°

80

handle

20°

9.3   **Vector Addition by Components**

1. $A = 1200 = A_x, B = 1750$
$Ay = 0$

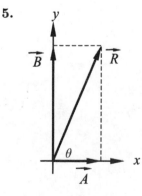

115.0°

$R_x = A_x + B_x = 1200 + 1750 \cos 115° = 460.4$
$R_y = A_y + B_y = 0 + 1750 \sin 115° = 1586$
$R = \sqrt{R_x^2 + R_y^2} = \sqrt{460.4^2 + 1586^2} = 1650$

$\theta = \tan^{-1} \dfrac{R_y}{R_x} = \tan^{-1} \dfrac{1586}{460.4} = 73.8°$

5.

$R = \sqrt{3.086^2 + 7.143^2} = \sqrt{60.54} = 7.781$

$\tan \theta = \dfrac{7.143}{3.086} = 2.315$

$\theta = 66.63°$ (with $\vec{A}$)

9.

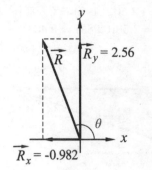

$R_x = -0.982, R_y = 2.56$

$R = \sqrt{R_x^2 + R_y^2} = \sqrt{(-0.982)^2 + 2.56^2} = 2.74$

$\tan \theta_{\text{ref}} = \left| \dfrac{2.56}{-0.982} \right| = 2.61$

$\quad \theta_{\text{ref}} = 69.0°$

$\qquad \theta = 180° - 69.0° = 111.0°$

(θ is in Quad II since R_x is negative and R_y is positive)

17.

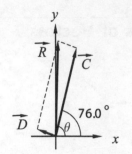

$C = 5650, \theta_C = 76.0°$
$C_x = 5650 \cos 76.0° = 1370$
$C_y = 5650 \sin 76.0° = 5480$
$D = 1280, \theta_D = 160.0°$
$D_x = 1280 \cos 160.0° = -1200$
$D_y = 1280 \sin 160.0° = 438$
$R_x = 1370 - 1200 = 170$
$R_y = 5480 + 438 = 5920$
$R = \sqrt{170^2 + 5920^2} = 5920$

$\tan \theta = \dfrac{R_y}{R_x} = \dfrac{5920}{170}, \theta = 88.4°$

13.

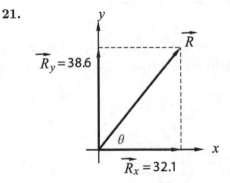

$R_x = 0.6941, R_y = -1.246$

$R = \sqrt{0.6941^2 + (-1.246)^2} = 1.426$

$\tan \theta_{\text{ref}} = \left| \dfrac{-1.246}{0.6941} \right| = 1.795$

$\quad \theta_{\text{ref}} = 60.88°$

$\qquad \theta = 360° - 60.88° = 299.12°$

(θ is in Quad IV since R_x is positive and R_y is negative)

21.

$R_x = A_x + B_x + C_x$
$R_x = 21.9 \cos 236.2° + 96.7 \cos 11.5°$
$\qquad + 62.9 \cos 143.4°$
$R_y = A_y + B_y + C_y$
$R_y = 21.9 \sin 236.2° + 96.7 \sin 11.5°$
$\qquad + 62.9 \sin 143.4°$
$R = \sqrt{R_x^2 + R_y^2} = 50.2$

$\theta = \tan^{-1} \dfrac{R_y}{R_x} = 50.3°$

25.

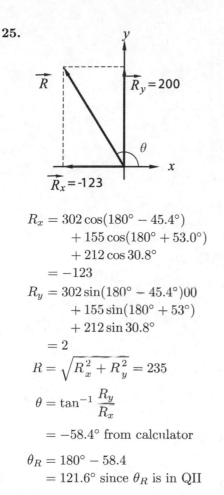

$R_x = 302 \cos(180° - 45.4°)$
$\quad + 155 \cos(180° + 53.0°)$
$\quad + 212 \cos 30.8°$
$\quad = -123$
$R_y = 302 \sin(180° - 45.4°)00$
$\quad + 155 \sin(180° + 53°)$
$\quad + 212 \sin 30.8°$
$\quad = 2$
$R = \sqrt{R_x^2 + R_y^2} = 235$

$\theta = \tan^{-1} \dfrac{R_y}{R_x}$

$\quad = -58.4°$ from calculator

$\theta_R = 180° - 58.4$
$\quad = 121.6°$ since θ_R is in QII

5.

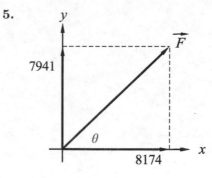

$F_x = 8300 \cos 10.0°$
$\quad = 8174$ N
$F_y = 8300 \sin 10.0° + 6500$
$\quad = 7941$ N
$F = \sqrt{8174^2 + 7941^2}$
$\quad = 11,000$ N

$\tan \theta = \dfrac{7941}{8174} = 0.97, \theta = 44°$ above horizontal

9.4   Applications of Vectors

1.

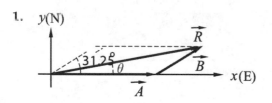

$R_x = A + B_x = 32.50 + 16.18 \cos 31.25°$
$\quad = 46.33$
$R_y = 16.18 \sin 31.25°$
$\quad = 8.394$
$R = \sqrt{46.33^2 + 8.394^2}$
$\quad = 47.08$ mi

$\theta = \tan^{-1} \dfrac{8.394}{46.33}$

$\quad = 10.27°$

The ship is 47.08 mi from start in direction 10.27°N of E.

9.

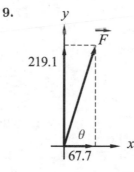

$F_x = 358.2 \cos 37.72° - 215.6$

$\quad = 67.7$
$F_y = 358.2 \sin 37.72°$
$\quad = 219.1$
$F = \sqrt{67.7^2 + 219.1^2}$
$\quad = 229.4$ ft

$\tan \theta = \dfrac{219.1}{67.74} = 3.234, \theta = 72.82°$, N of E

13.

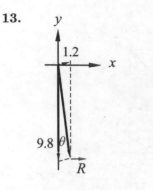

$R_x = 1.2\cos 15° = 1.2$
$R_y = 1.2\sin 15° - 9.8 = -9.5$
$R = \sqrt{R_x^2 + R_y^2} = \sqrt{1.2^2 + (-9.5)^2}$
$R = 9.6 \text{ m/s}^2$

$\theta = \tan^{-1}\dfrac{1.2}{9.5} = 7.0°$

17.

$R = \sqrt{R_x^2 + R_y^2}$
$R = \sqrt{(550 - 60\cos 78°)^2 + (60\sin 78°)^2}$
$R = 540 \text{ km/h}$

$\theta = \tan^{-1}\dfrac{60\sin 78°}{550 - 60\cos 78°}$

$\theta = 6°$

21. Assume that as the smoke pours out of the funnel it immediately takes up the velocity of the wind. Let $\vec{w}$ = velocity of wind, $\vec{u}$ = velocity of boat, $\vec{v}$ = velocity of smoke as seen by passenger.

$w\cos 45° + v\cos 15° = 32$
$w\sin 45° = v\sin 15°$

$v = \dfrac{w\sin 45°}{\sin 15°}$

$w\cos 45° + \dfrac{w\sin 45°}{\sin 15°}\cos 15° = 32$

$w = 9.6 \text{ km/h}$

25. $r = \dfrac{d}{2} = \dfrac{8.20}{2} = 4.10$

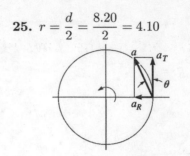

$a = \sqrt{a_T^2 + a_R^2} = \sqrt{(\alpha r)^2 + (w^2 r)^2}$
$a = \sqrt{(318(4.10))^2 + (212^2 \cdot 4.10)^2}$
$a = 184{,}000 \text{ in/min}^2$

$\theta = \tan^{-1}\dfrac{a_R}{a_T} = \tan^{-1}\dfrac{w_r^2 r}{\alpha r}$

$= \tan^{-1}\dfrac{212^2}{318}$

$\theta = 89.6°$

29. top view of plane

$V_H = \sqrt{75.0^2 + 15.0^2} = 76.5$

$\theta = \tan^{-1}\dfrac{15.0}{75.0} = 11.3°$

$V_v = 9.80(2.00) = 19.6$

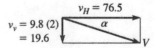

$V = \sqrt{76.5^2 + 19.6^2} = 79.0 \text{ m/s}$

$\alpha = \tan^{-1}\dfrac{19.6}{76.5} = 14.4°, \ 75.6° \text{ from vertical}$

9.5   Oblique Triangles, the Law of Sines

1.

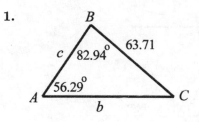

$$C = 180° - (56.29° - 82.94°) = 40.77°$$

$$\frac{b}{\sin 82.94°} = \frac{63.71}{\sin 56.29°} = \frac{c}{\sin 40.77°}$$

$$b = \frac{63.71 \sin 82.94°}{\sin 56.29°} = 76.01$$

$$c = \frac{63.71 \sin 40.77°}{\sin 56.29°} = 50.01$$

5.

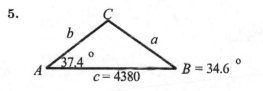

$c = 4380,\ A = 37.4°,\ B = 34.6°$
$C = 180.0° - (37.4° + 34.6°) = 108.0°$

$$\frac{b}{\sin B} = \frac{c}{\sin C}; \frac{b}{\sin 34.6°}$$

$$= \frac{4380}{\sin 108.0°}$$

$$b = \frac{4380 \sin 34.6°}{\sin 108.0°}$$

$$= 2620$$

$$\frac{a}{\sin A} = \frac{c}{\sin C}; \frac{a}{\sin 37.4°}$$

$$= \frac{4380}{\sin 108.0°}$$

$$a = \frac{4380 \sin 37.4°}{\sin 108.0°}$$

$$= 2800$$

9.

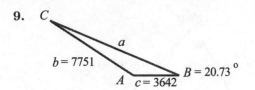

$b = 7751,\ c = 3642,\ B = 20.73°$

$$\frac{b}{\sin B} = \frac{c}{\sin C}; \frac{7751}{\sin 20.73°} = \frac{3642}{\sin C}$$

$$\sin C = \frac{3642 \sin 20.73°}{7751} = 0.1663$$

$$C = 9.57°$$

$$A = 180.0° - (20.73° - 9.57°) = 149.70°$$

$$\frac{a}{\sin A} = \frac{b}{\sin B}; \frac{a}{\sin 149.70°} = \frac{7751}{\sin 20.73°}$$

$$a = \frac{7751 \sin 149.70°}{\sin 20.73°} = 11,050$$

13.

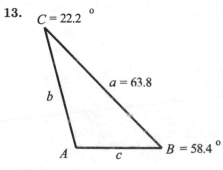

$a = 63.8,\ B = 58.4°,\ C = 22.2°$

$$A = 180.0° - 58.4° - 22.2° = 99.4°$$

$$\frac{a}{\sin A} = \frac{b}{\sin B}; \frac{63.8}{\sin 99.4°}$$

$$= \frac{b}{\sin 58.4°}$$

$$b = \frac{63.8 \sin 58.4°}{\sin 99.4°}$$

$$= 55.1$$

$$\frac{a}{\sin A} = \frac{c}{\sin C}; \frac{63.8}{\sin 99.4°}$$

$$= \frac{c}{\sin 22.2°}$$

$$c = \frac{63.8 \sin 22.2°}{\sin 99.4°}$$

$$= 24.4$$

17.

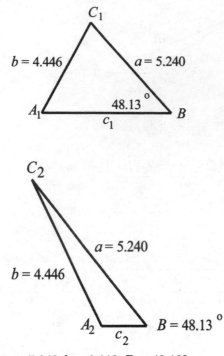

$$a = 5.240, b = 4.446, B = 48.13°$$

$$\frac{a}{\sin A} = \frac{b}{\sin B}; \frac{5.240}{\sin A} = \frac{4.446}{\sin 48.13°}$$

$$\sin A = \frac{5.240 \sin 48.13°}{4.446}$$

$$= 0.8776$$

$$A_1 = 61.36°$$
$$C_1 = 180.0° - 48.13° - 61.36° = 70.51°$$
or
$$A_2 = 180.0° - 61.36° = 118.64°$$
and
$$C_2 = 180.0° - 48.13° - 118.64° = 13.23°$$

$$\frac{b}{\sin B} = \frac{c_1}{\sin C_1}; \frac{4.446}{\sin 48.13°} = \frac{c}{\sin 70.51°}$$

$$c_1 = \frac{4.446 \sin 70.51°}{\sin 48.13°} = 5.628$$

or

$$\frac{b}{\sin B} = \frac{c_2}{\sin C_2}; \frac{4.446}{\sin 48.13°} = \frac{c_2}{\sin 13.23°}$$

$$c_2 = \frac{4.446 \sin 13.23°}{\sin 48.13°} = 1.366$$

21.

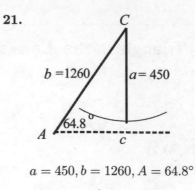

$$a = 450, b = 1260, A = 64.8°$$

$$\frac{a}{\sin A} = \frac{b}{\sin B}; \frac{450}{\sin 64.8°}$$

$$= \frac{1260}{\sin B}$$

$$\sin B = \frac{1260 \sin 64.8°}{450}$$

$$= 2.53 \ (\text{not } \leq 1)$$

Therefore, no solution.

25.

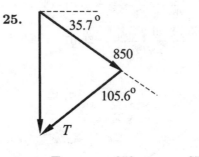

$$\frac{T}{\sin 54.3°} = \frac{850}{\sin 51.3°}; T = \frac{850 \sin 54.3°}{\sin 51.3°} = 880 \text{ N}$$

29.

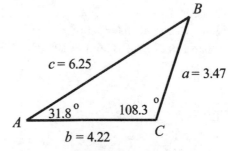

$$\frac{6.25}{\sin 108.3°} = \frac{a}{\sin 31.8°}$$

$$a = \frac{6.25 \sin 31.8°}{\sin 108.3°} = 3.47 \text{ cm}$$

$$B = 180° - 108.3° - 31.8° = 39.9°$$

$$\frac{6.25}{\sin 108.3°} = \frac{b}{\sin 39.9°}$$

$$b = \frac{6.25 \sin 39.9°}{\sin 108.3°} = 4.22 \text{ cm}$$

Perimeter $= 6.25 + 3.47 + 4.22 = 13.94$ cm

33.

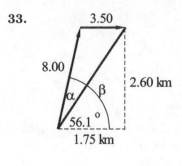

$$\theta = \tan^{-1} \frac{2.60}{1.75} = 56.1°$$

$$\frac{8.00}{\sin 56.1°} = \frac{3.50}{\sin \alpha}$$

$$\alpha = 21.3°,$$
$$\beta = 56.1° + 21.3° = 77.4°$$

with bank downstream

9.6   The Law of Cosines

1.

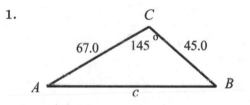

$$c = \sqrt{45.0^2 + 67.0^2 - 2(45.0)(67.0)\cos 145°}$$
$$= 107$$

$$\frac{45.0}{\sin A} = \frac{c}{\sin 145°} = \frac{67.0}{\sin B}$$

$$A = \sin^{-1} \frac{45.0 \sin 145°}{c} = 14.0°$$

$$B = \sin^{-1} \frac{67.0 \sin 145°}{c} = 21.0°$$

5.

$C = 98°$ 4530

924

A c B

$$a = 4530, b = 924, C = 98.0°$$

$$c = \sqrt{4530^2 + 924^2 + 2(4530)(924)(\cos 98.0°)}$$
$$= 4750$$

$$\frac{c}{\sin C} = \frac{b}{\sin B}; \frac{4750}{\sin 98.0°}$$
$$= \frac{924}{\sin B}$$

$$\sin B = \frac{924 \sin 98.0°}{4750}$$
$$= -0.193$$

$$B = 11.1°$$
$$A = 180° - 98.0° - 11.1°$$
$$= 70.9°$$

9.

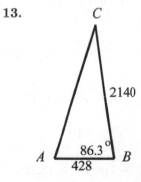

$$a = 385.4, b = 467.7, c = 800.9$$

$$\cos A = \frac{467.7^2 + 800.9^2 - 385.4^2}{2(467.7)(800.9)} = 0.9499$$

$$A = 18.21°$$

$$\cos B = \frac{385.4^2 + 800.9^2 - 467.7^2}{2(385.4)(800.9)} = 0.9253$$

$$B - 22.28°$$
$$C = 180° - 18.21° - 22.28° = 139.51°$$

13.

C

2140

A $86.3°$ B
428

$$a = 2140, c = 428, B = 86.3°$$

$$b = \sqrt{2140^2 + 428^2 - 2(2140)(428)(\cos 86.3°)}$$
$$= 2160$$

$$\frac{b}{\sin B} = \frac{c}{\sin C}; \frac{2160}{\sin 86.3°} = \frac{428}{\sin C}$$

$$\sin C = \frac{428 \sin 86.3°}{2160} = 0.198$$

$$C = 11.4°$$
$$A = 180° - 86.3° - 11.4° = 82.3°$$

17.

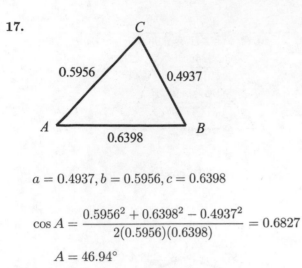

$a = 0.4937, b = 0.5956, c = 0.6398$

$$\cos A = \frac{0.5956^2 + 0.6398^2 - 0.4937^2}{2(0.5956)(0.6398)} = 0.6827$$

$A = 46.94°$

$$\cos B = \frac{0.4937^2 + 0.6398^2 - 0.5956^2}{2(0.4937)(0.6398)} = 0.4723$$

$B = 61.82°$
$C = 180° - 46.94° - 61.82° = 71.24°$

21.

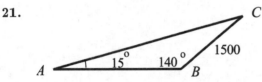

$a = 1500, A = 15°, B = 140°$

$$\frac{a}{\sin A} = \frac{b}{\sin B}; \ b = \frac{1500 \sin 140°}{\sin 15°} = 3700$$

$C = 180° - 15° - 140° = 25°$
$c = \sqrt{1500^2 + 3700^2 - 2(1500)(3700)(\cos 25°)}$
$= 2400$

25.

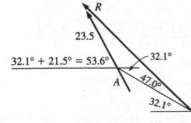

from $d = rt,$ $23.5(2.00) = 47.0$ and
$23.5(1.00) = 23.5$
$\sphericalangle = 32.1° + 90° + (90° - 53.6°)$
$\sphericalangle = 158.5°$
$R^2 = 23.5^2 + 47^2 - 2(23.5)(47) \cos 158.5°$
$R = 69.4$ miles from base

29.

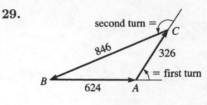

$846^2 = 624^2 + 326^2 - 2(624)(326) \cos A$
$\cos A = -0.5409$
$A = 122.7°$
first turn $= 180° - 122.7° = 57.3°$
$624^2 = 846^2 + 326^2 - 2(846)(326) \cos C$
$\cos C = 0.7843$
$C = 38.3°$
second turn $= 180° - 38.3° = 141.7°$

33.

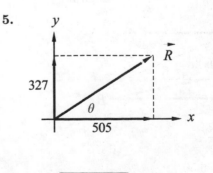

$c^2 = 12.7^2 + 11.5^2 - 2(12.7)(11.5) \cos 23.6°$
$c = 5.09$ km/h

Chapter 9 Review Exercises

1.

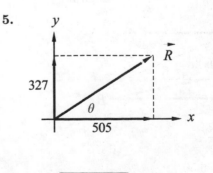

y-component $= 65.0 \cos 28.0° = 57.4$
x-component $= 65.0 \sin 28.0° = 30.5$

5.

$R = \sqrt{327^2 + 505^2} = 602$

$\theta = \tan^{-1} \dfrac{327}{505} = 32.9°$

9.

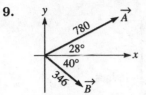

$$R_x = 780 \cos 28.0° + 346 \cos 40.0°$$
$$= 954$$
$$R_y = 780 \sin 28.0° - 346 \sin 40.0°$$
$$= 144$$

$$R = \sqrt{R_x^2 + R_y^2} = \sqrt{954^2 + 144^2}$$
$$= 965$$

$$\theta_R = \tan^{-1} \frac{144}{954} = 8.6°$$

13.

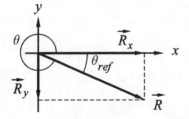

$$Y_x = 51.33 \cos 12.25° = 5016$$
$$Y_y = 51.33 \sin 12.25° = 10.89$$
$$Z_x = 42.61 \cos 68.23° = 15.80$$
$$Z_y = -42.61 \sin 68.23° = -39.57$$
$$R_x = 50.16 + 15.80 = 65.98$$
$$R_y = 10.89 - 39.57 = -28.68$$
$$R = \sqrt{R_x^2 + R_y^2}$$
$$= \sqrt{65.98^2 + (-28.68)^2}$$
$$= 71.94$$

$$\tan \theta = \frac{R_y}{R_x} = \frac{-28.68}{65.98}$$

$$\theta = 336.50°, \ \theta_{\text{ref}} = 23.50°$$

17.

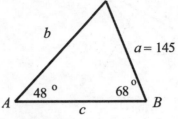

$$C = 180° - 48.0° - 68.0° = 64.0°$$

$$\frac{145}{\sin 48.0°} = \frac{b}{\sin 68.0°} = \frac{c}{\sin 64.0°}$$

$$b = \frac{145 \sin 68.0°}{\sin 48.0°} = 181,$$

$$c = \frac{145 \sin 64.0°}{\sin 48.0°} = 175$$

21.

$$C = 180° - 17.85° - 154.16° = 7.99°$$

$$\frac{a}{\sin 17.85°} = \frac{b}{\sin 154.16°} = \frac{7863}{\sin 7.99°}$$

$$b = \frac{7863 \sin 154.16°}{\sin 7.99°} = 24{,}660$$

$$a = \frac{7863 \sin 17.85°}{\sin 7.99°} = 17{,}340$$

25.

$$\frac{a}{\sin A} = \frac{14.5}{\sin B} = \frac{13.0}{\sin 56.6°}$$

$$\sin B = \frac{14.5 \sin 56.6°}{13.0}$$

$$B = 68.6° \quad \text{or} \quad 111.4°$$

Case I:

$$B = 68.6°, \ A = 180° - 68.6° - 56.6° = 54.8°$$

$$\frac{a}{\sin 54.8°} = \frac{13.0}{\sin 56.6°} \Rightarrow a = 12.7$$

Case II:

$$B = 111.4°, \ A = 180° - 111.4° - 56.6° = 12.0°$$

$$\frac{a}{\sin 12.0°} = \frac{13.0}{\sin 56.6°} \Rightarrow a = 3.24$$

29.

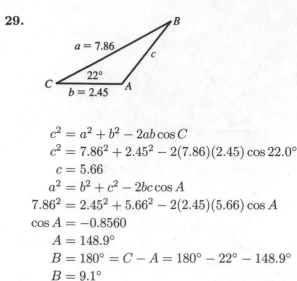

$$c^2 = a^2 + b^2 - 2ab\cos C$$
$$c^2 = 7.86^2 + 2.45^2 - 2(7.86)(2.45)\cos 22.0°$$
$$c = 5.66$$
$$a^2 = b^2 + c^2 - 2bc\cos A$$
$$7.86^2 = 2.45^2 + 5.66^2 - 2(2.45)(5.66)\cos A$$
$$\cos A = -0.8560$$
$$A = 148.9°$$
$$B = 180° = C - A = 180° - 22° - 148.9°$$
$$B = 9.1°$$

33.

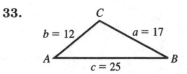

$$a^2 = b^2 + c^2 - 2bc\cos A$$
$$17^2 = 12^2 + 25^2 - 2(12)(25)\cos A$$
$$\cos A = 0.8$$
$$A = 37°$$
$$b^2 = a^2 + c^2 - 2ac\cos B$$
$$12^2 = 17^2 + 25^2 - 2(17)(25)\cos B$$
$$\cos B = 0.9059$$
$$B = 25°$$
$$C = 180° - 37° - 25° = 118°$$

37.

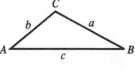

$$a^2 = b^2 + c^2 - 2bc\cos A$$
$$b^2 = a^2 + c^2 - 2ac\cos B$$
$$\underline{c^2 = a^2 + b^2 - 2ab\cos C \quad add}$$

$$a^2 + b^2 + c^2 = 2a^2 + 2b^2 + 2c^2 - 2bc\cos A$$
$$- 2ac\cos B - 2ab\cos C$$
$$a^2 + b^2 + c^2 = 2bc\cos A + 2ac\cos B + 2ab\cos G$$

$$\frac{a^2 + b^2 + c^2}{2abc} = \frac{\cos A}{a} + \frac{\cos}{b} + \frac{\cos C}{c}$$

41.

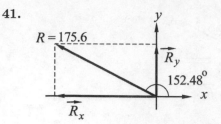

horizontal component $= 175.6\cos 152.48° = -155.7$ lb
vertical component $= 175.6\sin 152.48° = 81.14$ lb

45.

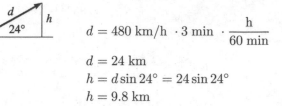

$$d = 480 \text{ km/h } \cdot 3 \text{ min } \cdot \frac{\text{h}}{60 \text{ min}}$$
$$d = 24 \text{ km}$$
$$h = d\sin 24° = 24\sin 24°$$
$$h = 9.8 \text{ km}$$

49.

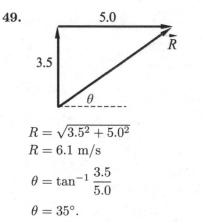

$$R = \sqrt{3.5^2 + 5.0^2}$$
$$R = 6.1 \text{ m/s}$$
$$\theta = \tan^{-1}\frac{3.5}{5.0}$$
$$\theta = 35°.$$

53.

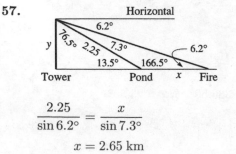

extra pipline
$$= 3.756 + 4.675 - c$$
$$= 3.756 + 4.675$$
$$- \sqrt{3.756^2 + 4.675^2 - 2(3.756)(4.675) \cdot \cos 168.85°}$$
$$= 0.0394 \text{ km}$$

57.

$$\frac{2.25}{\sin 6.2°} = \frac{x}{\sin 7.3°}$$
$$x = 2.65 \text{ km}$$

61.

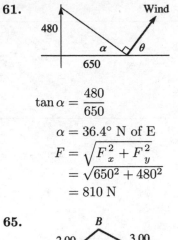

$$\tan \alpha = \frac{480}{650}$$

$$\alpha = 36.4° \text{ N of E}$$
$$F = \sqrt{F_x^2 + F_y^2}$$
$$= \sqrt{650^2 + 480^2}$$
$$= 810 \text{ N}$$

65.

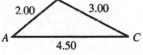

Use law of cosines three times.

$$2.00^2 + 4.50^2 - 2(2.00)(4.50)\cos A = 3.00^2$$
$$A = 32.1°$$
$$2.00^2 + 3.00^2 - 2(2.00)(3.00)\cos B = 4.50^2$$
$$B = 127.2°$$
$$3.00^2 + 4.50^2 - 2(3.00)(4.50)\cos C = 2.00^2$$
$$C = 20.7°$$

GRAPHS OF THE TRIGONOMETRIC FUNCTIONS

10.1   Graphs of $y = a \sin x$ and $y = a \cos x$

1. $y = 3 \cos x$

x	0	$\frac{\pi}{6}$	$\frac{\pi}{3}$	$\frac{\pi}{2}$	$\frac{2\pi}{3}$	$\frac{5\pi}{6}$	π	$\frac{7\pi}{6}$	$\frac{4\pi}{3}$	$\frac{3\pi}{2}$	$\frac{5\pi}{3}$	$\frac{11\pi}{6}$	2π
y	0	2.6	1.5	0	-1.5	-2.6	-3	-2.6	-1.5	0	1.5	2.6	3

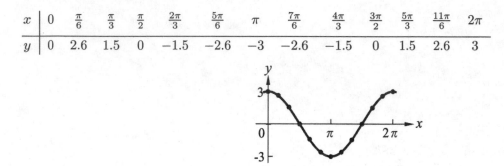

5. $y = 3 \cos x$

x	$-\pi$	$-\frac{3\pi}{4}$	$-\frac{\pi}{2}$	$-\frac{\pi}{4}$	0	$\frac{\pi}{4}$	$\frac{\pi}{2}$	$\frac{3\pi}{4}$	π
y	-3	-2.1	0	2.1	3	2.1	0	-2.1	-3

x	$\frac{5\pi}{4}$	$\frac{3\pi}{4}$	$\frac{7\pi}{4}$	2π	$\frac{9\pi}{4}$	$\frac{5\pi}{2}$	$\frac{11\pi}{4}$	3π
y	-2.1	0	2.1	3	2.1	0	-2.1	-3

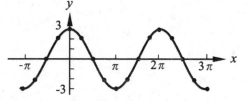

9. $y = \frac{5}{2} \sin x$; $\sin x$ has its amplitude value at $x = \frac{\pi}{2}$ and $x = \frac{3\pi}{2}$ and has intercepts at $x = 0, x = \pi$, and $x = 2\pi$. The graph can be sketched with these values.

x	0	$\frac{\pi}{2}$	π	$\frac{3\pi}{2}$	2π
y	0	$\frac{5}{2}$	0	$-\frac{5}{2}$	0

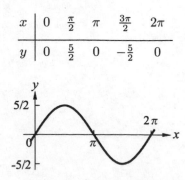

13. $y = 0.8 \cos$; $\cos x$ has its amplitude value at $x = 0$ and $x = \pi$, and $x = 2\pi$, and has intercepts at $x = \frac{\pi}{2}$ and $x = \frac{3\pi}{2}$. The graph can be sketched with these values.

x	0	$\frac{\pi}{2}$	π	$\frac{3\pi}{2}$	2π
y	0.8	0	-0.8	0	0.8

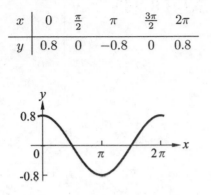

17. $y = -1500 \sin x = -1500(\sin x)$; $\sin x$ has its amplitude value at $x = \frac{\pi}{2}$ and $x = \frac{3\pi}{2}$ and has intercepts at $x = 0, x = \pi$, and $x = 2\pi$.
(The negative sign will invert the graph values.)

x	0	$\frac{\pi}{2}$	π	$\frac{3\pi}{2}$	2π
y	0	-1500	0	1500	0

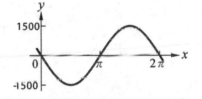

21. $y = -50 \cos x = -50(\cos x)$; $\cos x$ has its amplitude value at $x = 0, x = \pi$, and $x = 2\pi$, and has intercepts at $x = \frac{\pi}{2}$ and $x = \frac{3\pi}{2}$.
(The negative sign will invert the graph values.)

x	0	$\frac{\pi}{2}$	π	$\frac{3\pi}{2}$	2π
y	-50	0	50	0	-50

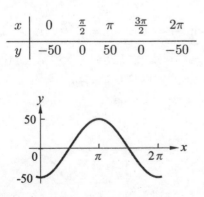

25. Sketch $y = 10 \cos x$ for $x = 0, 1, 2, 3, 4, 5, 6, 7$.

x	0	1	2	3	4
$10\cos x$	10	5.4	-4.2	-9.9	-6.5

x	5	6	7
$10\cos x$	2.8	9.6	7.5

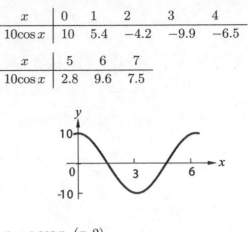

29. $y = a \cos x$, $(\pi, 2)$
$2 = a \cos \pi \Rightarrow a = -2$
$y = -2 \cos x$

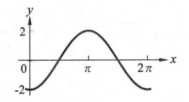

33. The graph passes through $(0,0), (\pi, 0)$, and $(2\pi, 0)$ with amplitude 4. The graph is $y = 4 \sin x$.

10.2   Graphs of $y = a \sin bx$ and $y = a \cos bx$

1. $y = 3 \sin 6x$, amplitude $= 3$, period $= \frac{2\pi}{6} = \frac{\pi}{3}$

x	0	$\frac{\pi}{12}$	$\frac{\pi}{6}$	$\frac{\pi}{4}$	$\frac{\pi}{3}$
y	0	3	0	-3	0

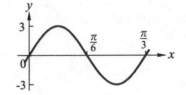

5. Since $\cos bx$ has period of $\frac{2\pi}{b}$, $y = 3 \cos 8x$ has a period of $\frac{2\pi}{8}$, or $\frac{\pi}{4}$.

9. $y = -\cos 16x$ has period of $\frac{2\pi}{16}$, or $\frac{\pi}{8}$

13. $y = 3 \cos 4\pi x$ has period of $\frac{2\pi}{4\pi}$, or $\frac{2}{4} = \frac{1}{2}$.

17. $y = -\frac{1}{2} \cos \frac{2}{3}x$ has period of $\frac{2\pi}{\frac{2}{3}} = \frac{2\pi}{1} \times \frac{3}{2} = 3\pi$.

21. $y = 3.3 \cos \pi^2 x$ has period of $\frac{2\pi}{\pi^2} = \frac{2}{\pi}$.

25. $y = 3 \cos 8x$ has amplitude of 3 and period of $\frac{\pi}{4}$.

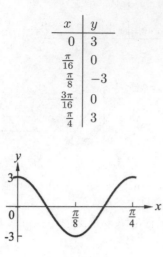

x	y
0	3
$\frac{\pi}{16}$	0
$\frac{\pi}{8}$	-3
$\frac{3\pi}{16}$	0
$\frac{\pi}{4}$	3

29. $y = -\cos 16x$ has amplitude of $|-1| = 1$, and period of $\frac{\pi}{8}$.

x	y
0	-1
$\frac{\pi}{32}$	0
$\frac{\pi}{16}$	1
$\frac{3\pi}{32}$	0
$\frac{\pi}{8}$	-1

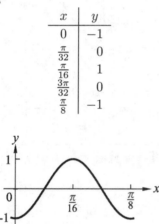

33. $y = 3 \cos 4\pi x$ has amplitude of 3, and period of $\frac{1}{2}$.

x	y
0	3
$\frac{1}{8}$	0
$\frac{1}{4}$	-3
$\frac{3}{8}$	0
$\frac{1}{2}$	3

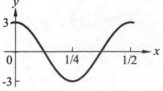
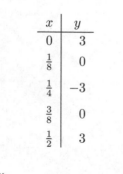

37. $y = -\frac{1}{2} \cos \frac{2}{3}x$ has amplitude of $\left|-\frac{1}{2}\right| = \frac{1}{2}$, and period of 3π.

x	y
0	$-\frac{1}{2}$
$\frac{3\pi}{4}$	0
$\frac{3\pi}{2}$	$\frac{1}{2}$
$\frac{9\pi}{4}$	0
3π	$-\frac{1}{2}$

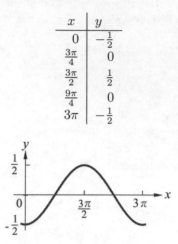

41. $y = 3.3 \cos \pi^2 x$ has amplitude of 3.3, and period of $\frac{2}{\pi}$.

x	0	$\frac{1}{2\pi}$	$\frac{1}{\pi}$	$\frac{3}{2\pi}$	$\frac{2}{\pi}$
$\pi^2 x$	0	$\frac{\pi}{2}$	π	$\frac{3\pi}{2}$	2π
$\cos \pi^2 x$	1	0	-1	0	1
$3.3 \cos \pi^2 x$	3.3	0	-3.3	0	3.3

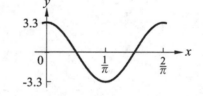

45. $b = \frac{2\pi}{2} = \pi; \ y = \sin \pi x$

49. $y = -2 \sin bx, \ \left(\frac{\pi}{4}, -2\right), b > 0$

$$-2 = -2 \sin b \cdot \frac{\pi}{4}$$

$$\sin \frac{b\pi}{4} = 1 \Rightarrow \frac{b\pi}{4} = \frac{\pi}{2} + 2\pi n$$

$$b = 2 + 8n \text{ of which}$$

the smallest is $b = 2$

$y = -2 \sin 2x$ is the function

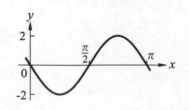
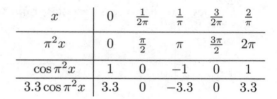
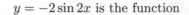

53. $V = 170\sin 120\pi t$

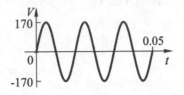

57. $y = \dfrac{1}{2}\cos 2x$ period of π,

(amplitude 0.5)

10.3 Graphs of $y = a\sin(bx+c)$ and $y = a\cos(bx+c)$

1. $y = -\cos\left(2x - \dfrac{\pi}{6}\right)$

(1) the amplitude is 1

(2) the period is $\dfrac{2\pi}{2} = \pi$

(3) the displacement is $-\dfrac{-\dfrac{\pi}{6}}{2} = \dfrac{\pi}{12}$

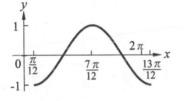

5. $y = \cos\left(x + \dfrac{\pi}{6}\right)$; $a = 1, b = 1, c = \dfrac{\pi}{6}$

Amplitude is $|a| = 1$; period is $\dfrac{2\pi}{b} = \dfrac{2\pi}{1} = 2\pi$;

displacement is $-\dfrac{c}{b} = -\dfrac{\pi}{6}$.

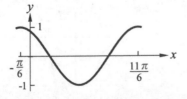

9. $y = -\cos(2x - \pi)$; $a = -1, b = 2, c = -\pi$

Amplitude is $|a| = 1$; period is $\dfrac{2\pi}{b} = \dfrac{2\pi}{1} = \pi$;

displacement is $-\dfrac{c}{b} = -\left(\dfrac{-\pi}{2}\right) = \dfrac{\pi}{2}$.

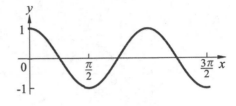

13. $y = 30\cos\left(\dfrac{1}{3}x + \dfrac{\pi}{3}\right)$; $a = 30, b = \dfrac{1}{3}, c = \dfrac{\pi}{3}$

Amplitude is $|a| = 30$; period is $\dfrac{2\pi}{b} = \dfrac{2\pi}{1/3} = 6\pi$;

displacement is $-\dfrac{c}{b} = \dfrac{-\pi/3}{1/3} = -\pi$.

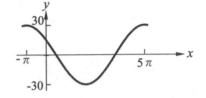

17. $y = \dfrac{3}{4}\cos\left(4\pi x - \dfrac{\pi}{5}\right)$; $a = \dfrac{3}{4}, b = 4\pi, c = -\dfrac{\pi}{5}$

Amplitude is $|a| = \dfrac{3}{4}$; period is $\dfrac{2\pi}{b} = \dfrac{2\pi}{4\pi} = \dfrac{1}{2}$;

displacement is $-\dfrac{c}{b} = -\left(-\dfrac{\pi/5}{4\pi}\right) = \dfrac{1}{20}$.

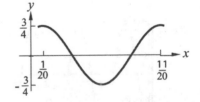

21. $y = 40\cos(3\pi x + 2)$; $a = 40, b = 3\pi, c = 2$

Amplitude is $|a| = 40$; period is $\dfrac{2\pi}{b} = \dfrac{2\pi}{3\pi} = \dfrac{2}{3}$;

displacement is $-\dfrac{c}{b} = -\dfrac{2}{3\pi}$.

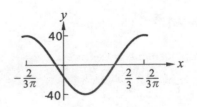

25. $y = -\dfrac{3}{2}\cos\left(\pi x + \dfrac{\pi^2}{6}\right)$; $a = -\dfrac{3}{2}, b = \pi, c = \dfrac{\pi^2}{6}$

Amplitude is $|a| = \dfrac{3}{2}$; period is $\dfrac{2\pi}{b} = \dfrac{2\pi}{\pi} = 2$;

displacement is $-\dfrac{c}{b} = -\dfrac{\pi^2/6}{\pi} = -\dfrac{\pi}{6}$.

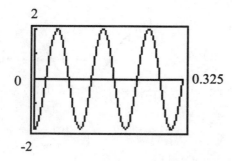

29. cosine, 12, $\dfrac{1}{2}, \dfrac{1}{8}$

$a = 12$

$\text{period} = \dfrac{1}{2} = \dfrac{2\pi}{b} \Rightarrow b = 4\pi$

$\text{displacement} = \dfrac{1}{8} = -\dfrac{c}{4\pi} \Rightarrow c = -\dfrac{\pi}{2}$

$y = 12\cos\left(4\pi x - \dfrac{\pi}{2}\right)$.

33. $y = 2.00\sin 2\pi\left(\dfrac{t}{0.100} - \dfrac{5.00}{20.0}\right)$; $a = 2.00$,

$b = \dfrac{2\pi}{0.100}, c = \dfrac{-5.00(2\pi)}{20.0}$

Amplitude $= |a| = 2.00$,

$\text{period} = \dfrac{2\pi}{b} = 0.100$

$\text{displacement} = -\dfrac{c}{b} = 0.025$

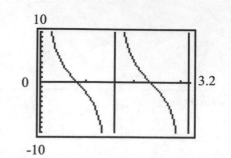

37. $y = a\sin(bx + c)$

Amplitude is 5,

$\text{period} = \dfrac{2\pi}{b} = 16, b = \dfrac{\pi}{8}$

$\text{displacement} = -\dfrac{c}{b} = -1, c = \dfrac{\pi}{8}$.

$y = 5\sin\left(\dfrac{\pi}{8}x + \dfrac{\pi}{8}\right)$

10.4 Graphs of $y = \tan x$, $y = \cot x$, $y = \sec x$, $y = \csc x$

1. $y = 5.0\cot 2x$. Graph $y_1 = \dfrac{5.0}{\tan 2x}$.

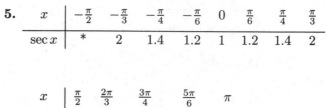

5.

x	$-\dfrac{\pi}{2}$	$-\dfrac{\pi}{3}$	$-\dfrac{\pi}{4}$	$-\dfrac{\pi}{6}$	0	$\dfrac{\pi}{6}$	$\dfrac{\pi}{4}$	$\dfrac{\pi}{3}$
$\sec x$	*	2	1.4	1.2	1	1.2	1.4	2

x	$\dfrac{\pi}{2}$	$\dfrac{2\pi}{3}$	$\dfrac{3\pi}{4}$	$\dfrac{5\pi}{6}$	π
$\sec x$	*	-2	-1.4	-1.2	-1

(* = undefined)

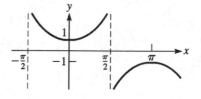

9. For $y = \frac{1}{2}\sec x$, first sketch the graph of $y = \sec x$, then multiply the y-values of the secant function by $\frac{1}{2}$ and graph.

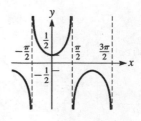

13. For $y = -3 \csc x$, sketch the graph of $y = \csc x$, multiply the y-values by -3, and resketch the graph. It will be inverted.

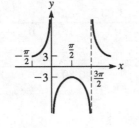

17. Since the period of $\sec x$ is 2π, the period of $y = \frac{1}{2}\sec 3x$ is $\frac{2\pi}{3}$. Graph $y_1 = 0.5(\cos 3x)^{-1}$, using $_{\min} = -0.5$, $x_{\max} = 4$, $y_{\min} = -5$, $y_{\max} = 5$.

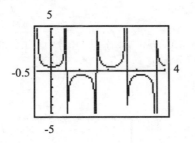

21. Since the period of $\csc x$ is 2π, the period of $y = 18\csc\left(3x - \frac{\pi}{3}\right)$ is $\frac{2\pi}{3}$. The displacement is $-\left(-\frac{\pi/3}{3}\right) = \frac{\pi}{9}$. Graph $y_1 = 18\left(\sin\left(3x - \frac{\pi}{3}\right)\right)^{-1}$, using $x_{\min} = -0.5$, $x_{\max} = 3.5$, $y_{\min} = -50$, $y_{\max} = 50$.

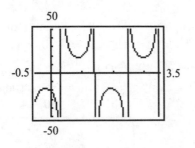

25. $x = 200\cot\theta$

θ	0	$\frac{\pi}{2}$
$\cot\theta$	*	0
$200\cot\theta$	*	0

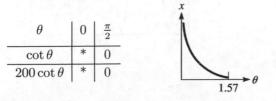

10.5　Applications of the Trigonometric Graphs

1. The displacement of the projection on the y-axis is d and is given by $d = R\cos wt$.

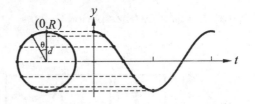

5. $y = R\cos\omega t$
$= 8.30\cos[(3.20)(2\pi)]t$

Amplitude is 8.30 cm:
period is $\frac{1}{3.20} = 0.3125$ s,
0.625 s for 2 cycles;
displacement is 0 s.

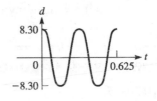

9. $e = E\cos(\omega t + \alpha)$

$= 170\cos\left[2\pi(60.0)t - \frac{\pi}{3}\right]$

Amplitude is 170 V

period is $\dfrac{2\pi}{2\pi(60.0)} = 0.016$ s, 0.033 s

for 2 cycles; displacement is $\dfrac{\pi/3}{2\pi(60.0)} = \dfrac{1}{360}$ s

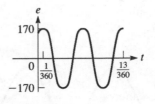

13. $p = p_0 \sin 2\pi ft$
$= 2.80 \sin[2\pi(2.30)]t$
$= 2.80 \sin 14.45t$
Amplitude is 2.80 lb/in^2
period is $\frac{2\pi}{14.45} = 0.435$ s
for 1 cycle, 0.87 s for 2
cycles; displacement is 0 s

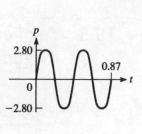

17. (a) $L = 12 \sec \pi t$ has period $= 2.0$ s

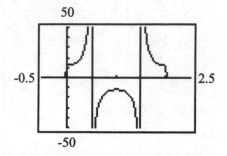

(b) Since L represents length, which is non-negative, only those parts of the graph where L is positive (above the x-axis) are meaningful.

10.6 Composite Trigonometric Curves

1. $y = 1 + \sin x$

x	y
-2π	1
$-\frac{3\pi}{2}$	2
$-\pi$	1
$-\frac{\pi}{2}$	0
0	1
$\frac{\pi}{2}$	2
π	1
$\frac{3\pi}{2}$	0
2π	1

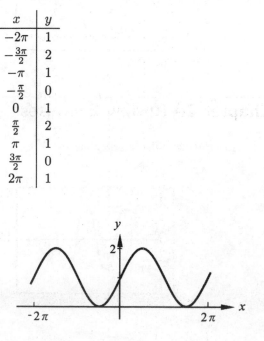

5. $y = \frac{1}{10}x^2 - \sin \pi x$

x	-4	-3.43	-2.55	-1.88	-1.47
y	1.60	0.20	1.64	0	-0.78

x	-1.03	-0.51	0	0.49	0.97	1.53
y	0	1.03	0	-0.98	0	1.23

x	2.15	2.45	2.73	0
y	0	-0.39	4	1.6

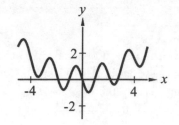

9. Graph $y_1 = x^3 + 10 \sin 2x$ on graphing calculator with $x_{\min} = -5, x_{\max} = 5, y_{\min} = -50, y_{\max} = 50$

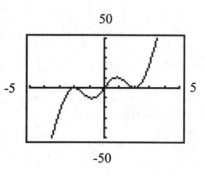

13. Graph $y_1 = 20 \cos 2x + 30 \sin x$ on graphing calculator with $x_{\min} = -10, x_{\max} = 10,$ $y_{\min} = -50, y_{\max} = 50.$

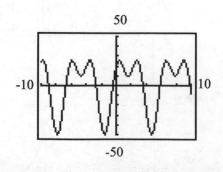

17. Graph $y_1 = \sin \pi x - \cos 2x$ on graphing calculator with $x_{min} = -8, x_{max} = 8, y_{min} = -3,$ $y_{max} = 3.$

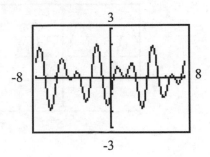

21. $x = \sin t, \ y = \sin t$

t	x	y
$-\frac{\pi}{2}$	-1	-1
$-\frac{\pi}{4}$	-0.71	-0.71
0	0	0
$\frac{\pi}{4}$	0.71	0.71
$\frac{\pi}{2}$	1	1

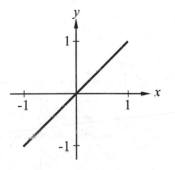

25. In parametric mode graph

$$x_{IT} = \cos \pi \left(t + \frac{1}{6} \right), \ y_{IT} = 2 \sin \pi t$$

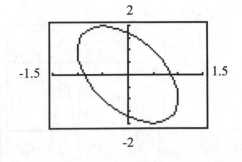

29. In parametric mode graph
$$x_{IT} = \sin t, \ y_{IT} = \sin 5t$$

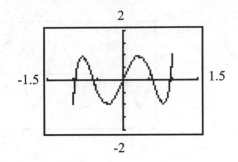

33. $T = 56 - 22 \cos \left[\dfrac{\pi}{6} (x - 0.5) \right]$

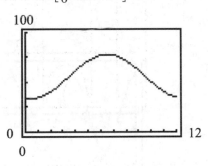

37. To graph $i = 0.32 + 0.50 \sin t - 0.20 \cos 2t$, let $y_1 = 0.32 + 0.50 \sin t - 0.20 \cos 2t$ on a graphing calculator with $x_{min} = -1, x_{max} = 12,$ $y_{min} = -0.1, y_{max} = 1.1.$

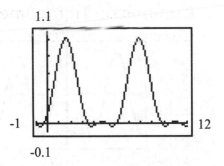

Chapter 10 Review Exercises

1. $y = \dfrac{2}{3} \sin x$

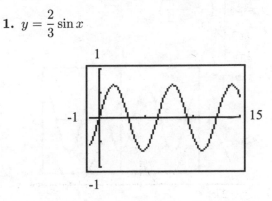

5. $y = 2 \sin 3x$

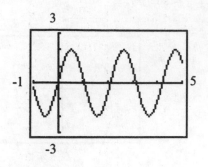

9. $y = 3 \cos \dfrac{1}{3}x$

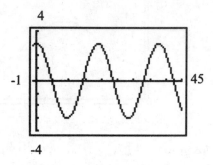

13. $y = 5 \cos 2\pi x$

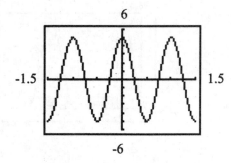

17. $y = 2 \sin \left(3x - \dfrac{\pi}{2}\right)$

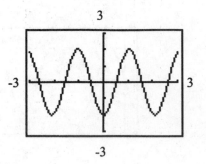

21. $y = -\sin \left(\pi x + \dfrac{\pi}{6}\right)$

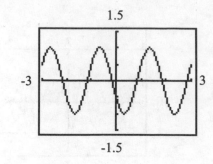

25. $y = 0.3 \tan 0.5x$

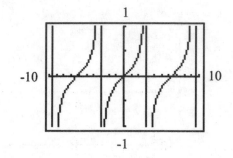

29. $y = 2 + \dfrac{1}{2} \sin 2x$

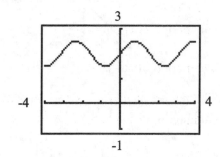

33. $y = 2 \sin x - \cos 2x$

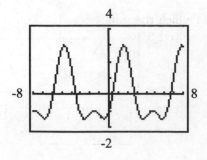

37. $y = \dfrac{\sin x}{x}$

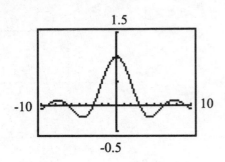

41. From the graph, $a = 2$, period $= \pi = \dfrac{2\pi}{b} \Rightarrow$

$b = 2$, and displacement $= -\dfrac{c}{b} = -\dfrac{\pi}{4} \Rightarrow c = \dfrac{\pi}{2}$.

$y = a\sin(bx + c)$ is $y = 2\sin\left(2x + \dfrac{\pi}{2}\right)$.

45. $x = -\cos 2\pi t$, $y = 2\sin \pi t$

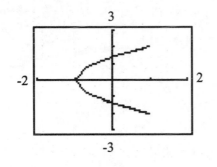

49. The period of $\cos 0.5x$ is $\dfrac{2\pi}{0.5} = 4\pi$.

The period of $\sin 3x$ is $\dfrac{2\pi}{3}$.

The period of $y = 2\cos 0.5x + \sin 3x$ is the least

common multiple of 4π and $\dfrac{2\pi}{3}$; 4π.

53. $y = 3\cos bx$, $\left(\dfrac{\pi}{3}, -3\right)$, $b > 0$

$-3 = 3\cos\left(b \cdot \dfrac{\pi}{3}\right) \Rightarrow b \cdot \dfrac{\pi}{3} = \pi + 2\pi \cdot n$

$b = 3 + 6 \cdot n$

of which the smallest is $b = 3$

$y = 3\cos 3x$

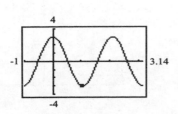

57. $v = wD\cos wt$

$w = 3000 \text{ r/min} \dfrac{2\pi}{r} \dfrac{\min}{60 \text{ s}} = 100\pi$

$v = 100\pi(3.6)\cos(100\pi t)$

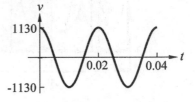

61. $y = 14.0\sin 40.0\pi t$

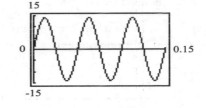

65. $d = a\sec\theta$, $a = 3.00$

$d = 3.00\sec\theta$

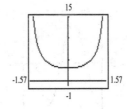

69. $y = 4\sin 2t - 2\cos 2t$

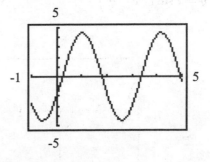

73. $Z = R \sec \theta$, $-\dfrac{\pi}{2} < \theta < \dfrac{\pi}{2}$. Graph shown is for an R value of 1. In general, the y-int would be R.

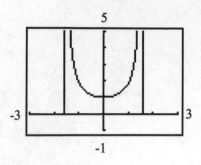

77. **(a)** If a is doubled in $y = a \sin(bx + c)$ the amplitude will be doubled.

(b) If b is doubled in $y = a \sin(bx + c)$ the period will be reduced by one half.

(c) If c is doubled in $y = a \sin(bx + c)$ the displacement will be doubled.

Chapter 11

EXPONENTS AND RADICALS

11.1 Simplifying Expressions with Integral Exponents

1. $(x^{-2}y)^2 \left(\dfrac{2}{x}\right)^{-2} = \dfrac{x^{-4}y^2}{\left(\dfrac{2}{x}\right)^2}$

$$= \dfrac{x^{-4}y^2}{\dfrac{4}{x^2}}$$

$$= \dfrac{x^{-4}y^2}{1} \times \dfrac{x^2}{4}$$

$$= \dfrac{x^{-2}y^2}{4}$$

$$= \dfrac{y^2}{4x^2}$$

5. $x^7 \cdot x^{-4} = x^{7+(-4)} = x^3$

9. $5 \cdot 5^{-3} = 5^{1+(-3)} = 5^{-2} = \dfrac{1}{5^2} = \dfrac{1}{25}$

13. $(5an^{-2})^{-1} = 5^{-1}a^{-1}n^{(-2)(-1)} = \dfrac{n^2}{5a}$

17. $-7x^0 = -7 \cdot 1 = -7$

21. $(7a^{-1}x)^{-3} = 7^{-3}a^3x^{-3} = \dfrac{a^3}{7^3x^3} = \dfrac{a^3}{343x^3}$

25. $\left(\dfrac{a}{b^{-2}}\right)^{-3} = \dfrac{a^{-3}}{(b^{-2})^{-3}} = \dfrac{\dfrac{1}{a^3}}{b^{(-2)(-3)}} = \dfrac{\dfrac{1}{a^3}}{b^6} = \dfrac{1}{a^3b^6}$

29. $3x^{-2} + 2y^{-2} = \dfrac{3}{x^2} + \dfrac{2}{y^2} = \dfrac{2x^2 + 3y^2}{x^2y^2}$

33. $\left(\dfrac{3a^2}{4b}\right)^{-3} \left(\dfrac{4}{a}\right)^{-5} = \dfrac{3^{-3}a^{-6}}{4^{-3}b^{-3}} \cdot \dfrac{4^{-5}}{a^{-5}}$

$$= \dfrac{4^3b^3}{3^3a^6} \cdot \dfrac{a^5}{4^5} = \dfrac{b^3}{432a}$$

37. $2a^{-2} + (2a^{-2})^4 = \dfrac{2}{a^2} + 2^4a^{-8} = \dfrac{2}{a^2} + \dfrac{16}{a^8}$

$$= \dfrac{2a^6 + 16}{a^8}$$

41. $(R_1^{-1} + R_2^{-1})^{-1} = \dfrac{1}{\dfrac{1}{R_1} + \dfrac{1}{R_2}} = \dfrac{R_1R_2}{R_1 + R_2}$

45. $\dfrac{6^{-1}}{4^{-2} + 2} = \dfrac{\dfrac{1}{6}}{\dfrac{1}{4^2} + 2} = \dfrac{\dfrac{1}{6}}{\dfrac{1}{16} + 2} \cdot \dfrac{48}{48}$

$$= \dfrac{8}{3 + 96} = \dfrac{8}{99}$$

49. $2t^{-2} + t^{-1}(t+1) = \dfrac{2}{t^2} + t^0 + t^{-1}$

$$= \dfrac{2}{t^2} + 1 + \dfrac{1}{t}$$

$$= \dfrac{2 + t^2 + t}{t^2}$$

53. **(a)** $4^2 \cdot 64 = 4^2 \cdot 4^3 = 4^5$

 (b) $4^2 \cdot 64 = (2^2)^2 \cdot 2^6 = 2^4 \cdot 2^6 = 2^{10}$

57. $x^\pi > \pi^x$. Graph $y_1 = x^\pi - \pi^x$ on a graphing calculator and use the zero feature to find the roots.

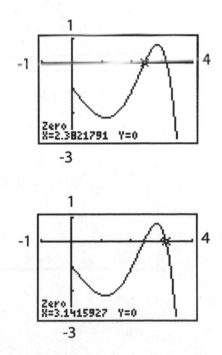

From the graph, $x^\pi > \pi^x$ in the interval $2.38 < x < \pi$. Therefoore, $n = 3$ is the only integral value for which $x^\pi > \pi^x$.

61. $\text{kg} \cdot \text{s}^{-2} \cdot \text{m}^2 = \dfrac{\text{kg} \cdot \text{m}^2}{\text{s}^2} = \dfrac{\text{kg} \cdot \text{m}}{\text{s}^2} \cdot \text{m} = \text{N} \cdot \text{m}$

65.
$$v = a^p t^r$$
$$m \cdot s^{-1} = (m \cdot s^{-2})^p \cdot s^r$$
$$m^1 \cdot s^{-1} = m^p \cdot s^{-2p+r} \Rightarrow p = 1$$
$$\text{and } -2p + r = -1 \Rightarrow -2(1) + r$$
$$= -1 \Rightarrow r = 1$$

11.2　Fractional Exponents

1. $8^{4/3} = (8^{1/3})^4 = (\sqrt[3]{8})^4 = 2^4 = 16$

5. $25^{1/2} = \sqrt{25} = 55$

9. $100^{25/2} = (100^{1/2})^{25} = (\sqrt{100})^{25} = 10^{25}$

13. $64^{-2/3} = \dfrac{1}{(64^{1/3})^2} = \dfrac{1}{(\sqrt[3]{64})^2} = \dfrac{1}{4^2} = \dfrac{1}{16}$

17. $(3^6)^{2/3} = 3^{6 \cdot 2/3} = 3^4 = 81$

21. $\dfrac{15^{2/3}}{5^2 \cdot 15^{-1/3}} = \dfrac{15^{2/3+1/3}}{5^2} = \dfrac{15^1}{25} = \dfrac{3}{5}$

25. $125^{-2/3} - 100^{-3/2} = \dfrac{1}{(125^{1/3})^2} - \dfrac{1}{(100^{1/2})^3}$

$$= \dfrac{1}{(\sqrt[3]{125})^2} - \dfrac{1}{(\sqrt{100})^3}$$

$$= \dfrac{1}{5^2} - \dfrac{1}{10^3}$$

$$= \dfrac{1}{25} - \dfrac{1}{1000}$$

$$= \dfrac{39}{1000}$$

29. $17.98^{1/4} = 2.059$

```
17.98^(1/4)
         2.059194748
```

33. $B^{2/3} \cdot B^{1/2} = B^{2/3+1/2} = B^{7/6}$

37. $\dfrac{x^{3/10}}{x^{-1/5}x^2} = x^{3/10+1/5-2} = x^{-3/2} = \dfrac{1}{x^{3/2}}$

41. $(16a^4b^3)^{-3/4} = 16^{-3/4}a^{4(-3/4)}b^{3(-3/4)}$

$$= \dfrac{1}{16^{3/4}a^3b^{9/4}} = \dfrac{1}{8a^3b^{9/4}}$$

45. $\dfrac{1}{2}(4x^2 + 1)^{-1/2}(8x) = \dfrac{4x}{(4x^2+1)^{1/2}}$

49. $(T^{-1} + 2T^{-2})^{-1/2} = \dfrac{1}{\left(\dfrac{1}{T} + \dfrac{2}{T^2}\right)^{1/2}}$

$$= \dfrac{1}{\left(\dfrac{T+2}{T^2}\right)^{1/2}}$$

$$= \dfrac{1}{\dfrac{(T+2)^{1/2}}{(T^2)^{1/2}}}$$

$$= \dfrac{T}{(T+2)^{1/2}}$$

53. $\left[(a^{1/2} - a^{-1/2})^2 + 4\right]^{1/2} = \left[\left(a^{1/2} - \dfrac{1}{a^{1/2}}\right)^2 + 4\right]^{1/2}$

$$= \left[\left(\dfrac{a-1}{a^{1/2}}\right)^2 + 4\right]^{1/2}$$

$$= \left[\dfrac{(a-1)^2}{a} + 4\right]^{1/2}$$

$$= \left[\dfrac{a^2 - 2a + 1 + 4a}{a}\right]^{1/2}$$

$$= \left[\dfrac{a^2 + 2a + 1}{a}\right]^{1/2}$$

$$= \left[\dfrac{(a+1)^2}{a}\right]^{1/2} = \dfrac{a+1}{a^{1/2}}$$

57. $f(x) = 3x^{1/2}$

x	0	1	2	4	9
y	0	3	4.24	6	9

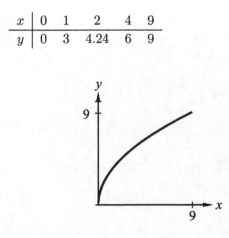

61. **(a)** $\sqrt[5]{x} = x^{1/5}$　　**(b)** $\sqrt[7]{T^3} = T^{3/7}$

65.
$$T^2 = kR^3 \left(1 + \frac{d}{R}\right)^3$$
$$\Rightarrow T^2 = kR^3 \left(\frac{R+d}{R}\right)^3$$
$$= kR^3 \frac{(R+d)^3}{R^3}$$
$$(R+d)^3 = \frac{T^2}{k} \Rightarrow R = -d\left(\frac{T^2}{k}\right)^{1/3}$$
$$= \frac{T^{2/3}}{k^{1/3}} - d$$

11.3   Simplest Radical Form

1. $\sqrt{a^3 b^4} = \sqrt{a^2 (b^2)^2 \cdot a} = ab^2 \sqrt{a}$

5. $\sqrt{24} = \sqrt{4 \cdot 6} = \sqrt{4} \cdot \sqrt{6} = 2\sqrt{6}$

9. $\sqrt{x^2 y^5} = \sqrt{x^2 y^4 y} = \sqrt{x^2}\sqrt{y^4}\sqrt{y} = xy^2\sqrt{y}$

13. $\sqrt{18 R^5 T V^4} = \sqrt{9 R^4 V^4 \cdot 2RT}$
$$= 3R^2 V^2 \sqrt{2RT}$$

17. $\sqrt[5]{96} = \sqrt[5]{32 \cdot 3} = \sqrt[5]{32}\sqrt[5]{3} = 2\sqrt[5]{3}$

21. $\sqrt[4]{64 r^3 s^4 t^5} = \sqrt[4]{16 \cdot 4 s^4 t^4 r^3 t}$
$$= \sqrt[4]{16}\sqrt[4]{s^4}\sqrt[4]{t^4}\sqrt[4]{4r^3 t}$$
$$= 2st\sqrt[4]{4r^3 t}$$

25. $\sqrt[3]{P^3}\sqrt[3]{P^2 V} = P\sqrt[3]{P^2 V}$

29. $\sqrt[3]{\frac{3}{4}} = \sqrt[3]{\frac{48}{64}} = \frac{\sqrt[3]{48}}{\sqrt[3]{64}} = \frac{\sqrt[3]{8 \cdot 6}}{4} = \frac{2\sqrt[3]{6}}{4} = \frac{\sqrt[3]{6}}{2}$

33. $\sqrt[4]{400} = \sqrt[4]{2^4 \cdot 5^2} = 2 \cdot \sqrt[4]{25} = 2\sqrt{5}$

37. $\sqrt{4 \times 10^4} = \sqrt{4} \cdot \sqrt{10^4} = 2 \times 10^2 = 200$

41. $\sqrt[4]{4a^2} = (4a^2)^{1/4} = (2^2)^{1/4}(a^2)^{1/4}$
$$= 2^{1/2} a^{1/2} = \sqrt{2a}$$

45. $\sqrt[4]{\sqrt[3]{16}} = \sqrt[4]{16^{1/3}} = \left(16^{1/3}\right)^{1/4}$
$$= \left(16^{1/4}\right)^{1/3} = 2^{1/3} = \sqrt[3]{2}$$

49. $\sqrt{\frac{n}{m^3}} = \sqrt{\frac{nm}{m^4}} = \frac{\sqrt{nm}}{m^2}$

53. $\sqrt{\frac{5}{4} - \frac{1}{8}} = \sqrt{\frac{5(2)}{4(2)} - \frac{1}{8}} = \sqrt{\frac{9}{8}}$
$$= \sqrt{\frac{3^2}{2^2(2)} \times \frac{2}{2}}$$
$$= \sqrt{\frac{3^2(2)}{2^4}} = \frac{3}{2^2}\sqrt{2}$$
$$= \frac{3}{4}\sqrt{2}$$

57. $\sqrt{\frac{C-2}{C+2}} = \sqrt{\frac{(C-2)(C+2)}{(C+2)^2}} = \frac{\sqrt{C^2-4}}{C+2}$

61. $\sqrt{9x^2 - 6x + 1} = \sqrt{(3x-1)^2} = 3x - 1$

65. $a\sqrt{\frac{2g}{a}} = a\sqrt{\frac{2g}{a} \times \frac{a}{a}} = a\sqrt{\frac{2ag}{a^2}}$
$$= \frac{a}{a}\sqrt{2ag} = \sqrt{2ag}$$

11.4   Addition and Subtraction of Radicals

1. $3\sqrt{125} - \sqrt{20} + \sqrt{45} = 3\sqrt{25(5)} - \sqrt{4(5)} + \sqrt{9(5)}$
$$= 15\sqrt{5} - 2\sqrt{5} + 3\sqrt{5}$$
$$= 15\sqrt{6} + \sqrt{5}$$
$$= 16\sqrt{5}$$

5. $2\sqrt{7} + \sqrt{5} - 3\sqrt{7} = \sqrt{5} + (2-3)\sqrt{7}$
$$= \sqrt{5} - \sqrt{7}$$

9. $2\sqrt{3t^2} - 3\sqrt{12t^2} = 2t\sqrt{3} - 3t\sqrt{3(4)}$
$$= 2t\sqrt{3} - 3(2)t\sqrt{3}$$
$$= (2-6)t\sqrt{3}$$
$$= -4t\sqrt{3}$$

13. $2\sqrt{28} + 3\sqrt{175}$
$$= 2\sqrt{4(7)} + 3\sqrt{25(7)} + 2(2)\sqrt{7} + 3(5)\sqrt{7}$$
$$(4+15)\sqrt{7} = 19\sqrt{7}$$

17. $3\sqrt{75R} + 2\sqrt{48R} - 2\sqrt{18R}$
$$= 3\sqrt{25(3)R} + 2\sqrt{16(3)R} - 2\sqrt{9(2)R}$$
$$= 3(5)\sqrt{3R} + 2(4)\sqrt{3R} - 2(3)\sqrt{2R}$$
$$= (15+8)\sqrt{3R} - 6\sqrt{2R}$$
$$= 23\sqrt{3R} - 6\sqrt{2R}$$

21. $\sqrt{\dfrac{1}{2}} + \sqrt{\dfrac{25}{2}} - \sqrt{18} = \sqrt{\dfrac{1(2)}{2(2)}} + \sqrt{\dfrac{25(2)}{4}} - \sqrt{(9)2}$

$\qquad\qquad = \sqrt{\dfrac{2}{4}} - \sqrt{\dfrac{25(2)}{4}} - 3\sqrt{2}$

$\qquad\qquad = \left(\dfrac{1}{2} + \dfrac{5}{2} - 3\right)\sqrt{2} = 0$

25. $\sqrt[4]{32} - \sqrt[8]{4} = \sqrt[4]{16(2)} - \sqrt[8]{2(2)}$

$\qquad\qquad = 2\sqrt[4]{2} - 2^{2/8} = 2\sqrt[4]{2} - 2^{1/4}$

$\qquad\qquad = 2\sqrt[4]{2} - \sqrt[4]{2} = (2-1)\sqrt[4]{2}$

$\qquad\qquad = \sqrt[4]{2}$

29. $\sqrt{6}\sqrt{5}\sqrt{3} - \sqrt{40a^2} = \sqrt{90} - \sqrt{4a^2(10)}$

$\qquad\qquad = \sqrt{9(10)} - 2a\sqrt{10}$

$\qquad\qquad = (3 - 2a)\sqrt{10}$

33. $\sqrt{\dfrac{a}{c^5}} - \sqrt{\dfrac{c}{a^3}} = \sqrt{\dfrac{a(c)}{c^5(c)}} - \sqrt{\dfrac{ca}{a^3(a)}}$

$\qquad\qquad = \sqrt{\dfrac{ac}{c^6}} - \sqrt{\dfrac{ac}{a^4}}$

$\qquad\qquad = \left(\dfrac{1}{c^3} - \dfrac{1}{a^2}\right)\sqrt{ac}$

$\qquad\qquad = \dfrac{(a^2 - c^3)\sqrt{ac}}{a^2c^3}$

37. $\sqrt{\dfrac{T-V}{T+V}} - \sqrt{\dfrac{T+V}{T-V}}$

$\qquad = \sqrt{\dfrac{(T-V)(T+V)}{(T+V)^2}} - \sqrt{\dfrac{(T+V)(T-V)}{(T-V)^2}}$

$\qquad = \dfrac{\sqrt{T^2 - V^2}}{T+V} - \dfrac{\sqrt{T^2 - V^2}}{T-V}$

$\qquad = \dfrac{(T-V)\sqrt{T^2 - V^2} - (T+V)\sqrt{T^2 - V^2}}{(T+V)(T-V)}$

$\qquad = \dfrac{(T-V-T-V)\sqrt{T^2 - V^2}}{T^2 - V^2}$

$\qquad = \dfrac{-2V\sqrt{T^2 - V^2}}{T^2 - V^2}$

$\qquad = \dfrac{-2V\sqrt{T^2 - V^2}}{T^2 - V^2}$

$\qquad = \dfrac{2V\sqrt{T^2 - V^2}}{V^2 - T^2}$

41. $2\sqrt{\dfrac{2}{3}} + \sqrt{24} - 5\sqrt{\dfrac{3}{2}} = 2\sqrt{\dfrac{2(3)}{3(3)}} + \sqrt{4(6)} - 5\sqrt{\dfrac{3(2)}{2(2)}}$

$\qquad\qquad = 2\sqrt{\dfrac{6}{9}} + 2\sqrt{6} - 5\sqrt{\dfrac{6}{4}}$

$\qquad\qquad = \dfrac{2}{3}\sqrt{6} + 2\sqrt{6} - \dfrac{5}{2}\sqrt{6}$

$\qquad\qquad = \dfrac{1}{6}\sqrt{6} = 0.40824829$

45. $10\sqrt{11} - \sqrt{1000} = 10\sqrt{11} - \sqrt{100(10)}$

$\qquad\qquad = 10\sqrt{11} - 10\sqrt{10}$

$\qquad\qquad = 10(\sqrt{11} - \sqrt{10})$

$\qquad\qquad > 0 \text{ since } \sqrt{11} > \sqrt{10}$

11.5   Multiplication and Division of Radicals

1. $\sqrt{2}(3\sqrt{5} - 4\sqrt{8}) = 3\sqrt{10} - 4\sqrt{16}$

$\qquad\qquad = 3\sqrt{10} - 4(4)$

$\qquad\qquad = 3\sqrt{10} - 16$

5. $\sqrt{3}\sqrt{10} = \sqrt{3 \cdot 10} = \sqrt{30}$

9. $\sqrt[3]{4} \cdot \sqrt[3]{2} = \sqrt[3]{4 \cdot 2} = \sqrt[3]{8} = 2$

13. $\sqrt{8} \cdot \sqrt{\dfrac{5}{2}} = \sqrt{\dfrac{40}{2}} = \sqrt{20} = \sqrt{4 \cdot 5} = 2\sqrt{5}$

17. $(2 - \sqrt{5})(2 + \sqrt{5}) = 2^2 - \sqrt{5}^2 = 4 - 5 = -1$

21. $(3\sqrt{11} - \sqrt{x})(2\sqrt{11} + 5\sqrt{x})$

$\qquad = 6\sqrt{11}^2 + 15\sqrt{11x} - 2\sqrt{11x} - 5\sqrt{x}^2$

$\qquad = 6 \cdot 11 + 13\sqrt{11x} - 5x$

$\qquad = 66 + 13\sqrt{11x} - 5x$

25. $\dfrac{\sqrt{6} - 3}{\sqrt{6}} = \dfrac{\sqrt{6} - 3}{\sqrt{6}} \cdot \dfrac{\sqrt{6}}{\sqrt{6}}\dfrac{\sqrt{6}^2 - 3\sqrt{6}}{\sqrt{6}^2}$

$\qquad\qquad = \dfrac{6 - 3\sqrt{6}}{6} = \dfrac{2 - \sqrt{6}}{2}$

29. $\sqrt{2}\sqrt[3]{3} = 2^{1/2}3^{1/3} = 2^{3/6}3^{2/6} = (2^3 3^2)^{1/6}$

$\qquad\qquad = \sqrt[6]{2^3 3^2} = \sqrt[6]{72}$

33. $\dfrac{\sqrt{2}-1}{\sqrt{7}-3\sqrt{2}} = \dfrac{\sqrt{2}-1}{\sqrt{7}-3\sqrt{2}} \cdot \dfrac{\sqrt{7}+3\sqrt{2}}{\sqrt{7}+3\sqrt{2}}$

$$= \dfrac{\sqrt{14}+3\sqrt{2}^2-\sqrt{7}-3\sqrt{2}}{\sqrt{7}^2-3^2\sqrt{2}^2}$$

$$= \dfrac{\sqrt{14}+3\cdot2-\sqrt{7}-3\sqrt{2}}{7-9\cdot2}$$

$$= \dfrac{\sqrt{14}+6-\sqrt{7}-3\sqrt{2}}{7-18}$$

$$= -\dfrac{\sqrt{14}+6-\sqrt{7}-3\sqrt{2}}{11}$$

37. $\dfrac{2\sqrt{x}}{\sqrt{x}-\sqrt{5}} = \dfrac{2\sqrt{x}}{\sqrt{x}-\sqrt{5}} \cdot \dfrac{\sqrt{x}+\sqrt{5}}{\sqrt{x}+\sqrt{5}}$

$$= \dfrac{2\sqrt{x}^2+2\sqrt{x}\sqrt{5}}{\sqrt{x}^2-\sqrt{5}^2} = \dfrac{2x+2\sqrt{5x}}{x-5}$$

41. $\left(\sqrt{\dfrac{2}{R}}+\sqrt{\dfrac{R}{2}}\right)\left(\sqrt{\dfrac{2}{R}}-2\sqrt{\dfrac{R}{2}}\right)$

$$= \dfrac{2}{R}-2\sqrt{\dfrac{2R}{2R}}+\sqrt{\dfrac{2R}{2R}}-2\left(\dfrac{R}{2}\right)$$

$$= \dfrac{2}{R}-2+1-R = \dfrac{2-2R+R-R^2}{R}$$

$$= \dfrac{2-R-R^2}{R}$$

45. $\dfrac{\sqrt{a}+\sqrt{a-2}}{\sqrt{a}-\sqrt{a-2}} \cdot \dfrac{\sqrt{a}+\sqrt{a-2}}{\sqrt{a}+\sqrt{a-2}}$

$$= \dfrac{a+2\sqrt{a}\sqrt{a-2}+a-2}{a-(a-2)}$$

$$= \dfrac{2a+2\sqrt{a}\sqrt{a-2}-2}{2}$$

$$= a+\sqrt{a}\sqrt{a-2}-1$$
$$= a-1+\sqrt{a(a-2)}$$

49. $\dfrac{2\sqrt{6}-\sqrt{5}}{3\sqrt{6}-4\sqrt{5}} = \dfrac{2\sqrt{6}-\sqrt{5}}{3\sqrt{6}-4\sqrt{5}} \times \dfrac{3\sqrt{6}+4\sqrt{5}}{3\sqrt{6}+4\sqrt{5}}$

$$= \dfrac{6(6)+8\sqrt{30}-3\sqrt{30}-4(5)}{9(6)-16(5)}$$

$$= -\dfrac{16+5\sqrt{30}}{26} = -1.6686962$$

53. $\dfrac{x^2}{\sqrt{2x+1}}+2x\sqrt{2x+1}$

$$= \dfrac{x^2}{\sqrt{2x+1}}+\dfrac{2x\sqrt{2x+1}\sqrt{2x+1}}{\sqrt{2x+1}}$$

$$= \dfrac{x^2+2x(2x+1)}{\sqrt{2x+1}} = \dfrac{x^2+4x^2+2x}{\sqrt{2x+1}}$$

$$= \dfrac{5x^2+2x}{\sqrt{2x+1}}$$

57. $\dfrac{\sqrt{x+h}-\sqrt{x}}{h} = \dfrac{\sqrt{x+h}-\sqrt{x}}{h} \times \dfrac{\sqrt{x+h}+\sqrt{x}}{\sqrt{x+h}+\sqrt{x}}$

$$= \dfrac{x+h-x}{h\sqrt{x+h}+h\sqrt{x}}$$

$$= \dfrac{h}{h(\sqrt{x+h}+\sqrt{x})}$$

$$= \dfrac{1}{\sqrt{x+h}+\sqrt{x}}$$

61. $m^2+bm+k^2=0;\ m=\dfrac{1}{2}(\sqrt{b^2-4k^2}-b)$

$$\left(\dfrac{1}{2}(\sqrt{b^2-4k^2}-b)\right)^2+b\left(\dfrac{1}{2}(\sqrt{b^2-4k^2}-b)\right)+k^2$$

$$= \dfrac{1}{4}(b^2-4k^2)-\dfrac{b}{2}\sqrt{b^2-4k^2}$$

$$+\dfrac{1}{4}b^2+\dfrac{b}{2}\sqrt{b^2-4k^2}-\dfrac{1}{2}b^2+k^2$$

$$= 0$$

65. $\dfrac{2Q}{\sqrt{\sqrt{2}-1}} = \dfrac{2Q}{\sqrt{\sqrt{2}-1}} \times \dfrac{\sqrt{\sqrt{2}+1}}{\sqrt{\sqrt{2}+1}}$

$$= \dfrac{2Q\sqrt{\sqrt{2}+1}}{\sqrt{2}-1}$$

$$= 2Q\sqrt{\sqrt{2}+1}$$

Chapter 11 Review Exercises

1. $2a^{-2}b^0 = 2a^{-2}\cdot1 = 2\cdot\dfrac{1}{a^2} = \dfrac{2}{a^2}$

5. $3(25)^{3/2} = 3\left[(25)^{1/2}\right]^3 = 3\left[\sqrt{25}\right]^3$
$$= 3\left[5\right]^3 = 3\cdot125 = 375$$

9. $\left(\dfrac{3}{t^2}\right)^{-2} = \dfrac{1}{\left(\dfrac{3}{t^2}\right)^2} = \dfrac{1}{\dfrac{3^2}{(t^2)^2}} = \dfrac{1}{\dfrac{9}{t^4}} = \dfrac{t^4}{9}$

13. $\left(2a^{1/3}b^{5/6}\right)^6 = 2^6 \cdot \left(a^{1/3}\right)^6 \cdot \left(b^{5/6}\right)^6 = 64 \cdot a^{6/3} \cdot b^{5/6 \cdot 6} = 64a^2b^5$

17. $2L^{-2} - 4C^{-1} = \dfrac{2}{L^2} - \dfrac{4}{C} = \dfrac{2C - 4L^2}{L^2C}$

21. $(a - 3b^{-1})^{-1} = \dfrac{1}{(a - 3b^{-1})^1} = \dfrac{1}{a - \dfrac{3}{b}} \cdot \dfrac{b}{b}$

$\qquad\qquad = \dfrac{b}{ab - 3}$

25. $(W^2 + 2WH + H^2)^{-1/2} = \dfrac{1}{((W+H)^2)^{1/2}}$

$\qquad\qquad\qquad\qquad\qquad = \dfrac{1}{W + H}$

29. $\sqrt{68} = \sqrt{4 \cdot 17} = \sqrt{4} \cdot \sqrt{17} = 2\sqrt{17}$

33. $\sqrt{9a^3b^4} = \sqrt{9a^2b^4 \cdot a} = 3ab^2\sqrt{a}$

37. $\dfrac{5}{\sqrt{2s}} = \dfrac{5}{\sqrt{2s}} \cdot \dfrac{\sqrt{2s}}{\sqrt{2s}} = \dfrac{5\sqrt{2s}}{2s}$

41. $\sqrt[4]{8m^6n^9} = \sqrt[4]{8m^4 \cdot m^2 \cdot n^8 \cdot n} = mn^2\sqrt[4]{8m^2n}$

45. $\sqrt{36 + 4} - 2\sqrt{10} = \sqrt{40} - 2\sqrt{10} = \sqrt{4(10)} - 2\sqrt{10} = 2\sqrt{10} - 2\sqrt{10} = 0$

49. $a\sqrt{2x^3} + \sqrt{8a^2x^3} = a\sqrt{2x^2 \cdot x} + \sqrt{4 \cdot 2 \cdot a^2x^2 \cdot x} = ax\sqrt{2x} + 2ax\sqrt{2x} = 3ax\sqrt{2x}$

53. $\sqrt{5}(2\sqrt{5} - \sqrt{11}) = 2\sqrt{5}^2 - \sqrt{5}\sqrt{11}$

$\qquad\qquad\qquad\quad = 2 \cdot 5 - \sqrt{55} = 10 - \sqrt{55}$

57. $(2 - 3\sqrt{17B})(3 + \sqrt{17B}) = 6 + 2\sqrt{17B} - 9\sqrt{17B} - 3(17B) = 6 - 51B - 7\sqrt{17B}$

61. $\dfrac{\sqrt{3x}}{2\sqrt{3x} - \sqrt{y}} = \dfrac{\sqrt{3x}}{(2\sqrt{3x} - \sqrt{y})} \cdot \dfrac{(2\sqrt{3x} + \sqrt{y})}{(2\sqrt{3x} + \sqrt{y})} = \dfrac{2\sqrt{3x}^2 + \sqrt{3x} \cdot \sqrt{y}}{4\sqrt{3x}^2 - \sqrt{y}^2} = \dfrac{2 \cdot 3x + \sqrt{3xy}}{4 \cdot 3x - y} = \dfrac{6x + \sqrt{3xy}}{12x - y}$

65. $\dfrac{\sqrt{7} - \sqrt{5}}{\sqrt{5} + 3\sqrt{7}} = \dfrac{(\sqrt{7} - \sqrt{5})}{(\sqrt{5} + 3\sqrt{7})} \cdot \dfrac{(\sqrt{5} - 3\sqrt{7})}{(\sqrt{5} - 3\sqrt{7})} = \dfrac{\sqrt{35} - 3 \cdot 7 - 5 + 3\sqrt{35}}{5 - 9 \cdot 7} = \dfrac{4\sqrt{35} - 26}{5 - 63} = \dfrac{4\sqrt{35} - 26}{-58}$

$\qquad\qquad = \dfrac{2(2\sqrt{35} - 13)}{2(-29)} = \dfrac{2\sqrt{35} - 13}{-29} = \dfrac{13 - 2\sqrt{35}}{29}$

69. $\sqrt{4b^2 + 1}$ is in simplest form

73. $\sqrt{3 + n}(\sqrt{3 + n} - \sqrt{n})^{-1} = \dfrac{\sqrt{3 + n}}{\sqrt{3 + n} - \sqrt{n}} \cdot \dfrac{\sqrt{3 + n} + \sqrt{n}}{\sqrt{3 + n} + \sqrt{n}} = \dfrac{3 + n + \sqrt{n}\sqrt{3 + n}}{3 + n - n} = \dfrac{3 + n + \sqrt{3n + n^2}}{3}$

77. $\sqrt{\sqrt{2} - 1}(\sqrt{2} + 1) = \sqrt{\sqrt{2} - 1}(\sqrt{2} + 1) \cdot \dfrac{\sqrt{\sqrt{2} + 1}}{\sqrt{\sqrt{2} + 1}} = \dfrac{\sqrt{\sqrt{2} - 1}(\sqrt{2} + 1)}{\sqrt{\sqrt{2} + 1}}$

$\qquad\qquad = \sqrt{\dfrac{(\sqrt{2} - 1)}{(\sqrt{2} + 1)} \cdot \dfrac{(\sqrt{2} - 1)}{(\sqrt{2} - 1)}} \cdot (\sqrt{2} + 1) \cdot \sqrt{\sqrt{2} + 1}$

$\qquad\qquad = \sqrt{\dfrac{2 - 2\sqrt{2} + 1}{2 - 1}} \cdot \sqrt{(\sqrt{2} + 1)^2} \cdot \sqrt{\sqrt{2} + 1}$

$\qquad\qquad = \sqrt{(3 - 2\sqrt{2})(2 + 2\sqrt{2} + 1)} \cdot \sqrt{\sqrt{2} + 1}$

$\qquad\qquad = \sqrt{6 + 6\sqrt{2} + 3 - 4\sqrt{2} - 8 - 2\sqrt{2}} \cdot \sqrt{\sqrt{2} + 1} = \sqrt{\sqrt{2} + 1}$

Evaluation of each ride separately gives same answer as following calculator screen shows.

```
√((√(2)-1)(√(2)+1
)
          1.553773974
√(√(2)+1
          1.553773974
```

81. (a) $v = k\sqrt[3]{\dfrac{P}{W}} = k\left(\dfrac{P}{W}\right)^{1/3}$

(b) $v = k\sqrt[3]{\dfrac{P}{W} \cdot \dfrac{W^2}{W^2}} = \dfrac{k}{W}\sqrt[3]{PW^2}$

85. $\dfrac{v}{n_2^{-2} - n_1^{-2}} = \dfrac{v}{\dfrac{1}{n_2^2} - \dfrac{1}{n_1^2}} \cdot \dfrac{n_1^2 n_2^2}{n_1^2 n_2^2} = \dfrac{v n_1^2 n_2^2}{n_1^2 - n_2^2}$

89. $\sqrt{3^2 + 3^2} + \sqrt{2^2 + 2^2} + \sqrt{1^2 + 1^2} = \sqrt{18} + \sqrt{8} + \sqrt{2} = \sqrt{9 \cdot 2} + \sqrt{4 \cdot 2} + \sqrt{2} = 3\sqrt{2} + 2\sqrt{2} + \sqrt{2} = 6\sqrt{2}$ cm

93. Answers may vary.

Chapter 12

COMPLEX NUMBERS

12.1   Basic Definitions

1. $-\sqrt{-3}\sqrt{-12} = -j\sqrt{3}(j\sqrt{12})$
$$= -j^2\sqrt{36}$$
$$= -(-1)6$$
$$= 6$$

5. $\sqrt{-81} = \sqrt{81(-1)} = \sqrt{81}\sqrt{-1} = 9j$

9. $\sqrt{-0.36} = \sqrt{0.36(-1)} = \sqrt{0.36}\sqrt{-1} = 0.6j$

13. $\sqrt{-\dfrac{7}{4}} = \dfrac{\sqrt{-7}}{\sqrt{4}} = \dfrac{\sqrt{7(-1)}}{2}$
$$= \dfrac{\sqrt{7}\sqrt{-1}}{2}$$
$$= j\dfrac{\sqrt{7}}{2}$$

17. (a) $(\sqrt{-7})^2 = (\sqrt{7(-1)})^2 = (\sqrt{7}\cdot\sqrt{-1})$
$$= (\sqrt{7}\cdot j)^2$$
$$= \sqrt{7}^2\cdot j^2$$
$$= 7(-1) = -7$$

(b) $(\sqrt{-7})^2 = \sqrt{49} = 7$

21. $\sqrt{-\dfrac{1}{15}}\sqrt{-\dfrac{27}{5}} = j\sqrt{\dfrac{1}{15}}j\sqrt{\dfrac{27}{5}}$
$$= j^2\sqrt{\dfrac{27}{75}}$$
$$= -\sqrt{\dfrac{9(3)}{25(3)}}$$
$$= -\dfrac{3}{5}$$

25. (a) $j^7 = j^4\cdot j^3 = (1)(-j) = -j$

(b) $j^{49} = j^{48}\cdot j^1 = (1)(j) = j$

29. $j^{15} - j^{13} = j^{12}\cdot j^3 - j^{12}\cdot j = (1)(-j) - (1)(j)$
$$= -j - j = -2j$$

33. $2 + \sqrt{-9} = 2 + \sqrt{9(-1)} = 2 + 3j$

37. $\sqrt{-4j^2} + \sqrt{-4} = \sqrt{(-4)(-1)} + 2j = 2 + 2j$

41. $\sqrt{18} - \sqrt{-8} = \sqrt{9\cdot 2} - \sqrt{4\cdot 2}j$
$$= 3\sqrt{2} - 2j\sqrt{2}$$

45. (a) the conjugate of $6 - 7j$ is $6 + 7j$

(b) the conjugate of $8 + j$ is $8 - j$

49. $7x - 2yj = 14 + 4j \Rightarrow 7x = 14$
$$x = 2$$

and $\quad -2y = 4$
$$y = -2$$

53. $\quad x - 2j^2 + 7y = yj + 2xj^3$
$$x - 2(-1) + 7j = yj + 2x(-j)$$
$$x + 2 + 7j = 0 + (y - 2x)j$$
$x + 2 = 0 \quad$ and $\quad 7 = y - 2x = y - 2(-2)$
$x = -2 \qquad\qquad 7 = y + 4$
$$y = 3$$

57. No. $x^4 + 16 = 0$

$2j$ is not a solution since

$$(2j)^4 + 16 = 0$$
$$16j^4 + 16 = 0$$
$$16(1) + 16 = 0$$
$$32 \neq 0.$$

$-2j$ is not a solution since

$$(-2j)^4 + 16 = 0$$
$$16j^4 + 16 = 0$$
$$16(1) + 16 = 0$$
$$32 \neq 0.$$

61. For a complex number and its conjugate to be equal, it must be a real number. $a + 0j = a - 0j$

12.2   Basic Operations with Complex Numbers

1. $(7 - 9j) - (6 - 4j) = 7 - 9j - 6 + 4j$
$$= 1 - 5j$$

5. $(3 - 7j) + (2 - j) = (3 + 2) + (-7 - 1)j = 5 - 8j$

9. $0.23 - (0.46 - 0.9j) + 0.67j$
$= 0.23 - 0.46 + 0.19j + 0.67j$
$= -0.23 + 0.86j$

13. $(7 - j)(7j) = 49j - 7j^2 = 49j - 7(-1) = 7 + 49j$

17. $(\sqrt{-18}\sqrt{-4})(3j) = (3\sqrt{2}j)(2j)(3j)$
$= 18\sqrt{2}j^3$
$= 18\sqrt{2}j^2j$
$= 18\sqrt{2}(-1)j$
$= -18j\sqrt{2}$

21. $j\sqrt{-7} - j^6\sqrt{112} + 3j = j\sqrt{7(-1)} - j^6\sqrt{16(7)} + 3j$
$= j^2\sqrt{7} - 4j^6\sqrt{7} + 3j$
$= (-1)\sqrt{7} - 4j^4(j^2)\sqrt{7} + 3j$
$= -\sqrt{7} - 4(1)(-1)\sqrt{7} + 3j$
$= -\sqrt{7} + 4\sqrt{7} + 3j$
$= 3\sqrt{7} + 3j$

25. $(1 - j)^3 - (1 - j)(1 - j)^2$
$= (1 - j)(1 - 2j + j^2)$
$= 1 - 2j + j^2 - j + 2j^2 - j^3$
$= 1 - 3j + 3j^2 - j^3$
$= 1 - 3j + 3(-1) - (-1)j$
$= -2 - 2j$

29. $\dfrac{1 - j}{3j} \times \dfrac{3j}{3j} = \dfrac{3j - 3j^2}{9(j^2)}$
$= \dfrac{3j - 3(-1)}{9(-1)}$
$= \dfrac{3j + 3}{-9}$
$= -\dfrac{1}{3}(1 + j)$

33. $\dfrac{j^2 - j}{2j - j^8} = \dfrac{-1 - j}{2j - 1} \cdot \dfrac{-2j - 1}{-2j - 1}$
$= \dfrac{1 + 3j + 2j^2}{1^2 + 2^2}$
$= \dfrac{1 + 3j - 2}{5}$
$= \dfrac{-1 + 3j}{5}$

37. Substituting $-1 - j$ into $x^2 + 2x + 2$ gives
$(-1 - j)^2 + 2(-1 - j) + 2 = 1 + 2j + j^2 - 2 - 2j + 2$
$= 1 + j^2$
$= 1 - 1$
$= 0$

41. $\dfrac{1}{3 - j} = \dfrac{1}{3 - j} \cdot \dfrac{3 + j}{3 + j} = \dfrac{3 + j}{9 + 1}$
$= \dfrac{1}{10}(3 + j)$
$= \dfrac{3}{10} + \dfrac{1}{10}j$

45. $E = I \cdot Z = (0.835 - 0.427j)(250 + 170j)$
$= 208.75 + 141.95j - 106.75j$
$= -72.59j^2$
$= 208.75 + 35.2j + 72.59$
$= 281.34 + 35.2j$

49. (a) $(a + bi) + (a - bi) = a + bi + a - bi = 2a$,
a real number

(b) $(a + bj) - (a - bj) = 2bj$

12.3   Graphical Representation of Complex Numbers

1. Add $5 - 2j$ and $-2 + j$ graphically.

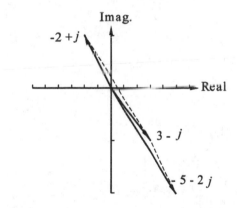

$5 - 2j + (-2 + j) = 3 - j$

5. $-4 - 3j$

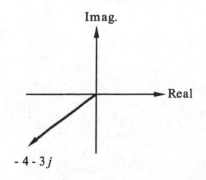

9. $2 + 3 + 4j = 5 + 4j$

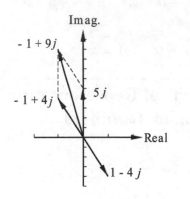

13. $5j - (1 - 4j) = 5j - 1 + 4j$
$$= -1 + 9j$$

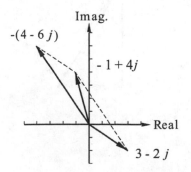

17. $(3 - 2j) - (4 - 6j) = 3 - 2j - 4 + 6j$
$$= -1 + 4j$$

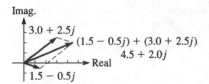

21. $(1.5 - 0.5j) + (3.0 + 2.5j) = 1.5 - 0.5j + 3.0 + 2.5j$
$$= 4.5 + 2.0j$$

25. $(2j + 1) - 3j - (j + 1) = (2j + 1) + (-3j) + (-(j + 1))$
$$= 2j + 1 - 3j - j - 1$$
$$= -2j$$

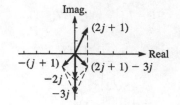

29. $3 + 2j$

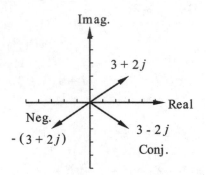

33. $a + bj = 3 - j$
$$3(a + bj) = 9 - 3j$$
$$-3(a + bj) = -9 + 3j$$

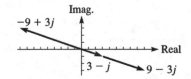

12.4   Polar Form of a Complex Number

1. $-3 + 4j \Rightarrow x = -3, y = 4 \Rightarrow r = \sqrt{(-3)^2 + 4^2} = 5$
$\tan \theta_{\text{ref}} = \dfrac{4}{3}, \theta_{\text{ref}} = 53.1°,$
$\theta = 180° - 53.1° = 126.9°$
$5(\cos 126.9° + j \sin 126.9°)$

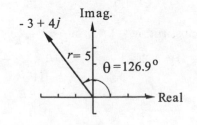

5. $3 - 4j$

$$r = \sqrt{3^2 + (-4)^2}$$
$$= 5$$

$$\tan \theta_{ref} = \left| \frac{-4}{3} \right|$$
$$= 1.33$$
$$\theta_{ref} = 53.1°$$
$$\theta = 306.9°$$

$$5(\cos 306.9° + j \sin 306.9°)$$

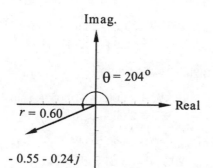

9. $-0.55 - 0.24j \Rightarrow x = -0.55, y = -0.24$
$$r = \sqrt{(-0.55)^2 + (-0.24)^2} = 0.60$$

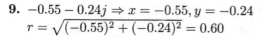

$$\tan \theta_{ref} = \frac{0.24}{0.55}, \theta_{ref} = 24°, \theta = 180° + 24° = 204°$$

$$0.60(\cos 204° + j \sin 204°)$$

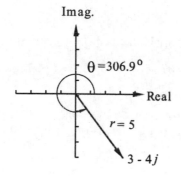

13. $3.514 - 7.256j$

$$r = \sqrt{(3.514)^2 + (-7.256)^2} = 8.062$$

$$\tan \theta_{ref} = \left| \frac{-7.256}{3.514} \right| = 2.065$$

$$\theta_{ref} = 64.16°$$
$$\theta = 295.84°$$

$$8.062(\cos 295.84° + j \sin 295.84°)$$

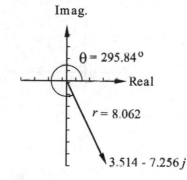

17. $9j = 0 + 9j$

$$r = \sqrt{0^2 + 9^2} = 9$$

$$\theta = 90° \text{ since } y \text{ is pos.}$$

$$9(\cos 90° + j \sin 90°)$$

21. $1.60(\cos 150.0° + j \sin 150.0°)$

$$x = 1.60 \cos 150.0 = 1.60(0.866) = -1.39$$
$$y = 1.60 \sin 150.0° = 1.60(0.5) = 0.800$$

$$-1.39 + 0.800j$$

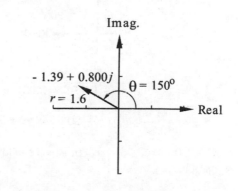

25. $0.08(\cos 360° + j \sin 360°)$

$x = 0.08 \cos 360°$
$\quad = 0.088(1) = 0.08$
$y = 0.088 \sin 360°$
$\quad = 0.088(0) = 0$

0.08

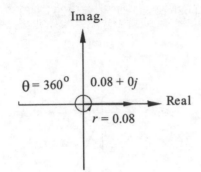

29. $4.75\angle 172.8°$
$\quad = 4.75(\cos 172.8° + j \sin 172.8°)$
$\quad = -4.71 + 0.595j$

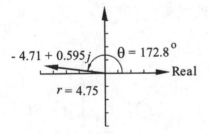

33. $7.32\angle -270° = 7.32(\cos(-270°) + j \sin(-270°))$
$\qquad\qquad\quad = 0 + 7.32j$

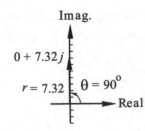

37.　　　　$r = \sqrt{2.84^2 + (-1.06)^2} = 3.03$

$\tan \theta_{\text{ref}} = \dfrac{-1.06}{2.84}, \ \theta_{\text{ref}} = -20.5°, \ \theta = 339.5°$

$2.84 - 1.06j = 3.03(\cos 339.5° + j \sin 339.5°)$
$3.03\angle 339.5° \text{ kV}$

12.5 Exponential Form of a Complex Number

1. $8.50\angle 226.3°, r = 8.50,$
$\theta = 226.3° \left(\dfrac{\pi}{180°}\right)$

$\theta = 3.95$
$8.50\angle 226.3° = 8.50e^{3.95j}$

5. $3.00(\cos 60.0° + j \sin 60.0°);$

$r = 3.00, \theta = 60.0° \cdot \left(\dfrac{\pi}{180°}\right) = 1.05 \text{ rad}$

$3.00e^{1.05j}$

9. $375.5(\cos 95.46° + j \sin 95.46°);$

$r = 375.5, \theta = 95.46° = 1.666 \text{ rad}$
$375.5e^{1.666j}$

13. $4.06\angle -61.4°; r = 4.06,$
$\theta = -61.4° = -1.07 \text{ rad}$

$4.06e^{-1.07j} = 4.06e^{5.21j}$

17. $3 - 4j; r = \sqrt{3^2 + (-4)^2} = 5,$

$\theta_{\text{ref}} = \tan^{-1} \dfrac{-4}{3} = -0.9273$

$\quad \theta = \theta_{\text{ref}} + 2\pi = 5.36 \text{ rad}$
$3 - 4j = 5e^{5.36j}$

21. $5.90 + 2.40j;$

$r = \sqrt{5.90^2 + 2.40^2} = 6.37$

$\theta = \tan^{-1} \dfrac{2.40}{5.90} = 0.386$

$5.90 + 2.40j = 6.37e^{0.386j}$

25. $3.00e^{0.500j}; r = 3, \theta = 0.500 \text{ rad} = 28.6°$

$3.00e^{0.500j} = 3(\cos 28.6° + j \sin 28.6°)$
$\qquad\qquad = 2.63 + 1.44j$

29. $3.20e^{5.41j}; r = 3.20, \theta = 5.41 \text{ rad} = 310.0°$

$3.20e^{5.41j} = 3.20(\cos 310.0° + j \sin 310.0°)$
$\qquad\qquad = 2.06 - 2.45j$

33. $(4.55e^{1.32j})^2 = 20.7e^{2.64j};$
$r = 20.7, \theta = 2.64 \text{ rad} = 151.3°$

$(4.55e^{1.32j})^2 = 20.7(\cos 151.3° + j \sin 151.3°)$
$\qquad\qquad\qquad = -18.2 + 9.94j$

37. $375 + 110j$; $r = \sqrt{375^2 + 110^2} = 391$

$$\theta = \tan^{-1}\frac{110}{375} = 0.285$$

$$375 + 110j = 391e^{0.285j}$$

The magnitude of the impedance is 391 ohms.

12.6   Products, Quotients, Powers, and Roots of Complex Numbers

1. $2 + 3j$: $r_1 = \sqrt{2^2 + 3^2} = 3.61$, $\tan\theta_1 = \dfrac{3}{2} \Rightarrow \theta_1 = 56.3°$

$1 + j$: $r_2 = \sqrt{1^1 + 1^2} = 1.41$, $\tan\theta_2 = \dfrac{1}{1} \Rightarrow \theta_2 = 45.0°$

$(2 + 3j)(1 + j) = 3.61(\cos 56.3° + j\sin 56.3°)(1.41)(\cos 45.5° + j\sin 45.0°)$
$$= 5.09(\cos 101.3° + j\sin 101.3°)$$

5. $[4(\cos 60° + j\sin 60°)][2(\cos 20° + j\sin 20°] = 4\cdot 2[(\cos(60° + 20°) + j\sin(60° + 20°)]$
$$= 8(\cos 80° + j\sin 80°)$$

9. $\dfrac{8(\cos 100° + j\sin 100°)}{4(\cos 65° + j\sin 65°)} = \dfrac{8}{4}(\cos(100° - 65°) + j\sin(100° - 65°)) = 2(\cos 35° + j\sin 35°)$

13. $[2(\cos 35° + j\sin 35°)]^3 = 2^3(\cos(3\cdot 35°) + j\sin(3\cdot 35°)) = 8(\cos 105° + j\sin 105°)$

17. $\dfrac{(50\angle 236°)^2(\angle 1840°)}{25\angle 47°} = \dfrac{100\angle 320°}{25\angle 47°} = 4\angle 273°$

21. $2.78\angle 56.8° + 1.37\angle 207.3° = 2.78(\cos 56.8° + j\sin 56.8°) + 1.37(\cos 207.3° + j\sin 207.3°)$

$$= 1.5222 + 2.3262j - 1.2174 - 0.6283j = 0.3048 + 1.6979j.$$
$r = \sqrt{0.3048^2 + 1.6979^2} = 1.73$, $\theta = \tan^{-1}\dfrac{1.6979}{0.3048} = 79.8°$.

$2.78\angle 56.8° + 1.37\angle 207.3° = 0.3048 + 1.6979j = 1.73\angle 79.8°$

25. $3 + 4j = \sqrt{3^2 + 4^2} = \left(\cos\left(\tan^{-1}\dfrac{4}{3}\right) + j\sin\left(\tan^{-1}\dfrac{4}{3}\right)\right) = 5(\cos 53.1° + j\sin 53.1°)$

$5 - 12j = \sqrt{5^2 + (-12)^2}\left(\cos\left(\tan^{-1}\dfrac{-12}{5} + 360°\right) + j\sin\left(\tan^{-1}\dfrac{-12}{5} + 360°\right)\right)$

$$= 13(\cos 292.6° - j\sin 292.6°)$$

polar form:

$(3 + 4j)(5 - 12j) = [5(\cos 53.1° + j\sin 53.1°)][13(\cos 292.6° + j\sin 292.6°)]$
$$= 65(\cos(53.1° + 292.6°) + j\sin(53.1° + 292.6°))$$
$$= 65(\cos(345.7°) + j\sin(345.7°))$$
$$= 63.0 - 16.1j$$

rectangular form:

$(3 + 4j)(5 - 12j) = 15 - 36j + 20j - 48j^2 = 15 - 16j + 48 = 63 - 16j$

29. $\dfrac{7}{1-3j} = \dfrac{7(\cos 0° + j \sin 0°)}{\sqrt{1^2 + (-3)^2}\left(\cos\left(\tan^{-1}\dfrac{-3}{1} + 360°\right) + j \sin\left(\tan^{-1}\dfrac{-3}{1} + 360°\right)\right)} = \dfrac{7(\cos 0° + j \sin 0°)}{3.16(\cos 288.4° + j \sin 288.4°)}$

$\qquad = \dfrac{7}{3.16}(\cos(0° - 288.4°) + j \sin(0 - 288.4°)) = 2.22(\cos(-288.4°) + j \sin(-288.4°))$

$\qquad = 2.22(\cos 71.6° + j \sin 71.6°) = 0.7 + 2.1j$

Rectangular form:

$\qquad \dfrac{7}{1-3j} = \dfrac{7}{(1-3j)} \cdot \dfrac{(1+3j)}{(1+3j)} = \dfrac{7+21j}{1^2+3^2} = \dfrac{7}{10} + \dfrac{21}{10}j$

33. $(3+4j) = \sqrt{3^2+4^2}\left(\cos\left(\tan^{-1}\dfrac{4}{3}\right) + j\sin\left(\tan^{-1}\dfrac{4}{3}\right)\right) = 5(\cos 53.1° + j \sin 53.1°)$

$\qquad (3+4j)^4 = [5(\cos 53.1° + j \sin 53.1°)]^4 5^4(\cos(4 \cdot 53.1°) + j \sin(4 \cdot 53.1°))$

$\qquad\qquad = 625(\cos 212.5° + j \sin 212.5°) = -527 - 336j$

rectangular form:

$\qquad (3+4j)^4 = [(3+4j)^2]^2 = (9 + 24j + (16j^2))^2 = (9 + 24j - 16)^2 = (-7+24j)^2$

$\qquad\qquad = 49 - 336j + 576j^2 49 - 336j - 576 = -527 - 336j$

37. The two square roots of $4(\cos 60° + j \sin 60°)$ are

$\qquad r_1 = \sqrt{4}\left(\cos\dfrac{60° + 0 \cdot 360°}{2} + j \sin\dfrac{60° + 0 \cdot 360°}{2}\right)$

$\qquad r_1 = 2(\cos 30° + j \sin 30°) = \sqrt{3} + j$

and

$\qquad r_2 = \sqrt{4}\left(\cos\dfrac{60° + 1 \cdot 360°}{2} + j \sin\dfrac{60° + 1 \cdot 360°}{2}\right)$

$\qquad r_2 = 2(\cos 210° + j \sin 210°) = -\sqrt{3} - j$

41. The two square roots of $1 + j = \sqrt{2}(\cos 45° + j \sin 45°)$ are

$\qquad r_1 = \sqrt{\sqrt{2}}\left(\cos\dfrac{45° + 0 \cdot 360°}{2} + j \sin\dfrac{4.5° + 0 \cdot 360°}{2}\right)$

$\qquad r_1 = 2^{1/4}(\cos 22.5° + j \sin 22.5°) = 1.0987 + 0.4551j$

and

$\qquad r_2 = 2^{1/4}\left(\cos\dfrac{45° + 1 \cdot 360°}{2} + j \sin\dfrac{4.5° + 1 \cdot 360°}{2}\right)$

$\qquad r_2 = 2^{1/4}(\cos 202.5° + j \sin 202.5°) = -1.0987 - 0.4551j$

45. $-27j$; $x = 0$, $y = -27$; $r = \sqrt{0^2 + 27^2} = 27$; $\theta = 270°$

First root: $(0 - 27j)^{1/3} = [27(\cos 270° + j \sin 270°)]^{1/3} = 3(\cos 90° + j \sin 90°) = 3j$

Second root: $\theta = 360° + 270° = 630°$

$(0 + 27j)^{1/3} = [27(\cos 630° + j \sin 630°)]^{1/3} = 3(\cos 210° + j \sin 210°) = \dfrac{-3\sqrt{3}}{2} - \dfrac{3}{2}j$

Third root: $\theta = 720° + 270° = 990°$

$(0 + 27j)^{1/3} = [27(\cos 990° + j \sin 990°)]^{1/3} = 3(\cos 330° + j \sin 330°) = \dfrac{3\sqrt{3}}{2} - \dfrac{3}{2}j$

49. $\left[\left(\dfrac{1}{2} - \dfrac{\sqrt{3}}{2}j\right)\right]^3 = \left[\dfrac{1}{2}(1 - \sqrt{3}j)\right]^3$

$\qquad = \dfrac{1}{8}(1 - \sqrt{3}j)^2(1 - \sqrt{3}j)$

$\qquad = \dfrac{1}{8}(1 - 2\sqrt{3}j + 3j^2)(1 - \sqrt{3}j)$

$\qquad = \dfrac{1}{8}(1 - 2\sqrt{3}j - 3)(1 - \sqrt{3}j)$

$\qquad = \dfrac{1}{8}(-2 - 2\sqrt{3}j)(1 - \sqrt{3}j)$

$\qquad = \dfrac{1}{8}(-2 - 2\sqrt{3}j + 2\sqrt{3}j + 2\sqrt{3}^2j^2)$

$\qquad = \dfrac{1}{8}(-2 + 2 \cdot 3(-1))$

$\qquad = \dfrac{1}{8}(-2 - 6) = \dfrac{1}{8}(-8) = -1$

53. $p = ei$

$p = (6.80\angle 56.3°)(7.05\angle - 15.8°)$

$\quad = 6.80(7.05)[\cos(56.3° - 15.8°)$
$\qquad + j\sin(56.3° - 15.8°)]$

$\quad = 47.9(\cos 40.5° + j\sin 40.5°)$

$\quad = 47.9\angle 40.5°$ watts

12.7 An Application to Alternating-Current (ac) Circuits

1. $V_R = IR = 2.00(12.0) = 24.0$ V
$Z = R + j(X_L - X_C) = 12.0 + j(16.0)$
$|Z| = \sqrt{12.0^2 + 16.0^2} = 20.0$ Ω
$V_L = IX_L = 2.00(16.0) = 32.0$ V
$V_{RL} = IZ = 2.00(20.0) = 40.0$ V

$\theta = \tan^{-1}\dfrac{X_L}{R} = \tan^{-1}\dfrac{16.0}{12.0} = 53.1°$, voltage
leads current.

5. (a) $|Z| = \sqrt{R^2 + X_L^2} = \sqrt{2250^2 + 1750^2} = 2850$ Ω

(b) $\tan\theta = \dfrac{1750}{2250}; \theta = 37.9°$

(c) $V_{RL} = IZ = (0.005\,75)(2850) = 16.4$ V

9. (a) $X_R = 45.0$ Ω

$\qquad X_L = 2\pi fL = 2\pi(60)(0.0429) = 16.2$ Ω

$\qquad Z = 45.0 + 16.2j$
$\qquad |Z| = \sqrt{45.0^2 + 16.2^2} = 47.8$ Ω

(b) $\tan\theta = \dfrac{16.2}{45.0}; \theta = 19.8°$

13. $R = 25.3$ Ω

$X_C = 1/(2\pi fC)$
$\quad = 1/(2\pi(1.2 \times 10^6)(2.75 \times 10^{-9})) = 48.2$ Ω
$f = 1200$ kHz $= 1.2 \times 10^6$ Hz
$Z = R - \overline{X}_{Cj} = 25.3 - 48.2j$
$|Z| = \sqrt{25.3^2 + (-48.2)^2} = 54.4$ Ω

$\tan\theta = \dfrac{-48.2}{25.3}; \theta = -62.3°$

17. $L = 12.5 \times 10^{-6}$ H
$C = 47.0 \times 10^{-9}$ F
$X_L = X_C$

$2\pi fL = \dfrac{1}{2\pi fC}$

$f = \sqrt{\dfrac{1}{4\pi^2 LC}}$

$\quad = \sqrt{\dfrac{1}{4\pi^2(12.5 \times 10^{-6})(4.70 \times 10^{-9})}}$

$\quad = 208$ kHz

21. $P = VI\cos\theta$
$V = 225$ mV
$\theta = -18.0° = 342°$
$Z = 47.3$ Ω
$V = IZ$

$I = \dfrac{225 \times 10^{-3}}{47.3} = 0.00476$ A

$P = (225 \times 10^{-3})(0.00476)\cos 342°$
$\quad = 0.00102$ W $= 1.02$ mW

Chapter 12 Review Exercises

1. $(6 - 2j) + (4 + j) = 6 - 2j + 4 + j$
$\qquad\qquad\qquad\quad = 10 - j$

5. $(2 + j)(4 - j) = 8 - 2j + 4j - j^2$
$\qquad\qquad\qquad = 8 + 2j + 1 = 9 + 2j$

9. $\dfrac{3}{7 - 6j} = \dfrac{3}{(7 - 6j)} \cdot \dfrac{(7 + 6j)}{(7 + 6j)}$

$\qquad = \dfrac{21 + 18j}{7^2 + 6^2}$

$\qquad = \dfrac{21}{85} + \dfrac{18}{85}j$

13. $\dfrac{5j - (3 - j)}{4 - 2j} = \dfrac{(-3 + 6j)}{(4 - 2j)} \cdot \dfrac{(4 + 2j)}{(4 + 2j)} = \dfrac{-12 - 6j + 24j + 12j^2}{4^2 + 2^2} = \dfrac{-12 + 18j - 12}{16 + 4} = \dfrac{-24 + 18j}{20} = -\dfrac{6}{5} + \dfrac{9}{10}j$

17. $3x - 2j = yj - 2 \Rightarrow 3x = -2, \quad -2y = yj$

$$x = -\frac{2}{3} \qquad -2 = y$$

$$x = -\frac{2}{3}, \, y = -2$$

21.

algebraically:

$$(-1 + 5j) + (4 + 6j) = -1 + 5j + 4 + 6j$$
$$= -1 + 4 + 5j + 6j$$
$$= 3 + 11j$$

25. $1 - j \Rightarrow r = \sqrt{1^2 + 1^2} = \sqrt{2}, \, \theta = \tan^{-1} \dfrac{-1}{1} + 360° = 315° = \dfrac{7\pi}{4}$ rad

polar: $1 - j = \sqrt{2}(\cos 315° + j \sin 315°)$

exponential: $1 - j = \sqrt{2}e^{7\pi/4j}$

29. $1.07 + 4.55j \Rightarrow r = \sqrt{1.07^2 + 4.55^2} = 4.67, \, \theta = \tan^{-1} \dfrac{4.55}{1.07} = 76.8° = 1.34$ rad

polar: $1.07 + 4.55j = 4.67(\cos 76.8° + j \sin 76.8°)$

exponential: $1.07 + 4.55j = 4.67e^{1.34j}$

33. $2(\cos 225° + j \sin 225°) = -\sqrt{2} - \sqrt{2}j$

37. $0.62\angle\underline{-72°} = 0.62(\cos(-72°) + j \sin(-72°))$
$$= 0.19 - 0.59j$$

41. $2.00e^{0.25j} = 2.00(\cos(0.25) + j \sin(0.25)$
$$= 1.94 + 0.495j$$

45. $[3(\cos 32° + j \sin 32°)] \cdot [5(\cos 52° + j \sin 52°)]$
$$= 3 \cdot 5(\cos(32° + 52°) + j \sin(32° + 52°))$$
$$= 15(\cos 84° + j \sin 84°)$$

49. $\dfrac{24(\cos 165° + j \sin 165°)}{3(\cos 106° + j \sin 106°)} = \dfrac{24}{3}(\cos(165° - 106°) + j \sin(165° - 106°) = 8(\cos 59° + j \sin 59°)$

53. $0.983\angle 47.2° + 0.366\angle 95.1° = 0.983(\cos 47.2° + j \sin 47.2°) + 0.366(\cos 95.1° + j \sin 95.1°)$
$$= 0.6679 + 0.7213j - 0.03254 + 0.3646j = 0.6354 + 1.0859j$$

in polar form: $r = \sqrt{0.6354^2 + 1.0859^2} = 1.26$

$$\theta = \tan^{-1} \frac{1.0859}{0.6354} = 59.7°, \, 1.26\angle 59.7°$$

57. $[2(\cos 16° + j \sin 16°)]^{10} = 2^{10}(\cos(10 \cdot 16°) + j \sin(10 \cdot 16°)] = 1024(\cos 160° + j \sin 160°)$

61. $\quad 1 - j = \sqrt{2}(\cos 315° + j \sin 315°)$ from problem 25.

$$(1 - j)^{10} = [\sqrt{2}(\cos 315° + j \sin 315°)]^{10} = \sqrt{2}^{10}(\cos(10 \cdot 315°) + j \sin(10 \cdot 315°))$$
$$= 32(\cos 3150° + j \sin 3150°), \text{ polar form}$$
$$= 0 - 32j, \text{ rectangular form}$$

$$(1 - j)^{10} = ((1 - j)^2)^5 = (1 - 2j + j^2)^5 = (1 - 2j - 1)^5 = (-2j)^5 = (-2)^5 \cdot j^5$$
$$= -32 \cdot j^4 \cdot j = -32j$$

65. $-8 = -8 + 0j = 8(\cos 180° + j \sin 180°)$

$$r_1 = \sqrt[3]{8}\left(\cos \frac{180° + 0 \cdot 360°}{3} + j \sin \frac{180° + 0 \cdot 360°}{3}\right) = 2(\cos 60° + j \sin 60°)$$

$$= 2\left(\frac{1}{2} + j \cdot \frac{\sqrt{3}}{2}\right) = 1 + j\sqrt{3}$$

$$r_2 = \sqrt[3]{8}\left(\cos \frac{180° + 1 \cdot 360°}{3} + j \sin \frac{180° + 1 \cdot 360°}{3}\right) = 2(\cos 180° + j \sin 180°)$$

$$= 2(-1 + j(0)) = -2$$

$$r_3 = \sqrt[3]{8}\left(\cos \frac{180° + 2 \cdot 360°}{3} + j \sin \frac{180° + 2 \cdot 360°}{3}\right) = 2(\cos 300° + j \sin 300°)$$

$$= 2\left(\frac{1}{2} - \frac{\sqrt{3}}{2}j\right) = 1 - j\sqrt{3}$$

69. Rectangular: $40 + 9j$ from the graph

polar: $40 + 9j \rightarrow r = \sqrt{40^2 + 9^2} = 41, \theta = \tan^{-1}\frac{9}{40} = 12.7°$

$$40 + 9j = 41(\cos 12.7° + j \sin 12.7°)$$

73. $x^2 - 2x + 4|_{x=5-2j} = (5 - 2j)^2 - 2(5 - 2j) + 4$
$$= 25 - 20j + 4j^2 - 10 + 4j + 4$$
$$= 19 - 16j - 4$$
$$= 15 - 16j$$

77. $x = 2 + j, x = 2 - j$
$x - (2 + j) = 0, x - (2 - j) = 0$
$(x - (2 + j))(x - (2 - j)) = 0$
$x^2 - (2 + j)x - (2 - j)x + (2 + j)(2 - j) = 0$
$x^2 - 2x - jx - 2x + jx + 4 - j^2 = 0$
$x^2 - 4x + 4 + 1 = 0$
$x^2 - 4x + 5 = 0$

81. $V_L = 60j, V_c = -60j$
$V = V_R + V_L + V_c$
$60 = V_R + 60j - 60j$
$V_R = 60$ volts

85. $2\pi f L = \frac{1}{2\pi f C} \Rightarrow f = \sqrt{\frac{1}{4\pi^2 LC}} = \sqrt{\frac{1}{4\pi^2 (2.65)(18.3 \times 10^{-6})}}$

$$f = 22.9 Hz$$

89. $\frac{1}{u + jwn} = \frac{1}{(u + jwn)} \cdot \frac{(u - jwn)}{(u - jwn)} = \frac{u - jwn}{u^2 + w^2 n^2}$

93. Answers may vary.

Chapter 13

EXPONENTIAL AND LOGARITHMIC FUNCTIONS

13.1 Exponential Functions

1. For $x = -\frac{3}{2}$, $y = -2(4^x) = -2(4^{-3/2}) = -\frac{1}{4}$

5. **(a)** $y = -7(-5)^{-x}, -5 < 0$, not an exponential function.

(b) $y = -7(5^{-x})$, real number multiple of an exponential function and therefore an exponential function.

9. $y = 9^x$; $x = -2, y = 9^{-2} = \frac{1}{9^2} = \frac{1}{81}$

13. $y = 4^x$

x	-3	-2	-1	0	1	2	3
y	$\frac{1}{64}$	$\frac{1}{16}$	$\frac{1}{4}$	1	4	16	64

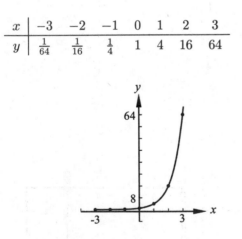

17. $y = -0.5\pi^x$

x	y
-3	27.000
-2	9.000
-1	3.000
0	1.000
1	0.333
2	0.111
3	0.037

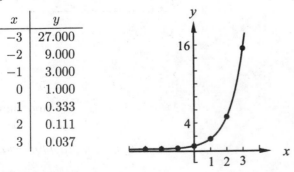

21. $y = 0.1(0.25)^x$

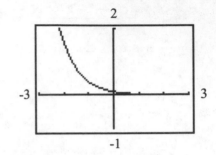

25. Since $x^2 = 2^x \Leftrightarrow x^2 - 2^x = 0$, graph $y_1 = x^2 - 2^x$.

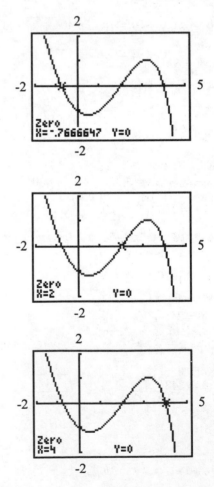

From the graph, $x^2 = 2^2$ for $x = -0.7667, 2, 4$.

29. $i = 2.5(1 - e^{-0.10t})$
$= 2.5(1 - e^{-0.10(5.5\times10^{-3})})$
$= 0.0012\,\text{mA}$

110

13.2   Logarithms Functions

1. $32^{4/5} = 16$ in logarithmic form is

$$\frac{4}{5} = \log_{32} 16.$$

5. $3^3 = 27$ has base 3, exponent 3, and number 27.

$\log_3 27 = 3.$

9. $4^{-2} = \dfrac{1}{16}$ has base 4, exponent -2, and number $\dfrac{1}{16}.$

$$\log_4 \frac{1}{16} = -2$$

13. $8^{1/3} = 2$ has base 8, exponent $\dfrac{1}{3}$, and number 2.

$$\log_8 2 = \frac{1}{3}$$

17. $\log_3 81 = 4$ has base 3, exponent 2, and number 81.

$3^4 = 81$

21. $\log_{25} 5 = \dfrac{1}{2}$ has base 25, exponent $\dfrac{1}{2}$, and number 5.

$25^{1/2} = 5$

25. $\log_{10} 0.1 = -1$ has base 10, exponent -1, and number 0.1.

$0.1 = 10^{-1}$

29. $\log_4 16 = x$ has base 4, exponent x, and number 16.

$4^x = 16$
$4^x = 4^2$
$x = 2$

33. $\log_7 y = 3$ has base 7, exponent 3, and number 3.

$7^3 = y$
$y = 343$

37. $\log_b 81 = 2$ has base b, exponent 2, and number 81.

$b^2 = 81 = 9^2$
$b = 9$

41. $\log_{10} 10^{0.2} = x$ has base 10, exponent x, and number $10^{0.2}$.

$10^x = 10^{0.2}$
$x = 0.2$

45. Write $y = \log_3 x$ as $3^y = x$ to find values in table.

x	y
0.19	-1.5
0.58	-0.5
1.00	0.0
1.93	0.6
3.00	1.0
5.20	1.5
9.00	2.0

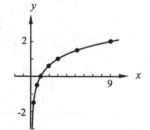

49. $N = 0.2 \log_4 v;\ \dfrac{N}{0.2} = \log_4 v;\ 4^{N/0.2} = v$

v	N
0.2	-0.232
0.6	-0.0737
0.8	-0.0322
1	0
2	0.1
3	0.159
4	0.2

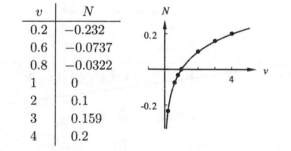

53. $y = -\log_{10}(-x)$

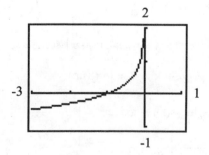

57. $m_1 - m_2 = 2.5 \log_{10}\left(\dfrac{b_2}{b_1}\right)$ or $\dfrac{m_1 - m_2}{2.5} = \log_{10}\left(\dfrac{b_2}{b_1}\right)$

has base 10, exponent $\dfrac{m_1 - m_2}{2.5}$ and number $\dfrac{b_2}{b_1}$.

$$10^{(m_1 - m_2)/2.5} = \frac{b_2}{b_1},\ b_2 = b_1(10)^{0.4(m_1 - m_2)}$$

61. $t = N + \log_2 N$ where $n > 0$ and $t > 0$.

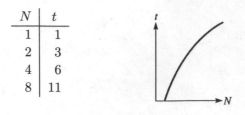

N	t
1	1
2	3
4	6
8	11

65. Solve $y = 10^{x/2}$ for x; $x = 2\log_{10} y$. Interchange x and y; $y = 2\log_{10} x$ which is the inverse function. Enter on graphing calculator $y_1 = 10^{x/2}$, $y_2 = 2\log_{10} x$.

For each graph to be the mirror image of the other across $y = x$ the calculator window must be "square." One way to do this is ZOOM 5: Square

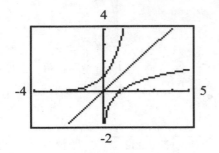

13.3   Properties of Logarithms

1. $\log_4 21 = \log_4(3(7)) = \log_4 3 + \log_4 7$

5. $\log_3 27 = \log_3 3^3 = 3\log_3 3 = 3(1) = 3$

9. $\log_5 33 = \log_5(3 \cdot 11) = \log_5 3 + \log_5 11$

13. $\log_2(a^3) = 3\log_2 a$

17. $\log_5 \sqrt[4]{y} = \log_5 y^{1/4} = \dfrac{1}{4}\log_5 y$

21. $\log_b a + \log_b c = \log_b(ac)$

25. $-\log_b \sqrt{x} + \log_b x^2 = \log_b \dfrac{x^2}{x^{1/2}}$
$$= \log_b x^{3/2}$$

29. $\log_2\left(\dfrac{1}{32}\right) = \log_2\left(\dfrac{1}{2^5}\right) = \log_2 2^{-5}$
$$= -5\log_2 2 = -5$$

33. $\log_7 \sqrt{7} = \log_7 7^{1/2}$
$$= \dfrac{1}{2}\log_7 7 = \dfrac{1}{2}$$

37. $\log_3 18 = \log_3(9 \cdot 2) = \log_3 9 + \log_3 2$
$$= \log_3 3^2 + \log_3 2 = 2\log_3 3 + \log_3 2$$
$$= 2 + \log_3 2$$

41. $\log_3 \sqrt{6} = \log_3(3 \cdot 2)^{1/2} = \dfrac{1}{2}\log_3(3 \cdot 2)$
$$= \dfrac{1}{2} \cdot [\log_3 3 + \log_3 2]$$
$$= \dfrac{1}{2} \cdot [1 + \log_3 2]$$

45. $\log_b y = \log_b 2 + \log_b x$
$\log_b y = \log_b(2x)$
$\quad y = 2x$

49. $\log_{10} y = 2\log_{10} 7 - 3\log_{10} x$
$$= \log_{10} 7^2 - \log_{10} x^3$$
$$= \log_{10} 49 - \log_{10} x^3$$
$\log_{10} y = \log_{10} \dfrac{49}{x^3}$
$$y = \dfrac{49}{x^3}$$

53. $\log_2 x + \log_2 y = 1$
$\log_2(xy) = 1 \Leftrightarrow 2^1 = xy$
$$y = \dfrac{2}{x}$$

57. $\log_{10}(x + 3) = \log_{10} x + \log_{10} 3 = \log_{10}(3x)$
$\quad x + 3 = 3x$
$\quad 2x = 3$
$$x = \dfrac{3}{2} \text{ is the only value for which}$$

$\log_{10}(x + 3) = \log_{10} x + \log_{10} 3$ is true.

For any other x-value $\log_{10}(x+3) = \log_{10} x + \log_{10} 3$ is false and thus not true in general. This can also be seen from the following graphs.

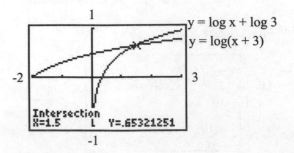

61.
$$\log_e D = \log_e a - br + cr^2$$
$$\log_e D - \log_e a = cr^2 - br$$
$$\log_e \frac{D}{a} = cr^2 - br$$
$$\frac{D}{a} = e^{cr^2 - br}$$
$$D = ae^{cr^2 - br}$$

13.4   Logarithms to the Base 10

1. $\log 0.3654 = -0.4372$

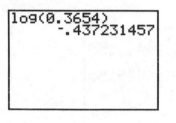

5. $\log 9.24 \times 10^6 = 6.966$

9. $\log(\cos 12.5°) = -0.0104$

13. $10^{4.437} = 27,400$

17. $10^{3.30112} = 2000.4$

21. $(5.98)(14.3) = 85.5$

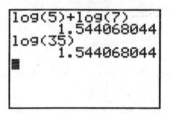

25. $\log 5 + \log 7 = \log 35$

29. $\log 9 \times 10^8 = 8.9542$

33. $\log T = 8$
$$T = 10^8 \text{ K}$$

37. $G = 10 \cdot \log\left(\dfrac{P_o}{P_i}\right) = 10 \cdot \log\left(\dfrac{25.0}{0.750}\right) = 15.2 \; dB$

13.5   Natural Logarithms

1. $\ln 200 = \dfrac{\log 200}{\log e} = 5.298$

5. $\ln 1.562 = \dfrac{\log 1.562}{\log e} = \dfrac{0.1937}{0.4343} = 0.4460$

9. $\log_7 42 = \dfrac{\log 42}{\log 7} = \dfrac{1.6232}{0.8451} = 1.92$

13. $\log_{40} 750 = \dfrac{\log 750}{\log 40} = \dfrac{2.875}{1.6021} = 1.795$

17. $\ln 1.394 = 0.3322$

21. $\ln 0.012937^4$
   $= -17.39066$

25. $\log 0.68528 = \dfrac{\ln 0.68528}{\ln 10}$
   $= -0.16413$

29. $e^{0.0084210} = 1.0085$

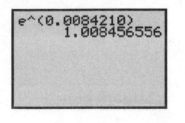

33. $e^{-23.504} = 6.20 \times 10^{-11}$

37. $y = 2^x \Leftrightarrow x = \log_2 y \Rightarrow y = \log_2 x$ is the inverse function.

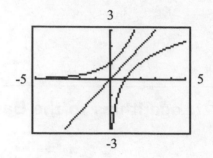

41. $4 \ln 3 = \ln 81$

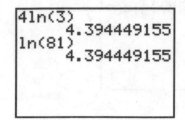

45. $\ln f = 21.619$
   $f = e^{21.619} = 2.45 \times 10^9$ Hz

49. $t = -\dfrac{L \cdot \ln\left(\dfrac{i}{I}\right)}{R} = -\dfrac{1.25 \ln\left(\dfrac{0.1I}{I}\right)}{7.5}$
   $t = 0.384$ s

13.6 Exponential and Logarithmic Equations

1. $3^{x+2} = 5$
                $\log 3^{x+2} = \log 5$
        $(x+2)\log 3 = \log 5$

                $x + 2 = \dfrac{\log 5}{\log 3}$

                $x = \dfrac{\log 5}{\log 3} - 2$

                $x = -0.535$

5. $5^x = 0.3$; $\log 5^x = \log 0.3$; $x \log 5 = \log 0.3$

   $x = \dfrac{\log 0.3}{\log 5} = \dfrac{-0.5229}{0.69897} = -0.748$

9.
$$6^{x+1} = 10$$
$$\ln 6^{x+1} = \ln 10$$
$$(x+1) \cdot \ln 6 = \ln 10$$
$$x + 1 = \frac{\ln 10}{\ln 6}$$
$$x = \frac{\ln 10}{\ln 6} - 1$$
$$x = 0.285$$

13.
$$0.6^x = 2^{x^2}$$
$$\ln(0.6^x) = \ln 2^{x^2}$$
$$x \cdot \ln 0.6 = x^2 \cdot \ln 2$$
$$x^2 \cdot \ln 2 - x \ln 0.6 = 0$$
$$x(x \cdot \ln 2 - \ln 0.6) = 0$$

$$x = 0 \quad \text{or} \quad x \cdot \ln 2 - \ln 0.6 = 0$$

$$x = \frac{\ln 0.6}{\ln 2} = -0.737$$

17. $2\ln x = 1$
$$\ln x = 0.5$$
$$x = e^{0.5} = 1.649$$

21. $2\log(3 - x) = 1$
$$\log(3 - x) = \frac{1}{2}$$
$$3 - x = 10^{1/2} = 3.162$$
$$-x = 3.162 - 3$$
$$= 0.162$$
$$x = -0.162$$

25. $3\ln 2 + \ln(x - 1) = \ln 24$
$$\ln 2^3 + \ln(x - 1) = \ln 24$$
$$\ln 8 + \ln(x - 1) = \ln 24$$
$$\ln[8(x - 1)] = \ln 24$$
$$8(x - 1) = 24$$
$$x - 1 = 3$$
$$x = 4$$

29. $\log(2x - 1) + \log(x + 4) = 1$
$$\log[(2x - 1)(x + 4)] = 1$$
$$(2x - 1)(x + 4) = 10$$
$$2x^2 + 7x - 4 = 10$$
$$2x^2 + 7x - 14 = 0$$

Use the quadratic formula to solve for x:

$$x = \frac{-7 \pm \sqrt{49 - 4(2)(-14)}}{2(2)} = \frac{-7 \pm \sqrt{161}}{4}$$

$$= \frac{-7 \pm 12.689}{4} = -4.92, 142$$

$x = 1.42$ (since logs are not defined on negatives.)

33. $4(3^x) = 5$. Graph $y_1 = 4(3^x) - 5$ and use the zero feature to solve.
$$x = 0.2031$$

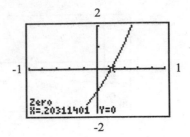

37. $2\ln 2 - \ln x = -1$. Graph $y_1 = 2\ln 2 - \ln x + 1$ and use the zero feature to solve.
$$x = 10.87$$

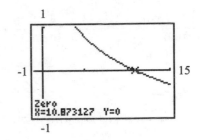

41. $N = 2^x \Rightarrow 2.6 \times 10^8 = 2^x$
$$\log 2^x = \log 2.6 \times 10^8$$
$$x \cdot \log 2 = \log 2.6 \times 10^8$$
$$x = \frac{\log 2.6 \times 10^8}{\log 2}$$
$$= 27.95393638 \cdots$$
$$x = 28$$

45.
$$pH = -\log(H^+)$$
$$4.764 = -\log(H^+)$$
$$-4.764 = \log(H^+)$$
$$H^+ = 10^{-4.764}$$
$$H^+ = 1.722 \times 10^{-5}$$

49.
$$\ln c = \ln 15 - 0.20t$$
$$\ln c - \ln 15 = -0.20t$$
$$\ln \frac{c}{15} = -0.20t$$
$$\frac{c}{15} = e^{-0.20t}$$
$$c = 15e^{-0.20t}$$

53. $2^x + 3^x = 50$. Graph $y_1 = 2^x + 3^x - 50$ and use zero feature to solve.
$x = 3.353$.

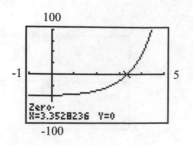

13.7 Graphs on Logarithmic and Semilogarithmic Paper

1. $y = 2(3^x)$

x	-1	0	2	3	4	5
y	0.67	2	18	54	162	486

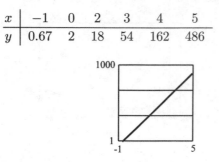

5. $y = 2(4^x)$

x	0	1	2	3	4	5
y	2	8	32	128	512	2048

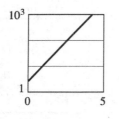

9. $y = 2x^3 + 4x$

x	0	1	2	4	6	8
y	0	6	24	144	456	1056

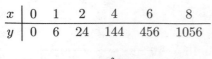

13. $y = x^{2/3}$

x	1	5	10	50	100	500	1000
y	1	2.9	4.6	13.6	21.5	63.0	100

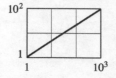

17. $x^2 y^3 = 25$; $y = \dfrac{5}{x}$

x	0.1	0.5	1	10	50
y	50	10	5	0.5	0.1

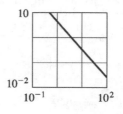

21. $y = 3x^6$, $\log - \log$ paper

x	1	2	3	4
y	3	192	2187	12,288

25. $x\sqrt{y} = 4$, $y = \dfrac{16}{x^2}$, $\log - \log$ paper

x	1	25	50	75	100
y	16	0.0256	0.0064	0.00284	0.0016

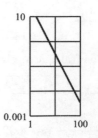

29. $N = N_0 e^{-0.028t}$, $N_0 = 1000$

t	0	25	50	75	100
N	1000	496.6	246.6	122.5	60.81

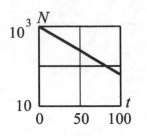

33.

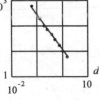

37.

d	0.63	1.3	1.9	2.5	3.8
R	600	190	100	72	46

d	5.0	7.5	10	15
R	29	17	10	6.0

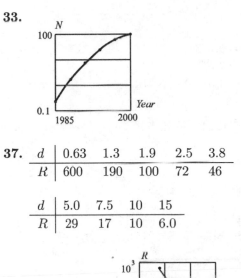

Chapter 13 Review Exercises

1. $\log_{10} x = 4 \Rightarrow x = 10^4 = 10{,}000$

5. $\log_2 64 = x \Rightarrow 2^x = 64 = 2^6$
$$x = 6$$

9. $\log_x 36 = 2 \Rightarrow x^2 = 36 = 6^2$
$$x = 6$$

13. $\log_3 2x = \log_3 2 + \log_3 x$

17. $\log_2 28 = \log_2(2^2 \cdot 7)$
$$= \log_2 2^2 + \log_2 7$$
$$= 2\log_2 2 + \log_2 7$$
$$= 2 \cdot 1 + \log_2 7$$
$$= 2 + \log_2 7$$

21. $\log_4 \sqrt{48} = \log_4 48^{1/2} = \dfrac{1}{2} \log_4(16 \cdot 3)$
$$= \frac{1}{2}\left[\log_4 16 + \log_4 3\right] = \frac{1}{2}\left[\log_4 4^2 + \log_4 3\right]$$
$$= \frac{1}{2}\left[2\log_4 4 + \log_4 3\right] = \frac{1}{2}\left[2 + \log_4 3\right]$$
$$= 1 + \frac{1}{2}\log_4 3$$

25. $\log_6 y = \log_6 4 - \log_{6x}$
$$\log_6 y = \log_6 \frac{4}{x}$$
$$y = \frac{4}{x}$$

29. $\log_5 x + \log_5 y = \log_5 3 + 1 = \log_5 3 + \log_5 5$
$$= \log_5(3 \cdot 5)$$
$$\log_5(x \cdot y) = \log_5(15)$$
$$xy = 15$$
$$y = \frac{15}{x}$$

33. $2(\log_4 y - 3\log_4 x) = 3$
$$\log_4 y - \log_4 x^3 = \frac{3}{2}$$
$$\log_4 \frac{y}{x^3} = \frac{3}{2}$$
$$\frac{y}{x^3} = 4^{3/2} = 8$$
$$y = 8x^3$$

37. $y = 0.5(5^x)$

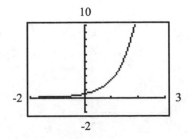

41. $y = \log_{3.15} x$

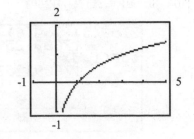

45. $\ln 8.86 = \dfrac{\log_{10} 8.86}{\log_{10} e}$

$\qquad = 2.18$

```
ln(8.86)
        2.181546765
log(8.86)/log(e^
(1)
        2.181546765
```

49. $\log_{10} 65.89 = \dfrac{\ln 65.89}{\ln 10}$

$\qquad\qquad = 1.819$

```
log(65.89)
        1.818819508
ln(65.89)/ln(10)

        1.818819508
```

53. $\qquad e^{2x} = 5$

$\ln e^{2x} = \ln 5$

$2x \cdot \ln e = \ln 5$

$2x \cdot 1 = \ln 5$

$\qquad x = \dfrac{\ln 5}{2}$

57. $\log_4 x + \log_4 6 = \log_4 12$

$\log(x \cdot 6) = \log_4 12$

$6x = 12$

$x = 2$

61. $y = 6^x$

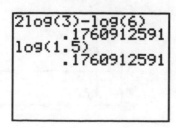

65. $10^{\log 4} = 4$

69. $2\log 3 - \log 6 = \log 1.5$

$0.1760912591 = 0.1760912591$

```
2log(3)-log(6)
        .1760912591
log(1.5)
        .1760912591
```

73. $\qquad V = P\left(1 + \dfrac{r}{n}\right)^{nt}$

$\qquad V = 1000\left(1 + \dfrac{0.06}{2}\right)^{2t}$

$\qquad \dfrac{V}{1000} = \left(1 + \dfrac{0.06}{2}\right)^{2t}$

$\log \dfrac{V}{1000} = \log(1.03)^{2t}$

$\log \dfrac{V}{1000} = 2t\log(1.03)$

$\qquad t = \dfrac{\log \frac{V}{1000}}{2\log 1.03}$

77. $\log M = 6.663$

$M = 10^{6.663}$

$M = 4{,}603{,}000 \text{ N} \cdot \text{m}$

81. $t = 2350(\ln 100 - \ln N)$

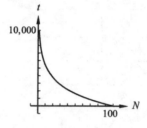

85. $C = B\log_2(1 + R)$

$\log_2(1 + R) = \dfrac{C}{B}$

$1 + R = 2^{C/B}$

$R = 2^{C/B} - 1$

89. $\qquad R = 4520(0.750)^{2.50t}$

$1950 = 4520(0.750)^{2.50t}$

$\dfrac{1950}{4520} = 0.750^{2.5t}$

$\ln \dfrac{1950}{4520} = \ln(0.750)^{2.5t} = 2.5t\ln(0.750)$

$2.5t = \dfrac{\ln \dfrac{1950}{4520}}{\ln(0.750)}$

$t = \dfrac{1}{2.5} \cdot \dfrac{\ln \dfrac{1950}{4520}}{\ln(0.750)}$

$t = 1.17 \text{ min}$

93.
$$\ln n = -0.04t + \ln 20$$
$$\ln n - \ln 20 = -0.04t$$
$$\ln \frac{n}{20} = -0.04t$$
$$\frac{n}{20} = e^{-0.04t}$$
$$n = 20e^{-0.04t}$$

97. $\log x^2$ exists for all values of x; $2\log x$ exists only for positive x-values. The graphs, shown below, are not the same.

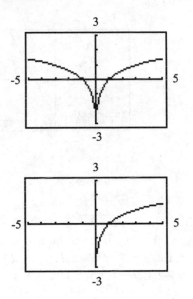

ADDITIONAL TYPES OF EQUATIONS AND SYSTEMS OF EQUATIONS

14.1 Graphical Solution of Systems of Equations

1. Graph $y_1 = 3x^2 + 6x$.

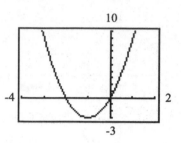

5.
$$y = 2x$$
$$x^2 + y^2 = 16 \Rightarrow y = \pm\sqrt{16 - x^2}.$$

Graph $y_1 = 2x$, $y_2 = \sqrt{16 - x^2}$, and $y_3 = -\sqrt{16 - x^2}$. Use the intersect feature to solve.
$x = 1.8, y = 3.6$; $x = -1.8, y = -3.6$.

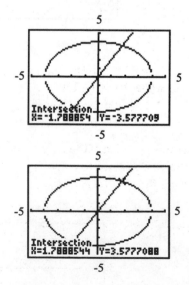

9. $y = x^2 - 2$
$$4y = 12x - 7 \Rightarrow y = \frac{12x - 7}{4}$$

Graph $y_1 = x^2 - 2$ and $y_2 = (12x - 7)/4$. Use the intersect feature to solve. $x = 1.5, y = 0.2$.

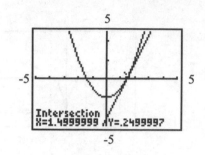

13. $x^2 + y^2 = 9 \Rightarrow y = \pm\sqrt{9 - x^2}$.
$$y = -x^2 + 4$$

Graph $y_1 = \sqrt{9 - x^2}$, $y_2 = -\sqrt{9 - x^2}$, $y_3 = -x^2 + 4$. Use the intersect feature to solve.
$x = 1.2, y = 2.8$, $x = -1.1, y = 2.8$,
$x = -2.4, y = -1.8$; $x = 2.3, y = -1.8$.

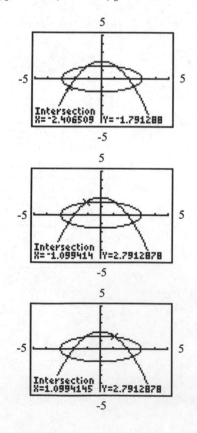

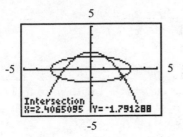

17. $2x^2 + 3y^2 = 19 \Rightarrow y = \pm\sqrt{(19 - 2x^2)/3}$
and $x^2 + y^2 = 9 \Rightarrow y = \pm\sqrt{9 - x^2}$. Graph
$y_1 = \sqrt{(19 - 2x^2)/3}$, $y_2 = -\sqrt{(19 - 2x^2)/3}$,
$y_3 = \sqrt{9 - x^2}$; $y_4 = -\sqrt{9 - x^2}$ and use the
intersect feature to solve. $x = -2.8, y = 1.0$;
$x = 2.8, y = 1.0$;
$x = -2.8, y = -1.0$; $x = 2.8, y = -1.0$.

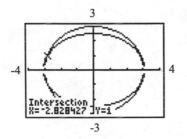

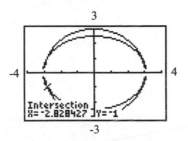

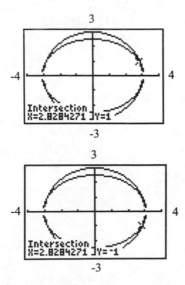

21. $y = x^2$
$y = \sin x$

Graph $y_1 = x^2$ and $y_2 = \sin x$ and use the
intersect feature to solve. $x = 0.0, y = 0.0$
and $x = 0.9, y = 0.8$.

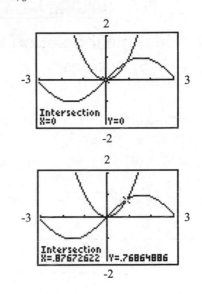

25. $x^2 - y^2 = 1 \Rightarrow y = \pm\sqrt{x^2 - 1}$ $y = \log_2 x = \frac{\ln x}{\ln 2}$.
Graph $y_1 = \sqrt{x^2 - 1}$, $y_2 = -\sqrt{x^2 - 1}$, and
$y_3 = \frac{\ln x}{\ln 2}$. Use the intersect feature to solve.
$x = 1.0, y$

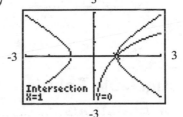

29. $10^{x+y} = 150$
$(x + y) \log 10 = \log 150$
$y = \log 150 - x$
$y = x^2$

Graph $y_1 = \log 150 - x$, $y_2 = x^2$ and use the
intersect feature to solve. $x = -2.06, y = 4.23$;
$x = 1.06, y = 1.12$

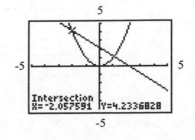

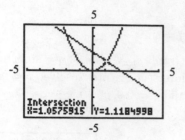

33. $P = i^2 R$; $R_1 = 2.0\ \Omega$, $R_2 = 3.0\ \Omega$

$$2.0i_1^2 + 3.0i_2^2 = 12;\quad i_2 = \sqrt{4.0 - 2.0i_1^2/3.0}$$

$$3.0i_1^2 + 2.0i_2^2 = 16;\quad i_2 = \sqrt{8.0 - 1.5i_1^2}$$

Graph $y_1 = \sqrt{4 - 2x^2/3}$, $y_2 = \sqrt{8 - 1.5x^2}$. Use the intersect feature to solve. The currents are $i_1 = 2.2$ A, $i_2 = 0.9$ A.

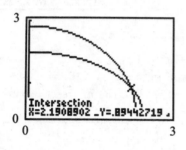

14.2   Algebraic Solution of Systems of Equations

1. $2x + y = 4 \Rightarrow y = 4 - 2x$, substitute into second equation $x^2 - y^2 = 4$

$$x^2 - (4 - 2x)^2 = 4$$
$$x^2 - (16 - 16x + 4x^2) = 4$$
$$x^2 - 16 + 16x - 4x^2 = 4$$
$$3x^2 - 16x + 20 = 0$$
$$(x - 2)(3x - 10) = 0$$
$$x - 2 = 0 \quad \text{or} \quad 3x - 10 = 0$$
$$x = 2 \qquad\qquad x = \frac{10}{3}$$
$$y = 4 - 2(2) = 0 \qquad y = 4 - 2\left(\frac{10}{3}\right) = -\frac{8}{3}$$

The solutions are $x = 2$, $y = 0$; $x = \dfrac{10}{3}$, $y = -\dfrac{8}{3}$

5. (1) $\quad y = x + 1$
    (2) $\quad y = x^2 + 1$

$$y = y$$
$$x^2 + 1 = x + 1 \text{ with } y \text{ from (1) and (2)}$$
$$x^2 - x = 0$$
$$x(x - 1) = 0$$
$$x = 0 \quad \text{or} \qquad x - 1 = 0$$
$$y = x + 1 = 1 \qquad\qquad x = 1$$
$$y = x + 1 = 2$$

The solutions are $x = 0$, $y = 1$; $x = 1$, $y = 2$.

9. (1) $\quad x + y = 1 \Rightarrow y = 1 - x$
    (2) $\quad x^2 - y^2 = 1$
    (2) $\quad x^2 - (1 - x)^2 = 1 \text{ with } y = 1 - x \text{ from (1)}$
$$x^2 - 1 + 2x - x^2 = 1$$
$$-1 + 2x = 1$$
$$2x = 2$$
$$x = 1 \quad y = 1 - (1) = 0$$

The solution is $x = 1$, $y = 0$.

13. (1) $\quad wh = 1$
    (2) $\quad w + h = 2 \Rightarrow h = 2 - w$

(1) $\quad w(2 - w) = 1 \text{ with } h \text{ from (2)}$
$$2w - w^2 = 1$$
$$w^2 - 2w + 1 = 0$$
$$(w - 1)^2 = 0$$
$$w - 1 = 0$$
$$w = 1 \Rightarrow (2)\ 1 + h = 2, h = 1$$

The solution is $w = 1$, $h = 1$.

17.
$$y = x^2$$
$$y = 3x^2 - 50$$
$$y = y \Rightarrow x^2 = 3x^2 - 50$$
$$2x^2 = 50$$
$$x^2 = 25$$
$$x = \pm 5$$
$$y = 25$$

The solutions are $x = 5$, $y = 25$, $x = -5$, $y = 25$.

21. (1) $D^2 - 1 = R \Rightarrow D^2 = 1 + R$

(2) $D^2 - 2R^2 = 1$

$$1 + R - 2R^2 = 1$$
$$R - 2R^2 = 0$$
$$R(1 - 2R) = 0$$

(2) with D^2 from (1)

$$R = 0 \quad \text{or} \quad 1 - 2R = 0$$
$$2R = 1$$
$$R = \frac{1}{2}$$

(1) with $R = 0$, $D^2 = 1 + 0$
$$D = \pm 1$$

(1) with $R = \frac{1}{2}$, $D^2 = 1 + \frac{1}{2}$
$$= \frac{3}{2}$$
$$= \frac{6}{4}$$
$$D = \frac{\pm\sqrt{6}}{2}$$

Solutions:

$R = 0, D = 1$

$R = 0, D = -1$

$R = \frac{1}{2}, D = \frac{\sqrt{6}}{2}$

$R = \frac{1}{2}, D = \frac{-\sqrt{6}}{2}$

25. (1) $x^2 + 3y^2 = 37$

(2) $2x^2 - 9y^2 = 14$

$3 \cdot (1) \Rightarrow \quad 3x^2 + 9y^2 = 111$

(2) $\qquad \underline{2x^2 - 9y^2 = \;\; 14}$

$\qquad\qquad 5x^2 \qquad\quad = 125$

$\qquad\qquad\quad x^2 = 25$

$\qquad\qquad\quad x = \pm 5$

(1) $(\pm 5)^2 + 3y^2 = 37$
$$25 + 3y^2 = 37$$
$$3y^2 = 12$$
$$y^2 = 4$$
$$y = \pm 2$$

Solution: $(5, 2), (5, -2), (-5, 2), (-5, -2)$

29. (1) $h = 3x - 0.05x^2$

(2) $h = 0.8x - 15 \Rightarrow$
$$h = h$$
$$3x - 0.05x^2 = 0.8x - 15$$
$$0.05x^2 - 2.2x - 15 = 0$$
$$5x^2 - 220x - 1500 = 0$$
$$x^2 - 44x - 300 = 0$$
$$(x - 50)(x + 6) = 0$$
$$x - 50 = 0 \quad \text{or} \quad x + 6 = 0$$
$$x = 50 \qquad\qquad x = -6 \text{ reject since } x > 0$$

(2) $h = 0.8(50) - 15$
$$h = 25$$

The rocket and missile cross when $h = 25$ mi and $x = 50$ mi.

33.

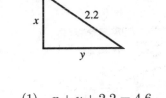

(1) $x + y + 2.2 = 4.6$
$$x + y = 2.4 \Rightarrow y = 2.4 - x$$

(2) $\qquad x^2 + y^2 = 2.2^2$
$$x^2 + y^2 = 4.84$$

(2) $x^2 + (2.4 - x)^2 = 4.84$, (2) with y from (1).

$$x^2 + 5.76 - 4.8x + x^2 = 4.84$$
$$2x^2 - 4.8x + 0.92 = 0$$

$$x = \frac{-(-4.8) \pm \sqrt{(-4.8)^2 - 4(2)(0.92)}}{2(2)}$$

$$= \frac{4.8 \pm \sqrt{15.68}}{4}$$

$$= \begin{array}{c} \nearrow 2.2 \\ \searrow 0.2 \end{array}$$

$x = 2.2$ in (1), $2.2 + y = 2.4$
$$y = 0.2$$
$x = 0.2$ in (1), $0.2 + y = 2.4$
$$y = 2.2$$

The lengths of the sides of the truss are 2.2 m and 0.2 m.

37. $A = lw = 560 \Rightarrow l = \dfrac{560}{w}$

$V = (l - 8)(w - 8)(4) = 960$

$$\left(\dfrac{560}{w} - 8\right)(w - 8) = 240$$

$$560 - \dfrac{560(8)}{w} - 8w + 64 = 240$$

$$-\dfrac{560(8)}{w} - 8w + 384 = 0$$

$$-8w^2 - 560(8) + 384w = 0$$
$$8w^2 - 384w + 560(8) = 0$$
$$w^2 - 48w + 560 = 0$$
$$(w - 20)(w - 28) = 0$$

$w - 20 = 0 \qquad$ or $\qquad w - 28 = 0$
$\quad w = 20 \qquad\qquad\qquad w = 28$

$l = \dfrac{560}{20} \qquad\qquad l = \dfrac{560}{20}$

$l = 28 \qquad\qquad\quad l = 20$

The dimensions of the original sheet are
$l = 80$ in.; $w = 20$ in.

14.3   Equations in Quadratic Form

1. $\qquad 2x^4 - 7x^2 = 4$
$2x^4 - 7x^2 - 4 = 0$, let $y = x^2$
$\qquad 2y^2 - 7y - 4 = 0$
$\qquad (y - 4)(2y + 1) = 0$
$y - 4 = 0 \qquad$ or $\quad 2y + 1 = 0$

$\qquad y = 4 \qquad\qquad\qquad y = -\dfrac{1}{2}$

$\qquad x^2 = 4 \qquad\qquad\quad x^2 = -\dfrac{1}{2}$

$\qquad x = \pm 2 \qquad\qquad\quad x = \pm\dfrac{\sqrt{2}}{2}j$

Check:

$$2(\pm 2)^4 - 7(\pm 2)^2 = 32 - 28 = 4$$

$$2\left(\pm\dfrac{\sqrt{2}}{2}j\right)^4 - 7\left(\pm\dfrac{\sqrt{2}}{2}j\right)^2 = \dfrac{1}{2} + \dfrac{7}{2} = 4$$

5. $x^{-2} - 2x^{-1} - 8 = 0$.

Let $y = x^{-1}, y^2 = x^{-2}$, then

$$y^2 - 2y - 8 = 0$$
$$(y - 4)(y + 2) = 0$$
$y - 4 = 0 \quad$ or $\quad y + 2 = 0$
$\quad y = 4 \qquad\qquad\quad y = -2$
$\quad x^{-1} = 4 \qquad\qquad x^{-1} = -2$

$\qquad x = \dfrac{1}{4} \qquad\qquad\quad x = \dfrac{-1}{2}$

Check:

$$\left(\dfrac{1}{4}\right)^{-2} - 2\left(\dfrac{1}{4}\right)^{-1} - 8 = 16 - 8 - 8 = 0$$

$$\left(-\dfrac{1}{2}\right)^{-2} - 2\left(-\dfrac{1}{2}\right)^{-1} - 8 = 4 + 4 - 8 = 0$$

9. $2x - 7\sqrt{x} + 5 = 0$.

Let $y = \sqrt{x}, y^2 = x$, then

$$2y^2 - 7y + 5 = 0$$
$$(2y - 5)(y - 1) = 0$$
$2y - 5 = 0 \quad$ or $\quad y - 1 = 0$
$\quad 2y = 5 \qquad\qquad\quad y = 1$

$\qquad y = \dfrac{5}{2} \qquad\qquad\quad \sqrt{x} = 1$

$\quad \sqrt{x} = \dfrac{2}{5} \qquad\qquad\quad x = 1$

$\qquad x = \dfrac{25}{4}$

Check:

$$2\left(\dfrac{25}{4}\right) - 7\sqrt{\dfrac{25}{4}} + 5 = \dfrac{25}{2} - \dfrac{35}{2} + \dfrac{35}{2} + \dfrac{10}{2} = 0$$

$$2(1) - 7\sqrt{1} + 5 = 2 - 7 + 5 = 0$$

13. $x^{2/3} - 2x^{1/3} - 15 = 0$.

Let $y = x^{1/3}, y^2 = x^{2/3}$, then

$$y^2 - 2y - 15 = 0$$
$$(y - 5)(y + 3) = 0$$
$y - 5 = 0 \quad$ or $\quad y + 3 = 0$
$\quad y = 5 \qquad\qquad\quad y = -3$
$\quad x^{1/3} = 5 \qquad\qquad x^{1/3} = -3$
$\qquad x = 125 \qquad\qquad x = -27$

Check:

$$125^{2/3} - 2(125)^{1/3} - 15 = 25 - 10 - 15 = 0$$
$$(-27)^{2/3} - 2(-27)^{1/3} - 15 = 9 + 6 - 15 = 0$$

17. $(x-1) - \sqrt{x-1} - 2 = 0.$

Let $y = \sqrt{x-1}, y^2 = x-1$, then

$$y^2 - y - 2 = 0$$
$$(y-2)(y+1) = 0$$
$$y - 2 = 0$$
$$y = 2$$
$$\sqrt{x-1} = 2$$
$$x - 1 = 4$$
$$x = 5$$

or

$$y + 1 = 0$$
$$y = -1, \text{ reject since}$$
$$y = \sqrt{x-1}$$
$$\text{requires } y \geq 0$$

Check:

$$(5-1) - \sqrt{5-1} - 2 = 4 - \sqrt{4} - 2$$
$$= 4 - 2 - 2$$
$$= 4 - 4$$
$$= 0$$

21. $x - 3\sqrt{x-2} = 6.$

Let $y = \sqrt{x-2}, y^2 = x-2 \Rightarrow y^2 + 2 = x$, then

$$y^2 + 2 - 3y = 6$$
$$y^2 - 3y - 4 = 0$$
$$(y-4)(y+1) = 0$$
$$y - 4 = 0$$
$$y = 4$$
$$\sqrt{x-2} = 4$$
$$x - 2 = 16$$
$$x = 18$$

or

$$y + 1 = 0$$
$$y = -1$$
$$\sqrt{x-2} = -1 \text{ has no solution}$$
$$\text{since } \sqrt{x-2} \geq 0$$

Check:

$$18 - 3\sqrt{18-2} = 18 - 3\sqrt{16}$$
$$= 18 - 3(4)$$
$$= 18 - 12$$
$$= 6$$

25. $e^{2x} - e^x = 0$

$$e^x(e^x - 1) = 0$$
$$e^x = 0, \text{ no solution}$$
$$e^x - 1 = 0$$
$$e^x = 1$$
$$x = 0$$

Check: $e^{2(0)} - e^0 = 1 - 1 = 0$

29. $x + 2 = 3\sqrt{x}$

$x - 3\sqrt{x} + 2 = 0$, let $y = \sqrt{x}, y \geq 0, x \geq 0$

$$y^2 - 3y + 2 = 0$$
$$(y-2)(y-1) = 0$$
$$y - 2 = 0 \quad \text{or} \quad y - 1 = 0$$
$$y = 2 \qquad\qquad y = 1$$
$$\sqrt{x} = 2 \qquad\qquad \sqrt{x} = 1$$
$$x = 4 \qquad\qquad x = 1$$

Check:

$$4 + 2 \overset{?}{=} 3\sqrt{4}$$
$$6 \overset{?}{=} 3(2)$$
$$6 = 6$$
$$1 + 2 \overset{?}{=} 3\sqrt{1}$$
$$3 = 3$$

33. $\sqrt{F} = 2\sqrt{p}/(1-p)$

$$\sqrt{16} = \frac{2\sqrt{p}}{1-p}$$

$$4(1-p) = 2\sqrt{p}$$
$$2(1-p) = \sqrt{p}$$
$$2 - 2p = \sqrt{p}$$

$2p + \sqrt{p} - 2 = 0$, let $x = \sqrt{p}, x \geq 0, p \geq 0$

$$2x^2 + x - 2 = 0$$

$$x = \frac{-1 \pm \sqrt{1^2 - 4(2)(-2)}}{2(2)} = \frac{-1 \pm \sqrt{17}}{4}$$

$$\sqrt{p} = \frac{-1 + \sqrt{17}}{4}$$

$$p = 0.610$$

14.4   Equations with Radicals

1. $2\sqrt{3x-1} = 3$

$$4(3x-1) = 9$$
$$12x - 4 = 9$$
$$12x = 13$$

$$x = \frac{13}{12}$$

Check: $2\sqrt{3\left(\dfrac{13}{12}\right) - 1} \overset{?}{=} 3$

$$3 = 3$$

5. $\sqrt{x-8} = 2$; squaring both sides
$$x - 8 = 4$$
$$x = 12$$
Check:
$$\sqrt{12 - 8} = \sqrt{4}$$
$$= 2$$

9.
$$\sqrt{3x + 2} = 3x$$
$$3x + 2 = 9x^2$$
$$9x^2 - 3x - 2 = 0$$
$$(3x + 1)(3x - 2) = 0$$
$$3x + 1 = 0 \quad \text{or} \quad 3x - 2 = 0$$
$$3x = -1 \qquad\qquad 3x = 2$$
$$x = \frac{-1}{3} \qquad\qquad x = \frac{2}{3}$$
Check:
$$\sqrt{3 \cdot \frac{1}{3} + 2} \quad \bigg| \quad 3 \cdot \frac{-1}{3}$$
$$\sqrt{-1 + 2} \qquad -1$$
$$\sqrt{1}$$
$$1$$
$$x = \frac{-1}{3} \text{ is not a solution.}$$
Check:
$$\sqrt{3 \cdot \frac{2}{3} + 2} \quad \bigg| \quad 3 \cdot \frac{2}{3}$$
$$\sqrt{2 + 2} \qquad 2$$
$$\sqrt{4}$$
$$2$$
$$x = \frac{2}{3} \text{ is the solution.}$$

13. $\sqrt[3]{y - 5} = 3$
$$y - 5 = 3^3 = 27$$
$$y = 32$$

The solution is $y = 32$, which checks.

17. $\sqrt{x^2 - 9} = 4$
$$x^2 - 9 = 16$$
$$x^2 = 25$$
$$x = \pm 5$$

Check:
$$\sqrt{(\pm 5)^2 - 9} \stackrel{?}{=} 4$$
$$\sqrt{25 - 9} \stackrel{?}{=} 4$$
$$\sqrt{16} \stackrel{?}{=} 4$$
$$4 = 4$$
$$x = \pm 5 \text{ is the solution.}$$

21.
$$\sqrt{5 + \sqrt{x}} = \sqrt{x} - 1$$
$$5 + \sqrt{x} = (\sqrt{x} - 1)^2$$
$$5 + \sqrt{x} = x - 2\sqrt{x} + 1$$
$$x - 3\sqrt{x} - 4 = 0$$
$$(\sqrt{x} - 4)(\sqrt{x} + 1) = 0$$
$$x = 16$$
$$\sqrt{x} = -1, \text{ not possible}$$

The solution is $x = 16$ since it checks.

25. $2\sqrt{x + 2} - \sqrt{3x + 4} = 1$
$$2\sqrt{x + 2} = 1 + \sqrt{3x + 4}$$
$$4(x + 2) = \left(1 + \sqrt{3x + 4}\right)^2$$
$$4x + 8 = 1 + 2\sqrt{3x + 4} + 3x + 4$$
$$x + 3 = 2\sqrt{3x + 4}$$
$$(x + 3)^2 = 4(3x + 4)$$
$$x^2 + 6x + 9 = 12x + 16$$
$$x^2 - 6x - 7 = 0$$
$$(x - 7)(x + 1) = 0$$

The solutions are $x = -1$ and $x = 7$, which check.

29. $\sqrt{2x - 1} - \sqrt{x + 11} = -1$
$$\sqrt{2x - 1} = \sqrt{x + 11} - 1$$
$$2x - 1 = (\sqrt{x + 11} - 1)^2$$
$$2x - 1 = x + 11 - 2\sqrt{x + 11} + 1$$
$$x - 13 = -2\sqrt{x + 11}$$
$$(x - 13)^2 = 4(x + 11)$$
$$x^2 - 26x + 169 = 4x + 44$$
$$x^2 - 30x + 125 = 0$$
$$(x - 25)(x - 5) = 0$$

The solution is $x = 5$, as $x = 25$ doesn't check.

33.
$$\sqrt{x - 2} = \sqrt[4]{x - 2} + 12$$
$$(\sqrt{x - 2} - 12)^2 = (\sqrt[4]{x - 2})^2$$
$$\sqrt{x - 2} = x - 2 - 24\sqrt{x - 2} + 144$$
$$(25\sqrt{x - 2})^2 = (x + 142)^2$$
$$625(x - 2) = x^2 + 284x + 20164$$
$$x^2 - 341x + 21414 = 0$$
$$(x - 258)(x - 83) = 0$$

The solution is $x = 258$ as $x = 83$ doesn't check.

37. $\sqrt{2x + 1} + 3\sqrt{x} = 9$
$$\sqrt{2x + 1} = 9 - 3\sqrt{x}$$
$$2x + 1 = 81 - 54\sqrt{x} + 9x$$
$$54\sqrt{x} = 7x + 80$$
$$2916x = 49x^2 + 1120x + 6400$$
$$49x^2 - 1796x + 6400 = 0$$
$$(x - 4)(49x - 1600) = 0$$

$$x - 4 = 0 \quad \text{or} \quad 49x = 1600$$

$$x = 4 \qquad x = \frac{1600}{49}$$

Check:

$$\sqrt{2(4) + 1} + 3\sqrt{4} \overset{?}{=} 9$$

$$3 + 6 \overset{?}{=} 9$$

$$9 = 9$$

$$\sqrt{2\left(\frac{1600}{49}\right) + 1} \overset{?}{=} 9$$

$$\frac{57}{7} + \frac{120}{7} \overset{?}{=} 9$$

$$\frac{177}{9} \ne 9$$

$x = 4$ is the solution

41. $k = \sqrt{2np + (np)^2} - np$
$(k + np)^2 = 2np + n^2p^2$
$k^2 + 2knp + n^2p^2 = 2np + n^2p^2$
$k^2 = 2np - 2knp$
$k^2 = p(2n - 2kn)$

$$p = \frac{k^2}{2n - 2kn}$$

$$= \frac{k^2}{2n(1 - k)}$$

45.

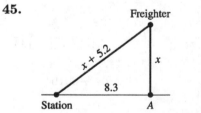

$$(x + 5.2)^2 = x^2 + 8.3^2$$
$$x^2 + 10.4x + 27.04 = x^2 + 68.89$$
$$10.4x = 41.85$$
$$x = 4.0$$
$$x + 5.2 = 4.0 + 5.2 = 9.2$$

The freighter is 9.2 km from the station.

Chapter 14 Review Exercises

1. $x + 2y = 6 \Rightarrow y = \dfrac{6 - x}{2}$

$$y = 4x^2$$

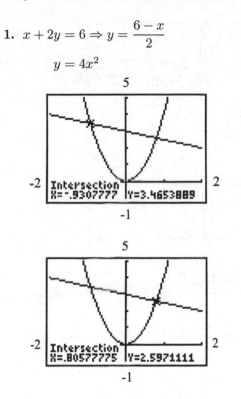

Solution: $x = -0.9, y = 3.5; x = 0.8, y = 2.6$

5. $y = x^2 + 1$
$2x^2 + y^2 = 4 \Rightarrow y \pm \sqrt{4 - 2x^2}$

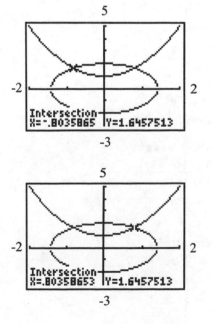

Solution: $x = 0.8, y = 1.6; x = -0.8, y = 1.6$

9. $y = x^2 - 2x$
$y = 1 - e^{-x}$

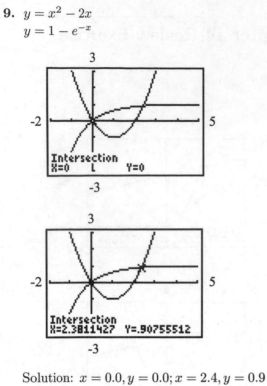

Solution: $x = 0.0, y = 0.0; x = 2.4, y = 0.9$

13. (1) $2L = R^2$

(2) $\qquad R^2 + L^2 = 3$
$\qquad\quad 2L + L^2 = 3$
$\qquad L^2 + 2L - 3 = 0$
$\qquad (L+3)(L-1) = 0$

$L + 3 = 0, \qquad L - 1 = 0$
$\quad L = -3, \qquad\quad L = 1$
$2(-3) = R^2, \qquad 2(1) = R^2$
$\quad$ no solution $\qquad R = \pm\sqrt{2}$

Solution: $(\sqrt{2}, 1), (-\sqrt{2}, 1)$

17. (1) $4x^2 - 7y^2 = 21$
$\quad$ (2) $x^2 + 2y^2 = 99$

$\quad$ (1) $\quad 8x^2 - 14y^2 = 42$
$\quad$ (2) $\quad \underline{7x^2 + 14y^2 = 693}$
$\qquad\qquad 15x^2 \qquad\quad = 735$
$\qquad\qquad\qquad x^2 = 49$
$\qquad\qquad\qquad\; x = \pm 7$

(2) $(\pm 7)^2 + 2y^2 = 99$
$\qquad 49 + 2y^2 = 99$
$\qquad\qquad 2y^2 = 50$
$\qquad\qquad\; y^2 = 25$
$\qquad\qquad\;\; y = \pm 5$

Solution: $(7, 5), (7, -5), (-7, 5), (-7, -5)$

21. $x^4 - 20x^2 + 64 = 0.$
Let $y = x^2, y^2 = x^4$

$y^2 - 20y + 64 = 0$
$(y - 16)(y - 4) = 0$
$y - 16 = 0 \quad$ or $\; y - 4 = 0$
$\quad y = 16 \qquad\qquad y = 4$
$\quad x^2 = 16 \qquad\qquad x^2 = 4$
$\quad\; x = \pm 4 \qquad\qquad x = \pm 2$

25. $D^{-2} + 4D^{-1} - 21 = 0.$

Let $x = D^{-1}, x^2 = D^{-2}$

$x^2 + 4x - 21 = 0$
$(x + 7)(x - 3) = 0$
$x + 7 = 0 \quad$ or $\; x - 3 = 0$
$\quad x = -7 \qquad\qquad x = 3$
$\; D^{-1} = -7 \qquad\; D^{-1} = 3$
$\quad D = \dfrac{-1}{7} \qquad\quad D = \dfrac{1}{3}$

29. $\dfrac{4}{r^2 + 1} + \dfrac{7}{2r^2 + 1} = 2$

$4(2r^2 + 1) + 7(r^2 + 1) = 2(r^2 + 1)(2r^2 + 1)$
$\quad 8r^2 + 4 + 7r^2 + 7 = 2(2r^4 + 3r^2 + 1)$
$\qquad\qquad 15r^2 + 11 = 4r^4 + 6r^2 + 2$
$\qquad 4r^4 - 9r^2 - 9 = 0.$ Let $x = r^2, x^2 = r^4$
$\qquad\quad 4x^2 - 9x - 9 = 0$
$\qquad\quad (4x + 3)(x - 3) = 0$

$4x + 3 = 0 \qquad$ or $\; x - 3 = 0$
$\quad 4x = -3 \qquad\qquad x = 3$
$\qquad x = \dfrac{-3}{4} \qquad\qquad r^2 = 3$

$\quad r^2 = \dfrac{-3}{4} \qquad\qquad r = \pm\sqrt{3}$

$\qquad r = \dfrac{\pm\sqrt{3}}{2} j$

33. $\sqrt{5x + 9} + 1 = x$
$\quad \sqrt{5x + 9} = x - 1$
$\qquad 5x + 9 = x^2 - 2x + 1$
$x^2 - 7x - 8 = 0$
$(x - 8)(x + 1) = 0$

$x - 8 = 0 \quad$ or $\; x + 1 = 0$
$\quad x = 0 \qquad\qquad x = -1$

Check: $\quad \dfrac{\sqrt{5 \cdot 8 + 9} + 1}{\sqrt{49} + 1} \,\Bigg|\, 8$
$$\sqrt{49} + 1$$
$$7 + 1$$
$$8$$

$\dfrac{\sqrt{5(-1) + 9} + 1}{\sqrt{-5 + 9} + 1} \,\Bigg|\, -1$
$$\sqrt{-5 + 9} + 1$$
$$\sqrt{4} + 1$$
$$2 + 1$$
$$3$$

$x = 8$ is a solution.

$x = -1$ is not a solution.

37. $\sqrt{n + 4} + 2\sqrt{n + 2} = 3$
$$\sqrt{n + 4} = 3 - 2\sqrt{n + 2}$$
$$n + 4 = 9 - 12\sqrt{n + 2} + 4(n + 2)$$
$$n + 4 = 9 - 12\sqrt{n + 2} + 4n + 8$$
$$12\sqrt{n + 2} = 13 + 3n$$
$$144(n + 2) = 169 + 78n + 9n^2$$
$$144n + 288 = 169 + 78n + 9n^2$$
$$9n^2 - 66n - 119 = 0$$

From the quadratic formula,

$$n = \frac{-(-66) \pm \sqrt{(-66)^2 - 4(9)(-119)}}{2(9)} = \frac{66 \pm \sqrt{8640}}{18}$$

Check:

$$\sqrt{\frac{66 + \sqrt{8640}}{18} + 4} + 2\sqrt{\frac{66 + \sqrt{8640}}{18} + 2} = 10.1639\cdots$$

$\dfrac{66 + \sqrt{8640}}{18}$ does not check

$$\sqrt{\frac{66 - \sqrt{8640}}{18} + 4} + 2\sqrt{\frac{66 - \sqrt{8640}}{18} + 2} = 3$$

$\dfrac{66 - \sqrt{8640}}{18}$ is the solution.

41. $x^3 - 2x^{3/2} - 48 = 0,$
$$x^3 - 2(x^3)^{1/2} - 48 = 0, \text{ let } x^3 = y$$
$$y - 2y^{1/2} - 48 = 0, \text{ let } z = y^{1/2}$$
$$z^2 - 2z - 48 = 0$$
$$(z - 8)(z + 6) = 0$$
$$z - 8 = 0 \quad \text{or} \quad z + 6 = 0$$
$$z = 8 \qquad\qquad z = -6$$
$$y^{1/2} = 8 \qquad\quad y^{1/2} = -6 \text{ reject}$$
$$y = 64$$
$$x^3 = 64$$
$$x = 4$$

Check:

$$4^3 - 2(4^{3/2}) - 48 \overset{?}{=} 0$$
$$64 - 2(8) - 48 \overset{?}{=} 0$$
$$64 - 16 - 48 \overset{?}{=} 0$$
$$0 = 0$$

$x = 4$ is the solution.

45.
$$\sqrt[3]{x^3 - 7} = x - 1$$
$$x^3 - 7 = x^3 - 3x^2 + 3x - 1$$
$$3x^2 - 3x - 6 = 0$$
$$x^2 - x - 2 = 0$$
$$(x - 2)(x + 1) = 0$$
$$x - 2 = 0 \qquad x + 1 = 0$$
$$x = 2 \qquad x = -1$$

Check:

$$\sqrt[3]{2^3 - 7} \overset{?}{=} 2 - 1$$
$$\sqrt[3]{8 - 7} \overset{?}{=} 1$$
$$\sqrt[3]{1} \overset{?}{=} 1$$
$$1 = 1$$
$$\sqrt[3]{-1 - 7} \overset{?}{=} -1 - 1$$
$$\sqrt[3]{-8} \overset{?}{=} -2$$
$$-2 = -2$$

$x = 2, x = -1$ is the solution.

49.
$$L = \frac{h}{2\pi}\sqrt{l(l + 1)}$$

$$L^2 = \frac{h^2}{4\pi^2} \cdot l(l + 1)$$

$$\frac{4\pi^2 L^2}{h^2} = l^2 + l$$

$l^2 + l - \dfrac{4\pi^2 L^2}{h^2} = 0$; from the quadratic formula,

$$l = \frac{-1 \pm \sqrt{1^2 - 4 \cdot 1\left(-\dfrac{4\pi^2 L^2}{h^2}\right)}}{2(1)} = \frac{-1 \pm \sqrt{1 + \dfrac{16\pi^2 L^2}{h^2}}}{2}$$

$l = \dfrac{-1 + \sqrt{1 + \dfrac{16\pi^2 L^2}{h^2}}}{2}$. The + was chosen because $l > 0$

53. (1) $16t_1^2 + 16t_2^2 = 45$ where $t_1, t_2 > 0$
    (2) $t_2 = 2t_1$

(1) with t_2 from (2)
$$16t_1^2 + 16(2t_1)^2 = 45$$
$$16t_1^2 + 64t_1^2 = 45$$
$$80t_1^2 = 45$$
$$t_1^2 = \frac{45}{80}$$
$$t_1 = 0.75s$$
$$t_2 = 2 \cdot t_1 = 2(0.75)$$
$$t_2 = 1.5 \text{ s}$$

57. $Z = \sqrt{R^2 + X^2}$, $Z = 2X^2$; $R = 0.800$
$2X^2 = \sqrt{R^2 + X^2}$ $R^2 = 0.640$
$4X^4 = R^2 + X^2$
$4X^4 - X^2 - R^2 = 0$
$4X^4 - X^2 - 0.640 = 0$. Let $X^2 = y$, $X^4 = y^2$
$4y^2 - y - 0.640 = 0$

$$y = \frac{-(-1) \pm \sqrt{(-1)^2 - 4(4)(-0.640)}}{2(4)} = \frac{1 \pm \sqrt{11.24}}{8}.$$ Choose $+$, $y > 0$

$y = 0.544 = X^2$
$X = 0.738\Omega$. Choose $+$, $X > 0$
$Z = 2X^2 = 2(0.738)^2$
$Z = 1.09 \ \Omega$

61. $A = \pi r^2 + s^2 = 40.0$
$2r + s = 7.00 \Rightarrow s = 7.00 - 2r$
$\pi r^2 + (7.00 - 2r)^2 = 40.0$
$\pi r^2 + 49.0 - 28.0r + 4r^2 = 40.0$
$(\pi + 4)r^2 - 28.0r + 9.00 = 0$

Solve with the quadratic formula,
$r = 0.353$, $r = 3.57$ reject since $2r < 7$
$r = 0.353$ cm, radius of circle
$s = 7.00 - 2r = 6.29$ cm, side of square

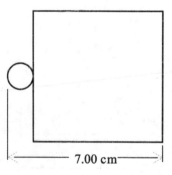

$\longleftarrow$ 7.00 cm $\longrightarrow$

65. $x + \sqrt{x - 1} + 4.00 = 9.00$ may be solved graphically or algebraically. To solve graphically, find the x-int of
$y = x + \sqrt{x - 1} - 5$

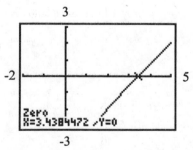

Algebraically, the solution is

$$x + \sqrt{x - 1} + 4 = 9$$
$$\sqrt{x - 1} = 5 - x$$
$$x - 1 = 25 - 10x + x^2$$
$$x^2 - 11x + 26 = 0$$

$$x = \frac{-(-11) \pm \sqrt{(-11)^2 - 4(1)(26)}}{2(1)} = \frac{11 \pm \sqrt{17}}{2}$$

$$x = \frac{11 + \sqrt{17}}{2} \quad \text{or} \quad x = \frac{11 - \sqrt{17}}{2}$$

Check: $\dfrac{11 + \sqrt{17}}{2} + \sqrt{\dfrac{11 + \sqrt{17}}{2} - 1} + 4 = 14.123 \cdots$

$\dfrac{11 + \sqrt{17}}{2}$ does not check

$\dfrac{11 - \sqrt{17}}{2} + \sqrt{\dfrac{11 - \sqrt{17}}{2} - 1} + 4 = 9$

$\dfrac{11 - \sqrt{17}}{2}$ checks.

$\dfrac{11 - \sqrt{17}}{2} = 3.438447 \cdots$ in agreement with the graphical solution..

The solution is 3.44 in.

EQUATIONS OF HIGHER DEGREE

15.1 The Remainder and Factor Theorems; Synthetic Division

1. Using the remainder theorem find the remainder, for $(3x^3 - x^2 - 20x + 5) \div (x + 3)$.

$$R = f(-3) = 3(-3)^3 - (-3)^2 - 20(-3) + 5 = -25$$

5.
$$\begin{array}{r} x^2 - x + 3 \\ x + 1)\overline{x^3 + 2x + 3} \\ \underline{x^3 + x^2} \\ -x^2 + 2x \\ \underline{-x^2 - x} \\ 3x + 3 \\ \underline{3x + 3} \\ 0 \end{array}$$

$$f(r) = R; \ r = -1$$
$$f(-1) = (-1)^3 + 2(-1) + 3$$
$$= -1 - 2 + 3$$
$$= 0$$

Therefore, $R = 0$

9.
$$\begin{array}{r} 3x^0 - x + 2 \\ x - 3)\overline{3x^4 - 9x^3 - x^2 + 5x - 10} \\ \underline{3x^4 - 9x^3} \\ -x^2 + 5x \\ \underline{-x^2 + 3x} \\ 2x - 10 \\ \underline{2x - 6} \\ -4 \end{array}$$

$$f(r) = R; \ r = 3$$
$$f(3) = 3(3)^4 - 9(3)^3 - (3)^2 + 5(3) - 10$$
$$= 243 - 243 - 9 + 15 - 10 = -4$$

Therefore, $R = -4$

13. $f(3) = 2 \cdot 3^4 - 7 \cdot 3^3 - 3^2 + 8 = -28$
$$R = -28$$

17. $4x^3 + x^2 - 16x - 4, x - 2; \ r = 2$
$$f(2) = 4(2)^3 + 2^2 - 16(2) - 4$$
$$= 32 + 4 - 32 - 4$$
$$= 0$$

$x - 2$ is a factor since $f(r) = R = 0$.

21. $x^6 + 1, x + 1; \ r = -1$
$$f(-1) = (-1)^6 + 1 = 2$$

$x + 1$ is not a factor since $f(r) = R \neq 0$.

25. $(x^3 + 2x^2 - 3x + 4) \div (x + 1)$
$$= x^2 + x - 4 + \frac{8}{x + 1}$$

$$\begin{array}{rrrr|r} 1 & 2 & -3 & 4 & \underline{-1} \\ & -1 & -1 & 4 & \\ \hline 1 & 1 & -4 & 8 & \end{array}$$

29. $(x^7 - 128) \div (x - 2)$
$$= x^6 + 2x^5 + 4x^4 + 8x^3 + 16x^2 + 32x + 64$$
$$R = 0$$

$$\begin{array}{rrrrrrrr|r} 1 & 0 & 0 & 0 & 0 & 0 & 0 & -128 & \underline{2} \\ & 2 & 4 & 8 & 16 & 32 & 64 & 128 & \\ \hline 1 & 2 & 4 & 8 & 16 & 32 & 64 & 0 & \end{array}$$

33.
$$\begin{array}{rrrrrr|r} 2 & 0 & -1 & 3 & 0 & -4 & \underline{-1} \\ & -2 & 2 & -1 & -2 & 2 & \\ \hline 2 & -2 & 1 & 2 & -2 & -2, & R = -2, \end{array}$$

$x + 1$ is not a factor.

37.
$$\begin{array}{rrrrr|r} 2 & -1 & -4 & 0 & 1 & \underline{\frac{1}{2}} \\ & 1 & 0 & -2 & -1 & \\ \hline 2 & 0 & -4 & -2 & 0, & R = 0, \end{array}$$

$Z - \frac{1}{2}$ is a factor $\Rightarrow 2z - 1$ is a factor.

41.
$$\begin{array}{rrrrr|r} 1 & -5 & -15 & 5 & 14 & \underline{7} \\ & 7 & 14 & -7 & -14 & \\ \hline 1 & 2 & -1 & -2 & 0, & R = 0, \ 7 \text{ is a zero.} \end{array}$$

45.
$$\begin{array}{r} 2x^2 + 5x + 2 \\ 2x - 1)\overline{4x^3 + 8x^2 - x - 2} \\ \underline{4x^3 - 2x^2} \\ 10x^2 - x \\ \underline{10x^2 - 5x} \\ 4x - 2 \\ \underline{4x - 2} \\ 0 \end{array}$$

$2x - 1$ is a factor of $4x^3 + 8x^2 - x - 2$.

We may not conclude $f(-1) = 0$ because $2x - 1$ is not in the form $x - r$.

49. $(x^3 - 3x^2 + x - 3) \div (x + j)$

$$
\begin{array}{rrrr|r}
1 & -3 & 1 & -3 & \underline{-j} \\
 & -j & -1+3j & 3 & \\
\hline
1 & -3-j & 3j & 0 &
\end{array}
$$

$(x^3 - 3x^2 + x - 3) \div (x + j)$
$= x^2 - (3 + j)x + 3j, \; R = 0$

53. (a) $(s^3 + 5s^2 + 4s + 20) \div (s - 2)$

$$
\begin{array}{rrrr|r}
1 & 5 & 4 & 20 & \underline{2} \\
 & 2 & 14 & 36 & \\
\hline
1 & 7 & 18 & 56 &
\end{array}
$$

$R = 56$, $s - 2$ is not a factor.

(b) $(s^3 + 5s^2 + 4s + 20) \div (s + 5)$

$$
\begin{array}{rrrr|r}
1 & 5 & 4 & 20 & \underline{-5} \\
 & -5 & 0 & -20 & \\
\hline
1 & 0 & 4 & 0 &
\end{array}
$$

$R = 0$, $s + 5$ is a factor.

15.2   The Roots of an Equation

1. $f(x) = (x - 1)^3(x^2 + 2x + 1) = 0$
$(x - 1)^3 = 0 \quad$ or $\quad x^2 + 2x + 1 = 0$
$x = 1, \qquad\qquad (x + 1)^2 = 0$
A triple root $\qquad\quad x + 1 = 0$
$\qquad\qquad\qquad\qquad\qquad x = -1$, a double root

the five roots are 1, 1, 1, -1, -1

5. $(x^2 + 6x + 9)(x^2 + 4) = 0$
$\quad (x + 3)^2(x^2 + 4) = 0$, by inspection
$x = -3$ double root, $x = \pm 2j$

9.
$$
\begin{array}{rrrr|r}
2 & 11 & 20 & 12 & \underline{-\frac{3}{2}} \\
 & -3 & -12 & -12 & \\
\hline
2 & 8 & 8 & 0 &
\end{array}
$$

$2x^3 + 11x^2 + 20x + 12 = \left(x + \dfrac{3}{2}\right)(2x^2 + 8x + 8)$

$\qquad\qquad\qquad\qquad\quad = 2\left(x + \dfrac{3}{2}\right)(x^2 + 4x + 4)$

$\qquad\qquad\qquad\qquad\quad = 2\left(x + \dfrac{3}{2}\right)(x + 2)(x + 2)$

$r_1 = -\dfrac{3}{2}, \; r_2 = r_3 = -2$

13.
$$
\begin{array}{rrrrr|r}
1 & 1 & -2 & 4 & -24 & \underline{2} \\
 & 2 & 6 & 8 & 24 & \\
\hline
1 & 3 & 4 & 12 & 0 &
\end{array}
$$

$t^4 + t^3 - 2t^2 + 4t - 24 = (t - 2)(t^3 + 3t^2 + 4t + 12)$

$$
\begin{array}{rrrr|r}
1 & 3 & 4 & 12 & \underline{-3} \\
 & -3 & 0 & -12 & \\
\hline
1 & 0 & 4 & 0 &
\end{array}
$$

$t^4 + t^3 - 2t^2 + 4t - 24 = (t - 2)(t + 3)(t^2 + 4)$
$\qquad\qquad\qquad\qquad\quad = (t - 2)(t + 3)(t - 2j)(t + 2j)$

$r_1 = 2, \; r_2 = -3, \; r_3 = -2j, \; r_4 = 2j$

17.
$$
\begin{array}{rrrrr|r}
6 & 5 & -15 & 0 & 4 & \underline{-\frac{1}{2}} \\
 & -3 & -1 & 8 & -4 & \\
\hline
6 & 2 & -16 & 8 & 0 &
\end{array}
$$

$6x^4 + 5x^3 - 15x^2 + 4$

$= \left(x + \dfrac{1}{2}\right)(6x^3 + 2x^2 - 16x + 8)$

$= 2\left(x + \dfrac{1}{2}\right)(3x^3 + x^2 - 8x + 4)$

$$
\begin{array}{rrrr|r}
3 & 1 & -8 & 4 & \underline{\frac{2}{3}} \\
 & 2 & 2 & -4 & \\
\hline
3 & 3 & -6 & 0 &
\end{array}
$$

$6x^4 + 5x^3 - 15x^2 + 4$

$= 2\left(x + \dfrac{1}{2}\right)\left(x - \dfrac{2}{3}\right)(3x^2 + 3x - 6)$

$= 6\left(x + \dfrac{1}{2}\right)\left(x - \dfrac{2}{3}\right)(x^2 + x - 2)$

$= 6\left(x + \dfrac{1}{2}\right)\left(x - \dfrac{2}{3}\right)(x + 2)(x - 1)$

$r_1 = -\dfrac{1}{2}, \; r_2 = \dfrac{2}{3}, \; r_3 = -2, \; r_4 = 1$

21. $x^5 - 3x^4 + 4x^3 - 4x^2 + 3x - 1 = 0$ (1 is a triple root)

$$
\begin{array}{rrrrrr|r}
1 & -3 & 4 & -4 & 3 & -1 & \underline{1} \\
 & 1 & -2 & 2 & -2 & 1 & \\
\hline
1 & -2 & 2 & -2 & 1 & 0 & \underline{1} \\
 & 1 & -1 & 1 & -1 & & \\
\hline
1 & -1 & 1 & 1 & 0 & & \underline{1} \\
 & 1 & 0 & 1 & & & \\
\hline
1 & 0 & 1 & 0 & & &
\end{array}
$$

$(x - 1)^3(x^2 + 1)$

The roots are 1, 1, 1, $-j, j$.

25. $x^6 + 2x^5 - 4x^4 - 10x^3 - 41x^2 - 72x - 36 = 0$

(-1 is a double root; $2j$ is a root)

$$
\begin{array}{rrrrrrr|r}
1 & 2 & -4 & -10 & -41 & -72 & -36 & \underline{-1} \\
  & -1 & -1 & 5 & 5 & 36 & 36 & \\
\hline
1 & 1 & -5 & -5 & -36 & -36 & 0 & \underline{-1} \\
  & -1 & 0 & 5 & 0 & 36 & & \\
\hline
1 & 0 & -5 & 0 & -36 & 0 & 0 & \underline{2j} \\
  & 2j & -4 & -18j & 36 & 0 & 0 & \\
\hline
1 & 2j & -9 & -18j & 0 & 0 & 0 & \underline{-2j} \text{ (conj.)} \\
  & -2 & 0 & 18j & 0 & 0 & 0 & \\
\hline
1 & 0 & -9 & 0 & 0 & 0 & 0 &
\end{array}
$$

$(x+1)^2(x-2j)(x+2j)(x^2-9)$
The roots are $-1, -1, 2j, -2j, , -3, 3$.

15.3   Rational and Irrational Roots

1. $f(x) = 4x^5 + x^4 + 4x^3 - x^2 + 5x + 6 = 0$ has two sign changes and thus no more than two positive roots.
$f(-x) = -4x^5 + x^4 - 4x^3 - x^2 - 5x + 6 = 0$ has three sign changes and thus no more than three negative roots.

5. $x^3 + 2x^2 - 5x - 6 = 0$; there are 3 roots.
$f(x) = x^3 + x^2 - 5x + 3$; there are at most 2 positive roots.
$f(-x) = -x^3 + x^2 + 5x + 3$; there is 1 negative root.
Possible rational roots are $\pm 1, \pm 2, \pm 3, \pm 6$.

Trying -1, we have

$$
\begin{array}{rrrr|r}
1 & 2 & -5 & -6 & \underline{-1} \\
  & -1 & -1 & 6 & \\
\hline
1 & 1 & -6 & 0 &
\end{array}
$$

Hence, -1 is a root and the remaining factor is
$x^2 + x - 6 = (x+3)(x-2)$.
The remaining roots are $-3, 2$.

9. $3x^3 + 11x^2 + 5x - 3 = 0$; there are 3 roots.
$f(x) = 3x^3 + 11x^2 + 5x - 3$; there is 1 positive root.
$f(-x) = -3x^3 + 11x^2 - 5x - 3$; there are at most 2 negative roots.
Possible rational roots are $\pm\frac{1}{3}, \pm 1, \pm 3$.
We try to find the one positive root first. $\frac{1}{3}$ is the first root with 0 remainder.

$$
\begin{array}{rrrr|r}
3 & 11 & 5 & -3 & \underline{\frac{1}{3}} \\
  & 1 & 4 & 3 & \\
\hline
3 & 12 & 9 & 0 &
\end{array}
$$

Thus, $\frac{1}{3}$ is the positive root. The remaining factor is
$3x^2 + 12x + 9 = 3(x^2 + 4x + 3) = 3(x+1)(x+3)$.
The remaining roots are $-1, -3$.

13. $N^4 - 2N^3 - 13N^2 + 14N + 24 = 0$; there are 4 roots.
$f(N) = N^4 - 2N^3 - 13N^2 + 14N + 24$; there are at most 2 positive roots.
$f(-N) = N^4 + 2N^3 - 13N^2 - 14N + 24$; there are at most 2 negative roots.
Possible rational roots are $\pm 1, \pm 2, \pm 3, \pm 4, \pm 6, \pm 8, \pm 12, \pm 24$.
We try to find a positive root first. 2 is the first root with 0 remainder.

$$
\begin{array}{rrrrr|r}
1 & -2 & -13 & 14 & 24 & \underline{2} \\
  & 2 & 0 & -26 & -24 & \\
\hline
1 & 0 & -13 & -12 & 0 &
\end{array}
$$

Now, we check other factors for rational roots. 4 is a root with 0 remainder.

$$
\begin{array}{rrrr|r}
1 & 0 & -13 & -12 & \underline{4} \\
  & 4 & 16 & 12 & \\
\hline
1 & 4 & 3 & 0 &
\end{array}
$$

The remaining factor is
$n^2 + 4n + 3 = (n+3)(n+1)$.
The remaining roots are $-3, -1$

17. $f(D) = D^5 + D^4 - 9D^3 - 5D^2 + 16D + 12 = 0$ has $n = 5$ and therefore five roots. $f(D)$ has two sign changes and therefore at most two positive roots.
$f(-D) = -D^5 + D^4 + 9D^3 - 5D^2 - 16D + 12$ has three sign changes and therefore at most three negative roots.

Possible rational roots

$$
= \frac{\text{factors of } 12}{\text{factors of } 1}
$$
$$
= \frac{\pm 1, \pm 2, \pm 3, \pm 4, \pm 6, \pm 12}{\pm 1}
$$

$$
\begin{array}{rrrrrr|r}
1 & 1 & -9 & -5 & 16 & 12 & \underline{2} \\
  & 2 & 6 & -6 & -22 & -12 & \\
\hline
1 & 3 & -3 & -11 & -6 & 0, & \quad 2 \text{ is a root}
\end{array}
$$

$D^5 + D^4 - 9D^3 - 5D^2 + 16D + 12$
$\quad = (D-2)(D^4 + 3D^3 - 3D^2 - 11D - 6)$

$$
\begin{array}{rrrrr|r}
1 & 3 & -3 & -11 & -6 & \underline{2} \\
  & 2 & 10 & 14 & 6 & \\
\hline
1 & 5 & 7 & 3 & 0, &
\end{array}
$$

2 is a root of $D^4 + 3D^3 - 3D^2 - 11D - 6$

$D^5 + D^4 - 9D^3 - 5D^2 + 16D + 12$
$= (D-2)(D-2)(D^3 + 5D^2 + 7D + 3)$

$$
\begin{array}{rrrr|r}
1 & 5 & 7 & 3 & \underline{-1} \\
  & -1 & -4 & -3 & \\
\hline
1 & 4 & 3 & 0 & , \\
\end{array}
$$

-1 is a root of $D^3 + 5D^2 + 7D + 3$

$D^5 + D^4 - 9D^3 - 5D^2 + 16D + 12$
$= (D-2)(D-2)(D+1)(D^2 + 4D + 3)$
$= (D-2)(D-2)(D+1)(D+1)(D+3)$

roots: $2, 2, -1, -1, -3$

21. $x^3 - 2x^2 - 5x + 4 = 0$.

Graph $y_1 = x^3 - 2x^2 - 5x + 4$ and use the zero feature to solve.

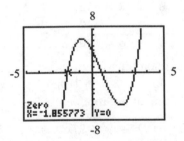

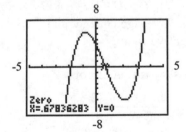

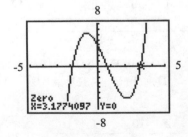

The zeros are -1.86, 0.68, 3.18.

25. $x^3 - 6x^2 + 10x - 4 = 0$ (0 and 1)

Graph $y_1 = x^3 - 6x^2 + 10x - 4$ and use the zero feature to solve.

$x = 0.59$

29. $f(x) = 4x^3 + 3x^2 - 20x - 15$.

Possible rational roots
$= \dfrac{\text{factors of } 15}{\text{factors of } 4}$
$= \dfrac{\pm 1, \ \pm 3, \ \pm 5, \ \pm 15}{\pm 1, \ \pm 2, \ \pm 4}$

$$
\begin{array}{rrrr|r}
4 & 3 & -20 & -15 & \underline{-\frac{3}{4}} \\
  & -3 & 0 & 15 & \\
\hline
4 & 0 & -20 & 0, & -\frac{3}{4} \text{ is a root} \\
\end{array}
$$

$4x^3 + 3x^2 - 20x - 15 = \left(x + \dfrac{3}{4}\right)(4x^2 - 20) = 0$

$4x^2 - 20 = 0$
$4x^2 = 20$
$x^2 = 5$
$x = \pm\sqrt{5}$

roots: $-\dfrac{3}{4}, \ \pm\sqrt{5}$

33.

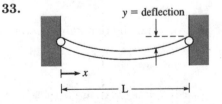

$y = k(x^4 - 2Lx^3 + L^3x) = 0$ for a deflection of zero.
$x^4 - 2Lx^3 + L^3x = 0$
$x(x^3 - 2Lx^2 + L^3) = 0, \ x = 0$ is a root
$x^3 - 2Lx^2 + L^3 = 0$

$$
\begin{array}{rrrr|r}
1 & -2L & 0 & L^3 & \underline{L} \\
  & L & -L^2 & -L^3 & \\
\hline
1 & -L & -L^2 & 0, & \\
\end{array}
$$

L is a root of $x^3 - 2Lx^2 + L^3 = 0$

$x^3 - 2Lx^2 + L^3 = (x - L)(x^2 - Lx - L^2)$

$x^2 - Lx - L^2 = 0$ has roots

$$= \frac{-(-L) \pm \sqrt{(-L)^2 - 4(1)(-L^2)}}{2} = \frac{L \pm L\sqrt{5}}{2} = \frac{L(1 \pm \sqrt{5})}{2}$$

$\dfrac{L}{2}(1 - \sqrt{5}) < 0$ and $\dfrac{L}{2}(1 + \sqrt{5}) > L$; reject both

Beam has a deflection of 0 for $x = 0$ and $x = L$.

37.

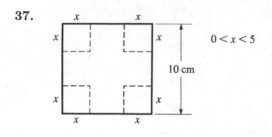

$V = (10 - 2x)^2 \cdot x = 70 \Rightarrow (100 - 40x + 4x^2) \cdot x = 70$

$4x^3 - 40x^2 + 100x - 70 = 0$

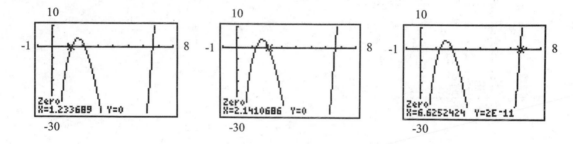

$6.62 > 5$ and must be rejected.

41. Let $x, x + 1, x + 4$ be the resistances.

$$\frac{1}{x} + \frac{1}{x + 1} + \frac{1}{x + 4} = 1$$

$(x + 1)(x + 4) + x(x + 4) + x(x + 1) = x(x + 1)(x + 4)$

$x^2 + 5x + 4 + x^2 + 4x + x^2 + x = x^3 + 5x^2 + 4x$

$x^3 + 2x^2 - 6x - 4 = 0$

Possible rational roots are $\pm 1, \pm 2, \pm 4$.
We find that 2 is the first root with 0 remainder.

$$
\begin{array}{rrrr|l}
1 & 2 & -6 & -4 & \underline{\,2\,} \\
  & 2 & 8 & 4 & \\
\hline
1 & 4 & 2 & 0 &
\end{array}
$$

Hence, 2 is a root. The remaining factor is $x^2 + 4x + 2$, which is solved by quadratic formula.

$$x = \frac{-4 \pm \sqrt{16 - 8}}{2} = \frac{-4 \pm 2\sqrt{2}}{2} = -2 \pm \sqrt{2}$$

Since the only positive root is $x = 2$, $R_1 = 2\,\Omega$,
$R_2 = 3\,\Omega$, $R_3 = 6\,\Omega$

Chapter 15 Review Exercises

1. $2(1)^3 - 4(1)^2 - (1) + 4 = 1$

$(2x^3 - 4x^2 - x + 4) \div (x - 1)$ has remainder 1.

5.
$$
\begin{array}{rrrrr|r}
1 & 1 & 1 & -2 & -3 & \underline{-1} \\
  & -1 & 0 & -1 & 3 & \\
\hline
1 & 0 & 1 & -3 & 0, &
\end{array}
$$
remainder $= 0$, therefore $x + 1$ is a factor of $x^4 + x^3 + x^2 - 2x - 3$

9.
$$
\begin{array}{rrrr|r}
1 & 3 & 6 & 1 & \underline{1} \\
  & 1 & 4 & 10 & \\
\hline
1 & 4 & 10 & 11 &
\end{array}
$$

$(x^3 + 3x^2 + 6x + 1) \div (x - 1)$

$\qquad = (x^2 + 4x + 10) + \dfrac{11}{x - 1}$

13.
$$
\begin{array}{rrrrr|r}
1 & -2 & -3 & -4 & -8 & \underline{-1} \\
  & -1 & 3 & 0 & 4 & \\
\hline
1 & -3 & 0 & -4 & -4 &
\end{array}
$$

$(x^4 - 2x^3 - 3x^2 - 4x - 8) \div (x + 1)$

$\qquad = x^3 - 3x^2 - 4 + \dfrac{-4}{x + 1}$

17.
$$
\begin{array}{rrrr|r}
1 & 5 & 0 & -6 & \underline{-3} \\
  & -3 & -6 & 18 & \\
\hline
1 & 2 & -6 & 12, &
\end{array}
$$
remainder $= 12$, therefore

-3 is not a root of $y^3 + 5y^2 - 6 = 0$

21.
$$
\begin{array}{rrrr|r}
1 & 8 & 17 & 6 & \underline{-3} \\
  & -3 & -15 & -6 & \\
\hline
1 & 5 & 2 & 0 &
\end{array}
$$

$x^3 + 8x^2 + 17x + 6 = (x + 3)(x^2 + 5x + 2)$

$x^2 + 5x + 2$ has roots $= \dfrac{-5 \pm \sqrt{5^2 - 4(1)(2)}}{2(1)} = \dfrac{-5 \pm \sqrt{17}}{2}$

roots: $-3,\ \dfrac{-5 \pm \sqrt{17}}{2}$

25.
$$
\begin{array}{rrrrr|r}
4 & 0 & -1 & -18 & 9 & \underline{\frac{1}{2}} \\
  & 2 & 1 & 0 & -9 & \\
\hline
4 & 2 & 0 & -18 & 0 &
\end{array}
$$

$4p^4 - p^2 - 18p + 9 = \left(p - \dfrac{1}{2}\right)(4p^3 + 2p^2 - 18)$

$$
\begin{array}{rrrr|r}
4 & 2 & 0 & -18 & \underline{\frac{3}{2}} \\
  & 6 & 12 & 18 & \\
\hline
4 & 8 & 12 & 0 &
\end{array}
$$

$4p^4 - p^2 - 18p + 9 = \left(p - \dfrac{1}{2}\right)\left(p - \dfrac{3}{2}\right)(4p^2 + 8p + 12) = 4\left(p - \dfrac{1}{2}\right)\left(p - \dfrac{3}{2}\right)(p^2 + 2p + 3)$

$p^2 + 2p + 3$ has roots $= -1 \pm \sqrt{2}j$

roots $\dfrac{1}{2}, \dfrac{3}{2}, -1 \pm \sqrt{2}j$

29.

$$
\begin{array}{rrrrrr|r}
1 & 3 & -1 & -11 & -12 & -4 & \underline{-1} \\
  & -1 & -2 & 3 & 8 & 4 & \\
\hline
1 & 2 & -3 & -8 & -4 & 0 &
\end{array}
$$

$$x^5 + 3x^4 - x^3 - 11x^2 - 12x - 4 = (x+1)(x^4 + 2x^3 - 3x^2 - 8x - 4)$$

$$
\begin{array}{rrrrr|r}
1 & 2 & -3 & -8 & -4 & \underline{-1} \\
  & -1 & -1 & 4 & 4 & \\
\hline
1 & 1 & -4 & -4 & 0 &
\end{array}
$$

$$x^5 + 3x^4 - x^3 - 11x^2 - 12x - 4 = (x+1)(x+1)(x^3 + x^2 - 4x - 4)$$

$$
\begin{array}{rrrr|r}
1 & 1 & -4 & -4 & \underline{-1} \\
  & -1 & 0 & 4 & \\
\hline
1 & 0 & -4 & 0 &
\end{array}
$$

$$x^5 + 3x^4 - 11x^3 - 11x^2 - 4 = (x+1)(x+1)(x+1)(x^2 - 4)$$
$$= (x+1)(x+1)(x+1)(x+2)(x-2)$$

roots: $-1, -1, -1, 2, -2$

33. $x^3 + x^2 - 10x + 8 = 0$ has three roots.

Possible rational roots $= \dfrac{\pm 1, \ \pm 2, \ \pm 4, \ \pm 8}{\pm 1}$

$$
\begin{array}{rrrr|r}
1 & 1 & -10 & 8 & \underline{1} \\
  & 1 & 2 & -8 & \\
\hline
1 & 2 & -8 & 0, & \text{1 is a root}
\end{array}
$$

$$x^3 + x^2 - 10x + 8 = (x-1)(x^2 + 2x - 8)$$
$$= (x-1)(x+4)(x-2)$$

roots: $1, -4, 2$

37. $6x^3 - x^2 - 12x - 5 = 0$ has three roots.

Possible rational roots $= \dfrac{\pm 1, \ \pm 5}{\pm 1, \ \pm 2, \ \pm 3, \ \pm 6}$

$$
\begin{array}{rrrr|r}
6 & -1 & -12 & -5 & \underline{\frac{5}{3}} \\
  & 10 & 15 & 5 & \\
\hline
6 & 9 & 3 & 0, & \frac{5}{3} \text{ is a root}
\end{array}
$$

$$6x^3 - x^2 - 12x - 5 = \left(x - \frac{5}{3}\right)(6x^2 + 9x + 3)$$

$$= 3\left(x - \frac{5}{3}\right)(2x^2 + 3x + 1)$$

$$= 3\left(x - \frac{5}{3}\right)(2x+1)(x+1)$$

roots: $\dfrac{5}{3}, \dfrac{-1}{2}, -1$

41. A polynomial of degree five with real coefficients has five zeros. Since the complex zeros occur in conjugate pairs, the possibilities are: real 5, complex 0; real 3, complex 2; and real 1, complex 4.

45.

$$
\begin{array}{cccc|}
3 & k & -8 & -8 \\
 & -6 & 12-2k & -8+4k \\
\hline
3 & -6+k & 4-2k & -16+4k \\
\end{array}
\quad \underline{-2}
$$

$$
\begin{aligned}
\text{remainder} = 4k - 16 &= 0 \\
4k &= 16 \\
k &= 4
\end{aligned}
$$

49. From the calculator, $x = 1.91$ is the irrational root between 1 and 2.

None of the possible rational roots $= \dfrac{\text{factors of 2}}{\text{factors of 3}} = \dfrac{\pm 1,\ \pm 2}{\pm 1,\ \pm 3}$ is a root.

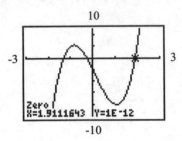

53. $f(d) = 64d^3 - 144d^2 + 108d - 27$ has $n = 3$ and therefore three roots at most. $f(d)$ has three sign changes and therefore at most three positive roots.

$f(-d) = -64d^3 - 144d^2 + 108d - 27$ has sign changes and therefore no negative roots.

Possible rational roots $= \dfrac{\text{factors of 27}}{\text{factors of 64}} = \dfrac{\pm 1,\ \pm 3,\ \pm 9,\ \pm 27}{\pm 1,\ \pm 2,\ \pm 4,\ \pm 8,\ \pm 16,\ \pm 32,\ \pm 64}$

From the graph, the root is between 0 and 1.

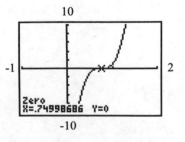

$$
\begin{array}{cccc|}
64 & -144 & 108 & -27 \\
 & 48 & -72 & 27 \\
\hline
64 & -96 & 36 & 0, \\
\end{array}
\quad \underline{\tfrac{3}{4}}
$$

$\tfrac{3}{4}$ is a repeated (multiplicity $= 3$) root.

$d = 0.75$ cm

57. $h = r + 3.2$, h and $r > 0$.

$V = \pi r^2 h = \pi r^2(r + 3.2) = \pi r^3 + 3.2\pi r^2 = 680$

$\pi r^3 + 3.2\pi r^2 - 680 = 0$ has one sign change and therefore one positive root. From the graph $r = 5.1$ m and $h = 5.1 + 3.2 = 8.3$ m.

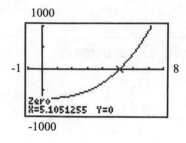

61. Perform synthetic division of $x^4 + r^4$ by $x + r$ for $n = 1, 2, 3, 4, 5$

$n = 1$

$$
\begin{array}{r|r}
1 \quad r & \underline{-r} \\
-r & \\
\hline
1 \quad 0, & x + r \text{ is a factor of } x + r
\end{array}
$$

$n = 2$

$$
\begin{array}{r|r}
1 \quad 0 \quad r^2 & \underline{-r} \\
-r \quad r^2 & \\
\hline
1 \quad -r \quad 2r^2, & x + r \text{ is not a factor of } x^2 + r^2
\end{array}
$$

$n - 3$

$$
\begin{array}{r|r}
1 \quad 0 \quad 0 \quad r^3 & \underline{-r} \qquad (x^3 + r^3) \div (x + r) \\
-r \quad r^2 \quad -r^3 & \\
\hline
1 \quad -r \quad r^2 \quad 0 & x + r \text{ is a factor of } x^3 + r^3
\end{array}
$$

$n = 4$

$$
\begin{array}{r|r}
1 \quad 0 \quad 0 \quad 0 \quad r^4 & \underline{-r} \qquad (x^4 + r^4) \div (x + r) \\
-r \quad r^2 \quad -r^3 \quad r^4 & \\
\hline
1 \quad -r \quad r^2 \quad -r^3 \quad 2r^4, & x + r \text{ is not a factor of } x^4 + r^4
\end{array}
$$

$n = 5$

$$
\begin{array}{r|r}
1 \quad 0 \quad 0 \quad 0 \quad 0 \quad r^5 & \underline{-r} \qquad (x^5 + r^5) \div (x + r) \\
-r \quad r^2 \quad -r^3 \quad r^4 \quad -r^5 & \\
\hline
1 \quad -r \quad r^2 \quad -r^3 \quad r^4 \quad 0, & x + r \text{ is a factor of } x^5 + r^5
\end{array}
$$

Apparently, $x + r$ is a factor of $x^n + r^n$ for $n = 1, 3, 5, 7, \cdots$.

MATRICES

16.1 Definitions and Basic Operations

1. $\begin{bmatrix} 8 & 1 & -5 & 9 \\ 0 & -2 & 3 & 7 \end{bmatrix} + \begin{bmatrix} -3 & 6 & 4 & 0 \\ 6 & 6 & -2 & 5 \end{bmatrix} = \begin{bmatrix} 8+(-3) & 1+6 & -5+4 & 9+0 \\ 0+6 & -2+6 & 3+(-2) & 7+5 \end{bmatrix} = \begin{bmatrix} 5 & 7 & -1 & 9 \\ 6 & 4 & 1 & 12 \end{bmatrix}$

5. $\begin{bmatrix} x & 2y & z \\ \frac{r}{4} & -s & -5t \end{bmatrix} = \begin{bmatrix} -2 & 10 & -9 \\ 12 & -4 & 5 \end{bmatrix}$

$x = -2, \quad 2y = 10, \quad z = -9$

$\qquad\qquad y = 5,$

$\dfrac{r}{4} = 12, \quad -s = -4, \quad -5t = 5$

$r = 48 \qquad s = 4 \qquad t = -1$

9. $\begin{bmatrix} x-3 & x+y \\ x-z & y+z \\ x+t & y-t \end{bmatrix} = \begin{bmatrix} 5 & 3 \\ 4 & -1 \end{bmatrix}$

13. $\begin{bmatrix} 50+(-55) & -82+82 \\ -34+45 & 57+14 \\ -15+26 & 62+(-67) \end{bmatrix} = \begin{bmatrix} -5 & 0 \\ 11 & 71 \\ 11 & -5 \end{bmatrix}$

17. The matrices are of different dimensions and cannot be added.

21. $A - 2B = \begin{bmatrix} -1-2 & 4-10 & -7+12 & 0-6 \\ 2-8 & -6+2 & -1-16 & 2+4 \end{bmatrix} = \begin{bmatrix} -3 & -6 & 5 & -6 \\ -6 & -4 & -17 & 6 \end{bmatrix}$

25. $-G - A = -\begin{bmatrix} 3 & -6 & 9 \\ -4 & 1 & 2 \end{bmatrix} - \begin{bmatrix} -1 & 4 & -7 & 0 \\ 2 & -6 & -1 & 2 \end{bmatrix}$

Cannot subtract, matrices have different dimensions.

29. $-(A-B) = -\begin{bmatrix} -1-4 & 2+1 & 3+3 & 7-0 \\ 0-5 & -3-0 & -1+1 & 4-1 \\ 9-1 & -1-11 & 0-8 & -2-2 \end{bmatrix} = \begin{bmatrix} 5 & -3 & -6 & -7 \\ 5 & 3 & 0 & -3 \\ -8 & 12 & 8 & 4 \end{bmatrix}$

$\qquad B - A = \begin{bmatrix} 4+1 & -1-2 & -3-3 & 0-7 \\ 5-0 & 0+3 & -1+1 & 1-4 \\ 1-9 & 11+1 & 8-0 & 2+2 \end{bmatrix} = \begin{bmatrix} 5 & -3 & -6 & -7 \\ 5 & 3 & 0 & -3 \\ -8 & 12 & 8 & 4 \end{bmatrix}$

33. Build 2 additional identical developments:

$\begin{pmatrix} 8 & 6 & 0 & 0 \\ 5 & 4 & 3 & 0 \\ 0 & 3 & 5 & 6 \end{pmatrix} + 2\begin{pmatrix} 8 & 6 & 0 & 0 \\ 5 & 4 & 3 & 0 \\ 0 & 3 & 5 & 6 \end{pmatrix} = 3\begin{pmatrix} 8 & 6 & 0 & 0 \\ 5 & 4 & 3 & 0 \\ 0 & 3 & 5 & 6 \end{pmatrix} = \begin{pmatrix} 24 & 18 & 0 & 0 \\ 15 & 12 & 9 & 0 \\ 0 & 9 & 15 & 18 \end{pmatrix}$

16.2   Multiplication of Matrices

1. $A = \begin{bmatrix} 1 & 2 \\ 0 & -3 \\ 2 & 1 \end{bmatrix}, B = \begin{bmatrix} -1 & 6 & 5 & -2 \\ 3 & 0 & 1 & -4 \end{bmatrix}$

$AB = \begin{bmatrix} 1 & 2 \\ 0 & -3 \\ 2 & 1 \end{bmatrix} \begin{bmatrix} -1 & 6 & 5 & -2 \\ 3 & 0 & 1 & -4 \end{bmatrix}$

$AB = \begin{bmatrix} (1)(-1)+(2)(3) & (1)(6)+(2)(0) & (1)(5)+(2)(1) & (1)(-2)+(2)(-4) \\ (0)(-1)+(-3)(3) & (0)(6)+(-3)(0) & (0)(5)+(-3)(1) & (0)(-2)+(-3)(-4) \\ (2)(-1)+(1)(3) & (2)(6)+(1)(0) & (2)(5)+(1)(1) & (2)(-2)+(1)(-4) \end{bmatrix}$

$AB = \begin{bmatrix} 5 & 6 & 7 & -10 \\ -9 & 0 & -3 & 12 \\ 1 & 12 & 11 & -8 \end{bmatrix}$

5. $\begin{bmatrix} 2 & -3 & 1 \\ 0 & 7 & -3 \end{bmatrix} \begin{bmatrix} 9 \\ -2 \\ 5 \end{bmatrix} = \begin{bmatrix} 2(9)+(-3)(-2)+1(5) \\ 0(9)+7(-2)+(-3)(5) \end{bmatrix} = \begin{bmatrix} 29 \\ -29 \end{bmatrix}$

9. $\begin{bmatrix} -1 & 7 \\ 3 & 5 \\ 10 & -1 \\ -5 & 12 \end{bmatrix} \begin{bmatrix} 2 & 1 \\ 5 & -3 \end{bmatrix} = \begin{bmatrix} -1(2)+7(5) & -1(1)+7(-3) \\ 3(2)+5(5) & 3(1)+5(-3) \\ 10(2)+(-1)(5) & 10(1)+(-1)(-3) \\ -5(2)+12(5) & -5(1)+12(-3) \end{bmatrix} = \begin{bmatrix} 33 & -22 \\ 31 & -12 \\ 15 & 13 \\ 50 & -41 \end{bmatrix}$

13.

```
[A]
[[-9.2 2.3  .5...
 [-3.8 -2.4 9.2...
[B]
  [[6.5  -5.2]
   [4.9  1.7 ]
   [-1.8 6.9 ]]
```

```
[A][B]
[[-49.43 55.2 ]
 [-53.02 79.16]]
■
```

17. $AB = \begin{bmatrix} -1 & 2 & 3 \\ 5 & -1 & 0 \end{bmatrix} \begin{bmatrix} 1 \\ -5 \\ 2 \end{bmatrix} = \begin{bmatrix} -1(1)+2(-5)+3(2) \\ 5(1)+(-1)(-5)+0(2) \end{bmatrix} = \begin{bmatrix} -5 \\ 10 \end{bmatrix}$

BA is not defined. B has 1 column; A has 2 rows.

21. $AI = \begin{bmatrix} 1 & 3 & -5 \\ 2 & 0 & 1 \\ 1 & -2 & 4 \end{bmatrix} \begin{bmatrix} 1 & 0 & 0 \\ 0 & 1 & 0 \\ 0 & 0 & 1 \end{bmatrix} = \begin{bmatrix} 1(1)+3(0)+(-5)(0) & 1(0)+3(1)+(-5)(0) & 1(0)+3(0)+(-5)(1) \\ 2(1)+0(0)+1(0) & 2(0)+0(1)+1(0) & 2(0)+0(0)+1(1) \\ 1(1)+(-2)(0)+4(0) & 1(0)+(-2)(1)+4(0) & 1(0)+(-2)(0)+4(1) \end{bmatrix}$

$= \begin{bmatrix} 1 & 3 & -5 \\ 2 & 0 & 1 \\ 1 & -2 & 4 \end{bmatrix}$

$IA = \begin{bmatrix} 1 & 0 & 0 \\ 0 & 1 & 0 \\ 0 & 0 & 1 \end{bmatrix} \begin{bmatrix} 1 & 3 & -5 \\ 2 & 0 & 1 \\ 1 & -2 & 4 \end{bmatrix} = \begin{bmatrix} 1(1)+0(2)+0(1) & 1(3)+0(0)+0(-2) & 1(-5)+0(1)+0(4) \\ 0(1)+1(2)+0(1) & 0(3)+1(0)+0(-2) & 0(-5)+1(1)+0(4) \\ 0(1)+0(2)+1(1) & 0(3)+0(0)+1(-2) & 0(-5)+0(1)+1(4) \end{bmatrix}$

$= \begin{bmatrix} 1 & 3 & -5 \\ 2 & 0 & 1 \\ 1 & -2 & 4 \end{bmatrix}$

Therefore, $AI = IA = A$

25. $AB = \begin{bmatrix} 1 & -2 & 3 \\ 2 & -5 & 7 \\ -1 & 3 & -5 \end{bmatrix} \begin{bmatrix} 4 & -1 & 1 \\ 3 & -2 & -1 \\ 1 & -1 & -1 \end{bmatrix}$

$= \begin{bmatrix} 1(4)+(-2)(3)+3(1) & 1(-1)+(-2)(-2)+3(-1) & 1(1)+(-2)(-1)+3(-1) \\ 2(4)+(-5)(3)+7(1) & 2(-1)+(-5)(-2)+7(-1) & 2(1)+(-5)(-1)+7(-1) \\ -1(4)+3(3)+(-5)(1) & -1(-1)+3(-2)+(-5)(-1) & -1(1)+3(-1)+(-5)(-1) \end{bmatrix}$

$= \begin{bmatrix} 1 & 0 & 0 \\ 0 & 1 & 0 \\ 0 & 0 & 1 \end{bmatrix}$

Therefore, $B = A^{-1}$ since $AB = I$

29. $\begin{bmatrix} 3 & 1 & 2 \\ 1 & -3 & 4 \\ 2 & 2 & 1 \end{bmatrix} \begin{bmatrix} -1 \\ 2 \\ 1 \end{bmatrix} = \begin{bmatrix} 3(-1)+1(2)+2(1) \\ 1(-1)+(-3)(2)+4(1) \\ 2(-1)+2(2)+1(1) \end{bmatrix} \neq \begin{bmatrix} 1 \\ -3 \\ 1 \end{bmatrix}$; A is not the proper matrix of solution

values.

33. $A^2 = \begin{bmatrix} 2 & 4 \\ 3 & 5 \end{bmatrix} \begin{bmatrix} 2 & 4 \\ 3 & 5 \end{bmatrix} = \begin{bmatrix} 2(2)+4(3) & 2(4)+4(5) \\ 3(2)+5(3) & 3(4)+5(5) \end{bmatrix} = \begin{bmatrix} 16 & 28 \\ 21 & 37 \end{bmatrix}$

$A^2 - I = \begin{bmatrix} 16 & 28 \\ 21 & 37 \end{bmatrix} - \begin{bmatrix} 1 & 0 \\ 0 & 1 \end{bmatrix} = \begin{bmatrix} 16-1 & 28-0 \\ 21-0 & 37-1 \end{bmatrix} = \begin{bmatrix} 15 & 28 \\ 21 & 36 \end{bmatrix}$

$A + I = \begin{bmatrix} 2+1 & 4+0 \\ 3+0 & 5+1 \end{bmatrix} = \begin{bmatrix} 3 & 4 \\ 3 & 6 \end{bmatrix}$

$A - I = \begin{bmatrix} 2-1 & 4-0 \\ 3-0 & 5-1 \end{bmatrix} - \begin{bmatrix} 1 & 4 \\ 3 & 4 \end{bmatrix}$

$(A+I)(A-I) = \begin{bmatrix} 3 & 4 \\ 3 & 6 \end{bmatrix} \begin{bmatrix} 1 & 4 \\ 3 & 4 \end{bmatrix} = \begin{bmatrix} 3(1)+4(3) & 3(4)+4(4) \\ 3(1)+6(3) & 3(4)+6(4) \end{bmatrix} = \begin{bmatrix} 15 & 28 \\ 21 & 36 \end{bmatrix}$

Therefore, $A^2 - I = (A+I)(A-I)$

37. $\begin{bmatrix} v_2 \\ i_2 \end{bmatrix} = \begin{bmatrix} 1 & 0 \\ -\frac{1}{R} & 1 \end{bmatrix} \begin{bmatrix} v_1 \\ i_1 \end{bmatrix}$

$\begin{bmatrix} v_2 \\ i_2 \end{bmatrix} = \begin{bmatrix} 1(v_1) + 0(i_1) \\ -\frac{1}{R}(v_1) + 1(i_1) \end{bmatrix}$

$v_2 = v_1$

$i_2 = -v_1/R + i_1$

16.3   Finding the Inverse of a Matrix

1. $A = \begin{bmatrix} 2 & -3 \\ 4 & -5 \end{bmatrix}$

$\det A = 2(-5) - (-3)(4) = -10 + 12 = 2$

$A^{-1} = \frac{1}{2} \begin{bmatrix} -5 & 3 \\ -4 & 2 \end{bmatrix} = \begin{bmatrix} -\frac{5}{2} & \frac{3}{2} \\ -2 & 1 \end{bmatrix}$

Check: $AA^{-1} = \begin{bmatrix} 2 & -3 \\ 4 & -5 \end{bmatrix} \begin{bmatrix} -\frac{5}{2} & \frac{3}{2} \\ -2 & 1 \end{bmatrix} = \begin{bmatrix} 1 & 0 \\ 0 & 1 \end{bmatrix}$

5. $\begin{bmatrix} -1 & 5 \\ 4 & 10 \end{bmatrix}$ Interchange the elements of the principal diagonal $\begin{bmatrix} 10 & -5 \\ -4 & -1 \end{bmatrix}$
and change the signs of the off-diagonal elements.

Find the determinant of the original matrix. $\begin{vmatrix} -1 & 5 \\ 4 & 10 \end{vmatrix} = -30$

Divide each element of the second matrix by -30. $-\frac{1}{30} \begin{bmatrix} 10 & -5 \\ -4 & -1 \end{bmatrix} = \begin{bmatrix} -\frac{1}{3} & \frac{1}{6} \\ \frac{2}{15} & \frac{1}{30} \end{bmatrix}$

9. $\begin{bmatrix} -50 & -45 \\ 26 & 80 \end{bmatrix}$ Interchange the elements of the principal diagonal $\begin{bmatrix} 80 & 45 \\ -26 & -50 \end{bmatrix}$
and change the signs of the off-diagonal elements.

Find the determinant of the original matrix. $\begin{vmatrix} -50 & -45 \\ 26 & 80 \end{vmatrix} = -2830$

Divide each element of the second matrix by -2830. $-\frac{1}{2830} \begin{bmatrix} 80 & 45 \\ -26 & -50 \end{bmatrix} = \begin{bmatrix} -\frac{8}{283} & -\frac{9}{566} \\ \frac{13}{1415} & \frac{5}{283} \end{bmatrix}$

13. $\begin{bmatrix} 2 & 4 & | & 1 & 0 \\ -1 & -1 & | & 0 & 1 \end{bmatrix}$ $R1 \rightarrow R1 + R2$ $\begin{bmatrix} 1 & 3 & | & 1 & 1 \\ -1 & -1 & | & 0 & 1 \end{bmatrix}$ $R2 \rightarrow R2 + R1$

$\begin{bmatrix} 1 & 3 & | & 1 & 1 \\ 0 & 2 & | & 1 & 2 \end{bmatrix}$ $R2 \rightarrow \frac{1}{2}R2$ $\begin{bmatrix} 1 & 3 & | & 1 & 1 \\ 0 & 1 & | & \frac{1}{2} & 1 \end{bmatrix}$ $R1 \rightarrow R1 - 3R2$ $\begin{bmatrix} 1 & 0 & | & -\frac{1}{2} & -2 \\ 0 & 1 & | & \frac{1}{2} & 1 \end{bmatrix}$;

$A^{-1} = \begin{bmatrix} -\frac{1}{2} & -2 \\ \frac{1}{2} & 1 \end{bmatrix}$

17. $\begin{bmatrix} 2 & -1 & | & 1 & 0 \\ 4 & 6 & | & 0 & 1 \end{bmatrix}$ $R1 \to \frac{1}{2}R1$ $\begin{bmatrix} 1 & \frac{-1}{2} & | & \frac{1}{2} & 0 \\ 4 & 6 & | & 0 & 1 \end{bmatrix}$ $R2 \to R2 - 4R1$

$\begin{bmatrix} 1 & \frac{-1}{2} & | & \frac{1}{2} & 0 \\ 0 & 8 & | & -2 & 1 \end{bmatrix}$ $R2 \to \frac{1}{8}R2$ $\begin{bmatrix} 1 & \frac{-1}{2} & | & \frac{1}{2} & 0 \\ 0 & 1 & | & \frac{-1}{4} & \frac{1}{8} \end{bmatrix}$ $R1 \to R1 + \frac{1}{2}R2$ $\begin{bmatrix} 1 & 0 & | & \frac{3}{8} & \frac{1}{16} \\ 0 & 1 & | & \frac{-1}{4} & \frac{1}{8} \end{bmatrix}$

$A^{-1} = \begin{bmatrix} \frac{3}{8} & \frac{1}{16} \\ \frac{-1}{4} & \frac{1}{8} \end{bmatrix}$

21. $\begin{bmatrix} 1 & 3 & 2 & | & 1 & 0 & 0 \\ -2 & -5 & -1 & | & 0 & 1 & 0 \\ 2 & 4 & 0 & | & 0 & 0 & 1 \end{bmatrix}$ $\begin{array}{l} R2 \to 2R1 + R2 \\ R3 \to -2R1 + R3 \end{array}$ $\begin{bmatrix} 1 & 3 & 2 & | & 1 & 0 & 0 \\ 0 & 1 & 3 & | & 2 & 1 & 0 \\ 0 & -2 & -4 & | & -2 & 0 & 1 \end{bmatrix}$ $\begin{array}{l} R1 \to -3R2 + R1 \\ R3 \to 2R2 + R3 \end{array}$

$\begin{bmatrix} 1 & 0 & -7 & | & -5 & -3 & 0 \\ 0 & 1 & 3 & | & 2 & 1 & 0 \\ 0 & 0 & 2 & | & 2 & 2 & 1 \end{bmatrix}$ $R3 \to \frac{1}{2}R3$ $\begin{bmatrix} 1 & 0 & -7 & | & -5 & -3 & 0 \\ 0 & 1 & 3 & | & 2 & 1 & 0 \\ 0 & 0 & 1 & | & 1 & 1 & \frac{1}{2} \end{bmatrix}$ $\begin{array}{l} R2 \to -3R3 + R2 \\ R1 \to 7R3 + R1 \end{array}$

$\begin{bmatrix} 1 & 0 & 0 & | & 2 & 4 & \frac{7}{2} \\ 0 & 1 & 0 & | & -1 & -2 & \frac{-3}{2} \\ 0 & 0 & 1 & | & 1 & 1 & \frac{1}{2} \end{bmatrix}$ $; A^{-1} = \begin{bmatrix} 2 & 4 & \frac{7}{2} \\ -1 & -2 & \frac{-3}{2} \\ 1 & 1 & \frac{1}{2} \end{bmatrix}$

25.

```
[A]
        [[2  8]
         [-1 6]]
[A]⁻¹▶Frac
   [[3/10 -2/5]
    [1/20 1/10]]
```

29.

```
[A]
      [[2  4  0 ]
       [3  4  -2]
       [-1 1  2 ]]
```

```
              [[2  4  0 ]
               [3  4  -2]
               [-1 1  2 ]]
[A]⁻¹
  [[2.5   -2    -2]
   [-1    1     1 ]
   [1.75  -1.5  -1]]
```

33.

```
[A]
[[.2  1.2  -.8…
 [-.4 3    -1.6…
 [1   -2.4 3.2 …
 [-.1 .4   0   …
```

```
[A]
…1.2  -.8  -.5]
…3    -1.6 .4 ]
…-2.4 3.2  1.5]
….4   0    3  ]]
```

```
[A]⁻¹
[[2.538   -.950 …
 [-.213   .687  …
 [-1.006  .870  …
 [.113    -.123 …
```

```
[A]⁻¹
…0  .159   .470 ]
…   .290   -.272]
…   .496   -.532]
…3  -.033  .385 ]]
```

$A^{-1} = \begin{bmatrix} 2.538 & -0.950 & 0.159 & 0.470 \\ -0.213 & 0.687 & 0.290 & -0.272 \\ -1.006 & 0.870 & 0.496 & -0.532 \\ 0.113 & -0.123 & -0.033 & 0.385 \end{bmatrix}$

37.
$$\frac{1}{ad-bc} \cdot \begin{bmatrix} a & b \\ c & d \end{bmatrix} \cdot \begin{bmatrix} d & -b \\ -c & a \end{bmatrix} = \frac{1}{ad-bc} \cdot \begin{bmatrix} ad-bc & -ab+ab \\ cd-cd & -bc+ad \end{bmatrix}$$

$$\frac{1}{ad-bc} \cdot \begin{bmatrix} ad-bc & 0 \\ 0 & ad-bc \end{bmatrix} = \begin{bmatrix} \frac{ad-bc}{ad-bc} & \frac{0}{ad-bc} \\ \frac{0}{ad-bc} & \frac{ad-bc}{ad-bc} \end{bmatrix} = \begin{bmatrix} 1 & 0 \\ 0 & 1 \end{bmatrix}$$

16.4   Matrices and Linear Equations

1. $2x - y = 7$
$5x - 3y = 19$

$$A = \begin{bmatrix} 2 & -1 \\ 5 & -3 \end{bmatrix}, C = \begin{bmatrix} 7 \\ 19 \end{bmatrix}, A^{-1} \begin{bmatrix} 3 & -1 \\ 5 & -2 \end{bmatrix}$$

$$A^{-1}C = \begin{bmatrix} 3 & -1 \\ 5 & -2 \end{bmatrix} \begin{bmatrix} 7 \\ 19 \end{bmatrix} = \begin{bmatrix} 2 \\ -3 \end{bmatrix} = \begin{bmatrix} x \\ y \end{bmatrix}$$

$x = 2, y = -3$ is the solution.

5. $x + 2y = 7$
$2x + 3y = 11$

$$A = \begin{bmatrix} 1 & 2 \\ 2 & 3 \end{bmatrix}, C = \begin{bmatrix} 7 \\ 11 \end{bmatrix}, A^{-1} = \begin{bmatrix} -3 & 2 \\ 2 & -1 \end{bmatrix}$$

$$A^{-1}C = \begin{bmatrix} -3 & 2 \\ 2 & -1 \end{bmatrix} \begin{bmatrix} 7 \\ 11 \end{bmatrix} = \begin{bmatrix} 1 \\ 3 \end{bmatrix} = \begin{bmatrix} x \\ y \end{bmatrix}$$

$x = 1, y = 3$ is the solution.

9. $C = \begin{bmatrix} 5 \\ -1 \\ -2 \end{bmatrix}$

$$A^{-1} = \begin{bmatrix} 2 & 4 & \frac{7}{2} \\ -1 & -2 & -\frac{3}{2} \\ 1 & 1 & \frac{1}{2} \end{bmatrix}; A^{-1}C = \begin{bmatrix} 2 & 4 & \frac{7}{2} \\ -1 & -2 & -\frac{3}{2} \\ 1 & 1 & \frac{1}{2} \end{bmatrix} \begin{bmatrix} 5 \\ -1 \\ -2 \end{bmatrix} = \begin{bmatrix} 10-4-7 \\ -5+2+3 \\ 5-1-1 \end{bmatrix} = \begin{bmatrix} -1 \\ 0 \\ 3 \end{bmatrix}$$

$x = -1, y = 0, z = 3$

13. $A = \begin{bmatrix} 2.5 & 2.8 \\ 3.5 & -1.6 \end{bmatrix}; C = \begin{bmatrix} -3.0 \\ 9.6 \end{bmatrix}; \begin{vmatrix} 2.5 & 2.8 \\ 3.5 & -1.6 \end{vmatrix} = -4 - 9.8 = -13.8; A^{-1} = -\frac{1}{13.8} \begin{bmatrix} -1.6 & -2.8 \\ -3.5 & 2.5 \end{bmatrix}$

$$A^{-1}C = -\frac{1}{13.8} \begin{bmatrix} -1.6 & -2.8 \\ -3.5 & 2.5 \end{bmatrix} \begin{bmatrix} -3.0 \\ 9.6 \end{bmatrix} = -\frac{1}{13.8} \begin{bmatrix} -22.08 \\ 34.5 \end{bmatrix} = \begin{bmatrix} -0.348+1.949 \\ -0.762-1.74 \end{bmatrix} = \begin{bmatrix} 1.6 \\ -2.5 \end{bmatrix}$$

$x = 1.6, y = -2.5$

17. $A = \begin{bmatrix} 2 & 4 & 1 \\ -2 & -2 & -1 \\ -1 & 2 & 1 \end{bmatrix}$; $C = \begin{bmatrix} 5 \\ -6 \\ 0 \end{bmatrix}$. To find A^{-1}: $\left[\begin{array}{ccc|ccc} 2 & 4 & 1 & 1 & 0 & 0 \\ -2 & -2 & -1 & 0 & 1 & 0 \\ -1 & 2 & 1 & 0 & 0 & 1 \end{array}\right]$ $\begin{array}{l} R1 \to \frac{1}{2}R1 \\ R2 \to R2 + R1 \\ R3 \to R3 + \frac{1}{2}R1 \end{array}$

$\left[\begin{array}{ccc|ccc} 1 & 2 & \frac{1}{2} & \frac{1}{2} & 0 & 0 \\ 0 & 2 & 0 & 1 & 1 & 0 \\ 0 & 4 & \frac{3}{2} & \frac{1}{2} & 0 & 1 \end{array}\right]$ $\begin{array}{l} R1 \to R1 - R2 \\ R2 \to \frac{1}{2}R2 \\ R3 \to R3 - 2R2 \end{array}$ $\left[\begin{array}{ccc|ccc} 1 & 0 & \frac{1}{2} & \frac{1}{2} & -1 & 0 \\ 0 & 1 & 0 & \frac{1}{2} & \frac{1}{2} & 0 \\ 0 & 0 & \frac{3}{2} & -\frac{3}{2} & -2 & 1 \end{array}\right]$ $\begin{array}{l} R1 \to R1 - \frac{1}{3}R3 \\ \\ R3 \to \frac{2}{3}R3 \end{array}$

$\left[\begin{array}{ccc|ccc} 1 & 0 & 0 & 0 & -\frac{1}{3} & -\frac{1}{3} \\ 0 & 1 & 0 & 0.5 & 0.5 & 0 \\ 0 & 0 & 1 & -1 & -\frac{4}{3} & \frac{2}{3} \end{array}\right]$

$A^{-1}C = \begin{bmatrix} 0 & -\frac{1}{3} & -\frac{1}{3} \\ \frac{1}{2} & \frac{1}{2} & 0 \\ -1 & -\frac{4}{3} & \frac{2}{3} \end{bmatrix} \begin{bmatrix} 5 \\ -6 \\ 0 \end{bmatrix} = \begin{bmatrix} 2 \\ 2.5 - 3 \\ -5 + 8 \end{bmatrix} = \begin{bmatrix} 2 \\ -\frac{1}{2} \\ 3 \end{bmatrix}$; $x = 2, y = -\frac{1}{2}, z = 3$

21. $\begin{bmatrix} u \\ v \\ w \end{bmatrix} = \begin{bmatrix} 1 & -3 & -2 \\ 3 & 2 & 6 \\ 4 & -1 & 3 \end{bmatrix}^{-1} \begin{bmatrix} 9 \\ 20 \\ 25 \end{bmatrix} = \begin{bmatrix} -\frac{12}{11} & -1 & \frac{14}{11} \\ -\frac{15}{11} & -1 & \frac{12}{11} \\ 1 & 1 & -1 \end{bmatrix} \begin{bmatrix} 9 \\ 20 \\ 25 \end{bmatrix} = \begin{bmatrix} 2 \\ -5 \\ 4 \end{bmatrix}$ (inverse from calculator)

```
[A]
    [[1  -3 -2]
     [3  2  6 ]
     [4  -1 3 ]]
```
```
[B]
              [[2 ]
               [-5]
               [4 ]]
```
```
[A][B]
              [[9 ]
               [20]
               [25]]
```

25. $\begin{bmatrix} v \\ w \\ x \\ y \\ z \end{bmatrix} = \begin{bmatrix} 2 & 3 & 1 & -1 & -2 \\ 6 & -2 & -1 & 3 & -1 \\ 1 & 3 & -4 & 2 & 3 \\ 3 & -1 & -1 & 7 & 4 \\ 1 & 6 & 6 & -4 & -1 \end{bmatrix}^{-1} \begin{bmatrix} 6 \\ 21 \\ -9 \\ 5 \\ -4 \end{bmatrix} = \begin{bmatrix} -\frac{97}{427} & \frac{107}{427} & \frac{43}{427} & -\frac{40}{427} & \frac{8}{61} \\ \frac{358}{1281} & -\frac{166}{1281} & \frac{19}{427} & \frac{86}{1281} & -\frac{5}{183} \\ -\frac{46}{1281} & -\frac{79}{2562} & -\frac{117}{854} & \frac{257}{2562} & \frac{17}{183} \\ \frac{571}{1281} & -\frac{551}{2562} & -\frac{135}{854} & \frac{625}{2562} & -\frac{32}{183} \\ -\frac{703}{1281} & \frac{190}{1281} & \frac{76}{427} & -\frac{83}{1281} & \frac{41}{183} \end{bmatrix} \begin{bmatrix} 6 \\ 21 \\ -9 \\ 5 \\ -4 \end{bmatrix}$

$= \begin{bmatrix} 2 \\ -1 \\ \frac{1}{2} \\ \frac{3}{2} \\ -3 \end{bmatrix}$ (inverse from calculator)

```
[A]
[[2 3  1  -1 -2...
 [6 -2 -1 3  -1...
 [1 3  -4 2  3 ...
 [3 -1 -1 7  4 ...
 [1 6  6  -4 -1...
```
```
[B]►Frac
              [[2  ]
               [-1 ]
               [1/2]
               [3/2]
               [-3 ]]
■
```
```
[A][B]
              [[6 ]
               [21]
               [-9]
               [5 ]
               [-4]]
```

29. $\begin{bmatrix} A \\ B \end{bmatrix} = \begin{bmatrix} \sin 47.2° & \sin 64.4° \\ \cos 47.2° & -\cos 64.4° \end{bmatrix}^{-1} \begin{bmatrix} 254 \\ 0 \end{bmatrix} = \begin{bmatrix} 118 \\ 186 \end{bmatrix}$; $A = 118$ N, $B = 186$ N

$$A^{-1}C = \begin{bmatrix} \frac{5}{17} & \frac{6}{17} & \frac{5}{17} \\ \frac{2}{17} & -\frac{1}{17} & \frac{2}{17} \\ \frac{10}{17} & -\frac{5}{17} & -\frac{7}{17} \end{bmatrix} \begin{bmatrix} 0 \\ 6 \\ -3 \end{bmatrix}$$

$$= \begin{bmatrix} 0 + \frac{36}{17} - \frac{15}{17} \\ 0 - \frac{6}{17} - \frac{6}{17} \\ 0 - \frac{30}{17} + \frac{21}{17} \end{bmatrix};$$

$$I_A = \frac{21}{17}\text{ A}, I_B = -\frac{12}{17}\text{ A}, I_C = -\frac{9}{17}\text{ A}$$

Chapter 16 Review Exercises

1. $\begin{pmatrix} 2a \\ a-b \end{pmatrix} = \begin{pmatrix} 8 \\ 5 \end{pmatrix}$; $2a = 8$;

$a = 4$; $a - b = 5$; $4 - b = 5$; $b = -1$

5. $\begin{bmatrix} \cos \pi & \sin \frac{\pi}{6} \\ x+y & x-y \end{bmatrix} = \begin{bmatrix} x & y \\ a & b \end{bmatrix}$

$x = \cos \pi = -1, y = \sin \frac{\pi}{6} = \frac{1}{2}$

$a = x + y = -1 + \frac{1}{2} = -\frac{1}{2}$

$b = x - y = -1 - \frac{1}{2} = -\frac{3}{2}$

9. $B - A = \begin{bmatrix} -1 & 0 \\ 4 & -6 \\ -3 & -2 \\ 1 & -7 \end{bmatrix} - \begin{bmatrix} 2 & -3 \\ 4 & 1 \\ -5 & 0 \\ 2 & -3 \end{bmatrix} = \begin{bmatrix} -3 & 3 \\ 0 & -7 \\ 2 & -2 \\ -1 & -4 \end{bmatrix}$

13.

```
[A]
      [[2  -1]
       [-2  1 ]]
[B]
      [[1  -1]
       [2  -2]]
```

```
[A]*[B]
        [[0 0]
         [0 0]]
```

17. $\begin{pmatrix} 2 & -5 \\ 2 & -4 \end{pmatrix}$

Interchange the elements of the principal diagonal and change the signs of the off-diagonal elements.

$\begin{pmatrix} -4 & 5 \\ -2 & 2 \end{pmatrix}$

Find the determinant of the original matrix.

$\begin{vmatrix} 2 & -5 \\ 2 & -4 \end{vmatrix} = 2$

Divide each element of the second matrix by 2.

$\frac{1}{2} \begin{pmatrix} -4 & 5 \\ -2 & 2 \end{pmatrix} = \begin{pmatrix} -2 & \frac{5}{2} \\ -1 & 1 \end{pmatrix}$

21. ① $\left(\begin{array}{ccc|ccc} 1 & 1 & -2 & 1 & 0 & 0 \\ -1 & -2 & 1 & 0 & 1 & 0 \\ 0 & 3 & 4 & 0 & 0 & 1 \end{array}\right)$; ② $\left(\begin{array}{ccc|ccc} 1 & 1 & -2 & 1 & 0 & 0 \\ 0 & -1 & -1 & 1 & 1 & 0 \\ 0 & 3 & 4 & 0 & 0 & 1 \end{array}\right)$; ③ $\left(\begin{array}{ccc|ccc} 1 & 1 & -2 & 1 & 0 & 0 \\ 0 & -1 & -1 & 1 & 1 & 0 \\ 0 & 0 & 1 & 3 & 3 & 1 \end{array}\right)$

④ $\left(\begin{array}{ccc|ccc} 1 & 0 & -3 & 2 & 1 & 0 \\ 0 & -1 & -1 & 1 & 1 & 0 \\ 0 & 0 & 1 & 3 & 3 & 1 \end{array}\right)$; ⑤ $\left(\begin{array}{ccc|ccc} 1 & 0 & -3 & 2 & 1 & 0 \\ 0 & -1 & 0 & 4 & 4 & 1 \\ 0 & 0 & 1 & 3 & 3 & 1 \end{array}\right)$; ⑥ $\left(\begin{array}{ccc|ccc} 1 & 0 & 0 & 11 & 10 & 3 \\ 0 & -1 & 0 & 4 & 4 & 1 \\ 0 & 0 & 1 & 3 & 3 & 1 \end{array}\right)$;

⑦ $\left(\begin{array}{ccc|ccc} 1 & 0 & 0 & 11 & 10 & 3 \\ 0 & 1 & 0 & -4 & -4 & -1 \\ 0 & 0 & 1 & 3 & 3 & 1 \end{array}\right)$

$A^{-1} = \begin{pmatrix} 11 & 10 & 3 \\ -4 & -4 & -1 \\ 3 & 3 & 1 \end{pmatrix}$

① Original setup.

② Row one added to row two.

③ 3 times row two added to row three.

④ Row two added to row one.

⑤ Row three added to row two.

⑥ 3 times row three added to row one.

⑦ -1 times row two.

25. $A = \begin{pmatrix} 2 & -3 \\ 4 & -1 \end{pmatrix}$; $C = \begin{pmatrix} -9 \\ -13 \end{pmatrix}$; $\begin{vmatrix} 2 & -3 \\ 4 & -1 \end{vmatrix} = 10$; $A^{-1} = \frac{1}{10}\begin{pmatrix} -1 & 3 \\ -4 & 2 \end{pmatrix} = \begin{pmatrix} -\frac{1}{10} & \frac{3}{10} \\ -\frac{4}{10} & \frac{2}{10} \end{pmatrix}$

$A^{-1}C = \begin{pmatrix} -\frac{1}{10} & \frac{3}{10} \\ -\frac{4}{10} & \frac{2}{10} \end{pmatrix} \begin{pmatrix} -9 \\ -13 \end{pmatrix} = \begin{pmatrix} \frac{9}{10} & -\frac{39}{10} \\ \frac{36}{10} & -\frac{26}{10} \end{pmatrix} \begin{pmatrix} -3 \\ 1 \end{pmatrix}$

$x = -3, y = 1$

29. $A = \begin{pmatrix} 2 & -3 & 2 \\ 3 & 1 & -3 \\ 1 & 4 & 1 \end{pmatrix}; C = \begin{pmatrix} 7 \\ -6 \\ -13 \end{pmatrix}$

① $\left(\begin{array}{ccc|ccc} 2 & -3 & 2 & 1 & 0 & 0 \\ 3 & 1 & -3 & 0 & 1 & 0 \\ 1 & 4 & 1 & 0 & 0 & 1 \end{array} \right)$; ② $\left(\begin{array}{ccc|ccc} 2 & -3 & -2 & 1 & 0 & 0 \\ 3 & 1 & -3 & 0 & 1 & 0 \\ 0 & -11 & -6 & 0 & 1 & -3 \end{array} \right)$; ③ $\left(\begin{array}{ccc|ccc} 2 & -3 & 2 & 1 & 0 & 0 \\ 0 & 11 & -12 & -3 & 2 & 0 \\ 0 & -11 & -6 & 1 & 0 & -3 \end{array} \right)$

④ $\left(\begin{array}{ccc|ccc} 1 & -\frac{3}{2} & 1 & \frac{1}{2} & 0 & 0 \\ 0 & -11 & -12 & -3 & 2 & 0 \\ 0 & -11 & -6 & 0 & 1 & -3 \end{array} \right)$; ⑤ $\left(\begin{array}{ccc|ccc} 1 & -\frac{3}{2} & 1 & \frac{1}{2} & 0 & 0 \\ 0 & 11 & -12 & -3 & 2 & 0 \\ 0 & 0 & -18 & -3 & 3 & -3 \end{array} \right)$;

⑥ $\left(\begin{array}{ccc|ccc} 1 & -\frac{3}{2} & 1 & \frac{1}{2} & 0 & 0 \\ 0 & 1 & -\frac{12}{11} & -\frac{3}{11} & \frac{2}{11} & 0 \\ 0 & 0 & -18 & -3 & 3 & -3 \end{array} \right)$; ⑦ $\left(\begin{array}{ccc|ccc} 1 & 0 & -\frac{7}{11} & \frac{1}{11} & \frac{3}{11} & 0 \\ 0 & 1 & -\frac{12}{11} & -\frac{3}{11} & \frac{2}{11} & 0 \\ 0 & 0 & -18 & -3 & 3 & -3 \end{array} \right)$;

⑧ $\left(\begin{array}{ccc|ccc} 1 & 0 & -\frac{7}{11} & \frac{1}{11} & \frac{3}{11} & 0 \\ 0 & 1 & -\frac{12}{11} & -\frac{3}{11} & \frac{2}{11} & 0 \\ 0 & 0 & 1 & \frac{1}{6} & -\frac{1}{6} & \frac{1}{6} \end{array} \right)$; ⑨ $\left(\begin{array}{ccc|ccc} 1 & 0 & -\frac{7}{11} & \frac{1}{11} & \frac{3}{11} & 0 \\ 0 & 1 & 0 & -\frac{1}{11} & 0 & \frac{2}{11} \\ 0 & 0 & 1 & \frac{1}{6} & -\frac{1}{6} & \frac{1}{6} \end{array} \right)$;

⑩ $\left(\begin{array}{ccc|ccc} 1 & 0 & 0 & \frac{13}{66} & \frac{11}{66} & \frac{7}{66} \\ 0 & 1 & 0 & -\frac{1}{11} & 0 & \frac{2}{11} \\ 0 & 0 & 1 & \frac{1}{6} & -\frac{1}{6} & \frac{1}{6} \end{array} \right)$;

$A^{-1}C = \begin{pmatrix} \frac{13}{66} & \frac{11}{66} & \frac{7}{66} \\ -\frac{1}{11} & 0 & \frac{2}{11} \\ \frac{1}{6} & -\frac{1}{6} & \frac{1}{6} \end{pmatrix} \begin{pmatrix} 7 \\ -6 \\ -13 \end{pmatrix} = \begin{pmatrix} \frac{91}{66} - \frac{66}{66} - \frac{91}{66} \\ -\frac{7}{11} + 0 - \frac{26}{11} \\ \frac{7}{6} + 1 - \frac{13}{6} \end{pmatrix} = \begin{pmatrix} -1 \\ -3 \\ 0 \end{pmatrix}$

① Original.

② Row three multiplied by −3 and added to row two.

③ Row two multiplied by 2. Row one multiplied by −3 and added to row two.

④ Row one divided by 2.

⑤ Row two added to row three.

⑥ Row two divided by 11.

⑦ Row two multiplied by $\frac{3}{2}$ and added to row one.

⑧ Row three divided by −18.

⑨ Row three multiplied by $\frac{12}{11}$ and added to row two.

⑩ Row three multiplied by $\frac{7}{11}$ and added to row one.

33. $3x - 2y + z = 6$
$2x + 0y + 3z = 3$
$4x - y + 5z = 6$

The denominator will be found first.

$$\begin{vmatrix} 3 & -2 & 1 \\ 2 & 0 & 3 \\ 4 & -1 & 5 \end{vmatrix} = -\begin{vmatrix} 3 & -2 & 1 \\ 2 & 0 & 3 \\ -4 & 1 & -5 \end{vmatrix} = (-1)\begin{vmatrix} -5 & 0 & -9 \\ 2 & 0 & 3 \\ -4 & 1 & -5 \end{vmatrix}$$

$$= -(-1)\begin{vmatrix} -5 & -9 \\ 2 & 3 \end{vmatrix} = (1)(-15 + 18) = 3$$

$$x = \frac{\begin{vmatrix} 6 & -2 & 1 \\ 3 & 0 & 3 \\ 6 & -1 & 5 \end{vmatrix}}{3} = (-1)\frac{\begin{vmatrix} 6 & -2 & 1 \\ 3 & 0 & 3 \\ -6 & 1 & -5 \end{vmatrix}}{3} = (-1)\frac{\begin{vmatrix} -6 & 0 & -9 \\ 3 & 0 & 3 \\ -6 & 1 & -5 \end{vmatrix}}{3}$$

$$= (-1)(-1)\frac{\begin{vmatrix} -6 & -9 \\ 3 & 3 \end{vmatrix}}{3} = \frac{-18 + 27}{3} = 3$$

Substitute the value for x into the second equation.

$2(3) + 3z = 3;\ 6 + 3z = 3;\ 3z = -3;\ z = -1$

Substitute the values of x and z into the first equation.

$3(3) - 2y + (-1) = 6;\ 9 - 2y - 1 = 6;\ -2y + 8 = 6;\ -2y = -2;\ y = 1$

37.

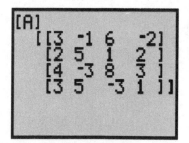 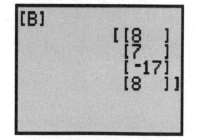 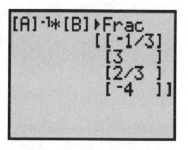

Check

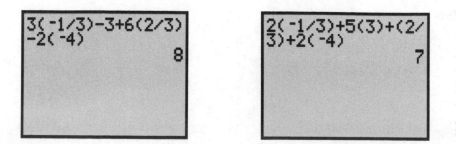

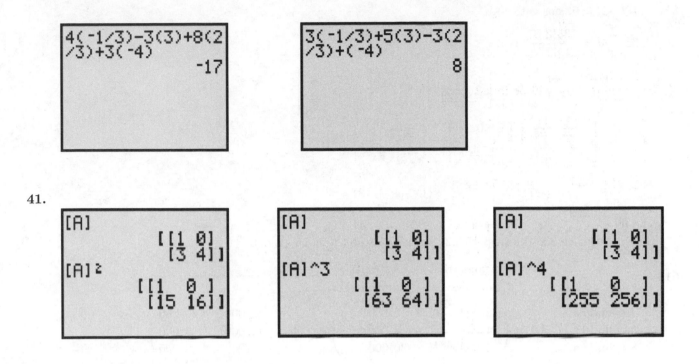

41.

45. $N = \begin{bmatrix} 0 & -1 \\ 1 & 0 \end{bmatrix}; N^{-1} \dfrac{1}{0-(-1)} \begin{bmatrix} 0 & 1 \\ -1 & 0 \end{bmatrix} = 1 \begin{bmatrix} 0 & 1 \\ -1 & 0 \end{bmatrix} = -1 \begin{bmatrix} 0 & -1 \\ 1 & 0 \end{bmatrix} = -N$

49. $A = \begin{bmatrix} 1 & -2 \\ 0 & 3 \end{bmatrix}, B = \begin{bmatrix} -3 & 1 \\ 2 & -1 \end{bmatrix}$

$(A+B)(A-B) = \left(\begin{bmatrix} 1 & -2 \\ 0 & 3 \end{bmatrix} + \begin{bmatrix} -3 & 1 \\ 2 & 1 \end{bmatrix} \right) \left(\begin{bmatrix} 1 & -2 \\ 0 & 3 \end{bmatrix} - \begin{bmatrix} -3 & 1 \\ 2 & -1 \end{bmatrix} \right)$

$\qquad = \begin{bmatrix} -2 & -1 \\ 2 & 2 \end{bmatrix} \begin{bmatrix} 4 & -3 \\ -2 & 4 \end{bmatrix} = \begin{bmatrix} -6 & 2 \\ 4 & 2 \end{bmatrix}$

$A^2 - B^2 = \begin{bmatrix} 1 & -2 \\ 0 & 3 \end{bmatrix}^2 - \begin{bmatrix} -3 & 1 \\ 2 & -1 \end{bmatrix}^2 = \begin{bmatrix} 1 & -8 \\ 0 & 9 \end{bmatrix} - \begin{bmatrix} 11 & -4 \\ -8 & 3 \end{bmatrix}$

$\qquad = \begin{bmatrix} -10 & -4 \\ 8 & 6 \end{bmatrix}$

$(A+B)(A-B) \neq A^2 - B^2$

53. $A = \begin{bmatrix} 2 & 3 \\ 3 & 2 \end{bmatrix}, C = \begin{bmatrix} 26 \\ 24 \end{bmatrix}, A^{-1} = \begin{bmatrix} -\frac{2}{5} & \frac{3}{5} \\ \frac{3}{5} & -\frac{2}{5} \end{bmatrix}$

$A^{-1}C = \begin{bmatrix} -\frac{2}{5} & \frac{3}{5} \\ \frac{3}{5} & -\frac{2}{5} \end{bmatrix} \begin{bmatrix} 26 \\ 24 \end{bmatrix} = \begin{bmatrix} 4 \\ 6 \end{bmatrix} = \begin{bmatrix} R_1 \\ R_2 \end{bmatrix}$

$R_1 = 4 \; \Omega, R_2 = 6 \; \Omega$

57. $110t - d = 0$, suspect

$$135t - d = \frac{135(3.0)}{60}, \text{ police}$$

$$A = \begin{bmatrix} 110 & -1 \\ 135 & -1 \end{bmatrix}, C = \begin{bmatrix} 0 \\ \frac{135(3.0)}{60} \end{bmatrix}, A^{-1} = \begin{bmatrix} -\frac{1}{25} & \frac{1}{25} \\ -\frac{27}{25} & \frac{22}{25} \end{bmatrix}$$

$$A^{-1}C = \begin{bmatrix} -\frac{1}{25} & \frac{1}{25} \\ -\frac{27}{25} & \frac{22}{25} \end{bmatrix} \begin{bmatrix} 0 \\ \frac{135(3.0)}{60} \end{bmatrix} = \begin{bmatrix} 0.27 \\ 5.94 \end{bmatrix} = \begin{bmatrix} t \\ d \end{bmatrix}$$

$$t = 0.27$$

$$t - \frac{3.0}{60} = 0.22$$

The police overtake the suspect 0.22 s after passing the intersection.

61.

	Standard Transmission	Automatic Transmission
4 cylinders	12,000	15,000
6 cylinders	24,000	8,000
8 cylinders	4,000	30,000

$$A = \begin{pmatrix} 12,000 & 15,000 \\ 24,000 & 8,000 \\ 4,000 & 30,000 \end{pmatrix} \quad B = \begin{pmatrix} 15,000 & 20,000 \\ 12,000 & 3,000 \\ 2,000 & 22,000 \end{pmatrix}$$

$$A + B = \begin{pmatrix} 27,000 & 35,000 \\ 36,000 & 11,000 \\ 6,000 & 52,000 \end{pmatrix}$$

65. Answers may vary, but the basic idea is that the matrix entries show the inventory of a particular product in a particular store in a compact way.

Chapter 17

INEQUALITIES

17.1 Properties of Inequalities

1. $x + 1 < 0$ is true for all values of x less than -1. Therefore, the values of x that satisfy this inequality are written as $x < -1$.

5. $4 + 3 < 9 + 3$; $7 < 12$; property 1

9. $\dfrac{4}{-1} > \dfrac{9}{-1}$; $-4 > -9$; property 3

13. $x > -2$

17. $1 < x < 7$

21. $x < 1$ or $3 < x \leq 5$

25. x is greater than 0 and less than or equal to 2

29. $x < 3$

33. $0 \leq x < 5$

37. $x < -1$ or $1 \leq x < 4$

41. $t < -3$ or $t > -3$

45.
$$
\begin{array}{ll}
0 < a < b & \text{given} \\
0 < a^2 < ab & \text{since } a > 0 \\
0 < ab < b^2 & \text{since } b > 0 \\
a^2 < ab < b^2 & \\
a^2 < b^2 & \text{is an absolute inequality}
\end{array}
$$

49. $2000 \leq M \leq 1{,}000{,}000$

53. $0 < n \leq 2565$ steps

17.2 Solving Linear Inequalities

1.
$$
\begin{aligned}
21 - 2x &\geq 15 \\
-2x &\geq -6 \\
x &\leq 3
\end{aligned}
$$

5.
$$
\begin{aligned}
x - 3 &> -4 \\
x &> -4 + 3 \\
x &> -1
\end{aligned}
$$

9.
$$
\begin{aligned}
3x - 5 &\leq -11 \\
3x &\leq -11 + 5 \\
3x &\leq -6 \\
x &\leq -2
\end{aligned}
$$

13.
$$
\begin{aligned}
4x - 5 &\leq 2x \\
4x - 2x &\leq 5 \\
2x &\leq 5 \\
x &\leq \frac{5}{2}
\end{aligned}
$$

17.
$$
\begin{aligned}
2.50(1.50 - 3.40x) &< 3.84 - 8.45x \\
3.75 - 8.50x &< 3.84 - 8.45x \\
-0.09 &< 0.05x \\
x &> -1.80
\end{aligned}
$$

21.
$$
\begin{aligned}
-1 &< 2x + 1 < 3 \\
-2 &< 2x < 2 \\
-1 &< x < 1
\end{aligned}
$$

155

25. $2x < x - 1 \leq 3x + 5$
$0 < -x - 1 \leq x + 5$
$0 < -x - 1$ and $-x - 1 \leq x + 5$
$x < -1$ and $-6 \leq 2x$
$x < -1$ and $x \geq -3$
$-3 \leq x < -1$

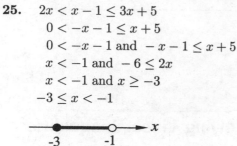

29. $3x - 2 < 8 - x$
$4x < 10$
$$x < \frac{5}{2}$$

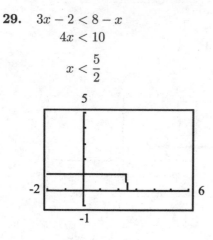

33. $1 < 5 - 2t < 9$
$-4 < -2t < 4$
$2 > t > -2$
or
$-2 < t < 2$

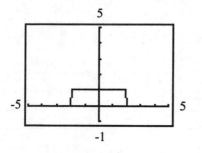

37. $f(x) = \sqrt{2x - 10}$
$2x - 10 \geq 0$
$2x \geq 10$
$x \geq 5$

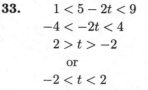

41. $100 < 130(1.42)w < 150$
$0.54\ \text{m} < w < 0.81\ \text{m}$

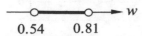

45. $0 \leq x \leq 800 - 300$
$0 \leq x \leq 500$
$y = x + 400 - 200 = x + 200$
$x = y - 200$
$0 \leq y - 200 \leq 500$
$200 \leq y \leq 700$

17.3   Solving Nonlinear Inequalities

1. $x^2 + 3 > 4x$
$x^2 - 4x + 3 > 0$
$(x - 3)(x - 1) > 0$

The critical values are 1, 3.

	$(x-3)(x-1)$		Sign
$x < 1$	$-$	$-$	$+$
$1 < x < 3$	$-$	$+$	$-$
$x > 3$	$+$	$+$	$+$

$x^2 - 4x + 3 > 0$ when $x < 1$ or $x > 3$.

5. $x^2 - 1 < 0$
$(x + 1)(x - 1) < 0$

The critical values are
$x = -1$ and $x = 1$.

	$(x+1)(x-1)$		Sign
$x < -1$	$-$	$-$	$+$
$-1 < x < 1$	$+$	$-$	$-$
$x > 1$	$+$	$+$	$+$

$(x + 1)(x - 1) < 0$ for $-1 < x < 1$

9. $2x^2 - 12 \leq -5x$
$2x^2 + 5x - 12 \leq 0$
$(2x - 3)(x + 4) \leq 0$

The critical values are $x = \dfrac{3}{2}, x = -4$.

	$(2x-3)(x+4)$		Sign
$x < -4$	$-$	$-$	$+$
$-4 < x < 3/2$	$-$	$+$	$-$
$0 < x < 3/2$	$+$	$+$	$+$

$(2x - 3)(x + 4) \leq 0$ for $-4 \leq x \leq \dfrac{3}{2}$

13. $R^2 + 4 > 0$

$R^2 + 4$ is never less than 4.

so all values of R are solutions.

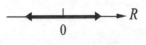

17.
$$s^3 + 2s^2 - s \geq 2$$
$$s^2(s+2) - 1(s+2) \geq 0$$
$$(s^2 - 1)(s + 2) \geq 0$$
$$(s+1)(s-1)(s+2) \geq 0$$

The critical values are $s = -1$,
$s = 1, s = -2$.

	$(s-1)(s+1)(s+2)$			Sign
$s < -2$	$-$	$-$	$-$	$-$
$-2 < s < -1$	$-$	$-$	$+$	$+$
$-1 < s < 1$	$-$	$+$	$+$	$-$
$s > 1$	$+$	$+$	$+$	$+$

$(s+1)(s-1)(s+2) \geq 0$
for $-2 \leq s \leq -1$ or $s \geq 1$

21.
$$\frac{x^2 - 6x - 7}{x + 5} > 0$$
$$\frac{(x-7)(x+1)}{x+5} > 0$$

The critical values are $x = 7$,
$x = -1, x = -5$.

	$(x-7)(x+1)(x+5)$			Sign
$x < -5$	$-$	$-$	$-$	$-$
$-5 < x < -1$	$-$	$-$	$+$	$+$
$-1 < x < 7$	$-$	$+$	$+$	$-$
$x > 7$	$+$	$+$	$+$	$+$

$$\frac{(x-7)(x+1)}{x+5} > 0 \text{ for } -5 < x < -1 \text{ or } x > 7$$

25.
$$3x^2 + 5x \geq 2$$
$$3x^2 + 5x - 2 \geq 0$$
$$(3x - 1)(x + 2) \geq 0$$

The critical values are $x = \dfrac{1}{3}$ and $x = -2$.

	$(3x-1)(x+2)$		Sign
$x < -2$	$-$	$-$	$+$
$-2 < x < 1/3$	$-$	$+$	$-$
$x > 1/3$	$+$	$+$	$+$

$(3x - 1)(x + 2) \geq 0$ for $x \leq -2$ or $x \geq \dfrac{1}{3}$

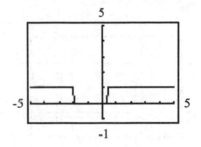

29.
$$\frac{6 - x}{3 - x - 4x^2} \geq 0$$
$$\frac{6 - x}{(1 + x)(3 - 4x)} \geq 0; \ \left(x \neq -1, x \neq \frac{3}{4}\right)$$

The critical values are $x = 6, x = -1$, and $x = \dfrac{3}{4}$.

	$(6-x)/(1+x)(3-4x)$			Sign
$x < -1$	$+$	$-$	$+$	$-$
$-1 < x < 3/4$	$+$	$+$	$+$	$+$
$3/4 < x < 6$	$+$	$+$	$-$	$-$
$x > 6$	$-$	$+$	$-$	$+$

$$\frac{6 - x}{(1 + x)(3 - 4x)} \geq 0 \text{ for } -1 < x < \frac{3}{4} \text{ or } x \geq 6$$

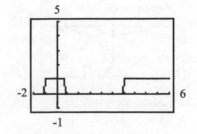

33. $\sqrt{(x-1)(x+2)}$ is real if $(x-1)(x+2) \geq 0$
The critical values are $x = 1$ and $x = -2$.

	$(x-1)(x+2)$		Sign
$x < -2$	$-$	$-$	$+$
$-2 < x < 1$	$-$	$+$	$-$
$x > 1$	$+$	$+$	$+$

$(x-1)(x+2) > 0$ for $x \leq -2$ or $x \geq 1$

37. To solve $x^3 - x > 2$ using a graphing
calculator, let $y_1 = x^3 - x - 2$.

$y > 0$ for $x > 1.52$

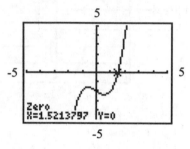

41. To solve $2^x > x + 2$ using a graphing
calculator, let $y_1 = 2^x - x - 2$.

$y > 0$ for $x < -1.69, x > 2.00$

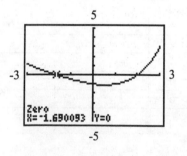

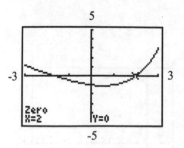

45. $\qquad x^2 > x$
$\qquad x^2 - x > 0$
$\qquad x(x-1) > 0$

The critical values are $x = 0, x = 1$.

	$x(x-1)$		Sign
$x < 0$	$-$	$-$	$+$
$0 < x < 1$	$+$	$-$	$-$
$x > 1$	$+$	$+$	$+$

$x(x-1) > 0$ for $x < 0$ or $x > 1$

Is $x^2 > x$ for all x? No.
$x^2 > x$ for $x < 0$ or $x > 1$.
$x^2 > x$ is not true for $0 \leq x \leq 1$.

49. $\qquad\qquad 2^{x+2} > 3^{2x-3}$
$\qquad\qquad \log 2^{x+2} > \log 3^{2x-3}$
$\qquad (x+2)\log 2 > (2x-3)\log 3$
$\qquad x\log 2 + 2\log 2 > 2x\log 3 - 3\log 3$
$\qquad x\log 2 + \log 4 > 2x\log 3 - \log 27$
$\qquad \log 4 + \log 27 > x(2\log 3 - \log 2)$
$\qquad\qquad \log 108 > x(\log 9 - \log 2)$

$$\log 108 > x\log \frac{9}{2}$$

$$x < \frac{\log 108}{\log \frac{9}{2}}$$

53. $63n = 2^x - 1, n < 100$
$\qquad 2^x - 1 < 63(100)$
$\qquad\quad 2^x < 6301$
$\qquad \log 2^x < \log 6301$
$\qquad x\log 2 < \log 6301$

$$x < \frac{\log 6301}{\log 2}$$

$x \leq 12$ (x is an integer)

57. $l = w + 2.0; w(w + 2.0) < 35; w \geq 3.0$ mm
$\qquad w^2 + 2.0w - 35 < 0$
$\qquad (w + 7.0)(w - 5.0) < 0$

The critical values are $w = -7.0$ and $w = 5.0$.

	$(w+7)(w-5)$		Sign
$w < -7$	$-$	$-$	$+$
$-7 < w < 5$	$+$	$-$	$-$
$w > 5$	$+$	$+$	$+$

$(w + 7.0)(w - 5.0) < 0$ for $-7.0 < w < 5.0$;
$w \geq 3.0$, so $3.0 \leq w < 5.0$ mm

17.4   Inequalities Involving Absolute Values

1. $|2x - 1| < 5$
$-5 < 2x - 1 < 5$
$-4 < 2x < 6$
$-2 < x < 3$

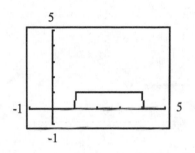

5. $|5x + 4| > 6$
$5x + 4 < -6$ or $5x + 4 > 6$
$5x < -10$ or $5x > 2$
$x < -2$ or $x > \dfrac{2}{5}$

9. $|3 - 4x| > 3$
$3 - 4x < -3$ or $3 - 4x > 3$
$-4x < -6$ or $-4x > 0$

$x > \dfrac{6}{4} = \dfrac{3}{2}$ or $x < 0$

13. $|20x + 85| \le 43$
$-43 \le 20x + 85 \le 43$
$-128 \le 20x \le -42$
$-6.4 \le x \le -2.1$

17. $8 + 3|3 - 2x| < 11$
$3|3 - 2x| < 3$
$|3 - 2x| < 1$
$-1 < 3 - 2x < 1$
$-4 < -2x < -2$
$2 > x > 1$
$1 < x < 2$

21. $\left|\dfrac{3R}{5} + 1\right| < 8$

$-8 < \dfrac{3R}{5} + 1 < 8$

$-15 < R < \dfrac{35}{3}$

25. $|2x - 5| < 3 \Leftrightarrow 1 < x < 4$

29. $|x^2 + x - 4| > 2$
$x^2 + x - 4 > 2$ or $x^2 + x - 4 < -2$
$x^2 + x - 6 > 0$ or $x^2 + x - 2 < 0$
(A) $(x + 3)(x - 2) > 0$
(B) $(x - 1)(x + 2) < 0$

(A) Critical values are $x = -3, x = 2$

	$(x+3)(x-2)$	Sign
$x < -3$	$-$ $-$	$+$
$-3 < x < 2$	$+$ $-$	$-$
$x > 2$	$+$ $+$	$+$

$(x + 3)(x - 2) > 0$ for $x < -3$ or for $x > 2$

(B) Critical values are $x = 1, x = -2$.

	$(x-1)(x+2)$	Sign
$x < -2$	$-$ $-$	$+$
$-2 < x < 1$	$-$ $+$	$-$
$x > 1$	$+$ $+$	$+$

$(x - 1)(x + 2) < 0$ for $-2 < x < 1$

The solution consists of values of x that are in (A) or (B): $x < -3, -2 < x < 1, x > 2$

33. Solve for x if $|x| < a$ and $a \le 0$.

$|x| < a \le 0$
$|x| < 0$, no values since $|x| \ge 0$.

37. $|p - 2,000,000| < 200,000$
$-200,000 < p - 2,000,000 < 200,000$
$1,800,000 < p < 2,200,000$ barrels

The production will be between 1,800,000 barrels and 2,200,000 barrels.

17.5 Graphical Solution of Inequalities with Two Variables

1. $y < 3 - x$

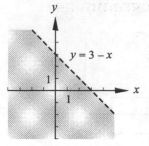

5. $y \geq 2x + 5$; graph $y = 2x + 5$. Use a solid line to indicate that points on it satisfy the inequality. Shade the region above the line.

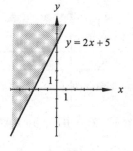

9. $y < x^2$; graph $y = x^2$. Use a dashed curve to indicated that points on it do not satisfy the inequality. Shade the region below the curve.

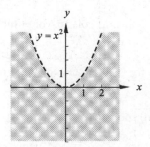

13. $y < 32x - x^4$; graph $y = 32x - x^4$. Use a dashed curve to indicated that points on it do not satisfy the inequality. Shade the region below the curve.

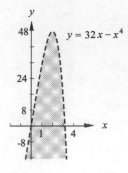

17. $y > 1 + \sin 2x$; graph $y = 1 + \sin 2x$. Use a dashed curve to indicate that the points on it do not satisfy the inequality. Shade the region above the curve.

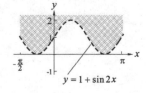

21. $y \leq 2x^2$ and $y > x - 2$. Graph $y = 2x^2$ using a solid curve. Shade the region below the curve. Graph $y = x - 2$ using a dashed line. Shade the region above the line. The region where the shadings overlap satisfies both inequalities.

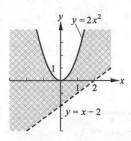

25. $y \geq 0$ and $y \leq \sin x$; $0 \leq x \leq 3\pi$. Graph $y = \sin x$ using a solid curve. Shade the region below the curve and above the x-axis for $0 \leq x \leq 3\pi$.

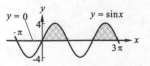

29. $2x + y < 5 \Rightarrow y < -2x + 5$ graph $y_1 = -2x + 5$.
The boundary line is dashed.

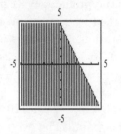

33. $y > 2x - 1$. Graph $y_1 = 2x - 1$.
$y < x^4 - 8$. Graph $y_2 = x^4 - 8$.

The boundary lines are dashed.

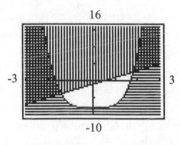

37. $y \le |2x - 3|$. Graph $y_1 = |2x - 3|$. The boundary
line is solid.
$y > 1 - 2x^2$. Graph $y_2 = 1 - 2x^2$. The boundary
line is dashed.

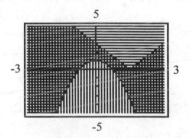

41. $y \ge 2x^2 - 6$ defines the region on and above the
parabola $y = 2x^2 - 6$. $y = x - 3$ defines all points
on the graph of the line $y = x - 3$. The solution
to the system $y \ge 2x^2 - 6$ and $y = x - 3$ is the
intersection of the graph of the parabola and the
line together with the points on the line above the
parabola.

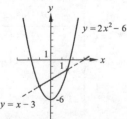

45. $p_R = Ri^2$; $R = 0.5\ \Omega$, $p > p_R$, $p > 0.5i^2$

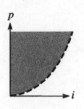

17.6   Linear Programming

1. Maximize $F = 2x + 3y$ subject to $x \ge 0$,
$y \ge 0$, $x + y \le 6$, $2x + y \le 8$.

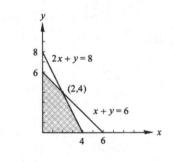

point	value of F
$(0,0)$	0
$(0,6)$	18
$(2,4)$	16
$(4,0)$	8

Maximum value of F is 18 at $(0,6)$.

5. maximum P: $P = 3x + 5y$ subject to

$x \ge 0, y \ge 0$
$2x + y \le 6$

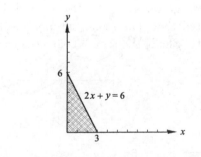

Vertex	$P = 3x + 5y$
$(0,0)$	0
$(0,6)$	30
$(3,0)$	9

max $P = 30$ at $(0,6)$

9. Maximim and minimum F: $F = x + 3y$ subject to

$$x \geq 1, y \geq 2$$
$$y - x \leq 3$$
$$y + 2x \leq 8$$

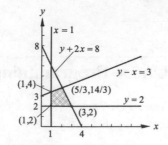

Vertex	$F = x + 3y$
$(1, 2)$	7
$(1, 4)$	13
$\left(\frac{5}{3}, \frac{14}{3}\right)$	$\frac{47}{3}$
$(3, 2)$	9

min $F = 7$ at $(1, 2)$

max $F = \dfrac{47}{3}$ at $\left(\dfrac{5}{3}, \dfrac{14}{3}\right)$

13. Minimum C: $C = 6x + 4y$ subject to

$$y \geq 2$$
$$x + y \leq 12$$
$$x + 2y \geq 12$$
$$2x + y \geq 12$$

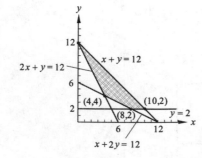

Vertex	$C = 6x + 4y$
$(0, 12)$	48
$(10, 2)$	68
$(8, 2)$	56
$(4, 4)$	40

min $C = 40$ at $(4, 4)$

17. Let x = the number of business models produced. Let y = the number of scientific models produced. Let p = the profit. $p = 8x + 10y$. The maximum time worked = 8 hours or 480 minutes. For the first operation, $3x + 6y \leq 480$. For the second operation, $6x + 4y \leq 480$. $3x + 6y \leq 480$; $y \leq -\frac{1}{2}x + 80$. Graph $y = -\frac{1}{2}x + 80$ and shade the region below the graph. $6x + 4y \leq 480$; $y \leq -\frac{3}{2}x + 120$; graph $y = -\frac{3}{2}x + 120$ and shade the region below the graph. The overlapping shaded regions satisfy both inequalities. Vertices of the region are $(80, 0), (0, 80)$ and the point p. p is the intersection of $y = -\frac{1}{2}x + 80$ and $y = -\frac{3}{2}x + 120$. Solve these equations simultaneously by substitution.

$$-\frac{1}{2}x + 80 = -\frac{3}{2}x + 120; x = 40, y = 60.$$

OR

The profit is calculated using the coordinates of the vertices. $p = 8(80) + 10(0) = 640$; $p = 8(0) + 10(80) = 800$; $p = 8(40) + 10(60) = 920$. The maximum profit occurs if 40 business models and 60 scientific models are produced.

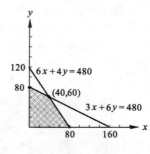

Chapter 17 Review Exercises

1. $2x - 12 > 0$; $2(x - 6) > 0$. The critical value is 6. If $x > 6$, $2x - 12 > 0$.

Thus the values which satisfy the inequality are $x > 6$.

5.
$$5x^2 + 9x < 2$$
$$(x + 2)(5x - 1) < 0$$
$$-2 < x < \frac{1}{5}$$

interval	$(x + 2)(5x - 1)$
$x < -2$	$(-)(-) = (+)$
$-2 < x < \dfrac{1}{5}$	$(+)(-) = (-)$
$x > \dfrac{1}{5}$	$(+)(+) = (+)$

9. $\dfrac{(2x-1)(3-x)}{(x+4)} > 0$

	-4	$\dfrac{1}{2}$	3	
$2x-1$	$-$	$-$	$+$	$+$
$3-x$	$+$	$+$	$+$	$-$
$x+4$	$-$	$+$	$+$	$+$
$\dfrac{(2x-1)(3-x)}{(x+4)}$	$+$	$-$	$+$	$-$
	$x < -4$		$\dfrac{1}{2} < x < 3$	

13.
$$|3x+2| \le 4$$
$$-4 \le 3x+2 \le 4$$
$$-6 \le 3x \le 2$$
$$-2 \le x \le \dfrac{2}{3}$$

17. $y = 5 - 3x < 0 \Leftrightarrow 3x > 5 \Leftrightarrow x > \dfrac{5}{3}$

21. $\dfrac{8-R}{2R+1} \le 0$

	$\dfrac{1}{2}$	8	
$8-R$	$+$	$+$	$-$
$2R+1$	$-$	$+$	$+$
$\dfrac{8-R}{2R+1}$	$-$	$+$	$-$
	$R < -\dfrac{1}{2}$		$R \ge 8$

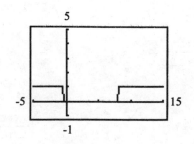

25. $x^3 + x + 1 < 0$; Graph $y_1 = x^3 + x + 1$ and use the zero feature to solve.

$x < -0.68$

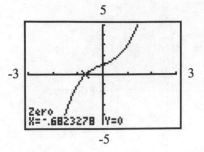

29. $y > 4 - x$. Graph $y = 4 - x$. Use a dashed line to indicate that points on it do not satisfy the inequality. Shade the region above the line.

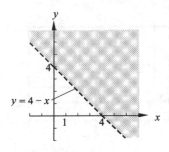

33. $y > x^2 + 1$. Graph $y = x^2 + 1$. Use a dashed line to indicate that points on it do not satisfy the inequality. Shade the region above the line.

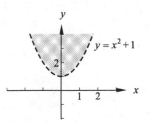

37. $y > x + 1$
  $y < 4 - x^2$

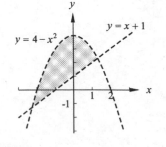

41. $y < 3x + 5$

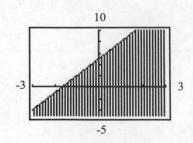

45. $y < 32x - x^4$

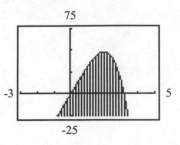

49. $\sqrt{3 - x}$ will be a real number if $3 - x \geq 0$. The critical values are is ± 3. If $x \leq 3$, $3 - x \geq 0$. Thus the values which satisfy the inequalities are $x \leq 3$.

53. Maximum P: $P = 2x + 9y$ subject to

$x \geq 0, y \geq 0$
$x + 4y \leq 13$
$3y - x \leq 8$

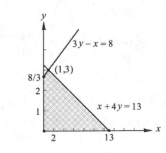

Vertex	$P = 2x + 9y$
$(0, 0)$	0
$(0, \frac{8}{3})$	24
$(1, 3)$	29
$(13, 0)$	26

max $P = 29$ at $(1, 3)$

57. When is $|a + b| < |a| + |b|$. There are 4 cases.

(1) $a \geq 0, b \geq 0 \Rightarrow a + b \geq 0$, the given inequality is

$$a + b < a + b$$
$$0 < 0, F$$

(2) $a < 0, b < 0 \Rightarrow a + b < 0$, the given inequality is

$$-(a + b) < -a + (-b)$$
$$-(a + b) < -(a + b)$$
$$0 < 0, F$$

(3) $a < 0, b > 0, |a| > b \Rightarrow a + b < 0$, the given inequality is

$$-(a + b) < -a + b$$
$$-a - b < -a + b$$
$$-b < b, T$$

(4) $a < 0, b > 0, |a| < b \Rightarrow a + b > 0$, the given inequality is

$$a + b < -a + b$$
$$a < -a, T$$

Note: in cases (3) and (4) a and b can be reversed without loss of generality.
$|a + b| < |a| + |b|$ when a and b have opposite signs.

61. $5F = 9C + 160, F \geq 98.6$

$$\frac{9C + 100}{5} > 98.6$$
$$9C + 160 > 493$$
$$C \geq 37°C$$

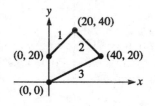

65. $101 + 10.1d > 500$
$$10.1d > 399$$
$$d > 39.5 \text{ m}$$

69. $p = Ri^2 = 12.0i^2; 2.50 < 12.0i^2 < 8.00$

$$\frac{2.50}{12.0} < i^2 < \frac{8.00}{12.0}$$
$$\sqrt{\frac{2.50}{12.0}} < i < \sqrt{\frac{8.00}{12.0}}$$
$$0.46 < i < 0.82 \text{ A}$$

73. Let $R =$ minutes research time
$D =$ minutes development time

$$R \leq 1200$$
$$D \leq 1000$$

77.

Write the equation of each line:

$\boxed{1}\ y = x + 20$

$\boxed{2}\ y = -x + 60$

$\boxed{3}\ y = \dfrac{1}{2}x$

The park region is described by the inequalities.

$$x \geq 0$$
$$y \geq 0$$
$$y \leq x + 20$$
$$y \leq -x + 60$$
$$y \geq \frac{1}{2}x$$

VARIATION

18.1 Ratio and Proportion

1. $\dfrac{3.5 \text{ in.}}{x} = \dfrac{1 \text{ in.}}{16 \text{ mi}}$

   $x = 56 \text{ mi}$

5. $\dfrac{96 \text{ h}}{3 \text{ days}} = \dfrac{96 \text{ h}}{72 \text{ h}} = \dfrac{4}{3}$

9. $\dfrac{0.14 \text{ kg}}{3500 \text{ mg}} = \dfrac{0.14 \text{ kg}}{0.0035 \text{ kg}} = 40$

13. $\dfrac{45 \text{ N}}{110 \text{ N}} = 0.41$

17. $\dfrac{487 \text{ lb/ft}^3}{62.4 \text{ lb/ft}^3} = 7.80$

21. $\dfrac{8460 \text{ N}}{9.80 \text{ m/s}^2} = \dfrac{8460 \text{ m} \cdot \text{kg/s}^2}{9.80 \text{ m/s}^2} = 863 \text{ kg}$

25. $\dfrac{36.6}{84.4} = \dfrac{0.0447}{V_1}$; $36.6 V_1 = 3.77$; $V_1 = 0.103 \text{ m}^3$

29. $\dfrac{1.00 \text{ hp}}{746 \text{ W}} = \dfrac{x}{250 \text{ W}}$; $746x = 250$; $x = 0.335 \text{ hp}$

33. $45.0 \text{ km/h} = 45.0\dfrac{\text{km}}{\text{h}} \times \dfrac{1000 \text{ m/km}}{3600 \text{ s/h}} = 12.5 \text{ m/s}$

37. $\dfrac{3.0 \text{ m}}{6.0 \text{ m}} = \dfrac{4.2 \text{ m}}{x}$

   $x = 8.4 \text{ m}$

41. $\dfrac{17}{595} = \dfrac{500}{x}$; $17x = 297,500$; $x = 17,500 \text{ chips}$

18.2 Variation

1. $C = kd = \pi d$

   $k = \pi$

5. $v = kr$

9. $P = \dfrac{k}{\sqrt{A}}$

13. The area varies directly as the square of the radius.

17. $V = kH^2$; $2 = k \cdot 64^2$

   $k = \dfrac{2}{64^2}$; $V = \dfrac{2H^2}{64^2} = \dfrac{H^2}{2048}$

21. $y = kx$; $20 = k(8)$; $k = 2.5$; $y = 2.5x$
    $y = 2.5(10) = 25$

25. $y = \dfrac{kx}{z}$; $60 = \dfrac{k(4)}{10}$; $k = 150$; $y = \dfrac{150x}{z}$

   $y = \dfrac{150(6)}{5} = 180$

29. $V = kV_0$; $75 = k(160)$; $k = \dfrac{15}{32}$; $V = \dfrac{15}{32}V_0$

   $V = \dfrac{15}{32}(130) = 61 \text{ ft}^3$

33. $H = kP$; $1800 = k \cdot 720$; $k = 2.5$

37. (a) a varies inversely with mass.

   (b) $a = \dfrac{k}{m}$; $30 = \dfrac{k}{2}$; $k = 60 \text{ g} \cdot \text{cm/s}^2$

   $a = \dfrac{60}{m}$

41. $F = kAv^2$; $19.2 = k(3.72)(31.4)^2$;
    $k = 5.23 \times 10^{-3} \text{ lb} \cdot \text{s/ft}^3$
    $F = 5.23 \times 10^{-3} Av^2$

45. $s = k\sqrt{T}$; $460 = k\sqrt{273}$; $k = \dfrac{460}{16.5} = 27.9 \text{ m/(s} \cdot \text{K}^{1/2})$

   $s = 27.9\sqrt{300} = 480 \text{ m/s}$

49. $P = kRi^2$; $10.0 = k(40.0)(0.500)^2$; $k = \dfrac{10.0}{10.0} = 1.00$

   $P = 20.0(2.00^2) = 80.0 \text{ W}$

53. Note: Make sure calculator is in rad mode.

   $x = k\omega^2(\cos \omega t)$
   $-11.4 = k(0.524^2) \cos[(1.00)(0.524)]$

   $k = \dfrac{-11.4}{0.238} = -48.0 \text{ ft}$

   $x = -48.0(0.524)^2 \cos[(2.00)(0.524)]$
   $\quad = -6.58 \text{ ft/s}^2$

Chapter 18 Review Exercises

1. $\dfrac{4\ \text{Mg}}{20\ \text{kg}} = \dfrac{4000\ \text{kg}}{20\ \text{kg}} = 200$

5. $\pi = \dfrac{c}{d}$

$\dfrac{4.2736}{1.3603} = 3.1417$

9. $p = \dfrac{F}{A} = \dfrac{37.4}{2.25^2}$

$p = 7.39\ \text{lb/in.}^2$

13. $\dfrac{1.3\ \text{in.}}{20.0\ \text{mi}} = \dfrac{6.0\ \text{in.}}{x}$

$x = 92\ \text{mi}$

17. $\dfrac{3600}{30\ \text{s}} = \dfrac{x}{300\ \text{s}}$ since $5\ \text{min} = 300\ \text{s}$

$30x = (360)(300)$

$x = 36{,}000$ characters in 5 min

21. $\dfrac{25.0\ \text{ft}}{2.00\ \text{in.}} = \dfrac{x}{5.75\ \text{in.}};\ x = 71.9\ \text{ft}$

25. $\dfrac{80.0}{98.0} = \dfrac{x}{37.0}$

$x = 30.2\ \text{kg}$

29. $y = kx^2;\ 27 = k(3^2);\ k = 3;\ y = 3x^2$

33. $\dfrac{F_1}{F_2} = \dfrac{L_2}{L_1};\ F_1 = 4.50\ \text{lb},\ F_2 = 6.75\ \text{lb},\ L_1 = 17.5\ \text{in}$

$\dfrac{4.50}{6.75} = \dfrac{L_2}{17.5}$

$(6.75)L_2 = (4.50)(17.5)$

$L_2 = 11.7\ \text{in.}$

37. $R = kA$

$850 = k(900)$

$k = 0.94$

$R = 0.94A$

41. $T = k\sqrt{L}$

$\dfrac{\pi}{2} = k\sqrt{2.00} \Rightarrow k = \dfrac{\pi}{2\sqrt{2.00}}$

$T = \dfrac{\pi}{2\sqrt{2.00}}\sqrt{L} = \dfrac{\pi}{2\sqrt{2.00}}\sqrt{4.00}$

$T = 2.22\ \text{s}$

45. $p = kA;\ 30.0 = k(8.00);\ k = 3.75\ \dfrac{\text{hp}}{\text{in}^2}.$

$p = 3.75A;\ p = 3.75(6.00) = 22.5\ \text{hp}$

49. $\dfrac{(\log 8000)^2}{(\log 2000)^2} = 1.4$ times longer to sort 8000 numbers.

53. $f = \dfrac{v}{\lambda};$

$v = f\lambda = 90.0 \times 10^6(3.29)$

$= 299 \times 10^6$

$= 2.99 \times 10^8\ \text{m/s}$

57. $R = kv_0^2 \sin 2\theta$

$5.12 \times 10^4 = k(850)^2 \sin(2(22.0°))$

$k = \dfrac{5.12 \times 10^4}{850^2 \sin(44.0°)}$

$R = \dfrac{5.12 \times 10^4}{850^2 \sin 44.0°}750^2(2(43.2°))$

$R = 5.73 \times 10^4\ \text{m}$

61. $V = \dfrac{kr^4}{d};\ V_1 = \dfrac{k(1.25r)^4}{0.98d}$

$= \dfrac{2.44kr^4}{0.98d}$

$= 2.49\left(\dfrac{kr^4}{d}\right)$

$= 2.49V$

An increase of $V_1 - V = 2.49V - V = 1.49V$ or 149% increase.

65. $L = \dfrac{kt}{d};\ 1200 = \dfrac{k \cdot 30}{8.0};\ k = 320\ \text{Btu} \cdot \text{in/min}$

$L = \dfrac{320t}{d} = \dfrac{320(90)}{6.0} = 4800\ \text{Btu}$

69. Let $V_1 = \pi r_1^2 h_1$ be the original volume then the new volume is

$V_2 = \pi r_2^2 h_2 = 0.9\pi r_1^2 h_1$ from which

$\left(\dfrac{r_2}{r_1}\right)^2 \cdot \dfrac{h_2}{h_1} = 0.9$ and since $\dfrac{r_2}{r_1} = \dfrac{h_2}{h_1}$

$\dfrac{r_2^3}{r_1^3} = 0.9$

$r_2 = \sqrt[3]{0.9}\,r_1 = 0.97r_1$

Reducing the radius and height by 3% will reduce the volume by 10%.

Chapter 19

SEQUENCES AND THE BINOMIAL THEOREM

19.1 Arithmetic Sequences

1. $a_1 = 5, a_{32} = -88, n = 32$

$-88 = 5 + (32 - 1)d$
$31d = -93$
$d = -3$

5. $4, 6, 8, 10, 12$

9. $a_8 = 1 + (8 - 1)(3) = 22$

13. $a_{80} = -0.7 + (80 - 1)0.4 = 30.9$

17. $S_{20} = \dfrac{20}{2}(4 + 40) = 440$

21. $45 = 5 + (n - 1)8$
$45 = 8n - 3$
$n = 6$

$S_6 = \dfrac{6}{2}(5 + 45) = 150$

25. $a_{30} = a_1 + (29)(3) = a_1 + 87$

$1875 = \dfrac{30}{2}(a_1 + a_1 + 87)$

$125 = 2a_1 + 87$
$a_1 = 19; a_{30} = 106$

29. $a_n = -5k + (n - 1)\left(\dfrac{1}{2}k\right)$

$S_n = \dfrac{n}{2}\left[-5k + \left(-5k + (n - 1)\left(\dfrac{1}{2}k\right)\right)\right]$

$\dfrac{23}{2}k = \dfrac{n}{2}\left(-5k - 5k + \dfrac{1}{2}kn - \dfrac{1}{2}k\right)$

$23k = n\left(-\dfrac{21}{2}k + \dfrac{1}{2}kn\right)$

$46k = n(-21k + kn)$
$46k = -21kn + kn^2$
$kn^2 - 21kn - 46k = 0$
$n^2 - 21n - 46 = 0$
$(n + 2)(n - 23) = 0$
$n = -2$ (not valid)

$n = 23; a_{23} = -5k + (22)\left(\dfrac{1}{2}k\right) = -5k + 11k = 6k$

33. $d = \dfrac{72 - 56}{10 - 6} = 4; a_6 = 56 = a_1 + (5)(4);$

$a_1 = 56 - 20 = 36$
$S_{10} = 5(36 + 72) = 540$

37. $\dfrac{a + b}{2} - a = -\dfrac{a}{2} + \dfrac{b}{2}$

$b - \dfrac{a + b}{2} = -\dfrac{a}{2} + \dfrac{b}{2}$

Thus, $a, \dfrac{a+b}{2}, b$ is an arithmetic sequence with

$d = -\dfrac{a}{2} + \dfrac{b}{2} = \dfrac{b-a}{2}$.

41. $3 - x, -x, \sqrt{9 - 2x}; 9 - 2x \geq 0 \Rightarrow x \leq \dfrac{9}{2}$

$3 - x + d = -x$
$d = -3$
$-x + (-3) = \sqrt{9 - 2x}$
$x^2 + 6x + 9 = 9 - 2x$
$x^2 + 8x + 9 = 0$
$x(x + 8) = 0 \Rightarrow x = -8; x = 0,$ reject

Check: $x = -8$

$3 - (-8), -(-8), \sqrt{9 - 2(-8)}$
$11, 8, 5, A.S.$ with $d = -3$

Check: $x = 0$

$3 - 0, -0, \sqrt{9 - 2(0)}$
$3, 0, 3$ is not an $A.S.$

45. $a_1 = 20, d = -1, n = 15$
$a_n = a_1 + (n - 1)d = 20 + (15 - 1)(-1)$
$a_{15} = 20 + (15 - 1)(-1) = 6$

$S_n = \dfrac{n}{2}(a_1 + a_n)$

$S_{15} = \dfrac{15}{2}(20 + 6)$

$S_{15} = 195$ logs in pile

49. $a_1 = 1800, d = -150, a_n = 0$
$0 = 1800 + (n - 1)(-150) = 1800 - 150n + 150$
$150n = 1800 + 150 = 1950; n = 13$ (12 more years)

$S_{13} = \dfrac{13}{2}(1800 + 0) = \$11,700,$ the sum of all depreciations, which is the cost of the car

53. $S_n = \dfrac{n}{2}(a_1 + a_n) = \dfrac{n}{2}[a_1 + (a_1 + (n-1))d]$

$= \dfrac{n}{2}[2a_1 + (n-1)d]$

19.2   Geometric Sequences

1. Find a_7 for $a_1 = \dfrac{8}{625}, r = -\dfrac{5}{2}$.

$a_n = a_1 r^{n-1}$

$a_7 = a_1 r^{7-1} = \dfrac{8}{625}\left(-\dfrac{5}{2}\right)^6$

$a_7 = \dfrac{25}{8}$

5. $\dfrac{1}{6}, \dfrac{1}{6}\cdot 3, \dfrac{1}{6}\cdot 3^2, \dfrac{1}{6}\cdot 3^3, \dfrac{1}{6}\cdot 3^4$

$\dfrac{1}{6}, \dfrac{1}{2}, \dfrac{3}{2}, \dfrac{9}{2}, \dfrac{27}{2}$

9. $r = -25 \div 125 = -0.2, a_1 = 125, n = 7$

$a_7 = 125(-0.2)^{7-1} = \dfrac{1}{125}$

13. $10^{100}, -10^{98}, 10^{96}, \ldots n = 51$

$r = \dfrac{-10^{98}}{10^{100}} = -10^{-2}$

$a_{51} = 10^{100}\cdot(-10^{-2})^{50} = 1$

17. $a_6 = 6 = 192r^5$

$r^5 = \dfrac{1}{32}$

$r = \left(\dfrac{1}{32}\right)^{1/5} = \dfrac{1}{2}$

$S_6 = \dfrac{192\left(1-\left(\dfrac{1}{2}\right)^6\right)}{1-\dfrac{1}{2}} = \dfrac{192\left(1-\dfrac{1}{64}\right)}{\dfrac{1}{2}}$

$= 192\left(\dfrac{63}{64}\right)\left(\dfrac{2}{1}\right) = 378$

21. $a_6 = \left(\dfrac{1}{16}\right)(4)^{6-1} = \left(\dfrac{1}{16}\right)(4)^5 = 64$

$S_6 = \dfrac{\frac{1}{16}(1-4^6)}{1-4} = \dfrac{\frac{1}{16}(1-4096)}{-3} = \dfrac{4095}{48} = \dfrac{1365}{16}$

25. $27 = a_1 r^{4-1}; a_1 = \dfrac{27}{r^3}$

$40 = a_1\dfrac{(1-r^4)}{1-r}$

$= a_1\dfrac{(1+r^2)(1+r)(1-r)}{1-r}$

$= a_1(1+r^2)(1+r)$

Substitute a from first equation in second equation:

$40 = \dfrac{27}{r^3}(1+r^2)(1+r); \; 40r^3 = 27 + 27r + 27r^2 + 27r^3;$

$13r^3 - 27r^2 - 27r - 27 = 0$

Using synthetic division, 3 gives a remainder of zero. Therefore, $r = 3$. $27 = a_1(3^{4-1}); 27a_1 = 27;$ $a_1 = 1$

29. $3, 3^{x+1}, 3^{2x+1}, \cdots$ is a GS, since $\quad 0$

$\dfrac{3^{x+1}}{3} = 3^x$

$\dfrac{3^{2x+1}}{3^{x+1}} = 3^x.$

$a_1 = 3, r = 3^x$
$a_{20} = 3\cdot(3^x)^{20-1} = 3^{19x+1}$

33. $S_n = \dfrac{a_1(1-r^n)}{1-r}, r \neq 1$

$S_3 = 7a_1 = \dfrac{a_1(1-r^3)}{1-r} \Rightarrow 7 - 7r = 1 - r^3$

$r^3 - 7r + 6 = 0$
$(r+3)(r-2)(r-1) = 0$

$r = -3, r = 2, r = 1$ reject since $r \neq 1$

37. $r = 1 - 0.125 = 0.875, a_1 = 3.27$ mA, $n = 9.2$

$a_{9.2} = 3.27(0.875)^{8.2} = 1.09$ mA

41. $0.9^5(9800) = 5800°$C

45. $a_1 = 80, r = 0.65$
$a_{11} = 80(0.65)^{10} = 1.1$
$20° + 1.1° = 21.1°$ C

49. $a_n = a_1 r^{n-1} = a_1 r^n r^{-1} = a_1 r^n/r$
$a_1 r^n = a_n r$

$S_n = \dfrac{a_1(1-r^n)}{1-r} = \dfrac{a_1 - a_1 r^n}{1-r} = \dfrac{a_1 - ra_n}{1-r}$

19.3   Infinite Geometric Series

1. Given the GS $4 + \dfrac{1}{2} + \dfrac{1}{16} + \dfrac{1}{128} + \cdots$ find the sum.

$a_1 = 4, r = \dfrac{1}{8}$

$S = \dfrac{a}{1-r} = \dfrac{4}{1 - \frac{1}{8}}$

$S = \dfrac{32}{7}$

5. $S = \dfrac{a_1}{1-r}$

$\dfrac{25}{0.6} = \dfrac{0.5}{1-r}$

$r = \dfrac{1}{5}$

9. $a_1 = 1, r = \dfrac{7}{8}, S = \dfrac{1}{1 - \frac{7}{8}} = 8$

13. $a_1 = 2 + \sqrt{3}, r = \dfrac{1}{2 + \sqrt{3}}$

$S = \dfrac{2+\sqrt{3}}{1 - \dfrac{1}{2+\sqrt{3}}} = \dfrac{2+\sqrt{3}}{\dfrac{2+\sqrt{3}-1}{2+\sqrt{3}}} = \dfrac{(2+\sqrt{3})(2+\sqrt{3})}{1+\sqrt{3}} = \dfrac{7+4\sqrt{3}}{1+\sqrt{3}} \times \dfrac{1-\sqrt{3}}{1-\sqrt{3}}$

$= \dfrac{7 - 7\sqrt{3} + 4\sqrt{3} - 12}{1 - 3} = \dfrac{-5 - 3\sqrt{3}}{-2} = \dfrac{1}{2}(5 + 3\sqrt{3})$

17. $0.49999\ldots = 0.4 + 0.09 + 0.009 + 0.0009 + \cdots = 0.4 + \dfrac{0.09}{1 - \frac{1}{10}} = 0.5$

21. $0.181818\ldots = 0.18 + 0.0018 + 0.000018 + \cdots$

$a_1 = 0.18, \ r = 0.01$

$S = \dfrac{0.18}{1 - 0.01} = \dfrac{2}{11}$

25. $0.36666\ldots = 0.3 + 0.06666\ldots$

For the GS $0.066\ldots$, $a = 0.06$, $r = 0.1$

$S = \dfrac{0.06}{1 - 0.1} = \dfrac{0.06}{0.9} = \dfrac{1}{15}$

Therefore,

$0.366\,66\ldots = \dfrac{3}{10} + \dfrac{1}{15} = \dfrac{11}{30}$

29. $r = 0.92, \ a_1 = 28.0$ gal

$S = \dfrac{28.0}{1 - 0.92} = \dfrac{28.0}{0.08} = 350$ gal

33. distance $= 10 + 10(0.9) + 10(0.9)^2 + \cdots$

distance $= \dfrac{10}{1 - 0.9}$

distance $= 100$ m

19.4   The Binomial Theorem

1. $(2x + 3)^5 = (2x)^5 + 5(2x)^4(3) + \dfrac{5(4)}{2!}(2x)^3(3)^2 + \dfrac{5(4)(3)}{3!}(2x)^2(3)^3 + \dfrac{5(4)(3)(2)}{4!}(2x)^1(3)^4 + (3)^5$

$(2x + 3)^5 = 32x^5 + 240x^4 + 720x^3 + 1080x^2 + 810x + 243$

5. $(2x - 1)^4 = (2x)^4 + 4(2x)^3(-1) + \dfrac{4(3)}{2}(2x)^2(-1)^2 + \dfrac{4(3)(2)}{6}(2x)(-1)^3 + \dfrac{4(3)(2)(1)}{24}(-1)^4$

$= 16x^4 - 32x^3 + 24x^2 - 8x + 1$

9. $(n + 2\pi)^5 = n^5 + 5n^4(2\pi) + \dfrac{5(4)}{2!}n^3(2\pi)^2 + \dfrac{5(4)(3)}{3!}n^2(2\pi)^3 + \dfrac{5(4)(3)(2)}{4!}n(2\pi)^4 + (2\pi)^5$

$(n + 2\pi)^5 = n^5 + 10\pi n^4 + 40\pi^2 n^3 + 80\pi^3 n^2 + 80\pi^4 n + 32\pi^5$

13. From Pascal's triangle, the coefficients for $n = 4$ are 1, 4, 6, 4, 1.

$(5x - 3)^4 = [5x + (-3)]^4$
$= 1(5x)^4 + 4(5x)^3(-3) + 6(5x)^2(-3)^2 + 4(5x)(-3)^3 + (-3)^4$
$= 625x^4 - 1500x^3 + 1350x^2 - 540x + 81$

17. $(x + 2)^{10} = x^{10} + 10x^9(2) + \dfrac{(10)(9)}{2}x^8(2^2) + \dfrac{(10)(9)(8)}{6}x^7(2)^3 + \cdots = x^{10} + 20x^9 + 180x^8 + 960x^7 + \cdots$

21. $(x^{1/2} - y)^{12} = (x^{1/2})^{12} - 12(x^{1/2})^{11}y + \dfrac{12 \cdot 11}{2!}(x^{1/2})^{10}y^2 - \dfrac{12 \cdot 11 \cdot 10}{3!}(x^{1/2})^9 y^3 + \cdots$

$= x^6 - 12x^{11/2}y + 66x^5y^2 - 220x^{9/2}y^3 + \cdots$

25. $(1.05)^6 = (1 + 0.05)^6$

$= 1^6 + 6(1)^5(0.05) + \dfrac{6(5)}{2!}(1)^4(0.05)^2 = 1.3375$

$= 1.338$ to 3 decimal places using three terms

29. $(1 + x)^8 = 1 + 8x + \dfrac{8(7)}{2}x^2 + \dfrac{8(7)(6)}{6}x^3 + \cdots = 1 + 8x + 28x^2 + 56x^3 + \cdots$

33. $\sqrt{1 + x} = (1 + x)^{1/2} = 1 + \dfrac{1}{2}x + \dfrac{\frac{1}{2}\left(-\frac{1}{2}\right)}{2}x^2 + \dfrac{\frac{1}{2}\left(-\frac{1}{2}\right)\left(-\frac{3}{2}\right)}{6}x^3 + \cdots$

$= 1 + \dfrac{1}{2}x - \dfrac{1}{8}x^2 + \dfrac{1}{16}x^3 - \cdots$

37. (a) $17! + 4! = 3.557 \times 10^{14}$

(b) $21! = 5.109 \times 10^{19}$

(c) $17! \times 4! = 8.536 \times 10^{15}$

(d) $68! = 2.480 \times 10^{96}$

```
17!+4!
      3.556874281E14
21!
      5.109094217E19
17!*4!
      8.536498274E15
```

```
68!
      2.480035542E96
```

41. The term involving b^5 will be the sixth term. $r = 5$, $n = 8$

The sixth term is $\dfrac{8(7)(6)(5)(4)}{5(4)(3)(2)}a^3b^5 = 56a^3b^5$.

45. $\sqrt{6} = \sqrt{4(1.5)} = 2\sqrt{1 + 0.5}$
$= 2(1 + 0.5)^{1/2}$

$= 2\left[1 + \dfrac{1}{2}(0.5) + \dfrac{\frac{1}{2}\left(\frac{1}{2} - 1\right)}{2!}(0.5)^2 + \dfrac{\frac{1}{2}\left(\frac{1}{2} - 1\right)\left(\frac{1}{2} - 2\right)}{3!}(0.5)^3\right]$

$= 2.453125$
$\sqrt{6} = 2.45$ to hundredths using four terms

49. $(a^2 + x^2)^{-1/2} = \dfrac{1}{a}\left[1 + \left(\dfrac{x}{a}\right)^2\right]^{-1/2} = \dfrac{1}{a}\left[1 - \dfrac{1}{2}\left(\dfrac{x^2}{a^2}\right) + \dfrac{3}{8}\left(\dfrac{x^4}{a^4}\right) + \cdots\right]$

$= 1 - x\left(\dfrac{1}{a}\right)\left[1 - \dfrac{x^2}{2a^2} + \dfrac{3x^4}{8a^4} + \cdots\right] = 1 - \dfrac{x}{a} + \dfrac{x^3}{2a^3} - \cdots$

Chapter 19 Review Exercises

1. $d = 5;\ a_n = 1 + (17 - 1)5 = 1 + 80 = 81$

5. $d = \dfrac{7}{2} - 8 = -\dfrac{9}{2};\ a_n = 8 + (16 - 1)\left(-\dfrac{9}{2}\right) = 8 - \dfrac{135}{2} = -\dfrac{119}{2}$

9. $s_n = \dfrac{15}{2}(-4 + 17) = \dfrac{15}{2}(13) = \dfrac{195}{2}$

13. $a_n = 17 + (9 - 1)(-2) = 17 - 16 = 1$

$s_n = \dfrac{9}{2}(1 + 17) = 81$

17. $s_n = \dfrac{n}{2}(a_1 + a_n);\ a_1 = 80,\ a_n = -25,\ s_n = 220$

$220 = \dfrac{n}{2}(80 - 25)$ $\qquad\qquad\qquad a_n = a_1 + (n - 1)d$

$440 = n(80 - 25) = 55n$ $\qquad\qquad -25 = 80 + (8 - 1)d = 80 + 7d$

$n = \dfrac{440}{55} = 8$ $\qquad\qquad\qquad\qquad d = \dfrac{-105}{7} = -15$

21. $s_{12} = \dfrac{12}{2}(-1 + 32) = 6(31) = 186$

25. $r = \dfrac{6}{9} = \dfrac{2}{3};\ s = \dfrac{a_1}{1 - r} = \dfrac{0.9}{1 - \frac{2}{3}} = 2.7$

29. $0.030303\ldots = 0.03 + 0.0003 + 0.000003\ldots$

$a_a = 0.03;\ r = 0.01$

$s = \dfrac{0.03}{1 - 0.01} = \dfrac{0.03}{0.99} = \dfrac{3}{99} = \dfrac{1}{33}$

33. $(x - 2)^4 = [x + (-2)]^4$

$\qquad = x^4 + 4x^3(-2) + \dfrac{4(3)x^2(-2)^2}{2} + \dfrac{4(3)(2)}{3(2)}x(-2)^3 + (-2)^4$

$\qquad = x^4 - 8x^3 + 24x^2 - 32x + 16$

37. $(a + 2e^2)^{10} = a^{10} + 10a^{10-1}(2e^2) + \dfrac{10(10 - 1)}{2!}a^{10-2}(2e^2)^2 + \dfrac{10(10 - 1)(10 - 2)}{3!}a^{10-3}(2e^2)^3 + \cdots$

$\qquad = a^{10} + 10a^9(2e^2) + 45a^8(4e^4) + 120a^7(8e^6) + \cdots$

$\qquad = a^{10} + 20a^9e^2 + 180a^8e^4 + 960a^7e^6 + \cdots$

41. $(1 + x)^{12} = 1 + 12x + \dfrac{12(12 - 1)}{2!}x^2 + \dfrac{12(12 - 1)(12 - 2)}{3!}x^3 + \cdots$

$\qquad = 1 + 12x + 66x^2 + 220x^3 + \cdots$

45. $[1 + (-a^2)]^{1/2} = 1 + \dfrac{1}{2}(-a^2) + \dfrac{\left(\frac{1}{2}\right)\left(-\frac{1}{2}\right)(-a^2)^2}{2} + \dfrac{\frac{1}{2}\left(-\frac{1}{2}\right)\left(-\frac{3}{2}\right)(-a^2)}{3(2)}$

$\qquad\qquad = 1 - \dfrac{1}{2}a^2 - \dfrac{1}{8}a^4 - \dfrac{1}{16}a^6 - \cdots$

49. $a = 2$, $d = 2$, $n = 1000$

$a_n = 2 + (1000 - 1)2 = 2 + 999(2) = 2000$

$s = \dfrac{1000}{2}(2 + 2000) = 1,001,000$

53. Let a_3, a_4, a_5, a_6, a_7 be the GS $6, a_4, 9, a_6, 12$

Suppose $r =$ common ratio, the GS is $6, 6r, 6r^2, 6r^3, 6r^4$ which gives

$9 = 6r^2$ and $6r^4 = 12$

$r^2 = \dfrac{9}{6}$ $r^4 = 2$

$r^2 = \sqrt{2}$

Since $\frac{9}{6} \neq \sqrt{2}$, $6, a_4, 9, a_6, 12$ cannot be a GS.

57. $\sqrt{30} = 5(1 + 0.2)^{1/2}$

$\sqrt{30} = 5\left[1 + \dfrac{1}{2}(0.2) + \dfrac{\frac{1}{2}\left(\frac{1}{2} - 1\right)}{2!}(0.2)^2\right]$

$\sqrt{30} = 5.475$ using three terms

61. $n =$ lens thickness in mm; $a_n = r^n$

$r = 0.88$ $0.20 = (0.88^n)$

$a_1 = 88\% = 0.88$ $\log 0.20 = n \log 0.88$

$a_n = 20\% = 0.20$ $n = \dfrac{\log 0.20}{\log 0.88}$

$n = 12.6$ mm

65. $V = 8600(0.99)^{60} = 4705.547125$

$V = \$4700$, value after 60 months.

69.   first second: $16(1)$

second second: $48 = 16(3)$

third second: $80 = 16(5)$

$\vdots$

nth second: $16(2n - 1)$

20th second: $16(2(20) - 1) = 624$ ft

73. The value of each investment is $a_n = 1000(1.0375)^n$; ($n =$ twice the number of invested years.) The total value is the sum of each investment value. Investment values (20 terms) are as follows:

$$1000(1.0375)^{40}, \ 1000(1.0375)^{38}, \ 1000(1.0375)^{36}, \ \ldots \ 1000(1.0375)^2$$

These terms are changing by a factor of 1.0375^{-2}

$$s = \frac{\left[1000(1.0375)^{40}\right]\left[1 - (1.0375^{-2})^{20}\right]}{1 - (1.0375)^{-2}} = \frac{\left[1000(1.0375)^{40}\right]\left[1 - 1.0375^{-40}\right]}{\left[1 - 1.0375^{-2}\right]}$$

$$\approx \frac{[4360.38]\,[0.7706621247]}{0.0709827261} = \$47,340.81$$

Value increases as additional decimal places are used.

77. Let $x = \dfrac{a-1}{2}m^2$ and $y = \dfrac{a}{a-1}$

$$(1+x)^y = 1 + yx + \frac{y(y-1)}{2}x^2 \ldots \text{(3 terms)}$$

$$= 1 + \left(\frac{a}{a-1}\right)\left(\frac{a-1}{2}m^2\right) + \frac{\left(\frac{a}{a-1}\right)\left(\frac{a}{a-1}-1\right)}{2}\left(\frac{a-1}{2}m^2\right)^2$$

$$= 1 + \frac{a}{2}m^2 + \frac{\left(\frac{a}{a-1}\right)\left(\frac{1}{a-1}\right)}{2}\left(\frac{(a-1)^2}{2^2}m^4\right)$$

$$= 1 + \frac{a}{2}m^2 + \frac{a}{2(a-1)^2}\left(\frac{(a-1)^2}{2^2}m^4\right)$$

$$= 1 + \frac{a}{2}m^2 + \frac{a}{2^3}m^4 = 1 + \frac{1}{2}am^2 + \frac{1}{8}am^4$$

81. Let $a_1 = 1000$ units. If 75% are killed, 25% remain after the first application.

$$r = \frac{a_2}{a_1} = \frac{250}{1000} = 0.25$$

If 99.9% are destroyed, 0.1% remain. $0.001 \times 1000 = 1$ insect remains.

$$1 = 1000(0.25)^n$$
$$0.001 = 0.25^n$$
$$\log 0.001 = \log 0.25^n$$
$$\log 0.001 = n \log 0.25$$

$$n = \frac{\log 0.001}{\log 0.25} = 5 \text{ applications}$$

85. Let $A = $ initial deposit, $t = $ time of a compounding period.
$V = A + Art = A(1 + rt)$, after one compounding period
$V = A(1 + rt) + A(1 + rt)rt = A(1 + rt)^2$, after two compounding periods

$\vdots$

$V = A(1 + rt)^n$, at the end of one year. For $A = \$1000$ and $r = 0.1 = 10\%$
$V = 1000(1 + 0.1t)^n$.

As n, the number of compounding periods, increases t, the length of a compounding period decreases. The product $nt = 1$. For example, if the compounding is done monthly $n = 12$ and $t = \frac{1}{12}$, so that $nt = 12 \cdot \frac{1}{12} = 1$. Thus, $V = 1000\left(1 + 0.1 \cdot \frac{1}{n}\right)^n$ which will increase as n increases-the more compounding periods the more interest. Write V as

$$V = 1000\left(1 + \frac{0.1}{n}\right)^{\frac{0.1}{0.1}} = 1000\left[\left(1 + \frac{0.1}{n}\right)^{\frac{1}{0.1}}\right]^{0.1}$$

As n increases $\left(1 + \dfrac{0.1}{n}\right)^{\frac{1}{0.1}}$ approaches e. Hence, the maximum value is $V_{\max} = 1000 \cdot e^{0.1} = \$1105.17$ as

compared with $V = 1000\left(1 + 0.1 \cdot \dfrac{1}{12}\right)^{12} = \$1104.71$ for monthly compounding.

ADDITIONAL TOPICS IN TRIGONOMETRY

20.1 Fundamental Trigonometric Identities

1. $\sin x = \dfrac{\tan x}{\sec x}$

$= \dfrac{\frac{\sin x}{\cos x}}{\frac{1}{\cos x}}$

$= \dfrac{\sin x}{\cos x} \cdot \dfrac{\cos x}{1}$

$= \sin x$

5. Verify $\sin^2 \theta + \cos^2 \theta = 1$ for $\theta = \dfrac{4\pi}{3}$

$\left(\sin \dfrac{4\pi}{3}\right)^2 = \left(-\dfrac{1}{2}\sqrt{3}\right)^2 = \dfrac{3}{4}$

$\left(\cos \dfrac{4\pi}{3}\right)^2 = \left(-\dfrac{1}{2}\right)^2 = \dfrac{1}{4}$

$\dfrac{3}{4} + \dfrac{1}{4} = 1$

9. $\dfrac{\sin x}{\tan x} = \sin x \times \dfrac{1}{\tan x} = \sin x \times \dfrac{\cos x}{\sin x} = \cos x$

13. $\sin x \sec x = \sin x \times \dfrac{1}{\cos x} = \dfrac{\sin x}{\cos x} = \tan x$

17. $\sin x(1 + \cot^2 x) = \sin x(\csc^2 x) = \sin x \left(\dfrac{1}{\sin^2 x}\right)$

$= \dfrac{1}{\sin x} = \csc x$

21. $\cos \theta \cot \theta + \sin \theta = \cos \theta \times \dfrac{\cos \theta}{\sin \theta} + \sin \theta$

$= \dfrac{\cos^2 \theta}{\sin \theta} + \sin \theta$

$= \dfrac{\cos^2 \theta + \sin^2 \theta}{\sin \theta}$

$= \dfrac{1}{\sin \theta} = \csc \theta$

25. $\tan x + \cot x = \dfrac{\sin x}{\cos x} + \dfrac{\cos x}{\sin x}$

$= \dfrac{\sin^2 x + \cos^2 x}{\cos x \sin x}$

$= \dfrac{1}{\cos x \sin x}$

$= \sec x \csc x$

29. $\dfrac{\sin x}{1 - \cos x} = \dfrac{\sin x(1 + \cos x)}{(1 - \cos x)(1 + \cos x)}$

$= \dfrac{\sin x(1 + \cos x)}{1 - \cos^2 x} = \dfrac{\sin x(1 + \cos x)}{\sin^2 x}$

$= \dfrac{1 + \cos x}{\sin x} = \dfrac{1}{\sin x} + \dfrac{\cos x}{\sin x}$

$= \csc x + \cot x$

33. $2\sin^4 x - 3\sin^2 x + 1 = (2\sin^2 x - 1)(\sin^2 x - 1)$

$= (2\sin^2 x - 1)(-\cos^2 x)$

$= \cos^2 x(1 - 2\sin^2 x)$

37. $1 + \sin^2 x + \sin^4 x \cdots + = $ infinite series

$a_1 = 1, r = \sin^2 x$

$S = \dfrac{1}{1 - \sin^2 x} = \dfrac{1}{\cos^2 x} = \sec^2 x$

41. $\cot x(\sec x - \cos x) = \dfrac{\cos x}{\sin x} \cdot \dfrac{1}{\cos x} - \dfrac{\cos x}{\sin x} \cdot \cos x$

$= \dfrac{1}{\sin x} - \dfrac{\cos^2 x}{\sin x}$

$= \dfrac{1 - \cos^2 x}{\sin x}$

$= \dfrac{\sin^2 x}{\sin x}$

$= \sin x$

45. $\dfrac{\cos x + \sin x}{1 + \tan x} = \dfrac{\cos x + \sin x}{1 + \frac{\sin x}{\cos x}} \cdot \dfrac{\cos x}{\cos x}$

$= \dfrac{(\cos x + \sin x) \cdot \cos x}{\cos x + \sin x}$

$= \cos x$

49.

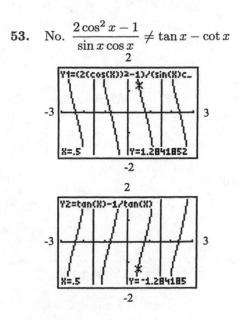

53. No. $\dfrac{2\cos^2 x - 1}{\sin x \cos x} \neq \tan x - \cot x$

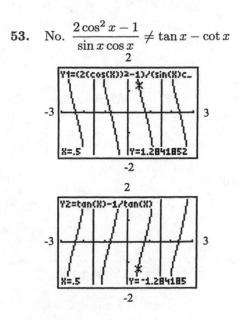

57. $l = a \csc \theta + a \sec \theta$

$= a(\csc \theta + \sec \theta)$

$= a\left(\dfrac{1}{\sin \theta} + \dfrac{1}{\cos \theta}\right)$

$= a\left(\dfrac{1}{\sin \theta} + \dfrac{\sin \theta}{\cos \theta} \times \dfrac{1}{\sin \theta}\right)$

$= a\left(\dfrac{1}{\sin \theta} + \dfrac{\tan \theta}{\sin \theta}\right)$

$= \dfrac{a(1 + \tan \theta)}{\sin \theta}$

61. $\sin^2 x(1 - \sec^2 x) + \cos^2 x(1 + \sec^4 x)$

$= \sin^2 x - \sin^2 x \sec^2 x + \cos^2 x + \cos^2 x \sec^4 x$

$= \sin^2 x - \dfrac{\sin^2 x}{\cos^2 x} + \cos^2 x + \dfrac{\cos^2 x}{\cos^4 x}$

$= \sin^2 x - \tan^2 x + \cos^2 x + \sec^2 x$

$= 1 - \tan^2 x + \sec^2 x$

$= 1 - (\sec^2 x - 1) + \sec^2 x$

$= 1 - \sec^2 x + 1 + \sec^2 x = 2$

65. $x = \cos \theta$;

$$\sqrt{1 - x^2} = \sqrt{1 - \cos^2 \theta} = \sqrt{\sin^2 \theta} = \sin \theta$$

20.2   The Sum and Difference Formulas

1. $\sin \alpha = \dfrac{12}{13}$ (α in first quadrant) and $\sin \beta = -\dfrac{3}{5}$ for β in third quadrant.

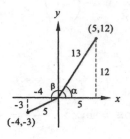

$\cos(\alpha + \beta) = \cos \alpha \cos \beta - \sin \alpha \sin \beta$

$= \dfrac{5}{13} \cdot \dfrac{-4}{5} - \dfrac{12}{13} \cdot \dfrac{-3}{5}$

$= \dfrac{16}{65}$

5. Given: $15° = 60° - 45°$

$\cos(\alpha - \beta) = \cos \alpha \cos \beta + \sin \alpha \sin \beta$

$\cos 15° = \cos(60° - 45°)$

$= \cos 60° \cos 45° + \sin 60° \sin 45°$

$= \dfrac{1}{2} \times \dfrac{\sqrt{2}}{2} + \dfrac{\sqrt{3}}{2} \times \dfrac{\sqrt{2}}{2}$

$= \dfrac{\sqrt{2}}{4} + \dfrac{\sqrt{6}}{4} = \dfrac{\sqrt{2} + \sqrt{6}}{4}$

$= 0.9659$

9. Using the results of exercise 7:

$$\cos\alpha = \frac{3}{5}$$

$$\cos\beta = -\frac{12}{13}$$

$$\sin\alpha = \frac{4}{5}$$

$$\sin\beta = \frac{5}{13}$$

$$\cos(\alpha+\beta) = \cos\alpha\cos\beta - \sin\alpha\sin\beta$$

$$= \frac{3}{5}\left(-\frac{12}{13}\right) - \frac{4}{5}\left(\frac{5}{13}\right)$$

$$= \frac{-36-20}{65} = -\frac{56}{65}$$

13. $\cos\alpha\cos\beta + \sin\alpha\sin\beta = \cos(\alpha-\beta);$
$\alpha = x+y, \beta = y$
$\cos(x+y)\cos y + \sin(x+y)\sin y$
$= \cos(x+y-y)$
$= \cos x$

17. $\sin\alpha\cos\beta - \cos\alpha\sin\beta = \sin(\alpha-\beta);$
$\alpha = 3x, \beta = 3x - \pi$
$\sin 3x\cos(3x-\pi) - \cos 3x\sin(3x-\pi)$
$\quad \sin(3x - 3x + \pi)$
$\quad = \sin\pi = 0$

21. $\cos\dfrac{\pi}{5}\cos\dfrac{3\pi}{10} - \sin\dfrac{\pi}{5}\sin\dfrac{3\pi}{10}$ is of the form
$\cos\alpha\cos\beta - \sin\alpha\sin\beta = \cos(\alpha+\beta)$ with
$\alpha = \dfrac{\pi}{5}$ and $\beta = \dfrac{3\pi}{10}$ so

$$\cos\frac{\pi}{5}\cos\frac{3\pi}{10} - \sin\frac{\pi}{5}\sin\frac{3\pi}{10} = \cos\left(\frac{\pi}{5} + \frac{3\pi}{10}\right)$$

$$= \cos\frac{\pi}{2} = 0$$

25. $\cos(-x) = \cos(0° - x)$
$\quad = \cos 0° \cos x + \sin 0° \sin x$
$\quad = (1)\cos x + (0)\sin x = \cos x$

29. $\cos\left(\dfrac{\pi}{3} + x\right) = \cos\dfrac{\pi}{3}\cos x - \sin\dfrac{\pi}{3}\sin x$

$$= \frac{1}{2}\cos x - \frac{\sqrt{3}}{2}\sin x$$

$$= \frac{\cos x - \sqrt{3}\sin x}{2}$$

33. $\cos(\alpha+\beta) + \cos(\alpha-\beta)$
$\quad = \cos\alpha\cos\beta - \sin\alpha\sin\beta + \cos\alpha\cos\beta + \sin\alpha\sin\beta$
$\quad = 2\cos\alpha\cos\beta$

37.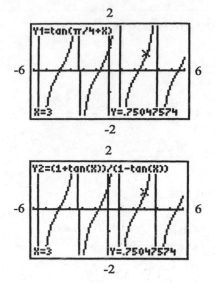

41. $\cos(\alpha+\beta) + \cos(\alpha-\beta)$
$\quad = \cos\alpha\cos\beta - \sin\alpha\sin\beta + \cos\alpha\cos\beta + \sin\alpha\sin\beta$
$\quad = 2\cos\alpha\cos\beta$

Therefore,

$$\cos\alpha\cos\beta = \frac{1}{2}[\cos(\alpha+\beta) + \cos(\alpha-\beta)]$$

45. $\cos x + \cos y$
$\quad = \cos(\alpha+\beta) + \cos(\alpha-\beta)$

$$= 2\left[\frac{1}{2}\cos(\alpha-\beta) + \frac{1}{2}\cos(\alpha-\beta)\right]$$

$$= 2\cos\alpha\cos\beta$$

$$= 2\cos\frac{1}{2}(x+y)\cos\frac{1}{2}(x-y)$$

49. $\sin 75° = \sin(30° + 45°)$
$\quad = \sin 30°\cos 45° + \sin 45°\cos 30°$

$$= \frac{1}{2}\cdot\frac{\sqrt{2}}{2} + \frac{\sqrt{2}}{2}\cdot\frac{\sqrt{3}}{2}$$

$$= \frac{\sqrt{2} + \sqrt{6}}{4}$$

$\sin 75° = \sin(135° - 60°)$
$\quad = \sin 135°\cos 60° - \sin 60°\cos 135°$

$$= \frac{\sqrt{2}}{2}\cdot\frac{1}{2} - \frac{\sqrt{3}}{2}\cdot\left(-\frac{\sqrt{2}}{2}\right)$$

$$= \frac{\sqrt{2} + \sqrt{6}}{4}$$

53. $i_0\sin(\omega t + \alpha) = i_0[\sin\omega t\cos\alpha + \sin\alpha\cos\omega t]$
$\quad = i_0\cos\alpha\sin\omega t + i_0\sin\alpha\cos\omega t$
$\quad = i_1\sin\omega t + i_2\cos\omega t$

20.3 Double-Angle Formulas

1. If $\alpha = \dfrac{\pi}{3}$,

$$\tan \dfrac{2\pi}{3} = \tan \left(2 \cdot \dfrac{\pi}{3}\right) = \dfrac{2 \tan \frac{\pi}{3}}{1 - \tan^2 \frac{\pi}{3}}$$

$$= \dfrac{2(\sqrt{3})}{1 - (\sqrt{3})^2}$$

$$= -\sqrt{3}$$

5. $60° = 2(30°);\ \sin 2\alpha = 2 \sin \alpha \cos \alpha$

$$\sin 2(30°) = 2 \sin 30° \cos 30°$$

$$= 2 \left(\dfrac{1}{2}\right) \left(\dfrac{\sqrt{3}}{2}\right)$$

$$= \dfrac{\sqrt{3}}{2} = \dfrac{1}{2}\sqrt{3}$$

9. $\sin 258° = -0.978147\ 6$

$$\sin 258° = \sin 2(129°)$$

$$= 2 \sin 129° \cos 129°$$

$$= -0.9781476$$

13. $\tan \dfrac{2\pi}{5} = \dfrac{2 \tan \frac{\pi}{5}}{1 - \tan^2 \frac{\pi}{5}} = 3.0777$

17. $\sin x = 0.5\ (\text{QII}) \Rightarrow x = \dfrac{5\pi}{6}$

$$\tan 2x = \dfrac{2 \tan x}{1 - \tan^2 x} = \dfrac{2 \tan \frac{5\pi}{6}}{1 - \tan^2 \frac{5\pi}{6}} = -\sqrt{3}$$

21. $1 - 2 \sin^2 4x = \cos 2(4x) = \cos 8x$

25. $4 \sin^2 2x - 2 = 2(2 \sin^2 2x - 1)$

$$= -2(1 - 2 \sin^2 2x)$$

$$= -2 \cos 2(2x)$$

$$= -2 \cos 4x$$

29. $\dfrac{\cos x - \tan x \sin x}{\sec x} = \dfrac{\cos x - \dfrac{\sin x \sin x}{\cos x}}{\dfrac{1}{\cos x}}$

$$= \dfrac{\cos^2 x - \sin^2 x}{\cos x} \times \dfrac{\cos x}{1}$$

$$= \cos^2 x - \sin^2 x$$

$$= \cos 2x$$

33. $\dfrac{\sin 2\theta}{1 + \cos 2\theta} = \dfrac{2 \sin \theta \cos \theta}{1 + (2 \cos^2 \theta - 1)}$

$$= \dfrac{2 \sin \theta \cos \theta}{2 \cos^2 \theta}$$

$$= \dfrac{\sin \theta}{\cos \theta} = \tan \theta$$

37. $\dfrac{\sin 3x}{\sin x} - \dfrac{\cos 3x}{\cos x} = \dfrac{\sin 3x \cos x - \cos 3x \sin x}{\sin x \cos x}$

$$= \dfrac{\sin(3x - x)}{\dfrac{1}{2} \sin 2x} = \dfrac{\sin 2x}{\dfrac{1}{2} \sin 2x} = 2$$

41. Both graphs are the same.

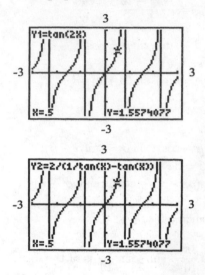

45. $\sin 3x$

$$= \sin(2x + x) = \sin 2x \cos x + \cos 2x \sin x$$

$$= (2 \sin x \cos x)(\cos x) + (\cos^2 x - \sin^2 x)(\sin x)$$

$$= 2 \sin x \cos^2 x + \sin x \cos^2 x - \sin^3 x$$

$$= 3 \sin x \cos^2 x - \sin^3 x$$

$$= 3 \sin x (1 - \sin^2 x) - \sin^3 x$$

$$= 3 \sin x - 4 \sin^3 x$$

49. $y = 4 \sin x \cos x = 2(2 \sin x \cos x)$

$$y = 2 \sin 2x$$

$$A = 2,\ \text{period} = \dfrac{2\pi}{2} = \pi$$

53. $R = vt \cos \alpha;\ t = \dfrac{(2v \sin \alpha)}{g}$

$$R = v \left(\dfrac{2v \sin \alpha}{g}\right) \cos \alpha = \dfrac{v^2 (2 \sin \alpha \cos \alpha)}{g}$$

$$= \dfrac{v^2 \sin 2\alpha}{g}$$

20.4   Half-Angle Formulas

1. $\sqrt{\dfrac{1+\cos 114°}{2}} = \cos \dfrac{1}{2}(114°) = \cos 57°$

$\sqrt{\dfrac{1+\cos 114°}{2}} = 0.544639035$, calculator

$\cos 57° = 0.544639035$, calculator

5. $\sin 75° = \sin \dfrac{150°}{2} = \sqrt{\dfrac{1-\cos 150°}{2}}$

$= \sqrt{\dfrac{1.8660}{2}} = 0.9659$

9. $\sqrt{\dfrac{1-\cos 236°}{2}} = \sin \dfrac{1}{2}(236°) = \sin 118°$

$= 0.8829476$

13. $\sin \dfrac{\alpha}{2} = \sqrt{\dfrac{1-\cos \alpha}{2}}$

$\sqrt{\dfrac{1-\cos 6x}{2}} = \sin \dfrac{6x}{2} = \sin 3x$

17. $\sqrt{4-4\cos 10\theta} = \sqrt{4(1-\cos(2(5\theta)))}$

$= 2\sqrt{2}\sqrt{\dfrac{1-\cos 5\theta}{2}}$

$= 2\sqrt{2}\sin 5\theta$

21. $\tan \alpha = -0.2917 \text{ (QII)}$
$\sec^2 \alpha = 1 + \tan^2 \alpha = 1 + 0.085 = 1.0851$

$\cos^2 \alpha = \dfrac{1}{\sec^2 \alpha} = \dfrac{1}{1.0851} = 0.921\,57$

$\cos \dfrac{\alpha}{2} = \sqrt{\dfrac{1+\cos \alpha}{2}} = \sqrt{\dfrac{1-0.95999}{2}}$

$= 0.1414$

25. $\tan \dfrac{\alpha}{2} = \dfrac{\sin \dfrac{\alpha}{2}}{\cos \dfrac{\alpha}{2}} = \dfrac{\sqrt{\dfrac{1-\cos \alpha}{2}}}{\sqrt{\dfrac{1+\cos \alpha}{2}}}$

$= \sqrt{\dfrac{1-\cos \alpha}{2}} \times \sqrt{\dfrac{2}{1+\cos \alpha}}$

$= \dfrac{\sqrt{1-\cos \alpha}}{\sqrt{1+\cos \alpha}} \times \dfrac{\sqrt{1+\cos \alpha}}{\sqrt{1+\cos \alpha}}$

$= \dfrac{\sqrt{1-\cos^2 \alpha}}{1+\cos \alpha} = \dfrac{\sin \alpha}{1+\cos \alpha}$

29. $2\sin^2 \dfrac{x}{2} + \cos x = 2\left(\sqrt{\dfrac{1-\cos x}{2}}\right)^2 + \cos x$

$= 2\left(\dfrac{1-\cos x}{2}\right) + \cos x$

$= 1 - \cos x + \cos x = 1$

33. $2\sin^2 \dfrac{\alpha}{2} - \cos^2 \dfrac{\alpha}{2} = \dfrac{1-3\cos \alpha}{2}$

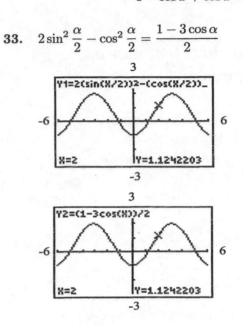

37. Find $\tan \theta$ if $\sin \dfrac{\theta}{2} = \dfrac{3}{5}$.

$\sin \dfrac{\theta}{2} = \dfrac{3}{5} \Rightarrow \dfrac{\theta}{2}$ in QI or $\dfrac{\theta}{2}$ in QII

For $\dfrac{\theta}{2}$ in QI, $\sin \dfrac{\theta}{2} = \dfrac{3}{5} \Rightarrow \cos \dfrac{\theta}{2} = \dfrac{4}{5}$

$\sin 2 \cdot \dfrac{\theta}{2} = \sin \theta = 2\sin \dfrac{\theta}{2}\cos \dfrac{\theta}{2} = 2 \cdot \dfrac{3}{5} \cdot \dfrac{4}{5} = \dfrac{24}{25}$

$\cos 2 \cdot \dfrac{\theta}{2} = \cos \theta = \cos^2 \dfrac{\theta}{2} - \sin^2 \dfrac{\theta}{2} = \dfrac{16}{25} - \dfrac{9}{25} = \dfrac{7}{25}$

$\tan \theta = \dfrac{\sin \theta}{\cos \theta} = \dfrac{\frac{24}{25}}{\frac{7}{25}} = \dfrac{24}{7}$

For $\dfrac{\theta}{2}$ in QII, $\sin \dfrac{\theta}{2} = \dfrac{3}{5} \Rightarrow \cos \dfrac{\theta}{2} = \dfrac{-4}{5}$

$\sin 2 \cdot \dfrac{\theta}{2} = \sin \theta = 2\sin \dfrac{\theta}{2}\cos \dfrac{\theta}{2} = 2 \cdot \dfrac{3}{5} \cdot \dfrac{-4}{5} = \dfrac{-24}{25}$

$\cos 2 \cdot \dfrac{\theta}{2} = \cos \theta = \cos^2 \dfrac{\theta}{2} - \sin^2 \dfrac{\theta}{2} = \dfrac{16}{25} - \dfrac{9}{25} = \dfrac{7}{25}$

$\tan \theta = \dfrac{\sin \theta}{\cos \theta} = \dfrac{-\frac{24}{25}}{\frac{7}{25}} = -\dfrac{24}{7}$

if $\sin \dfrac{\theta}{2} = \dfrac{3}{5}$, $\tan \theta = \pm \dfrac{24}{7}$

41. $\sin^2 \omega t = \sin^2 \left[\left(\dfrac{1}{2} \right) (2\omega t) \right]$

$\qquad = \left(\sqrt{\dfrac{1 - \cos 2\omega t}{2}} \right)^2$

$\qquad = \dfrac{1 - \cos 2\omega t}{2}$

20.5 Solving Trigonometric Equations

1. $2\sin^2 x - \sin x - 1 = 0;\ 0 \le x < 2\pi$

$(2\sin x + 1)(\sin x - 1) = 0$

$2\sin x + 1 = 0 \qquad$ or $\quad \sin x - 1 = 0$

$\qquad 2\sin x = -1 \qquad\qquad\qquad \sin x = 1$

$\qquad\quad \sin x = -\dfrac{1}{2} \qquad\qquad\qquad x = \dfrac{\pi}{2}$

$\qquad\qquad x = \dfrac{7\pi}{6}, \dfrac{11\pi}{6}$

$x = \dfrac{\pi}{2}, \dfrac{7\pi}{6}, \dfrac{11\pi}{6}$

5. $\sin x - 1 = 0,\ 0 \le x < 2\pi;\ \sin x = 1;\ x =$

9. $4\cos^2 x - 1 = 0;\ 0 \le x < 2\pi$

$4\cos^2 x = 1;\ \cos^2 x = \dfrac{1}{4};\ \cos x = \pm\dfrac{1}{2}$

$x = \dfrac{\pi}{3}, \dfrac{2\pi}{3}, \dfrac{4\pi}{3}, \dfrac{5\pi}{3}$

13. $\sin 2x \sin x + \cos x = 0,\ 0 \le x < 2\pi$

$(2\sin x \cos x)(\sin x) + \cos x = 0$

$2\sin^2 x \cos x + \cos x = 0;\ \cos x(2\sin^2 x + 1) = 0$

$\cos x = 0;\ x = \dfrac{\pi}{2}, \dfrac{3\pi}{2};\ 2\sin x + 1 = 0;\ 2\sin^2 x = -1$

$\sin^2 x = -\dfrac{1}{2}$, which has no real solution; thus,

$x = \dfrac{\pi}{2}, \dfrac{3\pi}{2}$

17. $4\tan x - \sec^2 x = 0;\ 4\tan x - (1 + \tan^2 x) = 0$

$4\tan x - 1 - \tan^2 x = 0;\ \tan^2 x - 4\tan x + 1 = 0$

$\tan^2 x - 4\tan x = -1;\ \tan^2 x - 4\tan x + 4 = -1 + 4$

(completing the square)

$(\tan x - 2)^2 = 3;\ \tan x - 2 = \pm\sqrt{3}$

$\tan x = 2 \pm \sqrt{3} = 3.732, 0.2679$

$x = \tan^{-1} 0.2679 = 0.2618,\ \pi + 0.2618 = 3.403$

$x = \tan^{-1} 3.732 = 1.309,\ \pi + 1.309 = 4.451$

$x = 0.2618, 1.309, 3.403, 4.451$

21. $\tan x + 1 = 0;\ \tan x = -1;\ x_{ref} = \dfrac{\pi}{4}$

(tan negative QII, QIV)

$x = \pi - \dfrac{\pi}{4} = \dfrac{3\pi}{4} \approx 2.36$ or

$x = 2\pi - \dfrac{\pi}{4} = \dfrac{7\pi}{4} \approx 5.50$

Graph $y_1 = \tan x + 1$. Use zero feature to solve. $x = 2.36, 5.50$.

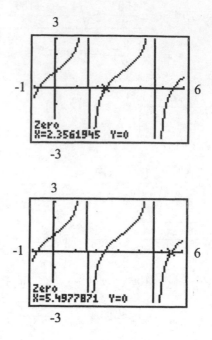

25. $4\sin^2 x - 3 = 0;\ 4\sin^2 x = 3;\ \sin^2 x = \dfrac{3}{4};$

$\sin x = \pm\sqrt{\dfrac{3}{4}} = \pm\dfrac{\sqrt{3}}{2};\ x_{ref} = \dfrac{\pi}{3}$

(sin positive or negative—all quadrants)

$x = \dfrac{\pi}{3} = 1.05;\ \pi - \dfrac{\pi}{3} = \dfrac{2\pi}{3} = 2.09$

$x = \pi + \dfrac{\pi}{3} = \dfrac{4\pi}{3} = 4.19;\ x = 2\pi - \dfrac{\pi}{3} = \dfrac{5\pi}{3} = 5.24$

Graph $y_1 = 4\sin^2 x - 3$. Use zero feature to solve. $x = 1.05, 2.09, 4.19$, and 5.24.

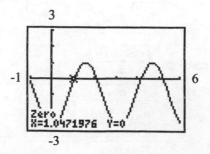

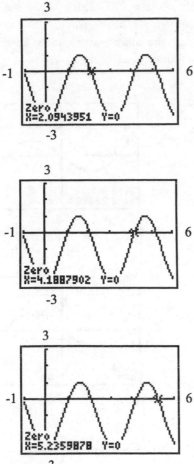

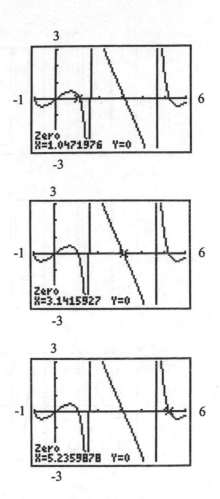

29. $2\sin x - \tan x = 0$; $2\sin x - \dfrac{\sin x}{\cos x} = 0$;

$\sin x \left(2 - \dfrac{1}{\cos x} \right) = 0$; $\sin x = 0$; $x = 0.00$;

$x = \pi = 3.14$

$2 - \dfrac{1}{\cos x} = 0$; $\dfrac{1}{\cos x} = 2$; $\cos x = \dfrac{1}{2}$; $x_{ref} = \dfrac{\pi}{3}$;

$x = \dfrac{\pi}{3} = 1.05$; $x = 2\pi - \dfrac{\pi}{3} = \dfrac{5\pi}{3} = 5.24$

Graph $y_1 = 2\sin x - \tan x$. Use zero feature to solve. $x = 0.00$, 1.05, 3.14, and 5.24.

33. $\tan x + 3\cot x = 4$; $\tan x + \dfrac{3}{\tan x} = 4$

$\tan^2 x + 3 = 4\tan x$; $\tan^2 x - 4\tan x + 3 = 0$;

$(\tan x - 1)(\tan x - 3) = 0$

$\tan x = 1$; $x = \dfrac{\pi}{4} = 0.7854$ or

$x = \pi + \dfrac{\pi}{4} = \dfrac{5\pi}{4} = 3.927$;

$\tan x - 3 = 0$; $\tan x = 3$; $x = 1.249$ or
$x = \pi + 1.249 = 4.391$

Graph $y_1 = \tan x + 3/\tan x - 4$.
Use zero feature to solve. $x = 0.79$, 1.25, 3.93, and 4.39.

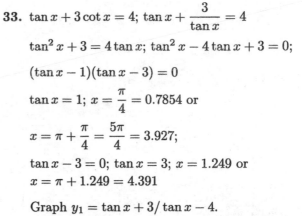

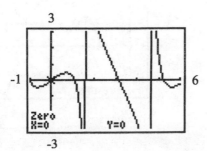

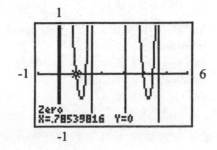

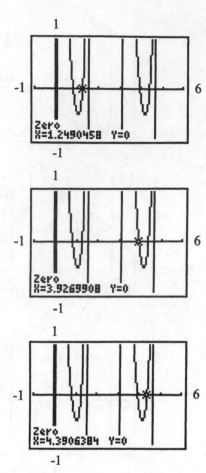

45. $3\sin x - x = 0$. Graph $y_1 = 3\sin x - x$.

Use zero feature to solve. $x = -2.28,\ 0.00,\ 2.28$.

Using the zoom feature, more accurate values can be found.

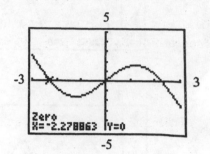

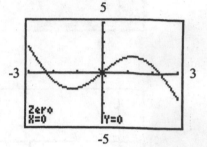

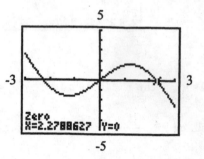

37. $\sin 3x + \sin x = 0,\ 0 \le x < 2\pi \Rightarrow 0 \le 3x < 6\pi$

$$2\sin\frac{3x+x}{2}\cos\frac{3x-x}{2} = 0$$

$$2\sin 2x\cos x = 0$$

$\sin 2x = 0$ $\qquad$ or $\qquad$ $\cos x = 0$

$2x = 0, \pi, 3\pi, 4\pi, 5\pi$ $\qquad$ $x = \dfrac{\pi}{2}, \dfrac{3\pi}{2},$

$x = 0, \dfrac{\pi}{2}, \pi, \dfrac{3\pi}{2}$ $\qquad$ $x = 0, \dfrac{\pi}{2}, \pi, \dfrac{3\pi}{2}$

41. $\dfrac{p^2\tan\theta}{0.0063 + p\tan\theta} = 1.6;\ p = 4.8$

$$\frac{4.8^2\tan\theta}{0.0063 + 4.8\tan\theta} = 1.6$$

$4.8^2\tan\theta = 1.6(0.0063 + 4.8\tan\theta) = 0.01008 + 7.68\tan\theta$

$4.8^2\tan\theta - 7.68\tan\theta = 0.01008$

$15.36\tan\theta = 0.01008$

$\tan\theta = \dfrac{0.01008}{15.36} = 6.5625 \times 10^{-4}$

$\theta = 6.56 \times 10^{-4}$

49. $2\ln x = 1 - \cos 2x;\ 2\ln x - 1 + \cos 2x = 0$

Graph $y_1 = 2\ln x - 1 + \cos 2x$.

Use zero feature to solve. $x = 2.10$.

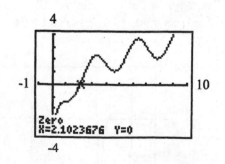

20.6   The Inverse Trigonometric Functions

1. $y = \tan^{-1} 3A$ is read as "y is the angle whose tangent is $3A$." In this case, $3A = \tan y$.

5. y is an angle whose tangent is x.

9. y is twice the angle whose sine is x.

13. $\cos^{-1} 0.5 = \dfrac{\pi}{3}$ since $\cos \dfrac{\pi}{3} = 0.5$ and

$0 \le \dfrac{\pi}{3} \le \pi$

17. $\tan^{-1}(-\sqrt{3}) = -\dfrac{\pi}{3}$ since $\tan\left(-\dfrac{\pi}{3}\right) = -\sqrt{3}$ and

$-\dfrac{\pi}{2} < -\dfrac{\pi}{3} < \dfrac{\pi}{2}$

21. $\sin^{-1}\left(-\dfrac{\sqrt{2}}{2}\right) = -\dfrac{\pi}{4}$ since $\sin\left(-\dfrac{\pi}{4}\right) = -\dfrac{\sqrt{2}}{2}$ and

$-\dfrac{\pi}{2} \le -\dfrac{\pi}{4} \le \dfrac{\pi}{2}$

25. $\cos[\tan^{-1}(-1)] = \cos\left(-\dfrac{\pi}{4}\right) = \dfrac{1}{2}\sqrt{2}$

29. $\tan^{-1} x = \sin^{-1}\dfrac{2}{5}$

$x = \tan\left(\sin^{-1}\dfrac{2}{5}\right)$

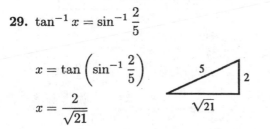

$x = \dfrac{2}{\sqrt{21}}$

33. $\tan^{-1}(-3.7321) = -1.3090$

37. $\tan[\cos^{-1}(-0.6281)] = \tan 2.250 = -1.2389$

41. $y = \sin 3x;\ 3x = \sin^{-1} y;\ x = \dfrac{1}{3}\sin^{-1} y$

45. $1 - y = \cos^{-1}(1 - x)$
$\cos(1 - y) = 1 - x$
$x = 1 - \cos(1 - y)$

49. Let $\alpha - \sin^{-1}, \beta = \cos^{-1} y$

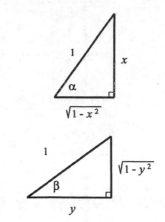

$\sin(\sin^{-1} x + \cos^{-1} y) = \sin(\alpha + \beta)$
$= \sin\alpha\cos\beta + \sin\beta\cos\alpha$
$= xy + \sqrt{1 - y^2}\sqrt{1 - x^2}$
$= xy + \sqrt{1 - y^2 - x^2 + x^2 y^2}$

53. $\sin(2\sin^{-1} x) = \sin 2\theta$
$= 2\sin\theta\cos\theta$

$= 2\left(\dfrac{x}{1}\right)\left(\dfrac{\sqrt{1 - x^2}}{1}\right)$

$= 2x\sqrt{1 - x^2}$

In a triangle, θ is set up such that its sine is $2x$. This gives an opposite side of $2x$, hypotenuse 1, and adjacent side $\sqrt{1 - 4x^2}$.

57. $i = I_m[\sin(\omega t + \alpha)\cos\phi + \cos(\omega t + \alpha)\sin\phi]$

$\dfrac{i}{I_m} = \sin(\omega t + \alpha + \phi)$

$\sin^{-1}\left(\dfrac{i}{I_m}\right) = \omega t + \alpha + \phi$

$\omega t = \sin^{-1}\left(\dfrac{i}{I_m}\right) - \alpha - \phi$

$t = \dfrac{1}{\omega}\left(\sin^{-1}\left(\dfrac{i}{I_m}\right) - \alpha - \phi\right)$

61. $\sin^{-1} 0.5 + \cos^{-1} 0.5 = \dfrac{\pi}{6} + \dfrac{\pi}{3} = \dfrac{\pi + 2\pi}{6} = \dfrac{3\pi}{6} = \dfrac{\pi}{2}$

65. Since $\sin A = \dfrac{a}{c},\ A = \sin^{-1}\left(\dfrac{a}{c}\right)$

69. Let $y =$ height to top of pedestal

$$\tan \alpha = \frac{151 + y}{d}$$

$$\tan \beta = \frac{y}{d}$$

$$y = d \tan \beta$$

$$\tan \alpha = \frac{151 + d \tan \beta}{d}$$

$$\alpha = \tan^{-1}\left(\frac{151 + d \tan \beta}{d}\right) = \tan^{-1}\left(\frac{151}{d} + \tan \beta\right)$$

Chapter 20 Review Exercises

1. $\sin 120° = \sin(90° + 30°) = \sin 90° \cos 30° + \cos 90° \sin 30°) = 1\left(\dfrac{\sqrt{3}}{2}\right) + 0\left(\dfrac{1}{2}\right) = \dfrac{\sqrt{3}}{2} = \dfrac{1}{2}\sqrt{3}$

5. $\cos \pi = \cos 2\left(\dfrac{\pi}{2}\right) = \cos^2 \dfrac{\pi}{2} - \sin^2 \dfrac{\pi}{2} = 0 - (1)^2 = -1$

9. $\sin 14° \cos 38° + \cos 14° \sin 38°$
      $= \sin(14° + 38°)$
      $= \sin 52°$
      $= 0.7880108$

13. $\cos 73° \cos 142° + \sin 73° \sin 142°$
      $= \cos(73° - 142°)$
      $= \cos(-69°)$
      $= 0.3583679495$

17. $\sin 2x \cos 3x + \cos 2x \sin 3x$
      $= \sin \alpha \cos \beta + \cos \alpha \sin \beta$
      $= \sin(\alpha + \beta)$ where $\alpha = 2x$, $\beta = 3x$
  $\sin(\alpha + \beta) = \sin(2x + 3x) = \sin 5x$

21. $2 - 4\sin^2 6x = 2(1 - 2\sin^2 6x) = 2(1 - 2\sin^2 \alpha) = 2(\cos 2\alpha) = 2\cos 12x$ where $\alpha = 6x$

25. $\sin^{-1}(-1) = -\dfrac{\pi}{2}$ since $\sin\left(-\dfrac{\pi}{2}\right) = -1$ and $-\dfrac{\pi}{2} \le -\dfrac{\pi}{2} \le \dfrac{\pi}{2}$

29. $\tan\left[\sin^{-1}(-0.5)\right] = \tan\left(-\dfrac{\pi}{6}\right) = -\dfrac{\sqrt{3}}{3} = -\dfrac{1}{3}\sqrt{3}$

33. $\dfrac{\sec y}{\csc y} = \sec y \times \dfrac{1}{\csc y} = \dfrac{1}{\cos y} \times \dfrac{\sin y}{1} = \dfrac{\sin y}{\cos y} = \tan y$

37. $\dfrac{\sec^4 x - 1}{\tan^2 x} = \dfrac{(\sec^2 x - 1)(\sec^2 x + 1)}{\tan^2 x}$

     $\dfrac{(\sec^2 x + 1)(\tan^2 x)}{\tan^2 x} = \sec^2 x + 1$

     $1 + \tan^2 x + 1 = 2 + \tan^2 x$

41. $\dfrac{1 - \sin^2 \theta}{1 - \cos^2 \theta} = \dfrac{\cos^2 \theta}{\sin^2 \theta}$ since $\sin^2 \theta + \cos^2 \theta = 1 = \left(\dfrac{\cos \theta}{\sin \theta}\right)^2 = (\cot \theta)^2 = \cot^2 \theta$

45. $\dfrac{\sec x}{\sin x} - \sec x \sin x = \dfrac{1}{\cos x \sin x} - \dfrac{\sin x}{\cos x} \cdot \dfrac{\sin x}{\sin x} = \dfrac{1 - \sin^2 x}{\sin x \cos x} = \dfrac{\cos^2 x}{\sin x \cos x} = \dfrac{\cos x}{\sin x} = \cot x$

49. $\dfrac{\sin x \cot x + \cos x}{2 \cot x} = \dfrac{\sin x \cdot \frac{\cos x}{\sin x} + \cos x}{2 \frac{\cos x}{\sin x}} \cdot \dfrac{\sin x}{\sin x} = \dfrac{\sin x \cos x + \sin x \cos x}{2 \cos x} = \dfrac{2 \sin x \cos x}{2 \cos x} = \sin x$

53.

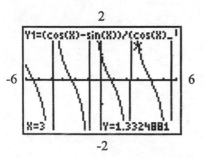
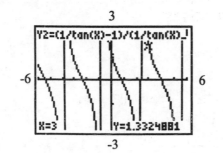

57.

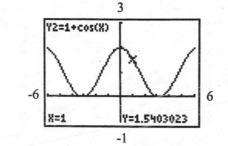

61. $y = 2 \cos 2x; \ \dfrac{y}{2} = \cos 2x$

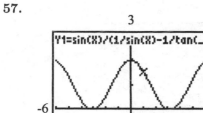

$\cos^{-1} \dfrac{y}{2} = 2x; \ \dfrac{1}{2} \cos^{-1} \dfrac{1}{2} y = x$

65. $3(\tan x - 2) = 1 + \tan x$

$3 \tan x - 6 = 1 + \tan x$

$2 \tan x = 7$

$\tan x = \dfrac{7}{2}$

$x = \tan^{-1} \dfrac{7}{2} = 1.2925$

Since $\tan x$ is positive in quadrant III also, $\pi + 1.2925 = 4.4341$ is also a value for x that is within the specified range of values for x.

69.

$$2\sin^2\theta + 3\cos\theta - 3 = 0, 0 \le \theta < 2\pi$$
$$2(1 - \cos^2\theta) + 3\cos\theta - 3 = 0$$
$$2 - 2\cos^2\theta + 3\cos\theta - 3 = 0$$
$$2\cos^2\theta - 3\cos\theta + 1 = 0$$
$$(\cos\theta - 1)(2\cos\theta - 1) = 0$$
$$\cos\theta - 1 = 0 \quad \text{or} \quad 2\cos\theta - 1 = 0$$

$$\cos\theta = 1 \qquad\qquad \cos\theta = \frac{1}{2}$$

$$\theta = 0 \qquad\qquad\quad \theta = \frac{\pi}{3}, \frac{5\pi}{3}$$

$$\theta = 0, \frac{\pi}{3}, \frac{5\pi}{3}$$

73. $\sin 2x = \cos 3x$

$$\sin 2x = \cos(2x + x)$$
$$2\sin x \cos x = \cos 2x \cos x - \sin 2x \sin x$$
$$2\sin x \cos x = \cos 2x \cos x - 2\sin x \cos x \sin x$$
$$2\sin x \cos x - \cos 2x \cos x + 2\sin^2 x \cos x = 0$$
$$\cos x(2\sin x - \cos 2x + \sin^z x) = 0$$
$$\cos x = 0 \qquad \text{or} \qquad 2\sin x - (1 - 2\sin^2 x) + 2\sin^2 x = 0$$

$$x = \frac{\pi}{2}, \frac{3\pi}{2} \qquad\qquad 2\sin x - 1 + 2\sin^2 x + 2\sin^2 x = 0$$

$$4\sin^2 x + 2\sin x - 1 = 0$$

$$\sin x = \frac{-2 \pm \sqrt{2^2 - 4(4)(-1)}}{2(4)} = \frac{-2 \pm 2\sqrt{5}}{8} = \frac{-1 \pm \sqrt{5}}{4}$$

$$\sin x = \frac{-1 + \sqrt{5}}{4} \quad \text{or} \quad \sin x = \frac{-1 - \sqrt{5}}{4}$$

$$= \frac{\pi}{10}, \frac{9\pi}{10} \qquad\qquad x = \frac{13\pi}{10}, \frac{17\pi}{10}$$

$$\sin 2x = \cos 3x \text{ has solutions} \left\{ \frac{\pi}{10}, \frac{\pi}{2}, \frac{9\pi}{10}, \frac{13\pi}{10}, \frac{3\pi}{2}, \frac{17\pi}{10} \right\}$$

77.

$$x + \ln x - 3\cos^2 x = 2$$
$$x + \ln x - 3\cos^2 x - 2 = 0$$

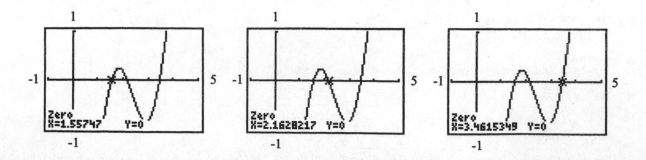

81. $\tan(\cot^{-1}x) = \tan\theta = \dfrac{1}{x}$

$\theta = \cot^{-1}x$

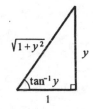

85. $\cos(\sin^{-1}x + \tan^{-1}y) = \cos(\sin^{-1}x)\cos(\tan^{-1}y) - \sin(\sin^{-1}x)\sin(\tan^{-1}y)$

$$= \sqrt{1-x^2}\cdot\dfrac{1}{\sqrt{1+y^2}} - x\cdot\dfrac{y}{\sqrt{1+y^2}} = \dfrac{\sqrt{1-x^2}-xy}{\sqrt{1+y^2}}$$

89.

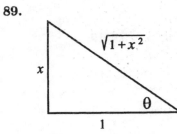

From the drawing $\tan\theta = x \Rightarrow \sin\theta = \dfrac{x}{\sqrt{x^2+1}}$

93. $$\sin 2x > 2\sin x$$
$$2\sin x\cos x - 2\sin x > 0$$
$$\sin x(\cos x - 1) > 0$$

   I. $\sin x > 0$ and $\cos x - 1 > 0$
        $0 \le x > \pi$ $\cos x > 1$, no solution

   II. $\sin x < 0$ and $\cos x - 1 < 0$
        $\pi < x < 2\pi$ $\cos x < 1$
                        $0 < x < 2\pi$

$\sin 2x > 2\sin x$ for $\pi < x < 2\pi$

97. $R = \sqrt{Rx^2 + Ry^2} = \sqrt{(A\cos\theta - B\sin\theta)^2 + (A\sin\theta + B\cos\theta)^2}$

$$= \sqrt{(A^2\cos^2\theta - 2AB\cos\theta\sin\theta + B^2\sin^2\theta) + (A^2\sin^2\theta + 2AB\cos\theta\sin\theta + B^2\cos^2\theta)}$$

$$= \sqrt{A^2\cos^2\theta + A^2\sin^2\theta + B^2\cos^2\theta + B^2\sin^2\theta}$$

$$= \sqrt{A^2(\cos^2\theta + \sin^2\theta) + B^2(\cos^2\theta + \sin^2\theta)}$$

$$= \sqrt{(\cos^2\theta + \sin^2\theta)(A^2 + B^2)} = \sqrt{1(A^2 + B^2)}$$

101.
$$\omega t = \sin^{-1}\frac{\theta - \alpha}{R}$$

$$\sin(\omega t) = \frac{\theta - \alpha}{R}$$

$$R\sin(\omega t) = \theta - \alpha$$

$$\theta = R\sin(\omega t) + \alpha$$

105.

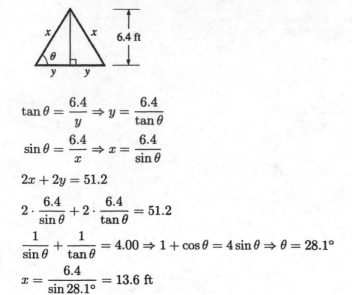

$$\tan\theta = \frac{6.4}{y} \Rightarrow y = \frac{6.4}{\tan\theta}$$

$$\sin\theta = \frac{6.4}{x} \Rightarrow x = \frac{6.4}{\sin\theta}$$

$$2x + 2y = 51.2$$

$$2 \cdot \frac{6.4}{\sin\theta} + 2 \cdot \frac{6.4}{\tan\theta} = 51.2$$

$$\frac{1}{\sin\theta} + \frac{1}{\tan\theta} = 4.00 \Rightarrow 1 + \cos\theta = 4\sin\theta \Rightarrow \theta = 28.1°$$

$$x = \frac{6.4}{\sin 28.1°} = 13.6 \text{ ft}$$

109. The equation $\tan\theta = 0.4250$ has an infinite number of solutions while $\tan^{-1} 0.4250 = 0.4019$.

Chapter 21

PLANE ANALYTIC GEOMETRY

21.1 Basic Definitions

1. The distance between $(3, -1)$ and $(-2, 5)$ is

$$d = \sqrt{(3 - (-2))^2 + (-1 - 5)^2}$$
$$= \sqrt{61}$$

5. Given: $(x_1, y_1) = (3, 8); (x_2, y_2) = (-1, -2)$

$$d = \sqrt{(x_2 - x_1)^2 + (y_2 - y_1)^2}$$
$$= \sqrt{(-1 - 3)^2 + (-2 - 8)^2}$$
$$= \sqrt{(-4)^2 + (-10)^2}$$
$$= \sqrt{16 + 100} = \sqrt{116} = \sqrt{4 \times 29} = 2\sqrt{29}$$

9. Given: $(x_1, y_1) = (-12, 20); (x_2, y_2) = (32, -13)$

$$d = \sqrt{(x_2 - x_1)^2 + (y_2 - y_1)^2}$$
$$= \sqrt{(32 + 12)^2 + (-13 - 20)^2}$$
$$= \sqrt{(44)^2 + (-33)^2}$$
$$= \sqrt{1936 + 1089} = \sqrt{3025} = 55$$

13. Given: $(x_1, y_1) = (1.22, -3.45);$
$(x_2, y_2) = (-1.07, -5.16)$

$$d = \sqrt{(x_2 - x_1)^2 + (y_2 - y_1)^2}$$
$$= \sqrt{(-1.07 - 1.22)^2 + (-5.16 - (-3.45))^2}$$
$$= \sqrt{(-2.29)^2 + (-5.16 + 3.45)^2}$$
$$= \sqrt{(-2.29)^2 + (-1.71)^2} = \sqrt{8.1682} = 2.86$$

17. Given: $(x_1, y_1) = (4, -5); (x_2, y_2) = (4. - 8)$

$$m = \frac{y_2 - y_1}{x_2 - x_1} = \frac{-8 - (-5)}{4 - 4}$$

Since $x_2 - x_1 = 4 - 4 = 0$, the slope is undefined.

21. Given: $(x_1, y_1) = (\sqrt{32}, -\sqrt{18});$
$(x_2, y_2) = (-\sqrt{50}, \sqrt{8})$

$$m = \frac{y_2 - y_1}{x_2 - x_1} = \frac{\sqrt{8} - (-\sqrt{18})}{-\sqrt{50} - \sqrt{32}} = \frac{-5}{9}$$

25. Given: $\alpha = 30°; m = \tan \alpha, 0° < \alpha < 180°$

$$\tan 30° = \frac{\sqrt{3}}{3} \text{ or } \frac{1}{3}\sqrt{3}$$

29. Given: $m = 0.364; m = \tan \alpha; 0.364 = \tan \alpha;$
$\alpha = 20.0°$

33. Given: $(x, y) = (6, -1); (x_1, y_1) = (4, 3)$
$(x_2, y_2) = (-5, 2); (x_3, y_3) = (-7, 6)$

$$m_1 = \frac{y - y_1}{x - x_1} = \frac{-1 - 3}{6 - 4} = \frac{-4}{2} = -2$$

$$m_2 = \frac{y_2 - y_3}{x_2 - x_3} = \frac{2 - 6}{-5 - (-7)} = \frac{-4}{-5 + 7}$$
$$= \frac{-4}{2} = -2$$

$m_3 = m_2$ for all parallel lines.

37. Given: distance between $(-1, 3)$ and $(11, k)$ is 13.

$$d = \sqrt{(x_1 - x_2)^2 + (y_1 - y_2)^2}$$
$$13 = \sqrt{(-1 - 11)^2 + (3 - k)^2}$$
$$= \sqrt{(-12)^2 + (3 - k)^2}$$
$$= \sqrt{144 + (3 - k)^2}$$
$$169 = 144 + (3 - k)^2;$$
$$(3 - k)^2 = 25; 3 - k = \pm 5$$
$$-k = -3 \pm 5; k = -2, 8$$

41. $d_1 = \sqrt{(9 - 7)^2 + [4 - (-2)]^2}$
$$= \sqrt{2^2 + 6^2} = \sqrt{40} = 2\sqrt{10}$$
$$d_2 = \sqrt{(9 - 3)^2 + (4 - 2)^2} = \sqrt{6^2 + 2^2}$$
$$= \sqrt{40} = 2\sqrt{10}$$

$d_1 = d_2$ so the triangle is isosceles.

45. $d_1 = \sqrt{(3 - 5)^2 + (-1 - 3)^2} = \sqrt{(-2)^2 + (-4)^2}$
$$= \sqrt{4 + 16} = \sqrt{20}$$

$$m_1 = \frac{y - y_1}{x - x_1} = \frac{5 - 3}{3 - (-1)} = \frac{5 - 3}{3 + 1} = \frac{2}{4} = \frac{1}{2}$$

$$d_2 = \sqrt{(5 - 1)^2 + (3 - 5)^2} = \sqrt{(4)^2 + (-2)^2}$$
$$= \sqrt{16 + 4} = \sqrt{20}$$

$$m_2 = \frac{y - y_1}{x - x_1} = \frac{5 - 1}{3 - 5} = \frac{4}{-2} = -2$$

$$m_1 = \frac{-1}{m_2}, m_1 \perp m_2$$

$$A = \frac{1}{2}d_1 d_2 = \frac{1}{2}\sqrt{20}\sqrt{20} = \frac{1}{2}(20) = 10$$

49. $\left(\frac{-4 + 6}{2}, \frac{9 + 1}{2}\right) = \left(\frac{2}{2}, \frac{10}{2}\right) = (1, 5)$

53. The distance between (x, y) and $(0, 0) = 3$.

$$\sqrt{(x - 0)^2 + (y - 0)^2} = 3$$
$$x^2 + y^2 = 9$$

21.2   The Straight Line

1. $m = -2, (x_1, y_1) = (4, -1)$

$$y - y_1 = m(x - x_1)$$
$$y - (-1) = -2(x - 4)$$
$$y + 1 = -2x + 8$$
$$y + 2x - 7 = 0$$

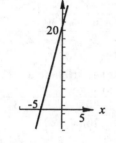

5. Given: $m = 4; (x_1, y_1) = (-3, 8)$

$$y - y_1 = m(x - x_1)$$
$$y - 8 = 4[x - (-3)] = 4(x + 3) = 4x + 12$$
$$y = 4x + 20 \text{ or } 4x - y + 20 = 0$$

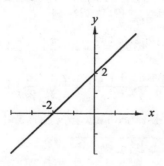

9. Given: $(x_1, y_1) = (1, 3); \alpha = 45°$

$$m = \tan \alpha = \tan 45° = 1$$
$$y - y_1 = m(x - x_1)$$
$$y - 3 = 1(x - 1) = x - 1; y = x + 2$$
$$\text{or } x - y + 2 = 0$$

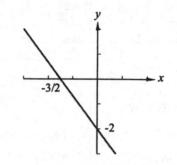

13. Parallel to y-axis and 3 units left of y-axis.

$$x = -3$$

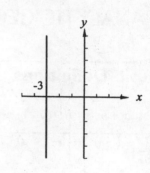

17. Parallel to a line through $(7, -1)$ and $(4, 3)$; y-intercept is -2

$$m = \frac{y_2 - y_1}{x_2 - x_1} = \frac{3 - (-1)}{4 - 7} = \frac{4}{-3} = -\frac{4}{3}$$

y-intercept is $b = -2$

$$y = mx + b; y = -\frac{4}{3}x - 2; 4x + 3y + 6 = 0$$

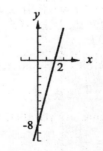

21. Given: $4x - y = 8, y = 4x - 8, m = 4, b = -8$
When $x = 0, y = -8$
$\qquad y = 0, x = 2$

25. Given: $3x - 2y - 1 = 0$

$3x - 2y - 1 = 0; -2y = -3x + 1$

$y = \frac{-3}{-2}x + \frac{1}{-2}; y = \frac{3}{2}x - \frac{1}{2}$

Slope $= \frac{3}{2} = m$;

y-intercept $= -\frac{1}{2} = b$

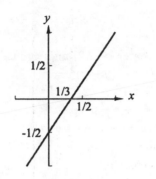

29. $3x - 2y + 5 = 0; -2y = -3x - 5;$

$y = \frac{-3}{-2}x + \frac{-5}{-2}; y = \frac{3}{2}x + \frac{5}{2};$

slope $= \frac{3}{2} = m_1$

$4y = 6x - 1; y = \frac{6}{4}x - \frac{1}{4};$

$y = \frac{3}{2}x - \frac{1}{4};$ slope $= \frac{3}{2} = m_2$

$m_1 = m_2$ for all parallel lines.

33. $5x + 2y = 3 \Rightarrow y = \frac{-5}{2} \cdot x + \frac{3}{2}$

$10y = 7 - 4x \Rightarrow y = \frac{-4}{10}x + \frac{7}{10}$

$m_1 \cdot m_2 = \frac{-5}{2} \cdot \frac{-4}{10} = 1 \neq -1$

$m_1 \neq m_2$

Lines are neither perpendicular nor parallel.

37. Given: $4x - ky = 6 \parallel 6x + 3y + 2 = 0$

$6x + 3y + 2 = 0; 3y = -6x - 2$

$y = \frac{-6}{3}x - \frac{2}{3}; y = -2x - \frac{2}{3};$ slope is -2

$4x - ky = 6; -ky = -4x + 6$

$y = \frac{-4}{-k}x + \frac{6}{-k}; y = \frac{4}{k}x - \frac{6}{k};$ slope is $\frac{4}{k}$

Since the lines are parallel, the slopes are equal.

$\frac{4}{k} = -2; 4 = -2k; k = -2$

41.

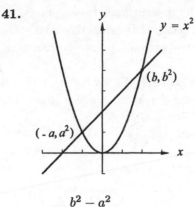

$m = \dfrac{b^2 - a^2}{b - (-a)}$

$m = \dfrac{(b + a)(b - a)}{b + a}$

$m = b - a$

45. $v = v_0 + at$

$35.4 = 12.2 + a(4.50)$

$4.50a = 35.4 - 12.2$

$a = 5.16 \text{ ft/s}^2$

$v = 12.2 + 5.16t$

49. $P = k(120 - T_s)$

$1.0 = k(120 - 80)$

$k = 0.025$

$P = 0.025(120 - T_s)$

$P = 3.0 - 0.025T_s$

53. $m = \tan(180° - 0.0032°)$

$b = 24\mu\text{m} = 24 \times 10^{-6} \text{ m} = 2.4 \times 10^{-5} \text{ m}$

$m = -5.6 \times 10^{-5}$

$y = mx + b = -5.6 \times 10^{-5}x + 2.4 \times 10^{-5}$

$y = (-5.6x + 2.4)10^{-5}$

57. $n = 1200\sqrt{t} + 0$

$m = 1200$

$b = 0$

t	$\sqrt{t}$	h
0	0	0
1	1	1200
4	2	2400

61. Slope is found by measuring between points. The vertical displacement and the horizontal displacement between the extreme points is in a 1 to 2 ratio; $m = \frac{1}{2}$.

Since the graph is linear, the log equation is of the form $\log y = m \log x + \log a$, where a is the intercept $(1, a)$.

$y = ax^n; y = 3x^4$
$a = 3, n = 4$

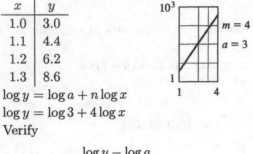

x	y
1.0	3.0
1.1	4.4
1.2	6.2
1.3	8.6

$\log y = \log a + n \log x$
$\log y = \log 3 + 4 \log x$
Verify

(1) Slope is $\dfrac{\log y - \log a}{\log x} = 4$.

Vertical and horizontal meaasures in millimeters between points are shown. Each slope is 4.

(2) The intercept is $a = 3$.
The line crosses the vertical axis at $x = 1.0$, $y = 3.0$.

21.3 The Circle

1. $(x-1)^2 + (y+1)^2 = 16$ has center at $(1, -1)$ and $r = 4$

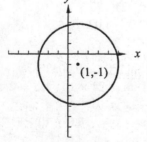

5. $(x-2)^2 + (y-1)^2 = 25$
Center at $(2, 1)$, radius is 5.

9. $(x-h)^2 + (y-k)^2 = r^2; C(0,0), r = 3$
$(x-0)^2 + (y-0)^2 = 3^2; x^2 + y^2 = 9$

13. $(x-12)^2 + (y-(-15))^2 = 18^2;$
$C(12, -15), r = 18$
$(x-12)^2 + (y+15)^2 = 324;$
$x^2 + y^2 - 24x + 30y + 45 = 0$

17. Concentric with $(x-2)^2 + (y-1)^2 = 4$ gives center at $(2, 1)$.

$r = \sqrt{(2-4)^2 + (1-(-1))^2} = 2\sqrt{2}$

The equation is $(x-2)^2 + (y-1)^2 = 8$

21. The center is $(2,2)$ and radius is 2.
$(x-h)^2 + (y-k)^2 = r^2$
$(x-2)^2 + (y-2)^2 = 2^2$
$x^2 - 4x + 4 + y^2 - 4y + 4 = 4$
$x^2 + y^2 - 4x - 4y + 4 = 0$

25. $x^2 + (y-3)^2 = 4$ is the same as
$(x-0)^2 + (y-3)^2 = 2^2$, so
Therefore, $h = 0, k = 3, r = 2$
$C(0,3)$

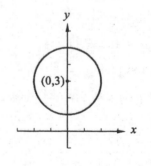

29. $x^2 + y^2 - 2x - 8 = 0$
$x^2 - 2x + 1 + y^2 = 9$
$(x-1)^2 + (y-0)^2 = 9$
$h = 1, k = 0, r = 3$
$C(1,0)$

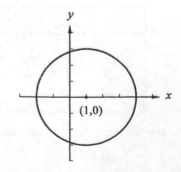

33. $4x^2 + 4y^2 - 16y = 9$

$4(x-0)^2 + 4(y^2 - 4y + 4) = 9 + 16$

$(x-0)^2 + (y-2) = \dfrac{25}{4}$

$h = 0, k = 2, r = \dfrac{5}{2}$

$C(0,2)$

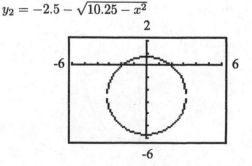

37. $(-x)^2 + y^2 = 100; \ x^2 + y^2 = 100$

Symmetrical to y-axis

$x^2 + (-y)^2 = 100; \ x^2 + y^2 = 100$

Symmetrical to x-axis

$(-x)^2 + (-y)^2 = 100; \ x^2 + y^2 = 100$

Symmetrical to origin

41. Find all points for which $y = 0$.

$x^2 - 6x + (0)^2 - 7 = 0; \ x^2 - 6x - 7 = 0 \Rightarrow$

$(x+1)(x-7) = 0; \ x = -1 \text{ or } x = 7;$

$(-1,0) \text{ and } (7,0)$

45. $x^2 + y^2 + 5y - 4 = 0$

$y^2 + 5y + (x^2 - 4) = 0;$ solve for y

$$y = \frac{-5 \pm \sqrt{5^2 - 4(x^2 - 4)}}{2} = \frac{-5 \pm \sqrt{41 - 4x^2}}{2}$$

$$= -2.5 \pm \sqrt{10.25 - x^2}$$

Set the range for

$x_{\min} = -6, x_{\max} = 6, y_{\min} = -6, y_{\max} = 2$

$y_1 = -2.5 + \sqrt{10.25 - x^2}$

$y_2 = -2.5 - \sqrt{10.25 - x^2}$

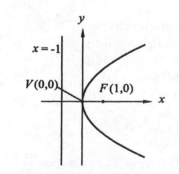

49. $x^2 + y^2 = 14.5$ is a circle with center $(0,0)$,

$r = \sqrt{14.5}$

$x^2 + y^2 - 19.6y + 86 = 0$

$x^2 + y^2 - 19.6y + 96.04 = -86 + 96.04 = 10.04$

$(x-0)^2 + (y - 9.8)^2 = 10.04,$ circle with center

$(0, 9.8),$

$r = \sqrt{10.04}$

distance between circles $= 9.8 - \sqrt{10.04} - \sqrt{14.5}$

$= 2.82$ in.

53. The center has coordinates $(0, -7)$ and the radius

$= 1.$

The equation is $x^2 + (y+7)^2 = 1.$

21.4　The Parabola

1. $y^2 = 20x \Rightarrow 4p = 20 \Rightarrow p = 5.$ The focus is

$F(5,0).$ The directrix is $x = -5.$

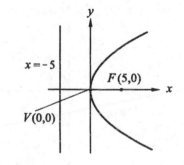

5. $y^2 = 4x$

$y^2 = 4px$

$y^2 = 4x = 4(1)x; p = 1$

$F(1,0);$ directrix $x = -1$

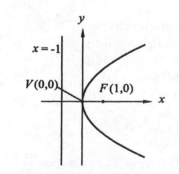

9. $x^2 = 8y$

$x^2 = 4py$

$x^2 = 8y = 4(2)y; p = 2$

$F(0,2)$; directrix $y = -2$

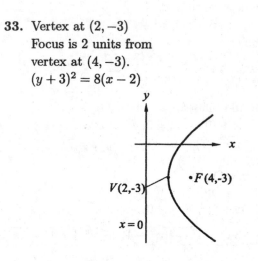

13. $2y^2 - 5x = 0$

$2y^2 = 5x$

$y^2 = \dfrac{5}{2}x = 4px$

$p = \dfrac{5}{8}$

$F(\dfrac{5}{8}, 0)$; directrix $x = -\dfrac{5}{8}$

17. $F(3,0)$; directrix $x = -3$; $p = 3$

$y^2 = 4px$

$y^2 = 4(3)x$;

$y^2 = 12x$

21. $V(0,0)$, directrix $y = -0.16$

$F(0, 0.16)$, $p = 0.16$

$x^2 = 4py = 4(0.16)y$

$x^2 = 0.64y$

25. $V(0,0)$

Therefore, $x^2 = 4py$

$(-1)^2 = 4p(8)$; $1 = 32p$; $p = \dfrac{1}{32}$

Therefore, $x^2 = \dfrac{1}{8}y$

29. $F(6,1)$; directrix $x = 0$; $V(3,1)$

$d_1 = d_2$

$d_1 = x$

$d_2 = \sqrt{(x-6)^2 + (y-1)^2}$

$x = \sqrt{(x-6)^2 + (y-1)^2}$

$x^2 = (x-6)^2 + (y-1)^2$

$x^2 = x^2 - 12x + 36 + y^2 - 2y + 1$

$0 = -12x + 36 + y^2 - 2y + 1$

$y^2 - 2y - 12x + 37 = 0$

33. Vertex at $(2, -3)$

Focus is 2 units from vertex at $(4, -3)$.

$(y+3)^2 = 8(x-2)$

37. $V(0,0), (2,2), (8,4)$. $y^2 = 4px, 2^2 = 4p(2), 4p = 2$

$y^2 = 2x$

41. $H = Ri^2$; $R = 6.0 \ \Omega$

Therefore, $H = 6.0i^2$; H vs i

of the form $y = 4px$

$4p = 6.0$; $p = \dfrac{3}{2}$

H and $i > 0$

45. $x^2 = 4py, 10^2 = 4p(3), 4p = \dfrac{100}{3}, x^2 = \dfrac{100}{3}y$

$\dfrac{100}{3}(340) = 11,333 \neq 110^2 = 12,100$. No, the path does not lead directly to the moon.

49. The graph is parabolic since it can be transformed into the form $f^2 = 4pA$.

$f = 0.065\sqrt{A} = 0.065\sqrt{200} = 0.92$

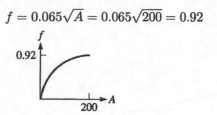

21.5   The Ellipse

1. $\dfrac{x^2}{25} + \dfrac{y^2}{36} = 1,$

$a^2 = 36, a = 6,$
$b^2 = 25, b = 5$
$V(0, \pm 6),$
minor axis: $(\pm 5, 0)$
$\quad a^2 = b^2 + c^2$
$\quad 36 = 25 + c^2$
$\quad c = \sqrt{11}$
$F(0, \pm\sqrt{11})$

5. $\dfrac{x^2}{25} + \dfrac{y^2}{144} = 1$

$a^2 = 144; a = 12$
$b^2 = 25; b = 5$
$V(0, \pm 12),$
minor axis: $(\pm 5, 0)$
$a^2 = b^2 + c^2$
$144 = 25 + c^2$
$c = \sqrt{119} \approx 10.9$
$F(0, \pm\sqrt{119})$
$V(0, \pm 6), F(0, \pm\sqrt{11}), x$-intercepts $(\pm 5, 0)$

9. $4x^2 + 9y^2 = 36$

$\dfrac{4x^2}{36} + \dfrac{9y^2}{36} = 1$

$\dfrac{x^2}{9} + \dfrac{y^2}{4} = 1$

$a^2 = 9, b^2 = 4$
$c^2 = 9 - 4 = 5; c = \sqrt{5}$
$V(\pm 3, 0), F(\pm\sqrt{5}, 0),$
y-intercepts $(0, \pm 2)$

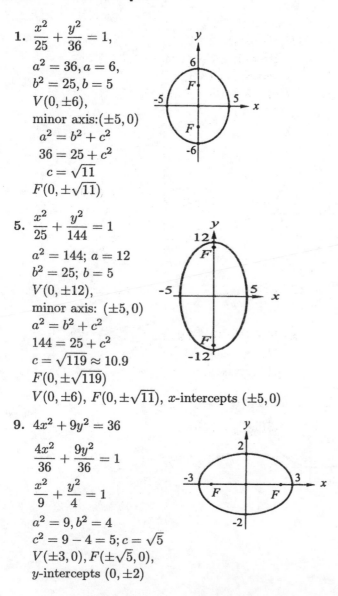

13. $y^2 = 8(2 - x^2)$
$\quad 8x^2 + y^2 = -16$

$\dfrac{8x^2}{16} + \dfrac{y^2}{16} = 1$

$\dfrac{x^2}{2} + \dfrac{y^2}{16} = 1$

$\dfrac{y^2}{16} + \dfrac{x^2}{2} = 1$

$a^2 = 16, b^2 = 2, c^2 = 16 - 2 = 14$
$V(0, \pm 4), F(0, \pm\sqrt{14}), x$-intercepts $(\pm\sqrt{2}, 0)$

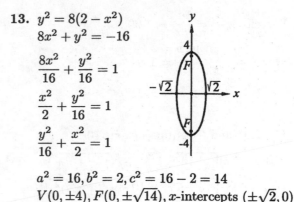

17. $V(15, 0); F(9, 0)$
$a = 15, a^2 = 225;$
$c = 9, c^2 = 81; a^2 - c^2 = b^2$

$b^2 = 144; \dfrac{x^2}{a^2} + \dfrac{y^2}{b^2} = 1;$

$\dfrac{x^2}{225} + \dfrac{y^2}{144} = 1$

$144x^2 + 225y^2 = 32,400$

21. $F(0, 2)$, therefore $c = 2$
Major axis 6, therefore $a = 3$
$c^2 = a^2 - b^2$
$b^2 = 9 - 4 = 5$
$b = \sqrt{5}$

$\dfrac{y^2}{9} + \dfrac{x^2}{5} = 1$ or $9x^2 + 5y^2 = 45$

25. $(x_1, y_1) = (2, 2), (x_2, y_2) = (1, 4)$

$\dfrac{x^2}{b^2} + \dfrac{y^2}{a^2} = 1$

Substitute: $\dfrac{4}{b^2} + \dfrac{4}{a^2} = 1$

Therefore, $4a^2 + 4b^2 = a^2 b^2$

$\dfrac{1}{b^2} + \dfrac{16}{a^2} = 1$

Therefore, $a^2 + 16b^2 = a^2 b^2$
$a^2 + 16b^2 = a^2 b^2$
$16b^2 = a^2 b^2 - a^2 = a^2(b^2 - 1)$

Therefore, $a^2 = \dfrac{16b^2}{b^2 - 1}$

Substitute:

$4a^2 + 4b^2 = a^2 b^2; \dfrac{64b^2}{b^2 - 1} + 4b^2 = \dfrac{16b^4}{b^2 - 1}$

$64b^2 + 4b^4 - 4b^2 = 16b^4; -12b^4 + 60b^2 = 0$
$12b^2(-b^2 + 5) = 0$
$b^2 = 5$

Therefore, $a^2 = \dfrac{16(5)}{4} = 20$

Therefore, $\dfrac{y^2}{20} + \dfrac{x^2}{5} = 1$

or: $5y^2 + 20x^2 = 100$; $4x^2 + y^2 = 20$

29. $F(-2, 1)$ and $(4, 1)$, major axis 10

$\sqrt{[x - (-2)]^2 + (y - 1)^2} + \sqrt{(x - 4)^2 + (y - 1)^2} = 10$

$\sqrt{(x + 2)^2 + (y - 1)^2} = 10 - \sqrt{(x - 4)^2 + (y - 1)^2}$

$(x + 2)^2 + (y - 1)^2 = 100 - 20\sqrt{(x - 4)^2 + (y - 1)^2} + (x - 4)^2 + (y - 1)^2$

$x^2 + 4x + 4 + y^2 - 2y + 1 = 100 - 20\sqrt{(x - 4)^2 + (y - 1)^2} + x^2 - 8x + 16 + y^2 - 2y + 1$

$x^2 + 4x + 4 + y^2 - 2y + 1 - 100 - x^2 + 8x - 16 - y^2 + 2y - 1 = -20\sqrt{(x - 4)^2 + (y - 1)^2}$

$12x - 112 = -20\sqrt{(x - 4)^2 + (y - 1)^2}$

$3x - 28 = -5\sqrt{(x - 4)^2 + (y - 1)^2}$

$(3x - 28)^2 = 25[(x - 4)^2 + (y - 1)^2]$

$9x^2 - 168x + 784 = 25(x^2 - 8x + 16 + y^2 - 2y + 1)$

$9x^2 - 168x + 784 = 25x^2 - 200x + 400 + 25y^2 - 50y + 25$

$-16x^2 - 25y^2 + 32x + 50y + 359 = 0$

$16x^2 + 25y^2 - 32x - 50y - 359 = 0$

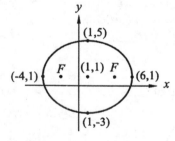

33. $2a = 6$; $a = 3$; $2b = 4$; $b = 2$; $(h, k) = (2, -1)$

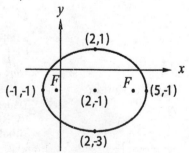

37. Given: $2x^2 + 3y^2 - 8x - 4 = 0$

$2x^2 + 3(-y)^2 - 8x - 4 = 2x^2 + 3y^2 - 8x - 4$

41. $P = Ri^2$

$P_T = R_1 i_1^2 + R_2 i_2^2$

$64 = 2i_1^2 + 8i_2^2$

$\dfrac{2}{64}i_1^2 + \dfrac{8}{64}i_2^2 = 1$

$\dfrac{i_1^2}{32} + \dfrac{i_2^2}{8} = 1$

$i_1^2 + 4i_2^2 = 32$

$a^2 = 32;\ a = \sqrt{32} \approx 5.7$

$b^2 = 8;\ b = \sqrt{8} \approx 2.8$

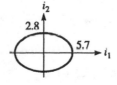

45. If the two vertices of each base are fixed at $(-3, 0)$ and $(3, 0)$, and the sum of the two leg lengths is also fixed, the third vertex lies on an ellipse. The base is 6 cm, so

$d_1 + d_2 = 14$ cm 6 cm $- 8$ cm

$(-3, 0)$ and $(3, 0)$ are foci $(\ c, 0)$ and $(c, 0)$

$d_1 + d_2 = 2a = 8;\ a = 4$

$a^2 - c^2 = b^2$

$4^2 - 3^2 = b^2$

$b^2 = 7,\ a^2 = 16$

The equation is $\dfrac{x^2}{16} + \dfrac{y^2}{7} = 1$, or $7x^2 + 16y^2 = 112$

49. $a = \dfrac{64}{2} = 32,\ b = 18$

Let the center be at the origin. The equation of the ellipse is

$\dfrac{x^2}{32^2} + \dfrac{y^2}{18^2} = 1;\ \dfrac{x^2}{1024} + \dfrac{y^2}{324} = 1$

If $x = 22,\ \dfrac{22^2}{1024} + \dfrac{y^2}{324} = 1$

$y = 13$ ft

21.6   The Hyperbola

1. $\dfrac{y^2}{16} - \dfrac{x^2}{4} = 1$

$a^2 = 16, a = 4$

$b^2 = 4, b = 2$

$c^2 = a^2 + b^2 = 20$

$c = 2\sqrt{5}$

$V(0, \pm 4)$

conjugate axis: $(\pm 2, 0)$

$F(0, \pm 2\sqrt{5})$

5. $\dfrac{y^2}{9} - \dfrac{x^2}{1} = 1$

$a^2 = 9;\ a = 3$

$b^2 = 1;\ b = 1$

$c^2 = 10;\ c = \sqrt{10}$

$V(0, \pm 3),\ F(0, \pm\sqrt{10})$

9. $4x^2 - y^2 = 4$

$\dfrac{4x^2}{4} - \dfrac{y^2}{4} = 1;$

$\dfrac{x^2}{1} - \dfrac{y^2}{4} = 1$

$a^2 = 1;\ b^2 = 4;\ c^2 = 5$

$V(\pm 1, 0);\ F(\pm\sqrt{5}, 0)$

13. $y^2 = 4(x^2 + 1)$

$4x^2 - y^2 + 4 = 0$

$4x^2 - y^2 = -4$

$\dfrac{4x^2}{-4} - \dfrac{y^2}{-4} = \dfrac{-4}{-4}$

$-x^2 + \dfrac{y^2}{4} = 1$

$\dfrac{y^2}{4} - \dfrac{x^2}{1} = 1$

$a^2 = 4;\ b^2 = 1;\ c^2 = 5$

$V(0, \pm 2),\ F(0, \pm\sqrt{5})$

17. $V(3, 0);\ F(5, 0)$

$a = 3;\ c = 5;\ a^2 = 9;\ c^2 = 25$

$b^2 = c^2 - a^2 = 25 - 9 = 16$

$\dfrac{x^2}{a^2} - \dfrac{y^2}{b^2} = 1;\ \dfrac{x^2}{9} - \dfrac{y^2}{16} = 1;$

$16x^2 - 9y^2 = 144$

21. (x,y) is $(2,3)$; $F(2,0), (-2,0)$; $c = \pm 2, c^2 = 4$

$$d_1 = \sqrt{(2-[-2])^2 + (3-0)^2}$$
$$= \sqrt{4^2 + 3^2} = \sqrt{16+9}$$
$$= \sqrt{25} = 5$$
$$d_2 = \sqrt{(2-2)^2 + (3-0)^2}$$
$$= \sqrt{0+9} = \sqrt{9} = 3$$
$$d_1 - d_2 = 2a; 5 - 3 = 2a; 2 = 2a; 1 = a; a^2 = 1$$
$$c^2 = 4; b^2 = c^2 - a^2 = 3$$
$$\frac{x^2}{a^2} - \frac{y^2}{b^2} = 1; \frac{x^2}{1} - \frac{y^2}{3} = 1$$
$$3x^2 - y^2 = 3$$

25. $V(1,0) \Rightarrow a = 1, a^2 = 1$

Asymptote $y = \dfrac{b}{a}x = \dfrac{b}{1}x = 2x \Rightarrow b = 2, b^2 = 4$

$$\frac{x^2}{1} - \frac{y^2}{4} = 1$$

29. $xy = 2; y = \dfrac{2}{x}$

x	y
$\pm\frac{1}{2}$	± 4
± 1	± 2
± 2	± 1
± 4	$\pm\frac{1}{2}$
± 8	$\pm\frac{1}{4}$

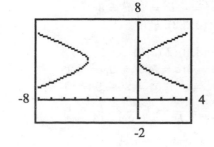

33. $x^2 - 4y^2 + 4x + 32y - 64 = 0$; solve for y

$$4y^2 - 34y + (-x^2 - 4x + 64) = 0$$

$$y = \frac{32 \pm \sqrt{(-32)^2 - 4(4)(-x^2 - 4x + 64)}}{2(4)}$$

$$= \frac{32 \pm \sqrt{16x^2 + 64x}}{8}$$

$$y_1 = 4 + 0.5\sqrt{x^2 + 4x}, y_2 = 4 - 0.5\sqrt{x^2 + 4x}$$

37. $V(0,1), F(0,\sqrt{3})$; $c^2 = a^2 + b^2$ where $c = \sqrt{3}$ and $a = 1; b^2 = \sqrt{3}^2 - 1^2 = 2$

$$\frac{y^2}{1^2} - \frac{x^2}{\sqrt{2}^2} = 1$$

The transverse axis of the first equation is length $2a = 2\sqrt{1}$ along the y-axis. Its conjugate axis is length $2b = 2\sqrt{2}$ along the x-axis.

The transverse axis of the conjugate hyperbola is length $2\sqrt{2}$ along the x-axis, and its conjugate axis is length $2\sqrt{1}$ along the y-axis.

The equation, then, is $\dfrac{x^2}{\sqrt{2}^2} - \dfrac{y^2}{\sqrt{1}^2} = 1$

$$\frac{x^2}{2} - \frac{y^2}{1} = 1 \text{ or } x^2 - 2y^2 = 2$$

41. For $a > 0, V(0,-a)$

For $c > 0, c = a + 3$

$$c^2 = a^2 + b^2$$
$$(a+3)^2 = a^2 + b^2$$
$$a^2 + 6a + 9 = a^2 + b^2$$
$$b^2 = 3(2a + 3)$$

$$\frac{y^2}{a^2} - \frac{x^2}{b^2} = 1$$
$$\frac{(-(a+3))^2}{a^2} - \frac{9^2}{b^2} = 1$$
$$\frac{(a+3)^2}{a^2} - \frac{81}{3(2a+3)} = 1$$

$$3(2a+3)(a+3)^2 - 81a^2 = 3a^2(2a+3)$$
$$(6a+9)(a^2 + 6a + 9) - 81a^2 = 6a^3 + 9a^2$$
$$6a^3 + 9a^2 + 36a^2 + 54a + 54a + 81 - 81a^2 = 6a^3 + 9a^2$$
$$45a^2 - 108a - 81 = 0$$
$$(a-3)(5a+3) = 0$$

$a - 3 = 0$ or $5a + 3 = 0$

$\quad a = 3 \qquad\qquad a = -\dfrac{3}{5}$ reject, $a > 0$

$\quad a^2 = 9$

$\quad b^2 = 3(2a + 3) = 3(2(3) + 3)$

$\quad b^2 = 27$

$$\frac{y^2}{9} - \frac{x^2}{27} = 1$$

45. $V = iR$ (Ohm's law)

$6.00 = iR$

Therefore, $i = \dfrac{6.00}{R}$

R	i
0.5	12
1	6
2	3
3	2
4	1.5
6	1
9	0.7
12	0.5

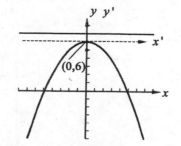

21.7   Translation of Axes

1. $\dfrac{(x-3)^2}{25} - \dfrac{(y-2)^2}{9} = 1$, hyperbola: $a = 5, b = 3$

Center: $(3, 2)$. Transverse axis parallel to x-axis.

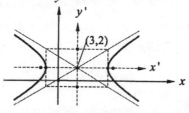

5. $\dfrac{(x-1)^2}{4} - \dfrac{(y-2)^2}{9} = 1$; eq. (21-32), hyperbola

Center $(1, 2)$; $a = 2$; $b = 3$

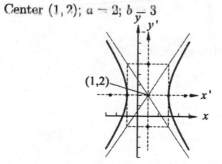

9. $(x+3)^2 = -12(y-1)$; eq. (21-29), parabola

$x' = x + 3$; $y' = y - 1$

$x'^2 = -12y'$

Origin at O' at $(h, k) = (-3, 1)$

$x'^2 = 4(3y')$; therefore $p = 3$

Vertex $(-3, 1)$, focus $(-3, -2)$, directrix $y = 4$

13. $F(12, 0), V(6, 0), p = 6$

$$(y-k)^2 = 4p(x-h)^2$$
$$(y-0)^2 = 4 \cdot 6(x-6)$$
$$y^2 = 24(x-6)$$

17. Ellipse: center $(-2, 1)$, vertex $(-2, 5)$, passes through $(0, 1)$

$$\frac{(y-1)^2}{4^2} + \frac{(x+2)^2}{b^2} = 1$$
$$\frac{(1-1)^2}{4^2} + \frac{(0+2)^2}{b^2} = 1$$
$$b^2 = 4$$
$$\frac{(y-1)^2}{16} + \frac{(x+2)^2}{4} = 1$$

21. Hyperbola: $V(2, 1), V(-4, 1), F(-6, 1)$

Center: $(h, k) = (-1, 1)$

$2a = 6$; $a = 3$; $c = 5$

Therefore, $b^2 = c^2 - a^2 = 25 - 9 = 16$

Transverse axis parallel to x-axis.

Therefore, $\dfrac{(x-h)^2}{a^2} - \dfrac{(y-k)^2}{b^2} = 1$

$$\frac{(x+1)^2}{9} - \frac{(y-1)^2}{16} = 1$$

or $16x^2 - 9y^2 + 32x + 18y - 137 = 0$

25. $x^2 + 4y = 24$

$x^2 = -4y + 24$

$x^2 = -4(y-6)$ is a parabola with $V(0, 6)$

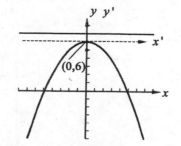

29. $9x^2 - y^2 + 8y = 7$

$9x^2 - y^2 + 8y - 7 = 0$

$9x^2 - (y^2 - 8y + 7 + 9) = -9$

$9x^2 - (y - 4)^2 = -9$

$$\frac{9x^2}{-9} + \frac{(y-4)^2}{-9} = 1$$

$$-x^2 + \frac{(y-4)^2}{9} = 1$$

$$\frac{(y-4)^2}{9} - \frac{x^2}{1} = 1$$

Hyperbola, (h, k) is $(0, 4)$; $a = 3$; $b = 1$

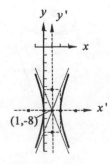

33. $4x^2 - y^2 + 32x + 10y + 35 = 0$

$4(x^2 + 8x) - (y^2 - 10y) = -35$

$4(x^2 + 8x + 16) - (y^2 - 10y + 25) = -35 + 64 - 25$

$$\frac{(x+4)^2}{1^2} - \frac{(y-5)^2}{2^2} = 1, \text{ hyperbola}$$

$C(-4, 5)$

37. $7x^2 - y^2 - 14x - 16y - 64 = 0$

$7x^2 - 14x - y^2 - 16y - 64 = 0$

$7(x^2 - 2x + 1) - (y^2 + 16y + 64) = 64 + 7 - 64$

$$\frac{(x-1)^2}{1^2} - \frac{(y+8)^2}{\sqrt{7}^2} = 1$$

hyperbola, $C(1, -8)$

41. Hyperbola: asymptotes: $x - y = -1$ or $x + 1 = y$, and $x + y = -3$ or $y = -x - 3$; vertices $(3, -1)$ and $(-7, -1)$. The center is at the point of interaction of the asymptotes. The equations for the asymptotes are solved simultaneously by adding, $2y = -2$; $y = -1$; $-1 = x + 1$; $x = -2$. Therefore, the coordinates of the center are $(-2, -1)$. Since the slopes are 1 and -1, $a = b$, where a is the distance from the center $(-2, -1)$ to the vertex $(3, -1)$; $a = 5$, $b = 5$.

$$\frac{(x-h)^2}{a^2} - \frac{(y-k)^2}{b^2} = 1;$$

$$\frac{[x-(-2)]^2}{25} - \frac{[y-(-1)]^2}{25} = 1$$

$$\frac{(x+2)^2}{25} - \frac{(y+1)^2}{25} = 1$$

$x^2 + 4x + 4 - (y^2 + 2y + 1) = 25;$

$x^2 + 4x + 4 - 2y - 1 = 25$

$x^2 - y^2 + 4x - 2y - 22 = 0$

45. Parabola: vertex and focus on x-axis.

$y^2 = 4p(x - h)$

49. $(x - h)^2 = 4p(y - k)$

$(x - 95)^2 = 4p(y - 60)$

Solve for $4p$ using $(x, y) = (0, 0)$.

$(-95)^2 = 4p(-60)$

$$4p = \frac{95^2}{-60}$$

$$(x - 95)^2 = \frac{95^2}{-60}(y - 60)$$

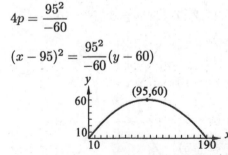

21.8   The Second-Degree Equation

1. $2x^2 = 3 + 2y^2$

$2x^2 - 2y^2 - 3 = 0$, A, C have different signs, $B = 0$, hyperbola

5. $2x^2 - y^2 - 1 = 0$

A and C have different signs, $B = 0$; hyperbola

9. $2.2x^2 - x - y = 1.6$

$A \neq 0$; $C = 0$; $B = 0$; parabola

13. $36x^2 = 12y(1 - 3y) + 1$
$36x^2 = 12y - 36y^2 + 1$
$36x^2 + 0 \cdot xy + 36y^2 - 12x - 0 \cdot y - 1 = 0, A = C, B = 0,$
circle

17. $2xy + x - 3y = 6$
$A = 0; B \neq 0; C = 0;$ hyperbola

21. $(x + 1)^2 + (y + 1)^2 = 2(x + y + 1)$
$x^2 + 2x + 1 + y^2 + 2y + 1 = 2x + 2y + 2$
$x^2 + y^2 = 0,$ none $((0, 0)$ is the only solution$)$

25. $x^2 = 8(y - x - 2)$
$x^2 = 8y - 8x - 16$
$x^2 + 8x - 8y + 16 = 0$
$A \neq 0; B = 0;$
$C = 0;$ parabola
$x^2 + 8x - 8y + 16 = 0$
$x^2 + 8x + 16 = 8y$
$(x + 4)^2 = 4(2)y; p = 2$
Vertex $(-4, 0),$ focus $(-4, 2)$
$a = 2\sqrt{2}, b = \sqrt{2},$ therefore $c = \sqrt{6}$
$V(3 \pm 2\sqrt{2}, 0)$

29. $y^2 + 42 = 2x(10 - x)$
$y^2 + 42 - 20x - 2x^2$
$y^2 + 2x^2 - 20x + 42 = 0;$ ellipse

$\dfrac{y^2}{2} + x^2 - 10x = -21$

$\dfrac{y^2}{2} + x^2 - 10x + 25 = -21 + 25$

$\dfrac{y^2}{2} + (x - 5)^2 = 4$

$\dfrac{y^2}{8} + \dfrac{(x - 5)^2}{4} = 1$

(h, k) at $(5, 0), V(5, \pm 2\sqrt{2})$
$a = \sqrt{8} = 2\sqrt{2}; b = 2$

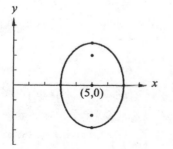

33. $x^2 + 2y^2 - 4x + 12y + 14 = 0;$ solve for y
$x^2 + 0xy + 2y^2 - 4x + 12y + 14 = 0$
$A \neq C,$ they have the same sign, and $B = 0;$ ellipse
Solve for y.

$2y^2 + 12 + (x^2 - 4x + 14) = 0$

$y = \dfrac{-12 \pm \sqrt{12^2 - 4(2)(x^2 - 4x + 14)}}{2(2)}$

$= \dfrac{-12 \pm \sqrt{-8x^2 + 32x + 32}}{4}$

$y_1 = -3 + 0.5\sqrt{-2x^2 + 8x + 8}$
$y_2 = -3 - 0.5\sqrt{-2x^2 + 8x + 8}$

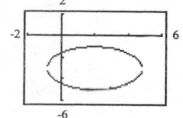

37. **(a)**   If $k = 1, x^2 + ky^2 = a^2; x^2 + (1)y^2 = a^2$
$x^2 + y^2 = a^2$(circle)

  (b)   If $k < 0, x^2 + ky^2 = a^2; x^2 - |k| y^2 = a^2$

$\dfrac{x^2}{a^2} - \dfrac{y^2}{a^2 / |k|} = 1$ (hyperbola)

  (c)   If $k > 0 \ (k \neq 1), x^2 + ky^2 = a^2$

$\dfrac{x^2}{a^2} + \dfrac{y^2}{a^2 / k} = 1$ (ellipse)

41. In $Ax^2 + Bxy + Cy^2 + Dx + Ey + F = 0,$
$A = B = C = 0, D \neq 0, E \neq 0, F \neq 0,$ then
the equation is $Dx + Ey + F = 0$ whose locus is a
straight line.

45. (a) Beam is perpendicular to floor. We have a
circle.

(b) Beam is not perpendicular to floor. We have
an ellipse.

* See conic section diagrams, Fig. 21-92, p. 595
of text.

21.9   Polar Coordinates

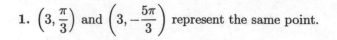

1. $\left(3, \dfrac{\pi}{3}\right)$ and $\left(3, -\dfrac{5\pi}{3}\right)$ represent the same point.

$\left(-3, \dfrac{\pi}{3}\right)$ and $\left(3, -\dfrac{2\pi}{3}\right)$ are on the opposite side of the pole.

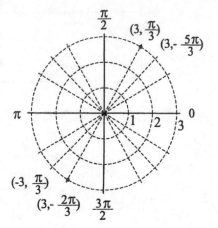

5. $\left(3, \dfrac{\pi}{6}\right)$; $r = 3$, $\theta = \dfrac{\pi}{6}$

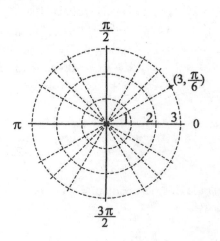

9. $\left(-2, \dfrac{7\pi}{6}\right)$; negative r is reversed in direction from positive r.

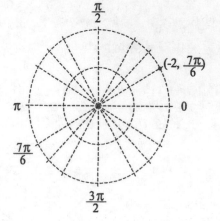

13. $(2,2)$; $\dfrac{\pi}{180°} = \dfrac{2}{\theta}$; $\theta = \dfrac{360}{\pi} = 114.6°$

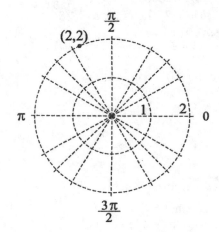

17. $(\sqrt{3}, 1)$ is (x, y), quadrant I

$\tan \theta = \dfrac{y}{x}$

$\theta = \tan^{-1} \dfrac{y}{x} = \tan^{-1} \dfrac{1}{\sqrt{3}} = \tan^{-1} \dfrac{\sqrt{3}}{3}$;

$\theta = 30° = \dfrac{\pi}{6}$

$r = \sqrt{x^2 + y^2} = \sqrt{(\sqrt{3})^2 + 1^2}$
$\quad = \sqrt{3 + 1} = \sqrt{4} = 2$

(r, θ) is $\left(2, \dfrac{\pi}{6}\right)$

21. (r, θ) is $\left(8, \dfrac{4\pi}{3}\right)$, quadrant III

$$x = r \cos \theta = 8 \cos \dfrac{4\pi}{3} = 8 \left(-\dfrac{1}{2}\right) = -4$$

$$y = r \sin \theta = 8 \left(-\dfrac{\sqrt{3}}{2}\right) = -4\sqrt{3}$$

(x, y) is $(-4, -4\sqrt{3})$

25. $x = 3$

$$r \cos \theta = x = 3; \quad r = \dfrac{3}{\cos \theta} = 3 \sec \theta$$

29. $\quad x^2 + (y - 2)^2 = 4$
$$x^2 + y^2 - 4y + 4 = 4$$
$$r^2 - 4 \cdot r \sin \theta = 0$$
$$r = 4 \sin \theta$$

33. $x^2 + y^2 = 6y$
$$r^2 = 6 \cdot r \sin \theta$$
$$r = 6 \sin \theta$$

37. $r = \sin \theta; \; r^2 = r \sin \theta; \; r^2 = x^2 + y^2$
$x^2 + y^2 = r^2 = r \sin \theta = y; \; x^2 + y^2 - y = 0$,
circle

41. $r = \dfrac{2}{\cos \theta - 3 \sin \theta}$

$$r \cos \theta - 3r \sin \theta = 2$$
$$x - 3y = 2, \text{ line}$$

45. $r = 2(1 + \cos \theta); \; x = r \cos \theta; \; \dfrac{x}{r} = \cos \theta$

$$r^2 = x^2 + y^2; \; r = \sqrt{x^2 + y^2}$$

$$r = 2(1 + \cos \theta) = 2\left(1 + \dfrac{x}{r}\right) = 2 + \dfrac{2x}{r}; \; r^2 = 2r + 2x$$

Multiply through by r.

$x^2 + y^2 = 2\sqrt{x^2 + y^2} + 2x; \; x^2 + y^2 - 2x = 2\sqrt{x^2 + y^2}$
$(x^2 + y^2 - 2x)^2 = 4(x^2 + y^2)$
$x^4 + y^4 - 4x^3 + 2x^2y^2 - 4xy^2 + 4x^2 = 4x^2 + 4y^2$
$x^4 + y^4 - 4x^3 + 2x^2y^2 - 4xy^2 + 4x^2 - 4x^2 - 4y^2 = 0$
$x^4 + y^4 - 4x^3 + 2x^2y^2 - 4xy^2 - 4y^2 = 0$

49. Each pair of vertices subtends a central angle of $\dfrac{\pi}{3}$ at the pole. The coordinates of the other vertices are $(2, 0), \left(2, \dfrac{\pi}{3}\right), \left(2, \dfrac{2\pi}{3}\right), \left(2, \dfrac{4\pi}{3}\right), \left(2, \dfrac{5\pi}{3}\right)$

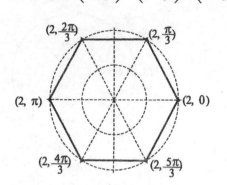

53. $r = 3 - \sin \theta; \; y = r \sin \theta$

$$\sqrt{x^2 + y^2} = 3 - \dfrac{y}{r} = 3 - \dfrac{y}{\sqrt{x^2 + y^2}}$$

$$\sqrt{x^2 + y^2} = \dfrac{3\sqrt{x^2 + y^2} - y}{\sqrt{x^2 + y^2}}$$

$x^2 + y^2 = 3\sqrt{x^2 + y^2} - y; \; x^2 + y^2 + y = 3\sqrt{x^2 + y^2}$

Square both sides.

$$x^4 + 2x^2y^2 + 2x^2y + y^4 + 2y^3 + y^2 = 9(x^2 + y^2)$$
$$= 9x^2 + 9y^2$$

Therefore,

$$x^4 + 2x^2y^2 + 2x^2y + y^4 + 2y^3 - 9x^2 - 8y^2 = 0$$

21.10   Curves in Polar Coordinates

1. The graph of $\theta = \dfrac{5\pi}{6}$ is a straight line through the pole. $\theta = \dfrac{5\pi}{6}$ for all possible values of r.

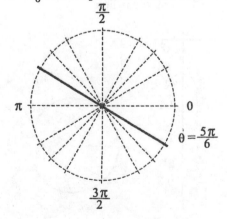

5. $r = 4$ for all θ. Graph is a circle with radius 4.

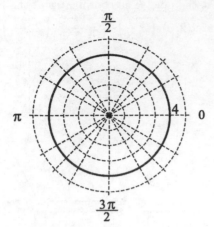

9. $r = 4\sec\theta = \dfrac{4}{\cos\theta}$; vertical line

θ	r
0	4
$\frac{\pi}{6}$	4.6
$\frac{\pi}{4}$	5.7
$\frac{\pi}{3}$	8
$\frac{\pi}{2}$	$*$
$\frac{2\pi}{3}$	-8
$\frac{3\pi}{4}$	-5.7
$\frac{5\pi}{6}$	4.6
π	-4
$\frac{5\pi}{4}$	-5.7
$\frac{3\pi}{2}$	$*$
$\frac{7\pi}{4}$	5.7
2π	4

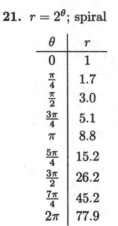

*denotes undefined

13. $r = 1 - \cos\theta$; cardioid

θ	r
0	0
$\frac{\pi}{4}$	0.3
$\frac{\pi}{2}$	1
$\frac{3\pi}{4}$	1.7
π	2
$\frac{5\pi}{4}$	1.7
$\frac{3\pi}{2}$	1
$\frac{7\pi}{4}$	0.3

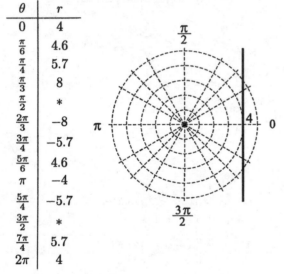

17. $r = 4\sin 2\theta$; rose (4 petals)

θ	r
0	0
$\frac{\pi}{8}$	2.8
$\frac{\pi}{4}$	4
$\frac{3\pi}{8}$	-2.8
$\frac{\pi}{2}$	0
$\frac{5\pi}{8}$	2.8
$\frac{3\pi}{4}$	-4
$\frac{7\pi}{8}$	-2.8
π	0
$\frac{9\pi}{8}$	2.8
$\frac{5\pi}{4}$	4
$\frac{11\pi}{8}$	2.8
$\frac{3\pi}{2}$	0
$\frac{13\pi}{8}$	-2.8
$\frac{7\pi}{4}$	-4
2π	-2.8

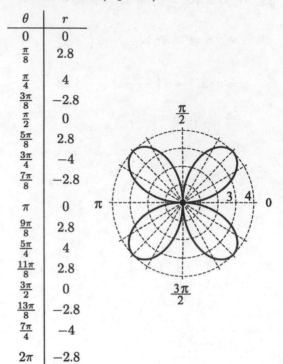

21. $r = 2^{\theta}$; spiral

θ	r
0	1
$\frac{\pi}{4}$	1.7
$\frac{\pi}{2}$	3.0
$\frac{3\pi}{4}$	5.1
π	8.8
$\frac{5\pi}{4}$	15.2
$\frac{3\pi}{2}$	26.2
$\frac{7\pi}{4}$	45.2
2π	77.9

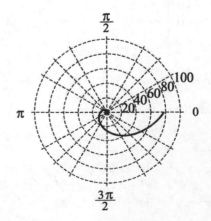

25. $r = \dfrac{1}{2 - \cos\theta}$; ellipse

θ	r
0	1
$\frac{\pi}{4}$	0.77
$\frac{\pi}{2}$	0.50
$\frac{3\pi}{4}$	0.37
π	0.33
$\frac{5\pi}{4}$	0.37
$\frac{3\pi}{2}$	0.50
$\frac{7\pi}{4}$	0.77
2π	1

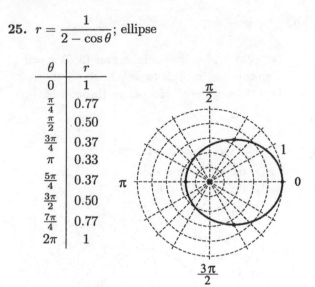

29. $r = 4\cos\dfrac{1}{2}\theta$

θ	r	θ	r
0	4.0	$\frac{13\pi}{6}$	-3.9
$\frac{\pi}{6}$	3.9	$\frac{9\pi}{4}$	-3.7
$\frac{\pi}{4}$	3.7	$\frac{7\pi}{3}$	-3.5
$\frac{\pi}{3}$	3.5	$\frac{5\pi}{2}$	-2.8
$\frac{\pi}{2}$	2.8	$\frac{8\pi}{3}$	-2.0
$\frac{2\pi}{3}$	2.0	$\frac{11\pi}{4}$	-1.5
$\frac{3\pi}{4}$	1.5	$\frac{17\pi}{6}$	-1.0
$\frac{5\pi}{6}$	1.0	3π	0
π	0	$\frac{19\pi}{6}$	1.0
$\frac{7\pi}{6}$	-1.0	$\frac{13\pi}{4}$	1.5
$\frac{5\pi}{4}$	-1.5	$\frac{10\pi}{3}$	2.0
$\frac{4\pi}{3}$	-2.0	$\frac{7\pi}{2}$	2.8
$\frac{3\pi}{2}$	-2.8	$\frac{11\pi}{3}$	3.5
$\frac{5\pi}{3}$	-3.5	$\frac{15\pi}{4}$	3.7
$\frac{7\pi}{4}$	-3.7	$\frac{23\pi}{6}$	3.9
$\frac{11\pi}{6}$	-3.9	4π	4.0
2π	-4.0		

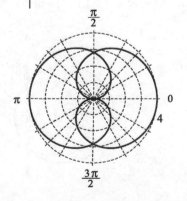

33. $r = \theta$ $(-20 \le \theta \le 20)$

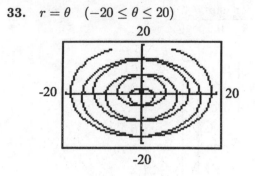

37. $r = 3\cos 4\theta$

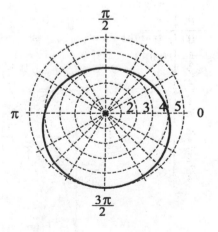

41. $r = 4.0 - \sin\theta$

θ	r
0	4.0
$\frac{\pi}{4}$	3.3
$\frac{\pi}{2}$	3.0
$\frac{3\pi}{4}$	3.3
π	4.0
$\frac{5\pi}{4}$	4.7
$\frac{3\pi}{2}$	5.0
$\frac{7\pi}{4}$	4.7

45. $R = \dfrac{\sin^2 \theta}{(1 - 0.5 \cos \theta)^2}$

θ	R	θ	R
0	0	$\frac{13\pi}{12}$	0.03
$\frac{\pi}{12}$	0.25	$\frac{7\pi}{6}$	0.12
$\frac{\pi}{6}$	0.78	$\frac{5\pi}{4}$	0.27
$\frac{\pi}{4}$	1.20	$\frac{4\pi}{3}$	0.48
$\frac{\pi}{3}$	1.33	$\frac{17\pi}{12}$	0.73
$\frac{5\pi}{12}$	1.23	$\frac{3\pi}{2}$	2
$\frac{\pi}{2}$	1	$\frac{19\pi}{12}$	1.23
$\frac{7\pi}{12}$	0.73	$\frac{5\pi}{3}$	1.33
$\frac{2\pi}{3}$	0.48	$\frac{7\pi}{4}$	1.20
$\frac{3\pi}{4}$	0.27	$\frac{11\pi}{6}$	0.78
$\frac{5\pi}{6}$	0.12	$\frac{23\pi}{12}$	0.25
$\frac{11\pi}{12}$	0.03	2π	0
π	0		

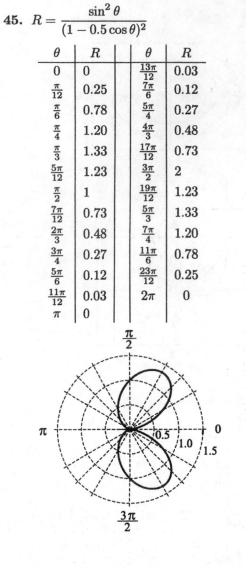

5. $x^2 + y^2 = 6x$
$x^2 - 6x + 9 + y^2 = 9$
$(x - 3)^2 + y^2 = 3^2$; circle, center $(3, 0), r = 3$
The concentric circle has equation
$(x - 3)^2 + y^2 = r^2$ and passes through $(4, -3)$

$$(4 - 3)^2 + (-3)^2 = r^2$$
$$r^2 = 10$$
$$(x - 3)^2 + y^2 = 10$$
$$x^2 - 6x + 9 + y^2 = 10$$
$$x^2 - 6x + y^2 - 1 = 0$$

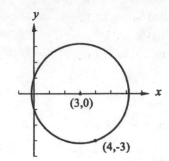

9. $a = 10, c = 8$
$$a^2 = b^2 + c^2$$
$$100 = b^2 + 8^2 \Rightarrow b^2 = 36$$
$$\frac{x^2}{100} + \frac{y^2}{36} = 1 \text{ or } 9x^2 + 25y^2 = 900$$

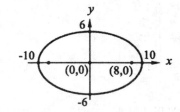

Chapter 21 Review Exercises

1. Given: straight line; (x_1, y_1) is $(1, -7)$; $m = 4$
$y - y_1 = m(x - x_1); \ y - (-7) = 4(x - 1)$
$y + 7 = 4x - 4; \ y = 4x - 4 - 7$
$y = 4x - 11 \text{ or } 4x - y - 11 = 0$

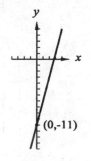

13. Given: $x^2 + y^2 + 6x - 7 = 0$
$(x^2 + 6x) + (y^2) = 7; \ (x^2 + 6x + 9) + y^2 = 7 + 9$
$(x + 3)^2 + (y + 0)^2 = 16$
$[x - (-3)]^2 + (y - 0)^2 = 4^2$
center $(h, k) = (-3, 0)$; radius $r = 4$

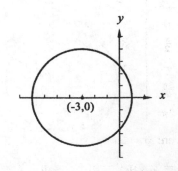

17. Given: $16x^2 + y^2 = 16$

$\dfrac{16x^2}{16} + \dfrac{y^2}{16} = 1; \dfrac{x^2}{1^2} + \dfrac{y^2}{4^2} = 1; \dfrac{y^2}{4^2} + \dfrac{x^2}{1^2} = 1$

$a = 4, b = 1, c = \sqrt{16 - 1} = \sqrt{15}$

vertices $(0, a)$, $(0, -a)$ or $(0, 4)$, $(0, -4)$

foci $(0, c)$, $(0, -c)$ or $(0, \sqrt{15})$, $(0, -\sqrt{15})$

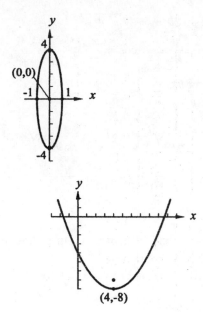

21. Given: $x^2 - 8x - 4y - 16 = 0$

$x^2 - 8x = 4y + 16; x^2 - 8x + 16 = 4y + 16 + 16$

$(x - 4)^2 = 4y + 32; (x - 4)^2 = 4(y + 8)$

$(x - 4)^2 = 4(1)(y + 8); p = 1$

vertex (h, k) is $(4, -8)$; focus is $(4, -7)$

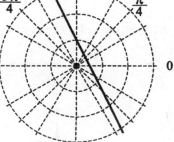

$(4, -8)$

25. Given: $r = 4(1 + \sin\theta)$

θ	r
0	4
$\frac{\pi}{4}$	6.8
$\frac{\pi}{2}$	8
$\frac{3\pi}{4}$	6.8
π	4
$\frac{5\pi}{4}$	1.2
$\frac{3\pi}{2}$	0
$\frac{7\pi}{4}$	1.2

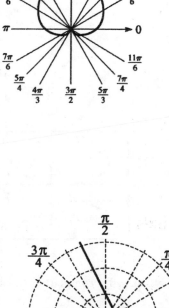

29. Given: $r = \dfrac{3}{\sin\theta + 2\cos\theta}$

θ	r
-2π	1.5
$-\frac{3\pi}{2}$	3
$-\pi$	-1.5
$-\frac{\pi}{2}$	-3
0	1.5
$\frac{\pi}{2}$	3
π	-1.5
$\frac{3\pi}{2}$	-3
2π	1.5

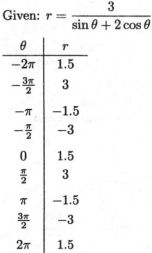

33. Given: $y = 2x$

$\dfrac{y}{x} = 2; \tan\theta = 2; \theta = \tan^{-1} 2 = 1.11$

37. Given: $r = 2\sin 2\theta$; $r = \sqrt{x^2 + y^2}$

$\sin\theta = \dfrac{y}{r} = \dfrac{y}{\sqrt{x^2 + y^2}}$; $\cos = \dfrac{x}{r} = \dfrac{x}{\sqrt{x^2 + y^2}}$

$r = 2(2\sin\theta\cos\theta)$

$r = 4\sin\theta\cos\theta$

$\sqrt{x^2 + y^2} = 4\dfrac{y}{\sqrt{x^2 + y^2}} \times \dfrac{x}{\sqrt{x^2 + y^2}}$; $\sqrt{x^2 + y^2} = \dfrac{4xy}{x^2 + y^2}$

$x^2 + y^2 = \dfrac{(4xy)^2}{(x^2 + y^2)^2} = \dfrac{16x^2y^2}{(x^2 + y^2)^2}$

$\left(x^2 + y^2\right)^3 = 16x^2y^2$

41. $x^2 + y^2 = 9$ circle; center $(0,0)$; radius 3

$x^2 + y^2 = 3^2$

$4x^2 + y^2 = 16$ ellipse; centered at $(0,0)$

$(\pm 2, 0)$ and $(0, \pm 4)$ vertices

$\dfrac{x^2}{4} + \dfrac{y^2}{16} = 1$

$\dfrac{x^2}{2^2} + \dfrac{y^2}{4^2} = 1$

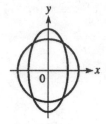

four real solutions

45. $x^2 + 3y + 2 - (1 + x)^2 = 0$

$3y = (1 + x)^2 - x^2 - 2$

$y = \dfrac{(1 + x)^2 - x^2 - 2}{3} - \dfrac{1 + 2x + x^2 - x^2 - 2}{3} = \dfrac{2x - 1}{3} = \dfrac{2}{3}x - \dfrac{1}{3}$

Graph $y_1 = \dfrac{2}{3}x - \dfrac{1}{3}$

49. $x^2 - 4y^2 + 4x + 24y - 48 = 0$. Solve for y by completing the square.

$y^2 - 6y = 0.25x^2 + x - 12$

$y^2 - 6y + 9 = 0.25x^2 + x - 3$

$(y - 3)^2 = 0.25x^2 + x - 3$

$y = \pm\sqrt{0.25x^2 + x - 3} + 3$

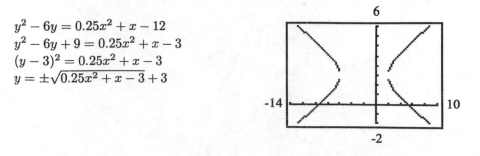

53. $r = 2 - 3\csc\theta = 2 - \dfrac{3}{\sin\theta}$

Graph $r_1 = 2 - \dfrac{3}{\sin\theta}$

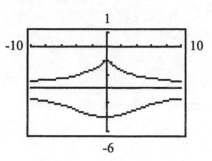

57.

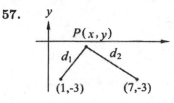

$d_1 + d_2 = 8$ describes an ellipse with center $(4, -3)$,
$a = 4 \Rightarrow a^2 = 16, c = 3 \Rightarrow c^2 = 9$.
$a^2 = b^2 + c^2 \Rightarrow 16 = b^2 + 9 \Rightarrow b^2 = 7$

$$\dfrac{(x-4)^2}{16} + \dfrac{(y+3)^2}{7} = 1$$

61. The boundary line is the dashed graph of the parabola $y = 4(x+2)^2$. Use $(0,0)$ as a test point in

$$y > 4(x+2)^2$$
$$0 > 4(0+2)^2$$
$$0 > 16, F$$

Solution region does not contain $(0,0)$. Shade region inside parabola.

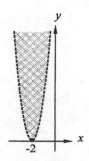

65.

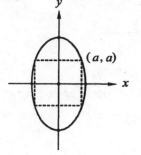

$$7a^2 + 2a^2 = 18$$
$$9a^2 = 18$$
$$a = \sqrt{2}$$

Square has side $= 2\sqrt{2}$
Area of square $= (2\sqrt{2})^2 = 8$

69. $R_T = R + 2.5$; linear function with slope 1 and y-int $= 2.5$

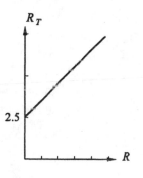

73. $y = 50.00 \text{ kg} \dfrac{2.010 \text{ kJ}}{1 \text{ kg} \cdot 1°\text{C}}(T - 100°\text{C})$

$y = 100.5T - 10{,}050$

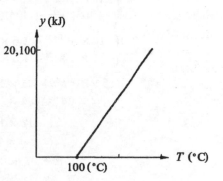
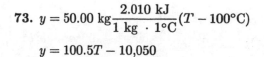

77.

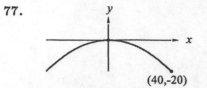

Choose the oriigin at top of arch.

$$4py = x^2$$
$$4p(-20) = 40^2$$
$$4p = -80$$
$$-80y = x^2$$

$$y = -\frac{1}{80}x^2$$

81.   Graph is parabolic in shape

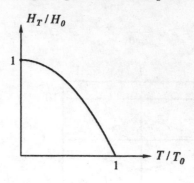

85. $a = \dfrac{120}{2} = 60$; $c = 60 - 15 = 45$; $b = \sqrt{a^2 - b^2} = \sqrt{60^2 - 45^2} = \sqrt{1575}$

$A = \pi ab = \pi \cdot 60 \cdot \sqrt{1575} = 7500 \text{ ft}^2$

89.

$$\frac{x^2}{a^2} - \frac{y^2}{b^2} = 1$$

$y = 40$ when $x = 40$

$y = 100$ when $x = 50$

$$\begin{cases} \dfrac{40^2}{a^2} - \dfrac{40^2}{b^2} = 1 \text{ or } 40^2b^2 - 40^2a^2 = a^2b^2 \\[2mm] \dfrac{50^2}{a^2} - \dfrac{100^2}{b^2} = 1 \text{ or } 50^2b^2 - 100^2a^2 = a^2b^2 \end{cases}$$

mult by 100^2
mult by -40^2
$$\begin{cases} 40^2b^2 - 40^2a^2 = a^2b^2 \\ 50^2b^2 - 100^2a^2 = a^2b^2 \end{cases}$$

$$\begin{cases} 100^2 40^2 b^2 - 100^2 40^2 a^2 = 100^2 a^2 b^2 \\ -40^2 50^2 b^2 + 40^2 100^2 a^2 = -40^2 a^2 b^2 \end{cases}$$

Add
$$\begin{cases} 16 \times 10^6 b^2 - 1.6 \times 10^7 a^2 = 10 \times 10^3 a^2 b^2 \\ 4 \times 10^6 b^2 + 1.6 \times 10^7 a^2 = -1.6 \times 10^3 a^2 b^2 \end{cases}$$

$$12 \times 10^6 b^2 = 8.4 \times 10^3 a^2 b^2$$
$$12 \times 10^6 = 8.4 \times 10^3 a^2$$

$$a^2 = \frac{12 \times 10^6}{8.4 \times 10^3} = 1.42 \times 10^3$$

$$a = 37.8 \text{ ft}$$

93. $r^2 = R^2 \cos 2\left(\theta + \dfrac{\pi}{2}\right)$

$r = R\sqrt{\cos 2\left(\theta + \dfrac{\pi}{2}\right)} = R\sqrt{\cos(2\theta + \pi)}$

Since the square root is real only when $\cos 2\left(\theta + \frac{\pi}{2}\right)$ is not negative, the range is $\dfrac{\pi}{4} \leq \dfrac{3\pi}{4}$ or $\dfrac{5\pi}{4} \leq r \leq \dfrac{7\pi}{4}$. (See Chapter 10.)

θ	r
$\frac{\pi}{4}$	0
$\frac{\pi}{3}$	$0.5R$
$\frac{\pi}{2}$	$1R$
$\frac{2\pi}{3}$	$0.5R$
$\frac{3\pi}{4}$	0
$\frac{5\pi}{4}$	0
$\frac{4\pi}{3}$	$0.5R$
$\frac{3\pi}{2}$	$1R$
$\frac{5\pi}{3}$	$0.5R$
$\frac{7\pi}{4}$	0

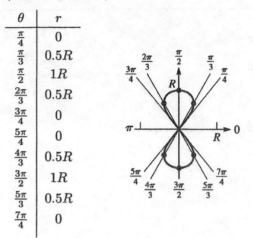

97. $\dfrac{1}{r} = a + b\cos\theta$

$1 = ar + br\cos\theta$

$1 = a\sqrt{x^2 + y^2} + bx$

$a\sqrt{x^2 + y^2} = 1 - bx$

$a^2(x^2 + y^2) = 1 - 2bx + b^2x^2$

$a^2x^2 + a^2y^2 + 2bx - b^2x^2 = 1$

$(a^2 - b^2)x^2 + 2bx + a^2y^2 = 1$

$x^2 + \dfrac{2b}{a^2 - b^2} \cdot x + \dfrac{a^2}{a^2 - b^2} \cdot y^2 = \dfrac{1}{a^2 - b^2}$

$x^2 + \dfrac{2b}{a^2 - b^2} \cdot x + \dfrac{b^2}{(a^2 - b^2)^2} + \dfrac{a^2}{a^2 - b^2} \cdot y^2 = \dfrac{1}{a^2 - b^2} + \dfrac{b^2}{(a^2 - b^2)^2}$

$\left(x + \dfrac{b}{a^2 - b^2}\right)^2 + \dfrac{a^2}{a^2 - b^2} \cdot y^2 = \dfrac{a^2 - b^2 + b^2}{(a^2 - b^2)^2} = \dfrac{a^2}{(a^2 - b^2)^2}$

$\dfrac{\left(x + \frac{b}{a^2 - b^2}\right)^2}{\dfrac{a^2}{(a^2 - b^2)^2}} + \dfrac{y^2}{\dfrac{1}{a^2 - b^2}} = 1$ which is the equation of a conic.

INTRODUCTION TO STATISTICS

22.1 Frequency Distributions

1.

Estimate (hours)	0-5	6-11	12-17	18-23	24-29
Frequency	5	12	19	9	5

5.

Number	103	104	105	106	107	108	109	110	111	112	113
Frequency	1	3	1	3	2	4	3	1	1	0	1

9.

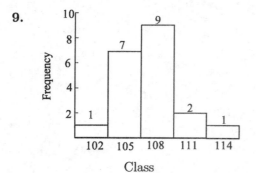

13.

Number	18	19	20	21	22	23	24	25
Frequency	1	3	2	4	3	1	0	1

17.

Time(s)	2.21	2.22	2.23	2.24	2.25	2.26	2.27	2.28	2.29
Frequency	2	7	18	41	56	32	8	3	3

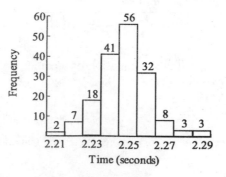

21.

Dist. (ft)	155 − 159	160 − 164	165 − 169	170 − 174	175 − 179	180 − 184	185 − 189
f, (%)	1.7	12.5	26.7	30.0	20.0	8.3	0.8

25.

Dosage (mR)	3.73-3.87	3.88-4.02	4.03-4.17	4.18-4.32	4.33-4.47	4.48-4.62
Frequency	1	2	2	7	7	1

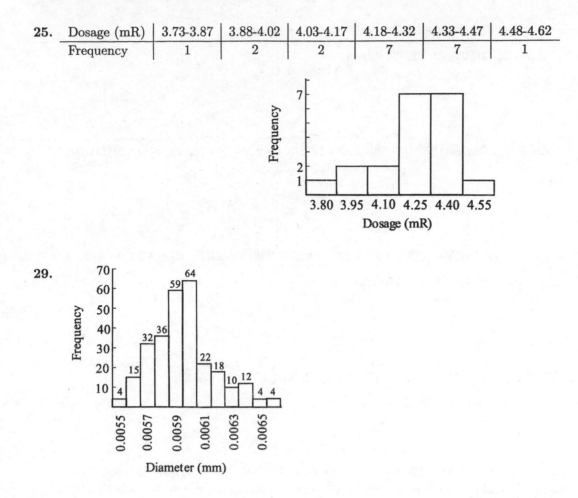

29.

22.2   Measures of Central Tendency

1. 1, 2, 2, 3, 4, 4, 4, 6, 7, 7, 8, 9, 9, 11

There are 14 numbers. The median is halfway between the seventh and eighth numbers.

$$\text{median} = \frac{4+6}{2} = 5$$

5. Arrange the numbers in numerical order:

2, 3, 3, 3, 4, 4, 4, 4, 5, 5, 6, 6, 6, 7, 7

There are 15 numbers. The middle number is eighth. Since the eighth number is 4, the median is 4.

9. The arithmetic mean is:

$$\overline{x} = \frac{2+3+3+3+4+4+4+4+5+5+6+6+6+7+7}{15} = \frac{69}{15} = 4.6$$

13. The mode is the number that occurs most frequently, which is 4 since it occurs 4 times.

17. Arrange in numerical order; find the value of the 8th (middle) number.

18, 19, 19, 19, 20, 20, 21, 21, 21, 21, 22, 22, 22, 23, 25

The median value is 21.

21. $\overline{T} = (2(2.21) + 7(2.22) + 18(2.23) + 41(2.24) + 56(2.25) + 32(2.26) + 8(2.27) + 3(2.28) + 3(2.29)/170)$

$\qquad = \dfrac{382.13}{170} = 2.248 \text{ s}$

25. $\overline{d} = (3.83 + 3.90 + 3.96 + 4.09 + 4.15 + 4.18 + 4.21 + 4.23 + 4.25 + 4.26 + 4.27 + 4.29 + 4.33$

$\qquad + 4.34 + 2(4.36) + 4.37 + 4.41 + 4.44 + 4.51/20)$

$\qquad = 4.237 \text{ mR}$

29. 25, 28, 28, 29, 29, 30, 30, 30, 30, 30, 31, 31, 31, 32, 32, 32, 33, 33, 34, 34, 34, 35, 36

The median value is the 12th number, which is 31 h.

33. Arrange the salaries in order: 375, 400, 425, 425, 450, 450, 475, 475, 500, 500, 500, 550, 550, 600

There are 14 numbers. The middle number is between the seventh and the eight, which are both 475. Therefore, the median is $475. The mode is $500, which occurs three times.

37. Arrange in order: 0.14, 0.15, 0.15, 0.17, 0.17, 0.18, 0.18, 0.18, 0.19, 0.20, 0.22, 0.22, 0.23, 0.23, 0.24, 0.26, 0.27, 0.32

The median is between the 9th and 10th.
Median $= (0.19 + 0.20) \div 2 = 0.195$
Mode $= 0.18$; $f = 3$

41. Add 100 to each number and arrange in order. 475, 500, 525, 525, 550, 550, 575, 575, 600, 600, 600, 650, 650, 700

The median is between the seventh and eighth number, both of which are $575. The mode is $600 since there are three of these. The mean is the sum divided by 14.

$\overline{x} = \dfrac{8075}{14} = \$577$

The mean, median, and mode are 100 more than the values in Exercise 33.

22.3   Standard Deviation

1.

x	$x - \bar{x}$	$(x - \bar{x})^2$
6	2	4
5	1	1
4	0	0
7	3	9
6	2	4
2	−2	4
1	−3	9
1	−3	9
5	1	1
3	−1	1
40		42

$\bar{x} = 40/10 = 4$

$$\frac{\sum(x - \bar{x})^2}{n - 1} = \frac{42}{10 - 1} = \frac{42}{9}$$

$$s = \sqrt{\frac{42}{9}} = 2.2$$

5.

x	$x - \bar{x}$	$(x - \bar{x})^2$	x^2
0.45	0.0525	0.00276	0.2025
0.46	0.0425	0.00181	0.2116
0.47	0.0325	0.00106	0.2209
0.48	0.0225	5.1×10^{-4}	0.2304
0.48	0.0225	5.1×10^{-4}	0.2304
0.49	0.0125	1.6×10^{-4}	0.2401
0.49	0.0125	1.6×10^{-4}	0.2401
0.51	−0.0075	5.6×10^{-5}	0.2601
0.53	−0.0275	7.6×10^{-4}	0.2809
0.55	−0.0475	0.00226	0.3025
0.55	−0.0475	0.00226	0.3025
0.57	−0.0675	0.00456	0.3249
$\sum x = 6.03$		$\sum(x - \bar{x})^2 = 0.016825$	$\sum x^2 = 3.0469$

$$\bar{x} = \frac{\sum x}{n} = \frac{6.03}{12} = 0.5025$$

$$s = \sqrt{\frac{\sum(x - x)^2}{n - 1}} = \sqrt{\frac{0.016825}{12 - 1}} = 0.039, \text{ equation 22.2}$$

9. Using equation 22-3

$$s = \sqrt{\frac{n\sum x^2 - (\sum x)^2}{n(n - 1)}} = \sqrt{\frac{12(3.0469) - 6.03^2}{12(12 - 1)}} = 0.039$$

13. $\overline{x} = 0.503, s = 0.039$

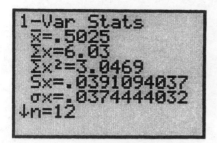

17. Battery lives, exercise 27,
section 22.1

$s = 2.6$ h

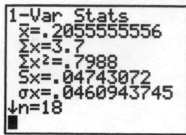

21. Air pollution data, exercise 37, section 22.2

$s = 0.047$ ppm

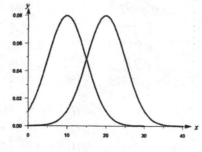

22.4   Normal Distributions

1. $\mu = 10, \alpha = 5$ and $\mu = 20, \alpha = 5$ are the same height with the first centered at $x = 10$ and the second centered at $x = 20$.

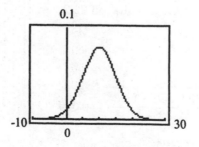

5. $\mu = 10, \sigma = 5$ is the graph in Fig. 22.9.

9. $200(0.68) = 136$

13. $\mu = 1.50, \sigma = 0.05.$ x between 1.45 and 1.55

$$z = \frac{1.45 - 1.50}{0.05} = -1, z = \frac{1.55 - 1.50}{0.05} = 1$$

$(0.3413 + 0.3413)(500) = 341.3$

341 batteries will have a voltage between 1.45 V and 1.55 V

17. $\mu = 100{,}000, \sigma = 10{,}000.$ x between 85,000 and 100,000

$$z = \frac{85{,}000 - 100{,}000}{10{,}000} = -1.5$$

$(0.4332)(5000) = 2166$

2166 tires will last bettween 85,000 km and 100,000 km

21. $\sigma_{\overline{x}} = \dfrac{\sigma}{\sqrt{n}} = \dfrac{10{,}000}{\sqrt{5000}} = 141.$ About 68% have a mean lifetime from 99,859 km to 100,141 km.

25. $\overline{x} + s = 2.262$ and $\overline{x} - s = 2.234.$ The readings within these bounds are 2.24, 2.25, and 2.26 with frequencies of $32 + 56 + 41 = 129.$ Thus 129 of the 170 readings or 76% fall within these bounds as compared to a normal distribution with 68%.

22.5   Statistical Process Control

1.

Subgroup	Amount of Drug (in mg) of five capacles					Mean x	Range R
1	497	499	502	493	498	497.8	9
2	497	499	500	495	502	498.6	7
3	496	500	507	503	502	501.6	11
4	512	503	488	500	497	500.0	24
5	504	505	500	508	502	503.8	8
6	495	495	501	497	497	497.0	6
7	503	500	507	499	498	501.4	9
8	494	498	497	501	496	497.2	7
9	502	504	505	500	502	502.6	5
10	500	502	500	496	497	499.0	6
11	502	498	510	503	497	502.0	13
12	497	498	496	502	500	498.6	6
13	504	500	495	498	501	499.6	9
14	500	499	498	501	494	498.4	7
15	498	496	502	501	505	500.4	9
16	500	503	504	499	505	502.2	6
17	487	496	499	498	494	494.8	12
18	498	497	497	502	497	498.2	5
19	503	501	500	498	504	501.2	6
20	496	494	503	502	501	499.2	9
					Sums	9993.6	174
					Means	499.7	8.7

$$UCL(\overline{x}) = \overline{\overline{x}} + A_2 R = 499.7 + 0.577(8.7) = 504.7 \text{ mg}$$
$$LCL(\overline{x}) = \overline{\overline{x}} - A_2 R = 499.7 - 0.577(8.7) = 494.7 \text{ mg}$$

5.

Hour	Torques (in N·m) of five engines					Mean x	Range R
1	366	352	354	360	362	358.8	14
2	370	374	362	366	356	365.6	18
3	358	357	365	372	361	362.6	15
4	360	368	367	359	363	363.4	9
5	352	356	354	348	350	352.0	8
6	366	361	372	370	363	366.4	11
7	365	366	361	370	362	364.8	9
8	354	363	360	361	364	360.4	10
9	361	358	356	364	364	360.6	8
10	368	366	368	358	360	364.0	10
11	355	360	359	362	353	357.8	9
12	365	364	357	367	370	364.6	13
13	360	364	372	358	365	363.8	14
14	348	360	352	360	354	354.8	12
15	358	364	362	372	361	363.4	14
16	360	361	371	366	346	360.8	25
17	354	359	358	366	366	360.6	12
18	362	366	367	361	357	362.6	10
19	363	373	364	360	358	363.6	15
20	372	362	360	365	367	365.2	12
					Sum	7235.8	248
					Mean	361.79	12.4

CL: $\overline{\overline{x}} = 361.79$ N·m

$$UCL(\overline{x}) = \overline{\overline{x}} + A_2\overline{R} = 361.79 + 0.577(12.4)$$
$$= 368.9 \text{ N} \cdot \text{m}$$
$$LCL(\overline{x}) = \overline{\overline{x}} - A_2\overline{R} = 361.79 - 0.577(12.4)$$
$$= 354.6 \text{ N} \cdot \text{m}$$

9.

Subgroup	Output voltages of five adapters						
1	9.03	9.08	8.85	8.92	8.90	8.956	0.23
2	9.05	8.98	9.20	9.04	9.12	9.078	0.22
3	8.93	8.96	9.14	9.06	9.00	9.018	0.21
4	9.16	9.08	9.04	9.07	8.97	9.064	0.19
5	9.03	9.08	8.93	8.88	8.95	8.974	0.20
6	8.92	9.07	8.86	8.96	9.04	8.970	0.21
7	9.00	9.05	8.90	8.94	8.93	8.964	0.15
8	8.87	8.99	8.96	9.02	9.03	8.974	0.16
9	8.89	8.92	9.05	9.10	8.93	8.978	0.21
10	9.01	9.00	9.09	8.96	8.98	9.008	0.13
11	8.90	8.97	8.92	8.98	9.03	8.960	0.13
12	9.04	9.06	8.94	8.93	8.92	8.978	0.14
13	8.94	8.99	8.93	9.05	9.10	9.002	0.17
14	9.07	9.01	9.05	8.96	9.02	9.022	0.11
15	9.01	8.82	8.95	8.99	9.04	8.962	0.22
16	8.93	8.91	9.04	9.05	8.90	8.966	0.15
17	9.08	9.03	8.91	8.92	8.96	8.980	0.17
18	8.94	8.90	9.05	8.93	9.01	8.966	0.15
19	8.88	8.82	8.89	8.94	8.88	8.882	0.12
20	9.04	9.00	8.98	8.93	9.05	9.000	0.12
21	9.00	9.03	8.94	8.92	9.05	8.988	0.13
22	8.95	8.95	8.91	8.90	9.03	8.948	0.13
23	9.12	9.04	9.01	8.94	9.02	9.026	0.18
24	8.94	8.99	8.93	9.05	9.07	8.996	0.14
					Sum	215.66	3.97
					Mean	8.986	0.1654

CL: $\overline{\overline{x}} = 8.986$ V

$$UCL(\overline{x}) = \overline{\overline{x}} + A_2\overline{R} = 8.986 + 0.577(0.1654)$$
$$= 9.081 \text{ V}$$
$$LCL(\overline{x}) = \overline{\overline{x}} - A_2\overline{R} = 8.986 - 0.577(0.1654)$$
$$= 8.891 \text{ V}$$

13. CL: $\mu = \overline{\overline{x}} = 2.725$ in.
$$UCL(\overline{x}) = \mu + A\sigma = 2.725 + 1.342(0.0032)$$
$$= 2.729 \text{ in.}$$
$$LCL(\overline{x}) = \mu - A\sigma = 2.725 - 1.342(0.0032)$$
$$= 2.721 \text{ in.}$$

17.

Week	Accounts with errors	Proportion with errors
1	52	0.052
2	36	0.036
3	27	0.027
4	58	0.058
5	44	0.044
6	21	0.021
7	48	0.048
8	63	0.063
9	32	0.032
10	38	0.038
11	27	0.027
12	43	0.043
13	22	0.022
14	35	0.035
15	41	0.041
16	20	0.020
17	28	0.028
18	37	0.037
19	24	0.024
20	42	0.042
Total	738	

$$CL: \quad \bar{p} = \frac{738}{1000(20)} = 0.0369$$

$$\sigma_p = \sqrt{\frac{\bar{p}(1-\bar{p})}{n}}$$

$$= \sqrt{\frac{0.0369(1-0.0369)}{1000}}$$

$$= 0.00596$$

$$UCL(p) = 0.0369 + 3(0.00596) = 0.0548$$
$$LCL(p) = 0.0369 - 3(0.00596) = 0.0190$$

22.6   Linear Regression

1.

x	y	xy	x^2
1	3	3	1
2	7	14	4
3	9	27	9
4	9	36	16
5	12	60	25
15	40	140	55

$n = 5$

$$m = \frac{n\sum xy - \sum x \sum y}{n\sum x^2 - (\sum x)^2} = \frac{5(140) - 15(40)}{5(55) - 15^2} = 2$$

$$b = \frac{\sum x^2 \sum y - \sum xy \sum x}{n\sum x^2 - (\sum x)^2} = \frac{55(40) - 140(15)}{5(55) - 15^2} = 2$$

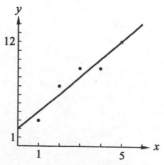

The equation of the least square line is $y = 2x + 2$.

5.

i	V	iV	i^2
15.0	3.00	45.00	225.00
10.8	4.10	44.28	116.64
9.30	5.60	52.08	86.49
3.55	8.00	28.40	12.60
4.60	10.50	48.30	21.16
43.25	31.20	218.06	461.89

$n = 5$

$$m = \frac{5(218.06) - (43.25)(31.20)}{5(461.89) - (43.25)^2} = -0.590$$

$$b = \frac{(461.89)(31.20) - (218.06)(43.25)}{5(461.89) - (43.25)^2} = 11.3$$

$$V = mi + b; \quad V = -0.590i + 11.3$$

Plot points:

i	V
2	10.1
10	5.3

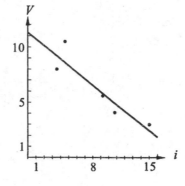

9.

x	p	xp	x^2
0	650	0	0
100	630	63,000	10,000
200	605	121,000	40,000
300	590	177,000	90,000
400	570	228,000	160,000
1000	3045	589,000	300,000

$n = 5$

$$m = \frac{5(589,000) - (1000)(3045)}{5(300,000) - (1000)^2} = -0.200$$

$$b = \frac{(300,000)(3045) - (589,000)(1000)}{5(300,000) - (1000)^2} = 649$$

$$p = mx + b; \quad p = -0.200x + 649$$

Plot points:

i	V
0	649
350	579

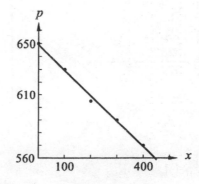

11. Plot points:

f (PHz)	V
0.600	0.562
0.800	1.426

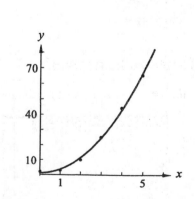

13.

x	y	x^2	y^2
1	3	1	9
2	7	4	49
3	9	9	81
4	9	16	81
5	12	25	144
15	40	55	364

$$\bar{x} = 3 \qquad \overline{x^2} = 11$$

$$\bar{y} = 8 \qquad \overline{y^2} = \frac{364}{5}$$

$$s_x = \sqrt{\overline{x^2} - (\bar{x})^2} = \sqrt{11 - 3^2} = 1.41$$

$$s_y = \sqrt{\overline{y^2} - (\bar{y})^2} = \sqrt{\left(\frac{364}{5}\right) - 8^2} = 2.97$$

$$m = 2$$

$$r = m\frac{s_x}{s_y} = 2\left(\frac{1.41}{2.97}\right)$$

$$r = 0.95$$

22.7   Nonlinear Regression

1.

x	$f(x) = x^2$	y	x^2y	$(x^2)^2$	
0	0	2	0	0	$n = 6$
1	1	3	3	1	
2	4	10	40	16	
3	9	25	225	81	
4	16	44	704	256	
5	25	65	1625	625	
	55	149	2597	979	

$$m = \frac{6(2597) - 55(149)}{6(979) - 55^2} = 2.59$$

$$b = \frac{979(149) - 2597(55)}{6(979) - 55^2} = 1.07$$

$$y = 2.59x^2 + 1.07$$

5. $y = mt^2 + b$

t	y	t^2	yt^2	$(t^2)^2$	
1.0	6.0	1.0	6.0	1.0	
2.0	23	4.0	92	16.0	
3.0	55	9.0	495	81.0	$n = 5$
4.0	98	16.0	1568	256	
5.0	148	25.0	3700	625	
	330	55.0	5861.0	979.0	

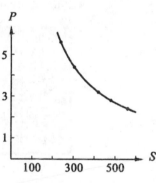

$$m = \frac{5(5861) - (55.0)(330)}{5(979.0) - 55.0^2} = 5.97$$

$$b = \frac{(979.0)(330) - (5861)(55.0)}{5(979.0) - 55.0^2} = 0.38$$

$$y = 5.97t^2 + 0.38$$

9.

S	$\frac{1}{S}$	P	$\left(\frac{1}{S}\right)P$	$\left(\frac{1}{S}\right)2$
240	0.00416666667	5.60	0.0233333333	1.736111×10^{-5}
305	0.00327868852	4.40	0.01442622951	1.074980×10^{-5}
420	0.00238095238	3.20	0.00761904762	5.668935×10^{-6}
480	0.0020833333	2.80	0.00583333333	4.340279×10^{-6}
560	0.00178571429	2.40	0.00428571429	3.188776×10^{-6}
2005	0.01369536	18.40	0.05549766	4.13089×10^{-5}

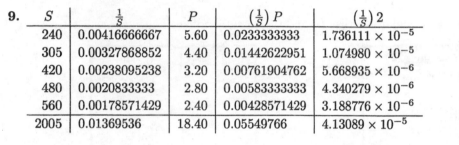

$$m = \frac{5(0.5549766) - (0.01369536)(18.40)}{5(4.13089 \times 10^{-5}) - (0.01369536)^2} = 1343$$

$$b = \frac{(4.13089 \times 10^{-5})(18.40) - (0.05549766)(0.01369536)}{5(4.13089 \times 10^{-5}) - (0.01369536)^2}$$

$$= 1.226612 \times 10^{-3} \text{ or } 0$$

$$P = 1343\left(\frac{1}{S}\right) + 0 = \frac{1343}{S}$$

Chapter 22 Review Exercises

1. Enter the 16 numbers as list L_1 in the calculator. Then $\boxed{\text{2nd}}$ $\boxed{\text{LIST}}$ $\boxed{\blacktriangleleft}$ to obtain

```
NAMES OPS MATH
1:min(
2:max(
3:mean(
4:median(
5:sum(
6:prod(
7↓stdDev(
```

```
median(L₁)
            1100
```

from which

5.

Number	1093-1095	1096-1098	1099-1101	1102-1104	1105-1107
Frequency	3	4	3	4	2

9.

Number	1093-1095	1096-1098	1099-1101	1102-1104	1105-1107
CF	3	7	10	14	16

13. Enter the 12 numbers as list L_1 in the calculator. Then ⌐STAT¬ ⌐▶¬ to obtain

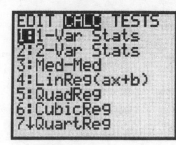 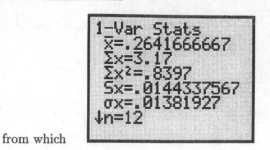   from which

0.014 Pa · s is the standard deviation

17. Enter the 9 power numbers in the calculator as list L_1 and the corresponding frequencies as list L_2, then

   from which

700 W is the median

21. Using L_1 & L_2 from problem 17,

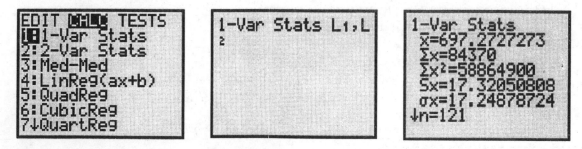

17.3 W is the standard deviation

25. $\sum f = 200$; the median is the mean of the 100th and 101st entries.

Counts	0	1	2	3	4	5	6	7	8	9	10
Intervals	3	10	25	45	29	39	26	11	7	2	3

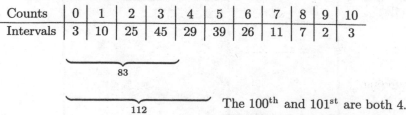

The 100th and 101st are both 4.
Therefore, the median is 4.

29. Enter speeds in L_1 and no. cars in L_2, then

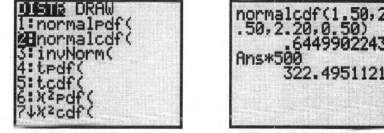

66.2 mi/h is the mean

33. CL; $\overline{p} = \dfrac{540}{500 \cdot 20} = 0.0540$

$$\sigma_p = \sqrt{\frac{\overline{p}(1 - \overline{p})}{n}} = \sqrt{\frac{0.054(1 - 0.054)}{500}} = 0.01011$$

$UCL(p) = 0.054 + 3(0.01011) = 0.0843$
$LCL(p) = 0.054 - 3(0.01011) = 0.0237$

37.

There are about 322 readings between 1.5 and 2.5 $\mu g/m^3$.

41.

T	R	TR	T^2
0.0	25.0	0	0
20.0	26.8	536	400
40.0	28.9	1156	1600
60.0	31.2	1872	3600
80.0	32.8	2624	6400
100	34.7	3470	10000
300	179.4	9658	22000

$\overline{T} = \dfrac{300}{6} = 50.0$ $(\overline{T})^2 = 2500$

$\overline{R} = \dfrac{179.4}{6} = 29.90$ $\overline{T}\,\overline{R} = 50.0(29.9) = 1495$

$\overline{TR} = \dfrac{9658}{6} = 1610$ $\overline{T^2} = \dfrac{22\,000}{6} = 3667$

$s_T^2 = \overline{T^2} - (\overline{T})^2 = 3667 - 2500 = 1167$

$m = \dfrac{\overline{TR} - \overline{T}\,\overline{R}}{s_T^2} = \dfrac{1610 - 1495}{1167} = 0.0985$

$b = \overline{R} - m\overline{T} = 29.90 - 0.0977(50.0) = 25.02$
$R = mT + b$; $R = 0.0985T + 25.0$

(Answers may vary due to rounding.)

45.

	x	y	xy	x^2
t	t^2	s	$(t^2)(s)$	$(t^2)^2$
0.0	0.0	3000	0	0
3.0	9.0	2960	26640	81
6.0	36.0	2820	101520	1296
9.0	81.0	2600	210600	6561
12.0	144.0	2290	329760	20736
15.0	225.0	1900	427500	50625
18.0	324.0	1410	456840	104976
63.0	819.0	16980	1552860	184275

$$m = \frac{n\sum xy - (\sum x)(\sum y)}{n\sum x^2 - (\sum x)^2} = \frac{7(1552860) - (819)(16980)}{7(184275) - (819)^2} = -4.90$$

$$b = \frac{(\sum x^2)(\sum y) - (\sum xy)(\sum x)}{n\sum x^2 - (\sum x)^2} = \frac{(184275)(16980) - 1552860(819)}{7(184275) - (819)^2} = 3000$$

$$s = -4.90t^2 + 3000$$

49. Enter x and y as L_1 and L_2 and use LinReg feature.

x	y
1.0	1.4
2.0	2.5
4.0	4.7
6.0	6.8
8.0	8.8
10.0	10.2

$y = 0.997x + 0.581$

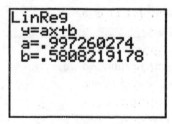

```
LinReg
 y=ax+b
 a=.997260274
 b=.5808219178
```

53. There are 7 numbers. The geometric mean is

$$\sqrt[7]{(8.0)(8.2)(8.8)(9.5)(9.7)(10.0)(10.7)} = \sqrt[7]{5692009.7} = 5692009.7^{1/7} = 9.2 \text{ ppm}$$

57. Answers may vary.

Chapter 23

THE DERIVATIVE

23.1 Limits

1. $f(x) = \frac{1}{x+2}$ is not continuous at $x = -2$ because $f(-2) = \frac{1}{-2+2}$ is a division by zero and the function is not defined. The condition that the function must exist is not satisfied.

5. $f(x) = 3x - 2$ is continuous for all real x since it is defined for all x, and any small change in x will produce only small change in $f(x)$.

9. $f(x) = \sqrt{\frac{x}{x-2}}$ is continuous for $x \le 0$ and $x > 2$. The function is not defined for $0 < x \le 2$. $0 < x < 2$ gives the square root of a negative and $x = 2$ gives division by zero.

13. The graph is not continuous at $x = 1$ since $f(0,9)$ is a value between -1 and -2, and $f(1.1)$ is a value greater than $+2$. This amount of change in y for a 0.2 change in x is not consistent with equivalent changes in x at other values in the function domain. A small change in x does not produce a small change in y at $x = 1$. The function is continuous for $x < 1$, and continuous for $x > 1$.

17. $f(x) = \begin{cases} x^2 & \text{for } x < 2 \\ 2 & \text{for } x \ge 2 \end{cases}$

Not continuous at $x = 2$. Small change in x around $x = 2$ produces a large change in $f(x)$.

21. $f(x) = \dfrac{x^3 - x}{x - 1}$

x	0.900	0.990	0.999
$f(x)$	1.7100	1.9701	1.9970

x	1.001	1.010	1.100
$f(x)$	2.0030	2.0301	2.3100

Therefore, $\lim\limits_{x \to 1} f(x) = 2$

25. $f(x) = \dfrac{2x + 1}{5x - 3}$

x	10	100	1000
$f(x)$	0.4468	0.4044	0.4004

Therefore, $\lim\limits_{x \to \infty} f(x) = 0.4$

29. $\lim\limits_{x \to 0} \dfrac{x^2 + x}{x} = \lim\limits_{x \to 0} \dfrac{x(x + 1)}{x}$

$\qquad = \lim\limits_{x \to 0} (x + 1)$

$\qquad = 0 + 1 = 1$

33. $\lim\limits_{h \to 3} \dfrac{h^3 - 27}{h - 3} = \lim\limits_{h \to 3} \dfrac{(h - 3)(h^2 + 3h + 9)}{h - 3}$

$\qquad = \lim\limits_{h \to 3} (h^2 + 3h + 9)$

$\qquad = 3^2 + 3(3) + 9$

$\qquad = 27$

37. For $p = -1$, $\sqrt{p} = \sqrt{-1} = i$. $\lim\limits_{p \to -1} \sqrt{p}(p + 1.3)$ does not exist.

41. $\lim\limits_{x \to \infty} \dfrac{\sqrt{t^2 + 16}}{t + 1} \cdot \dfrac{\frac{1}{t}}{\frac{1}{t}} = \lim\limits_{x \to \infty} \dfrac{\sqrt{\frac{t^2 + 16}{t^2}}}{1 + \frac{1}{t}}$

$\qquad = \lim\limits_{x \to \infty} \dfrac{\sqrt{1 + \frac{16}{t^2}}}{1 + \frac{1}{t}} = 1$

45. $\lim\limits_{x \to \infty} \dfrac{2x^2 + x}{x^2 - 3} = \lim\limits_{x \to \infty} \dfrac{2 + \frac{1}{x}}{1 - \frac{3}{x^2}} = \dfrac{2}{1} = 2$

x	10	100	1000
$f(x)$	2.1649	2.0106	2.0010

49.

t	T
0	100
1	90
2	81

etc.

This is a geometric progression
$a_n = a_1 r^{n-1}$, $r = 0.9$, $a_1 = 100$
Therefore, $T = 100(0.9)^t$

$$\lim_{t \to 10} 100(0.9)^t = 34.9°C$$
$$\lim_{t \to \infty} 100(0.9)^t = 100 \lim_{t \to \infty} (0.9)^t = 100(0) = 0°C$$

53. $f(x) = x\sqrt{16 - x^2}$ has domain $x \le 4$. The $\lim_{x \to 4^-} f(x)$ may be found by direct substitution.

$$\lim_{x \to 4^-} x\sqrt{16 - x^2} = -4\sqrt{16 - (-4)^2} = 0.$$

23.2   The Slope of a Tangent to a Curve

1. Find slope of tangent line to $y = x^2 + 3x$ at $(3, 18)$

$$m_{PQ} = \frac{f(3 + h) - f(3)}{h} = \frac{[(3 + h)^2 + 3(3 + h)] - [3^2 + 3(3)]}{h}$$

$$m_{PQ} = \frac{9 + 6h + h^2 + 9 + 3h - 9 - 9}{h} = \frac{h^2 + 9h}{h}$$

$$m_{PQ} = h + 9$$

$$m_{\tan} = \lim_{h \to 0} m_{PQ} = \lim_{h \to 0} (h + 9) = 9$$

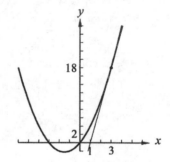

5. $y = 2x^2 + 5x$; $P = (-2, -2)$

	Q_1	Q_2	Q_3	Q_4	P
x_2	-1.5	1.9	1.99	1.999	-2
y_2	-3	-2.28	-2.0298	-2.002998	-2
$y_2 - (-2)$	-1	-0.28	-0.0298	-0.002998	
$x_2 - (-2)$	0.5	0.1	0.01	0.001	
$m = \frac{y_2 - (-2)}{x_2 - (-2)}$	-2	-2.8	-2.98	-2.998	

$m_{\tan} = -3$

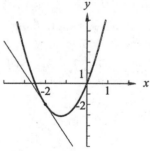

9. $y = 2x^2 + 5x$; $P(-2, 2)$

$$m_{PQ} = \frac{f(-2 + h) - f(-2)}{h} = \frac{2(-2 + h)^2 + 5(-2 + h) - [2(-2)^2 + 5(-2)]}{h}$$

$$m_{PQ} = \frac{8 - 8h + 2h^2 - 10 + 5h - 8 + 10}{h} = \frac{-3h + 2h^2}{h}$$

$$m_{PQ} = -3 + 2h$$
$$m_{\tan} = \lim_{h \to 0} (-3 + 2h) = -3$$

13. $y = 2x^2 + 5x$; $x = -2, x = 0.5$

$$m_{PQ} = \frac{f(x_1 + h) - f(x_1)}{h} = \frac{2(x_1 + h)^2 + 5(x_1 + h) - (2x_1^2 + 5x_1)}{h}$$

$$m_{PQ} = \frac{2x_1^2 + 4x_1 h + 2h^2 + 5x_1 + 5h - 2x_1^2 - 5x_1}{h}$$

$$m_{PQ} = \frac{4x_1 h + 2h^2 + 5h}{h} = 4x_1 + 2h + 5$$

$$m_{\tan} = \lim_{h \to 0} (4x_1 + 2h + 5) = 4x_1 + 5$$

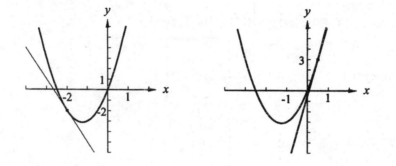

For $x_1 = -2, m_{\tan} = 4(-2) + 5 = -3$
For $x_1 = 0.5, m_{\tan} = 4(0.5) + 5 = 7$

17. $y = 6x - x^2$; $x = -2, x = 3$

$$m_{PQ} = \frac{f(x_1 + h) - f(x_1)}{h} = \frac{6(x_1 + h)^2 - (x_1 + h)^2 - (6x_1 - x_1^2)}{h} = \frac{6x_1 + 6h - x_1^2 - 2x_1 h + h^2 - 6x_1 + x_1^2}{h}$$

$$m_{PQ} = \frac{6h - 2x_1 h + h^2}{h} = 6 - 2x_1 + h$$

$$m_{\tan} = \lim_{h \to 0} (6 - 2x_1 + h) = 6 - 2x_1$$

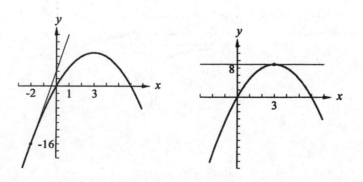

For $x_1 = -2, m_{\tan} = 6 - 2(-2) = 10$
For $x_1 = 3, m_{\tan} = 6 - 2(3) = 0$

21. $y = x^5$; $x = 0, x = 0.5, x = 1$

$$m_{PQ} = \frac{f(x_1 + h) - f(x_1)}{h} = \frac{(x_1 + h)^5 - x_1^5}{h} = \frac{(x_1^5 + 5x_1^4 h + 10x_1^3 h^2 + 10x_1^2 h^3 + 5x_1 h^4 + h^5 - x_1^5)}{h}$$

$$m_{PQ} = 5x_1^4 + 10x_1^3 h + 10x_1^2 h^2 + h^4$$

$$m_{tan} = \lim_{h \to 0} (5x_1^4 + 10x_1^3 h + 10x_1^2 h^2 + 5x_1 h^3 + h^4)$$
$$= 5x_1^4$$

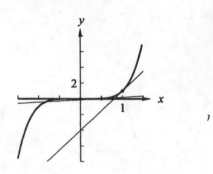

                                                                                                    ,

For $x_1 = 0, m_{tan} = 5(0)^4 = 0$

For $x_1 = 0.5, m_{tan} = 5(0.5)^4 = \dfrac{5}{16}$

For $x_1 = 1, m_{tan} = 5(1)^4 = 5$

22. $y = \dfrac{1}{x}$; $x = 0.5, x = 1, x = 2$

$$m_{PQ} = \frac{f(x_1 + h) - f(x_1)}{h} = \frac{\frac{1}{x_1 + h} - \frac{1}{x_1}}{h} = \frac{\frac{x_1 - x_1 - h}{x_1(x_1 + h)}}{h} = -\frac{1}{x_1(x_1 + h)}$$

$$m_{tan} = \lim_{h \to 0} -\frac{1}{x_1(x_1 + h)} = -\frac{1}{x_1^2}$$

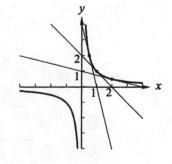

For $x_1 = 0.5, m_{tan} = -\dfrac{1}{0.5^2} = -4$

For $x_1 = 1, m_{tan} = -\dfrac{1}{1^2} = -1$

For $x_1 = 2, m_{tan} = -\dfrac{1}{2^2} = -\dfrac{1}{4}$

25. $y = x^6$; $x = 0, x = 0.5, x = 1$

Graph $y_1 = x^6$. Use DRAW feature to draw tangent line and dy/dx feature to find m_{tan}.

$x_1 = 0, m_{\text{tan}} = 0$
$x_1 = 0.5, m_{\text{tan}} = 0.19$
$x_1 = 1, m_{\text{tan}} = 6$

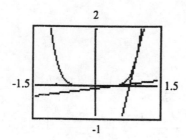

29. $y = 9 - x^3$; $P(2,1), Q(2.1, -0.261)$

From P to Q, x changes by 0.1 unit and $f(x)$ by -1.261 units. The average change in $f(x)$ for a 1 unit change in x is $\frac{-1.261}{0.1} = -12.61$.

$$m_{PQ} = \frac{f(x_1 + h) - f(x_1)}{h} = \frac{9 - (x_1 + h)^3 - (9 - x_1^3)}{h}$$

$$m_{PQ} = -3x_1^2 - 3x_1 h - h^2$$

$$m_{\text{tan}} = \lim_{h \to 0} (-3x_1^2 - 3x_1 h - h^2) = -3x_1^2$$

$x = 2, \quad m_{\text{tan}} = -12$ (instantaneous rate of change)
$\qquad m_{PQ} = -12.61$ (Average rate of change)

23.3   The Derivative

1. $y = 4x^2 + 3x$

$f(x + h) = 4(x + h)^2 + 3(x + h) = 4(x^2 + 2xh + h^2) + 3x + 3h$
$f(x + h) = 4x^2 + 8xh + 4h^2 + 3x + 3h$
$f(x + h) - f(x) = 4x^2 + 8xh + 4h^2 + 3x + 3h - 4x^2 - 3x = 8xh + 4h^2 + 3h$

$$\frac{f(x + h) - f(x)}{h} = \frac{8xh + 4h^2 + 3h}{h} = 8x + 4h + 3$$

$$\lim_{h \to 0} \frac{f(x + h) - f(x)}{h} = \lim_{h \to 0} (8x + 4h + 3) = 8x + 3$$

$$f'(x) = 8x + 3$$

5. $y = 1 - 2x$

$$f'(x) = \lim_{h \to 0} \frac{f(x + h) - f(x)}{h} = \lim_{h \to 0} \frac{1 - 2(x + h) - (1 - 2x)}{h}$$

$$f'(x) = \lim_{h \to 0} \frac{1 - 2x - 2h - 1 + 2x}{h} = \lim_{h \to 0} \frac{-2h}{h} = \lim_{h \to 0} -2 = -2$$

$$f'(x) = -2$$

9. $y = \pi x^2$

$$f'(x) = \lim_{h \to 0} \frac{f(x+h) - f(x)}{h} = \lim_{h \to 0} \frac{\pi(x+h)^2 - \pi x^2}{h} = \lim_{h \to 0} \frac{\pi x^2 + 2\pi x h + h^2 - \pi x^2}{h}$$

$$f'(x) = \lim_{h \to 0} \frac{2\pi x h + h^2}{h} = \lim_{h \to 0} (2\pi x + h)$$

$$f'(x) = 2\pi x$$

13. $y = 8x - 2x^2$

$$f'(x) = \lim_{h \to 0} \frac{f(x+h) - f(x)}{h} = \lim_{h \to 0} \frac{8(x+h)^2 - 2(x+h)^2 - (8x - 2x^2)}{h}$$

$$= \lim_{h \to 0} \frac{8x + 8h - 2x^2 - 4xh - 2h^2 - 8x + 2x^2}{h}$$

$$f'(x) = \lim_{h \to 0} \frac{8h - 4xh - 2h^2}{h} = \lim_{h \to 0} (8 - 4x - 2h)$$

$$f'(x) = 8 - 4x$$

17. $y = \dfrac{\sqrt{3}}{x+2}$

$$f'(x) = \lim_{h \to 0} \frac{f(x+h) - f(x)}{h} = \lim_{h \to 0} \frac{\dfrac{\sqrt{3}}{x+h+2} - \left(\dfrac{\sqrt{3}}{x+2}\right)}{h}$$

$$f'(x) = \lim_{h \to 0} \frac{\dfrac{\sqrt{3}}{x+h+2} - \left(\dfrac{\sqrt{3}}{x+2}\right)}{h} = \lim_{h \to 0} \frac{\dfrac{\sqrt{3}(x+2) - \sqrt{3}(x+h+2)}{(x+h+2)(x+2)}}{h}$$

$$f'(x) = \lim_{h \to 0} \frac{\dfrac{\sqrt{3}(x+2) - \sqrt{3}(x+h+2)}{(x+h+2)(x+2)}}{h} = \lim_{h \to 0} \frac{\dfrac{\sqrt{3}x + 2\sqrt{3} - \sqrt{3}x - \sqrt{3}h - 2\sqrt{3}}{(x+h+2)(x+2)}}{h}$$

$$f'(x) = \lim_{h \to 0} \frac{\dfrac{-\sqrt{3}h}{(x+h+2)(x+2)}}{h} = \lim_{h \to 0} \frac{-\sqrt{3}}{(x+h+2)(x+2)}$$

$$f'(x) = \frac{-\sqrt{3}}{(x+2)^2}$$

21. $y = \dfrac{2}{x^2}$

$$f'(x) = \lim_{h \to 0} \frac{f(x+h) - f(x)}{h} = \lim_{h \to 0} \frac{\dfrac{2}{(x+h)^2} - \dfrac{2}{x^2}}{h}$$

$$f'(x) = \lim_{h \to 0} \frac{2x^2 - 2(x^2 + 2xh + h^2)}{hx^2(x+h)^2} = \lim_{h \to 0} \frac{2x^2 - 2x^2 - 4xh - 2h^2}{hx^2(x+h)^2}$$

$$f'(x) = \lim_{h \to 0} \frac{-4x - 2h}{x^2(x+h)^2} = \frac{-4x}{x^4}$$

$$f'(x) = \frac{-4}{x^3}$$

25. $y = x^4 - \dfrac{2}{x}$

$$f(x+h) = (x+h)^4 - \frac{2}{x+h} = x^4 + 4x^3h + 6x^2h^2 + 4xh^2 + 4xh^3 + h^4 - \frac{2}{x+h}$$

$$f(x+h) - f(x) = x^4 + 4x^3h + 6x^2h^2 + 4xh^3 + h^4 - \frac{2}{x+h} - x^4 + \frac{2}{x}$$

$$f(x+h) - f(x) = 4x^3h + 6x^2h^2 + 4xh^3 + h^4 - \frac{2x - 2(x+h)}{x(x+h)}$$

$$f(x+h) - f(x) = 4x^3h + 6x^2h^2 + 4xh^3 + h^4 - \frac{-2h}{x(x+h)}$$

$$\frac{f(x+h) - f(x)}{h} = 4x^3 + 6x^2h + 4xh^2 + h^3 + \frac{2}{x(x+h)}$$

$$f'(x) = \lim_{h \to 0} \frac{f(x+h) - f(x)}{h} = 4x^3 + \frac{2}{x^2}$$

$$f'(x) = 4x^3 + \frac{2}{x^2}$$

29. $y = \dfrac{11}{3x+2}; \ (3,1)$

$$f(x+h) - f(x) = \frac{11}{3(x+h)} - \frac{11}{3x+2} = \frac{-33h}{(3x+2)(3(x+h)+2)}$$

$$\frac{f(x+h) - f(x)}{h} = \frac{-33}{(3x+2)(3(x+h)+2)}$$

$$f'(x) = \lim_{h \to 0} \frac{-33}{(3x+2)(3(x+h)+2)} = \frac{-33}{(3x+2)^2}$$

$$\frac{dy}{dx}\bigg|_{(3,1)} = \frac{-33}{(3(3)+2)^2} = \frac{-3}{11}$$

33. $y = \dfrac{3}{x^2 - 1}$

$$\frac{f(x+h) - f(x)}{h} = \frac{\dfrac{3}{(x+h)^2 - 1} - \dfrac{3}{x^2 - 1}}{h} = \frac{-3(2x+h)}{(x^2-1)(x^2 + 2xh + h^2 - 1)}$$

$$f'(x) = \lim_{h \to 0} \frac{-3(2x+h)}{(x^2-1)(x^2 + 2xh + h^2 - 1)} = \frac{-6x}{(x^2-1)^2}, \ x \neq \pm 1$$

Function is differentiable for all $x \neq \pm 1$.

37. $y = \sqrt{x+1}$

$$f'(x) = \lim_{h \to 0} \frac{\sqrt{x+h+1} - \sqrt{x+1}}{h} = \lim_{h \to 0} \frac{h}{h(\sqrt{x+h+1} + \sqrt{x+1})}$$

$$\frac{dy}{dx} = f'(x) = \lim_{h \to 0} \frac{1}{\sqrt{x+h+1} + \sqrt{x+1}} = \frac{1}{2\sqrt{x+1}}, \ x+1 > 0 \Rightarrow x > -1$$

Function is differentiable for $x > -1$.

23.4   The Derivative as an Instantaneous Rate of Change

1. $s = 48t - 16t^2$

$$v = \lim_{h \to 0} \frac{48(t+h) - 16(t+h)^2 - 48t + 16t^2}{h} = \lim_{h \to 0} (-16(h + 2t - 3)) = -32t + 48$$

$$\left.\frac{ds}{dt}\right|_{t=2} = -32(2) + 48 = -16 \text{ ft/s}$$

$$\left.\frac{ds}{dt}\right|_{t=4} = -32(4) + 48 = -80 \text{ ft/s}$$

5. $y = \dfrac{16}{3x+1}; \ (-3, -2)$

$$m_{\tan} = \lim_{h \to 0} \frac{\dfrac{16}{3(x+h)+1} - \dfrac{16}{3x+1}}{h}$$

$$m_{\tan} = \lim_{h \to 0} \frac{\dfrac{48x + 16 - 48x - 48h - 16}{(3(x+h)+1)(3x+1)}}{h}$$

$$m_{\tan} = \lim_{h \to 0} \frac{-48}{(3(x+h)+1)(3x+1)} = \frac{-48}{(3x+1)^2}$$

$$m_{\tan} = \left.\frac{dy}{dx}\right|_{(-3,-2)} = \frac{-48}{(3(-3)+1)^2} = -\frac{3}{4}$$

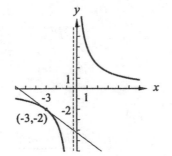

9. $s = 3t^2 - 4t; \ t = 2$

$s = 3(2)^2 - 4(2) = 4$

$t(s)$	1.0	1.5	1.9	1.99	1.999
$s(\text{ft})$	-1.0	0.75	3.23	3.9203	3.992003
$4 - s(\text{ft})$	5.0	3.25	0.77	0.0797	0.007997
$h = 2 - t(s)$	1.0	0.5	0.1	0.01	0.001
$v = \dfrac{4-s}{h}(\text{ft/s})$	5.0	6.5	7.7	7.97	7.997

$v = 8$ ft/s when $t = 2$ s

13. $s = 3t^2 - 4t; t = 2$

$$v = \lim_{h \to 0} \frac{3(t+h)^2 - 4(t+h) - 3t^2 + 4t}{h} = \lim_{h \to 0} \frac{3t^2 + 6th + 3h^2 - 4t - 4h - 3t^2 + 4t}{h}$$

$$v = \lim_{h \to 0} \frac{6th + 3h^2 - 4h}{h} = \lim_{h \to 0} (6t + 3 - 4) = 6t - 4$$

$$v = \frac{ds}{dt}\Big|_{t=2} = 6(2) - 4 = 8 \text{ ft/s}$$

17. $s = 4t^2 - t^4$

$$v = \frac{ds}{dt} = \lim_{h \to 0} \frac{4(t+h)^2 - (t+h)^4 - 4t^2 + t^4}{h}$$

$$v = \lim_{h \to 0} \frac{4(t^2 + 2th + h^2) - t^4 - 4t^3h - 6t^2h^2 - 4th^3 - t^4 - 4t^2 + t^4}{h}$$

$$v = \lim_{h \to 0} \frac{8th + 4h^2 - 4t^3h - 6t^2h^2 - 4th^3}{h}$$

$$v = \lim_{h \to 0} (8t + 4h - 4t^3 - 6t^2h - 4th^2) = 8t - 4t^3$$

21. $v = 6t^2 - 4t + 2$

$$a = \frac{dv}{dt} = \lim_{h \to 0} \frac{6(t+h)^2 - 4(t+h) + 2 - 6t^2 + 4t - 2}{h}$$

$$a = \lim_{h \to 0} \frac{6t^2 + 12th + 6t^2 - 4t - 4h + 2 - 6t^2 + 4t - 2}{h}$$

$$a = \lim_{h \to 0} (12t - 4)$$

$$a = 12t - 4$$

25. $s = 44t - 4.9t^2$

$$v = \frac{ds}{dt} = \lim_{h \to 0} \frac{44(t+h) - 4.9(t+h)^2 - 44t + 4.9t^2}{h}$$

$$v = \lim_{h \to 0} \frac{44t + 44h - 4.9t^2 - 9.8th - 4.9h^2 - 44t + 4.9t^2}{h}$$

$$v = 44 - 9.8t = 0$$

$$t = 4.5 \text{ s}$$

29. $A = l \cdot w; l = 3w \Rightarrow A = 3w \cdot w = 3w^2$

$$\frac{dA}{dw} = \lim_{h \to 0} \frac{3(w+h)^2 - 3w^2}{h} = \lim_{h \to 0} \frac{3w^2 + 6wh + 3h^2 - 3w^2}{h}$$

$$\frac{dA}{dw} = \lim_{h \to 0} \frac{6wh + 3h^2}{h} = \lim_{h \to 0} (6w + 3h)$$

$$\frac{dA}{dw} = 6w$$

33. $H = \dfrac{5000}{t^2 + 10}, -6 \le t \le 6$

$$\frac{dH}{dt} = \lim_{h \to 0} \frac{\dfrac{5000}{(t+h)^2 + 10} - \dfrac{5000}{t^2 + 10}}{h} = \frac{-10,000t}{(t^2 + 10)^2}$$

$$\frac{dH}{dt}\Big|_{t=3} = \frac{-10,000(3)}{(3^2 + 10)^2} = -83.1 \text{ W/(m}^2 \cdot \text{h)}$$

37. $V_{\text{cone}} = \frac{1}{3}\pi r^2 d$. From the figure $\frac{r}{d} = \frac{4}{4} \Rightarrow r = d$

$$V_{\text{cone}} = \frac{1}{3}\pi d^3$$

![figure of cone with dimensions 4, 4, r, d]

$$\frac{dV}{dd} = \lim_{h \to 0} \frac{\frac{1}{3}\pi(d+h)^3 - \frac{1}{3}\pi d^3}{h}$$

$$\frac{dV}{dd} = \lim_{h \to 0} \frac{\frac{1}{3}\pi(d^3 + 3d^2h + 3dh^2 + h^3) - \frac{1}{3}\pi d^3}{h}$$

$$\frac{dV}{dd} = \lim_{h \to 0} \frac{\pi d^2 h + \pi d h^2 + \frac{1}{3}\pi h^3}{h}$$

$$= \lim_{h \to 0} \left(\pi d^2 + \pi d h + \frac{1}{3}\pi h^2\right)$$

$$\frac{dV}{dd} = \pi d^2$$

23.5   Derivatives of Polynomials

1. $v = r^9$

$$\frac{dv}{dr} = 9r^{9-1}$$

$$\frac{dv}{dr} = 9r^8$$

5. $y = x^5$; $\dfrac{dy}{dx} = 5x^{5-1} = 5x^4$

9. $y = x^4 - 3\pi$; $\dfrac{dy}{dx} = 4x^{4-1} - 0 = 4x^3$

13. $p = 5r^3 - 2r + 1$; $\dfrac{dp}{dr} = 5(3r^2) - 2 + 0$

$$= 15r^2 - 2$$

17. $f(x) = -6x^7 + 5x^3 + \pi^2$

$$\frac{f(x)}{dx} = -6(7x^6) + 5(3x^2) + 0 = -42x^6 + 15x^2$$

21. $y = 6x^2 - 8x + 1$;

$$\frac{dy}{dx} = \frac{d(6x^2)}{dx} - \frac{d(8x)}{dx} + \frac{d(1)}{dx} = 12x - 8 + 0$$

Since the derivative is a function of only x, we now evaluate it for $x = 2$.

$$\left.\frac{dy}{dx}\right|_{x=2} = 12(2) - 8 = 24 - 8 = 16$$

25. $y = 2x^6 - 4x^2$; $m_{\text{tan}} = \dfrac{dy}{dx} = 12x^5 - 8x$

$$\left.\frac{dy}{dx}\right|_{x=-1} = m_{\text{tan}} = 12(-1)^5 - 8(-1) = -12 + 8$$
$$= -4$$

Move the trace to $x = -1$ and observe that the function is decreasing and that the slope is negative.

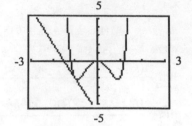

29. $s = 6t^5 - 5t + 2$; $v = \dfrac{ds}{dt} = 30t^4 - 5$

33. $s = 2t^3 - 4t^2$; $t = 4$

$$v = \frac{ds}{dt} = 2(3t^2) - 4(2t) = 6t^2 - 8t$$

$$v|_{t=4} = 6(4^2) - 8(4) = 64$$

37. $y = 3x^2 - 6x$; $m_{\text{tan}} = \dfrac{dy}{dx} = 6x - 6$

Tangent is parallel where slope is zero.
Therefore $6x - 6 = 0$; $x = 1$

41. $x - 3y = 16 \Rightarrow y = \dfrac{1}{3}x - \dfrac{16}{3}$; $m_\perp = -3$

$$y = 2x^2 - 7x$$

$$\frac{dy}{dx} = 4x - 7 = -3 \Rightarrow x = 1$$

$$y = 2(1)^2 - 7(1) = -5.$$

The tangent line to $y = 2x^2 - 7x$ at $(1, -5)$ is perpendicular to the line $x - 3y = 16$.

45. $V = \pi r^2 \cdot h$
$V = \pi r^2 \cdot r = r^3$

$$\frac{dV}{dr} = 3\pi r^2$$

49. $P = a(c_1 E + c_2 E^2 + c_3 E^3)$;

$$\frac{dP}{dE} = a(c_1 + 2c_2 E + 3c_3 E^2)$$

53. $h = 0.000104x^4 - 0.0417x^3 + 4.21x^2 - 8.33x$

$$\frac{dh}{dx} = 0.000416x^3 - 0.1251x^2 + 8.42x - 8.33\big|_{x=120}$$

$$\frac{dh}{dx} = -80.5 \text{ m/km}$$

23.6   Derivatives of Products and Quotients of Functions

1. $y = (x - 2x^2)(x^4 - x)$

$$\frac{dy}{dx} = (x - 2x^2)(4x^3 - 1) + (x^4 - x)(1 - 4x)$$

$$\frac{dy}{dx} = 4x^4 - x - 8x^5 + 2x^2 + x^4 - 4x^5 - x + 4x^2$$

$$\frac{dy}{dx} = -12x^5 + 5x^4 + 6x^2 - 2x$$

5. $s = (3t + 2)(2t - 5)$
   $u = 3t + 2,\ v = 2t - 5$

$$\frac{du}{dt} = 3 \qquad \frac{dv}{dt} = 2$$

$$\frac{ds}{dt} = (3t + 2)(2) + (2t - 5)(3)$$

$$= 6t + 4 + 6t - 15 = 12t - 11$$

9. $y = (2x - 7)(5 - 2x);\ u = (2x - 7);$
   $v = (5 - 2x)$

$$\frac{dy}{dx} = (2x - 7)(-2) + (5 - 2x)(2)$$

$$= -4x + 14 + 10 - 4x$$
$$= -8x + 24$$
$$y = (2x - 7)(5 - 2x)$$
$$= 10x - 4x^2 - 35 + 14x$$
$$= -4x^2 + 24x - 35$$

$$\frac{dy}{dx} = -8x + 24$$

13. $y = \dfrac{x}{2x + 3};\ u = x;\ \dfrac{du}{dx} = 1;\ v = 2x + 3;$

$$\frac{dv}{dx} = 2$$

$$\frac{dy}{dx} = \frac{(2x + 3)(1) - x(2)}{(2x + 3)^2}$$

$$= \frac{2x + 3 - 2x}{(2x + 3)^2}$$

$$= \frac{3}{(2x + 3)^2}$$

17. $y = \dfrac{x^2}{3 - 2x};\ u = x^2;$

$$\frac{dy}{dx} = 2x;\ v = 3 - 2x;\ \frac{dv}{dx} = -2$$

$$\frac{dy}{dx} = \frac{(3 - 2x)(2x) - (x^2)(-2)}{(3 - 2x)^2}$$

$$= \frac{6x - 4x^2 + 2x^2}{(3 - 2x)^2}$$

$$= \frac{6x - 2x^2}{(3 - 2x)^2}$$

21. $f(x) = \dfrac{3x + 8}{x^2 + 4x + 2}$

$$\frac{df(x)}{dx} = \frac{(x^2 + 4x + 2)(3) - (3x + 8)(2x + 4)}{(x^2 + 4x + 2)^2}$$

$$= \frac{-3x^2 - 16x - 26}{(x^2 + 4x + 2)^2}$$

25. $y = (3x - 1)(4 - 7x)$

$$\frac{dy}{dx} = (3x - 1)(-7) + (4 - 7x)(3)$$

$$= -21x + 7 + 12 - 21x$$
$$= -42x + 19$$

$$\left.\frac{dy}{dx}\right|_{x=3} = -42(3) + 19$$

$$= -126 + 19$$
$$= -107$$

29. $y = \dfrac{3x - 5}{2x + 3};\ y = 3x - 5;\ v = 2x + 3;$

$$du = 3dx;\ dv = 2dx$$

$$\frac{dy}{dx} = \frac{(2x + 3)(3) - (3x - 5)(2)}{(2x + 3)^2}$$

$$= \frac{6x + 9 - 6x + 10}{(2x + 3)^2}$$

$$= \frac{19}{(2x + 3)^2}$$

$$\left.\frac{dy}{dx}\right|_{x=-2} = \frac{19}{(2(-2) + 3)^2}$$

$$= \frac{19}{1} = 19$$

33. For $u = c$ the product rule $\dfrac{d(u \cdot v)}{dx} = u \cdot \dfrac{dv}{dx} + v \cdot \dfrac{du}{dx}$ becomes $\dfrac{d(cv)}{dx} = c\dfrac{dv}{dx} + v\dfrac{dc}{dx} = c\dfrac{dv}{dx} + v(0)$

$$\frac{d(cv)}{dx} = c\frac{dv}{dx}, \text{ Eq. 23.10}$$

37. **(1)** $y = \dfrac{x^2(1 - 2x)}{3x - 7}$

$$\frac{dy}{dx} = \frac{(3x-7)[x^2(-2) + (1-2x)(2x)] - x^2(1-2x)(3)}{(3x-7)^2} = \frac{(3x-7)(-6x^2 + 2x) - 3x^2 + 6x^3}{(3x-7)^2}$$

$$= \frac{-18x^3 + 6x^2 + 42x^2 - 14x - 3x^2 + 6x^3}{(3x-7)^2} = \frac{-12x^3 + 45x^2 - 14x}{(3x-7)^2}$$

(2) $y = \dfrac{x^2 - 2x^3}{3x - 7}$

$$\frac{dy}{dx} = \frac{(3x-7)(2x - 6x^2) - (x^2 - 2x^3)(3)}{(3x-7)^2} = \frac{-12x^3 + 45x^2 - 14x}{(3x-7)^2}$$

41. $y = \dfrac{x}{x^2 + 1}; \; y = x; \; \dfrac{du}{dx} = 1;$

$v = x^2 + 1; \; \dfrac{dv}{dx} = 2x$

$$\frac{dy}{dx} = \frac{(x^2+1)(1) - (x)(2x)}{(x^2+1)^2} = \frac{x^2 + 1 - 2x^2}{(x^2+1)^2} = \frac{-x^2 + 1}{(x^2+1)^2}$$

Therefore, $m_{\tan} = 0$ when $\dfrac{-x^2 + 1}{(x^2+1)^2} = 0$;

$-x^2 + 1 = 0; \; x^2 = 1; \; x = 1, -1$

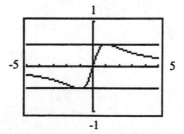

45. $i = \dfrac{8R}{7R + 12}$

$$\frac{di}{dR} = \frac{(7R+12)(8) - 8R(7)}{(7R+12)^2} = \frac{56R + 96 - 56R}{(7R+12)^2}$$

$$\frac{di}{dR} = \frac{96}{(7R+12)^2}$$

49. $r_f = \dfrac{2(R^2 + Rr + r^2)}{3(R+r)}$

$\dfrac{dr_f}{dR} = \dfrac{2(2R+r)(3)(R+r) - 2(R^2 + Rr + r^2)(3)}{9(R+r)^2} = \dfrac{6(2R+r)(R+r) - 6(R^2 + Rr + r^2)}{9(R+r)^2}$

$= \dfrac{12R^2 + 18Rr + 6r^2 - 6R^2 - 6Rr - 6r^2}{9(R+r)^2} = \dfrac{6R^2 + 12Rr}{9(R+r)^2} = \dfrac{6R(R+2)}{9(R+r)^2} = \dfrac{2R(R+2r)}{3(R+r)^2}$

23.7   The Derivative of a Power of a Function

1. $p(x) = (2 + 3x^3)^4$
$p'(x) = 4(2 + 3x^3)^3(9x^2)$
$p'(x) = 36x^2(2 + 3x^3)^3$

5. $y = \sqrt{x} = x^{1/2}$

$\dfrac{dy}{dx} = \dfrac{1}{2}x^{1/2-1} = \dfrac{1}{2}x^{-1/2} = \dfrac{1}{2}\left(\dfrac{1}{x^{1/2}}\right) = \dfrac{1}{2x^{1/2}}$

9. $y = \dfrac{3}{\sqrt[3]{x}} = \dfrac{3}{x^{1/3}} = 3x^{-1/3}, \dfrac{dy}{dx} = 3\left(-\dfrac{1}{3}x^{-1/3-1}\right)$

$= -1x^{-4/3} = -1\left(\dfrac{1}{x^{4/3}}\right) = -\dfrac{1}{x^{4/3}}$

13. $y = (x^2 + 1)^5;$

$\dfrac{dy}{dx} = 5(x^2 + 1)^4(2x) = 10x(x^2 + 1)^4$

17. $y = (2x^3 - 3)^{1/3};$

$\dfrac{dy}{dx} = \dfrac{1}{3}(2x^3 - 3)^{-2/3}(6x^2) = \dfrac{2x^2}{(2x^3 - 3)^{2/3}}$

21. $y = 4(2x^4 - 5)^{0.75}; u = 2x^4 - 5; \dfrac{du}{dx} = 8x^3$

$\dfrac{dy}{dx} = 4\left[0.75(2x^4 - 5)^{-0.25}(8x^3)\right] = \dfrac{24x^3}{(2x^4 - 5)^{0.25}}$

25. $y = x\sqrt{8x + 5} = x(8x + 5)^{1/2}$

$\dfrac{dy}{dx} = x\left(\dfrac{1}{2}\right)(8x + 5)^{-1/2}(8) + (8x + 5)^{1/2}(1) = 4x(8x + 5)^{-1/2} + (8x + 5)^{1/2}(1)$

$= \dfrac{4x}{(8x + 5)^{1/2}} + \dfrac{(8x + 5)}{(8x + 5)^{1/2}} = \dfrac{12x + 5}{(8x + 5)^{1/2}}$

29. $y = \dfrac{2x\sqrt{x + 2}}{x + 4}$

$\dfrac{dy}{dx} = \dfrac{(x + 4)\left[2x \cdot \dfrac{1}{2\sqrt{x + 2}} + 2\sqrt{x + 2}\right] - 2x\sqrt{x + 2}(1)}{(x + 4)^2}$

$\dfrac{dy}{dx} = \dfrac{x(x + 4) + 2(x + 4)(x + 2) - 2x(x + 2)}{(x + 4)^2\sqrt{x + 2}}$

$\dfrac{dy}{dx} = \dfrac{x^2 + 4x + 2x^2 + 12x + 16 - 2x^2 - 4x}{(x + 4)^2\sqrt{x + 2}}$

$\dfrac{dy}{dx} = \dfrac{x^2 + 12x + 16}{(x + 4)^2\sqrt{x + 2}}$

33. $\quad y = \sqrt{3x+4}; \; x = 7$

$$y = (3x+4)^{1/2}; \; u = 3x+4; \; n = \frac{1}{2}; \; \frac{du}{dx} = 3$$

$$\frac{dy}{dx} = \frac{1}{2}(3x+4)^{-1/2}(3) = \frac{3}{2}(3x+4)^{-1/2}$$

$$= \frac{3}{2\sqrt{3x+4}}$$

$$\left.\frac{dy}{dx}\right|_{x=7} = \frac{3}{2\sqrt{3(7)+4}} = \frac{3}{2\sqrt{25}} = \frac{3}{2(5)} = \frac{3}{10}$$

37. (a) $\quad y = \dfrac{1}{x^3}; \; u = 1; \; \dfrac{du}{dx} = 0$

$$= v = x^3; \; \frac{dv}{dx} = 3x^2$$

$$\frac{dy}{dx} = \frac{x^3(0) - 1(3x^2)}{x^6} = \frac{-3x^2}{x^6} = \frac{-3}{x^4}$$

(b) $\quad y = x^{-3}; \; \dfrac{dy}{dx} = -3x^{-3-1} = -3x^{-4} = \dfrac{-3}{x^4}$

41. $\quad x + 3y - 12 = 0 \Rightarrow y = -\dfrac{1}{3}x + 4 \Rightarrow m = -\dfrac{1}{3}$

$$y = \sqrt{2x+3} = (2x+3)^{1/2}$$

$$\frac{dy}{dx} = \frac{1}{2}(2x+3)^{-1/2}(2) = \frac{1}{\sqrt{2x+3}}$$

$$\frac{dy}{dx} = \frac{1}{\sqrt{2x+3}} = 3$$

$$x = -\frac{13}{9}$$

$$y = \sqrt{2\left(-\frac{13}{9}\right)+3} = \frac{1}{3}$$

The tangent line to $y = \sqrt{2x+3}$ at $\left(-\frac{13}{9}, \frac{1}{3}\right)$ is perpendicular to the line $x + 3y - 12 = 0$.

45. $\quad s = (8t - t^2)^{2/3}; \; t = 6.25$ s

$$\frac{ds}{dt} = \frac{2}{3}(8t - t^2)^{-1/3}(8 - 2t)$$

$$v = \frac{2(8 - 2t)}{3\sqrt[3]{8t - t^2}}; \; v|_{t=6.25} = -1.35 \text{ cm/s}$$

49. $v = \sqrt{\dfrac{l}{a} + \dfrac{a}{l}} = \left(\dfrac{l}{a} + \dfrac{a}{l}\right)^{1/2}$

$$\frac{dv}{dl} = \frac{1}{2}\left(\frac{l}{a} + \frac{a}{l}\right)^{-1/2}\left(\frac{1}{a} - \frac{a}{l^2}\right) = 0$$

$$\frac{1}{a} - \frac{a}{l^2} = 0$$

$$\frac{1}{a} = \frac{a}{l^2}$$

$$l^2 = a^2$$

$$l = a$$

53. $\quad \lambda_r = \dfrac{2a\lambda}{\sqrt{4a^2 - \lambda^2}} = \dfrac{2a\lambda}{(4a^2 - \lambda^2)^{1/2}}$

$$\frac{d\lambda_r}{d\lambda} = \frac{(4a^2 - \lambda^2)^{1/2}(2a) - 2a\lambda\left(\frac{1}{2}\right)(4a^2 - \lambda^2)^{-1/2}(-2\lambda)}{(4a^2 - \lambda^2)}$$

$$= \frac{2a(4a^2 - \lambda^2)^{1/2} + 2a\lambda^2(4a^2 - \lambda^2)^{-1/2}}{(4a^2 - \lambda^2)}$$

$$= \frac{(4a^2 - \lambda^2)^{-1/2}[(2a)(4a^2 - \lambda^2) + 2a\lambda^2]}{(4a^2 - \lambda^2)}$$

$$= \frac{8a^3}{(4a^2 - \lambda^2)^{3/2}}$$

23.8 Differentiation of Implicit Functions

1. $\quad y^3 + 2x^2 = 5$

$$3y^2 \cdot \frac{dy}{dx} + 4x = 0$$

$$\frac{dy}{dx} = \frac{-4x}{3y^2}$$

5. $4y - 3x^2 = x; \; \dfrac{d}{dx}(4y) - \dfrac{d}{dx}(3x^2) = \dfrac{d}{dx}(x)$

$$4\frac{dy}{dx} - 6x = 1; \; 4\frac{dy}{dx} = 1 + 6x; \; \frac{dy}{dx} = \frac{1 + 6x}{4}$$

9. $y^5 = x^2 - 1; \; \dfrac{d}{dx}(y^5) = 2x; \; 5x\dfrac{dy}{dx} = 2x; \; \dfrac{dy}{dx} = \dfrac{2x}{5y^4}$

13. $y + 3xy - 4 = 0$

$$\frac{dy}{dx} + 3\frac{d}{dx}(xy) = 0; \; \frac{dy}{dx} + 3\left(x\frac{dy}{dx} + y(1)\right) = 0$$

$$\frac{dy}{dx} + 3x\frac{dy}{dx} + 3y = 0; \; \frac{dy}{dx}(1 + 3x) = -3y$$

$$\frac{dy}{dx} = \frac{-3y}{1 + 3x}$$

17. $\dfrac{3x^2}{y^2 + 1} + y = 3x + 1$

$$\frac{(y^2 + 1)6x - 3x^2\left(2\frac{dy}{dx}\right)}{(y^2 + 1)^2} + \frac{dy}{dx} = 3$$

$$\frac{6x(y^2 + 1) - 6x^2y\frac{dy}{dx} + (y^2 + 1)^2\frac{dy}{dx}}{(y^2 + 1)^2} = 3$$

$$(y^2 + 1)^2\frac{dy}{dx} - 6x^2y\frac{dy}{dx} = 3(y^2 + 1)^2 - 6x(y^2 + 1)$$

$$= 3(y^2 + 1)(y^2 + 1 - 2x)$$

$$\frac{dy}{dx}[(y^2 + 1)^2 - 6x^2y] = 3(y^2 + 1)(y^2 - 2x + 1)$$

$$\frac{dy}{dx} = \frac{3(y^2 + 1)(y^2 - 2x + 1)}{(y^2 + 1)^2 - 6x^2 y}$$

21. $2(x^2 + 1)^3 + (y^2 + 1)^2 = 17$

$$6(x^2 + 1)^2(2x) + 2(y^2 + 1)^1 2y \frac{dy}{dx} = 0$$

$$4y(y^2 + 1)\frac{dy}{dx} = -12x(x^2 + 1)^2$$

$$\frac{dy}{dx} = \frac{-12x(x^2 + 1)^2}{4y(y^2 + 1)} = \frac{-3x(x^2 + 1)^2}{y(y^2 + 1)}$$

25. $5y^4 + 7 = x^4 - 3y;\ (3, -2)$

$$20y^3 \frac{dy}{dx} = 4x^3 - 3\frac{dy}{dx};\ 20y^3\frac{dy}{dx} + 3\frac{dy}{dx} = 4x^3$$

$$\frac{dy}{dx}(20y^3 + 3) = 4x^3;\ \frac{dy}{dx} = \frac{4x^3}{20y^3 + 3};$$

$$\left.\frac{dy}{dx}\right|_{(3,-2)} = -\frac{108}{157}$$

29. $x^2 + y^2 = 4x$

$$2x + 2y\frac{dy}{dx} = 4$$

$$\frac{dy}{dx} = \frac{2 - x}{y} = 0$$

$$x = 2$$
$$2^2 + y^2 = 4(2)$$
$$y^2 = 4$$
$$y = \pm 2$$

The graph of $x^2 + y^2 - 4x$ has a horizontal tangent line at $(2, 2)$ and $(2, -2)$.

33. $PV = n\left(RT + aP - \dfrac{bP}{T}\right)$

$$PV = nRT + naP - \frac{nbP}{T}$$

$$V\frac{dP}{dT} = nR + na\frac{dP}{dT} - \frac{nbT\frac{dP}{dT} - nbP}{T^2}$$

$$VT^2\frac{dP}{dT} = nRT^2 + naT^2\frac{dP}{dT} - nbT\frac{dP}{dT} + nbP$$

$$\frac{dP}{dT}(VT^2 - naT^2 + nbT) = nRT^2 + nbP$$

$$\frac{dP}{dT} = \frac{nRT^2 + nbP}{VT^2 - naT^2 + nbT}$$

37. $r^2 = 2rR + 2R - 2r;\ 2r = 2R + \dfrac{dR}{dr}(2r) + 2\dfrac{dR}{dr} - 2$

$$2r - 2R + 2 = 2r\frac{dR}{dr} + 2\frac{dR}{dr} = \frac{dR}{dr}(2r + 2)$$

$$\frac{dR}{dr} = \frac{2(r - R + 1)}{2(r + 1)} = \frac{r - R + 1}{r + 1}$$

23.9   Higher Derivatives

1. $y = 5x^3 - 2x^2$
$y' = 15x^2 - 4x$
$y'' = 30x - 4$
$y''' = 30$
$y^{(4)} = 0$
$y^{(n)}(x) = 0,\ n \ge 4$

5. $f(x) = x^3 - 6x^4;\ f'(x) = 3x^2 - 24x^3;$
$f''(x) = 6x - 72x^2;\ f'''(x) = 6 - 144x;$
$f^{(4)}(x) = -144;\ f^{(n)}(x) = 0,\ n \ge 5$

9. $f(r) = r(4r + 1)^3 = r(64r^3 + 48r^2 + 12r + 1)$
$f(r) = 64r^4 + 48r^3 + 12r^2 + r$
$f'(r) = 256r^3 + 144r^2 + 24r + 1$
$f''(r) = 768r^2 + 288r + 24$
$f'''(r) = 1536r + 288$
$f^{(4)}(r) = 1536$
$f^{(n)}(r) = 0,\ n \ge 5$

13. $y = 2x + \sqrt{x} = 2x + x^{1/2};\ y' = 2 + \dfrac{1}{2}x^{-1/2}$

$$y'' = \frac{1}{2}\left(-\frac{1}{2}\right)x^{-3/2} = \frac{-1}{4x^{3/2}}$$

17. $f(p) = \dfrac{4.8\pi}{\sqrt{1 + 2p}} = 4.8\pi(1 + 2p)^{-1/2}$

$$f'(p) = -2.4\pi(1 + 2p)^{-3/2}(2) = -4.8\pi(1 - 2p)^{-3/2}$$

$$f''(p) = 7.2\pi(1 + 2p)^{-5/2}(2) = \frac{14.4\pi}{(1 + 2p)^{5/2}}$$

21. $y = (3x^2 - 1)^5;\ y' = 5(3x^2 - 1)^4(6x) = 30x(3x^2 - 1)^4;$
$y'' = 30x(4)(3x^2 - 1)^3(6x) + (3x^2 - 1)^4(30)$
$\quad = 30(3x^2 - 1)^3(27x^2 - 1)$

25. $y = \dfrac{x^2}{x + 1}$

$$y' = \frac{(x + 1)2x - x^2}{(x + 1)^2} = \frac{x^2 + 2x}{(x + 1)^2}$$

$$y'' = \frac{(x + 1)^2(2x + 2) - (x^2 + 2x)(2)(x + 1)^1}{(x + 1)^4}$$

$$\quad = \frac{2(x + 1)[(x + 1)^2 - (x^2 + 2x)]}{(x + 1)^4}$$

$$y'' = \frac{2(1)}{(x + 1)^3}$$

$$\quad = \frac{2}{(x + 1)^3}$$

29. $x^2 - xy = 1 - y^2$; $2x - (xy' + y) = -2yy'$

$2x - xy' - y = -2yy'$; $2yy' - xy = y - 2x$

$y' = \dfrac{y - 2x}{2y - x}$;

$y'' = \dfrac{(2y - x)(y' - 2) - (y - 2x)(2y' - 1)}{(2y - x)^2}$

$y'' = \left[(2y - x)\left(\dfrac{y - 2x}{2y - x} - 2\right) - (y - 2x)\left(2\dfrac{y - 2x}{2y - x} - 1\right)\right]$

$\div (2y - x)^2$

$y'' = \left[y - 2x - 2(2 - y) - \dfrac{2(y - 2x)^2}{2y - x} + y - 2x\right]$

$\div (2y - x)^2$

$y'' = \left[-2(y + x) - \dfrac{2(y - 2x)^2}{(2y - x)}\right] \div (2y - x)^2$

$y'' = (-4y^2 - 2xy + 2x^2 - 2y^2 + 8xy - 8x^2) \div (2y - x)^3$

$y'' = \dfrac{-6(y^2 - xy + x^2)}{(2y - x)^3}$

33. $y = 3x^{2/3} - \dfrac{2}{x} = 3x^{2/3} - 2x^{-1}$

$y' = 2x^{-1/3} + 2x^{-2}$

$y'' = -\dfrac{2}{3}x^{-4/3} - 4x^{-3} = \dfrac{-2}{3x^{4/3}} - \dfrac{4}{x^3}$;

$y''|_{x=-8} = \dfrac{-2}{48} + \dfrac{4}{512}$

$y''|_{x=-8} = \dfrac{-2}{6 \times 8} + \dfrac{4}{8 \times 64} = -\dfrac{13}{384}$

37. $s = 26t - 4.9t^2, t = 3.0$ s

$v = 26 - 9.8t$

$a = -9.8$ m/s^2

41. $\dfrac{d}{dx}$ of $\dfrac{dy}{dx} = y''$; $x = 1$

$y = (1 - 2x)^4$

$y' = 4(1 - 2x)^3(-2) = -8(1 - 2x)^2$

$y'' = -24(1 - 2x)^2(-2) = 48(1 - 2x)^2$

$y''|_{x=1} = 48$

45. $V = L\left(\dfrac{d^2q}{dt^2}\right)$; $L = 1.60$ H

$q = \sqrt{2t + 1} - 1 = (2t + 1)^{1/2} - 1$

$\dfrac{dq}{dt} = \dfrac{1}{2}(2t + 1)^{-1/2}(2) = (2t + 1)^{-1/2}$

$\dfrac{d^2q}{dt^2} = -\dfrac{1}{2}(2t + 1)^{-3/2}(2) = \dfrac{-1}{(2t + 1)^{3/2}}$

$V = \dfrac{-1.60}{(2t + 1)^{3/2}}$

Chapter 23 Review Exercises

1. $\lim\limits_{x \to 4} (8 - 3x) = 8 - 3(4) = -4$

5. $\lim\limits_{x \to 2} \dfrac{4x - 8}{x^2 - 4} = \lim\limits_{x \to 2} \dfrac{4(x - 2)}{(x - 2)(x + 2)}$

$= \lim\limits_{x \to 2} \dfrac{4}{x + 2} = \dfrac{4}{2 + 2} = 1$

9. $\lim\limits_{x \to \infty} \dfrac{2 + \frac{1}{x+4}}{3 - \frac{1}{x^2}} = \dfrac{2 + 0}{3 - 0} = \dfrac{2}{3}$

13. $y = 7 + 5x$

$\dfrac{dy}{dx} = \lim\limits_{h \to 0} \dfrac{f(x + h) - f(x)}{h}$

$= \lim\limits_{h \to 0} \dfrac{7 + 5(x + h) - 7 - 5x}{h}$

$\dfrac{dy}{dx} = \lim\limits_{h \to 0} \dfrac{5h}{h} = \lim\limits_{h \to 0} 5 = 5$

17. $y = \dfrac{2}{x^2}$

$\dfrac{dy}{dx} = \lim\limits_{h \to 0} \dfrac{\dfrac{2}{(x + h)^2} - \dfrac{2}{x^2}}{h}$

$= \lim\limits_{h \to 0} \dfrac{2x^2 - 2(x + h)^2}{hx^2(x + h)^2}$

$= \lim\limits_{h \to 0} \dfrac{2x^2 - 2x^2 - 4xh - 2h^2}{hx^2(x + h)^2}$

$= \lim\limits_{h \to 0} \dfrac{-4xh - 2h^2}{hx^2(x + h)^2}$

$= \lim\limits_{h \to 0} \dfrac{-4x - 2h}{x^2(x + h)^2}$

$= \dfrac{-4x}{x^4}$

$= \dfrac{-4}{x^3}$

21. $y = 2x^7 - 3x^2 + 5$

$\dfrac{dy}{dx} = 2(7x^6) - 3(2x) + 0 = 14x^6 - 6x$

25. $f(y) = \dfrac{3y}{1 - 5y}$

$\dfrac{df(y)}{dy} = \dfrac{(1 - 5y)(3) - 3y(-5)}{(1 - 5y)^2} = \dfrac{3 - 15y + 15y}{(1 - 5y)^2}$

$\dfrac{df(y)}{dy} = \dfrac{3}{(1 - 5y)^2}$

29. $y = \dfrac{3\pi}{(5 - 2x^2)^{3/4}}$

$$\dfrac{dy}{dx} = \dfrac{(5 - 2x^2)^{3/4}(0) - 3\pi[-3x(5 - 2x^2)^{-1/4}]}{(5 - 2x^2)^{3/2}} = \dfrac{9\pi x(5 - 2x^2)^{-1/4}}{(5 - 2x^2)^{3/2}}$$

$$= \dfrac{9\pi x}{(5 - 2x^2)^{3/2}(5 - 2x^2)^{1/4}} = \dfrac{9\pi x}{(5 - 2x^2)^{7/4}}$$

33. $y = \dfrac{\sqrt{4x + 3}}{2x} = 2(4x + 3)^{-1/2}$

$$\dfrac{dy}{dx} = \dfrac{2x(2)(4x + 3)^{-1/2} - (4x + 3)^{1/2}(2)}{(2x)^2} = \dfrac{(4x + 3)^{-1/2}[4x - (4x + 3)(2)]}{4x^2}$$

$$= \dfrac{-4x - 6}{(4x + 3)^{1/2}(4x^2)} = \dfrac{2(-2x - 3)}{2(2x^2)(4x + 3)^{1/2}} = \dfrac{-2x - 3}{2x^2(4x + 3)^{1/2}}$$

37. $y = \dfrac{4}{x} + 2\sqrt[3]{x}, \; x = 8$

$$y = 4x^{-1} + 2x^{1/3}; \; \dfrac{dy}{dx} = 4(-1)x^{-2} + 2\left(\dfrac{1}{3}x^{-2/3}\right) = \dfrac{-4}{x^2} + \dfrac{2}{3x^{2/3}}$$

$$\dfrac{dy}{dx}\bigg|_{x=8} = \dfrac{-4}{8^2} + \dfrac{2}{3(8)^{2/3}} = \dfrac{-4}{64} + \dfrac{2}{3(4)} = \dfrac{-1}{16} + \dfrac{1}{6} = \dfrac{-3}{48} + \dfrac{8}{48} = \dfrac{5}{48}$$

41. $y = 3x^4 - \dfrac{1}{x} = 3x^4 - x^{-1}$

$$y' = 12x^3 + x^{-2}$$
$$y'' = 36x^2 - 2x^{-3}$$

45. $y = \dfrac{2(x^2 - 4)}{x - 2}$ does not have a y value for $x = 2$. Graph $y_1 = \dfrac{2(x^2 - 4)}{x - 2}$. Using the trace feature and the zoom feature y-values arbitrarily close to 8 may be found by making the x-values sufficiently close to 2.

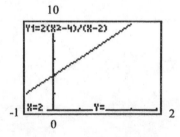

49. $y = 7x^4 - x^3; \; m_{\tan} = dy/dx = 28x^3 - 3x^2;$ when $x = -1, \; m_{\tan} = 28(-1)^3 - 3(-1)^2 = -31.$

53. $s = \sqrt{1 + 8t} = (1 + 8t)^{1/2}$

(a) $v = \dfrac{ds}{dt} = \dfrac{1}{2}(1 + 8t)^{-1/2}(8) = \dfrac{4}{\sqrt{1 + 8t}}$

(b) $a = \dfrac{dv}{dt} = \dfrac{d^2s}{dt^2} = 4\left(-\dfrac{1}{2}\right)(1 + 8t)^{-3/2}(8)$

$a = \dfrac{-16}{(1 + 8t)^{3/2}}$

57. $R = 1 - kt + \dfrac{k^2t^2}{2} - \dfrac{k^3t^3}{6} = 1 - kt + \dfrac{1}{2}(k^2t^2) - \dfrac{1}{6}(k^3t^3)$

$R' = -k + k^2t - \dfrac{1}{2}k^3t^2$

61. $E = \dfrac{L\,dI}{dt}$; $I = t(0.01t + 1)^3$; $\dfrac{dI}{dt} = (0.01t + 1)^2(0.04t + 1)$; $L = 0.4H$

$E = 0.4\dfrac{dI}{dt}$; substituting the value for $\dfrac{dI}{dt}$, $E = 0.04(0.01t + 1)^2(0.04t + 1)$

65. $E = t(1 + 2t)^2, t < 10$

$\dfrac{dE}{dt} = t[2(1 + 2t)(2)] + (1 + 2t)^2(1)$

$\dfrac{dE}{dt} = 4t(1 + 2t) + (1 + 2t)^2\big|_{t=8}$

$\dfrac{dE}{dt} = 4(8)(1 + 2(8)) + (1 + 2(8))^2$

$\dfrac{dE}{dt} = 830$ kW

69. $f = \dfrac{1}{2\pi\sqrt{C(L + 2)}} = \dfrac{1}{2\pi}(CL + 2C)^{-1/2}$

$\dfrac{df}{dL} = -\dfrac{1}{2}\left(\dfrac{1}{2\pi}\right)(CL + 2C)^{-3/2}(C) = -\dfrac{C}{4\pi}(CL + 2C)^{-3/2}$

$= -\dfrac{C}{4\pi\sqrt{C^3(L + 2)^3}} = -\dfrac{C}{4\pi C\sqrt{C(L + 2)^3}} = -\dfrac{1}{4\pi\sqrt{C(L + 2)^3}} = -\dfrac{1}{4\pi\sqrt{C}(L + 2)^{3/2}}$

73. $y = \dfrac{w}{24EI}(6L^2x^2 - 4Lx^3 + x^4)$

$y' = \dfrac{w}{24EI}(12L^2x - 12Lx^2 + 4x^3) = \dfrac{w}{6EI}(3L^2x - 3Lx^2 + x^3)$

$y'' = \dfrac{ww}{6EI}(3L^2 - 6Lx + 3x^2) = \dfrac{w}{2EI}(L - x)^2$

$y''' = \dfrac{w}{2EI}(-2L + 2x) = \dfrac{w}{EI}(x - L)$

$y^{iv} = \dfrac{w}{EI}$

77. $\quad A = xy = x(4 - x^2) = 4x - x^3$

$\quad \dfrac{dA}{dx} = 4 - 3x^2$

81. The angle at which they cross is the angle between the tangent lines and can be found from the derivatives.

APPLICATIONS OF THE DERIVATIVE

24.1 Tangents and Normals

1. $x^2 + 4y^2 = 17, (1, 2)$
$2x + 8yy' = 0$

$y' = \dfrac{-x}{4y}\Big|_{(1,2)} = \dfrac{-1}{4(2)} = -\dfrac{1}{8}$

$y - 2 = -\dfrac{1}{8}(x - 1)$
$8y - 16 = -x + 1$
$x + 8y - 17 = 0$

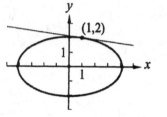

5. $y = \dfrac{1}{x^2 + 1}; \left(1, \dfrac{1}{2}\right); y = (x^2 + 1)^{-1}$

$\dfrac{dy}{dx} = m_{\tan} = -(x^2 + 1)^{-2}(2x); \; m_{\tan} = \dfrac{-2x}{(x^2 + 1)^2};$

$m_{\tan_{x=1}} = -\dfrac{1}{2}$

Eq. of T.L.: $y - \dfrac{1}{2} = -\dfrac{1}{2}(x - 1); \; 2y - 1 = -x + 1$

$y = -\dfrac{1}{2}x + 1$

Therefore, $x + 2y - 2 = 0$

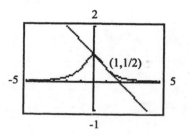

9. $y = \dfrac{6}{(x^2 + 1)^2}; \left(1, \dfrac{3}{2}\right); y = 6(x^2 + 1)^{-2}$

$\dfrac{dy}{dx} = m_{\tan} = -12(x^2 + 1)^{-3}(2x)$

$m_{\tan} = \dfrac{-24x}{(x^2 + 1)^3}; \; m_{\tan(1,3/2)}\big|_{x=1} = -3;$

$m_{\text{normal}} = \dfrac{1}{3}$

Eq. of normal: $y - \dfrac{3}{2} = \dfrac{1}{3}(x - 1)$

Therefore, $2x - 6y + 7 = 0$

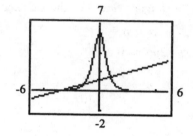

13. $y = (2x - 1)^3$; normal line $m = -\dfrac{1}{24}, x > 0$

Therefore, $m_{\tan} = 24$
$m_{\tan} = 3(2x - 1)^2(2) = 6(2x - 1)^2$
$6(2x - 1)^2 = 24; \; (2x - 1)^2 = 4; \; 2x - 1 = \pm 2$
$2x = \pm 2 + 1 = 3 \text{ and } -1$

$x = \dfrac{3}{2}, y = 8$

Eq. of N.L.: $y - 8 = -\dfrac{1}{24}\left(x - \dfrac{3}{2}\right);$

$24y - 192 = -x + \dfrac{3}{2}$

$48y - 384 = -2x + 3; \; 2x + 48y - 387 = 0$

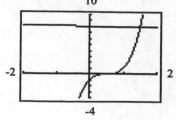

17. $y = x + 2x^2 - x^4$
$y' = 1 + 4x - 4x^3$
At $(1, 2), y' = 1 + 4(1) - 4(1)^3 = 1$
Eq of T.L: at $(1, 2)$: $y - 2 = 1(x - 1)$
$$y = x + 1$$

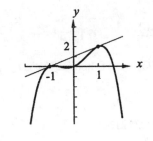

At $(-1, 0), y' = 1 + 4(1) - 4(-1)^3 = 1$
Equ of TL at $(-1, 0)$:

$y - 0 = 1(x - (-1))$
$\quad y = x + 1$

The tangent lines are the same: $y = x + 1$

21. $2x^2 + y^2 = 9$
$4x + 2yy' = 0$

$$y' = -\frac{2x}{y}\bigg|_{(2,1)} = -\frac{2(2)}{1} = -4$$

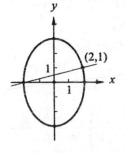

$$m_{\tan} = 4, m_{\mathrm{NL}} = \frac{1}{4}$$

Equ. of NL at $(2, 1)$:

$$y - 1 = \frac{1}{4}(x - 2)$$

$4y - 4 = x - 2$
$x - 4y + 2 = 0$

25. $y = \sqrt{2x^2 + 8} = (2x^2 + 8)^{1/2}$; $m = \tan 135° = -1$

$$\frac{dy}{dx} = \frac{1}{2}(2x^2 + 8)^{-1/2}(4x) = \frac{2x}{\sqrt{2x^2 + 8}} = 1$$

$2x = \sqrt{2x^2 + 8}$; $4x^2 = 2x^2 + 8$; $2x^2 = 8$; $x^2 = 4$
$x = \pm 2$; $y = \sqrt{2(4) + 8} = \sqrt{16} = 4$
$y - y_1 = m(x - x_1)$
$y - 4 = -1(x - 2)$
$y + x - 6 = 0$

24.2   Newtons Method for Solving Equations

1. $x^2 - 5x + 1 = 0, 0 < x < 1$, $f(x) = x^2 - 5x + 1$
$f(0) = 1, f(1) = -3$, choose $x_1 = 0.5$
$f'(x) = 2x - 5$

$$x_2 = x_1 - \frac{f(x_1)}{f'(x_1)} = 0.5 - \frac{0.5^2 - 5(0.5) + 1}{2(0.5) - 5} = 0.1875$$

$x_3 = 0.2086148649$, $x_4 = 0.2087121505$, $x_5 = 0.2087121525$, $x_6 = 0.2087121525$

Using quadratic formula,

$$x = \frac{(-5) - \sqrt{(-5)^2 - 4(1)(1)}}{2(1)} = 0.2087121525$$

5. $x^3 - 6x^2 + 10x - 4 = 0$ (between 0 and 1)
$f(x) = x^3 - 6x^2 + 10x - 4$; $f'(x) = 3x^2 - 12x + 10$; $f(0) = -4$; $f(1) = 1$

Let $x_1 = 0.7$

n	x_n	$f(x_n)$	$f'(x_n)$	$x_n - \frac{f(x_n)}{f'(x_n)}$
1	0.7	0.403	3.07	0.5687296
2	0.5687296	−0.0694666	4.1456049	0.5854863
3	0.5854863	−0.0012009	4.002547	0.5857863
4	0.5857863	−0.0000005	4.0000012	0.5857864

$x_4 = x_3 = 0.5857864$ to seven decimal places; $x = 0.58578644$, calculator

9. $x^4 - x^3 - 3x^2 - x - 4 = 0$; (between 2 and 3)
$f(x) = x^4 - x^3 - 3x^2 - x - 4$; $f'(x) = 4x^3 - 3x^2 - 6x - 1$
$f(2) = -10$; $f(3) = 20$.
Let $x_1 = 2.3$

n	x_n	$f(x_n)$	$f'(x_n)$	$x_n - \frac{f(x_n)}{f'(x_n)}$
1	2.3	−6.3529	17.998	2.6529781
2	2.6529781	3.0972725	36.657001	2.5684848
3	2.5684848	0.2175007	31.576097	2.5615967
4	2.5615967	0.0013683	−31.179599	2.5615528

$x_3 = x_4 = 2.5615528$ to seven decimal places; $x = 2.5615528$, calculator

13. $2x^2 = \sqrt{2x + 1}$ or $2x^2 - \sqrt{2x + 1} = 0$, (the positive real solution)
$4x^4 - 2x - 1 = 0$ (Square both sides.)
$f(x) = 4x^4 - 2x - 1$; $f'(x) = 16x^3 - 2$

Let $x_1 = 0.8$.

n	x_n	$f(x_n)$	$f'(x_n)$	$x_n - \frac{f(x_n)}{f'(x_n)}$
1	0.8	−0.9616	6.192	0.9552972
2	0.9552972	0.4207071	11.948757	0.9200879
3	0.9200879	0.0264914	10.462579	0.9175559
4	0.9175559	1.301096×10^{-4}	10.359975	0.9175433
5	0.9175433	3.1869×10^{-9}	10.3594671	0.9175433

The positive root is approximately 0.9175433; to seven decimal places. $x = 0.91754334$, calculator

17. $f(x) = x^3 - 2x^2 - 5x + 4$. From graph, one root lies between -1 and -2, a second between 0 and 1, and a third between 3 and 4

$f'(x) = 3x^2 - 4x - 5$

Let $x_1 = -1.7$

n	x_n	$f(x_n)$	$f'(x_n)$	$x_n - \frac{f(x_n)}{f'(x_n)}$
1	-1.7	1.807	10.47	-1.8725883
2	-1.8725883	-0.2166267	13.0101148	-1.8559377
3	-1.8559377	-0.0021074	12.7572652	-1.8557725
4	-1.8557725	$-2.0650050 \times 10^{-7}$	12.7547651	-1.8557725

Let $x_1 = 0.7$

1	0.7	-0.137	-6.33	0.6783570
2	0.6783570	3.6703855×10^{-5}	-6.3329233	0.6783628

Let $x_1 = 3.1$

1	3.1	-0.929	11.43	3.1812773
2	3.11812773	0.0487608	12.6364672	3.1774186
3	3.1774186	1.1226889×10^{-4}	12.5782926	3.1774097

The roots are $-1.8557725, 0.6783628$, and 3.1774097.

21. $f(x) = x^2 - a$
$f'(x) = 2x$

$$x_2 = x_1 - \frac{f(x_1)}{f'(x_1)} = x_1 - \frac{x_1^2 - a}{2x_1} = x_1 - \frac{x_1}{2} + \frac{a}{2x_1}$$

$x_2 = \frac{x_1}{2} + \frac{a}{2x_1}$. Similarly, $x_3 = \frac{x_2}{2} + \frac{a}{2x_2}$ which generalizes to $x_{n+1} = \frac{x_n}{2} + \frac{a}{2x_n}$.

25. $V = \frac{1}{6}\pi h(h^2 + 3r^2) = \frac{1}{6}\pi h^3 + \frac{1}{2}\pi r^2 h$

$180000 = \frac{1}{6}\pi h[h^2 + 3(60)^2] = \frac{1}{6}\pi h^3 + 1800\pi h$

$f(h) = \frac{1}{6}\pi h^3 + 1800\pi h - 180000$

$f'(h) = \frac{1}{2}\pi h^2 + \frac{1}{2}\pi r^2 = \frac{1}{2}\pi h^2 + 1800\pi$

n	h_n	$f(h_n)$	$f'(h_n)$	$h_n - \frac{f(h_n)}{f'(h_n)}$
1	29	-3238.813	6975.906	29.464286
2	29.464286	9.874670	7018.544	29.462879
3	29.462879			

$h_3 = 29.462879$; $h = 29.5$ m

24.3   Curvilinear Motion

1. $x = 4t^2$ $y = 1 - t^2$

$v_x = \dfrac{dx}{dt} = 8t|_{t=2} = 16 \quad \dfrac{dy}{dt} = -2t|_{t=2} = -4$

$v = \sqrt{16^2 + (-4)^2} = 16.5$

$\tan\theta = \dfrac{-4}{16}, \theta = -14.0°$

5. $x = t(2t + 1)^2$

$\dfrac{dx}{dt} = t(2)(2t + 1)(2) + (2t + 1)^2(1)$

$\quad = 12t^2 + 8t + 1 = v_x$

$y = 6(4t + 3)^{-1/2}$

$\dfrac{dy}{dt} = 6\left(-\dfrac{1}{2}\right)(4t + 3)^{-3/2}(4) = \dfrac{-12}{(4t + 3)^{3/2}} = v_y$

$v_x|_{t=0.5} = 8$
$v_y|_{t=0.5} = -1.0733$

$\quad v = \sqrt{8^2 + (-1.0773)^2}$
$\quad v = 8.07$

$\quad \alpha = \tan^{-1}\dfrac{1.0733}{8} = 7.641°$

t	x	y
0	0	3.464
0.5	2	2.683 ←
1	9	2.268

Therefore, $\theta = 360° - \alpha = 352.4°$
Therefore, v is 8.07 at $\theta = 352.4°$

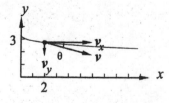

9. $x = t(2t + 1)^2; \; v_x = 12t^2 + 8t + 1; \; a_x = 24t + 8;$
$a_x|_{t=0.5} = 20.0$

$y = \dfrac{6}{\sqrt{4t + 3}}; \; v_y = -12(4t + 3)^{-3/2}$

$a_y = \dfrac{72}{(4t + 3)^{5/2}}; \; a_y|_{t=0.5} = 1.288$

$a = \sqrt{20.0^2 + 1.288^2}$
$a = 20.041$

$\theta = \tan^{-1}\dfrac{1.288}{20.0}$

$\theta = 3.68°$
Therefore, a is 20.0 at $\theta = 3.7°$.

13. $x = 0.2t^2; \; v_x = 0.4t; \; a_x = 0.4; \; a_x|_{t=2.0} = 0.4$

$y = -0.1t^3; \; v_y = -0.3t^2; \; a_y = -0.6t;$
$a_y|_{t=2.0} = -1.2$

$a = \sqrt{(0.4)^2 + (1.2)^2} = 1.3$

$\alpha = \tan^{-1}\left(\dfrac{1.2}{0.4}\right) = 71.6°$

$\theta = 288.4°$
Therefore, a is 1.3 ft/min^2 at $\theta = 288°$.

17. $x = 10(\sqrt{1 + t^4} - 1); \; v_x = \dfrac{20t^3}{\sqrt{1 + t^4}}$

$y = 40t^{3/2}; \; v_y = 60t^{1/2}; \; (0 \le t \le 100 \text{ s})$

For $t = 10$ s:

$v_x = \dfrac{20t^3}{\sqrt{1 + t^4}}\bigg|_{t=10.0\,s} = 200.0 \text{ m/s}$

$v_y = 60t^{1/2}|_{t=10.0\,s} = 189.7 \text{ m/s}$

$v = \sqrt{(200)^2 + (189.7)^2}$
$v = 276 \text{ m/s}$

$\theta = \tan^{-1}\dfrac{189.7}{200} = 43.5°$

For $t = 100$ s:

$v_x|_{t=100\,s} = 2000.0 \text{ m/s}$

$v_y = |_{t=100\,s} = 600 \text{ m/s}$

$v = \sqrt{(2000)^2 + (600)^2}$

$v = 2088 \text{ m/s}: \; \theta = \tan^{-1}\dfrac{600}{2000} = 16.7°$

At 10 s v is 276 m/s at $\theta = 43.5°$, and at 100 s v is
2090 m/s at $\theta = 16.7°$.

21. $x = 10(\sqrt{1+t^4} - 1) = 10(1+t^4)^{1/2} - 10;$
$y = 40t^{3/2}$

$\dfrac{dx}{dt} = 5(1+t^4)^{-1/2}(4t^3)$
$\quad = 20t^3(1+t^4)^{-1/2}$

$\quad = \dfrac{20t^3}{\sqrt{1+t^4}}$

$\dfrac{dy}{dt} = 60t^{1/2} = 60\sqrt{t}$

$ax = \dfrac{(1+t^4)^{1/2}(60t^2) - (20t^3)\left(\frac{1}{2}\right)(1+t^4)^{-1/2}(4t^3)}{1+t^4}$

$\quad = \dfrac{(1+t^4)^{-1/2}[60t^2(1+t^4) - 40t^6]}{(1+t^4)}$

$\quad = \dfrac{60t^2(1+t^4) - 40t^6}{(1+t^4)^{3/2}}$

$ay = 30t^{-1/2}$

$a_x\big|_{t=10.0} = \dfrac{6000(10,000) - 40,000,000}{1,000,000}$

$\quad = 20.0$

$a_y\big|_{t=10.0} = 30(10)^{-1/2} = \dfrac{30}{\sqrt{10}} = 9.5$

$a = \sqrt{(20)^2 + (9.5)^2} = 22.1 \text{ m/s}^2$

$\tan\theta = \dfrac{9.5}{20.0} = 0.475;\ \theta = 25.4°$

$a_x\big|_{t=100} = \dfrac{60(10^4)(10^8) - 40(10^{12})}{(10^8)^{3/2}}$

$\quad = \dfrac{6 \times 10^{13} - 4 \times 10^{13}}{10^{12}}$

$\quad = \dfrac{2 \times 10^{13}}{10^{12}} = 20.0$

$a_y\big|_{t=100} = 30(10^2)^{-1/2}$
$\quad = 30(10^{-1}) = 3.0$

$a = \sqrt{(20.0)^2 + (3.0)^2} = 20.2 \text{ m/s}^2$

$\tan\theta = \dfrac{3.0}{20.0}$
$\quad = 0.150;\ \theta = 8.5°$

25. $d = 3.50 \text{ in};\ r = 1.75 \text{ in};\ x^2 + y^2 = 1.75^2;$

$\dfrac{dy}{dx} = -\dfrac{x}{y}$

$3600 \text{ r/min} = 7200\pi \text{ rad/min} = \omega$
$v = \omega r = 7200\pi(1.75) = 12,600\pi \text{ in/min}$
$x^2 + y^2 = 1.75^2$

$y^2 = 1.75^2 - x^2 = 1.75^2 - 1.20^2$
$\quad = 3.062 - 1.44 = 1.622$
$y = 1.274 \text{ in}$

$\dfrac{dy}{dx} = -\dfrac{x}{y} = -\dfrac{1.20}{1.274} = -0.942 = \dfrac{v_y}{v_x};$

$v_y = -0.942v_x$

$v = 12,600\pi = \sqrt{v_x^2 + v_y^2}$

$\quad = \sqrt{(-0.942v_x)^2 + v_x^2}$

$\quad = \sqrt{1.893v_x^2} = 1.376v_x$

$v_x = 9158\pi = 28,800 \text{ in/min}$

$v_y = -0.942v_x = 8654\pi = -27,100 \text{ in/min}$

24.4   Related Rates

1. $E = 2.800T + 0.012T^2$

$\dfrac{dE}{dt} = 2.800\dfrac{dT}{dt} + 0.024T\dfrac{dT}{dt}$

$\dfrac{dE}{dt}\bigg|_{T=100°C} = 2.800(1.00) + 0.024(100)(1.00)$

$\dfrac{dE}{dt}\bigg|_{T=100°C} = 5.20 \text{ V/min}$

5. $R = 4.000 + 0.003T^2;\ \dfrac{dT}{dt} = 0.100°C/s$

$\dfrac{dR}{dt} = 0 + 0.006T\dfrac{dT}{dt}$

$\dfrac{dR}{dt}\bigg|_{T=150°C} = 0 + 0.006(150)(0.1)$
$\quad = 0.0900 \ \Omega/s$

9. $D = \sqrt{4.0 + x^2}$

$\dfrac{dD}{dt} = \dfrac{dD}{dx} \cdot \dfrac{dx}{dt} = \dfrac{x}{\sqrt{4.0 + x^2}} \cdot \dfrac{dx}{dt}\bigg|_{\substack{x=6.2 \\ \frac{dx}{dt}=350}}$

$\dfrac{dD}{dt} = \dfrac{6.2}{\sqrt{4 + 6.2^2}} \cdot 350 = 330 \text{ mi/h}$

13. $B = \dfrac{k}{\left[r^2 + \left(\frac{\ell}{2}\right)^2\right]^{3/2}} = k\left[r^2 + \left(\frac{\ell}{2}\right)^2\right]^{-3/2}$

$\dfrac{dB}{dt} = -\dfrac{3}{2}k\left[r^2 + \left(\frac{\ell}{2}\right)^2\right]^{-5/2}\left(2r\dfrac{dr}{dt}\right)$

$\dfrac{dB}{dt} = \dfrac{-3kr\dfrac{dr}{dt}}{\left[r^2 + \left(\frac{\ell}{2}\right)^2\right]^{5/2}}$

17. $A = \pi r^2; \dfrac{dr}{dt} = 0.020$ mm/mo; $\dfrac{dA}{dt} = 2\pi r\dfrac{dr}{dt}$

$\left.\dfrac{dA}{dt}\right|_{r=1.2} = 2\pi(1.2)(0.020) = 0.15$ mm²/month

21. $V = \dfrac{4}{3}\pi r^3$

$\dfrac{dV}{dt} = kA = k(4\pi r^2) = (4\pi r^2)\dfrac{dr}{dt}$

$\dfrac{dr}{dt} = k$

25. $V = \dfrac{4}{3}\pi r^3; \dfrac{dr}{dt} = 5.00$ mm/s; $r = 225$ mm

$\dfrac{dV}{dt} = 4\pi r^2\dfrac{dr}{dt}$

$\left.\dfrac{dV}{dt}\right|_{r=225} = 4\pi(225)^2(5.00) = 3.18 \times 10^6$ mm³/s

29. 0.5m³/min $\dfrac{x}{h} = \dfrac{1.15}{3.6}$

$V = \dfrac{1}{3}\pi r^2 h = \dfrac{1}{3}\pi\left(\dfrac{1.15}{3.6}\right)^2 h^3$

$\dfrac{dV}{dt} = \dfrac{dV}{dh}\cdot\dfrac{dh}{dt}$

$0.50 = \pi\cdot\left(\dfrac{1.15}{3.6}\right)^2\cdot h^2\cdot\dfrac{dh}{dt}$

$0.50 = \pi\left(\dfrac{1.15}{3.6}\right)^2(1.8)^2\cdot\dfrac{dh}{dt}$

$\dfrac{dh}{dt} = 0.48$ m/min

33. $z^2 = 20^2 + x^2; \dfrac{dz}{dt} = -10.0$ ft/s; $z = 36.0$ ft,

$x = 29.9$ ft

$2z\dfrac{dz}{dt} = 2x\dfrac{dx}{dt}$

$\dfrac{dx}{dt} = \dfrac{z}{x}\dfrac{dz}{dt}$

$\left.\dfrac{dx}{dt}\right|_{z=36.0} = \dfrac{36.0}{29.9}(-10.0)$

$\dfrac{dx}{dt} = -12.0$ ft/s

The negative sign indicates the boat is approaching the wharf.

24.5   Using Derivatives in Curve Sketching

1. $f(x) = x^3 - 6x^2$
$f'(x) = 3x^2 - 12x = 3(x-4)$ with $x = 0, x = 4$ as critical values.
If $x < 0, f'(x) = 3x(x-4) > 0$. $f(x)$ increasing
If $0 < x < 4, f'(x) = 3x(x-4) < 0$. $f(x)$ decreasing
If $x > 4, f'(x) = 3x(x-4) > 0$. $f(x)$ increasing
inc. $x < 0, x > 4$; dec. $0 < x < 4$

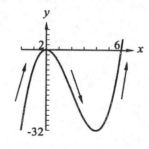

5. $y = x^2 + 2x; y' = 2x + 2; 2x + 2 > 0$
$2x > -2; x > -1; f(x)$ increases.
$2x + 2 < 0; 2x < -2; x < -1; f(x)$ decreases.

9. $y = x^2 + 2x; y' = 2x + 2; y' = 0$ at $x = 1$
$y'' = 2 > 0$ at $x = -1$ and $(-1, -1)$
is a relative minimum.

13. $y = x^2 + 2x; y' = 2x + 2; y'' = 2$
Thus, $y'' > 0$ for all x. The graph is concave up for all x and has no points of inflection.

17. $y = x^2 + 2x$

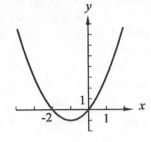

21. $y = 12x - 2x^2$; $y' = 12 - 4x$
$y' = 0$ at $x = 3$; for $x = 3$,
$y = 12(3) - 2(3)^2 = 18$
and $(3, 18)$ is a critical point. $12 - 4x < 0$ for $x > 3$
and the function decreases; $12 - 4x > 0$ for $x < 3$
and the function increases; $y'' = -4$; thus $y'' < 0$
for all x. There are no inflections; the graph is
concave down for all x, and $(3, 18)$ is a maximum
point.

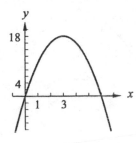

25. $y = x^3 + 3x^2 + 3x + 2$
$y' = 3x^2 + 6x = 3(x^2 + 2x + 1)$
   $= 3(x + 1)(x + 1)$
$3(x + 1)(x + 1) = 0$ for $x = -1$
$(-1, 1)$ is a critical point.
$3(x + 1)(x + 1) > 0$ for $x < -1$ and the slope is
positive.
$3(x + 1)(x + 1) > 0$ for $x > -1$ and the slope is
positive.
$y'' = 6x + 6$; $6x + 6 = 0$ for $x = 1$, and $(-1, 1)$ is
an inflection point.
$6x + 6 < 0$ for $x < -1$ and the graph is concave
down.
$6x + 6 > 0$ for $x > -1$ and the graph is concave
up.

Since there is no change in slope from positive to
negative or vice versa, there are no maximum or
minimum points.

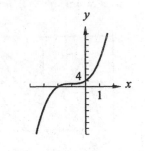

29. $y = 4x^3 - 3x^4$;
$y' = 12x^2 - 12x^3 = 12x^2(1 - x) = 0$
$12x^2(1 - x) = 0$ for $x = 0$ and $x = 1$
$(0, 0)$ and $(1, 1)$ are critical points.
$12x^2 - 12x^3 > 0$ for $x < 0$ and the slope is positive.
$12x - 12x^3 > 0$ for $0 < x < 1$ and the slope is
positive.
$12x - 12x^3 < 0$ for $x > 1$ and the slope is negative.
$y'' = 24x - 36x^2$; $24x - 36x^2 = 12x(2 - 3x) = 0$
for $x = 0$, $x = \frac{2}{3}$
$(0, 0)$ and $\left(\frac{2}{3}, \frac{16}{27}\right)$ are possible inflection points.
$24x - 36x^2 < 0$ for $x < 0$ and the graph is concave
down.
$24x - 36x^2 > 0$ for $0 < x < \frac{2}{3}$ and the graph is
concave up.
$24x - 36x^2 < 0$ for $x > \frac{2}{3}$ and the graph is concave
down.
$(1,1)$ is a relative maximum point since $y' = 0$
at $(1, 1)$ and the slope is positive for $x < 1$ and
negative for $x > 1$. $(0, 0)$ and $\left(\frac{2}{3}, \frac{16}{27}\right)$ are inflection
points since there is a concavity change.

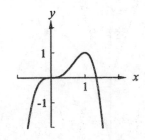

33. $y = x^3 - 12x$; $y' = 3x^2 - 12$; $y'' = 6x$. On graphing
calculator with $x_{\min} = -5$, $x_{\max} = 5$, $y_{\min} = -20$,
$y_{\max} = 20$, enter $y_1 = x^3 - 12x$; $y_2 = 3x^2 - 12$;
$y_3 = 6x$. From the graph is observed that the
maximum and minimum values of y occur when
y' is zero. A maximum value for y occurs when
$x = -2$, and a minimum value occurs when $x = 2$.

An inflection point (change in curvature) occurs when y'' is zero. x is also zero at this point. Where $y' > 0$, y inc.; $y' < 0$, y dec. $y'' > 0$, y conc. up; $y'' < 0$, y conc. down, $y'' = 0$, y has infl.

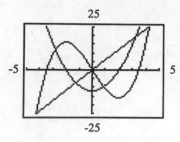

37. The left relative max is above the left relative min and below the right relative min.

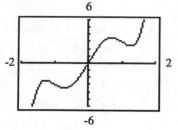

41. $P = 4i - 0.5i^2$
$P' = 4 - 1.0i = 0$ for $i = 4.0$
$P'' = -1.0 < 0$, conc. down everywhere
$P' > 0$ for $x < 4$, P inc.
$P' < 0$ for $x > 4$, P dec.
$P(4) = 8$, $(4,8)$ max.

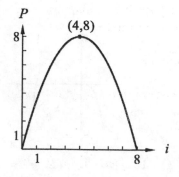

45. $R = 75 - 18i^2 + 8i^3 - i^4$
$R' = -36i + 24i^2 - 4i^3 = -4i(i^2 - 6i + 9)$
$\quad = -4i(i-3)^2$
$R' = 0$ for $i = 0$ and $i = 3$
$(0,75)$ and $(3,48)$ are critical points.
$R' > 0$ for $i < 0$, $R' < 0$ for $0 < i < 3$

$R' < 0$ for $i > 3$
Max. at $(0,75)$, no max. or min. at $(3,48)$
$R'' = -36 + 48i - 12i^2 = -12(i-1)(i-3)$
$(1,64)$ and $(3,48)$ are possible inflection points.
$R'' < 0$ for $i < 1$, concave down
$R'' > 0$ for $1 < i < 3$, concave up
$R'' < 0$ for $i > 3$, concave down
$(1,64)$ and $(3,48)$ are inflection points.
(From calculator graph, $R = 0$ for $i = -1.5$ and $i = 5.0$)

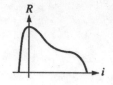

49. $f(1) = 0$; therefore $(1,0)$ is an x-intercept
$f'(x) > 0$ for all x; therefore curve rises left to right
$f''(x) < 0$ for all x; therefore concave down

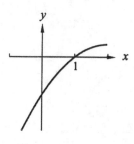

24.6   More on Curve Sketching

1. $y = x - \dfrac{4}{x}$

(1) Intercepts:

For $x = 0$, y is undefined which means curve is not continuous at $x = 0$ and there are no y-intercepts. For $y = 0$, $0 = x - \frac{4}{x}$, $x^2 - 4 = 0$, $x = \pm 2$ are the x-intercepts.

(2) Symmetry: none

(3) Behavior as x becomes large:

As $x \to \pm\infty$, $\dfrac{4}{x} \to 0$ and $y \to x$. $y = x$ is a slant asymptote.

(4) Vertical asymptotes:

y is undefined for $x = 0$. As $x \to 0^-, y \to \infty$ and as $x \to 0^+, y \to -\infty$. The x-axis is a vertical asymptote.

(5) Domain and range:

domain: $x \neq 0$, range: $-\infty < y < \infty$

(6) Derivatives:

$$y' = 1 + \frac{4}{x^2} > 0, y \text{ inc. for } x \neq 0$$

$$y'' = -\frac{8}{x^3} > 0 \text{ for } x < 0, y \text{ conc. up}$$

$$y'' = -\frac{8}{x^3} < 0 \text{ for } x > 0, y \text{ conc. down}$$

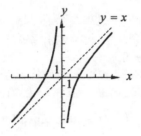

5. $y = x^2 + \dfrac{2}{x} = \dfrac{x^3 + 2}{x}$

(1) $\frac{2}{x}$ is undefined for $x = 0$, so the graph is not continuous at the y-axis; i.e., no y-intercept exists.

(2) $\frac{x^3+2}{x} = 0$ at $x = \sqrt[3]{-2} = -\sqrt[3]{2}$. There is an x-intercept at $(-\sqrt[3]{2}, 0)$.

(3) As $x \to \infty$, $x^2 \to \infty$ and $\frac{2}{x} \to 0$, so $x^2 + \frac{2}{x} \to \infty$.

(4) As $x \to 0$ through positive x, $x^2 \to 0$ and $\frac{2}{x} \to \infty$, so $x^2 + \frac{2}{x} \to \infty$.

(5) As $x \to -\infty$, $x^2 \to \infty$ and $\frac{2}{x} \to 0$ so $x^2 + \frac{2}{x} \to \infty$.

$x = 0$ is a vertical asymptote

(6) As $x \to 0$ through negative numbers, $x^2 \to 0$ and $\frac{2}{x} \to -\infty$, so $x^2 + \frac{2}{x} \to -\infty$.

(7) $y' = 2x - 2x^{-2} = 0$ at $x = 1$ and the slope is zero at $(1, 3)$.

(8) $y'' = 2 + 4x^{-3} = 0$ at $x = -\sqrt[3]{2}$ and $(-\sqrt[3]{2}, 0)$ is an inflection point.

(9) $y'' > 0$ at $x = 1$, so the graph is concave up and $(1, 3)$ is a relative minimum.

(10) Since $(-\sqrt[3]{2}, 0)$ is an inflection, $f''(-1) < 0$ and the graph is concave down. $f''(-2) > 0$ and the graph is concave up.

(11) Not symmetrical about the x- or y-axis.

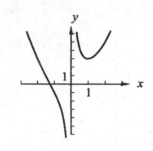

9. $y = \dfrac{x^2}{x+1}$

Intercepts:

(1) Function undefined at $x = -1$; not continuous at $x = -1$.

(2) At $x = 0$, $y = 0$. The origin is the only intercept. Behavior as x becomes large:

(3) As $x \to \infty$, $y \to x$, so $y = x$ is an asymptote. As $x \to \infty$, $y = -\infty$.

Vertical asymptotes:

(4) As $x \to -1$ from the left, $x + 1 \to 0$ through negative values and $\frac{x^2}{x+1} \to -\infty$ since $x^2 > 0$ for all x. As $x \to -1$ from the right, $x + 1 \to 0$ through positive values and $\frac{x^2}{x+1} \to +\infty$. $x = -1$ is an asymptote.

Symmetry:

(5) The graph is not symmetrical about the y-axis or the x-axis.

Derivatives:

(6) $y' = \frac{x^2+2x}{(x+1)^2}$; $y' = 0$ at $x = -2$, $x = 0$. $(-2, -4)$ and $(0, 0)$ are critical points. Checking the derivative at $x = -3$, the slope is positive, and at $x = -1.5$ the slope is negative. $(-2, -4)$ is a relative maximum point. Checking the derivative at $x = -0.5$, the slope is negative, and at $x = 1$ the slope is positive, so $(0, 0)$ is a relative minimum point.

Int. $(0,0)$, max. $(-2,-4)$, min $(0,0)$, asym. $x = -1$

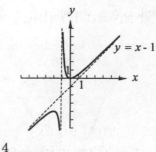

13. $y = \dfrac{4}{x} - \dfrac{4}{x^2}$

Intercepts:

(1) There are no y intercepts since $x = 0$ is undefined.

(2) $y = 0$ when $x = 1$ so $(1,0)$ is an x-intercept.

Asymptotes:

(3) $x = 0$ is an asymptote; the denominator is 0.
      $y = 0$ is an asymptote

Symmetry:

(4) Not symmetrical about the y-axis since $\frac{4}{x} - \frac{4}{x^2}$ is different from $\frac{4}{(-x)} - \frac{4}{(-x)^2}$

(5) Not symmetrical about the x-axis since

$y = \frac{4}{x} - \frac{4}{x^2}$ is different from $-y = \frac{4}{x} - \frac{4}{x^2}$

(6) Not symmetrical about the origin since

$y = \frac{4}{x} - \frac{4}{x^2}$ is different from $-y = \frac{4}{-x} - \frac{4}{(-x)^2}$

Derivatives:

(7) $y' = -4x^{-2} + 8x^{-3} = 0$ at $x = 2$; $(2,1)$ is a relative maximum.

(8) $y'' = 8x^{-3} - 24x^{-4} = 0$ at $x = 3$ so $\left(3, \frac{8}{9}\right)$ is a possible inflection.

$y'' < 0$ (concave down) for $x < 3$ and 0 (concave up) for $x > 3$ so $\left(3, \frac{8}{9}\right)$ is an inflection.

Behavior as x becomes large:

(9) As $x \to \infty$ or $-\infty$, $\frac{4}{x}$ and $-\frac{4}{x^2}$ each approach 0.

As $x \to 0$, $\frac{4}{x} - \frac{4}{x^2} = \frac{4x-4}{x^2}$ approaches $-\infty$, through positive or negative values of x.

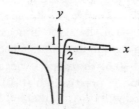

17. $y = \dfrac{9x}{9 - x^2}$

Intercept:

(1) Intercept at $x = 0, y = 0$ only

(2) Asymptotes at $x = -3, x = 3$

Derivatives:

(3) $y' = \dfrac{(9 - x^2)(9) - (9x)(-2x)}{(9 - x^2)^2} = \dfrac{81 + 9x^2}{(9 - x^2)^2}$

$81 + 9x^2 = 0$; $9x^2 = -81$; $x^2 = \sqrt{-9}$ (imaginary)
No real value max. or min., ± 3 are critical values.

(4) $y'' = \dfrac{(9 - x^2)^2(18x) - (81 + 9x^2)(2)(9 - x^2)(-2x)}{(9 - x^2)^2}$

$\qquad = \dfrac{-18x^5 - 324x^3 + 4374x}{(9 - x^2)^4}$

$-18x^5 - 324x^3 + 4374x = 0$;
$-18x(x^4 + 18x^2 - 243) = 0$
$-18x = 0$; $x = 0$
$x^4 + 18x^2 - 243 = 0$; $(x^2 + 27)(x^2 - 9) = 0$
(imaginary) $x^2 = 9$; $x = \pm 3$ (these are asymptotes)

$y|_{x=0} = 0$; a possible inflection is $(0,0)$

at $\left(-1, -\frac{9}{8}\right)$, $y'' = -4032$; concave down at $\left(1, \frac{9}{8}\right)$, $y'' = 4032$; concave up, and $(0,0)$ is an inflection point

Symmetry:

(5) There is symmetry to the origin.

(6) As $x \to +\infty$ and as $x \to -\infty$, $y \to 0$. Therefore, $y = 0$ is an asymptote.

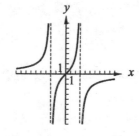

21. $C_T = \dfrac{6C}{6 + C}$; $\dfrac{dC_T}{dC} = \dfrac{36}{(6 + C)^2}$; $\dfrac{d^2C_T}{dC^2} = \dfrac{-72}{(6 + C)^3}$

$f'(C) \neq 0$; $f''(C) = 0$, therefore no max, no min, no infl. points

$f'(C) > 0$ for all C, therefore C_T is increasing for all C.

$f''(C) < 0$ for $C > -6$, therefore C_T is concave down for $C > -6$ (only values of $C \geq 0$ have physical significance.)

$C = 0, C_T = 0, (0,0)$ is the only intercept
No symmetry WRT axes or origin.

$\lim\limits_{x \to +\infty} \dfrac{6C}{6+C} = \lim\limits_{x \to +\infty} \dfrac{6}{\frac{6}{C}+1} = 6$, therefore, horizontal asymptote at $C_T = 6$.

Vertical asymptote at $C = -6$ (capacitance > 0)

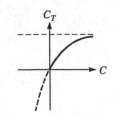

25. $v = k\left(r - \dfrac{1}{r^3}\right) = r - \dfrac{1}{r^3}$ for $k = 1$.

(1) Intercepts: For $r = 0$, v is undefined. There is no y-intercept. For $v = 0 = r - \frac{1}{r^3}$

$r^4 = 1, r = \pm 1$ are the x-intercepts.

(2) Symmetry: none

(3) Behavior as x becomes large:
As $x \to \pm\infty, v \to r$. $v = r$ is a slant asymptote.

(4) Vertical asymptotes: $r = 0$ is a vertical asymptote since v is undefined for $r = 0$.

(5) domain is all $r \neq 0$
range is $-\infty < v < \infty$

(6) Derivatives:

$v' = 1 + \dfrac{3}{r^4} > 0, v$ inc. everywhere

$v'' = -\dfrac{12}{r^5}, v'' < 0, r > 0, v$ conc. down

$v'' = -\dfrac{12}{r^5}, v'' > 0, r < 0, v$ conc. up.

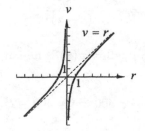

24.7 Applied Maximum and Minimum Problems

1. $A = xy, 2x + 2y = 2400 \Rightarrow x + y = 1200$
$A = (1200 - y)y = 1200y - y^2$
$A' = 1200 - 2y = 0 \Rightarrow y = 600$
$A'' = -2 < 0, y = 600$ is max.
$x + 600 = 1200 \Rightarrow x = 600$
$A_{\max} = 600(600) = 360{,}000 \text{ ft}^2$

5. $P = EI - RI^2; \dfrac{dP}{dI} = E - 2RI = 0; I = \dfrac{E}{2R}$

$\dfrac{d^2P}{dI^2} = -2R < 0$ for all I, therefore max. power
at $I = \dfrac{E}{2R}$

9. $Z = \sqrt{R^2 + (X_L + X_C)^2}; R = 2500\ \Omega;$
$X_L = 1500\ \Omega$
$Z = [R^2 + (X_L - X_C)^2]^{1/2}$

$\dfrac{dZ}{dX_C} = \dfrac{1}{2}[R^2 + (X_L - X_C)]^{-1/2}2(X_L - X_C)(-1)$

$= \dfrac{-(X_L - X_C)}{\sqrt{R^2 + (X_L - X_C)^2}}$

$= \dfrac{X_C - 1500}{\sqrt{2500^2 + (1500 - X_C)^2}}$

$= 0$

$X_C = 1500\ \Omega$

Test:

$\left.\dfrac{dZ}{dX_C}\right|_{X_C = 1400} < 0; \quad \left.\dfrac{dZ}{dX_C}\right|_{X_C = 1600} > 0.$

Therefore, concave up, minimum.
$X_C = 1500\ \Omega$ gives minimum impedance.

13.

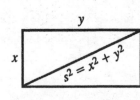

$P = 2x + 2y = 48$
$x + y = 24$

Diagonal will be a minimum if $l = s^2$ is a minimum.

$$l = x^2 + y^2$$
$$l = x^2 + (24 - x)^2$$
$$l = x^2 + 24^2 - 48x + x^2$$
$$l = 2x^2 - 48x + 24^2$$

$$\frac{dl}{dx} = 4x - 48 = 0$$
$$x = 12$$

from which $y = 12$

Dimensions are 12 in by 12 in, a square will minimize the diagonal.

17. $A = xy, P = 2x + 2y$

$$y = \frac{A}{x}$$

$$P = 2x + \frac{2A}{x}$$

$$P' = 2 - \frac{2A}{x^2} = 0 \Rightarrow x = \sqrt{A}$$

$$A = xy = \sqrt{A}y \Rightarrow y = \sqrt{A}$$

$$P'' = \frac{4A}{x^3}\bigg|_{x=\sqrt{A}} > 0 \Rightarrow P \text{ is a maximum for}$$
$$x = y = \sqrt{A}, \text{ a square.}$$

21. $A = \frac{1}{2}xy; \ 12.0^2 = x^2 + y^2$

$$y^2 = 144 - x^2; \ y = \sqrt{144 - x^2}$$

$$A = \frac{1}{2}x\sqrt{144 - x^2}$$

$$\frac{dA}{dx} = \frac{1}{2}\left[x \cdot \frac{1}{2}(144 - x^2)^{-1/2}(-2x) + \sqrt{144 - x^2}\right]$$

$$= \frac{1}{2}\left[\frac{-x^2}{\sqrt{144 - x^2}} + \sqrt{144 - x^2}\right]$$

$$= \frac{1}{2}\left[\frac{-x^2 + 144 - x^2}{\sqrt{144 - x^2}}\right] = \frac{1}{2}\frac{(144 - 2x^2)}{\sqrt{144 - x^2}}$$

$$\frac{dA}{dx} = 0 = 144 - 2x^2; \ x = \sqrt{72} = 8.49$$

Test $\sqrt{72}$: $f'\sqrt{71} > 0$; $f'\sqrt{73} < 0$
Therefore, max. $(\sqrt{72}, \sqrt{72})$.
Therefore, legs of triangle will be equal at 8.49 cm for max. area.

25. $V = (10 - 2x)(15 - 2x), 0 < x < 5$
$$V = 4x^3 - 50x^2 + 150x$$
$$V' = 8x^2 - 100x + 150 = 0$$
$$x = 1.96, 6.37 > 5, \text{ reject}$$
$$V'' = 12x^2 - 100x + 150\big|_{x=1.96} > 0,$$

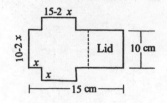

V is a maximum for $x = 2$ cm.

29. $y = k(2x^4 - 5Lx^3 + 3L^2x^2)$
$$= 2kx^4 - 5kLx^3 + 3kL^2x^2$$
$$y' = 8kx^3 - 15kLx^2 + 6kL^2x = 0$$
$$kx(8x^2 - 15Lx + 6L^2) = 0$$
$$kx = 0; \ x = 0$$
$$8x^2 - 15Lx + 6L^2 = 0$$

$$x = \frac{-(-15) \pm \sqrt{(-15)^2 - 4(8)(6)}}{2(8)}$$

$$= \frac{15 \pm \sqrt{33}}{16}$$

$$= \frac{15 \pm 5.75}{16}$$

$x = 0.58L, 1.30L$ (not valid—this distance is greater than L, the length of the beam)

33. $n(x) = \frac{k}{x^2} + \frac{8k}{(8 - x)^2}$

$n'(x) = \frac{-2k}{x^3} + \frac{8k \cdot (-2))(-1)}{(8 - x)^3} = 0 \Rightarrow 8x^3 = (8 - x)^3$
$$2x = 8 - x$$
$$3x = 8$$
$$x = \frac{8}{3}$$

$n''(x) = \frac{6k}{x^4} + \frac{48k}{(8 - x)^4}$

$n''\left(\frac{8}{3}\right) > 0 \Rightarrow n(x)$ is min at $x = \frac{8}{3}$ km from A.

37. $2x + \pi d = 400; \ \pi d = 400 - 2x; \ d = \frac{400 - 2x}{\pi}$

$$A = x(d) = x\left(\frac{400 - 2x}{\pi}\right) = \frac{400x - 2x^2}{\pi}$$

$$A' = \frac{400 - 4x}{\pi} = 0; \ 400 - 4x = 0; \ x = 100 \text{ m}$$

41. Let C = total cost

$$C = 50,000(10 - x) + 80,000(\sqrt{x^2 + 2.5^2})$$
$$= 500,000 - 50,000x + 80,000(x^2 + 6.25)^{1/2}$$
$$C' = -50,000 + 40,000(x^2 + 6.25)^{-1/2}(2x)$$
$$= -50,000 + 80,000x(x^2 + 6.25)^{-1/2}$$
$$= -50,000 + \frac{80,000x}{\sqrt{x^2 + 6.25}}$$
$$= \frac{-50,000\sqrt{x^2 + 6.25} + 80,000x}{\sqrt{x^2 + 6.25}} = 0$$

$$-50,000\sqrt{x^2 + 6.25} + 80,000x = 0$$

$$\sqrt{x^2 + 6.25} = \frac{-80,000x}{-50,000} = \frac{8x}{5}; \quad x^2 + 6.25 = \frac{64}{25}x^2$$

$$6.25 = \frac{64}{25}x^2 = \frac{39}{25}x^2; \quad x^2 = 6.25\left(\frac{25}{39}\right) = 4.00$$

$$x = 2.00 \text{ mi}; \; 10 - x = 8.00 \text{ mi}$$

24.8 Differentials and Linear Approximations

1. $y = \dfrac{4x}{x^3 + 4}$

$$dy = \frac{(x^3 + 4)(4) - 4x(3x^2)}{(x^3 + 4)^2}$$
$$= \frac{4x^3 + 16 - 12x^3}{(x^3 + 4)^2}dx$$
$$dy = \frac{-8x^3 + 16}{(x^3 + 4)^2}dx = \frac{-8(x^3 - 2)}{(x^3 + 4)^2}dx$$
$$dy = \frac{8(2 - x^3)}{(x^3 + 4)^2}dx$$

5. $y = x^5 + x;$

$$\frac{dy}{dx} = 5x^4 + 1$$
$$dy = (5x^4 + 1)dx$$

9. $s = 2(3t^2 - 5)^4;$

$$\frac{ds}{dt} = 8(3t^2 - 5)^3(6t)$$
$$ds = 8(3t^2 - 5)^3(6t)dt$$
$$ds = 48t(3t^2 - 5)^3 dt$$

13. $y = x^2(1 - x)^3$
$$dy = [x^2 \cdot 3(1 - x)^2(-1) + (1 - x)^3 \cdot 2x]dx$$
$$dy = (-3x^2(1 - x)^2 + 2x(1 - x)^3)dx$$
$$dy = (1 - x)^2(-3x^2 + 2x(1 - x))dx$$
$$dy = (1 - x)^2(-5x^2 + 2x)dx$$
$$dy = x(1 - x)^2(-5x + 2)dx$$

17. $y = f(x) = 7x^2 + 4x, dy = f'(x)dx$
$$= (14x + 4)dx$$
$$\Delta y = f(x + \Delta x) - f(x)$$
$$= 7(4.2)^2 + 4(4.2) - (7 \cdot 4^2 + 4 \cdot 4)$$
$$= 12.28$$
$$dy = (14 \cdot 4 + 4)(0.2) = 12$$

21. $f(x) = x^2 + 2x; f'(x) = 2x + 2$
$$L(x) = f(a) + f'(a)(x - a)$$
$$= f(0) + f'(0)(x - 0)$$
$$L(x) = 0^2 + 2 \cdot 0 + (2 \cdot 0 + 2)(x - 0)$$
$$L(x) = 2x$$

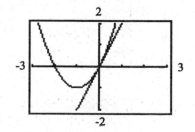

25. $C = 2\pi r, r = 6370, dr = 250$
$$dC = 2\pi dr = 2\pi(250) = 1570 \text{ km}$$

29. $\lambda = \dfrac{k}{f}, 685 = \dfrac{k}{4.38 \times 10^{14}};$

$$k = 3.00 \times 10^{17} \text{ mm} - \text{H}_z$$
$$\frac{d\lambda}{df} = \frac{-k}{f^2}$$
$$d\lambda = \frac{-k}{f^2}df$$
$$d\lambda = \frac{-3.00 \times 10^{17}}{(4.38 \times 10^{14})^2} \cdot (0.20 \times 10^{14})$$
$$d\lambda = -31 \text{ nm}$$

33. $A = s^2; dA = 2s\,ds; \dfrac{ds}{s} = 2\% = 0.02$

$$\frac{dA}{A} = \frac{2s\,ds}{s^2} = 2\frac{ds}{s}; \; \frac{dA}{A}\bigg|_{\frac{ds}{s}=0.02} = 2(0.02) = 4\%$$

37. $f(x) = \sqrt{2-x}; \; f'(x) = \dfrac{-1}{2\sqrt{2-x}}$

$L(x) = f(a) + f'(a)(x-a)$

$L(x) = f(1) + f'(1)(x-1) = \sqrt{2-1} + \dfrac{-1}{2\sqrt{2-1}}(x-1)$

$L(x) = 1 - \dfrac{1}{2}(x-1) = -\dfrac{1}{2}x + \dfrac{3}{2}$

$\sqrt{1.9} = f(0.1) \approx L(0.1) = 1 - \dfrac{1}{2}(0.1-1) = 1.45$

Chapter 24 Review Exercises

1. $y = 3x - x^2$ at $(-1,-4); \; y' = 3 - 2x$
$y'|_{x=-1} = 3 - 2(-1) = 5$

$m = 5$ for tangent line
$y - y_1 = 5(x - x_1)$
$y - (-4) = 5[x - (-1)]; \; y + 4 = 5x + 5$
$5x - y + 1 = 0$

5. $y = \sqrt{x^2 + 3}; \; m = \dfrac{1}{2}$

$y = (x^2 + 3)^{1/2}; \; \dfrac{dy}{dx} = \dfrac{1}{2}(x^2+3)^{-1/2}(2x) = \dfrac{x}{\sqrt{x^2+3}}$

$m_{\tan} = \dfrac{dy}{dx} = \dfrac{x}{\sqrt{x^2+3}} = \dfrac{1}{2}$

$2x = \sqrt{x^2+3}$

Squaring both sides, $4x^2 = x^2 + 3; \; 3x^2 = 3; \; x^2 = 1; \; x = 1$ and $x = -1$. Therefore, the abscissa of the point at which $m = \frac{1}{2}$ is 1 or -1. If $x = 1, y = \sqrt{1^2 + 3} = \sqrt{4} = 2$ or -2. If $x = -1, y = \sqrt{(-1)^2 + 3} = 2$ or -2. The possible points where the slope of the tangent line is $\frac{1}{2}$ are $(1,2), (1,-2), (-1,2), (-1,-2)$. A sketch of the curve shows that the only relative maximum or minimum point is at m(0,1.7). Therefore the point is $(1,2)$.

$y - 2 = \dfrac{1}{2}(x-1); \; y = \dfrac{1}{2}x + \dfrac{3}{2}$ is the equation of the tangent line.

9. $y = 0.5x^2 + x; \; v_y = \dfrac{dy}{dt} = \dfrac{x\,dx}{dt} + \dfrac{dx}{dt}; \; v_x = 0.5\sqrt{x}$

Substituting, $v_y = x(0.5\sqrt{x}) + 0.5\sqrt{x}$
Find v_y at $(2,4)$:

$v_y|_{x=2} = 2(0.5\sqrt{2}) + 0.5\sqrt{2} = \sqrt{2} + 0.5\sqrt{2} = 1.5\sqrt{2} = 2.12$

13. $x^3 - 3x^2 - x + 2 = 0$ (between 0 and 1)

$f(x) = x^3 - 3x^2 - x + 2;\ f'(x) = 3x^2 - 6x - 1$

$f(0) = 0^3 - 3(0^2) - 0 + 2 = 2;\ f(1) = 1^3 - 3(1^2) - 1 + 2 = -1$

The root is possibly closer to 1 than 0. Let $x_1 = 0.6$:

n	x_n	$f(x_n)$	$f'(x_n)$	$x_n - \dfrac{f(x_n)}{f'(x_n)}$
1	0.6	0.536	-3.52	0.7522727
2	0.7522727	-0.0242935	-3.8158936	0.7459063
3	0.7459063	-0.0000304	-3.8063092	0.7458983

$x_4 = x_3 = 0.7458983$

17. $y = 4x^2 + 16x$

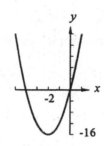

   (1)   The graph is continuous for all x.

   (2)   The intercepts are $(0,0)$ and $(-4,0)$.

   (3)   As $x \to +\infty$ and $-\infty, y \to +\infty$.

   (4)   The graph is not symmetrical about either axis or the origin.

   (5) $y' = 8x + 16;\ y' = 0$ at $x = -2$. $(-2, -16)$ is a critical point.

   (6) $y'' = 8 > 0$ for all x; the graph is concave up and $(-2, -16)$ is a minimum.

21. $y = x^4 - 32x$

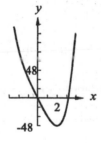

   (1)   The graph is continuous for all x.

   (2)   The intercepts are $(0,0)$ and $(2\sqrt[3]{4}, 0)$.

   (3)   As $x \to -\infty,\ y \to +\infty$; as $x \to +\infty,\ y \to +\infty$.

   (4)   The graph is not symmetrical about either axis or the origin.

   (5) $y' = 4x^3 - 32 = 0$ for $x = 2$

   (6) $y'' = 12x^2;\ y'' = 0$ at $x = 0$; $(0,0)$ is a possible point of inflection. Since $f''(x) > 0$; the graph is concave up everywhere and $(0,0)$ is not an inflection point. $(2, -48)$ is a minimum.

25. $y = f(x) = 4x^3 + \dfrac{1}{x}$

$dy = f'(x)dx$

$\quad = \left(12x^2 - \dfrac{1}{x^2}\right) dx$

29. $y = f(x) = x^3, x = 2, \Delta x = 0.1$

$\Delta y - dy = f(x + \Delta x) - f(x) - f'(x)dx$

$\quad = (x + \Delta x)^3 - x^3 - 3x^2 dx$

$\quad = 2.1^3 - 2^3 - 3 \cdot 2^2 (0.1)$

$\quad = 0.061$

33. $V = f(r) = \dfrac{4}{3}\pi r^3, r = 3.500, \Delta r = 0.012$

$dV = f'(r)dr = 4\pi r^2 \cdot dr = 4\pi (3.500)^2 (0.012)$

$dV = 1.847 \text{ m}^3$

37. $Z = \sqrt{R^2 + X^2}$

$$dZ = \frac{2R}{2\sqrt{R^2 + X^2}}dR$$

$$\frac{dZ}{Z} = \frac{R}{\sqrt{R^2 + X^2}\sqrt{R^2 + X^2}}dR$$

$$\frac{dZ}{Z} = \frac{RdR}{R^2 + X^2}$$

41. $y = x^2 + 2$ and $y = 4x - x^2$
$y' = 2x;\ y' = 4 - 2x$
$2x = 4 - 2x;\ 4x = 4;\ x = 1$

The point $(1, 3)$ belongs to both graphs; the slope of the tangent line is 2.

$y - y_1 = 2(x - x_1);\ y - 3 = 2(x - 1);\ y - 3 = 2x - 2$
$2x - y + 1 = 0$ is the equation of the tangent line.

45. $x = 8t$ $\qquad\qquad$ $y = -0.15t^2$ $\qquad$ $v = \sqrt{8^2 + (-3.6)^2}$

$\quad\dfrac{dx}{dt} = 8$ $\qquad\qquad$ $\dfrac{dy}{dt} = -0.30t$ $\qquad$ $v = \sqrt{64 + 12.96}$

$\quad v_x\big|_{t=12} = 8$ $\qquad$ $v_y\big|_{t=12} = -3.6$ $\qquad$ $v\big|_{t=12} = \sqrt{76.96} = 8.8$ m/s

$$\tan\theta = \frac{-3.6}{8} = -0.45;\ \theta = 336°$$

49. $y = x^2 - \dfrac{2}{x}$

(1) Intercepts: y is undefined for $x = 0 \Rightarrow$ no

y-intercept. $y = 0$ gives $0 = x^2 - \dfrac{2}{x}$

$$x^3 = 2$$
$$x = \sqrt[3]{2} \approx 1.26$$

(2) Symmetry: none

(3) Behavior as x becomes large: $y \to \infty$ as $x \to \pm\infty$

(4) Vertical asymptotes: $x = 0$ is a vertical asymptote

(5) Domain: $x \neq 0$; Range: $-\infty < y < \infty$

(6) Derivatives: $y' = 2x + \dfrac{2}{x^2} = 0$ for $x = -1$

$$y'' = 2 - \frac{4}{x^3}\bigg|_{x=-1} > 0 \Rightarrow (-1, 3) \text{ is a min}$$

$y'' = 0 = 2 - \dfrac{4}{x^3} \Rightarrow x^3 = 2 \Rightarrow x = \sqrt[3]{2}$

$y'' < 0$ for $x < \sqrt[3]{2}$; $y'' > 0$ for $x > \sqrt[3]{2} \Rightarrow (\sqrt[3]{2}, 0)$ is an infl. pt.

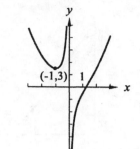

From the graph $y = x^2 - \dfrac{2}{x} > 0$ for $x < 0$ or $x > 1.26$

$x^2 - \dfrac{2}{x} > 0 \Rightarrow x^2 > \dfrac{2}{x}$ for $x < 0$ or $x > 1.26$

The graph of $x^2 > \dfrac{2}{x}$ is

$$\xleftarrow{\qquad} \overset{\circ}{\underset{0}{}} \; \overset{\circ}{\underset{1.26}{}} \xrightarrow{\qquad} x$$

53. $f(0) = 2 \Rightarrow y$-intercept is 2

$\left. \begin{array}{l} f'(x) < 0 \text{ for } x < 0 \Rightarrow f \text{ is dec. for } x < 0 \\ f'(x) > 0 \text{ for } x > 0 \Rightarrow f \text{ is inc. for } x > 0 \end{array} \right\}$ $(0, 2)$ is min.

$f''(x) > 0$ for all $x \Rightarrow f$ is conc. up for all x.

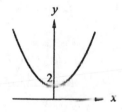

57. $A = \pi r^2$

$\dfrac{dA}{dt} = 2\pi r \dfrac{dr}{dt} = 2\pi(400)(15) = 38{,}000$

The area is changing 38,000 m^2/min when $r = 400$ m.

61. $y = \dfrac{300}{0.0005x^2 + 2} - 50, \, 0 < x < 100$

$y' = 300(0.0005x^2 + 2)^{-2}(0.001x)\big|_{x=50} = -1.42$

$y' < 0$ for $0 < x < 100 \Rightarrow y$ is dec. for $0 < x < 100$

$y' = \dfrac{-0.3x}{(0.0005x^2 + 2)^2}$

$y'' = \dfrac{(0.0005x^2 + 2)^2(-0.3) + 0.3x(2(0.0005x^2 + 2)^1(0.001x))}{(0.0005x^2 + 2)^4}$

$y'' = 0$ for $x = 37, y(37) = 63$

$y'' < 0$ for $x < 37$; $y'' > 0$ for $x > 37 \Rightarrow x = 37$ is infl.

y is conc. down for $x < 37$ and conc. up for $x > 37$.

$y(0) = 100, y$-intercept

$y = 0 \Rightarrow x = 89, x$-intercept

$L(x) = -1.42(x-50) + y(50) = -1.42x + 71 + 42$
$L(x) = -1.42x + 113$

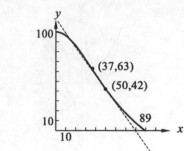

65. $\dfrac{1}{C_T} = \dfrac{1}{C_1} + \dfrac{1}{C_2} = \dfrac{C_1 + C_2}{C_1 C_2}, \quad C_1 + C_2 = 12$

$\hspace{8cm} C_2 = 12 - C_1$

$\dfrac{1}{C_T} = \dfrac{12}{C_1(12 - C_1)} = \dfrac{12}{12C_1 - C_1^2}$

$C_T = C_1 - \dfrac{1}{12}C_1^2$

$\dfrac{dC_T}{dC_1} = 1 - \dfrac{1}{6}C_1 = 0 \Rightarrow C = 6,$ a max. since

$\dfrac{d^2 C_T}{dC_1^2} = -\dfrac{1}{6} < 0.$

Each capacitor is 6 μF.

69. $t = \dfrac{\sqrt{16 + x^2}}{3} + \dfrac{5 - x}{5}$

$\dfrac{dt}{dx} = \dfrac{x}{3\sqrt{16 + x^2}} - \dfrac{1}{5} = 0$

$\hspace{3cm} 5x = 3\sqrt{16 + x^2}$

$\hspace{3cm} 25x^2 = 9(16 + x^2) = 144 + 9x^2$

$\hspace{3cm} 16x^2 = 144$

$\hspace{3cm} x^2 = 9$

$\hspace{3cm} x = 3,$ a min. since

$\dfrac{d^2 t}{dx^2} = \dfrac{16}{3(16 + x^2)^{3/2}}\bigg|_{x=3} > 0$

The boat should land 3 km from P toward A.

73. $V = \dfrac{1}{3}\pi r^2 h = \dfrac{1}{3}\pi r^2 \cdot r = \dfrac{1}{3}\pi r^3$

$\dfrac{dV}{dt} = \pi r^2 \dfrac{dr}{dt}$

$100 = \pi(10.0)^2 \dfrac{dr}{dt}$

$\dfrac{dr}{dt} = 0.318$ ft/min

77.

The amount of plastic used is determined by the surface area $S = 2 \cdot \pi r^2 + 2\pi r \cdot h$. $V = \pi r^2 h = $ constant from which $h = \frac{\text{constant}}{\pi r^2}$.

$$S = 2\pi r^2 + 2\pi r \cdot \frac{\text{constant}}{\pi r^2}$$

$$S(r) = 2\pi r^2 + \frac{2 \cdot \text{constant}}{r}$$

$$\frac{dS}{dr} = 4\pi r - \frac{2 \cdot \text{constant}}{r^2} = 0 \text{ for minimum}$$

$$4\pi r^3 = 2 \cdot \text{constant}$$

$$r^3 = \frac{\text{constant}}{2\pi}$$

$$\frac{h}{r} = \frac{\text{constant}}{\pi \cdot r^3} = \frac{\text{constant}}{\pi \frac{\text{constant}}{2\pi}} = 2$$

The height should be twice the radius to minimize the surface area. In finding the $\frac{h}{r}$ ratio, the constant volume divides out so it is not necessary to specify the volume.

INTEGRATION

25.1 Antiderivatives

1. $f(x) = 12x^3$; power of x required is 4, $F(x) = ax^4$
$F'(x) = 4ax^3 = 12x^3, 4a = 12, a = 3$
$F(x) = 3x^4$

5. $3x^2$; the power of x required in the antiderivative is 3. Therefore, we must multiply by $\frac{1}{3}$. The antiderivative of $3x^2$ is $\frac{1}{3}(3x^3) = x^3$. $a = 1$.

9. The power of x required in the antiderivative of $f(x) = 9\sqrt{x}$ is $\frac{3}{2}$. Multiply by $\frac{2}{3}$. The antiderivative of $9\sqrt{x}$ is $\frac{2}{3} \cdot 9x^{3/2}$. $a = 6$.

13. The power of x required in the antiderivative of $\frac{5}{2}x^{3/2}$ is $\frac{5}{2}$. Multiply by $\frac{2}{5}$. The antiderivative of $\frac{5}{2}x^{3/2}$ is $\frac{2}{5}\left(\frac{5}{2}\right)x^{5/2} = x^{5/2}$.

17. $f(x) = 2x^2 - x$; $2x^2 \to ax^3$; $\frac{d}{dx}(ax^3) = a3x^2$

$3a = 2$; $a = \frac{2}{3}$, therefore $\frac{2}{3}x^3$; $x \to ax^2$;

$\frac{d}{dx}(ax^2) = a2x$

$2a = 1$; $a = \frac{1}{2}$, therefore $\frac{1}{2}x^2$

Antiderivative of $2x^2 - x$ is $\frac{2}{3}x^3 - \frac{1}{2}x^2$.

21. $f(x) = \frac{-7}{x^6}$; $f(x) = -7x^{-6}$; power required is -5, therefore x^{-5};

$\frac{d}{dx}ax^{-5} = -5ax^{-6}$; $-5a = -7$; $a = \frac{7}{5}$, therefore $\frac{7}{5}x^{-5}$

Therefore, antiderivative is $\frac{7}{5x^5}$.

25. The power of x required for the antiderivative of x^2 is 3, so it will be multiplied by $\frac{1}{3}$, the power of x required for $2 = 2x^0$ is 1, and it will be multiplied by 1. The power of x required for x^{-2} is -1, and it will be multiplied by -1. The antiderivative of $x^2 + 2 + x^{-2}$ is $\frac{1}{3}x^3 + 2x - \frac{1}{x}$.

29. The antiderivative requires $(p^2 - 1)^4$. We multiply by $\frac{1}{4}$. Thus, we have $\frac{1}{4}[4(p^2 - 1)^4]$. The derivative of $(p^2 - 1)^4$ is $4(p^2 - 1)^3(2p)$. The antiderivative of $4(p^2 - 1)^3(2p)$ is $(p^2 - 1)^4$.

33. The antiderivative requires $(6x + 1)^{3/2}$. We multiply by $\frac{2}{3}$. Thus we have $\frac{2}{3}\left(\frac{3}{2}\right)(6x + 1)^{3/2}$. The derivative of $(6x + 1)^{3/2}$ is $\frac{3}{2}(6x + 1)^{1/2}(6)$. The antiderivative of $\frac{3}{2}(6x + 1)^{1/2}(6)$ is $(6x + 1)^{3/2}$.

25.2 The Indefinite Integral

1. $\int 8x\,dx = 8\int x^1 dx = 8\frac{x^{1+1}}{1+1} + C = 4x^2 + C$

5. $\int 2x\,dx = 2\int x\,dx$; $u = x$; $du = dx$; $n = 1$
$2\int x\,dx = 2\left(\frac{x^{1+1}}{1+1}\right) + C = x^2 + C$

9. $\int 2x^{3/2}dx$; $u = x$; $du = dx$; $n = \frac{3}{2}$

$\int 2x^{3/2}dx = \frac{2x^{(3/2)+1}}{\frac{3}{2}+1} + C$

$= \frac{2x^{5/2}}{\frac{5}{2}} + C$

$= \frac{4}{5}x^{5/2} + C$

13. $\int (x^2 - x^5)dx = \int x^2 d - x\int x^5 dx$

$= \frac{x^3}{3} - \frac{x^6}{6} + C$

$= \frac{1}{3}x^3 - \frac{1}{6}x^6 + C$

17. $\int \left(\frac{t^2}{2} - \frac{2}{t^2}\right)dt = \frac{t^{2+1}}{2(2+1)} - \frac{2t^{-2+1}}{-2+1} + C$

$= \frac{t^3}{6} + \frac{2}{t} + C$

21. $\int (2x^{-2/3} + 3^{-2})dx = \int 2x^{-2/3}dx + \int 3^{-2}x^0 dx$

$= 2\int x^{-2/3}dx + 3^{-2}\int x^0 dx$

$= 2 + \frac{1}{3}(3x^{1/3}) + 3^{-2}(x^1)$

$= 6x^{1/3} + \frac{1}{9}x + C$

25. $\int (x^2-1)^5(2x\,dx); \; u = x^2-1; \; du = 2x\,dx; \; n = 5$

$$\int (x^2-1)^5(2x\,dx) = \frac{(x^2-1)^6}{6} + C$$

$$= \frac{1}{6}(x^2-1)^6 + C$$

29. $\int (2\theta^5+5)^7\theta^4 d\theta = \frac{1}{10}\int (2\theta^5+5)^7\cdot (10\theta^4)d\theta$

$$= \frac{1}{10}\cdot\frac{(2\theta^5+5)^8}{8} + C$$

$$= \frac{(2\theta^5+5)^8}{80} + C$$

33. $\int \frac{x\,dx}{\sqrt{6x^2+1}} = \int (6x^2+1)^{-1/2}x\,dx$

$u = 6x^2+1; \; du = 12x; \; n = -\dfrac{1}{2}$

$$\int (6x^2+1)^{-1/2}x\,dx = \frac{1}{12}\int (6x^2+1)^{-1/2}(12x\,dx)$$

$$= \frac{1}{12}\frac{(6x^2+1)^{1/2}}{\frac{1}{2}} + C$$

$$= \frac{1}{6}\sqrt{6x^2+1} + C$$

37. $\dfrac{dy}{dx} = 6x^2; \; dy = 6x^2 dx$

$$y = \int 6x^2 dx = 6\int x^2 dx = \frac{6x^3}{3} + C = 2x^3 + C$$

The curve passes through $(0,2)$. $2 = 2(0^3) + C$, $C = 2; \; y = 2x^3 + 2$

41. $\int 3x^2 dx = x^3 + C$

$\int 3x^2 dx \neq x^3$ since the constant of integration must be included.

45. $\int 3(2x+1)^2 dx = \frac{3}{2}\int (2x+1)^2(2\,dx)$

$$= \frac{3}{2}\frac{(2x+1)^3}{3} + C$$

$$= \frac{(2x+1)^3}{3} + C.$$

$\int 3(2x+1)^2 dx \neq (2x+1)^3 + C$ because the factor of $\frac{1}{2}$ is missing.

49. $\dfrac{di}{dt} = 4t - 0.6t^2; \; di = (4t - 0.6t^2)dt$

$$i = \int (4t - 0.6t^2)dt = 2t^2 - 0.2t^3 + C$$

$i = 2A$ when $t = 0$ s; $2 = 2(0)^2 - 0.2(0)^3 + C$; $C = 2$
$i = 2t^2 - 0.2t^3 + 2$

53. $\dfrac{df}{dA} = \dfrac{0.005}{\sqrt{0.01A+1}} = 0.005(0.01A+1)^{-1/2}$

$f(A) = \int 0.005(0.01A+1)^{-1/2}dA + C$

$$= \frac{1}{2}\int (0.01A+1)^{-1/2}(0.01\,dA)$$

$$= (0.01A+1)^{1/2} + C$$

$f = 0$ for $A = 0$ m^2
$f(0) = 0 = (0.01(0)+1)^{1/2} + C; \; C = -1$
$f(A) = (0.01A+1)^{1/2} - 1 = \sqrt{0.01A+1} - 1$

25.3   The Area Under a Curve

1. (a)

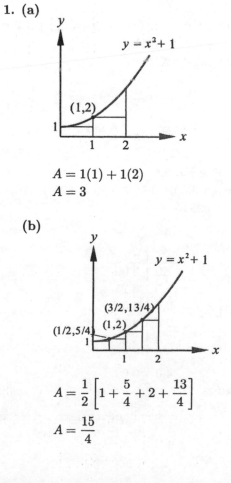

$A = 1(1) + 1(2)$
$A = 3$

(b)

$A = \dfrac{1}{2}\left[1 + \dfrac{5}{4} + 2 + \dfrac{13}{4}\right]$

$A = \dfrac{15}{4}$

5. $y = 3x$, between $x = 0$ and $x = 3$

(b) $n = 10, \Delta x = 0.3$
$$A = 0.3(3.00 + 3.51 + 3.84 + 3.96 + 3.75$$
$$+ 3.36 + 2.79 + 2.04 + 1.11)$$
$$A = 8.208$$

(a)

x	y
1	3
2	6
3	9

$n = 3$
$\Delta x = 1$

$A = 1(0 + 3 + 6) = 9$; (first rectangle has 0 height)

(b)

x	y
0	0
0.3	0.9
0.6	1.8
0.9	2.7
1.2	3.6
1.5	4.5
1.8	5.4
2.1	6.3
2.4	7.2
2.7	8.1
3.0	9.0

$n = 10$
$\Delta x = 0.3$

$$A = 0.3(0 + 0.9 + 1.8 + 2.7 + 3.6 + 4.5 + 5.4$$
$$+ 6.3 + 7.2 + 8.1)$$
$$= 0.3(40.5) = 12.15$$

9. $y = 4x - x^2$, between $x = 1$ and $x = 4$

(a) $n = 6, \Delta x = 0.5$
$$A = 0.5(3.00 + 3.75 + 3.75 + 3.00 + 1.75 + 0.00)$$
$$A = 7.625$$

x	y
1.0	3.00
1.5	3.75
2.0	4.00
2.5	3.75
3.0	3.00
3.5	1.75
4.0	0.00

($y = 4.00$ is not the height of any inscribed rectangle)

x	y
1.0	3.00
1.3	3.51
1.6	3.84
1.9	3.99
2.2	3.96
2.5	3.75
2.8	3.36
3.1	2.79
3.4	2.04
3.7	1.11
4.0	0.00

($y = 3.99$ is not the height of any inscribed rectangle)

13. $y = \dfrac{1}{\sqrt{x+1}}$, between $x = 3$ and $x = 8$

(a) $n = 5, \Delta x = \dfrac{8 - 3}{5} = 1$

$$A = \sum_{i=1}^{5} A_i = \sum_{i=1}^{5} y_i \Delta x$$

$y_1 = f(4)$
$$A = (0.447 + 0.408 + \cdots + 0.354 + 0.333)(1)$$
$$A = 1.92$$

x	y
3	0.5
4	0.447
5	0.408
6	0.378
7	0.355
8	0.333

(b) $n = 10$, $\Delta x = \dfrac{8-3}{10} = 0.5$

$$A = \sum_{i=1}^{10} A_i = \sum_{i=1}^{10} y_i \Delta x$$

$y_1 = f(3.5)$
$A = (0.471 + 0.447 + \cdots + 0.343 + 0.333)(0.5)$
$A = 1.96$

x	y
3	0.5
3.5	0.471
4	0.447
4.5	0.426
5	0.408
5.5	0.392
6	0.378
6.5	0.365
7	0.354
7.5	0.343
8	0.333

17. $y = x^2$, between $x = 0$ and $x = 2$

$$A_{0,2} = \left[\int x^2 dx \right]_0^2 = \frac{x^3}{3} \Big|_0^2 = \frac{8}{3} - 0 = \frac{8}{3}$$

21. $y - \dfrac{1}{x^2} = x^{-2}$, between $x = 1$ and $x = 5$

$$A_{1.5} = \left[\int x^{-2} dx \right]_1^5 = \frac{x^{-1}}{-1} \Big|_1^5 = \frac{-1}{x} \Big|_1^5$$

$$= -\frac{1}{5} - (-1) = \frac{4}{5} = 0.8$$

25. $y = 3x$, $x = 0$ to $x = 3$, $n = 10$, $\Delta x = 0.3$
Using the table in 5(b)

$$A = 0.3(0.9 + 1.8 + 2.7 + 3.6 + 4.5 + 5.4 + 6.3$$
$$+ 7.2 + 8.1 + 9.0)$$
$$A = 14.85$$

$A_{\text{inscribed}}$	$<$	A_{exact}	$<$	$A_{\text{circumscribed}}$
12.15	$<$	13.5	$<$	14.85

$\dfrac{12.15 + 14.85}{2} = 13.5$ because the extra area above
$y = 3x$ using circumscribed rectangles is the same
as the omitted area under $y = 3x$ using inscribed
rectangles.

25.4   The Definite Integral

1. $\displaystyle\int_1^4 (x^{-2} - 1)dx = -\frac{1}{x} - x \Big|_1^4$

$$= -\frac{1}{4} - 4 - \left(-\frac{1}{1} - 1 \right)$$

$$\int_1^4 (x^{-2} - 1)dx = -\frac{9}{4}$$

5. $\displaystyle\int_1^4 x^{5/2}dx = \frac{2}{7}x^{7/2} \Big|_1^4 = \frac{256}{7} - \frac{2}{7} = \frac{254}{7}$

9. $u = 1 - x$; $du = -dx$

$$\int_{-1.6}^{0.7} (1-x)^{1/3}dx = -\int_{-1.6}^{0.7} (1-x)^{1/3}(-dx)$$

$$= -\frac{3}{4}(1-x)^{4/3} \Big|_{-1.6}^{0.7}$$

$$= -\frac{3}{4}(0.2008 - 3.5752)$$

$$= 2.53$$

13. $\displaystyle\int_{0.5}^{2.2} (\sqrt[3]{x} - 2)dx = \int_{0.5}^{2.2} x^{1/3}dx - 2\int_{0.5}^{2.2} dx$

$$= \left(\frac{3}{4}x^{4/3} - 2x \right) \Big|_{0.5}^{2.2}$$

$$= (2.1460 - 4.4) - (0.2976 - 1)$$
$$= -1.5516 = -1.552$$

17. $u = 4 - x^2$; $du = -2x\,dx$

$$\int_{-2}^{-1} 2x(4 - x^2)^3dx = -\int_{-2}^{-1} (11 - x^2)^3(-2x\,dx)$$

$$= -\frac{(4 - x^2)^4}{4} \Big|_{-2}^{-1} = -\left(\frac{81}{4} - 0 \right)$$

$$= -\frac{81}{4}$$

21. $u = 6x + 1$; $du = 6\,dx$

$$\int_{2.75}^{3.25} \frac{dx}{\sqrt[3]{6x + 1}} = \int (6x + 1)^{-1/3}dx$$

$$= \frac{1}{6} \int (6x + 1)^{-1/3}(6\,dx)$$

$$= \frac{1}{6} \cdot \frac{3}{2}(6x + 1)^{2/3} \Big|_{2.75}^{3.25}$$

$$= \frac{1}{4}(6x + 1)^{2/3} \Big|_{2.75}^{3.25}$$

$$= \frac{1}{4}(7.4904 - 6.7405) = 0.1875$$

25. $u = 4t + 1; \, du = 4 \, dt$

$$\int_3^7 \sqrt{16t^2 + 8t + 1} \, dt = \int_3^7 \sqrt{(4t+1)^2} \, dt$$

$$= \int_3^7 \sqrt{(4t+1)} \, dt$$

$$= \frac{1}{4} \int_3^7 (4t+1)^1 4 \, dt$$

$$= \frac{1}{4} \frac{(4t+1)^2}{2}$$

$$= \frac{1}{8}(4t+1)^2 \Big|_3^7 = 84$$

29. $u = x^3 + 9x + 6; \, du = (3x^2 + 9)dx = 3(x^2 + 3)dx$

$$\int_0^1 (x^2+3)(x^3+9x+6)^2 \, dx$$

$$= \frac{1}{3} \int_0^1 (x^3+9x+6)^2(x^2+3)dx$$

$$= \frac{1}{3} \frac{(x^3+9x+6)^3}{3} = \frac{1}{9}(x^3+9x+6)^3 \Big|_0^1$$

$$= \frac{1}{9}(16^3 - 6^3) = \frac{3880}{9}$$

33. $\displaystyle\int_{\sqrt{5}}^3 2z \sqrt[4]{z^4 + 8z^2 + 16} \, dz$

$$= \int_{\sqrt{5}}^3 2z((z^2+4)^2)^{1/4} dz$$

$$= \int_{\sqrt{5}}^3 2z(z^2+4)^{1/2} dz$$

$$= \frac{2}{3}(z^2+4)^{3/2} \Big|_{\sqrt{5}}^3$$

$$= 13.25$$

37. Given that $\displaystyle\int_0^9 \sqrt{x} \, dx = 18,$

$$\int_0^9 2\sqrt{t} \, dt = 2 \int_0^9 \sqrt{x} \, dx = 2(18) = 36.$$

41. $u = 3x + 9; \, du = 3 \, dx$

$$A = 4\pi \int_0^2 \sqrt{3x+9} \, dx = 4\pi \cdot \frac{1}{3} \int_0^2 (3x+9)^{1/2} 3 \, dx$$

$$= \frac{4\pi}{3} \cdot \frac{2}{3}(3x+9)^{3/2} \Big|_0^2 = \frac{8\pi}{9}(3x+9)^{3/2} \Big|_0^2$$

$$= 86.8 \text{ m}^2$$

25.5 Numerical Integration: The Trapezoidal Rule

1. $\displaystyle\int_1^3 \frac{1}{x} dx, n = 2, h = \frac{b-a}{n} = \frac{3-1}{2} = 1$

x	y
1	1
2	$\frac{1}{2}$
3	$\frac{1}{3}$

$$A = \frac{1}{2}\left(1 + 2\left(\frac{1}{2}\right) + \frac{1}{3}\right) = \frac{7}{6}$$

5. $\displaystyle\int_1^4 (1 + \sqrt{x})dx; \, n = 6; \, h = \frac{4-1}{6} = \frac{1}{2}; \frac{h}{2} = \frac{1}{4}$

n	x_n	y_n
0	1	2
1	1.5	2.22
2	2	2.41
3	2.5	2.58
4	3	2.73
5	3.5	2.87
6	4	3

$$A_T = \frac{1}{4}[2 + 2(2.22) + 2(2.41) + 2(2.58)$$
$$+ 2(2.73) + 2(2.87) + 3]$$

$$A = \frac{1}{4}(30.646) = 7.661$$

$$A = \int_1^4 (1 + x^{1/2})dx = \left(x + \frac{2}{3}x^{3/2}\right)\Big|_1^4$$

$$A = 4 + \frac{16}{3} - \left(1 + \frac{2}{3}\right) = \frac{23}{3} = 7.667$$

9. $\int_0^5 \sqrt{25 - x^2} dx$; $n = 5$; $x = \dfrac{5}{5} = 1$; $\dfrac{h}{2} = \dfrac{1}{2}$

n	x_n	y_n
0	0	5
1	1	4.90
2	2	4.58
3	3	4
4	4	3
5	5	0

$$A_T = \frac{1}{2}[5 + 2(4.90) + 2(4.58) + 2(4) + 2(3) + 0]$$
$$= 18.98$$

13. $\int_0^4 2^x dx$; $n = 12$; $h = \dfrac{4}{12} = \dfrac{1}{3}$; $\dfrac{h}{2} = \dfrac{1}{6}$

x	y
0	1
$\frac{1}{3}$	1.260
$\frac{2}{3}$	1.587
1	2
$1\frac{1}{3}$	2.520
$1\frac{2}{3}$	3.175
2	4
$2\frac{1}{3}$	5.040
$2\frac{2}{3}$	6.350
3	8
$3\frac{1}{3}$	10.080
$3\frac{2}{3}$	12.699
4	16

$$A = \frac{1}{6}[1 + 2(1.260 + 2(1.587) + 2(2) + 2(2.520)$$
$$+ 2(3.175) + 2(4) + 2(5.040) + 2(6.350)$$
$$+ 2(8) + 2(10.080) + 2(12.699) + 16]$$
$$A = 21.74$$

17. The approximate value is less than the exact value because the tops of all the trapezoids are below the curve.

25.6 Simpson's Rule

1. $\int_0^1 \dfrac{dx}{x + 2}$, $n = 2$, $h = \dfrac{1 - 0}{2} = \dfrac{1}{2}$

x	y
0	$\frac{1}{2}$
$\frac{1}{2}$	$\frac{2}{5}$
1	$\frac{1}{3}$

$$\int_0^1 \frac{dx}{x + 2} = \frac{\frac{1}{2}}{3}\left(\frac{1}{2} + 4\left(\frac{2}{5}\right) + \frac{1}{3}\right) = 0.40\overline{5}$$

5. $\int_1^4 (2x + \sqrt{x})dx$; $n = 6$; $\Delta x = \dfrac{4 - 1}{6} = \dfrac{1}{2}$;

$$\frac{\Delta x}{3} = \frac{1}{6}$$

$$A_S = \frac{1}{6}[3 + 4(4.22) + 2(5.41) + 4(6.58)$$
$$+ 2(7.73) + 4(8.87) + 10]$$
$$A_S = \frac{1}{6}(117.999) = 19.67$$

n	x_n	y_n
1	1	3
2	1.5	4.22
3	2	5.41
4	2.5	6.58
5	3	7.73
6	3.5	8.87
7	4	10

$$A = \int_1^4 (2x + \sqrt{x})dx = 2\int_1^4 x\, dx + \int x^{1/2}dx$$
$$= \left(x^2 + \frac{2}{3}x^{3/2}\right)\Big|_1^4 = 16 + \frac{16}{3} + -\left(1 + \frac{2}{3}\right)$$
$$= \frac{59}{3} = 19.67$$

9. $\int_1^5 \dfrac{dx}{x^2 + x}$; $n = 10$; $\Delta x = 0.4$; $\dfrac{\Delta x}{3} = \dfrac{0.4}{3}$

$$A_s = \frac{0.4}{3}[0.5000 + 4(0.2976) + 2(0.1984)$$
$$+ 4(0.1420) + 2(0.1068) + 4(0.0833)$$
$$+ 2(0.0668) + 4(0.0548) + 2(0.0458)$$
$$+ 4(0.0388) + 0.0333]$$

$$= \frac{0.4}{3}(3.8349) = 0.5114$$

13. $\Delta x = 2; \dfrac{\Delta x}{3} = \dfrac{2}{3}$

x	y
2	0.67
4	2.34
6	4.56
8	3.67
10	3.56
12	4.78
14	6.87

$$\int_2^{14} y\,dx = \frac{2}{3}[0.67 + 4(2.34) + 2(4.56) + 4(3.67) + 2(3.56) + 4(4.78) + 6.87] = 44.63$$

Chapter 25 Review Exercises

1. $\displaystyle \int (4x^3 - x)\,dx = \int 4x^3\,dx - \int x\,dx = \frac{4x^4}{4} - \frac{x^2}{2} + C = x^4 - \frac{1}{2}x^2 + C$

5. $\displaystyle \int_1^4 \left(\frac{\sqrt{x}}{2} + \frac{2}{\sqrt{x}} \right) dx = \frac{1}{2}\int_1^4 x^{1/2}\,dx + 2\int_1^4 x^{-1/2}\,dx = \frac{1}{2}\frac{x^{3/2}}{\frac{3}{2}} + \frac{2x^{1/2}}{\frac{1}{2}}\Big|_1^4 = \frac{1}{3}x^{3/2} + 4x^{1/2}\Big|_1^4$

$$= \left[\frac{1}{3}(4)^{3/2} + 4(4)^{1/2} \right] - \left[\frac{1}{3}(1)^{3/2} + 4(1)^{1/2} \right] = \frac{19}{3}$$

9. $\displaystyle \int \left(3 + \frac{2}{x^3} \right) dx = \int 3\,dx + \int \frac{2}{x^3}\,dx = \int 3\,dx + \int 2x^{-3}\,dx = (3x) + \left(-\frac{2}{2}x^{-2} \right) = 3x - x^{-2} = 3x - \frac{1}{x^2} + C$

13. $\displaystyle \int \frac{dn}{(2 - 5n)^3} = \int (2 - 5n)^{-3}\,dn$

$$-\frac{1}{5}\int (2 - 5n)^{-3}(-5\,dn) = -\frac{1}{5} \times \frac{(2 - 5n)^{-2}}{-2} + C = \frac{1}{10} \times \frac{1}{(2 - 5n)^2} + C = \frac{1}{10(2 - 5n)^2} + C$$

17. $\displaystyle \int_0^2 \frac{3x\,dx}{\sqrt[3]{1 + 2x^2}} = \int_0^2 (1 + 2x^2)^{-1/3}(3x)\,dx$

$u = 1 + 2x^2; \ du = 4x\,dx; \ n = -\dfrac{1}{3}$

$$\frac{3}{4}\int_0^2 (1 + 2x^2)^{-1/3}(4x)\,dx = \frac{3}{4} \times \frac{(1 + 2x^2)^{2/3}}{\frac{2}{3}}\Big|_0^2 = \frac{9}{8}(1 + 2x^2)^{2/3}\Big|_0^2 = \frac{9}{8}[1 + 2(2^2)]^{2/3} - \frac{9}{8}[1 + 2(0)^2]^{2/3}$$

$$= \frac{9}{8}(9)^{2/3} - \frac{9}{8}(1)^{2/3} = \frac{9}{8}(\sqrt[3]{81} - 1) = \frac{9}{8}(3\sqrt[3]{3} - 1)$$

21. $\displaystyle \int \frac{(2 - 3x^2)\,dx}{(2x - x^3)^2} = \int (2x - x^3)^{-2}(2 - 3x^2)\,dx;$

$u = 2x - x^3; \ du = 2 - 3x^2; \ n = -2$

$$\int (2x - x^3)^{-2}(2 - 3x^2)\,dx = \frac{(2x - x^3)^{-1}}{-1} + C = -\frac{1}{(2x - x^3)} + C$$

25. $\dfrac{dy}{dx} = 3 - x^2, (-1, 3)$

$$y = 3x - \dfrac{x^3}{3} + C$$

$$3 = 3(-1) - \dfrac{(-1)^3}{3} + C$$

$$C = \dfrac{17}{3}$$

$$y = 3x - \dfrac{x^3}{3} + \dfrac{17}{3}$$

29. $\quad\displaystyle\int_0^1 x^3 dx = \dfrac{x^4}{4}\bigg|_0^1 = \dfrac{1}{4}$

$$\int_1^2 (x-1)^3 dx = \dfrac{(x-1)^4}{4}\bigg|_1^2 = \dfrac{(2-1)^4}{4} - \dfrac{(1-1)^4}{4} = \dfrac{1}{4}$$

which shows $\displaystyle\int_0^1 x^3 dx = \int_1^2 (x-1)^3 dx$

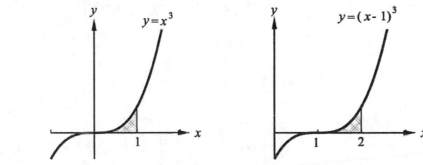

$y = (x-1)^3$ is $y = x^3$ shifted right one unit, so the areas are the same.

33. Since $f(x) > 0$, the graph is above x-axis.
Since $f''(x) < 0$, for $a \le x < b$, f is concave down for $a \le x \le b$.
The exact value of

$$\int_a^b f(x)dx > A_{\text{trapezoid}}$$

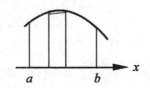

because the tops of trapezoids are all below the curve.

37. $h = \dfrac{3-1}{4} = \dfrac{1}{2}; \ x_0 = 1, x_1 = 1.5, x_2 = 2, x_3 = 2.5, x_4 = 3.0$

$$\int_1^3 \dfrac{dx}{2x-1} \approx \dfrac{h}{3}[y_0 + 4y_1 + 2y_2 + 4y_3 + y_4] \approx \dfrac{\frac{1}{2}}{3}\left[\dfrac{1}{2.1-1} + \dfrac{4}{2(1.5)-1} + \dfrac{2}{2(2)-1} + \dfrac{4}{2(2.5)-1} + \dfrac{1}{2(3)-1}\right]$$

$$\approx \dfrac{73}{90} = 0.811$$

41. $y = x\sqrt[3]{2x^2 + 1}, a = 1, b = 4, n = 3.$

$$h = \frac{b-a}{n} = \frac{4-1}{3} = 1$$

$$x_0 = 1, y_0 = 1\sqrt[3]{2 \cdot 1^2 + 1} = \sqrt[3]{3}$$
$$x_1 = 2, y_1 = 2\sqrt[3]{2 \cdot 2^2 + 1} = 2\sqrt[3]{9}$$
$$x_3 = 3, y_2 = 3\sqrt[3]{2 \cdot 3^2 + 1} = 3\sqrt[3]{19}$$
$$x_3 = 4, y_3 = 4\sqrt[3]{2 \cdot 4^2 + 1} = 4\sqrt[3]{33}$$

$$\int_1^4 x\sqrt[3]{2x^2 + 1}\,dx \approx \frac{h}{2}[y_0 + 2y_1 + 2y_2 + y_3] \approx \frac{1}{2}[\sqrt[3]{3} + 4\sqrt[3]{9} + 6\sqrt[3]{19} + 4\sqrt[3]{33}] \approx 19.30156604$$

45. $y(x) = 4 + \sqrt{1 + 8x - 2x^2}.$

$$A = \frac{1}{2}\left[y(0) + y\left(\frac{1}{2}\right) + y(1) + y\left(\frac{3}{2}\right) + y(2)\left(\frac{5}{2}\right) + y(3) + y\left(\frac{7}{2}\right) + y(4)\right]$$
$$A = 24.68 \text{ m}^2$$

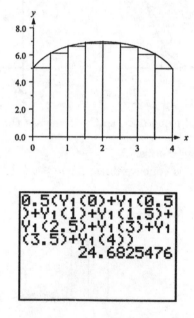

49. $\dfrac{dy}{dx} = k(2L^3 - 12Lx + 2x^4)$
$dy = k(2L^3x^0 - 12Lx + 2x^4)\,dx$

$$y = \int k(2L^3x^0 - 12Lx + 2x^4)\,dx = k\int(2L^3x^0 - 12Lx + 2x^4)\,dx = k\left(2L^3x^0 - \frac{12Lx}{2} + \frac{2x^5}{5}\right) + C$$

$y = 0$ for $x = 0$; $0 = k(0 - 0 + 0) + C$

$C = 0$; $y = k\left(2L^3x - 6Lx^2 + \dfrac{2}{5}x^5\right)$

53. The area of a quarter circle is $\frac{1}{4} \cdot \pi r^2$, thus $\pi = \frac{4 \cdot A}{r^2}$. The area of a quarter circle of radius one may be found from $\int_0^1 \sqrt{1-x^2}\,dx$. This may be evaluated using rectangles.

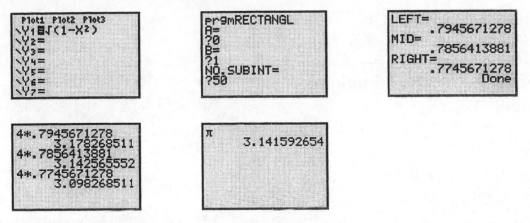

Multiplying each of these values by four gives an approximation for π. Increasing the number of subintervals will increase the accuracy of the approximation.

Chapter 26

APPLICATIONS OF INTEGRATION

26.1 Applications of the Indefinite Integral

1. $s = \displaystyle\int (v_0 - 32t)dt = v_0 t - 16t^2 + C$
$200 = v_0(0) - 16(0)^2 + C$
$200 = C$
$\quad s = v_0 t - 16t^2 + 200$
$\quad 0 = v_0(2.5) - 16(2.5)^2 + 200$
$\quad v_0 = -40 \text{ ft/s}$

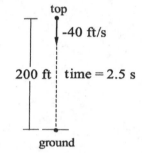

5. $\dfrac{ds}{dt} = -0.25 \text{ m/s}$

$ds = -0.25\,dt$
$s = -0.25 \int dt = -0.25t + C_1$
$t = 0, s = 8; \text{ therefore, } C_1 = 8$
$s = -0.25t + 8.00 = 8.00 - 0.25t$

9. At impact: $t = 0, a = -250 \text{ m/s}^2$,
$v_{\text{impact}} = 96 \text{ km/h} = 26.\overline{6} \text{ m/s}, s_{\text{impact}} = 0$

At stop: $t = t_{\text{stop}}, v = 0, s = 1.4 \text{ m}$
$a = -250$
$v = -250t + v_{\text{impact}} = -250t + 26.\overline{6}$
$s = -125t^2 + 26.\overline{6}t + s_{\text{impact}}, s_{\text{impact}} = 0$
$s = -125t^2 + 26.\overline{6}t$
$v = 0 = -250t_{\text{stop}} + 26.\overline{6}, t_{\text{stop}} = 0.10\overline{6}$
$s = -125(0.10\overline{6})^2 + 26.\overline{6} = 1.4 \text{ m}$

13. $v = \int -32\,dt = -32t + C; v = v_0; t = 0,$
$C = v_0; v = -32t + v_0;$

$s = \int (-32t + v_0)\,dt = -16t^2 + v_0 t + C_1$

$s = 0, t = 0; C_1 = 0; s = -16t^2 + v_0);$
$s = 90 \text{ ft when } v = 0$

$90 = -16t^2 + v_0 t; 0 = -32t + v_0; t = \dfrac{v_0}{32};$

$90 = -16\left(\dfrac{v_0}{32}\right)^2 + v_0\left(\dfrac{v_0}{32}\right); \dfrac{v_0^2}{64} = 90$

$v_0 = \sqrt{64(90)} = 76 \text{ ft/s}$

17. $q = \int i\,dt = \int 0.230 \times 10^{-6}dt = 0.230 \times 10^{-6}t + C;$

$q = 0, t = 0; C = 0; q = 0.230 \times 10^{-6}t$

Find q for $t = 1.50 \times 10^{-3}s$:

$q = 0.230 \times 10^{-6}(1.50 \times 10^{-3})$
$\quad = 0.345 \times 10^{-9} = 0.345 \text{ nC}$

21. $V_c = \dfrac{1}{C}\displaystyle\int i\,dt = \dfrac{1}{2.5 \times 10^{-6}}\int 0.025\,dt$

$\quad = \dfrac{1}{2.5 \times 10^{-6}}(0.025)t = 1.0 \times 10^4 t + C$

$v_c = 0, t = 0; C = 0; v_c = 1.0 \times 10^4 t$

Find v_c for $t = 0.012 \text{ s}: v_c = 1.0 \times 10^4(0.012)$
$\quad\quad\quad\quad\quad\quad = 120 \text{ V}$

25. $\omega = \dfrac{d\theta}{dt} = 16t + 0.5t^2; d\theta = (16t + 0.50t^2)\,dt$

$\theta = 8t^2 + \dfrac{0.50t^3}{3} + C; \theta = 0, t = 0; C = 0;$

$\theta = 8t^2 + \dfrac{0.50t^3}{3}; \text{ find } \theta \text{ for } t = 10.0 \text{ s}$

$\theta = 8(10.0)^2 + \dfrac{0.50}{3}(10.0)^3 = 970 \text{ rad}$

29. $\dfrac{dV}{dx} = \dfrac{-k}{x^2}; V = -\displaystyle\int \dfrac{k}{x^2}\,dx = kx^{-1} + C = \dfrac{k}{x} + C$

$\displaystyle\lim_{V \to 0} V = \lim_{x \to \infty} \dfrac{k}{x} + C; 0 = 0 + C; C = 0;$

therefore, $V|_{x=x_1} = \dfrac{k}{x_1}$

26.2   Areas by Integration

1. $A = \displaystyle\int_1^3 y\,dx = \int_1^3 2x^2\,dx$

$\quad = \dfrac{2x^3}{3}\Big|_1^3$

$A = \dfrac{2(3)^3}{3} - \dfrac{2(1)^3}{3}$

$A = \dfrac{52}{3}$

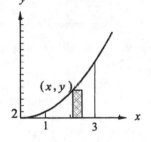

5. $y = 6 - 4x;\ x = 0, y = 0, y = 3$

$y - 6 = -4x,\ x = -\dfrac{1}{4}y + \dfrac{3}{2}$

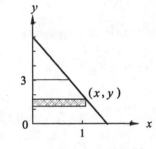

$A = \displaystyle\int_0^3 x\,dy = \int_0^3 \left(-\dfrac{1}{4}y + \dfrac{3}{2}\right)dy$

$\quad = -\dfrac{1}{8}y^2 + \dfrac{3}{2}y\,\Big|_0^3$

$\quad = -\dfrac{1}{8}(3)^2 + \dfrac{3}{2}(3) + \dfrac{1}{8}(0)^2 - \dfrac{3}{2}(0)$

$\quad = -\dfrac{9}{8} + \dfrac{9}{2} = -\dfrac{9}{8} + \dfrac{36}{8} = \dfrac{27}{8}$

9. $y = x^{-2};\ y = 0, x = 2, x = 3$

$A = \displaystyle\int_2^3 x^{-2}\,dy = -x^{-1}\Big|_2^3 = -\dfrac{1}{x}\Big|_2^3$

$\quad = -\dfrac{1}{3} - \left(-\dfrac{1}{2}\right) = \dfrac{1}{6}$

13. $y = \dfrac{2}{\sqrt{x}};\ x = 0, y = 1, y = 4$

$\sqrt{x} = \dfrac{2}{y};\ x = \dfrac{4}{y^2}$

$A = \displaystyle\int_1^4 x\,dy;\ A = 4\int_1^4 y^{-2}\,dy = -4y^{-1}\Big|_1^4$

$\quad = -\dfrac{4}{y}\Big|_1^4 = -\dfrac{4}{4} - \left(-\dfrac{4}{1}\right)$

$\quad = -1 + 4 = 3$

17. $A = \displaystyle\int_0^4 (0 - (x - 2\sqrt{x}))\,dx$

$A = -\dfrac{x^2}{2} + \dfrac{2x^{3/2}}{\frac{3}{2}}\,\Big|_0^4$

$A = \dfrac{8}{3}$

21. $y_1 = x^4 - 8x^2 + 16, y_2 = 16 - x^4$

$y_1 = (x^2 - 4)^2$

$y_2 = (4 - x^2)(4 + x^2)$

$dA = l\,dx; l = y_2 - y_1$

$l = 16 - x^4 - x^4 + 8x^2 - 16$

$\quad = 8x^2 - 2x^4$

$A = 2 \int_0^2 (8x^2 - 2x^4)dx = 2\left(\frac{8}{3}x^3 - \frac{2}{5}x^5\right)\Big|_0^2$

$\quad = \frac{256}{15}$

We could integrate from $x = -2$ to $x = 2$ or do as above because of symmetry with respect to y-axis.

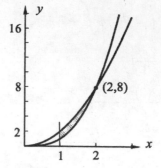

25. $y = x^5; x = -1, x = 2, y = 0$

$A_T = A_{((-1 \to 0)} + A_{(0 \to 2)}$

$\quad = \text{negative} + \text{positive}$

$\quad = -\left(A\Big|_{-1}^0\right) + A\Big|_0^2$

$l = y$

$A = -\int_{-1}^0 y\,dx + \int_0^2 y\,dx$

$\quad = -\int_{-1}^0 x^5 dx + \int_0^2 x^5 dx = -\frac{x^6}{6}\Big|_{-1}^0 + \frac{x^6}{6}\Big|_0^2$

$\quad = 0 - \left(-\frac{1}{6}\right) + \frac{64}{6} - 0 = \frac{65}{6}$

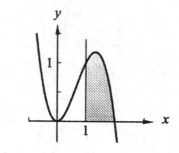

29. $\int_1^2 (2x^2 - x^3)dx = $ area bounded by $x = 1$, $y = 2x^2$, and $y = x^3$, the shaded area shown below.

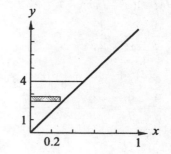

$\int_1^2 (2x^2 - x^3)dx = $ area bounded by $x = 1, y = 0$, and $y = 2x^2 - x^3$, the shaded area shown below.

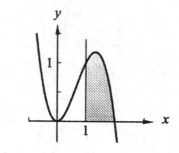

33. $y = 8x; x = 0, y = 4$

(a) Using horizontal elements,

$dA = x\,dy, y = 8x, x = \frac{1}{8}y$

$A = \int_0^4 x\,dy = \frac{1}{8}\int_0^4 y\,dy = \frac{1}{8}\cdot\frac{y^2}{2}\Big|_0^4$

$\quad = \frac{1}{16}y^2\Big|_0^4 = 1 - 0 = 1$

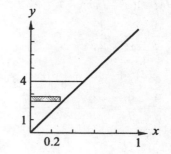

(b) Using vertical elements,

$$A = \int_0^{1/2} (4 - 8x)\, dx = 4x - 4x^2 \Big|_0^{1/2} = 1$$

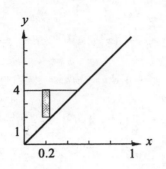

37. $dw = p\, dt;\ p = 12t - 4t^2$

$$w = \int_0^3 (12t - 4t^2)\, dt = 6t^2 - \frac{4}{3}t^3 \Big|_0^3$$

$$= 6(3)^2 - \frac{4}{3}(3)^3 - 0 = 54 - 36 = 18.0 \text{ J}$$

41. $y = x^3 - 2x^2 - x + 2$ and $y = x^2 - 1$

Find the points of intersection:

$$x^3 - 2x^2 - x + 2 = x^2 - 1$$

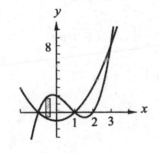

$$x^3 - 3x^2 - x + 3 = 0;\ (x^2 - 1)(x - 3) = 0$$
$$x^2 = 1;\ x = 3;\ x = \pm 1$$

$$A_1 = \int_{-1}^1 [(x^3 - 2x^2 - x + 2) - (x^2 - 1)]\, dx$$

$$= \int_{-1}^1 (x^3 - 3x^2 - x + 3)\, dx$$

$$= \frac{1}{4}x^4 - x^3 - \frac{1}{2}x^2 + 3x \Big|_{-1}^1$$

$$= \left(\frac{1}{4} - 1 - \frac{1}{2} + 3 \right) - \left(\frac{1}{4} + 1 - \frac{1}{2} - 3 \right)$$

$$= 4 \text{ cm}^2$$

26.3   Volumes by Integration

1. $y = x^3, x = 2, y = 0$ about x-axis.

$$V = \int_0^2 \pi y^2 dx = \pi \int_0^2 (x^3)^2 dx$$

$$V = \pi \frac{x^7}{7} \Big|_0^2 = \frac{128\pi}{7}$$

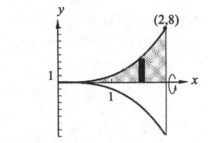

5. $V = \int_0^2 2\pi x(2 - x)\, dx = \frac{8\pi}{3}$

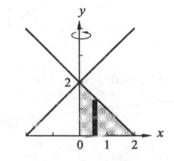

9. $y = 3\sqrt{x}, y = 0, x = 4$
Disk: $dV = \pi y^2 dx$

$$V = \pi \int_0^4 y^2 dx = \int_0^4 9x\, dx$$

$$= \pi \left(\frac{9}{2}x^2 \right) \Big|_0^4$$

$$= \pi \left[\frac{9}{2}(4)^2 - 0 \right] = 72\pi$$

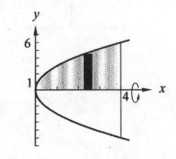

13. $y = x^2 + 1, x = 0, , x = 3, y = 0$
Disk: $dV = \pi y^2 dx$

$$V = \pi \int_0^3 (x^2 + 1)^2 dx$$

$$= \pi \int_0^3 (x^4 + 2x^2 + 1)dx$$

$$= \pi \left(\frac{1}{5}x^5 + \frac{2}{3}x^3 + x \right) \Big|_0^3$$

$$= \pi \left[\frac{1}{5}(3)^5 + \frac{2}{3}(3)^3 + 3 - 0 \right]$$

$$= \frac{348}{5}\pi$$

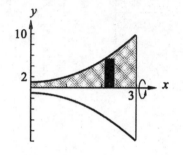

21. $x^2 - 4y^2 = 4, x = 3, h = 2y$
Shell: $dV = 2\pi x(2y)dx$

$$V = 4\pi \int_2^3 x\sqrt{\frac{x^2 - 4}{4}}dx$$

$$= \frac{2\pi}{2} \int_2^3 (x^2 - 4)^{1/2} 2x\, dx$$

$u = x^2 - 4, du = 2x\, dx$

$$V = \pi \cdot \frac{2}{3}(x^2 - 4)^{3/2} \Big|_2^3 = \frac{2\pi}{3}(5^{3/2}) - 0$$

$$= \frac{10\sqrt{5}}{3}\pi$$

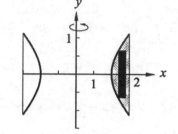

17. $y = x^{1/3}, x = 0, y = 2$
$x = y^3; x^2 = y^6$
Disk: $dV = \pi x^2 dy$

$$V = \pi \int_0^2 y^6 dy$$

$$= \frac{\pi}{7}y^7 \Big|_0^2 = \frac{128\pi}{7}$$

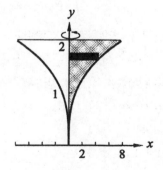

25. $y = \sqrt{4 - x^2}$, Quad I
Shell: $dV = 2\pi xy\, dx$

$$V = 2\pi \int_0^2 x\sqrt{4 - x^2}dx$$

$u = 4 - x^2, du = -2x\, dx$

$$V = -\pi \int_0^2 (4 - x^2)^{1/2}(-2x\, dx)$$

$$= -\pi \frac{2}{3}(4 - x^2)^{3/2} \Big|_0^2$$

$$= -\frac{2\pi}{3}(0 - 8) = \frac{16\pi}{3}$$

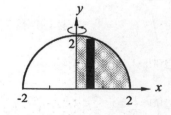

29. $y = 2x - x^2$, $y = 0$, rotated around

$x = 2$, using shells $r = 2 - x$

$h = y, t = dx$

$dV = 2\pi(2 - x)y\,dx$

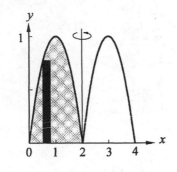

$$V = 2\pi \int_0^2 (2 - x)(2 - x^2)\,dx$$

$$= 2\pi \int_0^2 (4x - 4x^2 + x^3)\,dx$$

$$= 2\pi \left[2x^2 - \frac{4}{3}x^3 + \frac{1}{4}x^4\right]\Big|_0^2$$

$$= 2\pi \left[8 - \frac{32}{3} + 4\right] = \frac{8}{3}\pi$$

33. $y = 10(1 - 0.0001x^2)$

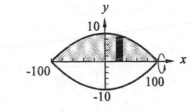

$$V = 2 \int_0^{100} \frac{\pi}{2} y^2\,dx$$

$$V = \pi \int_0^{100} (10(1 - 0.0001x^2))^2\,dx$$

$$V = 100\pi \int_0^{100} (1 - 0.0002x^2 + 1 \times 10^{-8}x^4)\,dx$$

$$V = 100\pi \left(x - 0.0002\frac{x^3}{3} + 1 \times 10^{-8}\frac{x^5}{5}\right)\Big|_0^{100}$$

$$V = 100\pi \left(100 - 0.0002\frac{100^3}{3} + 1 \times 10^{-8}\frac{100^5}{5}\right)$$

$$V = 16{,}800 \text{ m}^3$$

26.4   Centroids

1. $y = |x|$ is symmetric with respect to
y-axis. $\Rightarrow \overline{x} = 0$

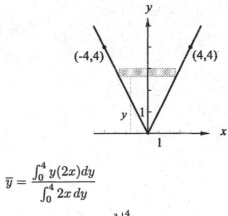

$$\overline{y} = \frac{\int_0^4 y(2x)\,dy}{\int_0^4 2x\,dy}$$

$$\overline{y} = \frac{\int_0^4 2y^2\,dy}{\int_0^4 2y\,dy} = \frac{\frac{y^3}{3}\big|_0^4}{\frac{y^2}{2}\big|_0^4}$$

$$= \frac{\frac{4^3}{3}}{\frac{4^2}{2}} = \frac{8}{3}$$

$$(\overline{x}, \overline{y}) = \left(0, \frac{8}{3}\right)$$

5. $M\overline{x} = m_1 x_1 + m_2 x_2 + m_3 x_3 + m_4 x_4$

$$(42 + 24 + 15 + 84)\overline{x} = 42(-3.5) + 24(0) + 15(2.6)$$
$$+ 84(3.7)$$
$$\overline{x} = 1.2 \text{ cm}$$

42 g		24 g		15 g 84 g

```
   -4 |-3 -2 -1  0  1  2 |3 |4
   -3.5            0      2.6 3.7
```

9. Break area into three rectangles.

First: center $(-1, -1)$; $A_1 = 4$

Second: center $\left(0, \frac{1}{2}\right)$; $A_2 = 4$

Third: center $\left(2\frac{1}{2}, 1\frac{1}{2}\right)$; $A_3 = 3$

Therefore,

$$4(-1) + 4(0) + 3\left(2\frac{1}{2}\right) = (4 + 4 + 3)\overline{x}$$

$$\overline{x} = 0.32$$

Therefore, $4(-1) + 4\left(\frac{1}{2}\right) + 3\left(1\frac{1}{2}\right) = 11\overline{y}$

$$\overline{y} = 0.23$$

Therefore, $(0.32 \text{ in}, 0.23 \text{ in})$ is the center of mass.

13. $y = 4 - x$, and axes

$$\overline{x} = \frac{\int_0^4 xy\,dx}{\int_0^4 y\,dx} = \frac{\int_0^4 x(4-x)dx}{\int_0^4 (4-x)dx} = \frac{\int_0^4 (4x - x^2)dx}{\int_0^4 (4-x)dx}$$

$$= \frac{(2x^2 - \frac{1}{3}x^3)\big|_0^4}{(4x - \frac{1}{2}x^2)\big|_0^4} = \frac{\frac{32}{3}}{8} = \frac{32}{24} = \frac{4}{3}$$

$$\overline{y} = \frac{\int_0^4 y(x)dy}{\int_0^4 x\,dy} = \frac{\int_0^4 y(4-y)dy}{\int_0^4 (4-y)dy} = \frac{\int_0^4 (4y - y^2)dy}{\int_0^4 y(4-y)dy}$$

$$= \frac{(2y^2 - \frac{1}{3}y^3)\big|_0^4}{(4y - \frac{1}{2}y^2)\big|_0^4} = \frac{4}{3}$$

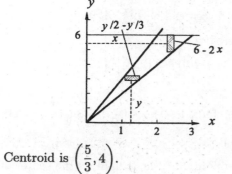

Therefore, centroid is $\left(\dfrac{4}{3}, \dfrac{4}{3}\right)$.

17. $A = \int_0^2 x\,dx + \int_2^3 (6 - 2x)dx = 3$

$$\overline{x} = \frac{\int_0^2 x(3x - 2x)dx + \int_2^3 x(6 - 2x)dx}{3} = \frac{5}{3}$$

$$\overline{y} = \frac{\int_0^6 y\left(\frac{y}{2} - \frac{y}{3}\right)dy}{3} = \frac{12}{3} = 4$$

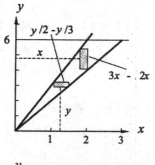

Centroid is $\left(\dfrac{5}{3}, 4\right)$.

21. $y = x^3, y = 0, x = 1$
Rotated about x-axis, $\overline{y} = 0$

$$\overline{x} = \frac{\int_a^b xy^2\,dx}{\int_a^b y^2\,dx} = \frac{\int_0^1 x(x^3)^2 dx}{\int_0^1 (x^3)^2 dx}$$

$$= \frac{\int_0^1 x^7 dx}{\int_0^1 x^6 dx} = \frac{\frac{x^8}{8}}{\frac{x^7}{7}}\Bigg|_0^1$$

$$= \frac{\frac{1}{8}}{\frac{1}{7}} = \frac{7}{8}$$

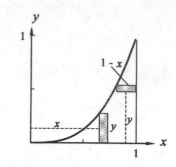

Centroid is $\left(\dfrac{7}{8}, 0\right)$.

25. $y^2 = 4x$; $x = 1$
Rotated about x-axis, $\overline{y} = 0$

$$\overline{x} = \frac{\int_a^b xy^2 dx}{\int_a^b y^2 dx} = \frac{\int_0^1 x(4x)\,dx}{\int_0^1 4x\,dx}$$

$$= \frac{\frac{4x^3}{3}}{2x^2}\Bigg|_0^1 = \frac{\frac{4}{3}}{2} = \frac{2}{3}$$

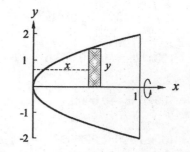

Centroid is $\left(\dfrac{2}{3}, 0\right)$.

29. $\dfrac{x^2}{5.00^2} + \dfrac{y^2}{1.00^2} = 1; \ y^2 = 1 - \dfrac{x^2}{25.0};$

$x^2 = 25.0 - 25.0y^2$

$$\int_0^{1.00} (yx^2)\,dy = \int_0^{1.00} y(25.0 - 25.0y^2)\,dy$$

$$= \int_0^{1.00} (25.0y - 25.0y^3)\,dy$$

$$= \left(\dfrac{25.0}{2}y^2 - \dfrac{25.0}{4}y^4 \right) \Bigg|_0^{1.00}$$

$$= \dfrac{25.0}{2} - \dfrac{25.0}{4} = \dfrac{25.0}{4}$$

$$\int_0^{1.00} x^2\,dy = \int_0^{1.00} (25.0 - 25.0y^2)\,dy$$

$$= \left(25.0y - \dfrac{25.0}{3}y^3 \right)\,dy \Bigg|_0^{1.00}$$

$$= \left(25.0 - \dfrac{25.0}{3} \right) = \dfrac{50.0}{3}$$

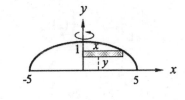

$$\overline{y} = \dfrac{25.0}{4} \div \dfrac{50.0}{3} = \dfrac{25.0}{4} \cdot \dfrac{3}{50.0}$$

$$= 0.375 \text{ cm above center of base}$$

26.5   Moments of Inertia

1. $\displaystyle I_y = k \int_0^1 x^2 y\,dx$

$\displaystyle I_y = k \int_0^1 x^2(4x)\,dx$

$\displaystyle I_y = 4k \dfrac{x^4}{4} \Bigg|_0^1$

$I_y = k$

$\displaystyle m = k \int_0^1 y\,dx = k \int_0^1 4x\,dx$

$\displaystyle m = 4k \dfrac{x^2}{2} \Bigg|_0^1 = 2k$

$$R_y^2 = \dfrac{I_y}{m} = \dfrac{k}{2k}$$

$$R_y = \dfrac{\sqrt{2}}{2}$$

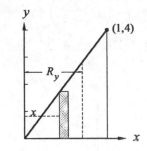

5. $I = m_1 x_1^2 + m_2 x_2^2 + m_3 x_3^2$
$I = 45.0(-3.80)^2 + 90.0(0.00)^2 + 62.0(5.50)^2$
$I = 2530 \text{ g} \cdot \text{cm}^2$

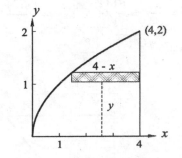

$I = MR^2$
$2530 = (45.0 + 9.0 + 62.0)R^2$
$\quad R = 3.58 \text{ cm}$

9. $y^2 = x, x = 4, x\text{-axis, with respect to the } x\text{-axis}$

$$I_x = k \int_0^2 y^2(4 - y^2)\,dy = k \int_0^2 (4y^2 - y^4)\,dy$$

$$= k \left(\dfrac{4}{3}y^3 - \dfrac{1}{5}y^5 \right) \Bigg|_0^2 = k \left(\dfrac{32}{3} - \dfrac{32}{5} \right) = \dfrac{64}{15}k$$

13. $y = \dfrac{b}{a}x;\ x = a, y = 0$

$$I_x = k \int_0^b y^2(a - x)\,dy = k \int_0^b y^2 \left(a - \frac{ay}{b}\right) dy$$

$$= ka \int_0^b \left(y^2 - \frac{y^3}{b}\right) dy = ka \left(\frac{1}{3}y^3 - \frac{1}{4b}y^4\right)\Big|_0^b$$

$$= \frac{kab^3}{12}$$

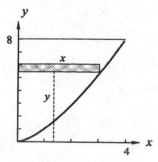

For $k = 1$; $m = \dfrac{1}{2}ab$ and

$$I_x = ab \left(\frac{b^2}{12}\right) = 2m \left(\frac{b^2}{12}\right) = \frac{1}{6}mb^2$$

17. $y^2 = x^3, y = 8, y$-axis, with respect to the x-axis

$$I_x = k \int_0^8 y^2 x\,dy = k \int_0^8 y^2 (y^{2/3})\,dy$$

$$= k \int_0^8 y^{8/3}dy = k\frac{3}{11}y^{11/3}\Big|_0^8$$

$$= \frac{3}{11}(8)^{11/3}k = \frac{3}{11}(2)^{11}k = \frac{6144}{11}k$$

$$m = k \int_0^8 x\,dy = k \int_0^8 y^{2/3}dy = k \left(\frac{3}{5}y^{5/3}\right)\Big|_0^8$$

$$= \frac{3}{5}(8)^{5/3}k = \frac{3}{5}(2)^5k = \frac{96k}{5}$$

$$R^2 = \frac{I_x}{m} = \frac{6144}{11} \div \frac{96k}{5} = \frac{64(5)}{11}$$

$$R = \sqrt{\frac{64(5)}{11}} = \frac{8}{11}\sqrt{55}$$

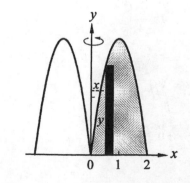

21. $y = 2x - x^2, y = 0$, rotated about y-axis

$$I_y = 2\pi k \int_0^2 (2x - x^2)(x^3)\,dx$$

$$= 2\pi k \int_0^2 (2x^4 - x^5)\,dx$$

$$= 2\pi k \left[\frac{2}{5}x^5 - \frac{1}{6}x^6\right]\Big|_0^2$$

$$= 2\pi k \left[\frac{2}{5}(2)^5 - \frac{1}{6}(2)^6\right]$$

$$= 2\pi k \left[\frac{64}{5} - \frac{64}{6}\right] = \frac{64\pi k}{15}$$

$$m = 2\pi k \int_0^2 (2x - x^2)(x)\,dx$$

$$= 2\pi k \int_0^2 (2x^2 - x^3)\,dx$$

$$= 2\pi k \left[\frac{2}{3}x^3 - \frac{1}{4}x^4\right]\Big|_0^2$$

$$= 2\pi k \left[\frac{2}{3}(2)^3 - \frac{1}{4}(2)^4\right]$$

$$= 2\pi k \left[\frac{16}{3} - \frac{16}{4}\right]$$

$$= \frac{8\pi k}{3}$$

$$R_y^2 = \frac{I_y}{m}$$

$$= \frac{65\pi k}{15} \div \frac{8\pi k}{3}$$

$$= \frac{8}{5};$$

$$R_y = \sqrt{\frac{8}{5}\left(\frac{5}{5}\right)}$$

$$= \frac{2}{5}\sqrt{10}$$

25. $r = 0.600$ cm, $h = 0.800$ cm, $m = 3.00$ g

$$y = \frac{0.600}{0.800}x = 0.750x; \quad x = 1.333y$$

$$I_x = 2\pi k \int_0^{0.600} (0.800 - 1.333y)y^3 \, dy$$

$$= 2\pi k (0.200y^4 - 0.2667y^5)\big|_0^{0.600}$$

$$= 2\pi k (0.005\,181)$$

$$m = \frac{k}{3}\pi r^2 h, \ 2\pi k = \frac{6m}{r^2 h} = \frac{6(3.00)}{(0.600^2)(0.800)}$$

$$= 62.5 \text{ g/cm}^3$$

$$I_x = (62.5)(0.005\,181) = 0.324 \text{ g} \cdot \text{cm}^2$$

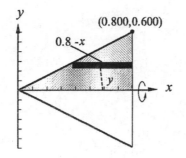

26.6   Other Applications

1. $f(x) = kx$
   $6.0 = k(2.0)$
   $k = 3.0$ lb/in.

$$W = \int_{3.0}^{6.0} 3.0x \, dx - 1.5x^2\big|_{3.0}^{6.0}$$

$$W = 41 \text{ lb} \cdot \text{in.}$$

5. $f(x) = kx; \ 6.0 = k(1.5); \ k = 4.0$ lb/in

$$w = \int_0^{2.0} 4.0x \, dx = 2.0x^2\big|_0^{2.0} = 2.0(2.0^2) - 0$$

$$= 8.0 \text{ lb} \cdot \text{in}$$

9. $f(x) = \dfrac{kq_1 q_2}{x^2}, 1.0$ pm $= 1.0 \times 10^{-12}$,

   4.0 pm $= 4.0 \times 10^{-12}$

$$W = \int_{1.0 \times 10^{-12}}^{4.0 \times 10^{-12}} \frac{9.0 \times 10^9 (1.6 \times 10^{-19})^2}{x^2} dx$$

$$= 9.0 \times 10^9 (1.6 \times 10^{-19})^2 \left(-\frac{1}{x}\right)\Big|_{1.0 \times 10^{-12}}^{4.0 \times 10^{-12}}$$

$$= -23.04 \times 10^{-29}[0.25 \times 10^{12} - 10^{12}]$$

$$= -23.04 \times 10^{-29}(-0.75 \times 10^{12})$$

$$= 1.7 \times 10^{-16} \text{ J}$$

13.   Weighs 100 lb: $\dfrac{100 \text{ lb}}{200 \text{ ft}} = 0.5$ lb/ft

   $f(x) = 0.5(200 - x)$

$$W = \int_0^{200} 0.5(200 - x)dx = \int_0^{200} (100 - 0.5x)dx$$

$$= 100x - 0.25x^2\big|_0^{200} = 10,000 \text{ ft} \cdot \text{lb}$$

17.   Weight of element $= dV(62.4)$
   $w = \pi 3.00^2 (62.4)dx = 9.00\pi(62.4)dx$

$$W = \int_0^{10.0} 9.00\pi(62.4)(10.0 - x)dx$$

$$= 9.00\pi\left(10.0x - \frac{x^2}{2}\right)\Big|_0^{10.0}$$

$$= 9.00\pi(62.4)(100 - 50)$$

$$= 8.82 \times 10^4 \text{ ft} \cdot \text{lb}$$

21. $F = w \displaystyle\int_a^b lh\,dh = 64.0 \int_{4.00}^{9.00} 10.0h\,dh$

$$= 64.0(10.0)\frac{h^2}{2}\Big|_{4.00}^{9.00}$$

$$= 640(40.5 - 8.0) = 20,800 \text{ lb}$$

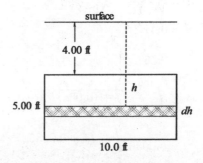

25. $y = x^2, y = 20$

$$F = 62.4 \int_0^4 2xy\,dy = 62.4(2) \int_0^4 \sqrt{y}(20-y)dy = 62.4(2) \int_0^4 (20\sqrt{y} - y\sqrt{y})dy$$

$$= 124.8 \left[20 \cdot \frac{2}{3}y^{3/2} - \frac{2}{5}y^{5/2} \right]\Big|_0^4 = 124.8 \left[\frac{40}{3}(8) - \frac{2}{5}(32) \right] = 11,700 \text{ lb}$$

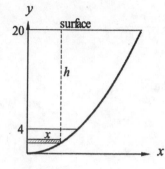

29. $i = 4t - t^2$. Find i_{av} with respect to time for $t = 0$ to $t = 4$.

$$i_{av} = \frac{\int_0^{4.0} i\,dt}{4.0 - 0} = \frac{\int_0^{4.0}(4t - t^2)\,dt}{4.0} = \frac{2t^2 - \frac{1}{3}t^3\big|_0^{4.0}}{4.0} = \frac{2(16) - \frac{1}{3}(64)}{4.0} = \frac{10.7}{4.0} = 2.7 \text{ A}$$

33. $\quad s = \int_a^b \sqrt{1 + \left(\frac{dy}{dx}\right)^2}\,dx;$

$y = 0.4x^{3/2};$

$\dfrac{dy}{dx} = 0.06x^{1/2}$

$$s = \int_0^{100} \sqrt{1 + (0.06x^{1/2})^2}dx = \int_0^{100} \sqrt{(1 + 0.0036x)}dx = \int_0^{100} (1 + 0.0036x)^{1/2}dx$$

$$= \frac{1}{0.0036} \int_0^{100} (1 + 0.0036x)^{1/2}(0.0036)(dx) = \frac{1}{0.0036} \left[\frac{2}{3}(1 + 0.0036x)^{3/2} \right]\Big|_0^{100}$$

$$= \frac{1}{0.0036} \left[\frac{2}{3}(1.586) - \frac{2}{3}(1)^{3/2} \right] = \frac{1}{0.0036} \left[\frac{2}{3}(0.586) \right] = \frac{1}{0.0036}[0.391] = 109 \text{ ft}$$

Chapter 26 Review Exercises

1. $v = \int a\,dt;\ a = 32 \text{ ft/s}^2;\ v = at + c,\ \text{at } t = 0, v = 0 \Rightarrow c = 0$

$v = at = 32t$

$140 = 32t$

$t = 4.4s$

5. $a = 12$

$v = 12t + v_0 = 12t \text{ since } v = 0,\ \text{at } t = 0.$

$s = 6t^2 + s_0 = 6t^2 \text{ since } s = 0 \text{ at } t = 0.$

$s = 6t^2$

9. $V_c = \dfrac{1}{c}\int i\,dt.$

$V_c = \dfrac{i}{c}\int dt = \dfrac{it}{c} + V_0 = \dfrac{it}{c} + 0$

$V_c = \dfrac{12 \times 10^{-3}(25 \times 10^{-6})}{5.5 \times 10^{-9}} = 55 \text{ V}$

13. $A = \displaystyle\int_0^1 y\,dx = \int_0^1 \sqrt{1-x}\,dx$

$A = -\displaystyle\int_0^1 (1-x)^{1/2}(-dx)$

$A = -\dfrac{2}{3}(1-x)^{3/2}\Big|_0^1$

$A = -\dfrac{2}{3}((1-1)^{3/2} - (1-0)^{3/2})$

$A = \dfrac{2}{3}$

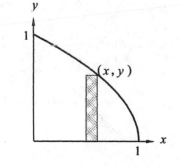

17. $A = \displaystyle\int_0^3 (x^2 - (x^3 - 2x^2))dx$

$A = \displaystyle\int_0^3 (3x^2 - x^3)dx$

$A = x^3 - \dfrac{x^4}{4}\Big|_0^3$

$A = \dfrac{27}{4}$

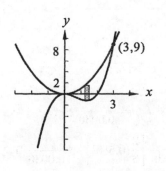

21.

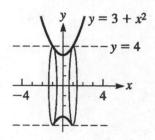

$$V = \pi \int_{-1}^{1} 4^2 dx - \pi \int_{-1}^{1} y^2 dx = \pi \int_{-1}^{1} (4^2 - y^2)\, dx = \pi \int_{-1}^{1} [16 - (3 + x^2)^2]\, dx$$

$$= \pi \int_{-1}^{1} (16 - 9 - 6x^2 - x^4)\, dx = \pi \int_{-1}^{1} (7 - 6x^2 - x^4)\, dx = \pi \left(7x - 2x^3 - \frac{1}{5}x^5 \right)\Big|_{-1}^{1}$$

$$= \pi \left(7 - 2 - \frac{1}{5} \right) - \pi \left(-7 + 2 + \frac{1}{5} \right) = \frac{24\pi}{5} + \frac{24\pi}{5} = \frac{48\pi}{5}$$

25.

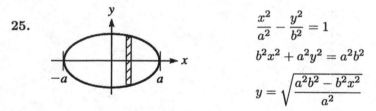

$$\frac{x^2}{a^2} - \frac{y^2}{b^2} = 1$$

$$b^2 x^2 + a^2 y^2 = a^2 b^2$$

$$y = \sqrt{\frac{a^2 b^2 - b^2 x^2}{a^2}}$$

$$V = \pi \int_{-a}^{a} y^2 dx = \pi \int_{-a}^{a} \left(\frac{a^2 b^2 - b^2 x^2}{a^2} \right) dx = \pi \int_{-a}^{a} \left(b^2 - \frac{b^2}{a^2} x^2 \right) dx = \pi \left(b^2 x - \frac{b^2}{3a^2} x^3 \right)\Big|_{-a}^{a}$$

$$= \pi \left[\left(ab^2 - \frac{ab^2}{3} \right) - \left(-ab^2 + \frac{ab^2}{3} \right) \right] = \pi \left(2ab^2 - \frac{2ab^2}{3} \right) = \pi \left(\frac{4ab^2}{3} \right) = \frac{4\pi ab^2}{3} = \frac{4}{3}\pi ab^2$$

29. $\overline{x} = \dfrac{\int_0^4 x(2x - x^{3/2})dx}{\int_0^4 (2x - x^{3/2})dx}$

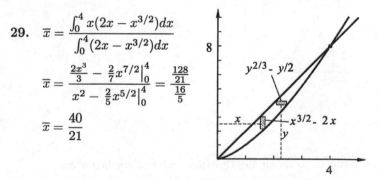

$$\overline{x} = \frac{\frac{2x^3}{3} - \frac{2}{7}x^{7/2}\big|_0^4}{x^2 - \frac{2}{5}x^{5/2}\big|_0^4} = \frac{\frac{128}{21}}{\frac{16}{5}}$$

$$\overline{x} = \frac{40}{21}$$

$$\overline{y} = \frac{\int_0^8 y(y^{2/3} - \frac{y}{2})dy}{\frac{16}{5}} = \frac{\int_0^8 (y^{5/3} - \frac{1}{2}y^2)dy}{\frac{16}{5}}$$

$$\overline{y} = \frac{\frac{3}{8}y^{8/3} - \frac{1}{6}y^3\big|_0^8}{\frac{16}{5}} = \frac{\frac{32}{3}}{\frac{16}{5}} = \frac{10}{3}$$

$$(\overline{x}, \overline{y}) = \left(\frac{40}{21}, \frac{10}{3} \right)$$

33. $I_y = k \int_0^2 x^2((3x - x^2) - x)dx$

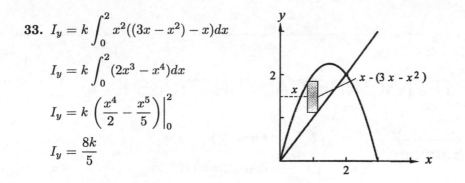

$I_y = k \int_0^2 (2x^3 - x^4)dx$

$I_y = k \left(\dfrac{x^4}{2} - \dfrac{x^5}{5} \right) \Big|_0^2$

$I_y = \dfrac{8k}{5}$

37. $W = 80(100) + \int_0^{100} \dfrac{10}{100}(100 - x)dx$

$W = 8000 + 10x - \dfrac{x^2}{20} \Big|_0^{100}$

$W = 8500 \text{ ft} \cdot \text{lb}$

41. Using disks and $\dfrac{x^2}{1.5^2} + \dfrac{y^2}{10^2} = 1$ as equation of ellipse

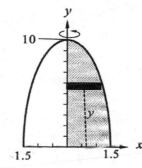

$V = \int_0^{10} \pi x^2 dy$

$V = \pi \int_0^{10} 1.5^2 \left(1 - \dfrac{y^2}{10^2} \right) dy$

$V = \pi (1.5)^2 \left(y - \dfrac{1}{3}\dfrac{y^3}{10^2} \right) \Big|_0^{10}$

$V = \pi (1.5)^2 \left(10 - \dfrac{1}{3}\dfrac{10^3}{10^2} \right)$

$V = 47 \text{ m}^3$

45. The circumference of the bottom, $c = 2\pi r = 9\pi$, equates to l, the length of the vertical surface area.

$F = 68.0 \int_0^{3.25} (9\pi h)\, dh = 68.0 \left[4.50\pi h^2 \right] \big|_0^{3.25} = 68.0[4.50\pi(3.25)^2 - 0] = 10,200 \text{ lb}$

49. The formula is $V = 2 \int_0^a (2 \cdot \sqrt{a^2 - x^2})^2\, dx$ where x is the distance from the center of the circular top to the cross section.

Chapter 27

DIFFERENTIATION OF TRANSCENDENTAL FUNCTIONS

27.1 Derivatives of the Sine and Cosine Functions

1. $r = \sin^2 2\theta^2$

$$\frac{dr}{d\theta} = 2\sin 2\theta^2 \cos 2\theta^2 (2(2\theta))$$

$$\frac{dr}{d\theta} = 8\theta \sin 2\theta^2 \cos 2\theta^2$$

$$\frac{dr}{d\theta} = 4\theta \sin 4\theta^2$$

5. $y = 2\sin(2x^3 - 1)$

$$\frac{dy}{dx} = 2\cos(2x^3 - 1)(6x^2) = 12x^2 \cos(2x^3 - 1)$$

9. $y = 2\cos(3x - \pi)$

$$\frac{dy}{dx} = 2\left[-\sin(3x - \pi)(3)\right] = -6\sin(3x - \pi)$$

13. $y = 3\cos^3(5x + 2)$;

$$\frac{dy}{dx} = 3.3\cos^2(5x + 2)[-\sin(5x + 2)(5)]$$

$$\frac{dy}{dx} = -45\cos^2(5x + 2)\sin(5x + 2)$$

17. $y = 3x^3 \cos 5x$;

$$\frac{dy}{dx} = 3[x^3(-5\sin 5x) + \cos 5x(3x^2)]$$

$$\frac{dy}{dx} = 9x^2 \cos 5x - 15x^3 \sin 5x$$

21. $y = \sqrt{1 + \sin 4x} = (1 + \sin 4x)^{1/2}$

$$\frac{dy}{dx} = \frac{1}{2}(1 + \sin 4x)^{-1/2}(4\cos 4x)$$

$$\frac{dy}{dx} = \frac{2\cos 4x}{\sqrt{1 + \sin 4x}}$$

25. $y = \dfrac{2\cos x^2}{3x - 1}$

$$\frac{dy}{dx} = \frac{(3x - 1)(2)(-\sin x^2)(2x) - 2\cos x^2(3)}{(3x - 1)^2}$$

$$\frac{dy}{dx} = \frac{-4x(3x - 1)\sin x^2 - 6\cos x^2}{(3x - 1)^2}$$

$$\frac{dy}{dx} = \frac{4x(1 - 3x)\sin x^2 - 6\cos x^2}{(3x - 1)^2}$$

29. $s = \sin(\sin 2t)$

$$\frac{ds}{dt} = \cos(\sin 2t)\cos(2t)(2)$$

$$\frac{ds}{dt} = 2\cos 2t \cos(\sin 2t)$$

33. $p = \dfrac{1}{\sin s} + \dfrac{1}{\cos s}$

$$\frac{dp}{ds} = \frac{\sin s(0) - \cos s}{\sin^2 s} + \frac{\cos s(0) - (-\sin s)}{\cos^2 s}$$

$$\frac{dp}{ds} = \frac{-\cos s}{\sin^2 s} + \frac{\sin s}{\cos^2 s}$$

37. (a) $\cos 1.0000 = 0.5403023$

Represents $\dfrac{d}{dx}(\sin x)$ at $x = 1$ (the derivative, slope of T.L. to sine curve at $x = 1$).

(b) $\dfrac{(\sin 1.0001 - \sin 1.0000)}{0.0001}$

$= 0.5402602$

$=$ slope of secant line through the two points on sine curve where $x = 1.000$ and $x = 1.0001$

41. $\sin(xy)\cos 2y = x^2$

$$\cos(xy)\left(x\frac{dy}{dx} + y\right) + (-\sin 2y)\left(2\frac{dy}{dx}\right) = 2x$$

$$x\frac{dy}{dx}\cos(xy) + y\cos(xy) - 2\frac{dy}{dx}\sin 2y = 2x$$

$$x\frac{dy}{dx}\cos(xy) - 2\frac{dy}{dx}\sin 2y = 2x - y\cos(xy)$$

$$\frac{dy}{dx}(x\cos(xy) - 2\sin 2y) = 2x - y\cos(xy)$$

$$\frac{dy}{dx} = \frac{2x - y\cos xy}{x\cos xy - 2\sin 2y}$$

45. $\cos 2x = 2\cos^2 x - 1$;

$-\sin 2x(2) = 2(2)\cos x(-\sin x) - 0$

$-2\sin 2x = -4\sin x \cos x$

$\sin 2x = 2\sin x \cos x$

49. $y = x \cos 2x;\ x = 1.20$

$$\frac{dy}{dx} = x(-2\sin 2x) + \cos 2x$$

$$m_{TL} = \cos 2x - 2x \sin x$$

$$m_{TL}|_{x=1.20} = -2.36$$

53. $y = 1.85 \sin 36\pi t;$

$$v = \frac{dy}{dx} = (1.85 \cos 36\pi t)(36\pi)$$

$$v|_{t=0.0250} = [1.85 \cos(36\pi \cdot 0.025)][36\pi]$$
$$= -199 \text{ cm/s}$$

27.2   Derivatives of the Other Trigonometric Functions

1. $y = 3 \sec^2 x^2$

$$\frac{dy}{dx} = 3(2)(\sec x^2)\frac{d}{dx}(\sec x^2)$$

$$\frac{dy}{dx} = 6 \sec x^2 \sec x^2 \tan x^2 (2x)$$

$$\frac{dy}{dx} = 12x \sec^2 x^2 \tan x^2$$

5. $y = 5 \cot(0.25\pi - \theta)$

$$\frac{dy}{d\theta} = -5 \csc^2(0.25\pi - \theta) \cdot (-1)$$

$$= 5 \csc^2(0.25\pi - \theta)$$

9. $y = -3 \csc \sqrt{2x+3}$

$$\frac{dy}{dx} = -3[-\csc \sqrt{2x+3} \cot \sqrt{2x+3}$$

$$\cdot \frac{1}{2}(2x+3)^{-1/2}(2)]$$

$$\frac{dy}{dx} = \frac{3 \csc \sqrt{2x+3} \cot \sqrt{2x+3}}{\sqrt{2x+3}}$$

13. $y = 2 \cot^4 \frac{1}{2}x$

$$\frac{dy}{dx} = 2(4) \cot^3 \frac{1}{2}x \left[-\csc^2 \frac{1}{2}x \left(\frac{1}{2} \right) \right]$$

$$= -4 \cot^3 \frac{1}{2}x \csc^2 \frac{1}{2}x$$

17. $y = 3 \csc^4 7x$

$$\frac{dy}{dx} = 3 \cdot 4 \csc^3 7x[-\csc 7x \cot 7x(7)$$

$$= -84 \csc^4 7x \cot 7x$$

21. $y = 4 \cos x \csc x^2$

$$\frac{dy}{dx} = 4[\cos x(-\csc x^2 \cot x^2 \cdot 2x) + \csc x^2(-\sin x)]$$

$$\frac{dy}{dx} = -4 \csc x^2 (2x \cos x \cot x^2 + \sin x)$$

25. $y = \dfrac{2 \cos 4x}{1 + \cot 3x}$

$$\frac{dy}{dx} = \frac{(1+\cot 3x)[-2\sin 4x(4)] - 2\cos 4x(-\csc^2 3x)(3)}{(1+\cot 3x)^2}$$

$$\frac{dy}{dx} = \frac{-8\sin 4x(1+\cot 3x) + 6\cos 4x \csc^2 3x}{(1+\cot 3x)^2}$$

$$\frac{dy}{dx} = \frac{2(-4\sin 4x - 4\sin 4x \cot 3x + 3\cos 4x \csc^2 3x)}{(1+\cot 3x)^2}$$

29. $r = \tan(\sin 2\pi\theta)$

$$\frac{dr}{d\theta} = \sec^2(\sin 2\pi\theta)\cos(2\pi\theta)(2\pi)$$

$$= 2\pi \cos 2\pi\theta \sec^2(\sin 2\pi\theta)$$

33. $x \sec y - 2y = \sin 2x$

$$x \sec y \tan y \frac{dy}{dx} + \sec y - 2\frac{dy}{dx} = 2 \cos 2x$$

$$x \sec y \tan y \frac{dy}{dx} - 2\frac{dy}{dx} = 2\cos 2x - \sec y$$

$$\frac{dy}{dx}(x \sec y \tan y - 2) = 2\cos 2x - \sec y$$

$$\frac{dy}{dx} = \frac{2\cos 2x - \sec y}{x \sec y \tan y - 2}$$

37. $y = \tan 4x \sec 4x$

$$\frac{dy}{dx} = \tan 4x \cdot 4 \sec 4x \tan 4x + \sec 4x \cdot 4\sec^2 4x$$

$$dy = 4\sec 4x(\tan^2 4x + \sec^2 4x)dx$$

41. (a)

(b)

The values are the same in the first four decimal places.

45. $y = 2\cot 3x$; $x = \dfrac{\pi}{12}$;

$$\frac{dy}{dx} = 2(-\csc^2 3x)(3) = -6\csc^2 3x;$$

$$\left.\frac{dy}{dx}\right|_{x=\pi/12} = -6\csc^2\frac{\pi}{4} = -6(\sqrt{2})^2 = -12$$

```
nDeriv(2/tan(3X)
,X,π/12)
          -12.000144
```

49. $y = 2t^{1.5} - \tan 0.1t$; $v = \dfrac{dy}{dt} = 3t^{0.5} - 0.1\sec^2 0.1t$;

$v|_{t=15} = 3(15)^{0.5} - 0.1\sec^2[0.1(15)] = -8.4$ cm/s

27.3 Derivatives of the Inverse Trigonometric Functions

1. $y = \sin^{-1} x^2$

$$\frac{dy}{dx} = \frac{1}{\sqrt{1-(x^2)^2}}(2x) = \frac{2x}{\sqrt{1-x^4}}$$

5. $y = 2\sin^{-1} 3x^3$

$$\frac{dy}{dx} = 2\frac{1}{\sqrt{1-9x^6}}(9x^2) = \frac{18x^2}{\sqrt{1-9x^6}}$$

9. $y = 2\cos^{-1}\sqrt{2-x}$

$$\frac{dy}{dx} = 2 \cdot \frac{-1}{\sqrt{1-(2-x)}} \cdot \frac{1}{2}(2-x)^{-1/2}(-1)$$

$$\frac{dy}{dx} = \frac{1}{\sqrt{x-1}\sqrt{2-x}} = \frac{1}{\sqrt{(x-1)(2-x)}}$$

13. $= 6\tan^{-1}\left(\dfrac{1}{x}\right)$

$$\frac{dy}{dx} = 6\frac{1}{1+\frac{1}{x^2}}\left(-\frac{1}{x^2}\right) = \frac{-\frac{6}{x^2}}{(x^2+1)/x^2} = \frac{-6}{x^2+1}$$

17. $y = 0.4u\tan^{-1} 2u$

$$\frac{dy}{du} = 0.4u \cdot \frac{2}{1+4u^2} + 0.4\tan^{-1} 2u$$

$$\frac{dy}{du} = \frac{0.8u}{1+4u^2} + 0.4\tan^{-1} 2u$$

21. $y = \dfrac{\sin^{-1} 2x}{\cos^{-1} 2x}$

$$\frac{dy}{dx} = \frac{\cos^{-1} 2x\frac{1}{\sqrt{1-4x^2}}(2) - \sin^{-1} 2x\frac{1}{\sqrt{1-4x^2}}(2)}{(\cos^{-1} 2x)^2}$$

$$\frac{dy}{dx} = \frac{2}{\sqrt{1-4x^2}}\left[\frac{\cos^{-1} 2x + \sin^{-1} 2x}{(\cos^{-1} 2x)^2}\right]$$

$$\frac{dy}{dx} = \frac{2(\cos^{-1} 2x + \sin^{-1} 2x)}{\sqrt{1-4x^2}(\cos^{-1} 2x)^2}$$

25. $y = [\sin^{-1}(4x+1)]^2$

$$\frac{dy}{dx} = 2[\sin^{-1}(4x+1)]^1\frac{1}{\sqrt{1-(4x+1)^2}}(4)$$

$$\frac{dy}{dx} = \frac{8\sin^{-1}(4x+1)}{\sqrt{1-16x^2-8x-1}}$$

$$= \frac{8\sin^{-1}(4x+1)}{\sqrt{4(-4x^2-2x)}}$$

$$\frac{dy}{dx} = \frac{4\sin^{-1}(4x+1)}{\sqrt{-4x^2-2x}}$$

29. $y = \dfrac{1}{1+4x^2} - \tan^{-1} 2x$

$$= (1+4x^2)^{-1} - \tan^{-1} 2x$$

$$\frac{dy}{dx} = -(1+4x^2)^{-2}(8x) - \frac{1}{1+4x^2}(2)$$

$$\frac{dy}{dx} = \frac{-8x}{(1+4x^2)^2} - \frac{2}{1+4x^2} = \frac{-8x-2(1+4x^2)}{(1+4x^2)^2}$$

$$\frac{dy}{dx} = \frac{-8x-2-8x^2}{(1+4x^2)^2} = \frac{-2(1+4x+4x^2)}{(1+4x^2)^2}$$

$$= \frac{-2(1+2x)^2}{(1+4x^2)^2}$$

33. $2\tan^{-1} xy + x = 3$

$$2\frac{1}{1+x^2y^2}\left(x\frac{dy}{dx}+y\right)+1 = 0$$

$$\frac{2x}{1+x^2y^2}\frac{dy}{dx} + \frac{2y}{1+x^2y^2} = -1$$

$$\frac{2x}{1+x^2y^2}\frac{dy}{dx} = -1 - \frac{2y}{1+x^2y^2}$$

$$\frac{2x}{1+x^2y^2}\frac{dy}{dx} = \frac{-1-x^2y^2-2y}{1+x^2y^2}$$

$$2x\frac{dy}{dx} = -1-x^2y^2-2y; \quad \frac{dy}{dx} = \frac{-(x^2y^2+2y+1)}{2x}$$

37. $y = (\sin^{-1} x)^3$

$$\frac{dy}{dx} = 3(\sin^{-1} x)^2 \frac{1}{\sqrt{1 - x^2}}$$

$$dy = \frac{3(\sin^{-1} x)^2 dx}{\sqrt{1 - x^2}}$$

41. $y_1 = \sin^{-1} x, y_2 = \dfrac{1}{\sqrt{(1 - x^2)}}$

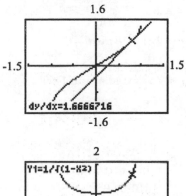

45. $\dfrac{d}{dx}(\sec^{-1} u) = \dfrac{1}{\sqrt{u^2(u^2 - 1)}} \dfrac{du}{dx}$

Let $\sec^{-1} u = y$, therefore $u = \sec y$,

therefore $\cos y = \dfrac{1}{u}$

Therefore, $\cos^{-1} \dfrac{1}{u} = y = \sec^{-1} u$.

$$\frac{dy}{dx} = \frac{-1}{\sqrt{1 - \frac{1}{u^2}}} \left(\frac{-1}{u^2}\right) \frac{du}{dx}$$

$$= \frac{1}{\frac{\sqrt{u^2 - 1}}{u}} \left(\frac{1}{u^2}\right) \frac{du}{dx}$$

$$\frac{dy}{dx} = \frac{1}{\sqrt{u^2 - 1}(u)} \frac{du}{dx}; u = \sqrt{u^2}$$

$$\frac{dy}{dx} = \frac{1}{\sqrt{u^2(u^2 - 1)}} \frac{du}{dx}$$

49. $\theta = \tan^{-1}[(X_L - X_C)/R]$

$$\frac{d\theta}{dX_C} = \frac{1}{1 + \left(\frac{X_L - X_C}{R}\right)^2} \left(\frac{-1}{R}\right)$$

$$\frac{d\theta}{dX_C} = -\frac{R}{R^2 + (X_L - X_C)^2}$$

27.4   Applications

1. Sketch the curve $y = \sin x - \dfrac{x}{2}, 0 \le x \le 2\pi$.

$x = 0 \Rightarrow y = 0, (0,0)$ is both x-intercept and y-intercept. Using Newton's method or zero feature on graphing calculator $(1.90, 0)$ is the only x-intercept for $0 \le x \le 2\pi$. For $x = 2\pi$
$y = \sin 2\pi - \dfrac{2\pi}{2} = -\pi \Rightarrow (2\pi, -\pi)$ is right hand end point.

$$\frac{dy}{dx} = \cos x - \frac{1}{2} = 0 \text{ for } x = \frac{\pi}{3}, \frac{5\pi}{3}$$

$$\frac{d^2 y}{dx^2} = -\sin x = \frac{-\sqrt{3}}{2} \text{ for } x = \frac{\pi}{3} \Rightarrow \max\left(\frac{\pi}{3}, 0.34\right)$$

$$\frac{d^2 y}{dx^2} = -\sin x = \frac{\sqrt{3}}{2} \text{ for } x = \frac{5\pi}{3} \Rightarrow \min\left(\frac{5\pi}{3}, -3.48\right)$$

$$\frac{d^2 y}{dx^2} = -\sin x = 0 \text{ for } x = 0, \pi$$

$$\frac{d^2 y}{dx^2} < 0 \text{ for } 0 < x < \pi \Rightarrow \text{infl } (0,0)$$

$$\frac{d^2 y}{dx^2} > 0 \text{ for } \pi < x < \frac{\pi}{2} \Rightarrow \text{infl }\left(\pi, -\frac{\pi}{2}\right)$$

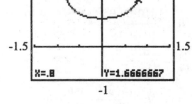

5. $y = \tan^{-1} x$

$$\frac{dy}{dx} = \frac{1}{1 + x^2} > 0 \text{ for all } x.$$

9. $y = \sin 2x$ at $x = \dfrac{5\pi}{8}$

$$\frac{dy}{dx} = 2\cos 2x = m_{TL}$$

$$m_{TL}|_{x=5\pi/8} = -1.414$$
$$= -\sqrt{2};$$

$$f\left(\frac{5\pi}{8}\right) = -0.707$$

$$= -\frac{\sqrt{2}}{2}$$

Equation of T.L.: $y + \dfrac{\sqrt{2}}{2} = -\sqrt{2}\left(x - \dfrac{5\pi}{8}\right)$

$8y + 4\sqrt{2} = -8\sqrt{2}x + 5\sqrt{2}\pi$
$8\sqrt{2}x + 8y + 4\sqrt{2} - 5\pi\sqrt{2} = 0$

13. $y = 6\cos x - 8\sin x$; minimum value occurs when
$f'(x) = 0$.
$f'(x) = -6\sin x - 8\cos x = 0$

$$\sin x = -\frac{8}{6}\cos x$$

$$\tan x = -\frac{8}{6} = -\frac{4}{3}$$

$\alpha = 0.927$ (a $3, 4, 5$ triangle)
$Q_1 = 2.214, Q_2 = 5.356$
$f''(x) = -6\cos x + 8\sin$
$f''(2.214) > 0,$min; $f''(5.356) < 0$, max.
Minimum occurs where $x = 2.214$ rad.

$$f(2.214) = 6\left(\frac{-3}{5}\right) - 8\left(\frac{4}{5}\right)$$

$$= \frac{-18}{5} + \frac{-32}{5}$$

$$= \frac{-50}{5} = -10$$

Minimum value of $y = -10$ units.

17. $T_x = 46.6\cos\theta$

$$\frac{dT_x}{dt} = 46.6\left(-\sin\theta\frac{d\theta}{dt}\right)$$

$$\frac{dT_x}{dt} = -46.6\sin\theta\frac{d\theta}{dt}$$

$$\frac{d\theta}{dt} = 0.36°/\text{s}; \; \theta = 14.2°; \; \frac{d\theta}{dt} = \frac{0.36°\pi}{180°} \text{ r/s}$$

$$\frac{dT_x}{dt} = -46.6(\sin 14.2°)\frac{0.36\pi}{180}$$

$$\frac{dT_x}{dt} = -0.072 \text{ lb/s}$$

21. $v_x = -6\sin 3t$; $a_x = -18\cos 3t$; $a_x|_{t=4.1} = -17.365$
$v_y = -2\sin 2t$; $a_y = -4\cos 2t$; $a_y = 1.357$
$a = 17.418$

$$\alpha = \tan^{-1}\frac{a_y}{a_x} = 0.078 = -4°$$

Therefore $a = 17.4 \text{ cm/s}^2$ at $\theta = 176°$

25. $\cos\theta = \dfrac{225}{x}$; $\dfrac{d\theta}{dt} = 1.5°/\text{s}$

$x = 225\sec\theta$; $x = 315, \theta = 44.415°$

$$\frac{dx}{dt} = 225\sec\theta\tan\theta\frac{d\theta}{dt}$$

$$\frac{dx}{dt} = 225\sec 44.4°\tan 44.4°\left(\frac{1.5\pi}{180}\right)$$

$$\frac{dx}{dt} = 8.08 \text{ ft/s}$$

29. $\sin\theta = \dfrac{R}{R + 610}$

$$R = \frac{610\sin\theta}{1 - \sin\theta}$$

$$\frac{dR}{d\theta} = \frac{610\cos\theta}{(1 - \sin\theta)^2}$$

$$\Delta R \approx dR = \frac{610\cos\theta}{(1 - \sin\theta)^2}d\theta$$

$$\Delta R = \frac{610\cos 65.8°}{(1 - \sin 65.8°)^2}\left(\pm 0.5°\left(\frac{\pi}{180°}\right)\right)$$

$$\Delta R = \pm 280 \text{ km}$$

33. $s = kwd^2$; $d^2 = 256 - w^2$; $\cos\theta = \dfrac{w}{16.0}$;

$w = 16.0\cos\theta$;

$S = k(16.0\cos\theta)[256 - (16.0\cos\theta)^2]$;

$S = 4100k[\cos\theta - \cos^3\theta]$;

$$\frac{dS}{d\theta} = 4100k[-\sin\theta - 3\cos^2\theta(-\sin\theta)];$$

$$\frac{dS}{d\theta} = 4100k(-\sin\theta + 3\sin\theta\cos^2\theta)$$

Maximum occurs when $\dfrac{dS}{d\theta} = 0$.

$4100k(-\sin\theta + 3\sin\theta\cos^2\theta) = 0;$

$-\sin\theta(1 - 3\cos^2\theta) = 0 - \sin\theta = 0;$

$\sin\theta = 0;\ \theta = 0, \theta = \pi;\ 1 - 3\cos^2\theta = 0;$

$\cos^2\theta = \dfrac{1}{3};\ \cos\theta = \sqrt{\dfrac{1}{3}}$

$w = 16.0\sqrt{\dfrac{1}{3}} = 9.24\ \text{in}$

$d = \sqrt{16.0^2 - 16.0^2\left(\dfrac{1}{3}\right)} = 13.1\ \text{in}$

27.5   Derivative of the Logarithmic Function

1. $y = \ln\cos 4x$

$\dfrac{dy}{dx} = \dfrac{1}{\cos 4x}(-\sin 4x)(4)$

$\dfrac{dy}{dx} = -4\tan x$

5. $y = 2\log_5(3x + 1)$

$\dfrac{dy}{dx} = 2\dfrac{1}{3x+1}\log_5 e(3) = \dfrac{6}{3x+1}\log_5 e$

9. $y = 2\ln\tan 2x$

$\dfrac{dy}{dx} = 2\dfrac{1}{\tan 2x}\sec^2 2x(2) = \dfrac{4\sec^2 2x}{\tan 2x} = \dfrac{4\sec^2 2x}{\dfrac{\sec 2x}{\csc 2x}}$

$\dfrac{dy}{dx} = 4\sec 2x\csc 2x$

13. $y = \ln(x^2 + 2x)^3$

$\dfrac{dy}{dx} = \dfrac{1}{(x^2+2x)^3}3(x^2+2x)^2(2x+2) = \dfrac{6(x+1)}{x^2+2x}$

17. $y = \dfrac{3x}{\ln(2x+1)}$

$\dfrac{dy}{dx} = \dfrac{\ln(2x+1)(3) - (3x)\dfrac{1}{2x+1}(2)}{[\ln(2x+1)]^2}$

$\dfrac{dy}{dx} = \dfrac{3\ln(2x+1) - \dfrac{6x}{2x+1}}{[\ln(2x+1)]^2}$

$\dfrac{dy}{dx} = \dfrac{3(2x+1)\ln(2x+1) - 6x}{(2x+1)[\ln(2x+1)]^2}$

21. $y = \ln\dfrac{2x}{1+x} = \ln 2x - \ln(1+x)$

$\dfrac{dy}{dx} = \dfrac{1}{2x}(2) - \dfrac{1}{1+x} = \dfrac{1+x-x}{x(1+x)}$

$= \dfrac{1}{x(1+x)} = \dfrac{1}{x^2+x}$

25. $u = 3v\ln^2 2v$

$\dfrac{du}{dv} = 3v\cdot 2\ln 2v\cdot\dfrac{1}{2v}\cdot 2 + 3\ln^2 2v$

$\dfrac{du}{dv} = 6\ln 2v + 3\ln^2 2v$

29. $r = \ln\dfrac{v^2}{v+2}$

$= \ln v^2 - \ln(v+2)$

$\dfrac{dr}{dv} = \dfrac{1}{v^2}(2v) - \dfrac{1}{v+2}$

$= \dfrac{2}{v} - \dfrac{1}{v+2}$

$= \dfrac{2v+4-v}{v(v+2)}$

$\dfrac{dr}{dv} = \dfrac{v+4}{v(v+2)}$

33. $y = x - \ln^2(x+y)$

$\dfrac{dy}{dx} = 1 - 2\ln(x+y)\dfrac{1}{x+y}\left(1 + \dfrac{dy}{dx}\right)$

$\dfrac{dy}{dx} = 1 - \dfrac{2\ln(x+y)}{x+y} - \dfrac{2\ln(x+y)}{x+y}\dfrac{dy}{dx}$

$\dfrac{dy}{dx} + \dfrac{2\ln(x+y)}{x+1} = 1 - \dfrac{2\ln(x+y)}{x+1}$

$= \dfrac{x+y-2\ln(x+y)}{x+y}$

$\dfrac{dy}{dx}\left[\dfrac{x+y+2\ln(x+y)}{x+y}\right] = \dfrac{x+y-2\ln(x+y)}{x+y}$

$\dfrac{dy}{dx} = \dfrac{x+y-2\ln(x+y)}{x+y+2\ln(x+y)}$

37. $y = (1 + x)^{(1/x)}$

(b) See table.

(a)

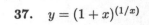

X	Y₁	Y₂
.1	2.5937	2.7183
.01	2.7048	2.7183
.001	2.7169	2.7183
1E-4	2.7181	2.7183
1E-5	2.7183	2.7183

X=

41. $y = \sin^{-1} 2x + \sqrt{1 - 4x^2};\ x = 0.250;$

$$\frac{dy}{dx} = \frac{2}{\sqrt{1 - (2x)^2}} + \frac{1}{2}(1 - 4x^2)^{-1/2}(-8x) = \frac{2 - 4x}{\sqrt{1 - 4x^2}}$$

$$\left.\frac{dy}{dx}\right|_{x=0.250} = \frac{2 - 4(0.250)}{\sqrt{1 - 4(0.250)^2}} = 1.15$$

45. $y = \tan^{-1} 2x + \ln(4x^2 + 1);$

$$m_{\tan} = \frac{dy}{dx} = \frac{1}{4x^2 + 1}(2) + \frac{1}{4x^2 + 1}(8x) = \frac{2}{1 + 4x^2} + \frac{8x}{4x^2 + 1} = \frac{2 + 8x}{1 + 4x^2}$$

When $x = 0.625$,

$$m_{\tan} = \frac{2 + 8(0.625)}{1 + 4(0.625)^2} = \frac{7}{2.5625} = 2.73$$

```
nDeriv(tan⁻¹(2X)+
ln(4X²+1),X,0.62
5)
           2.731707332
```

49. $y_1 = \ln(x^2),\ x^2 \neq 0$

$$\frac{dy_1}{dx} = \frac{1}{x^2}(2x) = \left.\frac{2}{x}\right|_{x=-1} = -2$$

$$y_2 = 2\ln x,\ x > 0$$

$$\frac{dy_2}{dx} = 2\left(\frac{1}{x}\right) = \left.\frac{2}{x}\right|_{x=-1}\quad \text{is not defined since}$$

$$-1 < 0$$

53. $y = \ln\left(\dfrac{1 + \sqrt{1 + x^2}}{x}\right) - \sqrt{1 - x^2}$

$$\frac{dy}{dx} = \frac{1}{\frac{1+\sqrt{1+x^2}}{x}}\left(\frac{x\left(0 + \frac{2x}{2\sqrt{1+x^2}}\right) - (1 + \sqrt{1+x^2})(1)}{x^2}\right) - \frac{-2x}{2\sqrt{1-x^2}}$$

$$\frac{dy}{dx} = \frac{x}{1+\sqrt{1+x^2}}\left(\frac{\frac{x^2}{\sqrt{1+x^2}} - 1 - \sqrt{1+x^2}}{x^2}\right) + \frac{x}{\sqrt{1-x^2}}$$

$$\frac{dy}{dx} = \frac{x^2 - \sqrt{1+x^2} - 1 - x^2}{x(1+\sqrt{1+x^2})\sqrt{1+x^2}} + \frac{x}{\sqrt{1-x^2}}$$

$$\frac{dy}{dx} = \frac{-1 - \sqrt{1+x^2}}{x\sqrt{1+x^2} + x + x^3} + \frac{x}{\sqrt{1-x^2}}$$

$$\frac{dy}{dx} = \frac{x^2 - x^2 - 1 - \sqrt{1+x^2}}{x(x^2 + 1 + \sqrt{1+x^2})} + \frac{x}{\sqrt{1-x^2}}$$

$$\frac{dy}{dx} = \frac{x^2 - (x^2 + 1 + \sqrt{1+x^2})}{x(x^2 + 1 + \sqrt{1+x^2})} + \frac{x}{\sqrt{1-x^2}}$$

$$\frac{dy}{dx} = \frac{x}{x^2 + 1 + \sqrt{1+x^2}} - \frac{1}{x} + \frac{x}{\sqrt{1-x^2}}$$

which may also be simplified to $\dfrac{dy}{dx} = \dfrac{-1}{x\sqrt{1+x^2}} + \dfrac{x}{\sqrt{1-x^2}}$

27.6   Derivative of the Exponential Function

1. $y = \ln\sin e^{2x}$

$$\frac{dy}{dx} = \frac{1}{\sin e^{2x}}(\cos e^{2x})(2e^{2x})$$

$$\frac{dy}{dx} = 2e^{2x}\cot e^{2x}$$

5. $y = e^{\sqrt{x}};$

$$\frac{dy}{dx} = e^{\sqrt{x}}\frac{1}{2}x^{-1/2} = \frac{e^{\sqrt{x}}}{2\sqrt{x}}$$

9. $R = Te^{-T}$

$$\frac{dR}{dT} = T(e^{-T})(-1) + (1)(e^{-T})$$

$$= e^{-T} - Te^{-T} = e^{-T}(1 - T)$$

13. $r = \dfrac{2(e^{2s} - e^{-2s})}{e^{2s}}$

$$r = 2(1 - e^{-4s})$$

$$\frac{dr}{ds} = 2(4e^{-4s})$$

$$\frac{dr}{ds} = 8e^{-4s}$$

17. $y = \dfrac{2e^{3x}}{4x + 3};$

$$\frac{dy}{dx} = \frac{(4x+3)(2e^{3x})(3) - (2e^{3x})(4)}{(4x+3)^2}$$

$$\frac{dy}{dx} = \frac{(12x+9)(2e^{3x}) - 8e^{3x}}{(4x+3)^2}$$

$$= \frac{2e^{3x}(12x+5)}{(4x+3)^2}$$

21. $y = (2e^{2x})^3\sin x^2$
    $= 8e^{6x}\sin x^2$

$$\frac{dy}{dx} = 8e^{6x}(\cos x^2)(2x) + \sin x^2(8e^{6x})(6)$$

$$= 16e^{6x}(x\cos x^2 + 3\sin x^2)$$

25. $y = xe^{xy} + \sin y$

$$\frac{dy}{dx} = x(e^{xy})\left(x\frac{dy}{dx} + y\right) + (1)e^{xy} + \cos y\frac{dy}{dx}$$

$$= x(e^{xy})\left(x\frac{dy}{dx}\right) + x(e^{xy})(y) + e^{xy} + \cos y\frac{dy}{dx}$$

$$\frac{dy}{dx} - x(e^{xy})\left(x\frac{dy}{dx}\right) - \cos y\frac{dy}{dx} = x(e^{xy})y + e^{xy}$$

$$\frac{dy}{dx}(1 - x(e^{xy})(x) - \cos y) = x(e^{xy})y + e^{xy}$$

$$\frac{dy}{dx} = \frac{xy(e^{xy}) + e^{xy}}{1 - x^2e^{xy} - \cos y} = \frac{e^{xy}(xy + 1)}{1 - x^2e^{xy} - \cos y}$$

29. $y = \ln\sin 2e^{6x}$

$$\frac{dy}{dx} = \frac{1}{\sin 2e^{6x}}(\cos 2e^{6x})(2e^{6x})(6)$$

$$\frac{dy}{dx} = \frac{12e^{6x}\cos 2e^{6x}}{\sin 2e^{6x}} = 12e^{6x}\cot 2e^{6x}$$

33. **(a)** $e = e^x = 2.7182818$ when $x = 1.0000$. This is the slope of a tangent line to the curve $f(x) = e^x$ when $x = 1.0000$. It is the value of $f'(x) = e^x$, since $\frac{de^x}{dx} = e^x$.

(b) $\dfrac{e^{1.0001} - e^{1.0000}}{0.0001} = 2.7184178$ This is the slope of a secant line through the curve $f(x) = e^x$ at $x = 1.0000$, where $\Delta x = 0.0001$.

$$\lim_{\Delta x \to 0}\frac{e^{(x+\Delta x)} - e^x}{\Delta x} = \frac{de^x}{dx} = e^x$$

For $\Delta x = 0.0001$, the slope of the tangent line is approximately equal to the slope of the secant line.

37. $y = e^{-2x}\cos 2x;\; x = 0.625$

$$\frac{dy}{dx} = e^{-2x}(-2\sin 2x) + \cos 2x(-2e^{-2x})$$

$$\frac{dy}{dx} = m_{TL} = -2e^{-2x}(\sin 2x + \cos 2x)$$

$$m_{TL}\big|_{x=0.625} = -0.724$$

41.

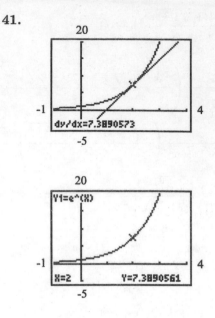

45. $y = \dfrac{e^{2x} - 1}{e^{2x} + 1}$

$$\frac{dy}{dx} = 1 - y^2$$

$$\frac{dy}{dx} = \frac{(e^{2x} + 1)2e^{2x} - (e^{2x} - 1)2e^{2x}}{(e^{2x} + 1)^2}$$

$$\frac{dy}{dx} = \frac{2e^{2x}(e^{2x} + 1 - e^{2x} + 1)}{(e^{2x} + 1)^2} = \frac{4e^{2x}}{(e^{2x} + 1)^2}$$

$$1 - y^2 = 1 - \frac{(e^{2x} - 1)^2}{(e^{2x} + 1)^2}$$

$$= \frac{(e^{2x} + 1)^2 - (e^{2x} - 1)^2}{(e^{2x} + 1)^2}$$

$$1 - y^2 = \frac{e^{4x} + 2e^{2x} + 1 - e^{4x} + 2e^{2x} - 1}{(e^{2x} + 1)^2}$$

$$= \frac{4e^{2x}}{(e^{2x} + 1)^2}$$

Q.E.D

49. $R = e^{-0.002t}; t = 100\ h: R(0 \le R \le 1)$

$$\frac{dR}{dt} = e^{-0.002t}(-0.002)$$

$$\frac{dR}{dt} = -0.002e^{-0.002t};\; \frac{dR}{dt}\bigg|_{t=100} = -0.00164/h$$

53. $\cosh^2 u - \sinh^2 u$

$$= \frac{1}{4}(e^u + e^{-u})^2 - \frac{1}{4}(e^u - e^{-u})^2$$

$$= \frac{1}{4}(e^{2u} + 2e^0 + e^{-2u}) - \frac{1}{4}(e^{2u} - 2e^0 + e^{-2u})$$

$$= \frac{1}{4}[0 + 2e^0 + 2e^0 + 0]$$

$$= \frac{1}{4}(4e^0) = \frac{1}{4}(4) = 1$$

27.7   Applications

1. $y = e^{-x} \sin x, 0 \le x \le 2\pi$

$y = 0$ for $x = 0, \pi, 2\pi$. Intercepts: $(0,0)$, $(\pi,0), (2\pi, 0)$

$$\frac{dy}{dx} = e^{-x} \cos x - e^{-x} \sin x = 0 \text{ for } \sin x = \cos x$$

$$x = \frac{\pi}{4}, \frac{5\pi}{4}$$

$$\frac{d^2 y}{dx^2} = e^{-x}(-\sin x - \cos x) - e^{-x}(\cos x - \sin x)$$

$$\frac{d^2 y}{dx^2} = e^{-x}(-2\cos x) = 0 \text{ for } x = \frac{\pi}{2}, \frac{3\pi}{2}$$

$$\left.\frac{d^2 y}{dx^2}\right|_{x=\frac{\pi}{4}} = -2e^{-\pi/4} \cos \frac{\pi}{4}$$

$$= -0.64 < 0 \Rightarrow \left(\frac{\pi}{4}, 0.322\right) \text{ is a max}$$

$$\left.\frac{d^2 y}{dx^2}\right|_{\frac{5\pi}{4}} = -2e^{-5\pi/4} \cos \frac{5\pi}{4}$$

$$= 0.03 > 0 \Rightarrow \left(\frac{5\pi}{4}, -0.014\right) \text{ is a min}$$

$\frac{d^2 y}{dx^2}$ changes from negative to positive at $x = \frac{\pi}{2}$

$(\frac{\pi}{2}, 0.208))$ is an infl. point

$\frac{d^2 y}{dx^2}$ changes from positive to negative at $x = \frac{3\pi}{2}$

$(\frac{3\pi}{2}, -0.009)$ is an infl. point

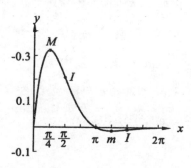

5. $y = xe^{-x} = \frac{x}{e^x}$

$$\frac{dy}{dx} = x(-e^{-x}) + e^{-x} = e^{-x}(1 - x)$$

$$\frac{d^2 y}{dx^2} = e^{-x}(-1) + (1 - x)(-e^{-x})$$

$$= e^{-x} - e^{-x} + xe^{-x} = e^{-x}(x - 2)$$

(1) Intercepts: $x = 0, y = 0$ (origin)

(2) Symmetry: none

(3) As $x \to +\infty, y \to 0$ positively. Horizontal asymptote $y = 0$. As $x \to -\infty, y \to -\infty$.

(4) Vertical asymptote: none

(5) Domain: all x, range to be determined.

(6) $\frac{dy}{dx} = 0; e^{-x}(1 - x) = 0; x = 1; f''(1) < 0$,

max. $\left(1, \frac{1}{e}\right)$

$\frac{d^2 y}{dx^2} = 0; e^{-x}(x - 2) = 0; x = 2;$ infl. $\left(2, \frac{2}{e^2}\right)$

Therefore, range: $-\infty < y \le \frac{1}{e}$

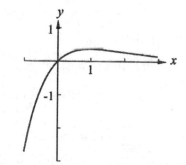

9. $y = 4e^{-x^2}; \frac{dy}{dx} = 4e^{-x^2}(-2x) = \frac{-8x}{e^{x^2}}$

$$\frac{d^2 y}{dx^2} = \frac{e^{x^2}(-8) + 8x(2xe^{x^2})}{e^{2x^2}} = 8e^{x^2}(2x^2 - 1)$$

(1) Intercepts: $x = 0, y = 4, (0, 4)$ intercept.

(2) Symmetry: yes, with respect to y-axis.

(3) As $x \to \pm\infty, y \to 0$ positively; x-axis is a horizontal asymptote.

(4) No vertical asymptote.

(5) Domain: all x; range: to be determined.

(6) $\dfrac{dy}{dx} = 0$; $\dfrac{-8x}{e^{x^2}} = 0$; $f''(0) < 0$, max. $(0,4)$

$\dfrac{d^2y}{dx^2} = 0$; $2x^2 - 1 = 0$; $x = \pm\sqrt{\dfrac{1}{2}} = \pm\dfrac{\sqrt{2}}{2}$;

$\left(-\dfrac{\sqrt{2}}{2}, \dfrac{4}{\sqrt{e}}\right)$, $\left(\dfrac{\sqrt{2}}{2}, \dfrac{4}{\sqrt{e}}\right)$ are inflection points.

Range: $0 < y \le 4$

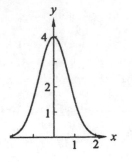

13. $y = \dfrac{1}{2}(e^x - e^{-x})$; $\dfrac{dy}{dx} = \dfrac{1}{2}(e^x + e^{-x})$

$\dfrac{d^2y}{dx^2} = \dfrac{1}{2}(e^x - e^{-x})$

(1) Intercepts: $x = 0, y = 0, (0,0)$

(2) No symmetry.

(3) As $x \to +\infty, y \to +\infty, x \to -\infty, y \to -\infty$

(4) No vertical asymptote.

(5) Domain: all x; range: all y.

(6) $\dfrac{dy}{dx} = 0$; $e^x = -e^{-x} = -\dfrac{1}{e^x}$; $(e^x)^2 = -1$;

$e^x = \sqrt{-1}$. $\dfrac{dy}{dx} > 0$, inc for all x.

(imaginary), no max,. no min.

$\dfrac{d^2y}{dx^2} = 0, e^x = e^{-x} = \dfrac{1}{e^x}$; $(e^x)^2 = 1$; $e^x = \pm 1$

$e^x \ne -1$; $e^x = 1$; $x = 0$, therefore infl. at $(0,0)$

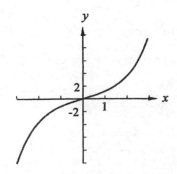

17. $y = x^2 \ln x$;

$\dfrac{dy}{dx} = x^2\left(\dfrac{1}{x}\right) + (\ln 2)(2x) = x + 2x \ln x$;

$\dfrac{dy}{dx}\bigg|_{x=1} = 1 + 2\ln 1 = 1 + 2(0) = 1$

Slope is 1, $x = 1, y = 0$; using slope intercept form of the equation and substituting gives $0 = 1(1) + b$ or $b = 1$. The equation is $y = (1)x - 1$ or $y = x - 1$.

21. $f(x) = x^2 - 2 + \ln x$; $f'(x) = 2x + \dfrac{1}{x}$;

$f(1) = 1^2 - 2 + \ln 1 = -1$;

$f(2) = 2^2 - 4 + \ln 2 = 0.69$

Therefore we choose $x_1 = 1.5$

n	x_n	$f(x_n)$	$f'(x_n)$	$x_n - \dfrac{f(x_n)}{f'(x_n)}$
1	1.5	0.6554651	3.6666667	1.3212368
2	1.3212368	0.0242349	3.3993402	1.3141075
3	1.3141075	0.0000362	3.3891878	1.3140968

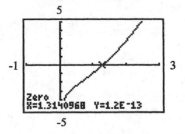

Therefore, the root is 1.3140968, which is correct to the number of decimal places shown.

25. $P = 100e^{-0.005t}$; $t = 100$ days;

$\dfrac{dP}{dt} = 100e^{-0.005t}(-0.005)$

$\dfrac{dP}{dt} = -0.5e^{-0.005t}\big|_{t=100} = -0.303$ W/day

29. $F = ka$; $x = ae^{kt} + be^{-kt}$

$\dfrac{dx}{dt} = ae^{kt} \cdot k + be^{-kt}(-k)$

$v = ake^{kt} - bke^{-kt} = k(ae^{kt} - be^{-kt})$

$\dfrac{d^2x}{dt^2} = k[ae^{kt} \cdot k - be^{-kt}(-k)]$

$a = k(ake^{kt} + bke^{-kt}) = k^2(ae^{kt} + be^{-kt}) = k^2x$

$F = ka = k(k^2a) = k^3a$; therefore, $F \propto a$ given $x = ae^{kt} + be^{-kt}$

33. $y = 6.0e^{-0.020x} \sin(0.20x), 0 \le x \le 60$

$$\frac{dy}{dx} = e^{-0.020x}\left[\frac{6\cos(0.2x)}{5} - \frac{3\sin(0.2x)}{25}\right] = 0$$

$\tan 0.2x = 10$

$\qquad 0.2x = \tan^{-1} 10 + k\pi$

$\qquad\quad x = 5\tan^{-1} 10 + 5k\pi$

$k = 0 \quad x_1 = 7.355638372, y_1 = 5.153476505$
$k = 1 \quad x_2 = 23.06360164, y_2 = -3.764113107$
$k = 2 \quad x_3 = 38.77156491, y_3 = 2.749318343$
$k = 3 \quad x_4 = 54.47952818, y_4 = -2.008109516$

$(x_1, y_1) - 117.6°$ W $50.2°$N, maximum
$(x_2, y_2) = 101.9°$ W $41.2°$ N, minimum
$(x_3, y_3) = 86.2°$ W $47.7°$ N, maximum
$(x_4, y_4) = 70.5°$ W $43.0°$ N, minimum

37. $s = kx^2 \ln\dfrac{1}{x} = k[x^2(\ln 1 - \ln x)] = -kx^2 \ln x$

$$\frac{ds}{dx} = -k\left(x^2\frac{1}{x} + \ln x\, 2x\right) = -k(x + 2x\ln x)$$

$$\frac{ds}{dx} = -kx(1 + 2\ln x) = 0$$

For max., min.:

$$x = 0;\ \ln x = -\frac{1}{2};\ x = e^{-1/2} = \frac{1}{\sqrt{e}} - 0.607$$

Chapter 27 Review Exercises

1. $y = 3\cos(4x - 1); \dfrac{dy}{dx} = [-3\sin(4x - 1)][4] = -12\sin(4x - 1)$

5. $y = \csc^2(3x + 2); \dfrac{dy}{dx} = 2\csc(3x + 2)[-\csc(3x + 2)\cot(3x + 2)](3)$

$\qquad\qquad\qquad\qquad\qquad = -6\csc^2(3x + 2)\cot(3x + 2)$

9. $y = (e^{x-3})^2; \dfrac{dy}{dx} = 2(e^{x-3})(e^{x-3})(1) = 2e^{2(x-3)}$

13. $y = 3\tan^{-1}\left(\dfrac{x}{3}\right); \dfrac{dy}{dx} = 3\left[\dfrac{1}{1 + \left(\frac{x}{3}\right)^2}\right]\dfrac{1}{3} = \dfrac{1}{1 + \left(\frac{x}{3}\right)^2} = \dfrac{1}{1 + \frac{x^2}{9}} = \dfrac{9}{9 + x^2}$

17. $y = \sqrt{\csc 4x + \cot 4x} = (\csc 4x + \cot 4x)^{1/2}$

$$\frac{dy}{dx} = \frac{1}{2}(\csc 4x + \cot 4x)^{-1/2}(-4\csc 4x \cot 4x - 4\csc^2 4x)$$

$$= \frac{1}{2}(\csc 4x + \cot 4x)^{-1/2}(-4\csc 4x)(\csc 4x + \cot 4x)$$

$$= -2\csc 4x(\csc 4x + \cot 4x)^{1/2} = (-2\csc 4x)\sqrt{\csc 4x + \cot 4x}$$

21. $y = \dfrac{\cos^2 x}{e^{3x} + 1}$

$$\frac{dy}{dx} = \frac{(e^{3x} + 1)[2\cos x(-\sin x)] - (\cos^2 x)(e^{3x})(3)}{(e^{3x} + 1)^2} = \frac{(e^{3x} + 1)[-2\sin x \cos x] - 3e^{3x}\cos^2 x}{(e^{3x} + 1)^2}$$

$$= \frac{-\cos x[(e^{3x} + 1)(2\sin x) + 3e^{3x}\cos x]}{(e^{3x} + 1)^2} = \frac{-\cos x[2e^{3x}\sin x + 2\sin x + 3e^{3x}\cos x]}{(e^{3x} + 1)^2}$$

$$= \frac{-\cos x(2e^{3x}\sin x + 3e^{3x}\cos x + 2\sin x)}{(e^{3x} + 1)^2}$$

25. $y = \ln(\csc x^2);\ \dfrac{dy}{dx} = \dfrac{1}{\csc x^2}(-\csc x^2 \cot x^2)(2x) = -2x\cot x^2$

29. $L = 0.1e^{-2t}\sec(\pi t)$

$$\frac{dL}{dt} = 0.1e^{-2t}\sec(\pi t)\tan(\pi t)\cdot \pi + \sec(\pi t)\cdot 0.1(-2)e^{-2t}$$

$$\frac{dL}{dt} = 0.1\pi e^{-2t}\sec(\pi t)\tan(\pi t) - 0.2e^{-2t}\sec(\pi t)$$

$$\frac{dL}{dt} = e^{-2t}\sec(\pi t)\cdot [0.1\pi \tan(\pi t) - 0.2]$$

33. $\tan^{-1}\dfrac{y}{x} = x^2 e^y;\ u = \dfrac{y}{x} = yx^{-1};\ \dfrac{du}{dx} = -yx^{-2} + x^{-1}\dfrac{dy}{dx}$

$$\frac{1}{1 + (yx^{-1})^2}\left(-yx^{-2} + x^{-1}\right)\frac{dy}{dx} = x^2 e^y \frac{dy}{dx} + 2xe^y$$

$$\frac{\frac{-y}{x^2} + \frac{1}{x}\frac{dy}{dx}}{1 + y^2 x^{-2}} = x^2 e^y \frac{dy}{dx} + 2xe^y$$

$$\frac{-y}{x^2} + \frac{1}{x}\frac{dy}{dx} = \left(x^2 e^y \frac{dy}{dx} + 2xe^y\right)(1 + y^2 x^{-2})$$

$$\frac{-y}{x^2} + \frac{1}{x}\frac{dy}{dx} = x^2 e^y \frac{dy}{dx} + 2xe^y + y^2 e^y \frac{dy}{dx} + 2x^{-1}y^2 e^y$$

$$\frac{1}{x}\frac{dy}{dx} - x^2 e^y \frac{dy}{dx} - y^2 e^y \frac{dy}{dx} = 2xe^y + 2x^{-1}y^2 e^y + \frac{y}{x^2}$$

$$\frac{dy}{dx}\left(\frac{1}{x} - x^2 e^y - y^2 e^y\right) = 2xe^y + \frac{2y^2 ey}{x} + \frac{y}{x^2}$$

$$\frac{dy}{dx}\left(\frac{1 - x^3 e^y - xy^2 e^y}{x}\right) = \frac{2xe^y + 2xy^2 e^y + y}{x^2}$$

$$\frac{dy}{dx} = \frac{2x^3 e^y + 2xy^2 e^y + y}{x^2}\cdot\frac{x}{1 - x^3 e^y - xy^2 e^y}$$

$$\frac{dy}{dx} = \frac{2x^3 e^y + 2xy^2 e^y + y}{x - x^4 e^y - x^2 y^2 e^y}$$

37. $\ln xy + ye^{-x} = 1$

Using implicit differentiation, $\dfrac{d\ln xy}{dx} + \dfrac{dye^{-x}}{dx} = \dfrac{d(1)}{dx}$

$$\frac{1}{xy}\left(x\frac{dy}{dx} + y\frac{dx}{dy}\right) + y\frac{de^{-x}}{dx} + e^{-x}\frac{dy}{dx} = 0$$

$$\frac{1}{xy}\left(x\frac{dy}{dx} + y\right) + ye^{-x}(-1) + e^{-x}\frac{dy}{dx} = 0$$

$$\frac{1}{y}\frac{dy}{dx} + \frac{1}{x} - ye^{-x} + e^{-x}\frac{dy}{dx} = 0$$

$$\frac{1}{y}\frac{dy}{dx} + e^{-x}\frac{dy}{dx} = ye^{-x} - \frac{1}{x}$$

$$\frac{dy}{dx}\left(\frac{1}{y} + e^{-x}\right) = ye^{-x} - \frac{1}{x}$$

$$\frac{dy}{dx}\left(\frac{1 + ye^{-x}}{y}\right) = \frac{xye^{-x} - 1}{x}$$

$$\frac{dy}{dx} = \left(\frac{xye^{-x} - 1}{x}\right)\left(\frac{y}{1 + ye^{-x}}\right) = \frac{y(xye^{-x} - 1)}{x(1 + ye^{-x})}$$

41. $y = x - \cos x;\ \dfrac{dy}{dx} = 1 + \sin x;\ \dfrac{d^2y}{dx^2} = \cos x$ Infl.: $\left(\dfrac{1}{2}\pi, \dfrac{1}{2}\pi\right), \left(\dfrac{3}{2}\pi, \dfrac{3}{2}\pi\right)$

(a) $x = 0, y = 0 - \cos 0 = 0 - 1 = -1;\ (0, -1)$ is an intercept. $x - \cos x = 0$ when $x = \cos x$; $x = 0.74$ (see Table 3); $(0.74, 0)$ is an intercept.

(b) y is defined for all x; no asymptotes.

(c) Critical points occur at $1 + \sin x = 0$, $\sin x = -1$, $x = -\dfrac{\pi}{2}, \dfrac{3\pi}{2}, \dfrac{7\pi}{2}$, etc.

(d) Inflections occur at $\cos x = 0$, $x = -\dfrac{\pi}{2}, \dfrac{\pi}{2}, \dfrac{3\pi}{2}, \dfrac{5\pi}{2}$, etc., since the second derivative undergoes a change of sign at each of these points.

(e) All critical points are inflections; no maximum or minimum points.

(f) Checking concavity at $x = 0, -\cos 0 = -1$; the graph is concave up at $(0, -1)$ and on each side of this point up to the inflection points at $\left(-\frac{\pi}{2}, -\frac{\pi}{2}\right)$ and $\left(\frac{\pi}{2}, \frac{\pi}{2}\right)$. It will switch concavity again at each subsequent inflection point.

x	$-\frac{3\pi}{2}$	$-\pi$	$-\frac{\pi}{2}$	0	0.7	$\frac{\pi}{2}$	π	$\frac{3\pi}{2}$
y	-4.7	-4.1	-1.6	-1	0	1.6	4.1	4.7

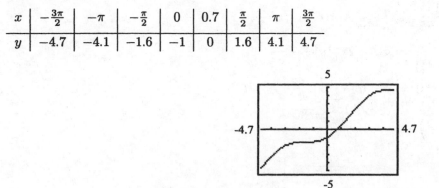

45. $y = 4\cos^2(x^2)$; slope $= \dfrac{dy}{dx} = 2[4\cos(x^2)][-\sin(x^2)](2x) = -16x\cos x^2 \sin x^2$

$$\left.\dfrac{dy}{dx}\right|_{x=1} = -16\cos(1^2)\sin(1^2) = -16(0.5403)(0.8415) = -7.27$$

$$f(1) = 4\cos^2(1^2) = 4(0.5403)^2 = 1.168$$

By Eq. (21-9), $y = -7.27x + b$; $1.168 = -7.27(1) + b$, $b = 8.44$; $y = -7.27x + 8.44$; $7.27x + y - 8.44 = 0$

49. $\sin^2 x + \cos^2 x = 1$

$$\dfrac{d(\sin^2 x + \cos^2 x)}{dx} = \dfrac{d(1)}{dx}$$

$$\dfrac{d\sin^2 x}{dx} + \dfrac{d\cos^2 x}{dx} = 0$$

$$2\sin x \cos x + 2\cos x(-\sin x) = 0$$

$$2\sin x \cos x - 2\cos x \sin x = 0;\ 0 = 0$$

53. $y = e^x - 2e^{-x}$

$$\dfrac{dy}{dx} = e^x + 2e^{-x}$$

$$\dfrac{d^2y}{dx^2} = e^x - 2e^{-x} > 0$$

$$e^{2x} > 2$$

$$2x > \ln 2$$

$$x > \dfrac{1}{2}\ln 2 \approx 0.3466$$

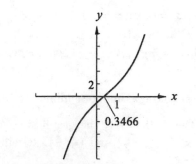

$y = e^x - 2e^{-x}$ is concave up for $x > \dfrac{1}{2}\ln 2$

57. $y = 0.75(\sec\sqrt{0.15t} - 1)$

$$\dfrac{dy}{dt} = 0.75\sec\sqrt{0.15t}\,\tan\sqrt{0.15t}\,\left.\dfrac{0.15}{2\sqrt{0.15t}}\right|_{t=5.0}$$

$$\left.\dfrac{dy}{dt}\right|_{t=5.0} = 0.12\ \text{m/s}$$

61. $W = 10\cos 2t$

$$P = \dfrac{dW}{dt} = -20\sin 2t$$

65. $\quad I = kE_0^2 \cos^2 \dfrac{1}{2}\theta$

$$\frac{dI}{d\theta} = ke_0^2 \left(2\cos\frac{1}{2}\theta\right)\left(-\sin\frac{1}{2}\theta\right)\left(\frac{1}{2}\right)$$

$$\frac{dI}{d\theta} = -kE_0^2 \sin\frac{1}{2}\theta \cos\frac{1}{2}\theta$$

69. $\quad w = \sqrt{\dfrac{g}{l\cos\theta}}, g = 9.800 \text{ m/s}^2, l = 0.6375 \text{ m}$
$\theta = 32.50°, d\theta = 0.25°$

$$\Delta w \approx dw = \frac{1}{2}\sqrt{\frac{g}{l\cos\theta}}\tan\theta\, d\theta$$

$$\Delta w \approx \frac{1}{2}\sqrt{\frac{9.800}{0.6375\cos 32.5°}}\tan 32.5° \left(\frac{\pi}{180°}\right)$$

$$\Delta w \approx 0.005934 \text{ rad/s}$$

73. $\quad n = 160 - 140e^{-0.30t}$

$$\frac{du}{dt} = 42e^{-0.30t}\Big|_{t=10} = 2.091056871$$

In 2010 the annual rate of increase of Internet users will be 2,100,000/year

77.

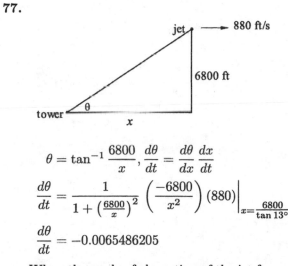

$$\theta = \tan^{-1}\frac{6800}{x}, \frac{d\theta}{dt} = \frac{d\theta}{dx}\frac{dx}{dt}$$

$$\frac{d\theta}{dt} = \frac{1}{1+\left(\frac{6800}{x}\right)^2}\left(\frac{-6800}{x^2}\right)(880)\Big|_{x=\frac{6800}{\tan 13°}}$$

$$\frac{d\theta}{dt} = -0.0065486205$$

When the angle of eleveation of the jet from the control tower is 13°, the angle of elevation is changing -0.0065 rad/s

81. $\quad x = r(\theta - \sin\theta); y = r(1-\cos\theta); r = 5.00 \text{ cm}; \dfrac{d\theta}{dt} = 0.12 \text{ rad/s}; \theta = 35°$

horizontal component of velocity,

$$v_x = \frac{dx}{dt} = \frac{d[5.5(\theta - \sin\theta]}{dt} = 5.5\left(\frac{d\theta}{dt} - \cos\theta\frac{d\theta}{dt}\right) = 5.5(0.12 - 0.12\cos 35°) = 0.119 \text{ cm/s}$$

vertical component of velocity,

$$v_y = \frac{dy}{dt} = \frac{d[5.5(1-\cos\theta)]}{dt} = 5.5\sin\theta\frac{d\theta}{dt} = (5.5)(0.12)\sin 35° = 0.379$$

$$v = \sqrt{0.119^2 + 0.379^2} = 0.4 \text{ cm/s}. \quad \theta = \tan^{-1}\frac{0.379}{0.119} = 72.5°$$

83. $I = \dfrac{k\cos\theta}{r^2}, \cos\theta = \dfrac{h}{r}$

   $I = \dfrac{kh}{r^3}, r^2 = h^2 + 10.0^2 \Rightarrow r^3 = (h^2 + 100)^{3/2}$

   $I = \dfrac{kh}{(h^2 + 100)^{3/2}}$

   $\dfrac{dI}{dh} = \dfrac{2k(50 - h^2)}{(h^2 + 100)^{5/2}} = 0$

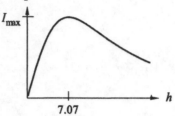

   for $h^2 = 50$

   $\qquad h = 7.07$

The illuminance at the circumference will be a max for a light placed 7.07 in. above the center of the circle.

87. $y = \dfrac{H}{w}\cosh\dfrac{wx}{H}$

   $\dfrac{dy}{dx} = \sinh\dfrac{wx}{H}$

   $\dfrac{d^2y}{dx^2} = \dfrac{w}{H}\cosh\dfrac{wx}{H}$

   $\dfrac{w}{H}\sqrt{1 + \left(\dfrac{dy}{dx}\right)^2} = \dfrac{w}{H}\sqrt{1 + \left(\dfrac{\sinh wx}{H}\right)^2}$

   $\qquad\qquad\qquad = \dfrac{w}{H}\sqrt{\left(\cosh\dfrac{wx}{H}\right)^2}$

   $\qquad\qquad\qquad = \dfrac{w}{H}\cosh\dfrac{wx}{H}$

   $\qquad\qquad\qquad = \dfrac{d^2y}{dx^2}$

METHODS OF INTEGRATION

28.1 The General Power Formula

1. Change $\cos x$ to $-\sin x$, then

$$\int \cos^3 x(-\sin x\, dx) = \frac{1}{4}\cos^4 x + C$$

5. $u = \cos x$; $n = \frac{1}{2}$; $du = -\sin x\, dx$

$$0.4\int \sqrt{\cos x}\,\sin x\, dx = 0.4\int (\cos x)^{1/2}(-\sin x\, dx)$$

$$= -\frac{0.8}{3}(\cos x)^{3/2} + C$$

9. Let $u = \cos 2x$; $n = 1$; $du = -2\sin 2x\, dx$

$$\int_0^{\pi/8} \cos 2x \sin 2x\, dx$$

$$= -\frac{1}{2}\int_0^{\pi/8} (\cos 2x)^{-1}(-2\sin 2x\, dx)$$

$$= -\frac{1}{2}\frac{(\cos 2x)^2}{2}\Big|_0^{\pi/8}$$

$$= -\frac{1}{4}\cos^2 2x\Big|_0^{\pi/8}$$

$$= -\frac{1}{4}\left(\cos^2\frac{\pi}{4} - \cos^2 0\right)$$

$$= -\frac{1}{4}\left(\frac{1}{2} - 1\right) = \frac{1}{8}$$

13. $u = \tan^{-1} 5x$; $du = \dfrac{1}{1+25x^2}(5\, dx)$; $n = 1$

$$\int \frac{5\tan^{-1} 5x}{1+25x^2}dx = \int (\tan^{-1} 5x)^1\frac{5\, dx}{1+25x^2}$$

$$= \frac{1}{2}(\tan^{-1} 5x)^2 + C$$

17. $u = \ln(2x+3)$; $du = \dfrac{1}{2x+3}(2\, dx)$; $n = 1$

$$\frac{1}{2}\int_0^{1/2}[\ln(2x+3)]\frac{2\, dx}{2x+3} = \frac{1}{2}\frac{[\ln(2x+3)]^2}{2}\Big|_0^{1/2}$$

$$= \frac{1}{4}\ln^2(2x+3)\Big|_0^{1/2}$$

$$= \frac{1}{4}(\ln^2 4 - \ln^2 3)$$

$$= 0.179$$

21. $\displaystyle\int \frac{e^{2t}}{(1-e^{2t})^3}dt$. Let $u = 1-e^{2t}$, $du = -2e^{2t}\, dt$.

$$\int \frac{e^{2t}}{(1-e^{2t})^3}dt = -\frac{1}{2}\int (1-e^{2t})^{-3}(-2e^{2t}\, dt)$$

$$= -\frac{1}{2}\int u^{-3}du = -\frac{1}{2}\cdot\frac{u^{-3+1}}{-3+1} + C$$

$$= -\frac{1}{2}\cdot\frac{1}{-2(u^2)} + C$$

$$= \frac{1}{4(1-e^{2t})^2 + C}$$

25. $\displaystyle\int_{\pi/6}^{\pi/4}(1+\cot x)^2\csc^2 x\, dx$

$$= \int_{\pi/6}^{\pi/4}(1+\cot x)^2(-\csc^2 x\, dx)$$

$$= -\frac{(1+\cot x)^3}{3}\Big|_{\pi/6}^{\pi/4}$$

$$= -\frac{(1+\cot\frac{\pi}{4})^3}{3} + \frac{(1+\cot\frac{\pi}{6})^3}{3}$$

$$= 2\sqrt{3} + \frac{2}{3}$$

$$= 4.1308$$

29. $\displaystyle\int \frac{\sqrt{(1+e^{-r})(1-e^{-r})}}{e^{2r}}dr$

$$= \int \frac{\sqrt{1-e^{-r}+e^{-r}-e^{-2r}}}{e^{2r}}dr$$

$$= \int \frac{\sqrt{1-e^{-2r}}}{e^{2r}}dr$$

$$= \int (1-e^{-2r})^{1/2}(e^{-2r}dr)$$

which has the form $\displaystyle\int u^n du$ with $u = 1-e^{-2r}$,

$$n = \frac{1}{2}, du = 2e^{-2r}dr$$

33. $P = mnv^2 \displaystyle\int_0^{\pi/2} \sin\theta \cos^2\theta \, d\theta; \quad n = 2;$

$\mu = \cos\theta; \; du = -\sin\theta \, d\theta$

$P = mnv^2 \displaystyle\int_0^{\pi/2} \cos^2\theta(-\sin\theta \, d\theta)$

$= -mnv^2 \left[\dfrac{\cos^3\theta}{3} \right]\Big|_0^{\pi/2}$

$= -mnv^2 \left[\dfrac{1}{3}\left(\cos^3\dfrac{\pi}{2} - \cos^3 0 \right) \right]$

$= -mnv^2 \left[\dfrac{1}{3}(0 - 1) \right]$

$= -mnv^2 \left(-\dfrac{1}{3} \right) = \dfrac{1}{3}mnv^2$

28.2   The Basic Logarithmic Form

1. Add $2x$ to the integrand, then

$\displaystyle\int \frac{2x \, dx}{x^2 + 1} = \ln|x^2 + 1| + C$

5. $\displaystyle\int \frac{2x \, dx}{4 - 3x^2}; \; u = 4 - 3x^2; \; du = -6x \, dx$

$-\dfrac{1}{3}\displaystyle\int \frac{-6x \, dx}{4 - 3x^2} = -\dfrac{1}{3}\ln|4 - 3x^2| + C$

9. $0.4\displaystyle\int \frac{\csc^2 2\theta \, d\theta}{\cot 2\theta}; \; u = \cot 2\theta; \; du = -2\csc^2 2\theta \, d\theta$

$\dfrac{0.4}{2}\displaystyle\int \frac{2\csc^2 2\theta \, d\theta}{\cot 2\theta} = -0.2\ln|\cot 2\theta| + C$

13. $u = 1 - e^{-x}; \; du = e^{-x}dx$

$\displaystyle\int \frac{e^{-x}dx}{1 - e^{-x}} = \ln|1 - e^{-x}| + C$

17. $u = 1 + 4\sec x; \; du = 4\sec x \tan x \, dx$

$\displaystyle\int \frac{\sec x \tan x \, dx}{1 + 4\sec x} = \dfrac{1}{4}\displaystyle\int \frac{4\sec x \tan x \, dx}{1 + 4\sec x}$

$= \dfrac{1}{4}\ln|1 + 4\sec x| + C$

21. $u = \ln r; \; du = \dfrac{dr}{r}$

$0.5\displaystyle\int \frac{dr}{r \ln r} = 0.5\displaystyle\int \frac{\frac{dr}{r}}{\ln r} = 0.5\ln|\ln r| + C$

25. $n = -\dfrac{1}{2}; \; u = 1 - 2x; \; du = -2\,dx$

$\displaystyle\int \frac{2\,dx}{\sqrt{1 - 2x}} = -\displaystyle\int (1 - 2x)^{-1/2} = 2\,dx$

$= -(1 - 2x)^{1/2} \cdot 2 + C$

$= -2\sqrt{1 - 2x} + C$

29. $u = 4 + \tan 3x; \; du = 3\sec^2 3x \, dx$

$\displaystyle\int_0^{\pi/12} \frac{\sec^2 3x}{4 + \tan 3x}dx = \dfrac{1}{3}\displaystyle\int_0^{\pi/12} \frac{3\sec^2 3x \, dx}{(4 + \tan 3x)}$

$= \dfrac{1}{3}\ln|4 + \tan 3x|\Big|_0^{\pi/12}$

$= \dfrac{1}{3}(\ln 5 - \ln 4) = \dfrac{1}{3}\ln\dfrac{5}{4}$

$= 0.0744$

33.

$\begin{array}{r} 1 \\ x + 4 \overline{)\, x - 4} \\ \underline{x + 4} \\ -8 \end{array}$

$\displaystyle\int \frac{x - 4}{x + 4}dx = \displaystyle\int dx - \displaystyle\int \frac{8}{x + 4}dx$

$= x - 8\ln|x + 4| + C$

37. $m = \dfrac{dy}{dx} = \dfrac{\sin x}{3 + \cos x}; \; y = \displaystyle\int \frac{1}{3 + \cos x} \times \sin x \, dx$

$y = -\displaystyle\int \frac{1}{3 + \cos x}(-\sin x)\,dx;$

let $u = 3 + \cos x; \; du = -\sin x \, dx$

$y = -\displaystyle\int \frac{1}{u}du = -\ln|u| + C$

$= -\ln(3 + \cos x) + C$

$2 = -\ln\left(3 + \cos\dfrac{\pi}{3}\right) + C;$ substitute values of x

and y

$2 = -\ln(3 + 0.5) + C; \; C = 2 + \ln 3.5$

$y = -\ln(3 + \cos x) + \ln 3.5 + 2;$ substituting for C

$y = \ln\dfrac{3.5}{3 + \cos x} + 2$

41. $t = L \int \dfrac{di}{E - iR}$; $u = E - iR$; $du = -R\,di$

$t = -\dfrac{L}{R} \int \dfrac{-R\,di}{E - iR} = \dfrac{-L}{R} \ln|E - iR| + C$;

$t = 0$ for $i = 0$

$0 = -\dfrac{L}{R} \ln E + C$; $C = \dfrac{L}{R} \ln|E|$

$t = \dfrac{L}{R}(-\ln|E - iR| + \ln|E|)$

$t = \dfrac{L}{R} \ln \dfrac{E}{E - iR}$; $\dfrac{R}{L}t = \ln \dfrac{E}{E - iR}$; $e^{Rt/L} = \dfrac{E}{E - iR}$

$i = \dfrac{E}{R} - \dfrac{E}{R}e^{-Rt/L}$; $i = \dfrac{E}{R}(1 - e^{-Rt/L})$

28.3   The Exponential Form

1. $\displaystyle\int 3x^2 e^{x^3}\,dx = \int e^{x^3}(3x^2\,dx)$

$\qquad = e^{x^3} + C$

5. $u = 2x + 5$; $du = 2\,dx$

$\displaystyle\int e^{2x+5}\,dx = \frac{1}{2} \int e^{2x+5}(2\,dx) = \frac{1}{2}e^{2x+5} + C$

9. $y = x^3$; $du = 3x^2\,dx$

$\displaystyle\int 6r^2 e^{r^3}\,dr = 6 \int e^{r^3}(r^2\,dr) = \frac{6}{3} \int e^{r^3}(3r^2\,dr)$

$\qquad = 2e^{x^3} + C$

13. $u = 2\sec\theta$; $du = 2\sec\theta\tan\theta\,d\theta$

$\displaystyle\int 4(\sec\theta\tan\theta)e^{2\sec\theta}\,d\theta = \frac{4}{2} \int e^{2\sec\theta}2\sec\theta\tan\theta\,d\theta$

$\qquad = 2e^{2\sec\theta} + C$

17. $u = -2x$; $du = -2\,dx$

$\displaystyle\int_1^3 3e^{2x}(e^{-2x} - 1)\,dx = 3 \int (e^0 - e^{2x})\,dx$

$\qquad = 3 \int dx - \frac{3}{2} \int e^{2x}(2\,dx)$

$\qquad = 3x - \frac{3}{2}e^{2x}\Big|_1^3$

$\qquad = \left[9 - \frac{3}{2}e^6 - \left(3 - \frac{3}{2}e^2\right)\right]$

$\qquad = 9 - 3 - \frac{3}{2}e^6 + \frac{3}{2}e^2$

$\qquad = 6 - \frac{3}{2}(e^6 - e^2) = -588.06$

21. $u = \tan^{-1}x$; $du = \dfrac{1}{1 + x^2}\,dx$

$\displaystyle\int \frac{e^{\tan^{-1}x}}{x^2 + 1}\,dx = \int e^{\tan^{-1}x}\frac{dx}{x^2 + 1} = e^{\tan^{-1}x} + C$

25. $u = \cos^2 x$;

$du = 2\cos x(-\sin x)\,dx = -2\sin x\cos x\,dx$

$\qquad = -2\sin 2x\,dx$

$\displaystyle\int_0^\pi (\sin 2x)e^{\cos^2 x}\,dx = -\frac{1}{2} \int_0^\pi e^{\cos^2 x}(-2\sin 2x\,dx)$

$\qquad = -\frac{1}{2}e^{\cos^2 x}\Big|_0^\pi$

$\qquad = -\frac{1}{2}[(\cos\pi)^2 - (\cos 0)^2]$

$\qquad = -\frac{1}{2}[(-1)^2 - 1^2] = 0$

29. Let $y = e^{\ln x}$

$\qquad \ln y = \ln e^{\ln x} = \ln x\ln e$

$\qquad \ln y = \ln x$

$\qquad y = x$

$\qquad e^{\ln x} = x$

$\displaystyle\int 2e^{x^2 + \ln x}\,dx = \int 2e^{x^2}e^{\ln x}\,dx$

$\qquad = \int 2e^{x^2}x\,dx = \int 2e^{x^2}(2x\,dx)$

$\qquad = e^{x^2} + C$

33. $y_{av} = \dfrac{\displaystyle\int_0^4 e^{2x}\,dx}{4 - 0} = \dfrac{\dfrac{1}{2}\displaystyle\int e^{2x}(2\,dx)}{4}$

$\qquad = \dfrac{\dfrac{1}{2}e^{2x}\Big|_0^4}{4} = \dfrac{1}{8}e^{2x}\Big|_0^4$

$\qquad = \dfrac{1}{8}(e^8 - 1) = 372$

37. $qe^{t/RC} = \dfrac{E}{R} \int e^{t/RC}\,dt$; $u = \dfrac{t}{RC}$; $du = \dfrac{1}{RC}\,dt$

$qe^{t/RC} = RC \cdot \dfrac{E}{R} \int e^{t/RC}\left(\dfrac{1}{RC}\right)\,dt$

$qe^{t/RC}EC(e^{t/RC}) + C_1$, where C_1 is the constant of integration.

$\qquad q = 0$ for $t = 0$; $0 = EC + C_1$; $C_1 = -EC$;

$qe^{t/RC} = EC(r^{t/RC}) - EC$

$\qquad q = EC - \dfrac{EC}{e^{t/RC}}$; $q = EC(1 - e^{-t/RC})$

28.4   Basic Trigonometric Forms

1. Change $x\,dx$ to $3x^2\,dx$ then

$$\int \sec^2 x^3 (3x^2 dx) = \tan x^3 + C$$

5. $u = 3\theta;\ du = 3\,d\theta$

$$\int 0.3 \sec^2 3\theta\,d\theta = 0.3 \int \sec^2 3\theta (3\,d\theta)$$

$$= 0.1 \tan 3\theta + C$$

9. $u = x^3;\ du = 3x^2 dx$

$$\int_{0.5}^{1} x^2 \cot x^3 dx = \frac{1}{3} \int_{0.5}^{1} \cot x^3 (3x^2 dx)$$

$$= \frac{1}{3} \ln \left| \sin x^3 \right| \Big|_{0.5}^{1}$$

$$= \frac{1}{3} \left(\ln |\sin 1| - \ln \left| \sin \frac{1}{8} \right| \right)$$

$$= 0.6365$$

13. $u = \dfrac{1}{x} = x^{-1};$

$$du = -1x^{-2}dx = -\frac{dx}{x^2}$$

$$\int \frac{\sin\left(\frac{1}{x}\right)}{x^2}dx = -\int \sin\left(\frac{1}{x}\right)\left(-\frac{dx}{x^2}\right)$$

$$= -\left[-\cos\left(\frac{1}{x}\right) \right] + C$$

$$= \cos\left(\frac{1}{x}\right) + C$$

17. $u = 5x;\ du = 5\,dx$

$$\int \frac{\sec 5x}{\cot 5x}dx = \int \sec 5x \tan 5x\,dx$$

$$= \frac{1}{5} \int \sec 5x \tan 5x (5\,dx)$$

$$= \frac{1}{5} \sec 5x + C$$

21. $\displaystyle\int \frac{1 + \sin 2T}{\tan 2T}dT$

$$= \int \frac{dT}{\tan 2T} + \int \frac{\sin 2T}{\tan 2T}dT$$

$$= \int \cot 2T\,dT + \int \cos 2T\,dT$$

$u = 2T;\ du = 2\,dT$

$$= \frac{1}{2} \int \cot 2T (2\,dT) + \frac{1}{2} \int \cos 2T (2\,dT)$$

$$= \frac{1}{2} \ln |\sin 2T| + \frac{1}{2} \sin 2T + C$$

$$= \frac{1}{2} (\ln |\sin 2T| + \sin 2T) + C$$

25. $\sin 3x \left(\dfrac{1}{\sin 3x} + \dfrac{1}{\cos 3x} \right) = 1 + \tan 3x;$

$u = 3x;\ du = 3\,dx$

$$\int_{0}^{\pi/9} \sin 3x (\csc 3x + \sec 3x)dx$$

$$= \int_{0}^{\pi/9} (1 + \tan 3x)dx$$

$$= \int_{0}^{\pi/9} dx + \int_{0}^{\pi/9} \tan 3x\,dx$$

$$= \int_{0}^{\pi/9} dx + \frac{1}{3} \int_{0}^{\pi/9} \tan 3x (3\,dx)$$

$$= \left(x - \frac{1}{3} \ln |\cos 3x| \right) \Big|_{0}^{\pi/9}$$

$$= \frac{\pi}{9} - \frac{1}{3} \ln \left| \cos \frac{\pi}{3} \right| - \left(0 - \frac{1}{3} \ln |\cos 0| \right)$$

$$= \frac{\pi}{9} - \frac{1}{3} \ln \left(\frac{1}{2} \right) = \frac{\pi}{9} + \frac{1}{3} \ln 2$$

$$= 0.580$$

29. $\displaystyle\int \frac{dx}{1 + \sin x} = \int \frac{dx}{1 + \sin x} \cdot \frac{1 - \sin x}{1 - \sin x}$

$$= \int \frac{(1 - \sin x)}{1 - \sin^2 x}dx$$

$$= \int \frac{1 - \sin x}{\cos^2 x}dx$$

$$= \int \frac{1}{\cos^2 x}dx + \int \frac{-\sin x\,dx}{\cos^2 x}$$

$$= \int (\sec^2 x\,dx - \sec x \tan x)dx$$

$$= \tan x - \sec x + C$$

33. $\omega = -0.25\sin 2.5t$

$$\theta = \int -0.25\sin 2.5t\,dt;\ u = 2.5t;\ du = 2.5\,dt$$

$$\theta = -0.10\int \sin 2.5t(2.5\,dt) = -0.10(-\cos 2.5t) + C$$

$\theta = 0.10\cos 2.5t + C$

$0.10 = 0.10\cos 0 + C;\ C = 0;\ \theta = 0.10\cos 2.5t$

28.5   Other Trigonometric Forms

1. Change dx to $\cos 2x\,dx$, then

$$\int \sin^2 2x(\cos 2x\,dx) = \frac{1}{2}\int \sin^2 2x(2\cos 2x\,dx) = \frac{1}{2}\cdot\frac{\sin^3 2x}{3} + C = \frac{\sin^3 2x}{6} + C$$

5. $u = 2x;\ du = 2\,dx;\ u = \cos 2x;\ du = -2\sin 2x\,dx$

$$\int \sin^3 2x\,dx = \int \sin^2 2x\sin 2x\,dx = \int(1 - \cos^2 2x)\sin 2x\,dx = \int \sin 2x\,dx - \int \cos^2 2x\sin 2x\,dx$$

$$= \frac{1}{2}\int \sin 2x(2\,dx) + \frac{1}{2}\int \cos^2 2x(-2\sin 2x\,dx) = -\frac{1}{2}\cos 2x + \frac{1}{2}\frac{\cos^3 2x}{3} + C$$

$$= -\frac{1}{2}\cos 2x + \frac{1}{6}\cos^3 2x + C$$

9. $u = \cos x;\ du = -\sin x\,dx$

$$\int_0^{\pi/4} 5\sin^5 x\,dx = 5\int_0^{\pi/4} \sin x\sin^4 x\,dx = 5\int_0^{\pi/4} \sin x(1 - \cos^2 x)^2 dx = 5\int_0^{\pi/4} \sin x(1 - 2\cos^2 x + \cos^4 x)dx$$

$$= 5\left(\int \sin x\,dx - 2\int \cos^2 x\sin x\,dx + \int \cos^4 x\sin x\,dx\right) - 5(-\cos x) + 10\frac{\cos^3 x}{3} - 5\left.\frac{\cos^5 x}{5}\right|_0^{\pi/4}$$

$$= 5\left(-\frac{1}{\sqrt{2}}\right) + \frac{10}{3}\left(\frac{1}{\sqrt{2}}\right)^3 - \left(\frac{1}{\sqrt{2}}\right)^5 - \left[5(-1) + \frac{10}{3}(1) - 1\right]$$

$$= -\frac{5}{\sqrt{2}} + \frac{10}{3}\frac{1}{2\sqrt{2}} - \frac{1}{4\sqrt{2}} - \left(-5 + \frac{10}{3} - 1\right) = \frac{-60 + 10(2) - 3}{12\sqrt{2}} - \left[\frac{-15 + 10 - 3}{3}\right]$$

$$= \frac{-43 + 32\sqrt{2}}{12\sqrt{2}} = \frac{64 - 43\sqrt{2}}{24} = 0.1329$$

13. $$\int 2(1 + \cos 3\phi)^2 d\phi = \int 2(1 + 2\cos 3\phi + \cos^2 3\phi)d\phi = \int(2 + 4\cos 3\phi + 2\cos^2 3\phi)d\phi$$

$$= 2\phi + \frac{4\sin 3\phi}{3} + \int(1 + \cos 6\phi)d\phi = 2\phi + \frac{4\sin 3\phi}{3} + \phi + \frac{1}{6}\int \cos 6\phi(6\,d\phi)$$

$$= 3\phi + \frac{4\sin 3\phi}{3} + \frac{\sin 6\phi}{6} + C = \frac{1}{3}(9\phi + 4\sin 3\phi + \sin 3\phi\cos 3\phi) + C$$

17. $u = \tan x;\ du = \sec^2 x\,dx$

$$\int_0^{\pi/4} \tan x\sec^4 x\,dx = \int_0^{\pi/4} \tan x\sec^2 x(1 + \tan^2 x)dx = \int_0^{\pi/4}(\tan x)^1\sec x\,dx + \int_0^{\pi/4} \tan^3 x\sec^2 x\,dx$$

$$= \frac{1}{2}(\tan x)^2 + \left.\frac{1}{4}(\tan x)^4\right|_0^{\pi/4} = \frac{1}{2}(1)^2 + \frac{1}{4}(1)^4 = \frac{1}{2} + \frac{1}{4} = \frac{3}{4}$$

21. $\displaystyle\int 0.5 \sin s \sin 2s \, ds = \int 0.5 \sin s \cdot 2 \sin s \cos s \, ds = \int \sin^2 s \cos s \, ds = \frac{\sin^3 s}{3} + C$

25. $\displaystyle\int \frac{1 - \cot x}{\sin^4 x} dx$

$\displaystyle = \int (1 - \cot x) \csc^4 x \, dx = \int (1 - \cot x) \csc^2 x (1 + \cot^2 x) dx = \int (1 - \cot x + \cot^2 x - \cot^3 x \csc^2 x \, dx)$

$\displaystyle = \int \csc^2 x \, dx - \int \cot x \csc^2 x \, dx + \int \cot^2 x \csc^2 x \, dx - \int \cot^3 x \csc^2 x \, dx$

$\displaystyle = \int \csc^2 x \, dx + \int \cot x(-\csc^2 x \, dx) - \int \cot^2 x(-\csc^2 x \, dx) + \int \cot^3 x(-\csc^2 x \, dx)$

$\displaystyle = -\cot x + \frac{\cot^2 x}{2} - \frac{\cot^3 x}{3} + \frac{\cot^4 x}{4} + C = \frac{1}{4}\cot^4 x - \frac{1}{3}\cot^3 x + \frac{1}{2}\cot^2 x - \cot x + C$

29. $\displaystyle\int \sec^6 x \, dx = \int \sec^4 x(1 + \tan^2 x) dx = \int \sec^4 x \, dx + \int \sec^4 x \tan^2 x \, dx$

$\displaystyle = \int \sec^2 x(1 + \tan^2 x) dx + \int \sec^2 x(1 + \tan^2 x) x \, dx$

$\displaystyle = \int \sec^2 x \, dx + \int \tan^2 x \sec^2 x \, dx + \int \tan^2 x \sec^2 x \, dx + \int \tan^4 x \sec^2 x \, dx$

$\displaystyle = \tan x + \frac{1}{3}\tan^3 x + \frac{1}{3}\tan^3 x + \frac{1}{5}\tan^5 + C = \frac{1}{5}\tan^5 x + \frac{2}{3}\tan^3 x + \tan x + C$

33. $y = \sin x; \; y = \cos x, x = 0; \text{ Quad I}$

$\sin x = \cos x$

$\tan x = 1; \; x = \dfrac{\pi}{4}$

$\displaystyle A_{0,\pi 4} = \int_0^{\pi/4} (y_1 - y_2) dx = \int_0^{\pi/4} (\cos x - \sin x) dx; \; A = \int_0^{\pi/4} \cos x \, dx - \int_0^{\pi/4} \sin x \, dx = \sin x + \cos x \Big|_0^{\pi/4} = 0.414$

37. $\displaystyle\int_0^{\pi} \sin^2 nx \, dx = \int_0^{\pi} \frac{1 - \cos 2nx}{2} dx = \int_0^{\pi} \frac{1}{2} dx - \frac{1}{2n} \int_0^{\pi} (\cos 2nx)(2n \, dx) = \frac{x}{2}\Big|_0^{\pi} - \frac{1}{2n}\sin 2nx \Big|_0^{\pi}$

$\displaystyle = \frac{\pi}{2} - \frac{1}{2n}(\sin 2n\pi - \sin 0) = \frac{\pi}{2}$

41. $\displaystyle V_{rms} = \sqrt{\frac{1}{1/60.0} \int_0^{1/60.0} (340 \sin 120\pi t)^2 dt} = \sqrt{60}\sqrt{\int_0^{1/60.0} 340^2 \frac{1 - \cos 240\pi t}{2} dt}$

$\displaystyle = \sqrt{60}\sqrt{\frac{340^2}{2}\left(t - \frac{1}{240\pi}\sin 240\pi t\right)\Big|_0^{1/60.0}} = 240 \text{ V}$

28.6   Inverse Trigonometric Forms

1. Change dx to $-x \, dx$, then

$\displaystyle\int \frac{-x \, dx}{\sqrt{9 - x^2}} = \frac{1}{2}\int (9 - x^2)^{-1/2}(-2x \, dx) = \frac{1}{2}\frac{(9 - x^2)^{1/2}}{\frac{1}{2}} + C = \sqrt{9 - x^2} + C$

5. $a = 8; u = x; du = dx;$

$$\int \frac{dx}{64 + x^2} = \frac{1}{8} \tan^{-1} \frac{x}{8} + C$$

9. $\int_0^2 \frac{3e^{-t} dt}{1 + 9e^{-2t}}$

$$= -\int_0^2 \frac{-3e^{-t} dt}{1 + (3e^{-t})^2} \text{ which has form } \int \frac{dx}{1 + x^2}$$

$$= -\tan^{-1}(3e^{-t})\big|_0^2$$

$$= -\tan^{-1} \frac{3}{e^2} + \tan^{-1} 3$$

$$= 0.8634$$

13. $u = 9x^2 + 16; du = 18x\, dx$

$$\int \frac{8x\, dx}{9x^2 + 16} = \frac{8}{18} \int \frac{18x\, dx}{9x^2 + 16}$$

$$= \frac{4}{9} \ln |9x^2 + 16| + C$$

17. $a = 1; u = e^x; du = e^x dx$

$$\int \frac{e^x dx}{\sqrt{1 - e^{2x}}} = \sin^{-1} e^x + C$$

21. $a = 2; u = x + 2; du = dx$

$$\int \frac{4\, dx}{\sqrt{-4x - x^2}} = \int \frac{4\, dx}{\sqrt{4 - (x+2)^2}}$$

$$= 4 \int \frac{dx}{\sqrt{4 - (x+2)^2}}$$

$$= 4 \sin^{-1} \left(\frac{x+2}{2} \right) + C$$

25. $a = 2; u = x; du = dx; n = -\frac{1}{2}; u = 4 - x^2;$

$du = -2x\, dx$

$$\int \frac{2 - x}{\sqrt{4 - x^2}} dx = \int \frac{2\, dx}{\sqrt{4 - x^2}} - \int \frac{x\, dx}{\sqrt{4 - x^2}}$$

$$= 2 \int \frac{dx}{\sqrt{4 - x^2}} + \frac{1}{2} \int \frac{(-2x\, dx)}{(4 - x^2)^{1/2}}$$

$$= 2 \sin^{-1} \frac{x}{2} + \frac{1}{2}(4 - x^2)^{1/2} \cdot 2 + C$$

$$= 2 \sin^{-1} \frac{x}{2} + \sqrt{4 - x^2} + C$$

29. (a) General power, $\int u^{-1/2} du$ where $u = 4 - 9x^2$.

$du = -18x\, dx$; numerator can fit du of denominator.
Square root becomes $-1/2$ power.
Does not fit inverse sine form.

(b) Inverse sine; $a = 2; u = 3x; du = 3\, dx$

(c) Logarithmic; $u = 4 - 9x; du = -9\, dx$

33. $y = \frac{1}{1 + x^2}; A = \int_0^2 \frac{1}{1 + x^2} dx;$

$a = 1; u = x; du = dx$

$$A = \frac{1}{1} \tan^{-1} \frac{x}{1} \Big|_0^2 = \tan^{-1} 2 - \tan^{-1} 0 = 1.11$$

37. $\int \frac{dx}{\sqrt{A^2 - x^2}} = \int \sqrt{\frac{k}{m}} dt; \sin^{-1} \frac{x}{A} = \sqrt{\frac{k}{m}} t + C$

Solve for C by letting $x = x_0$ and $t = 0$.

$$\sin^{-1} \frac{x_0}{A} = \sqrt{\frac{k}{m}}(0) + C; C = \sin^{-1} \frac{x_0}{A};$$

therefore, $\sin^{-1} \frac{x}{A} = \sqrt{\frac{k}{m}} t + \sin^{-1} \frac{x_0}{A}$

28.7   Integrations by Parts

1. $u = \sqrt{1 - x}, dv = x\, dx$

$$du = \frac{-1}{2\sqrt{1 - x}} dx, v = \frac{x^2}{2}$$

$$\int x\sqrt{1 - x}\, dx = \frac{x^2}{2} \sqrt{1 - x} - \int \frac{x^2}{2} \frac{-dx}{2\sqrt{1 - x}}$$

$$= \frac{x^2}{2} \sqrt{1 - x} + \frac{1}{4} \int \frac{x^2 dx}{\sqrt{1 - x}}$$

No, the substitution $u = \sqrt{1 - x}, dv = x\, dx$ does not work since $\int \frac{x^2 dx}{\sqrt{1 - x}}$ is more complex than $\int x\sqrt{1 - x}\, dx$.

5. $\int xe^{2x} dx; u = x; du = dx; dv = e^{2x} dx$

$$v = \frac{1}{2} \int e^{2x} (2\, dx) = \frac{1}{2} e^{2x}$$

$$\int xe^{2x} dx = \frac{1}{2} xe^{2x} - \frac{1}{2} \int e^{2x} dx$$

$$= \frac{1}{2} xe^{2x} - \frac{1}{4} \int e^{2x} (2\, dx)$$

$$= \frac{1}{2} xe^{2x} - \frac{1}{4} e^{2x} + C$$

9. $\int 2\tan^{-1} x\, dx$; $u = \tan^{-1} x$; $du = \dfrac{1}{1+x^2} dx$;

$dv = dx$;

$v = x$

$2\int \tan^{-1} x\, dx = 2\left(x\tan^{-1} x - \int \dfrac{x\, dx}{1+x^2}\right)$

$u = x^2; du = 2x\, dx = 2\left(x\tan^{-1} x - \dfrac{1}{2}\int \dfrac{2x\, dx}{1+x^2}\right) = 2x\tan^{-1} x - \ln\left|1+x^2\right| + C$

OR

$\quad = 2x\tan^{-1} x - 2\ln\sqrt{1+x^2} + C$

13. $\int x\ln x\, dx$; $u = \ln x$; $du = \dfrac{dx}{x}$; $dv = x\, dx$; $v = \dfrac{x^2}{2}$

$\int x\ln x\, dx = \dfrac{1}{2}x^2\ln x - \dfrac{1}{2}\int x^2\dfrac{dx}{x} = \dfrac{1}{2}x^2\ln x - \dfrac{1}{2}\int x\, dx = \dfrac{1}{2}x^2\ln x - \dfrac{1}{2}\cdot\dfrac{x^2}{2} + C = \dfrac{1}{2}x^2\ln x - \dfrac{1}{4}x^2 + C$

17. $\int_0^{\pi/2} e^x\cos x\, dx$; $u = e^x$; $du = e^x dx$; $dv = \cos x\, dx$;

$v = \sin x$

$\int_0^{\pi/2} e^x\cos x\, dx = e^x\sin x - \int \sin x e^x dx$

$u = e^x$; $du = e^x dx$; $dv = \sin x\, dx$; $v = -\cos x$

$\int_0^{\pi/2} e^x\cos x\, dx = e^x\sin x - \left(-e^x\cos x + \int e^x\cos x\, dx\right)$

$\int_0^{\pi/2} e^x\cos x\, dx = e^x\sin x + e^x\cos x - \int e^x\cos x\, dx$

$2\int e^x\cos x\, dx = e^x\sin x + e^x\cos x$

$\int_0^{\pi/2} e^x\cos x\, dx = \dfrac{1}{2}e^x(\sin x + \cos x)\Big|_0^{\pi/2} = \dfrac{1}{2}e^{\pi/2}(1+0) - \dfrac{1}{2}e^0(0+1)$

$\qquad\qquad = \dfrac{1}{2}e^{\pi/2} - \dfrac{1}{2} = \dfrac{1}{2}(e^{\pi/2} - 1) = 1.91$

21. $A = \int_0^2 xe^{-x}dx$; $u = x$; $du = dx$; $dv = e^{-x}dx$;

$v = \int e^{-x}dx = -e^{-x}$

$A = -xe^{-x}\Big|_0^2 = \int_0^2 -e^{-x}dx = -xe^{-x} - e^{-x}\Big|_0^2 = -2e^{-2} - e^{-2} - (0-1) = 1 - \dfrac{3}{e^2} = 0.594$

25. $\overline{x} = \dfrac{\displaystyle\int_0^{\pi/2} x(\cos x)\, dx}{\displaystyle\int_0^{\pi/2} \cos x\, dx}$

Let $u = x$; $du = dx$; $dv = \cos x$; $v = \sin x$

$\overline{x} = \dfrac{x\sin x\big|_0^{\pi/2} - \displaystyle\int_0^{\pi/2}\sin x\, dx}{\sin x\big|_0^{\pi/2}} = \dfrac{x\sin x\big|_0^{\pi/2} - (-\cos x)\big|_0^{\pi/2}}{1} = x\sin x + \cos x\big|_0^{\pi/2} = \dfrac{\pi}{2} - 1 = 0.571$

29. $v = \dfrac{ds}{dt} = \dfrac{t^3}{\sqrt{t^2+1}}; \ s = \displaystyle\int \dfrac{t^3 \, dt}{\sqrt{t^2+1}}$

Let $u = t^2; \ du = 2t \, dt; \ dv = \dfrac{t \, dt}{(t^2+1)^{1/2}}$

$v = \dfrac{1}{2} \displaystyle\int \dfrac{2t \, dt}{(t^2+1)^{1/2}} = \dfrac{1}{2}(2)(t^2+1)^{1/2} = (t^2+1)^{1/2}$

$s = t^2(t^2+1)^{1/2} - \displaystyle\int (t^2+1)^{1/2}(2t \, dt) = t^2(t^2+1)^{1/2} - \dfrac{2}{3}(t^2+1)^{3/2} + C$

$s = 0$ for $t = 0; \ 0 = -\dfrac{2}{3} + C; \ C = \dfrac{2}{3}$

$s = \dfrac{1}{3}[3t^2(t^2+1)^{1/2} - 2(t^2+1)^{3/2} + 2] = \dfrac{1}{3}[(t^2-2)(t^2+1)^{1/2} + 2]$

28.8   Integration by Trigonometric Substitution

1. Delete the x^2 before the radical in the denominator.

$\displaystyle\int \dfrac{dx}{\sqrt{1-x^2}} = \sin^{-1} x + C$

5. $\displaystyle\int \dfrac{dx}{x^2\sqrt{x^2+1}}$. Let $x = \tan\theta, \ dx = \sec\theta\tan\theta \, d\theta$

$\displaystyle\int \dfrac{dx}{x^2\sqrt{x^2+1}} = \int \dfrac{\sec\theta\tan\theta \, d\theta}{\tan^2\theta\sqrt{\tan^2\theta+1}} = \int \dfrac{\sec\theta\tan\theta \, d\theta}{\tan^2\theta\sqrt{\sec^2\theta}} = \int \dfrac{\sec\theta \, d\theta}{\tan\theta\sec\theta} = \int \dfrac{d\theta}{\tan\theta} = \int \cot\theta \, d\theta$

9. Let $x = \sin\theta; \ dx = \cos\theta \, d\theta$

$\displaystyle\int \dfrac{\sqrt{1-x^2}}{x^2} \, dx = \int \dfrac{\sqrt{1-\sin^2\theta}}{\sin^2\theta} \cos\theta \, d\theta = \int \dfrac{\cos^2\theta}{\sin^2\theta} \, d\theta = \int \cot^2\theta \, d\theta = \int (\csc^2\theta - 1) \, d\theta$

$= \displaystyle\int \csc^2\theta \, d\theta - \int d\theta = -\cot\theta - \theta + C = \dfrac{-\sqrt{1-x^2}}{x} - \sin^{-1}x + C$

13. Let $z = 3\tan\theta; \ dz = 3\sec^2\theta \, d\theta$

$\displaystyle\int \dfrac{6 \, dz}{z^2\sqrt{z^2+9}} = 6\int \dfrac{3\sec^2\theta \, d\theta}{9\tan^2\theta\sqrt{9\tan^2\theta+9}} = 6\int \dfrac{3\sec^2\theta \, d\theta}{27\tan^2\theta\sqrt{\tan^2\theta+1}} = \dfrac{6}{9}\int \dfrac{\sec\theta \, d\theta}{\tan^2\theta} = \dfrac{6}{9}\int \dfrac{\cos\theta \, d\theta}{\sin^2\theta}$

$= \dfrac{6}{9}\displaystyle\int \csc\theta\cot\theta \, d\theta = -\dfrac{6}{9}\csc\theta + C = \dfrac{-6}{9\sin\theta} + C$

$\tan\theta = \dfrac{z}{3}; \ \sin\theta = \dfrac{z}{\sqrt{9+z^2}}$

$\dfrac{-6}{9\sin\theta} + C = \dfrac{-6}{\dfrac{9z}{\sqrt{9+z^2}}} + C = -\dfrac{2\sqrt{z^2+9}}{3z} + C$

17. $\displaystyle\int_0^{0.5} \dfrac{x^3 \, dx}{\sqrt{1-x^2}}, \ x = \sin\theta; \ dx = \cos\theta \, d\theta$

$\displaystyle\int \dfrac{\sin^3\theta\cos\theta \, d\theta}{\sqrt{1-\sin^2\theta}} = \int \sin^3\theta \, d\theta = \int \sin\theta\sin^2\theta \, d\theta = \int \sin\theta(1-\cos^2\theta) \, d\theta = \int \sin\theta \, d\theta - \int \cos^2\theta\sin\theta \, d\theta$

$= -\cos\theta + \dfrac{\cos^3\theta}{3}$

$\cos\theta = \sqrt{1-x^2}; \ \left. -\sqrt{1-x^2} + \dfrac{1}{3}(\sqrt{1-x^2})^3 \right|_0^{0.5} = -\sqrt{1-0.5^2} + \dfrac{1}{3}(\sqrt{1-0.5^2})^3 + \sqrt{1} - \dfrac{1}{3}\sqrt{1} = 0.017$

21. $\int \dfrac{dy}{y\sqrt{4y^2-9}}$; $2y = 3\sec\theta$; $y = \dfrac{3}{2}\sec\theta$; $dy = \dfrac{3}{2}\sec\theta\tan\theta\,d\theta$

$$\int \frac{\frac{3}{2}\sec\theta\tan\theta\,d\theta}{\frac{3}{2}\sec\theta\sqrt{4\left(\frac{3}{2}\sec\theta\right)^2-9}} = \int \frac{\tan\theta\,d\theta}{\sqrt{9\sec^2\theta-9}} = \int \frac{\tan\theta\,d\theta}{3\sqrt{\sec^2\theta-1}} = \int \frac{\tan\theta\,d\theta}{3\tan\theta} = \frac{1}{3}\int d\theta$$

$$= \frac{1}{3}\theta + C = \frac{1}{3}\sec^{-1}\frac{2}{3}y + C$$

$$\int_{2.5}^{3} \frac{dy}{y\sqrt{4y^2-9}} = \frac{1}{3}\sec^{-1}\left(\frac{2y}{3}\right)\bigg|_{2.5}^{3} = \frac{1}{3}\cos^{-1}\left(\frac{3}{2y}\right)\bigg|_{2.5}^{3} = 0.03997$$

25. $A = 4\displaystyle\int_0^1 y\,dx = 4\int_0^1 \sqrt{1-x^2}\,dx$

Let $x = \sin\theta$, $dx = \cos\theta\,d\theta$

$$\int \sqrt{1-x^2}\,dx = \int \sqrt{1-\sin^2\theta}\cos\theta\,d\theta = \int \cos^2\theta\,d\theta = \frac{1}{2}\int(1+\cos 2\theta)\,d\theta$$

$$= \frac{1}{2}\theta + \frac{1}{4}\sin 2\theta + C = \frac{1}{2}\theta + \frac{1}{2}\sin\theta\cos\theta + C$$

$$= \frac{1}{2}\sin^{-1}x + \frac{1}{2}x\sqrt{1-x^2} + C$$

$$A = 4\int_0^1 \sqrt{1-x^2}\,dx = 4\left(\frac{1}{2}\sin^{-1}x + \frac{1}{2}x\sqrt{1-x^2}\right)\bigg|_0^1 = 2\sin^{-1}1 + 2(1)\sqrt{0} - [2\sin^{-1}0 + 2(0)]$$

$$= 2\sin^{-1}1 = 2\left(\frac{\pi}{2}\right) = \pi$$

29. $V = 2\pi\displaystyle\int_4^5 \dfrac{x(\sqrt{x^2-16})}{x^2}\,dx$, disks

(The limits of integration are $x = 4$ since $x = 4$ when $y = 0$; and $x = 5$.)

Let $x = 4\sec\theta$; $dx = 4\sec\theta\tan\theta\,d\theta$

$$V = 2\pi\int_4^5 \frac{\sqrt{x^2-16}}{x}\,dx$$

$$2\pi\int \frac{\sqrt{x^2-16}}{x}\,dx = 2\pi\int \frac{\sqrt{16\sec^2\theta-16}}{4\sec\theta}(4\sec\theta\tan\theta\,d\theta) = 2\pi\int \sqrt{16\sec^2\theta-16}\tan\,d\theta$$

$$= 2\pi\int 4\sqrt{\sec^2\theta-1}\tan\theta\,d\theta = 8\pi\int(\tan\theta)\tan\theta\,d\theta = 8\pi\int\tan^2\theta\,d\theta$$

$$= 8\pi\int(\sec^2\theta-1)\,d\theta = 8\pi(\tan\theta-\theta)$$

Since $x = 4\sec\theta$; $\sec = \dfrac{x}{4}$; and $\tan\theta = \dfrac{\sqrt{x^2-16}}{4}$; and

$$2\pi\int \frac{\sqrt{x^2-16}}{x}\,dx = 8\pi(\tan\theta-\theta) = 8\pi\left(\frac{\sqrt{x^2-16}}{4} - \sec^{-1}\frac{x}{4}\right)$$

$$V = 2\pi\int_4^5 \frac{x\sqrt{x^2-16}}{x^2}\,dx = 8\pi\left(\frac{\sqrt{x^2-16}}{4} - \sec^{-1}\frac{x}{4}\right)\bigg|_4^5 = 8\pi\left(\frac{3}{4} - \sec^{-1}\frac{5}{4} - 0\right) = 2.68$$

28.9   Integration by Partial Fractions: Nonrepeated Linear Factors

1. $\dfrac{10-x}{x^2+x-2} = \dfrac{10-x}{(x-1)(x+2)} = \dfrac{A}{x-1} + \dfrac{B}{x+2}$

$10 - x = A(x+2) + B(x-1)$

for $x = -2$:

$10 - (-2) = A(-2+2) + B(-2-1)$

$\qquad 12 = -3B$

$\qquad B = -4$

for $x = 1$:

$10 - 1 = A(1+2) + B(1-1)$

$\qquad 9 = 3A$

$\qquad A = 3$

$\dfrac{10-x}{x^2+x-2} = \dfrac{3}{x-1} + \dfrac{-4}{x+2}$

5. $\dfrac{x^2-6x-8}{x^3-4x} = \dfrac{x^2-6x-8}{x(x^2-4)}$

$\qquad = \dfrac{x^2-6x-8}{x(x+2)(x-2)}$

$\qquad = \dfrac{A}{x} + \dfrac{B}{x+2} + \dfrac{C}{x-2}$

9. $\displaystyle\int \dfrac{dx}{x^2-4} = \int \dfrac{dx}{(x+2)(x-2)}$

$\qquad = \displaystyle\int \dfrac{-\frac{1}{4}}{x+2}\,dx + \int \dfrac{\frac{1}{4}}{x-2}\,dx$

$\qquad = -\dfrac{1}{4}\ln|x+2| + \dfrac{1}{4}\ln|x-2| + C$

$\qquad = \dfrac{1}{4}\ln\left|\dfrac{x-2}{x+2}\right| + C$

13. $\displaystyle\int_0^1 \dfrac{2t+4}{3t^2+5t+2}\,dt$

$\qquad = \displaystyle\int_0^1 \dfrac{8}{3t+2}\,dt - \int_0^1 \dfrac{2}{t+1}\,dt$

$\qquad = \dfrac{8\ln(3t+2)}{3}\bigg|_0^1 - 2\ln(t+1)\bigg|_0^1$

$\qquad = \dfrac{8\ln 5}{3} - \dfrac{8\ln 2}{3} - 2\ln 2 + 2\ln 1$

$\qquad = 1.057$

17. $\displaystyle\int \dfrac{6x^2-2x-1}{4x^3-x}\,dx$

$= \displaystyle\int \dfrac{6x^2-2x-1}{x(4x^2-1)}\,dx = \int \dfrac{6x^2-2x-1}{x(2x+1)(2x-1)}\,dx$

$= \displaystyle\int \dfrac{dx}{x} + \int \dfrac{\frac{3}{2}}{2x+1}\,dx - \dfrac{\frac{1}{2}}{2x-1}\,dx$

$= \ln|x| + \dfrac{3\ln|2x+1|}{4} - \dfrac{\ln|2x-1|}{4} + C$

$= \dfrac{4\ln|x|}{4} + \dfrac{3\ln|2x+1|}{4} - \dfrac{\ln|2x-1|}{4} + C$

$= \dfrac{1}{4}\ln\left|\dfrac{x^4(2x+1)^3}{2x-1}\right| + C$

21. $\displaystyle\int \dfrac{dV}{(V^2-4)(V^2-9)}$

$= \displaystyle\int \dfrac{dV}{(V-2)(V+2)(V+3)(V-3)}$

$= \displaystyle\int \dfrac{\frac{1}{30}}{V-3}\,dV - \int \dfrac{\frac{1}{30}dV}{V+3} - \int \dfrac{\frac{1}{20}dV}{V-2} + \int \dfrac{\frac{1}{20}dV}{V+2}$

$= \dfrac{1}{30}\ln|V-3| - \dfrac{1}{30}\ln|V+3|$

$\quad - \dfrac{1}{20}\ln|V-2| + \dfrac{1}{20}\ln|V+2| + C$

$= \dfrac{2}{60}\ln|V-3| - \dfrac{2}{60}\ln|V+3| - \dfrac{3}{60}\ln|V-2|$

$\quad + \dfrac{3}{60}\ln|V+2| + C$

$= \dfrac{1}{60}\ln\left|\dfrac{(V+2)^3(V-3)^2}{(V-2)^3(V+3)^2}\right| + C$

25. $A = \displaystyle\int_2^4 \dfrac{x-16}{x^2-5x-14}\,dx$

$= \displaystyle\int_2^4 \dfrac{-1}{x-7}\,dx + \int_2^4 \dfrac{2}{x+2}\,dx$

$= 1.322$

29. $\dfrac{3x+5}{x^2+5x} = \dfrac{3x+5}{x(x+5)} = \dfrac{A}{x} + \dfrac{B}{x+5} = \dfrac{A(x+5)+Bx}{x(x+5)}$

$3x+5 = A(x+5) + Bx$

$x = 0, \qquad 5 = 5A, \quad A = 1$

$x = -5, \; -10 = -5B, \; B = 2$

$y = \displaystyle\int \dfrac{3x+5}{x^2+5x}\,dx$

$y = \displaystyle\int \dfrac{dx}{x} + \int \dfrac{2}{x+5}\,dx$

$0 = \ln|x| + 2\ln|x+5| + C = \ln|1| + 2\ln|6| + C, \; C = -2\ln 6$

$y = \ln|x| + 2\ln|x+5| - 2\ln 6$

$y = \ln|x| + \ln|x+5|^2 - \ln 36$

$y = \ln \dfrac{|x|(x+5)^2}{36}$

28.10   Integration by Partial Fractions: Other Cases

1. $\dfrac{2}{x(x+3)^2} = \dfrac{A}{x} + \dfrac{B}{x+3} + \dfrac{C}{(x+3)^2}$

5. $\displaystyle\int \dfrac{x-8}{x^3-4x^2+4x} = \int \dfrac{-2}{x}\,dx + \int \dfrac{2}{x-2}\,dx - \int \dfrac{3}{(x-2)^2}\,dx = -2\ln|x| + 2\ln|x-2| + \dfrac{3}{x-2} + C$

$\qquad\qquad = 2\ln\left|\dfrac{x-2}{x}\right| + \dfrac{3}{x-2} + C$

9. $\dfrac{2s}{(s-3)^3} = \dfrac{A}{s-3} + \dfrac{B}{(s-3)^2} + \dfrac{C}{(s-3)^3} = \dfrac{A(s-3)^2 + B(s-3) + C}{(s-3)^3}$

$\qquad 2s = A(s-3)^2 + B(s-3) + C$

$s = 3, \quad 6 = C$

$\qquad 2s = A(s-3)^2 + B(s-3) + 6$

$\left. \begin{array}{ll} s=1, & 2 = 4A - 2B + 6 \\ s=2, & 4 = A - B + 6 \end{array} \right\} A = 0, \; B = 2$

$\displaystyle\int_1^2 \dfrac{2s}{(s-3)^3}\,ds = \int_1^2 \dfrac{2}{(s-3)^3}\,ds + \int_1^2 \dfrac{6}{(s-3)^3}\,ds = 2 \cdot \dfrac{(s-3)^{-2+1}}{-2+1} + 6 \cdot \dfrac{(s-3)^{-3+1}}{-3+1}\Big|_1^2$

$\qquad\qquad = \dfrac{-2}{(s-3)} - \dfrac{3}{(s-3)^2}\Big|_1^2 = -\dfrac{5}{4}$

13. $\dfrac{x^2+x+5}{(x+1)(x^2+4)} = \dfrac{A}{x+1} + \dfrac{Bx+C}{x^2+4} = \dfrac{A(x^2+4) + (Bx+C)(x+1)}{(x+1)(x^2+4)}$

$\qquad x^2 + x + 5 = A(x^2+4) + (Bx+C)(x+1)$

$\left. \begin{array}{ll} x=0, & 5 = 4A + \qquad C \\ x=1, & 7 = 5A + 2B + 2C \\ x=2, & 11 = 8A + 6B + 3C \end{array} \right\} A = 1, \; B = 0, \; C = 1$

$\displaystyle\int_0^2 \dfrac{x^2+x+5}{(x+1)(x^2+4)}\,dx = \int_0^2 \dfrac{dx}{x+1} + \int_1^2 \dfrac{1}{x^2+4}\,dx \; \ln|x+1| + \dfrac{\tan^{-1}\frac{x}{2}}{2}\Big|_0^2 = 1.491$

17. $\dfrac{10x^3 + 40x^2 + 22x + 7}{(4x^2 + 1)(x^2 + 6x + 10)} = \dfrac{Ax + B}{4x^2 + 1} + \dfrac{Cx + D}{x^2 + 6x + 10}$

$10x^3 + 40x^2 + 22x + 7 = (Ax + B)(x^2 + 6x + 10) + (Cx + D)(4x^2 + 1)$

$10x^3 + 40x^2 + 22x + 7 = Ax^3 + 6Ax^2 + 10Ax + Bx^2 + 6Bx + 10B + 4Cx^3 + Cx + 4Dx^2 + D$

$10x^3 + 40x^2 + 22x + 7 = (A + 4C)x^3 + (6A + B + 4D)x^2 + (10A + 6B + C)x + 10B + D$

(1) $A + 4C \qquad\quad = 10$
(2) $6A + B + 4D \ = 40$
(3) $10A + 6B + C = 22$
(4) $10B + D \qquad = 7$

$\left.\right\}\ A = 2, B = 0, C = 2, D = 7$

$$\int \frac{10x^3 + 40x^2 + 22x + 7}{(4x^2 + 1)(x^2 + 6x + 10)}\, dx = \int \frac{2x}{4x^2 + 1}\, dx + \int \frac{2x + 7}{x^2 + 6x + 10}\, dx$$

$$\int \frac{2x}{4x^2 + 1}\, dx = \frac{1}{4} \int \frac{8x}{4x^2 + 1}\, dx = \frac{\ln(4x^2 + 1)}{4}$$

$$\int \frac{2x + 7}{x^2 + 6x + 10}\, dx = \int \frac{2x + 7}{x^2 + 6x + 9 + 1}\, dx = \int \frac{2x + 7}{(x + 3)^2 + 1}\, dx \quad \text{let} \quad u = x + 3,\ x = u - 3$$
$$du = dx$$

$$\int \frac{2x + 7}{x^2 + 6x + 10}\, dx = \int \frac{2(u - 3) + 7}{u^2 + 1}\, du$$

$$\int \frac{2x + 7}{x^2 + 6x + 10}\, dx = \int \frac{2u - 6 + 7}{u^2 + 1}\, du$$

$$\int \frac{2x + 7}{x^2 + 6x + 10}\, dx = \int \frac{2u}{u^2 + 1}\, du + \int \frac{1}{u^2 + 1}\, du$$

$$\int \frac{2x + 7}{x^2 + 6x + 10}\, dx = \ln(u^2 + 1) + \tan^{-1} u + C$$

$$\int \frac{2x + 7}{x^2 + 6x + 10}\, dx = \ln(x^2 + 6x + 10) + \tan^{-1}(x + 3) + C$$

$$\int \frac{10x^3 + 40x^2 + 22x + 7}{(4x^2 + 1)(x^2 + 6x + 10)}\, dx = \frac{\ln(4x^2 + 1)}{4} + \ln(x^2 + 6x + 10) + \tan^{-1}(x + 3) + C$$

21. $\qquad A = -\displaystyle\int_1^3 \frac{x - 3}{x^3 + x^2}\, dx = -\int_1^3 \frac{x - 3}{x^2(x + 1)}\, dx$

$\dfrac{x - 3}{x^2(x + 1)} = \dfrac{Ax + B}{x^2} + \dfrac{C}{x + 1} = \dfrac{(Ax + B)(x + 1) + Cx^2}{x^2(x + 1)} = \dfrac{Ax^2 + Ax + Bx + B + Cx^2}{x^2(x + 1)}$

$x - 3 = (A + C)x^2 + (A + B)x + B$

(1) $A + C = 0,\ C = -4$
(2) $A + B = 1,\ A = 4$
(3) $\qquad\quad B = -3$

$$\frac{x - 3}{x^2(x + 1)} = \frac{4x - 3}{x^2} - \frac{4}{x + 1} = \frac{4}{x} - \frac{3}{x^2} - \frac{4}{x + 1}$$

$$\int_1^3 \frac{x - 3}{x^3 + x^2}\, dx = \int_1^3 \frac{4}{x}\, dx - 3\int_1^3 \frac{dx}{x^2} - 4\int_1^3 \frac{dx}{x + 1} = 4\ln|x|\Big|_1^3 + \frac{3}{x}\Big|_1^3 - 4\ln(x + 1)\Big|_1^3$$

$$= 4(\ln 3 - \ln 1) + \frac{3}{3} - \frac{3}{1} - 4\ln(4) + 4\ln 2 = \ln 3^4 + 1 - 3 - \ln 4^4 + \ln 2^4$$

$$= -2 + \ln 81 - \ln 256 + \ln 16 = -2 + \ln \frac{81 \cdot 16}{256} = -2 + \ln \frac{81}{16} = -0.3781$$

$$A = 2 - \ln \frac{81}{16} = 0.3781$$

25. $\dfrac{t^2 + 14t + 27}{(2t+1)(t+5)^2} = \dfrac{A}{2t+1} + \dfrac{B}{t+5} + \dfrac{C}{(t+5)^2}$

$\dfrac{t^2 + 14t + 27}{(2t+1)(t+5)^2} = \dfrac{A(t+5)^2 + B(t+5)(2t+1) + C(2t+1)}{(2t+1)(t+5)^2}$

$t^2 + 14t + 27 = At^2 + 10At + 25A + 2Bt^2 + 11Bt + 5B + 2Ct + C$

$t^2 + 14t + 27 = (A + 2B)t^2 + (10A + 11B + 2C)t + 25A + 5B + C$

$\left.\begin{array}{ll}(1) & A + 2B = 1 \\ (2) & 10A + 11B + 2C = 14 \\ (3) & 25A + 5B + C = 27\end{array}\right\} A = 1,\ B = 0,\ C = 2$

$\dfrac{ds}{dt} = \dfrac{t^2 + 14t + 27}{(2t+1)(t+5)^2} = \dfrac{1}{2t+1} + \dfrac{2}{(t+5)^2}$

$s = \dfrac{1}{2}\displaystyle\int_0^{2.00} \dfrac{2}{2t+1}\,dt + \int_0^{2.00} \dfrac{2}{(t+5)^2}\,dt; \quad s = \dfrac{1}{2}\ln|2t+1|\Big|_0^{2.00} - 2\cdot\dfrac{1}{(t+5)}\Big|_0^{2.00}$

$s = \dfrac{1}{2}\ln 5.00 - \dfrac{1}{2}\ln 1 - \dfrac{2}{7.00} + \dfrac{2}{5.00} = 0.919 \text{ m}$

28.11   Integration by Use of Tables

1. $\displaystyle\int \dfrac{x\,dx}{(2+3x)^2}$ is formula 3 with $u = x$, $du = dx$, $a = 2$, $b = 3$.

5. Formula #1; $u = x$; $a = 2$; $b = 5$; $du = dx$

$\displaystyle\int \dfrac{3x\,dx}{2+5x} = 3\int \dfrac{3x\,dx}{2+5x} = 3\left\{\dfrac{1}{25}[(2+5x) - 2\ln|2+5x|]\right\} + C = \dfrac{3}{25}[2 + 5x - 2\ln|2+5x|] + C$

9. Formula #24; $u = y$, $a = 2$

$\displaystyle\int \dfrac{dy}{(y^2+4)^{3/2}} = \dfrac{y}{4\sqrt{y^2+4}} + C$

13. Formula #17; $u = 2x$; $du = 2\,dx$; $a = 3$

$\displaystyle\int \dfrac{\sqrt{4x^2-9}}{x}\,dx = \int \dfrac{\sqrt{(2x)^2-3^2}}{2x}\,dx = \sqrt{4x^2-9} - 3\sec^{-1}\left(\dfrac{2x}{3}\right) + C$

17. Formula #52; $u = r^2$; $du = 2r\,dr$

$6\displaystyle\int \tan^{-1} r^2 (r\,dr) = 3\int \tan^{-1} r^2 (2r\,dr) = 3\left[r^2\tan^{-1} r^2 - \dfrac{1}{2}\ln(1+r^4)\right] + C = 3r^2\tan^{-1} r^2 - \dfrac{3}{2}\ln(1+r^4) + C$

21. Formula #11; $u = 2x$; $du = 2\,dx$; $a = 1$

$\displaystyle\int \dfrac{dx}{x\sqrt{4x^2+1}} = \int \dfrac{2\,dx}{2x\sqrt{(2x)^2+1^2}} = -\ln\left(\dfrac{1+\sqrt{4x^2+1}}{2x}\right) + C$

25. Formula #40; $a = 1$; $u = x$; $du = dx$; $b = 5$

$$\int_0^{\pi/12} \sin\theta \cos 5\theta \, d\theta = -\frac{\cos(-4\theta)}{2(-4)} - \frac{\cos 6\theta}{12} = \frac{1}{8}\cos 4\theta - \frac{1}{12}\cos 6\theta \Big|_0^{\pi/12} = 0.0208$$

29. let $u = x^2$, $du = 2x\,dx$

  $\quad u^2 = x^4$

$$\int \frac{2x\,dx}{(1-x^4)^{3/2}} = \int \frac{du}{(1-u^2)^{3/2}}$$

Formula #25: $a = 1$

$$\int \frac{2x\,dx}{(1-x^4)^{3/2}} = \frac{u}{\sqrt{1-u^2}} + C;$$
$$\int \frac{2x\,dx}{(1-x^4)^{3/2}} = \frac{x^2}{\sqrt{1-x^4}} + C$$

33. Formula #46; $u = x^2$; $du = 2x\,dx$; $n = 1$

$$\int x^3 \ln x^2 dx = \frac{1}{2}\int x^2 \ln x^2 (2x\,dx) = \frac{1}{2}\left[(x^2)^2\left(\frac{\ln x^2}{2} - \frac{1}{4}\right)\right] = \frac{1}{2}\left[\frac{x^4}{2}\left(\ln x^2 - \frac{1}{2}\right)\right] = \frac{1}{4}x^4\left(\ln x^2 - \frac{1}{2}\right) + C$$

37. From Exercise 17 of Section 26-6,

$$s = \int_a^b \sqrt{1 + \left(\frac{dy}{dx}\right)^2}\,dx; \quad y = x^2; \quad \frac{dy}{dx} = 2x;$$
$$s = \int_0^1 \sqrt{1 + (2x)^2}\,dx) = \frac{1}{2}\int_0^1 \sqrt{(2x)^2 + 1}\,(2dx)$$

Formula #14; $u = 2x$; $du = 2\,dx$

$$s = \frac{1}{2}\left[\frac{2x}{2}\sqrt{4x^2+1} + \frac{1}{2}\ln(2x + \sqrt{4x^2+1})\right]\Big|_0^1 = \frac{1}{2}\left[\left(1\sqrt{5} + \frac{1}{2}\ln(2 + \sqrt{5})\right) - \frac{1}{2}\ln 1\right]$$

$$= \frac{1}{4}[2\sqrt{5} + \ln(2 + \sqrt{5})] = 1.479$$

41. $F = w\displaystyle\int_0^3 lh\,dh = w\int_0^3 x(3-y)\,dy = w\int_0^3 \frac{3-y}{\sqrt{1+y}}\,dy$

(Formula #6)

$$\int \frac{3-y}{\sqrt{1+y}}\,dy = 3\int \frac{dy}{\sqrt{1+y}} - \int \frac{y\,dy}{\sqrt{1+y}} = 3\frac{(1+y)^{1/2}}{\frac{1}{2}} - \left[\frac{-2(2-y)\sqrt{1+y}}{3(1)^2}\right] + C$$

$$F = w\int_0^3 \frac{3-y}{\sqrt{1+y}}\,dy = w\left[6(1+y)^{1/2} + \frac{2}{3}(2-y)(1+y)^{1/2}\right]\Big|_0^3 = w\left[6(2) + \frac{2}{3}(-1)(2) - 6(1) - \frac{2}{3}(2)(1)\right]$$

$$F = w\left(12 - \frac{4}{3} - 6 - \frac{4}{3}\right) = \frac{10w}{3} = \frac{10(62.4)}{3} = 208\text{ lb}$$

Chapter 28 Review Exercises

1. $u = -2x$, $du = -2\,dx$

$$\int e^{-2x}dx = -\frac{1}{2}\int e^{-2x}(-2\,dx) = -\frac{1}{2}e^{-2x} + C$$

5. $\displaystyle\int_0^{\pi/2}\frac{4\cos\theta\,d\theta}{1+\sin\theta} = 4\int_0^{\pi/2}\frac{\cos\theta\,d\theta}{1+\sin\theta}$; $u = 1 + \sin\theta$, $du = \cos\theta = 4\ln(1+\sin\theta)\Big|_0^{\pi/2} = 2.77$

9. $\displaystyle\int_0^{\pi/2}\cos^3 2\theta\,d\theta = \int_0^{\pi/2}\cos^2 2\theta\cos 2\theta\,d\theta = \int_0^{\pi/2}(1-\sin^2 2\theta)\cos 2\theta\,d\theta$

$$= \int_0^{\pi/2}\cos 2\theta\,d\theta - \int_0^{\pi/2}\sin^2 2\theta\cos 2\theta\,d\theta$$

$$= \frac{1}{2}\int_0^{\pi/2}\cos 2\theta(2\,d\theta) - \frac{1}{2}\int_0^{\pi/2}\sin^2 2\theta\cos 2\theta(2\,d\theta)$$

$$= \frac{1}{2}\left[\sin 2\theta - \frac{1}{3}\sin^3 2\theta\right]\Big|_0^{\pi/2}$$

$$= \frac{1}{2}\left[\left(\sin\pi - \frac{1}{3}\sin^3\pi\right) = \left(\sin 0 - \frac{1}{3}\sin^3 0\right)\right] = \frac{1}{2}(0) = 0$$

13. $\displaystyle\int(\sin t + \cos t)^2\cdot\sin t\,dt = \int(\sin^2 t + 2\sin t\cos t + \cos^2 t)\cdot\sin t\,dt$

$$= \int(1 + 2\sin t\cos t)\cdot\sin t\,dt$$

$$= \int(\sin t + 2\sin^2 t\cos t)dt$$

$$= \int\sin t\,dt + 2\int\sin^2 t(\cos t\,dt)$$

$$= -\cos t + \frac{2\sin^3 t}{3} + C$$

17. $\displaystyle\int\sec^4 3x\,dx = \int\sec^2 3x\sec^2 3x\,dx = \int(1 + \tan^2 3x)\sec^2 3x\,dx$

$$= \frac{1}{3}\int\sec^2 3x(3\,dx) + \frac{1}{3}\int\tan^2 3x\sec^2 3x(3\,dx)$$

$$= \frac{1}{3}\tan 3x + \frac{1}{3}\frac{\tan^3 3x}{3} + C = \frac{1}{9}\tan^3 3x + \frac{1}{3}\tan 3x + C$$

21. $\int \dfrac{3x\,dx}{4+x^4} = 3\int \dfrac{x\,dx}{4+x^4} = 3\int \dfrac{1}{2^2+(x^2)^2}\,x\,dx = \dfrac{3}{2}\int \dfrac{1}{2^2+(x^2)^2}\,2x\,dx$

$$= \dfrac{3}{2}\left(\dfrac{1}{2}\tan^{-1}\dfrac{x^2}{2}+C_1\right) = \dfrac{3}{4}\tan^{-1}\dfrac{x^2}{2}+C \text{ where } C = \dfrac{3}{2}C_1.$$

25. $u = e^{2x},\, du = e^{2x}(2\,dx)$

$$\int \dfrac{e^{2x}\,dx}{\sqrt{e^{2x}+1}} = \dfrac{1}{2}\int (e^{2x}+1)^{-1/2}e^{2x}(2\,dx) = \dfrac{1}{2}(e^{2x}+1)^{1/2}(2)+C = \sqrt{e^{2x}+1}+C$$

29. $\displaystyle\int_0^{\pi/6} 3\sin^2 3\phi\,d\phi = \int_0^{\pi/6} 3\cdot\dfrac{(1-\cos 6\phi)}{2}\,d\phi = \int_0^{\pi/6}\dfrac{3}{2}\,d\phi - \dfrac{1}{4}\int_0^{\pi/6}\cos 6\phi(6\,d\phi)$

$$= \dfrac{3}{2}\phi\Big|_0^{\pi/6} - \dfrac{1}{4}\sin 6\phi\Big|_0^{\pi/6} = \dfrac{3}{2}\left[\dfrac{\pi}{6}-0\right] - \dfrac{1}{4}[\sin\pi - \sin 0] = \dfrac{\pi}{4}$$

33. $\dfrac{3u^2-6u-2}{u^2(3u+1)} = \dfrac{Au+B}{u^2} + \dfrac{C}{3u+1} = \dfrac{(Au+B)(3u+1)+Cu^2}{u^2(3u+1)}$

$3u^2-6u-2 = 3Au^2+Au+3Bu+B+Cu^2$
$3u^2-6u-2 = (3A+C)u^2+(A+3B)u+B$

(1) $3A+C = 3,\ 3(0)+C = 3,\ C = 3$
(2) $A+3B = -6;\ A+3(-2) = -6,\ A = 0$
(3) $B = -2$

$$\int \dfrac{3u^2-6u-2}{u^2(3u+1)}\,du = \int \dfrac{-2}{u^2}\,du + \int \dfrac{3}{3u+1}\,du = \dfrac{2}{u} + \ln|3u+1| + C$$

37. $\displaystyle\int_1^e 3\cos(\ln x)\cdot\dfrac{dx}{x} = 3\sin(\ln x)\Big|_1^e = 3\sin(\ln e) - 3\sin(\ln 1) = 3\sin(1) - 3\sin(0)$

$$= 3\sin 1 - 3\cdot 0 = 3\sin 1 \approx 2.52$$

41. $x = \sqrt{2}\sin\theta,\, dx = \sqrt{2}\cos\theta\,d\theta$

$$\int \dfrac{dx}{x\sqrt{2-x^2}} = \int \dfrac{\sqrt{2}\cos\theta\,d\theta}{\sqrt{2}\sin\theta\sqrt{2-2\sin^2\theta}} = \dfrac{1}{\sqrt{2}}\int \dfrac{\cos\theta\,d\theta}{\sin\theta\sqrt{\cos^2\theta}} = \dfrac{1}{\sqrt{2}}\int \csc\theta\,d\theta$$

45. (a) $\displaystyle\int \sin^2 x\,dx = \dfrac{1}{2}\int (1-\cos 2x)\,dx = \dfrac{x}{2} - \dfrac{1}{4}\int(\cos 2x)(2\,dx) = \dfrac{x}{2} - \dfrac{1}{4}\sin 2x + C$

(b) $\displaystyle\int \sin^2 x\,dx = \int (\sin x)(\sin x\,dx)$

$u = \sin x,\qquad dv = \sin x\,dx$
$du = \cos x\,dx\qquad v = -\cos x$

$$\int \sin^2 x\,dx = -\sin x\cos x - \int(-\cos x)(\cos x\,dx)$$

$$= -\sin x\cos x + \int(1-\sin^2 x)\,dx$$

$$= -\sin x\cos x + x - \int \sin^2 x\,dx$$

$$2\int \sin^2 x\,dx = x - \sin x\cos x$$

$$\int \sin^2 x\,dx = \dfrac{x}{2} - \dfrac{\sin 2x}{4} + C$$

49. $\int \sec^4 x \, dx = \dfrac{\sec^2 \tan x}{3} + \dfrac{2}{3} \int \sec^2 x \, dx$ Formula 37 in table of integrals.

$$y = \frac{\sec^2 x \tan x}{3} + \frac{2}{3} \tan x + C = \frac{1}{3}(1 + \tan^2 x)(\tan x) + \frac{2}{3} \tan x + C$$

$$= \frac{1}{3} \tan x + \frac{1}{3} \tan^3 x + \frac{2}{3} \tan x + C = \frac{1}{3} \tan^3 x + \frac{2}{3} \tan x + C$$

$$0 = \frac{1}{3} \tan^3(0) + \frac{2}{3} \tan 0 + C$$

$$0 = 0 + 0 + C; \; C = 0; \; y = \frac{1}{3} \tan^3 x + \tan x$$

53. $x^2 + y^2 = 5^2$; $y = \sqrt{25 - x^2}$; $A = 2 \displaystyle\int_3^5 \sqrt{25 - x^2} \, dx$

$$A = 2 \left[\frac{x}{2}\sqrt{25 - x^2} + \frac{25}{2} \sin^{-1} \frac{x}{5} \right]\Bigg|_3^5$$ Formula 15 in table of integrals.

$$A = 2 \left[\frac{5}{2}\sqrt{0} + \frac{25}{2} \sin^{-1} 1 \right] - 2 \left[\frac{3}{2}\sqrt{16} + \frac{25}{2} \sin^{-1} \frac{3}{5} \right]$$

$$= 2 \left[\frac{25}{2}\left(\frac{\pi}{2}\right) \right] - 2 \left[6 + \frac{25}{2}(0.6435) \right]$$

$$= 2[19.63] - 2[14.04] = 11.18$$

57. $y = xe^x, y = 0, x = 2$

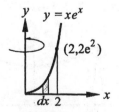

shells: $V = \displaystyle\int_0^2 2\pi xy \, dx = 2\pi \int_0^2 x(xe^x) \, dx$

$$V = 2\pi \int_0^2 x^2 e^x \, dx, \; \#45$$

$$V = 2\pi \left[e^x(x^2 - 2x + 2) \right]\Big|_0^2$$

$$V = 2\pi \left[e^2(4 - 4 + 2) - e^0(0 - 0 + 2) \right]$$

$$V = 2\pi \left[2e^2 - 2 \right] = 4\pi \left[e^2 - 1 \right]$$

$$V = 80.29$$

61. $y = \ln \sin x, x = \dfrac{\pi}{3}$ to $x = \dfrac{2\pi}{3}$

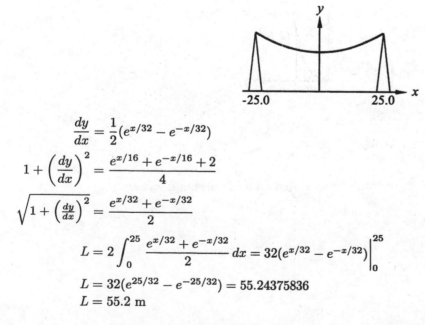

$$\frac{dy}{dx} = \frac{1}{\sin x}(\cos x) = \cot x$$

$$\sqrt{1 + \left(\frac{dy}{dx}\right)^2} = \sqrt{1 + \cot^2 x}$$

$$= \sqrt{\csc^2 x}$$

$$= \csc x$$

$$L = \int_{\pi/3}^{2\pi/3} \csc x\, dx = \ln\left|\frac{\sin x}{\cos x + 1}\right|\;\Bigg|_{\pi/3}^{2\pi/3}$$

$$L = \ln \frac{\sin \frac{2\pi}{3}}{\cos \frac{2\pi}{3} + 1} - \ln \frac{\sin \frac{\pi}{3}}{\cos \frac{\pi}{3} + 1}$$

$$L = \ln \frac{\frac{\sqrt{3}}{2}}{-\frac{1}{2} + 1} - \ln \frac{\frac{\sqrt{3}}{2}}{\frac{1}{2} + 1}$$

$$L = \ln \frac{\frac{\sqrt{3}}{2}}{\frac{1}{2}} - \ln \frac{\frac{\sqrt{3}}{2}}{\frac{3}{2}}$$

$$L = \ln \sqrt{3} - \ln \frac{\sqrt{3}}{3} = \ln \frac{\sqrt{3}}{\frac{\sqrt{3}}{3}}$$

$$L = \ln 3 = 1.10$$

65. $y = 16.0(e^{x/32} + e^{-x/32}), x = -25.0$ to $x = 25.0$

$$\frac{dy}{dx} = \frac{1}{2}(e^{x/32} - e^{-x/32})$$

$$1 + \left(\frac{dy}{dx}\right)^2 = \frac{e^{x/16} + e^{-x/16} + 2}{4}$$

$$\sqrt{1 + \left(\frac{dy}{dx}\right)^2} = \frac{e^{x/32} + e^{-x/32}}{2}$$

$$L = 2\int_0^{25} \frac{e^{x/32} + e^{-x/32}}{2}\, dx = 32(e^{x/32} - e^{-x/32})\;\Big|_0^{25}$$

$$L = 32(e^{25/32} - e^{-25/32}) = 55.24375836$$

$$L = 55.2 \text{ m}$$

69.
$$y_{rms} = \sqrt{\frac{1}{T} \int i^2 dt} = \sqrt{\frac{1}{T} \int (2\sin t)^2 dt}$$

$$\int_0^{2\pi} (2\sin t)^2 dt = \int_0^{2\pi} 4\sin^2 t\, dt = 4 \int_0^{2\pi} \sin^2 t\, dt$$

$$= 4\left(\frac{t}{2} - \frac{1}{2}\sin t \cos t\right)\Bigg|_0^{2\pi} \qquad \text{Formula 29 in table of integrals.}$$

$$= 2t - 2\sin t \cos t \Big|_0^{2\pi} = 4\pi;\ T = 2\pi$$

$$y_{rms} = \sqrt{\frac{1}{2\pi}(4\pi)} = \sqrt{2}$$

73. $V = \pi \displaystyle\int_{2.00}^{4.00} y^2 dx = \pi \int_{2.00}^{4.00} e^{-0.2x} dx;$ and $u = -0.2x\ du = -0.2\,dx$

$$= -\frac{\pi}{0.2} \int_{2.00}^{4.00} e^{-0.2x}(-0.2)dx = \frac{-\pi}{0.2} e^{-0.2x}\Big|_{2.00}^{4.00}$$

$$= -\frac{\pi}{2}[e^{-0.8} - e^{-0.4}] = 3.47 \text{ cm}^3$$

77. (a) $\displaystyle\int_0^{2.8} \frac{4}{1+e^x} dx = \int_0^{2.8} \frac{-4e^{-x}}{e^{-x}+1} \cdot (-e^{-x}dx) = -4\ln(e^{-x}+1)\big|_0^{2.8} = 2.536$

    (b) let $u = e^x$

$$du = e^x dx$$

$$du = u\, dx$$

$$\frac{1}{u} du = dx$$

$$\int \frac{4}{1+e^x} dx = \int \frac{4}{1+u} \cdot \frac{du}{u} = \int \frac{4}{u(u+1)} du$$

$$\int \frac{4}{1+e^x} dx = \int \left(\frac{4}{u} - \frac{4}{u+1}\right) du$$

$$\int \frac{4}{1+e^x} dx = 4\ln|u| - 4\ln|u+1|$$

$$\int \frac{4}{1+e^x} dx = 4\ln\left(\frac{u}{u+1}\right) = 4 \cdot \ln\left(\frac{e^x}{e^x+1}\right)$$

$$\int \frac{4}{1+e^x} dx = 4\ln\left(\frac{e^x}{e^x+1}\right)\Bigg|_0^{2.8} = 2.536$$

In (a) the integrand was multiplied by $\dfrac{e^{-x}}{e^{-x}}$.

In (b) a u-substitution led to an integral which was evaluated using partial fractions.

Chapter 29

EXPANSION OF FUNCTIONS IN SERIES

29.1   Infinite Series

1. $\displaystyle\sum_{u=1}^{\infty} 0.5^n = 0.5 + 0.5^2 + 0.5^3 + 0.5^4 + \cdots + 0.5^n + \cdots$

$s_1 = 0.5, s_2 = 0.75, s_3 = 0.875, s_4 = 0.9375.$
Converges

5. $a_n = \dfrac{1}{n+2};\ n = 0, 1, 2, 3, \ldots$

$a_0 = \dfrac{1}{0+2} = \dfrac{1}{2}$ $\qquad a_2 = \dfrac{1}{2+2} = \dfrac{1}{4}$

$a_1 = \dfrac{1}{1+2} = \dfrac{1}{3}$ $\qquad a_3 = \dfrac{1}{3+2} = \dfrac{1}{5}$

9. $a_n = \cos\dfrac{n\pi}{2}, n = 0, 1, 2, 3, \ldots$

$a_0 = \cos\dfrac{0\cdot\pi}{2} = 1$

$a_1 = \cos\dfrac{1\cdot\pi}{2} = 0$

$a_2 = \cos\dfrac{2\cdot\pi}{2} = -1$

$a_3 = \cos\dfrac{3\cdot\pi}{2} = 0$

(a) $1, 0, -1, 0$

(b) $1 + 0 - 1 + 0 - \cdots$

13. $\dfrac{1}{2\times 3} + \dfrac{1}{3\times 4} + \dfrac{1}{4\times 5} + \dfrac{1}{5\times 6} + \cdots$

$n = 1, a_2 = \dfrac{1}{(1+1)(1+2)} = \dfrac{1}{2\times 3}$

$n = 2, a_3 = \dfrac{1}{(2+1)(2+2)} = \dfrac{1}{3\times 4}$

$a_n = \dfrac{1}{(n+1)(n+2)}$

17. $1 + \dfrac{1}{2} + \dfrac{2}{3} + \dfrac{3}{4} + \dfrac{4}{5} + \cdots$

$S_0 = 1;\ S_1 = 1 + \dfrac{1}{2} = \dfrac{3}{2} = 1.5$

$S_2 = 1 + \dfrac{1}{2} + \dfrac{2}{3} = \dfrac{13}{6} = 2.1666667$

$S_3 = 1 + \dfrac{1}{2} + \dfrac{2}{3} + \dfrac{3}{4} = \dfrac{35}{12} = 2.9166667$

$S_4 = 1 + \dfrac{1}{2} + \dfrac{2}{3} + \dfrac{3}{4} + \dfrac{4}{5} = \dfrac{223}{60} = 3.7166667$

Divergent

21. $\displaystyle\sum_{n=1}^{\infty} \dfrac{2n+1}{n^2(n+1)^2}$

First five terms:

$a_1 = \dfrac{3}{4};\ a_2 = \dfrac{5}{36};\ a_3 = \dfrac{7}{144};\ a_4 = \dfrac{9}{400};\ a_5 = \dfrac{11}{900}$

First five partial sums:

$S_1 = 0.75;$

$S_2 = \dfrac{3}{4} + \dfrac{5}{36} = 0.8888889$

$S_3 = \dfrac{3}{4} + \dfrac{5}{36} + \dfrac{7}{144} = 0.9375000$

$S_4 = \dfrac{3}{4} + \dfrac{5}{36} + \dfrac{7}{144} + \dfrac{9}{400} = 0.9600000$

$S_5 = \dfrac{3}{4} + \dfrac{5}{36} + \dfrac{7}{144} + \dfrac{9}{400} + \dfrac{11}{900} - 0.9722222$

Convergent, converging to 1 (approx. sum)

25. $1 - \dfrac{1}{3} + \dfrac{1}{9} - \cdots + \left(-\dfrac{1}{3}\right)^n + \cdots$

$S = \lim_{n\to\infty} S_n = \lim_{n\to\infty}\left(-\dfrac{1}{3}\right)^n = \lim_{n\to\infty}\dfrac{(-1)^n}{3^n} = 0$

Convergent. $a = 1, n = -\dfrac{1}{3}$

$S = \dfrac{a}{1-r} = \dfrac{1}{1-\left(-\frac{1}{3}\right)} = \dfrac{1}{\frac{4}{3}} = \dfrac{3}{4}$

29. $512 - 64 + 8 - 1 + \dfrac{1}{8} - \cdots$

$a_n = \dfrac{512}{(-8)^n};\ n = 0, 1, 2, 3, \ldots$

$S = \lim_{n\to\infty}\dfrac{512}{(-8)^n} = 0;$ convergent.

$a = 512, r = -\dfrac{1}{8};\ S = \dfrac{512}{1+\frac{1}{8}} = \dfrac{512(8)}{9} = \dfrac{4096}{9}$

33. $S_n = \dfrac{a_1(1 - r^n)}{(1 - r)}$; $r \neq 1$; geometric series

Series: $\dfrac{1}{2} + \dfrac{1}{4} + \dfrac{1}{8} + \cdots$; $a_n = \dfrac{1}{2^n}, a = \dfrac{1}{2}, r = \dfrac{1}{2}$

$f(x) = \dfrac{a_1(1 - r^x)}{(1 - r)}$; $f(x) = \dfrac{\frac{1}{2}(1 - r^x)}{\left(1 - \frac{1}{2}\right)} = (1 - r^x)$

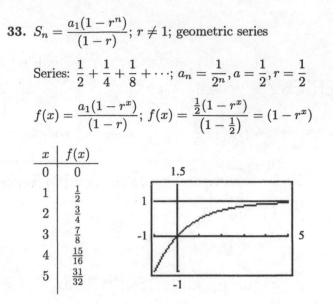

x	$f(x)$
0	0
1	$\frac{1}{2}$
2	$\frac{3}{4}$
3	$\frac{7}{8}$
4	$\frac{15}{16}$
5	$\frac{31}{32}$

The infinite series approaches 1.

37. $\displaystyle\sum_{n=0}^{\infty} x^n = 1 + x + x^2 + \cdots + x^n + \cdots$

For $|x| < 1, a_1 = 1, r = x$,

$S = \dfrac{1}{1 - x}$

$\displaystyle\sum_{n=0}^{\infty} x^n = \dfrac{1}{1 - x}$

29.2   Maclaurin's Series

1. $f(x) = \dfrac{2}{2 + x}, f(0) = 1$

$f'(x) = \dfrac{-2}{(2 + x)^2}, f'(0) = -\dfrac{1}{2}$

$f''(x) = \dfrac{4}{(2 + x)^3}, f''(0) = \dfrac{1}{2}$

$f'''(x) = \dfrac{-12}{(2 + x)^4}, f'''(0) = -\dfrac{3}{4}$

$f(x) = \dfrac{2}{2 + x} = 1 - \dfrac{1}{2}x + \dfrac{1}{2}x^2 - \dfrac{3}{4}x^3 + \cdots$

5. $f(x) = \cos x$ $\qquad f(0) = 1$
 $f'(x) = -\sin x$ $\qquad f'(0) = 0$
 $f''(x) = -\cos x$ $\qquad f''(0) = -1$
 $f'''(x) = \sin x$ $\qquad f'''(0) = 0$
 $f^{iv}(x) = \cos x$ $\qquad f^{iv}(0) = 1$

$f(x) = \cos x = f(0) + f''(0)\dfrac{x^2}{2!} + f^{iv}(0)\dfrac{x^4}{4!} - \cdots$

$\cos x = 1 - 1\dfrac{x^2}{2} + 1\dfrac{x^4}{24} - \cdots$

$\cos x = 1 - \dfrac{1}{2}x^2 + \dfrac{1}{24}x^4 - \cdots$

9. $f(x) = \cos 4\pi x$
 $f'(x) = -4\pi \sin 4\pi x$
 $f''(x) = -16\pi^2 \cos 4\pi x$
 $f'''(x) = 64\pi^3 \sin 4\pi x$
 $f^{iv}(x) = 256\pi^4 \cos 4\pi x$
 $f(0) = 1$
 $f'(0) = 0$
 $f''(0) = -16\pi^2$
 $f'''(0) = 0$
 $f^{iv}(0) = 256\pi^4$

$f(x) = 1 + 0 \cdot x - \dfrac{16\pi^2}{2!} \cdot x^2 + 0 \cdot \dfrac{x^3}{3!}$

$\qquad + \dfrac{256\pi^4}{4!}x^4 + \cdots$

$= f(x) = 1 - 8\pi^2 x^2 + \dfrac{32\pi^4 x^4}{3} - \cdots$

13. $f(x) = \ln(1 - 2x)$

$f'(x) = \dfrac{1}{1 - 2x}(-2)$

$\qquad = \dfrac{-2}{1 - 2x}$

$f''(x) = \dfrac{0 - (-2)(-2)}{(1 - 2x)^2}$

$\qquad = \dfrac{-4}{(1 - 2x)^2}$

$f'''(x) = \dfrac{0 - (-4)2(1 - 2x)(-2)}{(1 - 2x)^4}$

$\qquad = \dfrac{-16(1 - 2x)}{(1 - 2x)^4}$

$f(0) = \ln 1 = 0$

$f'(0) = -2$

$f''(0) = -4$

$f'''(0) = -16$

$\ln(1 - 2x) = 0 + (-2)x + (-4)\dfrac{x^2}{2!} + (-16)\dfrac{x^3}{3!} + \cdots$

$\qquad = -2x - 2x^2 - \dfrac{8}{3}x^3 - \cdots$

17. $f(x) = \tan^{-1} x$

$$f'(x) = \frac{1}{1+x^2} = (1+x^2)^{-1}$$

$$f''(x) = -(1+x^2)^{-2}2x = -2x(1+x^2)^{-2}$$
$$f'''(x) = -2x[-2(1+x^2)^{-3}(2x)] + (1+x^2)^{-2}(-2)$$
$$f(0) = 0$$

$$f'(0) = 1$$

$$f''(0) = 0$$
$$f'''(0) = -2$$

$$f(x) = 0 + 1x + \frac{0x^2}{2!} - \frac{2x^3}{3!} + \cdots = x - \frac{1}{3}x^3 + \cdots$$

21. $f(x) = \ln \cos x$

$$f'(x) = -\frac{1}{\cos x}\sin x = -\tan x$$

$$f''(x) = -\sec^2 x$$
$$f'''(x) = -2\sec x \sec x \tan x = -2\sec^2 x \tan x$$
$$f^{iv}(x) = -2\sec^2 x \sec^2 x - 2\tan x(2\sec x \sec x \tan x)$$
$$f(0) = \ln 1 = 0$$

$$f'(0) = 0$$

$$f''(0) = -1$$
$$f'''(0) = 0$$
$$f^{iv}(0) = -2 - 0 = -2$$

$$f(x) = 0 + 0x - \frac{1x^2}{2!} + \frac{0x^3}{3!} - \frac{2x^4}{4!} + \cdots$$

$$= -\frac{1}{2}x^2 - \frac{1}{12}x^4 - \cdots$$

25. (a) $f(x) = e^x \qquad f(0) = 1$
$\qquad\qquad f'(x) = e^x \qquad f'(0) = 1$
$\qquad\qquad f''(x) = e^x \qquad f''(0) = 1$

$$e^x = 1 + x + \frac{1}{2}x^2 + \cdots$$

(b) $f(x) = e^{x^2} \qquad\qquad\qquad f(0) = 1$
$\qquad\quad f'(x) = 2xe^{x^2} \qquad\qquad\quad f'(0) = 0$
$\qquad\quad f''(x) = 2e^{x^2}(2x^2+1) \qquad f''(0) = 2$
$\qquad\quad f'''(x) = 4xe^{x^2}(2x^2+3) \qquad f'''(0) = 0$
$\qquad\quad f^{iv}(x) = 4e^{x^2}(4x^4+12x^2+3) \quad f^{iv}(0) = 12$

$$e^{x^2} = 1 + \frac{2x^2}{2} + \frac{12x^4}{4!} + \cdots = 1 + x^2 + \frac{1}{2}x^4 + \cdots$$

29. $f(x) = x^2, f'(x) = 2x, f''(x) = 2, f^{(n)}(x) = 0,$
$\quad n \geq 3$
$\quad f(0) = 0, f'(0) = 0, f''(0) = 2, f^{(n)}(x) = 0, n \geq 3$
$$x^2 = 0 + 0(x) + 2\frac{x^2}{2!} + 0\frac{x^3}{3!} + \cdots$$

$$x^2 = x$$

29.3   Certain Operations with Series

1. $e^x = 1 + x + \frac{x^2}{2!} + \frac{x^3}{3!} + \cdots$

$$e^{2x^2} = 1 + 2x^2 + \frac{(2x^2)^2}{2!} + \frac{(2x^2)^3}{3!} + \cdots$$

$$e^{2x^2} = 1 + 2x^2 + 2x^4 + \frac{4}{3}x^6 + \cdots$$

5. $f(x) = \sin\left(\frac{1}{2}x\right);\ \sin x = x - \frac{x^3}{3!} + \frac{x^5}{5!} - \frac{x^7}{7!} + \cdots$

$$f(x) = \sin\left(\frac{1}{2}x\right)$$

$$= \frac{1}{2}x - \frac{\left(\frac{1}{2}x\right)^3}{6} + \frac{\left(\frac{1}{2}x\right)^5}{120} - \frac{\left(\frac{1}{2}x\right)^7}{7!} + \cdots$$

$$= \frac{1}{2}x - \frac{x^3}{2^3 3!} + \frac{x^5}{2^5 5!} - \frac{x^7}{2^7 7!} + \cdots$$

9. $f(x) = \ln(1+x^2);\ \ln(1+x) = x - \frac{x^2}{2} + \frac{x^3}{3} - \frac{x^4}{4} + \cdots$

$$\ln(1+x^2) = x^2 - \frac{(x^2)^2}{2} + \frac{(x^2)^3}{3} - \frac{(x^2)^2}{4} + \cdots$$

$$= x^2 - \frac{1}{2}x^4 + \frac{1}{3}x^6 - \frac{1}{4}x^8 + \cdots$$

13. $\displaystyle\int_0^{0.2} \cos\sqrt{x}\,dx = \int_0^{0.2}\left(1 - \frac{(\sqrt{x})^2}{2} + \frac{(\sqrt{x})^4}{24}\right)dx$

$$= \int_0^{0.2}\left(1 - \frac{1}{2}x - \frac{1}{24}x^2\right)dx$$

$$= \left(x - \frac{1}{4}x^2 + \frac{1}{72}x^3\right)\Big|_0^{0.2}$$

$$= 0.2 - \frac{1}{4}(0.2)^2 + \frac{1}{72}(0.2)^3$$

$$= 0.1901$$

17. $e^x \sin x = f(x)$

$$e^x = 1 + x + \frac{x^2}{2!} + \frac{x^3}{3!} + \cdots \quad (1)$$

$$\sin x = x - \frac{x^3}{3!} + \frac{x^5}{5!} - \cdots \quad (2)$$

Multiply (1) by x from (2): $x + x^2 + \frac{x^3}{2!} + \frac{x^4}{3!} + \cdots$

Multiply (1) by $-\frac{x^3}{3!}$ from (2): $-\frac{x^3}{3!} - \frac{x^4}{3!} - \cdots$

Combine:

$$e^x \sin x = x + x^2 + \frac{x^3}{2!} + \frac{x^4}{3!} - \frac{x^3}{3!} - \frac{x^4}{3!}$$

$$= x + x^2 + \frac{1}{2}x^3 - \frac{1}{6}x^3$$

$$= x + x^2 + \frac{2}{6}x^3 + \cdots$$

$$= x + x^2 + \frac{1}{3}x^3 + \cdots$$

21. $\dfrac{d(\sin x)}{dx} = \dfrac{d}{dx}\left(x - \dfrac{x^3}{3!} + \dfrac{x^5}{5!} - \cdots \right)$

$$= 1 - \frac{3x^2}{3!} + \frac{5x^4}{4!} - \cdots$$

$$= 1 - \frac{x^2}{2} + \frac{x^4}{24} - \cdots = \cos x$$

25. $\displaystyle\int_0^1 e^x\,dx = e^x\Big|_0^1 = e - e^0 = e - 1$

$$= 2.7182818 - 1 = 1.7182818$$

$$\begin{array}{ll} f(x) = e^x & f(0) = e^0 = 1 \\ f'(x) = e^x & f'(0) = 1 \\ f''(x) = e^x & f''(0) = 1 \\ f'''(x) = e^x & f'''(0) = 1 \end{array}$$

$$e^x = 1 + x + \frac{x^2}{2!} + \frac{x^3}{3!} + \cdots$$

$$\int_0^1 \left(1 + x + \frac{x^2}{2} + \frac{x^3}{6} \right) dx$$

$$= x + \frac{x^2}{2} + \frac{x^3}{6} + \frac{x^4}{24}\Big|_0^1$$

$$= 1 + \frac{1}{2} + \frac{1}{6} + \frac{1}{24}$$

$$= 1.7083333$$

29. $\displaystyle\int_0^x \cos t^2\,dt = \int_0^{0.2} \left[1 - \frac{(t^2)^2}{2!} \right] dt$

$$= \int_0^{0.2} \left(1 - \frac{t^4}{2} \right) dt$$

$$\left(t - \frac{t^5}{10} \right)\Big|_0^{0.2} = 0.199968$$

33. $y_1 = e^x$, $y_2 = 1$, $y_3 = 1 + x$, $y_4 = 1 + x + \dfrac{1}{2}x^2$;
$x_{\min} = -5$, $x_{\max} = 5$, $y_{\min} = -1$, $y_{\max} = 3$

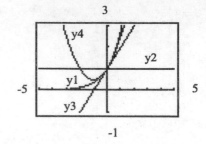

29.4   Computations by Use of Series Expansions

1. $e^x = 1 + x + \dfrac{x^2}{2!} + \cdots$

$$e^{-0.1} = 1 + (-0.1) + \frac{(-0.1)^2}{2!} + \cdots$$

$$e^{-0.1} = 0.905$$

5. $\sin 0.1$, (2 terms); $\sin x = x - \dfrac{x^3}{3!}$

$$\sin 0.1 = 0.1 - \frac{(0.1)^3}{6} = 0.09983333$$

(0.0998334 calculator)

9. $\cos 3°$, (2 terms); $3° = \dfrac{3}{180}\pi$ radians

$$\cos x = 1 - \frac{x^2}{2!}$$

$$\cos 3° = 1 - \frac{\left(\frac{3\pi}{180} \right)^2}{2} = 0.9986292$$

(0.9986295 calculator)

13. $\sin 0.3625$, (3 terms): $\sin x = x - \dfrac{x^3}{3!} + \dfrac{x^5}{5!}$

$$\sin 0.3625 = 0.3625 - \frac{(0.3625)^3}{6} + \frac{(0.3625)^5}{5!}$$

$$= 0.3546130$$

(0.3546129 calculator)

17. $(1 + x)^6 = 1 + 6x + 15x^2 + 20x^3 + 15x^4$
$\qquad\qquad + 6x^5 + x^6$

$$(1.032)^6 = 1 + 6(0.032) + 15(0.032)^2$$

$$= 1.20736$$

$(1.032)^6 = 1.20803$, calculator

21. $\sqrt[3]{1+x} = (1+x)^{1/3} = 1 + \dfrac{1}{3}x + \dfrac{\frac{1}{3}\left(-\frac{2}{3}\right)x^2}{2!}$

$= 1 + \dfrac{1}{3}x - \dfrac{1}{9}x^2$

$\sqrt[3]{0.9628} = (1 - 0.0372)^{1/3}$

$= 1 + \dfrac{1}{3}(-0.0372) - \dfrac{1}{9}(-0.0372)^2$

$= 0.9874462$

(0.9874430 calculator)

25. $\cos 3° = 0.9986292$ to 2 terms.

Max. error is 3rd term $= \left| \dfrac{\left(\frac{3\pi}{180}\right)^4}{4!} \right| = 3.1 \times 10^{-7}$

29. $e^x = 1 + x + \dfrac{x^2}{2} + \dfrac{x^3}{3!} + \dfrac{x^4}{4!} + \cdots > 1 + x + \dfrac{x^2}{2}$

for $x > 0$ since the terms of the expansion for e^x after those on right hand side of the inequality have a positive value.

33. $f(t) = \dfrac{E}{R}(1 - e^{-Rt/L});\ e^x = 1 + x + \dfrac{x^2}{2} + \cdots$

$e^{-Rt/L} = 1 - \dfrac{Rt}{L} + \dfrac{R^2 t^2}{2L^2} + \cdots$

$i = \dfrac{E}{R}\left[1 - \left(1 - \dfrac{Rt}{L} + \dfrac{R^2 t^2}{2L^2}\right)\right] = \dfrac{E}{L}\left(t - \dfrac{Rt^2}{2L}\right)$

The approximation will be valid for small values of t.

29.5   Taylor Series

1. $f(x) = x^{1/2}, f(1) = 1$

$f'(x) = \dfrac{1}{2x^{1/2}}, f'(1) = \dfrac{1}{2}$

$f''(x) = -\dfrac{1}{4x^{3/2}}, f''(1) = -\dfrac{1}{4}$

$f'''(x) = \dfrac{3}{8x^{5/2}}, f'''(1) = \dfrac{3}{8}$

$\sqrt{x} = 1 + \dfrac{1}{2}(x-1) + \dfrac{-\frac{1}{4}(x-1)^2}{2!} + \dfrac{\frac{3}{8}(x-1)^3}{3!} + \cdots$

$\sqrt{x} = 1 + \dfrac{1}{2}(x-1) - \dfrac{1}{8}(x-1)^2 + \dfrac{1}{16}(x-1)^3 - \cdots$

5. $\sqrt{4.2};\ \sqrt{x} = 2 + \dfrac{(x-4)}{4} - \dfrac{(x-4)^2}{64} + \dfrac{(x-3)^3}{512}$

$\sqrt{4.2} = 2 + \dfrac{(4.2-4)}{4} - \dfrac{(4.2-4)^2}{64} + \dfrac{(4.2-4)^3}{512}$

$= 2.049;\ (2.04939 \text{ calculator})$

9. $\sin x = \dfrac{1}{2} + \dfrac{\sqrt{3}}{2}\left(x - \dfrac{\pi}{6}\right) - \dfrac{1}{4}\left(x - \dfrac{\pi}{6}\right)^2$

$\sin 29.53°$

$= \dfrac{1}{2} + \dfrac{\sqrt{3}}{2}\left(\dfrac{29.53\pi}{180} - \dfrac{\pi}{6}\right)$

$- \dfrac{1}{4}\left(\dfrac{29.53\pi}{180} - \dfrac{\pi}{6}\right)^2$

$= 0.49288;\ (0.4928792 \text{ calculator})$

13. $\sin x;\ a = \dfrac{\pi}{3}$

$f(x) = \sin x \qquad\qquad f\left(\dfrac{\pi}{3}\right) = \dfrac{\sqrt{3}}{2}$

$f'(x) = \cos x \qquad\qquad f'\left(\dfrac{\pi}{3}\right) = \dfrac{1}{2}$

$f''(x) = -\sin x \qquad\quad f''\left(\dfrac{\pi}{3}\right) = -\dfrac{\sqrt{3}}{2}$

$\sin x = \dfrac{\sqrt{3}}{2} + \dfrac{1}{2}\left(x - \dfrac{\pi}{3}\right) - \dfrac{\sqrt{3}}{2!}\left(x - \dfrac{\pi}{3}\right)^2 - \cdots$

$= \dfrac{1}{2}\left[\sqrt{3} + \left(x - \dfrac{\pi}{3}\right) - \dfrac{\sqrt{3}}{2!}\left(x - \dfrac{\pi}{3}\right)^2 - \cdots\right]$

17. $\tan x;\ a = \dfrac{\pi}{4}$

$f(x) = \tan x \qquad\qquad f\left(\dfrac{\pi}{4}\right) = 1$

$f'(x) = \sec^2 x \qquad\quad f'\left(\dfrac{\pi}{4}\right) = (\sqrt{2})^2 = 2$

$f''(x) = 2\sec x \sec x \tan x = 2\sec^2 x \tan x$

$f''(x) = 2(\sqrt{2})^2(1) = 4$

$\tan x = 1 + 2\left(x - \dfrac{\pi}{4}\right) + \dfrac{4\left(x - \frac{\pi}{4}\right)^2}{2!} + \cdots$

$= 1 + 2\left(x - \dfrac{\pi}{4}\right) + 2\left(x - \dfrac{\pi}{4}\right)^2 + \cdots$

21. $\sqrt{9.3};\ a = 9$

$f(x) = \sqrt{x} \qquad\qquad f(9) = 3$

$f'(x) = \dfrac{1}{2\sqrt{x}} \qquad\qquad f'(9) = \dfrac{1}{6}$

$f''(x) = -\dfrac{1}{4x^{3/2}} \qquad\quad f''(9) = -\dfrac{1}{108}$

$\sqrt{x} = 3 + \dfrac{1}{6}(x-9) - \dfrac{1}{108}\dfrac{(x-9)^2}{2!}$

$\sqrt{9.3} = 3 + \dfrac{1}{6}(0.3) - \dfrac{1}{108}\dfrac{(0.3)^2}{2} = 3.0496$

25. $\sin x = \dfrac{1}{2}\left[\sqrt{3} + \left(x - \dfrac{\pi}{3}\right) - \dfrac{\sqrt{3}}{2}\left(x - \dfrac{\pi}{3}\right)^2\right]; \ a = \dfrac{\pi}{3}$

$61° = 60° + 1° = \dfrac{\pi}{3} + \dfrac{\pi}{180}$

$\sin 61° = \dfrac{1}{2}\left[\sqrt{3} + \dfrac{\pi}{180} - \dfrac{\sqrt{3}}{2}\left(\dfrac{\pi}{180}\right)^2\right] = 0.87462$

29. Expand $\quad f(x) = 2x^3 + x^2 - 3x + 5$ about $x = 1$

$\qquad\quad f'(x) = 6x^2 + 2x - 3$

$\qquad\quad f''(x) = 12x + 2$

$\qquad\quad f'''(x) = 12$

$f(x) = f(1) + f'(1)(x-1)\dfrac{f''(1)(x-1)^2}{2!} + \dfrac{f'''(1)(x-1)^3}{3!}$

$\quad = 2(1)^3 + 1^2 - 3(1) + 5 + (6(1)^2 + 2(1) - 3)(x-1) + \dfrac{(12(1)+2)(x-1)^2}{2!} + \dfrac{12(x-1)^3}{3!}$

$\quad = 5 + 5(x-1) + 7(x-1)^2 + 2(x-1)^3$

33. $f(x) = \sin x; \ x = 0$ to $x = 2$

(a) $y_1 = \sin x$

(b) $y_2 = \dfrac{\sqrt{3}}{2} + \dfrac{1}{2}\left(x - \dfrac{\pi}{3}\right)$

$\qquad x_{\min} = 0, \ x_{\max} = 2, \ y_{\min} = 0, \ y_{\max} = 1.2$

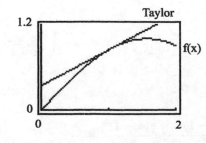

The series gives a good approximation near $x = \dfrac{\pi}{3}$ and deteriorates as x moves away from $x = \dfrac{\pi}{3}$.

29.6   Introduction to Fourier Series

1. $f(x) = \begin{cases} -2, & -\pi \leq x < 0 \\ 2, & 0 \leq x < \pi \end{cases}$

$a_0 = \dfrac{1}{2\pi}\displaystyle\int_{-\pi}^{0}(-2)dx + \dfrac{1}{2\pi}\displaystyle\int_{0}^{\pi}2\,dx = 0$

$a_n = \dfrac{1}{\pi}\displaystyle\int_{-\pi}^{0}-2\cos nx\,dx + \dfrac{1}{\pi}\displaystyle\int_{0}^{\pi}2\cos nx\,dx = 0$

$b_n = \dfrac{1}{\pi}\displaystyle\int_{-\pi}^{0}-2\sin nx\,dx + \dfrac{1}{\pi}\displaystyle\int_{0}^{\pi}2\sin nx\,dx$

$= \dfrac{4}{\pi}\left(\dfrac{1}{n} - \dfrac{\cos(\pi n)}{n}\right)$

$b_n = \dfrac{4}{\pi}(1 - \cos \pi n) = \begin{cases} \dfrac{8}{n\pi}, & n \text{ odd} \\ \\ 0, & n \text{ neven} \end{cases}$

$b_1 = \dfrac{8}{\pi}, \; b_3 = \dfrac{8}{3\pi}, \; b_5 = \dfrac{8}{5\pi}$

$f(x) = \dfrac{8}{\pi}\sin x + \dfrac{8}{3\pi}\sin 3x + \dfrac{8}{5\pi}\sin 5x + \cdots$

$f(x) = \dfrac{8}{\pi}\left(\sin x + \dfrac{1}{3}\sin 3x + \dfrac{1}{5}\sin 5x + \cdots\right)$

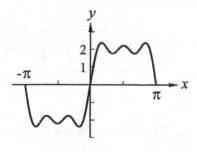

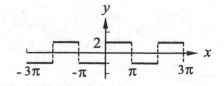

5. $f(x) = \begin{cases} 1 & -\pi \leq x < 0 \\ 2 & 0 \leq x < \pi \end{cases}$

$a_0 = \dfrac{1}{2\pi}\displaystyle\int_{-\pi}^{0}1\,dx + \dfrac{1}{2\pi}\displaystyle\int_{0}^{\pi}2\,dx$

$= \dfrac{x}{2\pi}\Big|_{-\pi}^{0} + \dfrac{2x}{2\pi}\Big|_{0}^{\pi}$

$= 0 + \dfrac{\pi}{2\pi} + \dfrac{2\pi}{2\pi} - 0 = \dfrac{1}{2} + 1 = \dfrac{3}{2}$

$a_1 = \dfrac{1}{\pi}\displaystyle\int_{-\pi}^{0}1\cos x\,dx + \dfrac{1}{\pi}\displaystyle\int_{0}^{\pi}2\cos x\,dx$

$= \dfrac{1}{\pi}\sin x\Big|_{-\pi}^{0} + \dfrac{2}{\pi}\sin x\Big|_{0}^{\pi}$

$= \dfrac{1}{\pi}(0 - 0) + \dfrac{2}{\pi}(0 - 0) = 0$

$a_n = 0$ since $\sin n\pi = 0$

$b_1 = \dfrac{1}{\pi}\displaystyle\int_{-\pi}^{0}1\sin x\,dx + \dfrac{1}{\pi}\displaystyle\int_{0}^{\pi}2\sin x\,dx$

$= -\dfrac{1}{\pi}\cos x\Big|_{-\pi}^{0} - \dfrac{2}{\pi}\cos x\Big|_{0}^{\pi}$

$= -\dfrac{1}{\pi}(1 + 1) - \dfrac{2}{\pi}(-1 - 1)$

$= -\dfrac{2}{\pi} + \dfrac{4}{\pi} = \dfrac{2}{\pi}$

$b_2 = \dfrac{1}{\pi}\displaystyle\int_{-\pi}^{0}1\sin 2x\,dx + \dfrac{1}{\pi}\displaystyle\int_{0}^{\pi}2\sin x\,dx$

$= -\dfrac{1}{2\pi}\cos 2x\Big|_{-\pi}^{0} - \dfrac{1}{\pi}\cos 2x\Big|_{0}^{\pi}$

$= -\dfrac{1}{2\pi}(1 - 1) - \dfrac{1}{\pi}(1 - 1) = 0$

$b_3 = \dfrac{1}{\pi}\displaystyle\int_{-\pi}^{0}\sin 3x\,dx + \dfrac{1}{\pi}\displaystyle\int_{0}^{\pi}2\sin 3x\,dx$

$= -\dfrac{1}{3\pi}\cos 3x\Big|_{-\pi}^{0} - \dfrac{2}{3\pi}\cos 3x\Big|_{0}^{\pi}$

$= -\dfrac{1}{3\pi}(1 + 1) - \dfrac{2}{3\pi}(-1 - 1) = \dfrac{2}{3\pi}$

Therefore, $b_n = 0$ for n even; $b_n = \dfrac{2}{n\pi}$ for n odd.

Therefore, $f(x) = \dfrac{3}{2} + \dfrac{2}{\pi}\sin x + \dfrac{2}{3\pi}\sin 3x + \cdots$

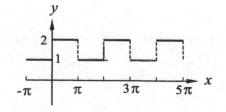

9. $f(x) = \begin{cases} -1 & -\pi \le x < 0 \\ 0 & 0 \le x < \frac{\pi}{2} \\ 1 & \frac{\pi}{2} \le x < \pi \end{cases}$

$a_0 = \dfrac{1}{2\pi} \displaystyle\int_{-\pi}^{0} -dx + \dfrac{1}{2\pi} \displaystyle\int_{\pi/2}^{\pi} dx$

$= \dfrac{1}{2\pi} x \Big|_{-\pi}^{0} + \dfrac{1}{2\pi} x \Big|_{\pi/2}^{\pi}$

$= -\dfrac{1}{2\pi} \left(x \Big|_{-\pi}^{0} - x \Big|_{\pi/2}^{\pi} \right)$

$= -\dfrac{1}{2\pi} \left[\pi - \left(\pi - \dfrac{\pi}{2} \right) \right] = -\dfrac{1}{4}$

$a_1 = \dfrac{1}{\pi} \displaystyle\int_{-\pi}^{0} - \cos x\, dx + \dfrac{1}{\pi} \displaystyle\int_{\pi/2}^{\pi} c \cos x\, dx$

$= -\dfrac{1}{\pi} \sin x \Big|_{-\pi}^{0} + \dfrac{1}{\pi} \sin x \Big|_{\pi/2}^{\pi}$

$= -\dfrac{1}{\pi} \left(\sin x \Big|_{-\pi}^{0} - \sin x \Big|_{\pi/2}^{\pi} \right) = -\dfrac{1}{\pi}$

$a_2 = \dfrac{1}{\pi} \displaystyle\int_{-\pi}^{0} - \cos 2x\, dx + \dfrac{1}{\pi} \displaystyle\int_{\pi/2}^{\pi} \cos 2x\, dx$

$= -\dfrac{1}{2\pi} \sin 2x \Big|_{-\pi}^{0} + \dfrac{1}{2\pi} \sin 2x \Big|_{\pi/2}^{\pi}$

$= -\dfrac{1}{2\pi} \left(\sin 2x \Big|_{-\pi}^{0} - \sin 2x \Big|_{\pi/2}^{\pi} \right) = 0$

$a_3 = \dfrac{1}{\pi} \displaystyle\int_{-\pi}^{0} - \cos 3x\, dx + \dfrac{1}{\pi} \displaystyle\int_{\pi/2}^{\pi} \cos 3x\, dx$

$= -\dfrac{1}{3\pi} \sin 3x \Big|_{-\pi}^{0} + \dfrac{1}{3\pi} \sin 3x \Big|_{\pi/2}^{\pi}$

$= -\dfrac{1}{3\pi} \left(\sin 3x \Big|_{-\pi}^{0} - \sin 3x \Big|_{\pi/2}^{\pi} \right) = \dfrac{1}{3\pi}$

Therefore, $a_n = \pm \dfrac{1}{n\pi}$ for n odd; $a_n = 0$ for n even.

$b_1 = \dfrac{1}{\pi} \displaystyle\int_{-\pi}^{0} - \sin x\, dx + \dfrac{1}{\pi} \displaystyle\int_{\pi/2}^{\pi} \sin x\, dx$

$= \dfrac{1}{\pi} \cos x \Big|_{-\pi}^{0} - \dfrac{1}{\pi} \cos x \Big|_{\pi/2}^{\pi}$

$= \dfrac{1}{\pi} \left(\cos x \Big|_{-\pi}^{0} - \cos x \Big|_{\pi/2}^{\pi} \right) = \dfrac{3}{\pi}$

$b_2 = \dfrac{1}{\pi} \displaystyle\int_{-\pi}^{0} - \sin 2x\, dx + \dfrac{1}{\pi} \displaystyle\int_{\pi/2}^{\pi} \sin 2x\, dx$

$= \dfrac{1}{2\pi} \cos 2x \Big|_{-\pi}^{0} - \dfrac{1}{2\pi} \cos 2x \Big|_{\pi/2}^{\pi}$

$= \dfrac{1}{2\pi} \left(\cos x \Big|_{-\pi}^{0} - \cos 2x \Big|_{\pi/2}^{\pi} \right) = -\dfrac{1}{\pi}$

$b_3 = \dfrac{1}{\pi} \displaystyle\int_{-\pi}^{0} - \sin 3x\, dx + \dfrac{1}{\pi} \displaystyle\int_{\pi/2}^{\pi} \sin 3x\, dx$

$= \dfrac{1}{3\pi} \cos 3x \Big|_{-\pi}^{0} - \dfrac{1}{3\pi} \cos 3x \Big|_{\pi/2}^{\pi}$

$= \dfrac{1}{3\pi} \left(\cos 3x \Big|_{-\pi}^{0} - \cos 3x \Big|_{\pi/2}^{\pi} \right) = -\dfrac{1}{\pi}$

$b_n = \pm \dfrac{1}{\pi}$ for $n > 1$

$f(x) = -\dfrac{1}{4} - \dfrac{1}{\pi} \cos x + \dfrac{1}{3\pi} \cos 3x - \cdots$

$\qquad + \dfrac{3}{\pi} \sin x - \dfrac{1}{\pi} \sin 2x + \dfrac{1}{\pi} \sin 3x - \cdots$

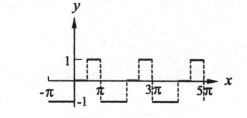

13. $f(x) = \begin{cases} -1 & -\pi \le x < 0 \\ 1 & 0 \le x < \pi \end{cases}$

Graph $y_1 = \dfrac{4}{\pi} \left(\sin x + \dfrac{1}{3} \sin 3x + \dfrac{1}{5} \sin 5x \right)$

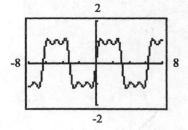

17. $f(x) = \begin{cases} -x, -\pi \le x < 0 \\ x, 0 \le x < \pi \end{cases}$

Graph $y_1 = \dfrac{\pi}{2} - \dfrac{4}{\pi}\left(\cos x + \dfrac{1}{9}\cos 3x\right)$

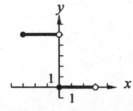

29.7   More About Fourier Series

1. $f(x) = \begin{cases} 2 & -\pi \le x < -\dfrac{\pi}{2}, \dfrac{\pi}{2} \le x < \pi \\ 3 & -\dfrac{\pi}{2} \le x < \dfrac{\pi}{2} \end{cases}$

From Example 2,

$f(x) = \dfrac{1}{2} + \dfrac{2}{\pi}\left(\cos x - \dfrac{\cos 3x}{3} + \dfrac{\cos 5x}{5} - \cdots\right) + 2.$

$= \dfrac{5}{2} + \dfrac{2}{\pi}\left(\cos x - \dfrac{\cos 3x}{3} + \dfrac{\cos 5x}{5} - \cdots\right)$

5. $f(x) = \begin{cases} 5 & -3 \le x < 0 \\ 0 & 0 \le x < 3 \end{cases}$

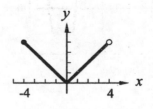

from the graph $f(x)$ is
neither odd nor even.

9. $f(x) = |x| \quad -4 \le x < 4$

is even from the graph.

13. $f(x) \begin{cases} 5 & -3 \le x < 0 \\ 0 & 0 \le x < 3 \end{cases}$

period $= 6 = 2L$, $L = 3$

$a_0 = \dfrac{1}{2L}\int_{-L}^{L} f(x)\,dx$

$= \dfrac{1}{6}\int_{-3}^{0} 5\,dx + \dfrac{1}{6}\int_{0}^{3} 0 \cdot dx = \dfrac{5}{2}$

$a_n = \dfrac{1}{L}\int_{-L}^{L} f(x)\cos\dfrac{n\pi x}{L}\,dx$

$= \dfrac{1}{3}\int_{-3}^{0} 5\cos\dfrac{n\pi x}{3}\,dx + \dfrac{1}{3}\int_{0}^{3} 0\cdot\cos\dfrac{n\pi x}{3}\,dx$

$a_n = \dfrac{5\sin(n\pi)}{n\pi} = 0, n = 1, 2, 3\cdots$

$b_n = \dfrac{1}{L}\int_{-L}^{L} f(x)\sin\dfrac{n\pi x}{L}\,dx$

$= \dfrac{1}{3}\int_{-3}^{0} 5\sin\dfrac{n\pi x}{3}\,dx + \dfrac{1}{3}\int_{0}^{3} 0\cdot\sin\dfrac{2\pi x}{3}\,dx$

$b_n = \dfrac{5\cos(n\pi) - 5}{n\pi} = \dfrac{5}{\pi}\left(\dfrac{\cos(n\pi) - 1}{n}\right)$

n	b_n
1	$\dfrac{5}{\pi}\cdot(-2) = \dfrac{-10}{\pi}$
2	0
3	$\dfrac{5}{\pi}\left(-\dfrac{2}{3}\right) = \dfrac{-10}{3\pi}$
4	0
5	$\dfrac{5}{\pi}\left(-\dfrac{2}{5}\right) = \dfrac{-10}{5\pi}$

$f(x) = a_0 + a_1\cos\dfrac{\pi x}{L} + a_2\cos\dfrac{2\pi x}{L} + a_3\cos\dfrac{3\pi x}{L} + \cdots$
$+ b_1,\sin\dfrac{\pi x}{L} + b_2\dfrac{2\pi x}{L} + b_3\dfrac{3\pi x}{L} + \cdots$

$f(x) = \dfrac{5}{2}$

$- \dfrac{10}{\pi}\left(\sin\dfrac{\pi x}{3} + \dfrac{1}{3}\sin\dfrac{3\pi x}{3} + \dfrac{1}{5}\sin\dfrac{5\pi x}{3} + \cdots\right)$

17. $f(x) = \begin{cases} -x & -4 \le x < 0 \\ x & 0 \le x < 4 \end{cases}$

$$a_0 = \frac{1}{8} \int_{-4}^{0} -x\,dx + \frac{1}{8} \int_{0}^{4} x\,dx = -\frac{1}{16}x^2 \Big|_{-4}^{0} + \frac{1}{16}x^2 \Big|_{0}^{4} = 2$$

$$a_n = \frac{1}{4} \int_{-4}^{0} -x \cos \frac{n\pi x}{4}\,dx + \frac{1}{4} \int x \cos \frac{n\pi x}{4}\,dx$$

$$= -\frac{1}{4}\frac{16}{(n\pi)^2} \int_{-4}^{0} \frac{n\pi}{4}x \cos \frac{n\pi}{4}x\frac{n\pi}{4}\,dx + \frac{1}{4}\frac{16}{(n\pi)^2} \int_{0}^{4} \frac{n\pi}{4}x \cos \frac{n\pi}{4}x\frac{n\pi}{4}\,dx$$

$$= -\frac{4}{(n\pi)^2} \left(\cos \frac{n\pi x}{4} + \frac{n\pi x}{4} \sin \frac{n\pi x}{4} \right)\Big|_{-4}^{0} + \frac{4}{(n\pi)^2} \left(\cos \frac{n\pi x}{4} + \frac{n\pi x}{4} \sin \frac{n\pi x}{4} \right)\Big|_{0}^{4}$$

$$\quad - \frac{4}{(n\pi)^2}(\cos 0 - [\cos(-n\pi) + n\pi \sin n\pi]) + \frac{4}{(n\pi)^2}(\cos n\pi + n\pi \sin n\pi - [\cos 0])$$

$$= -\frac{4}{(n\pi)^2}(1 - \cos n\pi - n\pi \sin n\pi) + \frac{4}{(n\pi)^2}(\cos n\pi + n\pi \sin n\pi - 1)$$

$$= -\frac{4}{(n\pi)^2}(1 - \cos n\pi - n\pi \sin n\pi - \cos n\pi - n\pi \sin n\pi + 1)$$

$$= -\frac{4}{(n\pi)^2}(2 - 2\cos n\pi - 2n\pi \sin n\pi)$$

$$a_1 = -\frac{16}{\pi^2}; \quad a_2 = 0; \quad a_3 = -\frac{16}{9\pi^2}$$

$$b_n = \frac{1}{4} \int_{-4}^{0} -x \sin \frac{n\pi x}{4}\,dx + \frac{1}{4} \int_{0}^{4} x \sin \frac{n\pi x}{4}\,dx$$

$$= -\frac{1}{4}\frac{16}{(n\pi)^2} \int_{-4}^{0} \frac{n\pi x}{4} \sin \frac{n\pi x}{4} \left(\frac{n\pi}{4}\,dx\right) + \frac{1}{4}\frac{16}{(n\pi)^2} \int_{0}^{4} \frac{n\pi x}{4} \sin \frac{n\pi x}{4} \cdot \frac{n\pi\,dx}{4}$$

$$= -\frac{4}{(n\pi)^2} \left(\sin \frac{n\pi x}{4} - \frac{n\pi x}{4} \cos \frac{n\pi x}{4} \right)\Big|_{-4}^{0} + \frac{4}{(n\pi)^2} \left(\sin \frac{n\pi x}{4} - \frac{n\pi x}{4} \cos \frac{n\pi x}{4} \right)\Big|_{0}^{4}$$

$$= -\frac{4}{(n\pi)^2} \{-[\sin(-n\pi) + n\pi \cos(-n\pi)]\} + \frac{4}{(n\pi)^2}(\sin n\pi - n\pi \cos n\pi)$$

$$= -\frac{4}{(n\pi)^2}(\sin n\pi - n\pi \cos n\pi) + \frac{4}{(n\pi)^2}(\sin n\pi - n\pi \cos n\pi) = 0, \text{ for all } n.$$

Therefore,

$$f(x) = 2 - \frac{16}{\pi^2} \cos \frac{\pi x}{4} - \frac{16}{9\pi^2} \cos \frac{3\pi x}{4} = 2 - \frac{16}{\pi^2} \left(\cos \frac{\pi x}{4} + \frac{1}{9} \cos \frac{3\pi x}{4} + \cdots \right)$$

and comparing with calculator,

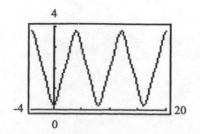

21. Expand $f(x) = x^2$ in a half-range cosine series for $0 \le x < 2$.

$$a_0 = \frac{1}{L}\int_0^L f(x)dx = \frac{1}{2}\int_0^2 x^2 dx = \frac{1}{2}\left.\frac{x^3}{3}\right|_0^2 = \frac{1}{6}(2^3 - 0) = \frac{4}{3}$$

$$a_n = \frac{2}{L}\int_0^L f(x)\cos\frac{n\pi x}{L}dx, (n = 1, 2, 3, \ldots)$$

$$a_n = \frac{2}{2}\int_0^2 x^2\frac{n\pi x}{2}dx = \frac{2x}{\frac{n^2\pi^2}{4}}\cos\frac{n\pi x}{2} + \left(\frac{x^2}{\frac{n\pi}{2}} - \frac{2}{\frac{n^3\pi^3}{8}}\right)\sin\frac{n\pi x}{2}\bigg|_0^2$$

$$a_n = \frac{8x}{n^2\pi^2}\cos\frac{n\pi x}{2} + \left(\frac{2x^2}{n\pi} - \frac{16}{n^3\pi^3}\right)\sin\frac{n\pi x}{2}\bigg|_0^2$$

$$a_n = \frac{16}{n^2\pi^2}\cos n\pi + \left(\frac{8}{n\pi} - \frac{16}{n^3\pi3}\right)\sin n\pi$$

$$a_n = \frac{16}{n^2\pi^2}\cos n\pi$$

$$a_1 = \frac{16}{1^2\pi^2}\cos\pi = \frac{-16}{\pi^2}$$

$$a_2 = \frac{16}{2^2\pi^2}\cos 2\pi = \frac{4}{\pi^2}$$

$$a_3 = \frac{16}{3^2\pi^2}\cos 3\pi = \frac{-16}{9\pi^2}$$

$$f(x) = \frac{4}{3} - \frac{16}{\pi^2}\cos\frac{\pi x}{2} + \frac{4}{\pi^2}\cos\frac{2\pi x}{2} - \frac{16}{9\pi^2}\cos\frac{3\pi x}{2} + \cdots$$

$$f(x) = \frac{4}{3} - \frac{16}{\pi^2}\left(\cos\frac{\pi x}{2} - \frac{1}{4}\cos\pi x + \frac{1}{9}\cos\frac{3\pi x}{2} - \cdots\right)$$

Chapter 29 Review Exercises

1. $f(x) = \dfrac{1}{1 + e^x} = (1 + e^x)^{-1}$

$f'(x) = -(1 + e^x)^{-2}(e^x) = e^x(1 + e^x)^{-2}$

$f''(x) = -(1 + e^x)^{-2}e^x + e^x(2)(1 + e^x)^{-3}(e^x)$

$f'''(x) = -(1 + e^x)^{-2}e^x + e^x(2)(1 + e^x)^{-3}(e^x) + 2e^{2x}(-3)(1 + e^x)^{-4}e^x + (1 + e^x)^{-3}(2e^{2x})(2)$

$f(0) = \dfrac{1}{1 + 1} = \dfrac{1}{2}$

$f'(0) = -1(2^{-2}) = -\dfrac{1}{4}$

$f''(0) = -\dfrac{1}{4} + \dfrac{1}{4} = 0$

$f'''(0) = -\dfrac{1}{4} + \dfrac{1}{4} - \dfrac{3}{8} + \dfrac{1}{2} = \dfrac{1}{8}$

$f(x) = \dfrac{1}{2} - \dfrac{1}{4}x + \dfrac{0x^2}{2!} + \left(\dfrac{1}{8}\right)\dfrac{x^3}{3!} + \cdots$

$= \dfrac{1}{2} - \dfrac{1}{4}x + \dfrac{1}{48}x^3 - \cdots$

5. $f(x) = (x+1)^{1/3}$ $f(0) = 1$ $f(x) = 1 + \dfrac{1}{3}x - \dfrac{2x^2}{9(2)} + \cdots$

$\qquad f'(x) = \dfrac{1}{3}(x+1)^{-2/3}$ $f'(0) = \dfrac{1}{3}$ $= 1 + \dfrac{1}{3}x - \dfrac{1}{9}x^2 + \cdots$

$\qquad f''(x) = -\dfrac{2}{9}(x+1)^{-5/3}$ $f''(0) = -\dfrac{2}{9}$

9. In $e^x = 1 + x + \dfrac{x^2}{2} + \cdots$ Let $x = -0.2$

$\qquad e^{-0.2} = 1 - 0.2 + \dfrac{(0.2)^2}{2} + \cdots = 0.82$

13. Taylor Series: $f(x) = f(a) + f'(a)(x-a) + \dfrac{f''(a)(x-a)^2}{2!} + \cdots$

$\qquad$ Let $f(x) = \dfrac{1}{x}$

$\qquad\qquad f'(x) = -\dfrac{1}{x^2}$

$\qquad\qquad f''(x) = \dfrac{2}{x^3}$

$\qquad$ and $a = 1$, then

$\qquad\qquad f(x) = 1 - (x-1) + 2 \cdot \dfrac{(x-1)^2}{2!} + \cdots$ from which

$\qquad f(1.086) = \dfrac{1}{1.086} = 1 - (1.086 - 1) + (1.086 - 1)^2$

$\qquad 1.986^{-1} = 0.9214$

17. $f(x) = \tan x;\ a = \dfrac{\pi}{4}$ $f\left(\dfrac{\pi}{4}\right) = 1$

$\qquad f'(x) = \sec^2 x = 1 + \tan^2 x$ $f'\left(\dfrac{\pi}{4}\right) = 2$

$\qquad f''(x) = 2\tan x \sec^2 x$ $f''\left(\dfrac{\pi}{4}\right) = 4$

$\qquad f(x) = 1 + 2\left(x - \dfrac{\pi}{4}\right) + \dfrac{4\left(x - \frac{\pi}{4}\right)^2}{2!} + \cdots$

$\qquad \tan 43.62° = \tan(45° - 1.38°) = \tan\left(\dfrac{\pi}{4} - \dfrac{1.38\pi}{180}\right) = 1 + 2\left(\dfrac{\pi}{4} - \dfrac{1.38\pi}{180} - \dfrac{\pi}{4}\right) + 2\left(\dfrac{\pi}{4} - \dfrac{1.38\pi}{180} - \dfrac{\pi}{4}\right)^2 + \cdots$

$\qquad\qquad = 1 + 2(-0.0240855) + 2(0.0005801) = 0.953$

21. $\displaystyle\int_{0.1}^{0.2} \dfrac{1 - \dfrac{x^2}{2} + \dfrac{x^4}{24} + \cdots}{\sqrt{x}}\, dx = \int_{0.1}^{0.2}\left(x^{-1/2} - \dfrac{x^{3/2}}{2} + \dfrac{x^{7/2}}{24} + \cdots\right) dx$

$\qquad\qquad\qquad = \displaystyle\int_{0.1}^{0.2} x^{-1/2}dx - \dfrac{1}{2}\int_{0.1}^{0.2} x^{3/2}dx + \dfrac{1}{24}\int_{0.1}^{0.2} x^{7/2}dx$

$\qquad\qquad\qquad = 2x^{1/2} - \dfrac{1}{5}x^{5/2} + \dfrac{1}{108}x^{9/2} + \cdots \Big|_{0.1}^{0.2} = 0.259$

25. $f(x) \begin{cases} 0 & -\pi \le x < 0 \\ x - 1 & 0 \le x < \pi \end{cases}$

is Example 2 of section 29-6 shifted down 1 unit. The Fourier series is

$$f(x) = -1 + \frac{2 + \pi}{4} - \frac{2}{\pi} \cos x - \frac{2}{9\pi} \cos 3x - \cdots + \left(\frac{\pi - 2}{\pi}\right) \sin x - \frac{1}{2} \sin 2x + \cdots$$

29. From example 2, $f(x) = \frac{1}{2} + \frac{2}{\pi}\left(\cos x - \frac{1}{3}\cos 3x + \frac{1}{5}\cos 5x - \cdots\right)$

33. It is a geometric series for which $|r| < 1 = 0.80$. Therefore the series converges.

$$S = \frac{1000}{1 - 0.80} = 5000$$

37. $\sin x = x - \frac{x^3}{3!} + \cdots$

$$\sin(x + h) - \sin(x - h) = (x + h) - \frac{(x+h)^3}{3!} + \cdots - (x - h) + \frac{(x-h)^3}{3!} - \cdots$$

$$= x + h - \frac{x^3 + 3h^2h + 3xh^2 + h^3}{3!} + \cdots - x + h + \frac{x^3 - 3h^2h + 3xh^2 - h^3}{3!} - \cdots$$

$$= 2h - \frac{6x^2h}{3!} - \frac{2h^3}{3!} + \cdots = 2h\left(1 - \frac{x^2}{2} + \cdots\right) - \frac{2h^3}{3!} + \cdots$$

$$= 2h\cos x \text{ for small } h$$

41. $\cos^2 x = \frac{1}{2}(1 + \cos 2x) - \frac{1}{2}\left(1 + 1 - \frac{(2x)^2}{2!} + \frac{(2x)^4}{4!} - \frac{(2x)^6}{6!} + \cdots\right)$

$$- \frac{1}{2}\left(2 - \frac{4x^2}{2} + \frac{16x^4}{24} - \frac{64x^6}{720} + \cdots\right) = 1 - x^2 + \frac{1}{3}x^4 - \frac{2}{45}x^6 + \cdots$$

45. $f(x) = \frac{1}{1 - x} = 1 + x + x^2 + \cdots$

$$\frac{1}{1 + x} = \frac{1}{1 - (-x)} = 1 + (-x) + (-x)^2 + \cdots = 1 - x + x^2 - \cdots$$

49. $e^x = 1 + x + \frac{x^2}{2!} + \frac{x^3}{3!}$

$$e^{0.9} = 1 + (0.9) + \frac{0.9^2}{2} + \frac{0.9^3}{6} = 2.4265$$

$$e^x = e\left[1 + (x - 1) + \frac{(x-1)^2}{2}\right]$$

$$e^{0.9} = e\left[1 + (0.9 - 1) + \frac{(0.9 - 1)^2}{2}\right] = 2.4600$$

$$e^{0.9} = 2.459603 \text{ directly from calculator}$$

53. $\tan^{-1} x = \int \frac{1}{1 + x^2}\,dx = \int(1 - x^2 + x^4 - x^6 + \ldots)dx$

$$\tan^{-1} x = x - \frac{x^3}{3} + \frac{x^5}{5} - \frac{x^7}{7} + \cdots$$

57. $\cos\theta = \dfrac{r}{r+h}, r = 4000$ mi

$10 = r\theta, \theta = \dfrac{10}{r}$

$\cos\dfrac{10}{4000} = \dfrac{4000}{4000+h}$

$h = 0.0125$ mi $\left(\dfrac{5280 \text{ ft}}{\text{mi}}\right)$

$h = 66$ ft

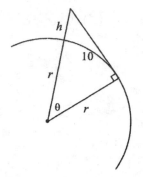

61. $\dfrac{N_0}{1-e^{-kt}} = N_0\left(\dfrac{1}{1-e^{-kt}}\right)$; Let $x = e^{-kt}$

$N_0\left(\dfrac{N_0}{1-e^{-kt}}\right) = N_0\left(\dfrac{1}{1-x}\right)$

The Maclaurin's expansion for $f(x) = \dfrac{1}{1-x}$ is:

$f(x) = \dfrac{1}{1-x};$ \qquad\qquad $f(0) = 1$

$f'(x) = \dfrac{1}{(1-x)^2};$ \qquad\qquad $f'(0) = 1$

$f''(x) = \dfrac{2}{(1-x)^3}:$ \qquad\qquad $f''(0) = 2$

$f(x) = 1 + x + \dfrac{2x^2}{2!} + \cdots = 1 + x + x^2 + \cdots$

Substituting $e^{-k/t}$ for x; $f(x) = 1 + e^{-kt} + e^{-2kt} + \cdots$;

$\therefore \dfrac{N_0}{1-e^{-kt}} = N_0(1 + e^{-kt} + e^{-2kt} + \cdots)$

65. Answers may vary. One way would be to use a Taylor Series and choosing an a-value from the known values which is close the angle for the particular trig function being computed.

Chapter 30

DIFFERENTIAL EQUATIONS

30.1 Solutions of Differential Equations

1. $y = c_1 e^{-x} + c_2 e^{2x}$

$$\frac{dy}{dx} = -c_1 e^{-x} + 2c_2 e^{2x}$$

$$\frac{d^2 y}{dx^2} = c_1 e^{-x} + 4c_2 e^{2x}$$

$$\frac{d^2 y}{dx^2} - \frac{dy}{dx} = c_1 e^{-x} + 4c_2 e^{2x} - (-c_1 e^{-x} + 2c_2 e^{2x})$$
$$= c_1 e^{-x} + 4c_2 e^{2x} + c_1 e^{-x} - 2c_2 e^{2x}$$
$$= 2c_1 e^{-x} + 2c_2 e^{2x} = 2(c_1 e^{-x} + c_2 e^{2x})$$
$$= 2y$$

$y = 4e^{-x}, \dfrac{dy}{dx} = -4e^{-x}, \dfrac{d^2 y}{dx^2} = 4e^{-x}$

$$\frac{d^2 y}{dx^2} - \frac{dy}{dx} = 4e^{-x} - (-4e^{-x}) = 8e^{-x}$$
$$= 2(4e^{-x}) = 2y$$

5. $y'' + 3y' - 4y = 3e^x; \ y = c_1 e^x + c_2 e^{-4x} + \dfrac{3}{5}xe^x$

$$y' = c_1 e^x - 4c_2 e^{-4x} + \frac{3}{5}(xe^x + e^x)$$

$$= c_1 e^x - 4c_2 e^{-4x} + \frac{3}{5}xe^x + \frac{3}{5}e^x$$

$$y'' = c_1 e^x + 16c_2 e^{-4x} + \frac{3}{5}e^x + \frac{3}{5}(xe^x + e^x)$$

$$= c_1 e^x + 16c_2 e^{-4x} + \frac{3}{5}e^x + \frac{3}{5}xe^x + \frac{3}{5}e^x$$

$$= c_1 e^x + 16c_2 e^{-4x} + \frac{3}{5}xe^x + \frac{6}{5}e^x$$

Substitute y, y', y'' into differential equation.

$$c_1 e^x + 16c_2 e^{-4x} + \frac{3}{5}xe^x + \frac{6}{5}e^x$$

$$+ 3\left(c_1 e^x - 4c_2 e^{-4x} + \frac{3}{5}xe^x + \frac{3}{5}e^x\right)$$

$$- 4\left(c_1 e^x + c_2 e^{-4x} + \frac{3}{5}xe^x\right) = 3e^x$$

$$c_1 e^x + 16c_2 e^{-4x} + \frac{3}{5}xe^x + \frac{6}{5}e^x$$

$$+ 3c_1 e^x - 12c_2 e^{-4x} + \frac{9}{5}xe^x + \frac{9}{5}e^x$$

$$- 4c_1 e^x - 4c_2 e^{-4x} - \frac{12}{5}xe^x = 3e^x$$

$\dfrac{15}{5}e^x = 3e^x; \ 3e^x = 3e^x$ identity

General solution; order two, c_1 and c_2

9. $y = 3\cos 2x; \ y'' = -12\cos 2x$
$y'' + 4y = -12\cos 2x + 4(3\cos 2x) = 0$
$y = c_1 \sin 2x + c_2 \cos 2x;$
$y'' = -4c_1 \sin 2x - 4c_2 \cos 2x$
$y'' + 4y = -4c_1 \sin 2x - 4c_2 \cos 2x$
$\qquad + 4(c_1 \sin 2x + c_2 \cos 2x)$
$\qquad = 0$

13. $\dfrac{dy}{dx} - 3 = 2x; \ y = x^2 + 3x; \ \dfrac{dy}{dx} = 2x + 3$

Substitute. $2x + 3 - 3 = 2x; \ 2x = 2x$ identity

17. $y'' + 9y = 4\cos x; \ 2y = \cos x; \ y = \dfrac{1}{2}\cos x;$

$y' = -\dfrac{1}{2}\sin x; \ y'' = -\dfrac{1}{2}\cos x$

Substitute y and y''.

$$-\frac{1}{2}\cos x + 9\left(\frac{1}{2}\cos x\right) = 4\cos x$$

$$-\frac{1}{2}\cos x + \frac{9}{2}\cos x = 4\cos x$$

$\dfrac{8}{2}\cos x = 4\cos x; \ 4\cos x = 4\cos x$ identity

21. $x\dfrac{d^2 y}{dx^2} + \dfrac{dy}{dx} = 0; \ y = c_1 \ln x + c_2$

$\dfrac{dy}{dx} = \dfrac{c_1}{x} = c_1 x^{-1}; \ \dfrac{d^2 y}{dx^2} = -c_1 x^{-2} = -\dfrac{c_1}{x^2}$

Substitute $\dfrac{dy}{dx}$ and $\dfrac{d^2 y}{dx^2}$.

$$x\left(\frac{-c_1}{x^2}\right) + c_1 x^{-1} = 0; \ -\frac{c_1}{x} + \frac{c_1}{x} = 0$$

$0 = 0$ identity

25. $y'' + y' = 6\sin 2x$

$$y = e^{-x} - \frac{3}{5}\cos 2x - \frac{6}{5}\sin 2x$$

$$y' = -e^{-x} + \frac{6}{5}\sin 2x - \frac{12}{5}\cos 2x$$

$$y'' = e^{-x} + \frac{12}{5}\cos 2x + \frac{24}{5}\sin 2x$$

Substitute y' and y''.

$$e^{-x} + \frac{12}{5}\cos 2x + \frac{24}{5}\sin 2x - e^{-x}$$

$$+ \frac{6}{5}\sin 2x - \frac{12}{5}\cos 2x = 6\sin 2x$$

$$\frac{30}{5}\sin 2x = 6\sin 2x; \ 6\sin 2x = 6\sin 2x \text{ identity}$$

29. $(y')^2 + xy' = y$
$y = cx + c^2; \ y' = c$

Substitute.

$$(c)^2 + x(c) = y; \ c^2 + cx = y; \ y = y \text{ identity}$$

30.2 Separation of Variables

1. $2xy\,dx + (x^2+1)dy = 0$

$$\frac{2x\,dx}{x^2+1} + \frac{dy}{y} = 0$$

$$\ln(x^2+1) + \ln y = \ln c$$
$$\ln(y(x^2+1)) = \ln c$$
$$y(x^2+1) = c$$

5. $y^2dx + dy = 0$; divide by y^2;

$$dx + \frac{dy}{y^2} = 0; \text{ integrate}$$

$$x + \frac{y^{-1}}{-1} = c; \ x - \frac{1}{y} = c$$

9. $x^2 + (x^3+5)y' = 0; \ (x^3+5)\frac{dy}{dx} = -x^2$

$$(x^3+5)dy = -x^2dx; \ dy = \frac{-x^2dx}{x^3+5}; \text{ integrate}$$

$$y = -\frac{1}{3}\ln(x^3+5) + c$$

$$3y + \ln(x^3+5) = 3c_1; \ 3c_1 \text{ is constant}$$
$$3y + \ln(x^3+5) = c$$

13. $e^{x^2}dy = x\sqrt{1-y}\,dx; \ \dfrac{dy}{\sqrt{1-y}} = \dfrac{x\,dx}{e^{x^2}}$

$$\frac{dy}{(1-y)^{1/2}} = e^{-x^2}x\,dx; \text{ integrate}$$

$$-\frac{(1-y)^{1/2}}{\frac{1}{2}} = -\frac{1}{2}e^{-x^2} + c$$

$$-2\sqrt{1-y} = -\frac{1}{2}e^{-x^2} + c; \text{ multiply by } -2$$

$$4\sqrt{1-y} = e^{-x^2} - 2c_1; \ -2c_1 = c$$
$$4\sqrt{1-y} = e^{-x^2} + c$$

17. $y' - y = 4; \ \dfrac{dy}{dx} = 4 + y; \ \dfrac{dy}{4+y} = dx; \text{ integrate}$

$$\ln(4+y) = x + c$$

21. $y\tan x\,dx + \cos^2 x\,dy = 0; \ \dfrac{\tan x\,dx}{\cos^2 x} + \dfrac{dy}{y} = 0$

$$(\tan x)^1\sec^2 x\,dx + \frac{dy}{y} = 0; \text{ integrate}$$

$$\frac{1}{2}\tan^2 x + \ln y = c_1; \ 2c_1 = c; \ \tan^2 x + 2\ln y = c$$

25. $y\sqrt{1-x^2}dy + 2\,dx = 0; \ y\,dy + \dfrac{2}{\sqrt{1-x^2}}dx = 0$

Integrate: $\dfrac{1}{2}y^2 + 2\sin^{-1}x = c_1;$

$$y^2 + 4\sin^{-1}x = 2c_1; \ y^2 + 4\sin^{-1}x = c$$

29. $2\ln t\,dt + t\,di = 0;$

$$2\ln t\frac{dt}{t} + di = 0; \text{ integrate}$$

$$\frac{2(\ln t)^2}{2} + i = 0; \ (\ln t)^2 + i = c;$$
$$i = c - (\ln t)^2$$

33. $\dfrac{dy}{dx} + yx^2 = 0; \ \dfrac{dy}{y} + x^2dx = 0$

Integrate: $\ln y + \dfrac{x^3}{3} + c$

Substitute $x = 0, y = 1; \ \ln 1 = c; \ c = 0$
$3\ln y + x^3 = 0$

37. $\dfrac{dy}{dx} = (1 - y)\cos x$; $x = \dfrac{\pi}{6}$ when $y = 0$

$dy = (1 - y)\cos x\,dx$

$\dfrac{1}{1 - y}\,dy = \cos x\,dx$; integrate

$-\ln(1 - y) = \sin x + c$; $\sin x + \ln(1 - y) = c$

Substitute $x = \dfrac{\pi}{6}$, $y = 0$; $\sin\dfrac{\pi}{6} + \ln 1 = c$; $c = \dfrac{1}{2}$

$\sin x + \ln(1 - y) = \dfrac{1}{2}$; $2\ln(1 - y) = 1 - 2\sin x$

30.3   Integrating Combinations

1. $x\,dy + y\,dx + 2xy^2\,dy = 0$

$\dfrac{x\,dy + y\,dx}{xy} + 2y\,dy = 0$

$\dfrac{d(xy)}{xy} + 2y\,dy = 0$

$\ln xy + y^2 = c$

5. $y\,dx - x\,dy + x^3\,dx = 2\,dx$;

$x\,dy - y\,dx - x^3\,dx = -2\,dx$

$\dfrac{(x\,dy - y\,dx)}{x^2} - x\,dx = -\dfrac{2\,dx}{x^2}$

$\dfrac{y}{x} - \dfrac{1}{2}x^2 = 2x^{-1} = \dfrac{2}{x} + c_1$; $y - \dfrac{1}{2}x^3 = 2 + c_1 x$

$2y - x^3 = 4 + 2c_1 x$; $x^3 - 2y = -2c_1 x - 4$; $-2c_1 = c$

$x^3 - 2y = cx - 4$

9. $x^3 y^4(x\,dy + y\,dx) = 3\,dy$;

$\displaystyle\int x^3 y^3(x\,dy + y\,dx) = \int \dfrac{3}{y}\,dy$

$(xy)^3(x\,dy + y\,dx) = 3\dfrac{dy}{y}$; $\dfrac{(xy)^4}{4} = 3\ln y + c_1$

$(xy)^4 = 12\ln y + 4c_1$; $4c_1 = c$; $(xy)^4 = 12\ln y + c$

13. $\tan(x^2 + y^2)\,dy + x\,dx + y\,dy = 0$;

$dy + \dfrac{x\,dx + y\,dy}{\tan(x^2 + y^2)} = 0$

$d(x^2 + y^2) = 2x\,dx + 2y\,dy = 2(x\,dx + y\,dy)$

$dy + \cot(x^2 + y^2)(x\,dx + y\,dy) = 0$

$dy + \dfrac{1}{2}\cot(x^2 + y^2)^2 d(x^2 + y^2)$

$y + \dfrac{1}{2}\ln\sin(x^2 + y^2) = c$; $y = c - \dfrac{1}{2}\ln\sin(x^2 + y^2)$

---

17. $10x\,dy + 5y\,dx + 3y\,dy = 0$

$5(2x\,dy + y\,dx) + 3y\,dy = 0$; multiply by y

$5(2xy\,dy + y^2\,dx) + 3y^2\,dy = 0$; $5d(xy^2) + 3y^2\,dy = 0$

$5xy^2 + y^3 = c$

21. $y\,dx - x\,dy = y^3\,dx + y^2 x\,dy$; $x = 2, y = 4$

$\dfrac{y\,dx - x\,dy}{y^2} = y\,dx + x\,dy$; $d\left(\dfrac{x}{y}\right) = d(xy)$

$\dfrac{x}{y} = xy + c$; $x = 2, y = 4$; $\dfrac{2}{4} = 2(4) + c$; $c = -\dfrac{15}{2}$

$\dfrac{x}{y} = xy - \dfrac{15}{2}$; multiply by $2y$

$2x = 2xy^2 - 15y$

30.4   The Linear Differential Equations of the First Order

1. $dy + \left(\dfrac{2}{x}\right)y\,dx = 3\,dx$

$ye^{\int \frac{2}{x}dx} = \displaystyle\int 3e^{\int \frac{2}{x}dx}\,dx + c$

$ye^{2\ln x} = \displaystyle\int 3e^{2\ln x}\,dx + c$

$ye^{\ln x^2} = \displaystyle\int 3e^{\ln x^2}\,dx + c$

$yx^2 = \displaystyle\int 3x^2\,dx + c$

$yx^2 = x^3 + c$

$y = x + cx^{-2}$

5. $dy + 2y\,dx = e^{-4x}dx$; $P = 2, Q = e^{-4x}$;

$e^{\int 2dx} = e^{2x}$

$ye^{2x} = \displaystyle\int e^{-4x}e^{2x}\,dx = -\dfrac{1}{2}\int e^{-2x}(-2\,dx)$

$\qquad = -\dfrac{1}{2}e^{-2x} + c$

$y = -\dfrac{1}{2}e^{-2x}e^{-2x} + ce^{-2x} = -\dfrac{1}{2}e^{-4x} + ce^{-2x}$

9. $x\,dy - y\,dx = 3x\,dx$; $dy - \left(\dfrac{y}{x}\right)dx = 3\,dx$

$P = -\dfrac{1}{x}, Q = 3$; $e^{-\int (dx/x)} = e^{-\ln x} = \dfrac{1}{x}$

$dy + \left(-\dfrac{1}{x}\right)y\,dx = 3\,dx$; $y\left(\dfrac{1}{x}\right) = \displaystyle\int 3\dfrac{1}{x}\,dx + c$

$\dfrac{y}{x} = 3\ln x + c$; $y = x(3\ln x + c)$

13. $dr + r \cot \theta \, d\theta = d\theta$; $dr + \cot \theta r \, d\theta = d\theta$

$P = \cot \theta, Q = 1, e^{\int \cot \theta \, d\theta} = e^{\ln \sin \theta} = \sin \theta$

$r \sin \theta = \displaystyle\int \sin \theta \, d\theta + c$; $r \sin \theta = -\cos \theta + c$

$r = -\dfrac{\cos \theta}{\sin \theta} + \dfrac{c}{\sin \theta} = -\cot \theta + c \csc \theta$

17. $y' + y = 3$; $\dfrac{dy}{dx} + y = 3$; $dy + y \, dx = 3 \, dx$

$P = 1, Q = 3$; $e^{\int dx} = e^{x}$

$ye^{x} = \displaystyle\int 3e^{x} dx + c = 3e^{x} + c$; $y = 3 + ce^{-x}$

21. $y' = x^3(1 - 4y)$; $\dfrac{dy}{dx} = x^3 - 4x^3 y$;

$dy = x^3 dx - 4x^3 y \, dx$

$dy + 4x^3 y \, dx = x^3 dx$; $P = 4x^3, Q = x^3$;

$e^{4\int x^3 dx} = e^{x^4}$

$ye^{x^4} = \displaystyle\int x^3 e^{x^4} dx + c = \dfrac{1}{4} e^{x^4} 4x^3 dx + c$

$\qquad = \dfrac{1}{4} e^{x^4} + c$

$y = \dfrac{1}{4} + ce^{-x^4}$

25. $x \, dy + (1 - 3x)y \, dx = 3x^2 e^{3x} dx$

$dy + \left(\dfrac{1 - 3x}{x}\right) y \, dx = 3x e^{3x} dx$

$P = \dfrac{1}{x} - 3$; $Q = 3x e^{3x}$

$e^{\int ((1/x)-3)dx} = e^{\int (dx/x) - \int 3 \, dx} = e^{\ln x - 3x} = \dfrac{e^{\ln x}}{e^{3x}} = \dfrac{x}{e^{3x}}$

$y\dfrac{x}{e^{3x}} = \displaystyle\int 3x e^{3x} \dfrac{x}{e^{3x}} dx + c = 3 \int x^2 dx + c = x^3 + c$

$xy = e^{3x}(x^3 + c)$

29. $y' = 2(1 - y)$; solve by separation of variables.

$\dfrac{dy}{1 - y} = 2 \, dx$; $-\ln(1 - y) = 2x - \ln c$;

$\ln \dfrac{c}{1 - y} = 2x$;

$c = (1 - y)e^{2x}$; $1 - y = ce^{-2x}$; $y = 1 - ce^{-2x}$

Solve as a first order equation.

$dy = 2 \, dx - 2y \, dx$; $dy + 2y \, dx = 2 \, dx$

$ye^{\int 2dx} = \displaystyle\int e^{\int 2dx} dx$; $ye^{2x} = \int 2e^{2x} dx$

$ye^{2x} = e^{2x} + c$; $y = 1 + ce^{-2x}$

33. $\dfrac{dy}{dx} + 2y \cot x = 4 \cos x$; $x = \dfrac{\pi}{2}, y = \dfrac{1}{3}$;

$dy + 2y \cot x \, dx = 4 \cos x \, dx$; $P = 2 \cot x$;

$Q = 4 \cos x$

$e^{\int P dx} = e^{\int 2 \cot x dx} = 2^{2 \ln |\sin x|} = e^{\ln |\sin x|^2}$

$\qquad = |\sin x|^2$

$y(\sin x)^2 = \displaystyle\int 4 \cos x (\sin x)^2 dx + c = \dfrac{4(\sin x)^3}{3} + c$

$y = \dfrac{4}{3} \sin x + c(\csc^2 x)$

$x = \dfrac{\pi}{2}$ when $y = \dfrac{1}{3}$; $\dfrac{1}{3} = \dfrac{4}{3} \sin \dfrac{\pi}{2} + c$; $c = -1$

$y = \dfrac{4}{3} \sin x - \csc^2 x$

30.5   Elementary Applications

1. $\qquad y^2 = cx$

$2y\dfrac{dy}{dx} = c = \dfrac{y^2}{x}$

$\dfrac{dy}{dx} = \dfrac{y}{2x}$ for slope of any member of family.

$\dfrac{dy}{dx} = -\dfrac{2x}{y}$ for slope of orthogonal trajectories.

$y \, dy = -2x \, dx$

$\dfrac{y^2}{2} = -x^2 + \dfrac{c}{2}$

$y^2 + 2x^2 = c$

5. $\dfrac{dy}{dx} = \dfrac{2x}{y}$; $y \, dy = 2x \, dx$; $\dfrac{1}{2} y^2 = x^2 + c$

Substitute $x = 2, y = 3$; $\dfrac{1}{2}(9) = 4 + c$; $c = 0.5$

$\dfrac{1}{2} y^2 = x^2 + 0.5$; $y^2 = 2x^2 + 1$; $y = \pm\sqrt{2x^2 + 1}$

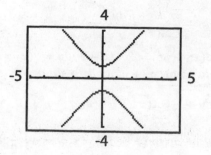

9. See Example 2; $\dfrac{dy}{dx} = ce^x$; $y = ce^x$; $c = \dfrac{y}{e^x}$

Substitute for c in the equation for the derivative.

$\dfrac{dy}{dx} = \dfrac{y}{e^x}e^x = y$; $\left.\dfrac{dy}{dx}\right|_{OT} = -\dfrac{1}{y}$; $y\,dy = -dx$

Integrating, $\dfrac{y^2}{2} = -x + \dfrac{c}{2}$; $y^2 = c - 2x$

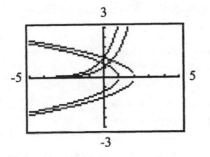

13. See Example 3; $N = N_o e^{kt}$

Use the condition that half this isotope decays in 40.0 s.

$N = \dfrac{N_0}{2}$ when $t = 40.0$ s. $\dfrac{N_0}{2} = N_0 e^{40.0k}$;

$0.5 = e^{40.0k}$; $0.5^{1/40.0} = e^k$; $0.5^{0.025} = e^k$;
$N = N_0(0.5)^{0.025}$

Evaluating when $t = 60.0$ s,

$N = N_0(0.5)^{0.025(60.0)} = N_0(0.5)^{1.50} = 0.354N_0$

Therefore, 35.4% remains after 60.0 s.

17. $\dfrac{dN}{dt} = r - kN$

$\dfrac{dN}{r - kN} = dt$

$-\dfrac{1}{k}\ln(r - kN) = t + c$

$N = 0$ for $t = 0$

$c = -\dfrac{1}{k}\ln r$

$-\dfrac{1}{k}\ln(r - kN) = t - \dfrac{1}{k}\ln r$

$\ln\dfrac{r - kN}{r} = -kt$

$r - kN = re^{-kt}$

$N = \dfrac{r}{k}(1 - e^{-kt})$

21. $r\dfrac{dS}{dr} = 2(a - S)$; $r\,dS = 2a\,dr - 2S\,dr$;

$dS + \dfrac{2}{r}S\,dx = 2a\dfrac{dr}{r}$; $y = S$, $x = r$, $P = \dfrac{2}{r}$,

$Q = \dfrac{2a}{r}$

$e^{\int P\,dx} = e^{\int (2/r)\,dr} = e^{2\ln x} = e^{\ln r^2} = r^2$

$Sr^2 = \int\left(2a\dfrac{dr}{r}\right) - 2a\ln r + c = \int 2ar\,dr$

$Sr^2 = ar^2 + c$; $S = a + \dfrac{c}{r^2}$

25. $\dfrac{dT}{dt} = k(T - 80.0)$; $\dfrac{dT}{T - 80.0} = k\,dt$;

$\ln(T - 80.0) = kt + \ln c$; $T = 80.0 + ce^{kt}$;
$200 = 80.0 + c$; $T = 80.0 + 120e^{kt}$;
$140 = 80.0 + 120e^{5k}$; $e^{5k} = 0.5$; $e^k = (0.5)^{1/5}$;
$T = 80.0 + 120(0.5)^{t/5}$; $100 = 80.0 + 120(0.5)^{t/5}$;

$0.5^{t/5} = \dfrac{1}{6.0}$; $t = 5\dfrac{\ln\frac{1}{6.0}}{\ln\frac{1}{2}} = 13$ min

29. See Example 4; $i = \dfrac{E}{R}(1 - e^{-(R/L)t})$

$\lim_{t\to\infty}\left(\dfrac{E}{R} - \dfrac{E}{R}e^{-(R/L)t}\right) = \dfrac{E}{R} - 0 = \dfrac{E}{R}$

33. $Ri + \dfrac{q}{C} = 0$; $i = \dfrac{dq}{dt}$; $R\dfrac{dq}{dt} + \dfrac{q}{C} = 0$;

$\dfrac{dq}{q} + \dfrac{1}{RC}\,dt = 0$

Integrating, $\ln q = -\dfrac{1}{RC}t + c$

Let $q = q_0$ when $t = 0$; $\ln q_0 = c$;

$\ln q = -\dfrac{1}{RC}t + \ln q_0$; $\ln q - \ln q_0 = -\dfrac{1}{RC}t$;

$\ln\dfrac{q}{q_0} = -\dfrac{1}{RC}t$; $\dfrac{q}{q_0} = e^{(-1/RC)t}$; $q = q_0 e^{-t/RC}$

37. $\dfrac{dv}{dt} = 32 - v$; $\dfrac{dv}{32 - v} = dt$; $-\dfrac{-dv}{32 - v} = dt$

Integrating, $(-1)\ln(32 - v) = t - \ln c$;

$\ln\dfrac{32 - v}{c} = -t$;

$32 - v = ce^{-t}$; $-v = -32 + ce^{-t}$; $v = 32 - ce^{-t}$

Starting from rest means $v = 0$ when $t = 0$;
$0 = 32 - c$; $c = 32$; $v = 32 - 32e^{-t} = 32(1 - e^{-t})$

$\lim_{t\to\infty} 32(1 - e^{-t}) = 32$

41. $\dfrac{dx}{dt} = 6t - 3t^2$; $dx = (6t - 3t^2)$;

$x = \dfrac{6t^2}{2} - \dfrac{3t^3}{3} + c$; $x = 3t^2 - t^3 + c$;

$x = 0$ for $t = 0$; $0 = c$; $x = 3t^2 - t^3$;

$y = 2(3t^2 - t^3) - (3t^2 - t^3)^2$;

$y = -t^6 + 6t^5 - 9t^4 - 2t^3 + 6t^2$

45. $\dfrac{dv}{dt} = kv$; $\dfrac{dv}{v} = k\,dt$; integrating, $\ln v = kt + \ln c$

Let $v = 16\,500$ when $t = 0$; $16\,500 = c$;

$\ln v = kt + 16500$; $\ln v - \ln 16\,500 - kt$;

$\ln \dfrac{v}{16\,500} = kt$; $\dfrac{v}{16\,500} = e^{kt}$; $v = 16\,500e^{kt}$

Let $v = 9850$ when $t = 3$; $9850 = 16\,500e^{3k}$;

$e^k = (0.597)^{1/3}$; $v = 16\,500(0.597)^{t/3}$

After 11 years, $v = 16\,500(0.597)^{11/3} = \$2490$

30.6   Higher-Order Homogeneous Equations

1. $D^2y - 5Dy = 0$

     $m^2 - 5m = 0$

     $m(m - 5) = 0$

   $m = 0$, $m = 5$

   $y = c_1 + c_2e^{5x}$

5. $3\dfrac{d^2y}{dx^2} + 4\dfrac{dy}{dx} + y = 0$

$3D^2y + 4Dy + y = 0$;; $3m^2 + 4m + 1 = 0$

$(3m + 1)(m + 1) = 0$; $m_1 = -\dfrac{1}{3}$, $m_2 = -1$

$y = c_1e^{-(1/3)x} + c_2e^{-x}$

9. $2D^2y - 3y = Dy$

   $2D^2y - Dy - 3y = 0$

     $2m^2 - m - 3 = 0$

   $(2m - 3)(m + 1) = 0$

$m = \dfrac{3}{2}$, $m = -1$

$y = c_1e^{\frac{3x}{2}} + c_2e^{-x}$

13. $3D^2y + 8Dy - 3y = 0$; $3m^2 + 8m - 3 = 0$;

     $(3m - 1)(m + 3) = 0$; $m_1 = \frac{1}{3}$ and $m_2 = -3$;

     $y = c_1e^{x/3} + c_2e^{-3x}$

17. $2\dfrac{d^2y}{dx^2} - 4\dfrac{dy}{dx} + y = 0$; $2D^2y - 4Dy + y = 0$;

$2m^2 - 4m + 1 = 0$

Quadratic formula: $m = \dfrac{4 \pm \sqrt{16 - 8}}{4}$;

$m_1 = 1 + \dfrac{\sqrt{2}}{2}$,

$m_2 = 1 - \dfrac{\sqrt{2}}{2}$

$y = c_1e^{(1 + (\sqrt{2}/2))x} + c_2e^{(1 - (\sqrt{2}/2))x}$;

$y = c_1e^xe^{(\sqrt{2}/2)x} + c_2e^xe^{-(\sqrt{2}/2)x}$

   $= e^x(c_1e^{x(\sqrt{2}/2)} + c_2e^{-x(\sqrt{2}/2)})$

21. $y'' = 3y' + y$; $D^2y - 3Dy - y = 0$; $m^2 - 3m - 1 = 0$

Quadratic formula:

$m = \dfrac{3 \pm \sqrt{9 + 4}}{2}$; $m_1 = \dfrac{3}{2} + \dfrac{\sqrt{13}}{2}$; $m_2 = \dfrac{3}{2} - \dfrac{\sqrt{13}}{2}$

$y = c_1e^{((3/2) + (\sqrt{13}/2))x} + c_2e^{((3/2) - (\sqrt{13}/2))x}$;

$y = e^{3x/2}(c_1e^{x(\sqrt{13}/2)} + c_2e^{-x(\sqrt{13}/2)})$

25. $D^2y - 4Dy - 21y = 0$; $m^2 - 4m - 21 = 0$;

     $(m - 7)(m + 3) = 0$; $m_1 = 7$ and $m_2 = -3$;

     $y = c_1e^{7x} + c_2e^{-3x}$

The derivative of the general equation is:

$Dy = 7c_1e^{7x} - 3c_2e^{-3x}$

Substituting $Dy = 0$, $y = 2$ when $x = 0$:

$c_1 + c_2 = 2$ and $7c_1 - 3c_2 = 0$.

Solving this system: $c_1 = \dfrac{3}{5}$ and $c_2 = \dfrac{7}{5}$.

Therefore, $y = \dfrac{3}{5}e^{7x} + \dfrac{7}{5}e^{-3x}$; $y = \dfrac{1}{5}(3e^{7x} + 7e^{-3x})$

29. $D^3y - 2D^2y - 3Dy = 0$; $m^3 - 2m^2 - 3m = 0$;

     $m(m + 1)(m - 3) = 0$; $m_1 = 0$, $m_2 = -1$, and

     $m_3 = 3$; $y = c_1e^0 + c_2e^{-x} + c_3e^{3x}$;

     $y = c_1 + c_2e^{-x} + c_3e^{3x}$

30.7 Auxiliary Equations with Repeated or Complex Roots

1. $\dfrac{d^2y}{dx^2} + 10\dfrac{dy}{dx} + 25y = 0$

   $D^2y + 10Dy + 25y = 0$
   $m^2 + 10m + 25 = 0$
   $(m+5)^2 = 0$
   $m = -5,\ -5$
   $y = e^{-5x}(c_1 + c_2x)$

5. $D^2y - 2Dy + y = 0;\ m^2 - 2m + 1 = 0;$
   $(m-1)^2 = 0;\ m = 1,\ 1$
   $y = e^x(c_1 + c_2x);\ y = (c_1 + c_2x)e$

9. $D^2y + 9y = 0;\ m^2 + 9 = 0;\ m_1 = 3j$
   and $m_2 = -3j,\ \alpha = 0,\ \beta = 3$

   $y = e^{0x}(c_1 \sin 3x + c_2 \cos 3x);$
   $y = c_1 \sin 3x + c_2 \cos 3x$

13. $D^4y - y = 0$
   $m^4 - 1 = 0$
   $(m^2 - 1)(m^2 + 1) = 0$
   $(m-1)(m+1)(m^2+1) = 0$
   $m = \pm 1,\ m = \pm j$
   $y = c_1e^x + c_2e^{-x} + c_3 \sin x + c_4 \cos(-x)$
   $y = c_1e^x + c_2e^{-x} + c_3 \sin x + c_4 \cos x$

17. $16D^2y - 24Dy + 9y = 0;\ 16m^2 - 24m + 9 = 0;$

   $(4m - 3)^2 = 0;\ m = \dfrac{3}{4}, \dfrac{3}{4}$

   $y = e^{3x/4}(c_1 + c_2x)$

21. $2D^2y + 5y = 4Dy;\ 2D^2y + 5y - 4Dy = 0;$
   $2m^2 - 4m + 5 = 0$

   Quadratic formula:

   $m = \dfrac{4 \pm \sqrt{16 - 40}}{4} = \dfrac{4 \pm 2\sqrt{-6}}{4}$

   $m_1 = 1 + \dfrac{\sqrt{6}}{2}j;\ m_2 = 1 - \dfrac{\sqrt{6}}{2}j;\ \alpha = 1, \beta = \dfrac{1}{2}\sqrt{6}$

   $y = e^x\left(c_1 \cos \dfrac{1}{2}\sqrt{6}x + c_2 \sin \dfrac{1}{2}\sqrt{6}x\right)$

25. $2D^2y - 3Dy - y = 0;\ 2m^2 - 3m - 1 = 0$

   By the quadratic formula, $m = \dfrac{3 \pm \sqrt{9 + 8}}{4}$

   $m_1 = \dfrac{3}{4} + \dfrac{\sqrt{17}}{4},\ m_2 = \dfrac{3}{4} - \dfrac{\sqrt{17}}{4}$
   $y = c_1e^{((3/4)+(\sqrt{17}/4))x} + c_2e^{((3/4)+(\sqrt{17}/4))x};$
   $y = e^{(3/4)x}(c_1e^{x(\sqrt{17}/4)} + c_2e^{-x(\sqrt{17}/4)})$

29. $D^3y - 6D^2y + 12Dy - 8y = 0$
   $m^3 - 6m^2 + 12m - 8 = 0$
   $(m-2)(m^2 - 4m + 4) = 0$
   $(m-2)(m-2)(m-2) = 0$
   $m = 2, 2, 2$ repeated root
   $y = e^{2x}(c_1 + c_2x + c_3x^2)$

33. $D^2y + 2Dy + 10y = 0;\ m^2 + 2m + 10 = 0$

   By the quadratic formula, $m = \dfrac{-2 \pm \sqrt{4 - 40}}{2}$

   $m_1 = -1 + 3j;\ m_2 = -1 - 3j,\ \alpha = -1,\ \beta = 3;$
   $y = e^{-x}(c_1 \sin 3x + c_2 \cos 3x)$

   Substituting $y = 0$ when $x = 0$;

   $0 = e^0(c_1 \sin 0 + c_2 \cos 0);\ c_2 = 0$

   Substituting $y = e^{-\pi/6},\ x = \dfrac{\pi}{6}$;

   $e^{-\pi/6} = e^{-\pi/6}\left(c_1 \sin \dfrac{\pi}{2}\right);\ e^{-\pi/6} = e^{-\pi/6}c_1;$
   $c_1 = 1$
   $y = e^{-x} \sin 3x$

37. $y = c_1e^{3x} + c_2e^{-3x}$
   $(m-3)(m+3) = 0$
   $m^2 - 9 = 0;\ (D^2 - 9)y = 0$

30.8 Solutions of Nonhomogeneous Equations

1. b: $x^2 + 2x + e^{-x}$
   $y_p = A + Bx + Cx^2 + Ee^{-x}$

5. $D^2y - Dy - 2y = 4;\ m^2 - m - 2 = 0$
   $(m-2)(m+1) = 0;\ m_1 = 2,\ m_2 = -1$
   $y_c = c_1e^{2x} + c_2e^{-x}$
   $y_p = A;\ Dy_p = 0;\ D^2y_p = 0$

   Substituting in diff. equation, $0 - 0 - 2A = 4$;
   $A = -2$
   Therefore, $y_p = -2;\ y = c_1e^{2x} + c_2e^{-x} - 2$

9. $y'' - 3y' = 2e^x + xe^x;\ D^2y - 3Dy = 2e^x + xe^x$
   $m^2 - 3m = 0;\ m(m-3) = 0;\ m_1 = 0,\ m_2 = 3$
   $y_c = c_1e^0 + c_2e^{3x} = c_1 + c_2e^{3x};\ y_p = Ae^x + Bxe^x$
   $Dy_p = Ae^x + B(xe^x + e^x) = Ae^x + Bxe^x + Be^x$
   $D^2y_p = Ae^x + Be^x + B(xe^x + e^x)$
   $\quad\quad = Ae^x + Be^x + Bxe^x + Be^x$
   $D^2y_p = Ae^x + 2Be^x + Bxe^x$

Substituting in diff. equation:

$$Ae^x + 2Be^x + Bxe^x - 3(Ae^x + Bxe^x + Be^x)$$
$$= 2e^x + xe^x$$
$$Ae^x + 2Be^x + Bxe^x - 3Ae^x - 3Bxe^x - 3Be^x$$
$$= 2e^x + xe^x$$
$$-2Ae^x - Be^x - 2Bxe^x$$
$$= 2e^x + xe^x$$
$$e^x(-2A - B) + xe^x(-2B)$$
$$2e^x + xe^x$$
$$-2A - B = 2; \quad -2A + \frac{1}{2} = 2; \quad -2A = \frac{3}{2};$$

$$A = -\frac{3}{4}; \quad -2B = 1; \quad B = -\frac{1}{2}$$

$$y = c_1 + c_2 e^{3x} - \frac{3}{4}e^x - \frac{1}{2}xe^x$$

13. $\dfrac{d^2y}{dx^2} - 2\dfrac{dy}{dx} + y = 2x + x^2 + \sin 3x$

$$D^2y - 2Dy + y = 2x + x^2 + \sin 3x$$

$$m^2 - 2m + 1 = 0; \quad (m-1)^2 = 0; \quad m = 1, 1$$
$$y_c = e^x(c_1 + c_2 x);$$
$$y_p = A + Bx + Cx^2 + E\sin 3x + F\cos 3x$$
$$Dy_p = B + 3Cx + 3E\cos 3x - 3F\sin 3x$$
$$D^2y_p = 2c - 9E\sin 3x - 9F\cos 3x$$

Substituting in diff. equation:

$$2C - 9E\sin 3x - 9F\cos 3x$$
$$\quad - 2(B + 2Cx + 3E\cos 3x - 3F\sin 3x)$$
$$\quad + A + Bx + Cx^2 + E\sin 3x + F\cos 3x$$
$$\quad = 2x + x^2 + \sin 3x$$
$$2C - 9E\sin 3x - 9F\cos 3x - 2B - 4Cx - 6E\cos 3x$$
$$\quad + 6F\sin 3x + A + Bx + Cx^2 + E\sin 3x + F\cos 3x$$
$$\quad = 2x + x^2 + \sin 3x$$
$$2C - 2B + A - 8E\sin 3x + 6F\sin 3x - 8F\cos 3x$$
$$\quad - 6E\cos 3x - 4Cx + Bx + Cx^2$$
$$\quad = 2x + x^2 + \sin 3x$$
$$(2C - 2B + A) + \sin 3x(6F - 8E) + \cos 3x(-8F - 6E)$$
$$\quad + x(B - 4) + Cx^2$$
$$\quad = 2x + x^2 + \sin 3x$$
$$2C - 2B + A = 0; \quad A = 10$$

$$6F - 8E = 1; \quad -8F - 6E = 0; \quad E = -\frac{2}{25};$$

$$F = \frac{3}{50}; \quad B - 4 = 2; \quad B = 6; \quad C = 1$$

$$y = e^x(c_1 + c_2 x) + 10 + 6x + x^2$$

$$\quad - \frac{2}{25}\sin 3x + \frac{3}{50}\cos 3x$$

17. $D^2y - Dy - 30y = 10; \quad m^2 - m - 30 = 0;$
$(m - 6)(m + 5) = 0; \quad m_1 = -5; \quad m_2 = 6$
$y_c = c_1 e^{-5x} + c_2 e^{6x}; \quad y_p = A; \quad Dy_p = 0;$

$$D^2y_p = 0; \quad 0 = 0 - 30A = 10; \quad A = -\frac{1}{3};$$

$$y_p = -\frac{1}{3}; \quad y = c_1 e^{-5x} + c_2 e^{6x} - \frac{1}{3}$$

21. $D^2y - 4y = \sin x + 2\cos x; \quad m^2 - 4 = 0;$
$m_1 = 2; \quad m_2 = -2$
$y_c = c_1 e^{2x} + c_2 e^{-2x}$
$y_p = A\sin x + B\cos x; \quad Dy_p = A\cos x - B\sin x$
$D^2y_p = -A\sin x - B\cos x$
$-A\sin x - B\cos x - 4A\sin x - 4B\cos x$
$\quad = \sin x + 2\cos x$
$-5A\sin x - 5B\cos x$
$\quad = \sin x + 2\cos x$

$$-5A = 1; \quad A = -\frac{1}{5}; \quad -5B = 2; \quad B = -\frac{2}{5}$$

$$y_p = -\frac{1}{5}\sin x - \frac{2}{5}\cos x$$

$$y = c_1 e^{2x} + c_2 e^{-2x} - \frac{1}{5}\sin x - \frac{2}{5}\cos x$$

25. $D^2y + 5Dy + 4y = xe^x + 4; \quad m^2 + 5m + 4 = 0;$
$(m + 1)(m + 4) = 0; \quad m_1 = -1, \quad m_2 = -4$
$y_c = c_1 e^{-x} + c_2 e^{-4x}; \quad y_p = Ae^x + Bxe^x + C$
$Dy_p = Ae^x + B(xe^x + e^x) = Ae^x + Bxe^x + Be^x$
$D^2y_p = Ae^x - B(xe^x + e^x) + Be^x$
$\quad = Ae^x + 2Be^x + Bxe^x$
$Ae^x + 2Be^x + Bxe^x + 5(Ae^x + Bxe^x + Be^x)$
$\quad + 4(Ae^x + Bxe^x + C) = xe^x + 4$
$(10A + 7B)e^x + 10Bxe^x + 4C = xe^x + 4$

$$10A + 7B = 0; \quad 10B = 1; \quad B = \frac{1}{10}$$

$$4C = 4; \quad C = 1; \quad 10A + 7\left(\frac{1}{10}\right) = 0$$

$$A = -\frac{7}{100}; \quad y_p = -\frac{7}{100}e^x + \frac{1}{10}e^x + 1$$

$$y = c_1 e^{-x} + c_2 e^{-4x} - \frac{7}{100}e^x + \frac{1}{10}xe^x + 1$$

29. $D^2y + y = \cos x$

$$m^2 + 1 = 0$$
$$m = \pm i$$

$$y_c = c_1 \sin x + c_2 \cos x$$

let $\quad y_p = x(A\sin x + B\cos x)$
$$Dy_p = x(A\cos x - B\sin x) + A\sin x + B\cos x$$
$$D^2y_p = x(-A\sin x - B\cos x) + A\cos x$$
$$\qquad\qquad - B\sin x + A\cos x - B\sin x$$

$$D^2y_p + y_p = \cos x$$

$$-x(A\sin x + B\cos x) + 2A\cos x - 2B\sin x$$
$$\qquad + x(A\sin x + B\cos x) = \cos x$$
$$2A\cos x - 2B\sin x = \cos x$$
$$2A = 1, B = 0$$

$$A = \frac{1}{2}$$

$$y_p = \frac{1}{2}x\sin x$$

$$y = y_c + y_p$$

$$y = c_1\sin x + c_2\cos x + \frac{1}{2}x\sin x$$

33. $D^2y - Dy - 6y = 5 - e^x; \ m^2 - m - 6 = 0;$
$(m-3)(m+2) = 0; \ m_1 = 3, \ m_2 = -2$
$y_c = c_1 e^{3x} + c_2 e^{-2x}$
$y_p = A + Be^x; \ Dy_p = Be^x; \ D^2y_p = Be^x$
$Be^x - Be^x - 6(A + Be^x) = 5 - e^x$

$$-6A - 6Be^x = 5 - e^x; \ -6A = 5; \ A = -\frac{5}{6};$$

$$-6B = -1; \ B = \frac{1}{6}$$

$$y_p = -\frac{5}{6} + \frac{1}{6}e^x; \ y = c_1 e^{3x} + c_2 e^{-2x} + \frac{1}{6}e^x - \frac{5}{6}$$

Substituting $x = 0$ when $y = 2$; $3c_1 + 3c_2 = 8$

$$Dy = 3c_1 e^{3x} - 2c_2 e^{-2x} + \frac{1}{6}e^x$$

Substituting, $Dy = 4$ when $x = 0$, $18c_1 - 12c_2 = 23$

Solving the two linear equations simultaneously,

$$c_1 = \frac{11}{6}, \ c_2 = \frac{5}{6}$$

$$y = \frac{11}{6}e^{3x} + \frac{5}{6}e^{-2x} + \frac{1}{6}e^x - \frac{5}{6}$$

$$= \frac{1}{6}(11e^{3x} + 5e^{-2x} + e^x - 5)$$

30.9 Applications of Higher-Order Equations

1. $x = c_1 \sin 4t + c_2 \cos 4t; \ x = 0, Dx = 2$ for $t = 0$
$0 = c_1 \sin(4(0)) + c_2 \cos(4(0)) \Rightarrow c_2 = 0$
$x = c_1 \sin 4t$
$Dx = 4c_1 \cos 4t$

$$4c_1 \cos(4(0)) = 2 \Rightarrow c_1 = \frac{1}{2}$$

$$x = \frac{1}{2}\sin 4t$$

5. $D^2\theta + \dfrac{g}{l}\theta = 0; \ g = 9.8 \text{ m/s}^2, \ l = 0.1 \text{ m};$
$D^2\theta + 9.8\theta = 0; \ m^2 + 9.8 = 0$

$m_1 = \sqrt{9.8}j, \ m_2 = -\sqrt{9.8}j; \ \alpha = 0, \beta = \sqrt{9.8}$
$x = c_1 \sin\sqrt{9.8}t + c_2 \cos\sqrt{9.8}t$

Substituting $\theta = 0.1$ when $t = 0$;
$0.1 = c_1 \sin 0 + c_2 \cos 0; \ 0.1 = c_2;$
$D_x = c_1 \cos\sqrt{9.8}t - c_2 \sin\sqrt{9.8}t$
Substituting $D\theta = 0$ when $t = 0$;
$0 = c_1 \cos 0 - c_2 \sin 0; \ c_1 = 0;$
$\theta = 0.1 \cos\sqrt{9.8}t = 0.1\cos 3.1t$

$\sqrt{9.8}t$	t	$\cos\sqrt{9.8}t$	$0.1\cos\sqrt{9.8}t$
0	0	1	0.1
$\frac{\pi}{2}$	0.50	0	0
π	1.00	-1	-0.1
$\frac{3\pi}{2}$	1.50	0	0
2π	2.00	1	0.1

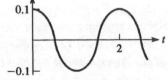

9. To get spring constant: $F = kx; \ 4.00 = k(0.125);$
$k = 32.0 \text{ lb/ft}$
To get mass of object: $F = ma; \ 4.00 = m(32.0);$

$$m = 0.125\frac{\text{lb} \cdot \text{s}^2}{\text{ft}} \text{ (a slug)}$$

Using Newton's Second Law:
mass × accel. = restoring force

$$0.125\frac{d^2x}{dt^2} = -32.0x; \ D^2x + 256x = 0;$$

$m^2 + 256 = 0;$

$m = \pm 16.0j; \; x = c_1 \sin 16.0t + c_2 \cos 16.0t$

$D_x = 16.0c_1 \cos 16.0t - 16.0c_2 \sin 16.0t$

Let $x = 0.250$ ft when $t = 0$;

$0.250 = c_1 \sin 0 + c_2 \cos 0;$

$c_2 = 0.250$

Let $Dx = 0$ when $t = 0$,

$0 = 16.0c_1 \cos 0 - 16.0c_2 \sin 0;$

$c_1 = 0; \; x = 0.250 \cos 16.0t$

13.
$$L\frac{d^2q}{dt^2} + R\frac{dq}{dt} + \frac{q}{C} = E$$

$$0.200\frac{d^2\theta}{dt^2} + 8.00\frac{dq}{dt} + 10^6 q = 0$$

$$0.200m^2 + 8.00m + 10^6 = 0$$

$$m = \frac{-8.00 \pm \sqrt{64.0 - 0.800 \times 10^6}}{0.400};$$

$m = -20.0 \pm 2240j; \; \alpha = -20.0, \; \beta = 2240$

$q = e^{-20.0t}(c_1 \sin 2240t + c_2 \cos 2240t); \; t = 0, \; q = 0$

Therefore, $c_2 = 0$

$$\frac{dq}{dt} = e^{-20.0t}(2240c_1 \cos 2240t - 2240c_2 \sin 2240t)$$
$$+ (c_1 \sin 2240t + c_2 \cos 2240t)(-20.0e^{-20.0t})$$

$t = 0, \; i = 0.500;$ therefore, $c_1 = 2.24 \times 10^{-4};$

$q = e^{-20.0t}(2.24 \times 10^{-4}) \sin 2240t$

$q = 2.24 \times 10^{-4}e^{-20.0t} \sin 2240t$

17. $0.500D^2q + 10.0Dq + \dfrac{q}{200 \times 10^6} = 120 \sin 120\pi t$

$1.00D^2q + 20.0Dq + 10^4 q = 240 \sin 120\pi t$

$1.00m^2 + 20.0m + 10^4 = 0$

$$m = \frac{-20.0 \pm \sqrt{400 - 4 \times 10^4}}{200} = -10.0 \pm 99.5j;$$

$q_c = e^{-10.0t}(c_1 \sin 99.5t + c_2 \cos 99.5t);$

$q_p = A \sin 120\pi t + B \cos 120\pi t$

$Dq_p = 120\pi A \cos 120\pi t - 120\pi B \sin 120\pi t$

$D^2q_p = -142\,000 \, A \sin 120\pi t - 142\,000B \cos 120\pi t$

$\qquad -142\,000 \, A120\pi t - 142\,000 \, B \cos 120\pi t$

$\qquad + 7540A \cos 120\pi t - 7540B \sin 120\pi t$

$\qquad + 10\,000A \sin 120\pi t + 10\,000B \cos 120\pi t$

$\qquad = 240 \sin 120\pi t$

$-132\,000A - 7540B = 240$

$-132\,000B + 7540A = 0$

$A = -1.81 \times 10^{-3}, B = -1.03 \times 10^{-4}$

$q = e^{-10.0t}(c_1 \sin 99.5t + c_2 \cos 99.5t)$

$\qquad -1.81 \times 10^{-3} \sin 120\pi t - 1.03 \times 10^{-4} \cos 120\pi t$

21. $1.00D^2q + 5.00Dq + \dfrac{q}{150 \times 10^{-6}} = 120 \sin 100t$

$\qquad 1.00D^2q + 5.00Dq + 6670q = 120 \sin 100t$

$q_p = A \sin 100t + B \cos 100t$

$Dq_p = 100A \cos 100t - 100B \sin 100t$

$D^2q_p = -10^4 A \sin 100t - 10^4 B \cos 100t$

$-10^4 A \sin 100t - 10^4 B \cos 100t$

$\quad + 5.00(100A \cos 100t - 100B \sin 100t)$

$\quad + 6670(A \sin 100t + B \cos 100t)$

$\quad = 120 \sin 100t$

$(-10^4 A - 500B + 6670A) \sin 100t$

$\quad + (-10^4 B + 500A + 6670B) \cos 100t$

$\quad = 120 \sin 100t$

$3330A + 500B = -120$

$500A - 3330B = 0$

$A = -0.0352; \; B = 0.005\,28;$

$q_p = -0.0352 \sin 100t + 0.005\,28 \cos 100t;$

$i_p = -3.52 \cos 100t + 0.528 \sin 100t$

30.10   Laplace Transforms

1. $\quad f(t) = 1, t > 0$

$$L(f) = \int_0^\infty e^{-st} \cdot 1 \, dt$$

$$= \lim_{c \to \infty} \frac{-1}{s} \int_0^c e^{-st}(-s \, dt)$$

$$L(f) = -\frac{1}{s} \lim_{c \to \infty} e^{-st} \Big|_0^c$$

$$= -\frac{1}{s} \left[\lim_{c \to \infty} (e^{-sc} - e^{-s(0)}) \right]$$

$$= -\frac{1}{s} \lim_{c \to \infty} (0 - 1)$$

$$L(f) = \frac{1}{s}$$

5. $f(t) = e^{3t};$ from transform (3) of the table,

$$a = -3; \; L(3t) = \frac{1}{s - 3}$$

9. $f(t) = \cos 2t - \sin 2t; \; L(f) = L(\cos 2t) - L(\sin 2t)$

By transforms (5) and (6),

$$L(f) = \frac{s}{s^2 + 4} - \frac{2}{s^2 + 4}; \; L(f) = \frac{s - 2}{s^2 + 4}$$

13. $y'' + y'$; $f(0) = 0$; $f'(0) = 0$
$$L[f''(y) + f'(y)]$$
$$= L(f'') + L(f')$$
$$= s^2 L(f) - s f(0) - f'(0) + s L(f) - f(0)$$
$$= s^2 L(f) - s(0) - 0 + s L(f) - 0$$
$$= s^2 L(f) + s L(f)$$

17. $L^{-1}(F) = L^{-1}\left(\dfrac{2}{s^3}\right) = 2L^{-1}\left(\dfrac{1}{s^3}\right)$;

$$L^{-1}(F) = \frac{2t^2}{2} = t^2; \text{ transform (2)}$$

21. $L^{-1}(F) = L^{-1}\dfrac{1}{(s+1)^3} = L^{-1}\dfrac{1}{2}\left[\dfrac{2}{(s+1)^3}\right]$

$$= \frac{1}{2}t^2 e^{-t};$$

transform (12)

25. $F(s) = \dfrac{4s^2 - 8}{(s+1)(s-2)(s-3)} = \dfrac{-\frac{1}{3}}{s+1} + \dfrac{-\frac{8}{3}}{s-2} + \dfrac{7}{s-3}$

$$L^{-1}(F) = -\frac{1}{3}L^{-1}\left(\frac{1}{s+1}\right) - \frac{8}{3}L^{-1}\left(\frac{1}{s-2}\right)$$

$$+ 7L^{-1}\frac{1}{s-3}$$

$$f(t) = -\frac{1}{3}e^{-t} - \frac{8}{3}e^{2t} + 7e^{3t}$$

30.11   Solving Differential Equations by Laplace Transforms

1. $2y' - y = 0$; $y(0) = 2$
$$L(2y') - L(y) = L(0)$$
$$2L(y') - L(y) = 0$$
$$2sL(y) - 2(2) - L(y) = 0$$

$$L(y) = \frac{4}{2s-1} = 2\frac{1}{s-\frac{1}{2}}, \text{ from transform 3,}$$

$$y = 2e^{\frac{1}{2}t}$$

5. $y' + y = 0$; $y(0) = 1$; $L(y') + L(y) = L(0)$;
$$L(y') + L(y) = 0; \quad sL(y) - y(0) + L(y) = 0$$
$$sL(y) - 1 + L(y) = 0; \quad (s+1)L(y) = 1;$$

$$L(y) = \frac{1}{s+1}; \quad a = -1, \text{ transforms (3)}; \quad y = e^{-t}$$

9. $y' + 3y = e^{-3t}$; $y(0) = 1$; $L(y') + L(3y) = L(e^{-3t})$;

$$L(y') + 3L(y) = L(3^{-3t});$$

$$[sL(y-1] + 3L(y) = \frac{1}{s+3}$$

$$(s+3)L(y) = \frac{1}{s+3} + 1; \quad L(y) = \frac{1}{(s+3)^2} + \frac{1}{s+3}$$

The inverse is found from transforms (11) and (3).

$$y = te^{-3t} + e^{-3t} = (1+t)e$$

13. $y'' + 2y' = 0$; $y(0) = 0$, $y'(0) = 2$;
$$L(y'') + L(2y') = 0;$$
$$L(y'') + 2L(y') = 0$$
$$[s^2 L(y) - 0 - 2] + 2sL(y) - 0 = 0;$$
$$(s^2 + 2s)L(y) = 2;$$

$$L(y) = \frac{2}{s^2 + 2s} = \frac{2}{s(s+2)}$$

By transform (4), $a = 2$; $y = 1 - e^{-2t}$

17. $y'' + y = 1$; $y(0) = 1$; $y'(0) = 1$;
$$L(y'') + L(y) = L(1);$$

$$s^2 L(y) - s - 1 + L(y) = \frac{1}{s}$$

$$(s^2 + 1)L(y) = \frac{1}{s} + s + 1;$$

$$L(y) = \frac{1}{s(s^2 + 1)} + \frac{s}{s^2 + 1} + \frac{1}{s^2 + 1}$$

By transforms (7), (5), and (6),
$$y = 1 - \cos t + \cos t + \sin t; \quad y = 1 + \sin t$$

21. $y'' - 4y = 10e^{3t}$, $y(0) = 5$, $y'(0) = 0$;
$$L(y'') - 4L(y) = 10 \cdot L(e^{3t})$$

$$s^2 L(y) - s \cdot y(0) - y'(0) - 4L(y) = \frac{10}{s-3};$$

$$s^2 L(y) - 5s - 0 - 4L(y) = \frac{10}{s-3}$$

$$(s^2 - 4)L(y) = 5s + \frac{10}{s-3}$$

$$L(y) = \frac{5s}{(s+2)(s-2)} + \frac{10}{(s+2)(s-2)(s-3)}$$

$$L(y) = \frac{\frac{5}{2}}{s+2} + \frac{\frac{5}{2}}{s-2} + \frac{\frac{1}{2}}{s+2} + \frac{-\frac{5}{2}}{s-2} + \frac{2}{s-3}$$

$$L(y) = \frac{3}{s+2} + \frac{2}{s-3}$$

$$y = 3e^{-2t} + 2e^{3t}$$

25. $2v' = 6 - v$; since the object starts from rest,
$f(0) = 0,\ f'(0) = 0$

$$2L(v') + L(v) = 6L(1);\ 2sL(v) - 0 + L(v) = \frac{6}{s};$$

$$(2s + 1)L(v) = \frac{6}{s}$$

$$L(v) = \frac{6}{s(2s + 1)} = 6\left[\frac{\frac{1}{2}}{s\left(s + \frac{1}{2}\right)}\right]$$

By transforms (4), $v = 6(1 - e^{-t/2})$

29. $10\dfrac{d^2q}{dt^2} + \dfrac{q}{4 \times 10^{-5}} = 100\sin 50t;\ q(0) = 0$ and

$q'(0) = 0$
$10L(q'') + 2.5 \times 10^4 L(q) = L(100\sin 50t)$
$10s^2 L(q) + 2.5 \times 10^4 L(q) = L(100\sin 50t)$

$$(s^2 + 2.5 \times 10^3)L(q) = 10\left(\frac{50}{s^2 + 50}\right);$$

$$L(q) = \frac{500}{(s^2 + 50^2)^2};\ L(q) = \frac{1}{500}\frac{2(50)^3}{(s^2 + 50^2)^2}$$

By transforms (15),

$$q = \frac{1}{500}(\sin 50t - 50t\cos 50t)$$

$$i = \frac{dq}{dt} = \frac{1}{500}\{50\cos 50t - [50t(-50\sin 50t) + (\cos 50t)50]\} = \frac{1}{500}(2500t\sin 50t) = 5t\sin 50t$$

33. $0.2Di + 10i = 50e^{-100t},\ i(0) = 0$

$$0.2L(Di) + 10L(i) = 50L(e^{-100t});$$

$$0.2(s \cdot L(i) - i(0)) + 10L(i) = 50 \cdot \frac{1}{s + 100};$$

$$\frac{s}{5}L(i) + 10L(i) = \frac{50}{s + 100};$$

$$sL(i) + 50L(i) = \frac{250}{s + 100};\ (s + 50) \cdot L(i) = \frac{250}{s + 100}$$

$$L(i) = \frac{250}{(s + 50)(s + 100)} = \frac{5}{s + 50} + \frac{-5}{s + 100};$$

$$i = 5e^{-50t} - 5e$$

Chapter 30 Review Exercises

1. $4xy^3\,dx + (x^2 + 1)dy = 0$; divide by y^3 and $x^2 + 1$

$$\frac{4x}{x^2 + 1}\,dx + \frac{dy}{y^3} = 0;\ \text{integrating, } 2\ln(x^2 + 1) - \frac{1}{2y^2} = c$$

5. $2D^2y + Dy = 0$. The auxiliary equation is $2m^2 + m = 0$

$$m(2m + 1) = 0;\ m_1 = 0 \text{ and } m_2 = -\frac{1}{2}$$

$$y = c_1 e^0 + c_2 e^{-1/2x};\ y = c_1 + c_2 e^{-x/2}$$

9. $(x+y)dx + (x+y^3)dy = 0$; $x\,dx + y\,dx + x\,dy + y^3\,dy = 0$; $x\,dx + d(xy) + y^3\,dy = 0$

Integrating, $\dfrac{1}{2}x^2 + xy + \dfrac{1}{4}y^4 = c_1$; $2x^2 + 4xy + y^4 = c$

13. $dy = (2y + y^2)dx$; $\dfrac{dy}{(2y + y^2)} = dx$

$-\dfrac{1}{2}\ln\left(\dfrac{2+y}{y}\right) = x + \ln c_1$; $\ln\dfrac{2+y}{y} = -2x - \ln c_1^2$; $\left(\dfrac{2+y}{y}\right) = -2x$; $\dfrac{2+y}{y} = \dfrac{e^{-2x}}{c_1^2}$;

$y = c_1^2(y+2)c^{2x}$; $y = c(y+2)e^{2x}$

17. $y' + 4y = 2e^{-2x}$; $\dfrac{dy}{dx} + 4y = 2e^{-2x}$; $dy + 4 \cdot y\,dx = 2e^{-2x}\,dx$

$e^{\int 4dx} = e^{4x}$; $e^{4x}dy + 4ye^{4x}dx = 2e^{-2x} \cdot e^{4x}dx$; $d(ye^{4x}) = 2e^{2x}dx$; $\displaystyle\int d(ye^{4x}) = \int e^{2x} \cdot (2\,dx)$; $ye^{4x} = e^{2x} + c$;

$y = e^{-2x} + ce^{-4x}$

21. $2D^2s + Ds - 3s = 6$; $2m^2 + m - 3 = 0$; $(m-1)(2m+3) = 0$; $m_1 = 1$, $m_2 = -\dfrac{3}{2}$

$s_c = c_1e^t + c_2e^{-3t/2}$; $s_p = A$; $s_p' = 0$; $s_p'' = 0$

Substituting into the differential equation, $2(0) + 0 - 3A = 6$; $A = -2$; $s_p = -2$.
$s = c_1e^t + c_2e^{-3t/2} - 2$

25. $9D^2y - 18Dy + 8y = 16 + 4x$

$D^2y - 2Dy + \dfrac{8}{9}y = \dfrac{16}{9} + \dfrac{4}{9}x$

$m^2 - 2m + \dfrac{8}{9} = 0$; $m = \dfrac{2 \pm \sqrt{4 - 4\left(\frac{8}{9}\right)}}{2}$; $m_1 = \dfrac{2}{3}$; $m_2 = \dfrac{4}{3}$

$y_c = c_1e^{2x/3} + c_2e^{4x/3}$; $y_p = A + Bx$; $y_p' = B$; $y_p'' = 0$

Substituting into the differential equation,

$$0 - 2B + \dfrac{8}{9}(A + Bx) = \dfrac{16}{9} + \dfrac{4}{9}x$$

$$\left(-2B + \dfrac{8}{9}A\right) + \dfrac{8}{9}Bx = \dfrac{16}{9} + \dfrac{4}{9}x; \quad -2B + \dfrac{8}{9}A = \dfrac{16}{9};$$

$$\dfrac{8}{9}B = \dfrac{4}{9}; \ B = \dfrac{1}{2}; \ -2\left(\dfrac{1}{2}\right) + \dfrac{8}{9}A = \dfrac{16}{9}; \ A = \dfrac{25}{8}; \ y_p = \dfrac{1}{2}x + \dfrac{25}{8}$$

$$y = c_1e^{2x/3} + c_2e^{4x/3} + \dfrac{1}{2}x + \dfrac{25}{8}$$

29.
$$y'' - 7y' - 8y = 2e^{-x}$$
$$D^2 y_c - 7Dy_c - 8y_c = 0$$
$$m^2 - 7m - 8 = 0$$
$$(m+1)(m-8) = 0$$
$$m = -1, \; m = 8$$
$$y_c = c_1 e^{-x} + c_2 e^{8x}$$

Let $y_p = Axe^{-x}$, $y_p' = Ae^{-x}(1-x)$, $y_p'' = Ae^{-x}(x-2)$

$$Ae^{-x}(x-2) - 7Ae^{-x}(1-x) - 8Axe^{-x} = 2e^{-x}$$
$$A(x-2) - 7A(1-x) - 8Ax = 2$$
$$-9A = 2$$
$$A = \frac{-2}{9}$$

$$y_p = \frac{-2}{9} xe^{-x}$$

$$y = y_c + y_p$$

$$y = c_1 e^{-x} + c_2 e^{8x} + \frac{-2}{9} xe^{-x}$$

33.
$$3y' = 2y \cot x; \quad \frac{dy}{dx} = \frac{2}{3} y \cot x; \quad \frac{dy}{y} = \frac{2}{3} \cot x \, dx; \text{ integrating,}$$

$$\ln y = \frac{2}{3} \ln \sin x + \ln c; \quad \ln y - \ln \sin^{2/3} x = \ln c;$$

$$\ln \frac{y}{\sin^{2/3} x} = \ln c; \quad \frac{y}{\sin^{2/3} x} = c; \; y = c \sin^{2/3} x$$

Substituting $y = 2$ when $x = \dfrac{\pi}{2}$, $2 = c \sin^{2/3} \dfrac{\pi}{2}$; $c = 2$

Therefore $y = 2 \sin^{2/3} x = 2 \sqrt[3]{\sin^2 x}$; $y^3 = 8 \sin^2 x$

37. $D^2 y + Dy + 4y = 0$. $m^2 + m + 4 = 0$; $m = \dfrac{-1 \pm \sqrt{-15}}{2}$

$$m_1 = -\frac{1}{2} + \frac{\sqrt{15}}{2} j; \; m_2 = -\frac{1}{2} - \frac{\sqrt{15}}{2} j; \; \alpha = -\frac{1}{2}, \; \beta = \frac{\sqrt{15}}{2}; \text{ by Eq. (30-17)}$$

$$y = e^{-x/2} \left(c_1 \sin \frac{\sqrt{15}}{2} x + c_2 \cos \frac{\sqrt{15}}{2} x \right)$$

$$Dy = e^{-x/2} \left(\frac{\sqrt{15}}{2} c_1 \cos \frac{\sqrt{15}}{2} x - c_2 \sin \frac{\sqrt{15}}{2} x \right) + \left(c_1 \sin \frac{\sqrt{15}}{2} x + c_2 \cos \frac{\sqrt{15}}{2} x \right) \left(-\frac{1}{2} e^{-x} \right)$$

Substituting $Dy = \sqrt{15}$, $y = 0$ when $x = 0$; $c_2 = 0$; $c_1 = 2$.

$$y = 2 e^{-x/2} \sin \left(\frac{1}{2} \sqrt{15} x \right)$$

41. $L(4y') - L(y) = 0$; $4L(y') - L(y) = 0$; $4sL(y) - 1 - L(y) = 0$, by Eq. (30-24)

$$(4s - 1)L(y) = 1; \; L(y) = \frac{1}{4s - 1} = \frac{\frac{1}{4}}{s - \frac{1}{4}}$$

By transform (3), $y = e^{t/4}$.

45. $L(y'') + L(y) = 0$; $y(0) = 0$,
$y'(0) = -4$, Eq. (30-25)

$s^2 L(y) + 4 + L(y) = 0$; $(s^2 + 1)L(y) = -4$;

$L(y) = -4 \left(\dfrac{1}{s^2 + 1} \right)$

By transform (6), $y = -4 \sin t$.

49. $\dfrac{dx}{dt} = 2t$

$x = t^2 + c$
$1 = 0^2 + c \Rightarrow c = 1$
$x = t^2 + 1$
$xy = 1$

$x \dfrac{dy}{dt} + y \dfrac{dx}{dt} = 0$

$x \dfrac{dy}{dt} + y(2t) = 0$

$\dfrac{x}{y} dy + 2t\, dt = 0$

$\dfrac{1}{y^2} dy + 2t\, dt = 0$

$-\dfrac{1}{y} + t^2 = c$

$-\dfrac{1}{1} + 0^2 = c \Rightarrow c = -1$

$-\dfrac{1}{y} + t^2 = -1$

$-1 + yt^2 = -y$
$y(t^2 + 1) = 1$

$y = \dfrac{1}{t^2 + 1}$

In terms of t, $x = t^2 + 1$ and $y = \dfrac{1}{t^2 + 1}$.

53. $\dfrac{dm}{dt} = km$

$\dfrac{dm}{m} = k\, dt$

$\ln m = kt + c$
$\ln m_0 = k(0) + c \Rightarrow c = \ln m_0$
$\ln m = kt + \ln m_0$

$\ln \dfrac{m}{m_0} = kt$

$\dfrac{m}{m_0} = e^{kt}$

$m = m_0 e^{kt}$

57. $N = N_0 e^{kt}$
$0.9 N_0 = N_0 e^{k(1.0)}$
$k = \ln 0.9$

$\dfrac{N_0}{2} = N_0 e^{(\ln 0.9)t}$

$t = \dfrac{\ln \frac{1}{2}}{\ln 0.9} = 6.6$

The half-life is 6.6 h.

61. $\dfrac{dP}{dt} = kP, P = P_0 = 5.0$ billion when $t = 0, 1987$

$P = P_0 e^{kt}$
$P = 5.0 e^{kt}$ $P = 6.0$ when $t = 12, 1999$

$6.0 = 5.0 e^{k(12)} \Rightarrow k = \dfrac{1}{12} \ln \dfrac{6.0}{5.0}$

$P = 5.0 e^{(1/12) \ln(6.0/5.0)t}$; in 2010, $t = 23$

$P = 5.0 e^{(1/12) \ln(6.0/5.0)(23)} = 7.1$

In 2010 the world's population will be 7.1 billion.

65. $\dfrac{dT}{dt} = k(T - 20)$

$\dfrac{dT}{T - 20} = k\, dt$

$\ln(T - 20) = kt + C$, at $t = 0$, T=100
$\ln(100 - 20) = k(0) + C \Rightarrow C = \ln 80$

$\ln \dfrac{T - 20}{80} = kt$

$\dfrac{T - 20}{80} = e^{kt}$

$T = 20 + 80 e^{kt}$, at $t = 5$, $T = 90$

$90 = 20 + 80 e^{k(5)} \Rightarrow k = \dfrac{1}{5} \ln \dfrac{70}{80}$

$T = 20 + 80 e^{(1/5) \ln(7/8)t}$, at $t = 60$ min $= 1$ h
$T = 20 + 80 e^{(1/5) \ln(7/8)(60)}$
$T = 36.1°C$

69. $F = kx$; $40 = 0.50k$; $k = 80$ N/m; $m = 4\,kg$; $4\dfrac{d^2x}{dt^2} = -16\dfrac{dx}{dt} - 80x$; $4D^2x + 16Dx + 80 = 0$; $D^2x + 4Dx + 20 = 0$; $4m^2 + 16m + 80 = 0$; $m_1 = -2 + 4j$; $m_2 = -2 - 4j$; $x = e^{-2t}(c_1 \sin 4t + c_2 \cos 4t)$

Let $x = 0.50$ when $t = 0$; $0.50 = c_2$

$Dx = e^{-2t}(4c_1 \cos 4t - 4c_2 \sin 4t) + (c_1 \sin 4t + c_2 \cos 4t)(-2)e^{-2t}$
Let $Dx = 0$ when $t = 0$; $0 = 4c_1 - 2c_2$; $0 = 4c_1 - 1$; $c_1 = 0.25$

$x = e^{-2t}(0.25 \sin 4t + 0.5 \cos 4t) = 0.25e^{-2t}(\sin 4t + 2 \cos 4t)$ underdamped

73. $R = 20\ \Omega$, $L = 4$ H, $C = 10^{-4}$ F; $V = 100$ V; $q(0) = 10^{-2}$ C; $4q'' + 20q' + 10^4 q = 100$;

$$\frac{1}{25}q'' + \frac{1}{5}q' + 100q = 1$$

$$\frac{1}{25}[s^2 L(q) - s(10^{-2})] + \frac{1}{5}[sL(q) - 10^{-2}] + 100L(q) = L(1)$$

$$\frac{1}{25}s^2 L(q) - \frac{1}{2500}s + \frac{1}{5}sL(q) - \frac{1}{500} + 100L(q) = \frac{1}{s}$$

$$L(q)\left(\frac{1}{25}s^2 + \frac{1}{5}s + 100\right) = \frac{1}{s} + \frac{1}{2500}s + \frac{1}{500}$$

$$L(q)\left(\frac{s^2 + 5s + 2500}{25}\right) = \frac{2500 + s^2 + 5s}{2500s}$$

$$L(q) = \frac{1}{100s}; \quad q = \frac{1}{100}; \quad i = \frac{dq}{dt} = 0$$

77. $0.25\dfrac{d^2q}{dt^2} + \dfrac{4.0\,dq}{dt} + \dfrac{q}{10^{-4}} = 0$; $q(0) = 400\ \mu C = 4.0 \times 10^{-4}$ C

$i = \dfrac{dq}{dt} = q'(0)$; $0.25L(q'') + 4.0L(q') + 10^4 L(q) = 0$; $L(q'') + 16L(q') + 4.0 \times 10^4 L(q) = 0$
$s^2 L(q) - 4.0 \times 10^{-4}s - 0 + 16sL(q) - 4.0 \times 10^{-4} + 4.0 \times 10^4 L(q) = 0$
$(s^2 + 16s + 4.0 \times 10^{-4})L(q) = 4.0 \times 10^{-4}s + 64 \times 10^{-4}$
$L(q) = 4.0 \times 10^{-4}\left[\dfrac{s + 16}{s^2 + 16s + 64 + 4 \times 10^4}\right]$

$= 4.0 \times 10^{-4}\left[\dfrac{s + 8}{(s + 8)^2 + 200^2} + \dfrac{8}{(s + 8)^2 + 200^2}\right]$

$= 4.0 \times 10^{-4}\left[\dfrac{s + 8}{(s + 8)^2 + 200^2} + \dfrac{8}{200} \times \dfrac{200}{(s + 8)^2 + 200^2}\right]$

$q = 4.0 \times 10^{-4}(e^{-8t} \cos 200t + 0.04e^{-8t} \sin 200t)$
$q = 10^{-4}e^{-8t}(4.0 \cos 200t + 0.16 \sin 200t)$

81. R = rate in L/t at which mixtures flow in/out of container
$V(t)$ = volume of O_2 in L in container at time t

$V(0) = 5.00$ L. When 5.00 L of air passed into the container, $Rt = 5, t = \dfrac{R}{5}$. Find $V\left(\dfrac{R}{5}\right)$.

$\dfrac{dV}{dt} = 0.20R - \dfrac{V}{5.00}R = -0.20R(V - 1)$

$\dfrac{dV}{V - 1} = -0.20\,R\,dt$

$\ln(V - 1) = -0.20\,Rt + C$
$\ln(5.00 - 1) = -0.20R(0) + C \Rightarrow C = \ln 4.00$
$\ln(V - 1) = -0.20Rt + \ln 4.00$

$$\ln(V - 1) = -0.20R\left(\frac{5}{R}\right) + 4.00$$

$$\ln\frac{V - 1}{4.00} = -0.20R\left(\frac{5}{R}\right)$$

$$e^{\ln\frac{V-1}{4.00}} = e^{-0.20R\left(\frac{5}{R}\right)} \Rightarrow \frac{V - 1}{4.00} = e^{-0.20R\left(\frac{5}{R}\right)}$$

$$V = 4.00e^{-0.20R\left(\frac{5}{R}\right)} + 1$$
$$V = 2.47 \text{ L}$$

85.

$$L \cdot \frac{di}{dt} + iR = E$$
$$i(0) = 0$$

(a) separation of variables.

$$L\,di + iR\,dt = E\,dt$$
$$L\,di = (E - iR)\,dt$$

$$\int \frac{L}{E - iR}\,di = \int dt$$

$$-\frac{L}{R}\int \frac{-R\,di}{E - iR} = \int dt$$

$$-\frac{L}{R}\ln(E - iR) = t + \ln C$$

$$-\frac{L}{R}\ln(E - 0\cdot R) = 0 + \ln C$$

$$\ln E^{-L/R} = \ln C$$
$$C = E^{-L/R}$$

$$-\frac{L}{R}\cdot\ln(E - iR) = t + \ln E^{-L/R}$$
$$\ln(E - iR)^{L/R} + \ln E^{-L/R} = -t$$
$$\ln[(E - iR)^{L/R}\cdot E^{-L/R}] = -t$$
$$(E - iR)^{L/R}\cdot E^{-L/R} = e^{-t}$$
$$(E - iR)^{L/R} = E^{L/R}\cdot e^{-t}$$
$$E - iR = E\cdot e^{-(R/L)\cdot t}$$
$$iR = E - E\cdot e^{-(R/L)\cdot t}$$

$$i = \frac{E}{R}(1 - e^{-(R/L)\cdot t})$$

(b)   linear differential equation of first order, use integrating factor

$$L\,di + iR\,dt = E\,dt$$

$$di + \frac{R}{L}\cdot i\,dt = \frac{E}{L}\,dt$$

$$e^{\int R/L\,dt} = e^{(R/L)t}$$

$$e^{R/Lt}\cdot di + \frac{R}{L}\cdot e^{(R/L)t}\cdot i\,dt = \frac{E}{L}e^{(R/L)t}dt$$

$$\int d(ie^{(R/L)t}) = \int \frac{E}{L}e^{(R/L)t}dt = \frac{E}{R}\int e^{(R/L)t}\cdot\frac{R}{L}dt$$

$$i\cdot e^{(R/L)t} = \frac{E}{R}e^{(R/L)t} + C$$

$$0\cdot e^{R/L\cdot 0} = \frac{E}{R}e^{R/L\cdot 0} + C$$

$$C = \frac{-E}{R}$$

$$i\cdot e^{(R/L)t} = \frac{E}{R}e^{(R/L)t} - \frac{E}{R}$$

$$i = \frac{E}{R}(1 - e^{-(R/L)t})$$

(c)   Laplace transforms: use L for inductance and $\mathcal{L}$ for the Laplace transform

$$L\frac{di}{dt} + iR = E$$

$$L\mathcal{L}(i') + R\mathcal{L}(i) = \mathcal{L}(E)$$

$$L\cdot(s\mathcal{L}(i) - i(0)) + R\mathcal{L}(i) = \frac{E}{s}$$

$$Ls\mathcal{L}(i) + R\mathcal{L}(i) = \frac{E}{s}$$

$$\mathcal{L}(i)(Ls + R) = \frac{E}{s}$$

$$\mathcal{L}(i) = \frac{E}{s(Ls + R)} = \frac{E}{Ls\cdot\left(s + \frac{R}{L}\right)} = \frac{\frac{E}{L}}{s\left(s + \frac{R}{L}\right)}$$

$$\mathcal{L}(i) = \frac{\frac{E}{R}}{s} - \frac{\frac{E}{R}}{s + \frac{R}{L}}$$

$$i = \frac{E}{R}(1 - e^{-(R/L)t})$$